7

THE KING'S ENGLAND

Edited by Arthur Mee

In 41 Volumes

ENCHANTED LAND (INTRODUCTORY VOLUME)

Bedfordshire and
  Huntingdonshire
Berkshire
Buckinghamshire
Cambridgeshire
Cheshire
Cornwall
Derbyshire
Devon
Dorset
Durham
Essex
Gloucestershire
Hampshire with the Isle of
  Wight
Herefordshire
Hertfordshire
Kent
Lake Counties
Lancashire
Leicestershire and
  Rutland

Lincolnshire
London
Middlesex
Monmouthshire
Norfolk
Northamptonshire
Northumberland
Nottinghamshire
Oxfordshire
Shropshire
Somerset
Staffordshire
Suffolk
Surrey
Sussex
Warwickshire
Wiltshire
Worcestershire
Yorkshire—East Riding
Yorkshire—North Riding
Yorkshire—West Riding

THE KING'S ENGLAND

LINCOLNSHIRE

By
ARTHUR MEE

fully revised and edited by
F. T. BAKER

Illustrated with new photographs by
A. F. KERSTING

HODDER AND STOUGHTON

*Printed in Great Britain
for Hodder and Stoughton Ltd.,
St. Paul's House, Warwick Lane, London, E.C.4,
by Richard Clay (The Chaucer Press), Ltd.,
Bungay, Suffolk*

INTRODUCTION TO REVISED EDITION

In preparing the new edition of THE KING'S ENGLAND care has been taken to bring the books up to date as far as possible within the changes which have taken place since the series was originally planned. In addition the editor has made his revisions both in text and illustrations with a view to keeping the price of the books within reasonable limits, in spite of greatly increased production costs. But throughout the book, it has been the editor's special care to preserve Mr Arthur Mee's original intention of providing something more than just another guide book giving archaeological, ecclesiastical, and topographical information.

In the case of every town and village mentioned in the King's England Series, it has been the intention not only to indicate its position on the map, but to convey something of its atmosphere. And the biographical selections about people who are ever associated with that part of the country in which they lived, or who are commemorated in the parish church—which was such a popular feature of the former edition—have been retained and in some cases supplemented.

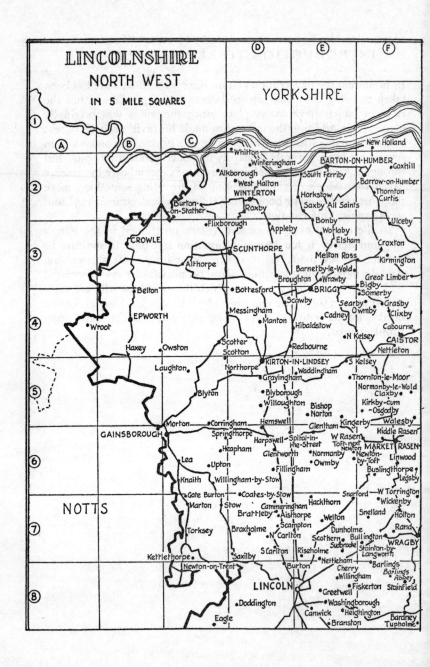

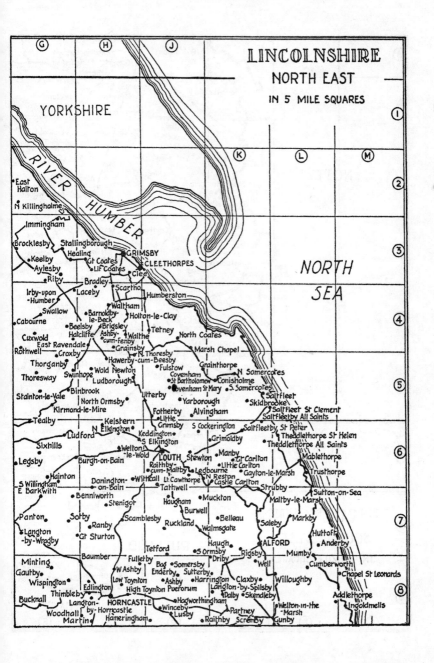

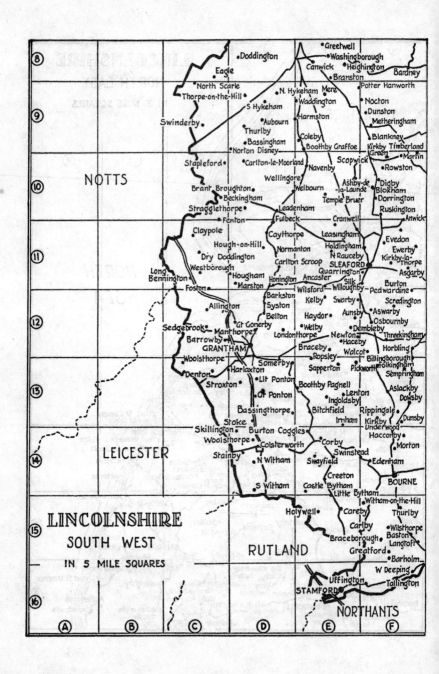

LINCOLNSHIRE

SOUTH WEST

IN 5 MILE SQUARES

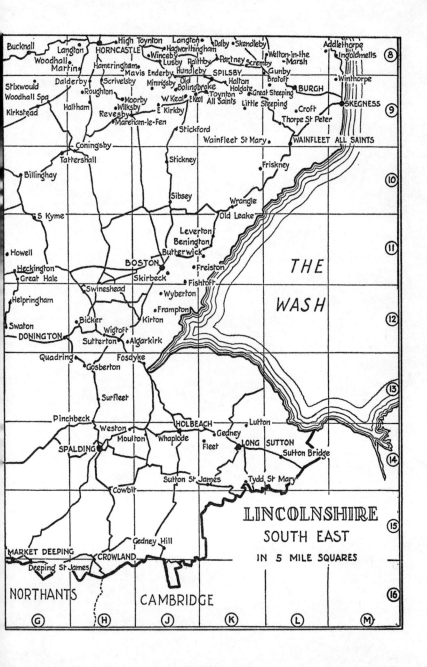

ILLUSTRATIONS

DISCOVERING LINCOLNSHIRE

A JOURNEY away from the main lines of communication into one of the least known of the English counties is a rewarding experience. Lincolnshire fulfils all the expectations of the traveller who looks for new things in a quiet and attractive countryside. Apart from the world-renowned Cathedral at Lincoln and its wealth of fine churches, of which Boston Stump, a magnificent 15th century parish church is perhaps the outstanding example, little is known of this large county, second only to Yorkshire in size. To most people the mention of Lincolnshire produces an immediate picture of a flat and wet county. But the tourist will find that, apart from the Fens, it is not flat and meteorological records prove it to be one of the driest counties of England.

Throughout its history Lincolnshire has been an insular county. Natural barriers have made entry into this part of England difficult. Its eastern boundary is the North Sea open only to invaders coming from the Continent. The Fens in the south-east have for much of their history been impassable swamps and meres; the River Trent on the west is a major river divide and in the north the River Humber has effectively limited north–south movement. The one great corridor of overland migration into the County has been along the limestone ridge extending from north Lincolnshire across England to the Cotswolds. In prehistoric times, many of the earliest settlers from the populous and developing region of Wessex found their way along this highway into the County. The other points for the reception of immigrants have been the estuaries of the Humber and the Wash and from the Bronze Age onwards seafaring peoples, looking for a landfall in eastern England, found a haven in these estuaries and moved up the rivers to settle in Lincolnshire. This picture of an insular and inaccessible county, although modified by the Romans with their fine roads, drainage, and canal systems, remained basically true until the advent of motor transport, and even today it is pleasant to take a journey on the roads of Lincolnshire which are far less congested than those of many other counties.

Lincolnshire is divided into three administrative counties, similar to the Ridings of Yorkshire, and known as the Parts of Holland, the Parts of Kesteven, and the Parts of Lindsey, each with its own County Council. Their names are interesting: Holland means "hollow land" and although it appeared in Domesday Book it has not very much early history, for it was largely under water for long periods of time; Kesteven includes a Celtic word "coed" meaning wood and was clearly a richly wooded territory and had a royal forest within its boundaries from Norman times until the 13th century; Lindsey, whose name means "the island of the Lindissi", was the territory of the people who lived near Lincoln (*Lindum colonia* of the Romans). It enjoyed the status of a kingdom and its list of kings has come down to us from Anglo-Saxon times. One of the early Anglian kings of Lindsey, who was probably born *c.* AD 570, has an interesting name, Coedbead. The first syllable is Celtic *Cad*, a battle, and may point to intermarriage between the Celts of Lindsey and their Anglian conquerors. Lindsey never was an important kingdom though in area it was as large as others that played a significant part in recorded history. When the Anglian population responded to the Christian Gospel, Lindsey received Paulinus, who came from Rome with St Augustine in 597. He baptised people in the Trent and preached in Lincoln. Shortly afterwards Lindsey had its bishop and we have a list from 678 to 869 and again from 953 to 1004. Lindsey's boundaries then were much the same as the boundaries today; it was surrounded for the most part by sea and fen which isolation helped to preserve its identity as a distinct kingdom or district.

In area, Lincolnshire comprises approximately 1,700,000 acres— 270,000 in Holland; 470,000 in Kesteven and 960,000 in Lindsey. Apart from the larger centres of population in Lincoln, Scunthorpe, Grimsby, Cleethorpes, Louth, Grantham, Stamford, and Boston, the rural parish with under 300 inhabitants is typical of Lincolnshire. Their character clearly reflects the agricultural history of the region. They have evolved as centres of population serving the farming community: their physical form has changed very little with the passage of time. The church and the manor have been the two central features and life has revolved around them. The present movement away from the land stimulated by the mechanisation of the farms is creating a new situation. Some villages are shrinking and the problem of redundant churches and houses is pressing. Many villages will disappear as they did under economic and other pressures in the late Middle Ages, but in time a balance must be found and it is hoped that many of the fine churches and houses will be saved. Some of the wold and cliff villages, particularly those nearer to the towns, are being repopulated by those wishing to live in the countryside or to spend their leisure in these pleasant situations.

Each administrative division has its own natural characteristics.

Holland is a flat area of fenland and marsh with deep dykes that provide drainage for the rich agricultural land which produces some of the finest crops of wheat, sugar beet, and potatoes in the County. Kesteven is extremely varied and still has many acres of attractive woodland. Its low hills and pleasant villages are set among warm brown soils that are so typical of this part of the County. The limestone plateau in Kesteven is wide and wooded but narrows northwards until north of Lincoln, in Lindsey, it is only a few miles wide. Lindsey is as diverse as it is large. Some of the finest scenic areas are in the Wolds and it is a moving experience to travel along the Blue Stone Heath road to enjoy the long and changing vistas across the rolling chalk country. Many of its roads along the ridges originated as prehistoric trackways, following the highest ground in the County. The Lincolnshire Edge, a steep escarpment on the west, overlooking the broad Trent Valley, is another route that is worthy of special note and offers a magnificent panorama including in the north-west the surprise view of the confluence of the rivers Trent, Humber, and Ouse at Alkborough which is worth the long journey needed to discover it. Lindsey also has its carr-land with deep rich black soils in the Ancholme Valley and the Isle of Axholme. This "island" is cut off from the rest of the County by the lower course of the Trent and has as its other boundaries the rivers Idle, Torne, and Don with connective drainage channels. The area is nearly 50,000 acres. Drainage in this region has changed low-lying meres and peat fen into a fertile agricultural and horticultural area. The story began in the 17th century when Vermuyden was commissioned to employ Dutch methods of drainage. This was at first sternly resisted by the local people and there were riotous scenes. The Dutchmen were attacked and the work held up. However, after a long and difficult struggle the operation was successful and the benefits that it brought to this part of the County were enormous.

The coast of Lindsey has undergone many changes due to incursions of the sea on to the marshland. At one time the eastern edge of the Wolds formed a chalk cliff but the wave-cut platform is now covered with rich marshland clay which provides some of the finest grazing in the County. The coast between Mablethorpe and Skegness is still exposed to the erosion of the sea. A single line of sand-dunes, now reinforced by great concrete sea-walls, many built after the serious flooding of 1953, protect the marshland from inundation. Farther north there is an area where mud and sand are deposited to form great salt-marshes and a similar area of deposition occurs south of Skegness and includes the famous Skegness and

Gibraltar Point Nature Reserve, one of the finest stretches of natural beauty in the County.

The area of the County that has undergone the most revolutionary changes is the fenland. The Romans first effectively brought this part of the County into cultivation. They realised its potential and their engineers devised a series of wide canals to serve both for drainage and transport. As drains, with subsidiary channels, they acted as catch-waters and took the water from the uplands and as canals they linked the fenland with the Witham at Lincoln which was in turn joined by means of the Fossdyke canal with the Trent which gave barges laden with corn access to the Ouse and so to York. This must have been an important government-sponsored scheme using native labour, and the mosaic of farms to be seen from the air bear an unmistakable native appearance indicating that the Romans allowed them to use farming methods with which they were familiar. After reverting to swamps again in Saxon times, the Holland and Witham Fens were finally drained during the second half of the 18th century, but it was not until the early years of the 19th century that the enormous east and west fens were drained and brought under cultivation. In 1799, Arthur Young described a visit to the East Fen: "Sir Joseph Banks had the goodness to order a boat, and accompanied me into the heart of the fen, which in the wet season had appeared as a chain of lakes, bordered by great crops of reeds." It was rich in fauna and flora and the bird-life included many of the rarest species then found in the County. The ten duck decoys in the East Fen are said to have sent as many as 31,000 ducks to London markets in one season in *c.* 1800. Today, there is little evidence of this former fenland and to discover a corner suitable as a nature reserve is impossible. All is cultivated but along the margins are remnants of fen-carr with characteristic plants and insects that recapitulate its former history.

It is evident that agriculture dominates the life and activity of the County. Lincolnshire is the principal agricultural County of England with 80% of the total area of nearly 1,700,000 acres under cultivation. The principal crops are barley, wheat, potatoes and sugar beet, and the farms are also noted for the Lincoln Red Shorthorn cattle which has been bred in the County since the middle of the 19th century; the Lincolnshire Longwool sheep is typical of the farms on the wolds and heath and the Lincolnshire Curly Coat pig is favoured by the pig farmers. Modern farming methods are altering the character of the farms and the landscape is changing. It is now quite common to see field boundaries being changed; hedges uprooted and drainage improved. Large units suitable for machines are now replacing the smaller farms and the buildings have altered in character and appearance.

In a county with such varied geological structure, the surface extraction of minerals is a considerable industry. Ironstone is quarried from rich beds in several places. The Frodingham ironstone is worked along 7 miles of outcrop near Scunthorpe and forms the major supply for the steel industry which has some of the most up-to-date rolling mills in Europe. Near Grantham and Colsterworth the Marlstone and Northampton beds yield rich deposits and near Caistor underground mining is employed to obtain Claxby ironstone. There are enormous reserves sufficient for almost 200 years. Large cement works at Kirton Lindsey using Lincolnshire Limestone and at Barton-upon-Humber using chalk are important industrial processes. The extraction of sand and gravel is now a feature of the river valleys and there is still a little quarrying of clay for brick-making though this use of the County's abundant supply of natural clay suitable for this purpose has greatly reduced. All the natural resources have contributed to the industrial life of the principal towns but many raw materials now have to be brought into the County by rail, road, and shipping. Immingham now accepts major imports of oil and petroleum, iron ore for Scunthorpe's steel mills, pyrites, ilmenites, and sulphur for factories on the Humber Bank, and great quantities of timber and pit wood. It is interesting to recall that this rapidly developing industrial zone and seaport was in 1609 the scene of the quiet departure of the Pilgrim Fathers for Holland.

But not only is the land of Lincolnshire full of interest—the towns and villages all have something to offer to the visitor. Dominant in the landscape, with its characteristic long vistas, is the village church, many with fine towers and spires. The finest Saxon church is at Barton-upon-Humber and is one of the most remarkable buildings of its period in England. In the Middle Ages Barton's busy port received ferries from across the Humber which made it a focal point for trade and travellers and brought considerable wealth to the town. Indeed, Barton has two major churches and offers the tourist a feast of good things. Another rich example of the massive monumental parish church of England, built in Saxon times, is to be found at Stow. It was further developed by the Normans and may well be more than a parish church and have served as the base of missionary enterprise in the region. These are outstanding examples and in themselves make a visit to Lincolnshire memorable, but other

5

parish churches have their Saxon work, mainly in the shape of long-and-short quoins at the angles of naves or towers or the decorative inter-lace work that may be seen on stone built into the later fabric. The one area where no Saxon work survives is in the fens. Much of the fenland was flooded at this time but evidence may yet be found to show that where the ground was above flood level early Saxon buildings existed, to be replaced by such magnificent churches as those at Sutterton and Algarkirk. Around the fens there are many fine Norman features in the churches and at Crowland, the most important abbey in the County, the west front of the south aisle is rich in Norman work and the naves of Frieston, Deeping St James, and Bourne are all Norman survivals of great monastic churches.

Other features, almost confined to Lindsey, are the impressive Saxo-Norman towers of such churches as Clee, Rothwell near Caistor, Marton in the Trent Valley, and two outstanding examples in Lincoln High Street—St Mary-le-Wigford and St Peter-at-Gowts—with another striking example at Bracebridge on the Brant Road just within the City boundary. An example in Kesteven may be seen at Great Hale. The great wealth of architecture is, however, of the 13th, 14th, and 15th centuries and few counties can boast of more fine examples of mediaeval churches than Lincolnshire. The area south of Lincoln to Grantham and again into the south-east to include Sleaford, Heckington, Boston, and Spalding is very rewarding. Many reflect the great wealth of the County derived from the wool trade in the Middle Ages. The list of fine churches is considerable but Stamford, Pinchbeck, Moulton, Holbeach, Long Sutton, Swineshead, Helpringham, Deeping St James, Gedney, Tattershall, Thornton Curtis, Louth, and Bottesford all demand a visit. The marshland has its own outstanding examples—Theddle-thorpe All Saints, known as the Cathedral of the marshland and South Somercotes, the Queen of the marsh.

The visitor to Lincolnshire must look further than the wealth of parish churches. There are other architectural treasures to be discovered and these are not alone in Lincoln and the larger towns in the County. Castles are not numerous, but Ralph Cromwell's elaborate brick-built moated castle near the River Witham at Tattershall, now in the care of the National Trust, is quite outstanding and possibly the finest tower of its period in England. It is unusual in being built in the fenland area and it is still not clear why the site was chosen. Fifteenth century in date, it formed part of a group of buildings which included a collegiate church, a school, and almshouses. The collegiate buildings have recently been seen by excavation and they too show the same dignified use of brick for walls, gateways, and turrets. In the north, Thornton Abbey with its moats and magnificent brick gatehouse and barbican with two rounded turrets, leads into a fascinating site where excavations undertaken by the Ministry of Public Building and Works have opened up the church with its chapels, the monastic quarters, and the octagonal chapter-house. An excellent guide book is available. Another architectural gem is the Old Hall at Gainsborough; notable among its 15th century features is the Great Hall with its fine open timber roof with arched braces nearly up to the ridge. Again much brick was employed in this building and the tower, although smaller and later in date, is reminiscent of Tattershall Castle. The only stonework is in the bay window of the Great Hall. The west and east ranges are of the 16th century with Elizabethan features and some impressive timber-framing. Again the care of the Ministry of Public Building and Works in restoration and the local enthusiasm of the members of the Gainsborough Old Hall Trust has contributed to the survival and use of this splendid hall which was generously made available to them by its owner Sir Edmund Bacon. Old Bolingbroke is another site worth seeing. Here a castle that goes back to William de Roumare, 1st earl of Lincoln, in the 11th century and later was associated with John of Gaunt and the birth of his son Henry of Bolingbroke, is slowly emerging from its grass mounds as the Ministry excavators carefully uncover its defences. In Kesteven, there is another similar example at Somerton Castle with a square plan and prominent towers built in the late 13th century. Here more of the castle is standing; one of the corner towers is more or less complete and there are remains of another. Not far away from it at Temple Bruer, where excavations have proved the presence of a Round Church of the Knights Templars, a 13th century tower has recently been restored through the co-operation of the owner, the Kesteven County Council and the Ministry.

Of the great houses of Lincolnshire, the one that immediately springs to mind is Grimsthorpe Castle, home of the Earl of Ancaster, Lord Lieutenant of Lincolnshire. This is unquestionably the greatest country house of the County and is associated with one of the County's most distinguished families. The magnificent Vanbrugh north front is fine in its proportions and widely accepted as one of the architect's best designs. Belton House, home of Lord Brownlow, is a good late 17th century house built in rich Ancaster stone and with few rivals in the country. It is open to visitors and in its furnishings and pictures has many national treasures. The Earl of Yarborough lives at Brocklesby House in the north-east of the County. It has been extensively altered but is basically 18th century in date. Standing in a fine park it has many interesting ancillary buildings including a majestic classical mausoleum built in the late 18th century on a low mound to the south of the Park. Gunby Hall, built in 1700 for Sir William Massingberd, is another of the less pretentious country houses, now in the care of the National Trust, but illustrating the restrained use of brick to produce a simple but satisfying design. Of the earlier houses, Doddington Hall is an outstanding example of the Elizabethan house and belongs to a famous group including Wollaton Hall, Nottingham, and Hardwick Hall. Surrounded by large trees, it is quite exciting to discover this magnificent brick house with its turrets and domed cupolas. Knaith Hall is another Elizabethan brick house with later modifications including a 19th century timber-framed front. In the Wolds, Harrington Hall has Elizabethan work in its west front but was developed in the 17th century: it is a fine house with Tennyson associations and set in a beautiful garden associated with "Maud".

All the towns of Lincolnshire have their gems of domestic architecture. The list is too long to give in any detail but Stamford, one of the finest stone-built towns in England, has impressive buildings and churches in abundance; Boston, already noted in connection with its church, has many fine houses and historic buildings to reward the visitor; Spalding, famous for its bulb industry, has streets and riverside that include terraces of attractive houses and individual buildings of note; Grantham, a town with a wealth of history stretching back into the Middle Ages, is a busy centre studded with historic buildings waiting to be discovered among later developments; Louth has a charm of its own with many quaint vistas and buildings of great interest presided over by the glorious church with its majestic spire set right at the heart of the town and dominating the scene for miles around. The market centres at Brigg, Caistor, Horncastle, Spilsby, Alford, and Sleaford each have their own appeal and here and there fragments that remind the visitor of their ancient history.

For those who prefer to discover their local history in terms of the personalities involved Lincolnshire offers characters widespread in time and interest. Literature is represented by Alfred Lord Tennyson, Victoria's Poet Laureate, who was born at Somersby and deeply influenced by the Lincolnshire landscape and its people; science claims Sir Isaac Newton, distinguished early 18th century President of the Royal Society, born at Woolsthorpe and an original member of the Spalding Gentlemen's Society; exploration is immortally linked with many famous names, among whom are Sir Joseph Banks of Revesby, naturalist and associate of Captain Cook in his journeys round the world; Matthew Flinders of Donington and George Bass of Aswarby named many of their places of discovery in Australia after Lincolnshire towns and villages. Sir John Franklin of Spilsby was another pioneer explorer and disappeared in his attempt to discover the North-West Passage. Religious leaders have come from this County: Saint Gilbert, founder of the Gilbertine Order came from Sempringham; John Wesley, who was born at Epworth, was the founder of Methodism; Archbishop Stephen Langton, associated with Magna Carta, came from Langton-by-Wragby; Archbishop John Whitgift, was born at Grimsby and Thomas Cooper, the Chartist, originated at Gainsborough. The list could be greatly extended. Churches throughout the County hold memorials to many of its distinguished sons and daughters—the personalities of the County who have contributed to the history of England and the discovery of the world.

This is a fascinating county to explore and it is hoped that this new edition of Arthur Mee's popular guide book will encourage many to make journeys into its countryside and towns. This revision could not have been undertaken without the help of many friends. In the midst of a very busy life to travel up and down the County to check up all the facts involved was impossible but members of the Lincolnshire Local History Society have generously helped by supplying notes and criticisms of the earlier editions. These have been incorporated, but the reviser is conscious that much still remains to be done. Further notes will be welcomed for future editions: the County is constantly changing—development is taking its toll of older buildings despite every effort to save those of historic interest. To all who have helped and by their efforts are contributing in so many ways to the life and study of this County, the writer offers a warm expression of thanks.

Addlethorpe. It lies in the flat country round Skegness, and is a mile from the sea.

The finely embattled marshland church is a rich example of a 15th century building, though it lost its chancel in 1706, traces of the old chancel arch being visible in the brick walling at the east end. Pinnacles and gargoyles adorn the sturdy tower, and surmounting the six pinnacled buttresses on the north side of the church are winged figures, human and grotesque; some hold scrolls now hard to read, one of them proclaiming: "Of God's saying comes no ill."

The porch is a joy to behold—its buttresses adorned with angels, its moulding with flowers and heads below a parapet carved with trailing foliage, and its gable cross adorned with sculptures of the Crucifixion and the Madonna and Child. Its outer doorway is dotted with flowers, and above it is a lovely niche; within are fine old roof beams, a holy water stoup, a niche, and a stone inscribed with a prayer for the soul of John Godard "that this porch made".

An old traceried door with a wicket opens to an interior which is filled with light streaming through unstained glass and is rich with fine old woodwork. The clerestoried nave, with its arcades of five bays, has a partly-restored roof enriched with traceried arcading, floral bosses, and nine long-skirted wooden figures. The roof of the south aisle is largely old work and has floral bosses and figures of men and women. The old oak benches have carved arm-rests and poppyheads, one showing two birds in a tree preening their feathers and a quaint little man in the tree-top. Rising from the poppyheads in the nave are 11 old candlesticks. The chancel screen, now spanning the blocked arch, is coloured and gilded. The tower screen has a raised inscription asking a prayer for John Dudeck and his wife, and there are screens enclosing chapels in the aisles.

Other relics of the past are the traceried font with an embattled edge; piscinas in the aisles; fragments of fine glass showing angels and priests and elaborate canopy-work; and 15th century floorstones. Of an 18th century gentleman who lies in the north aisle we read that he was plain in his form but rich in mind, and religious, quiet, honest, meek, and kind.

In the churchyard is a fragment of an old cross.

Aisthorpe. Lying at the foot of the Cliff, 6 miles north of Lincoln, it has a church which was rebuilt in 1867 and ministers also to Thorpe-in-the-Fallows, a hamlet which lost its own church long ago. Standing in the fields, with its imposing broach spire rising grey above dark and trim churchyard yews, Aisthorpe Church crowns a pleasant landscape of green and fertile countryside. Its registers reflect the story of the parish from as far back as 1593.

Alford. Busy with the flourishing market held in its spacious square, and with its annual bull fair, this pleasant little marshland town just below the Wolds has a long main street still wearing the gracious air of more leisurely days. Here are bow-windowed shops and Georgian houses, and thatched cottages all in haphazard array. There is even a white-walled thatched inn with a prancing White Horse sign, and, most charming of all, an old thatched manor house shaped like the letter H that has recently been given to the town by a generous local resident and is now managed by the Alford and District Civic Trust. Recent work on the building has revealed a major part of the timber-frame of a house built about 1540. Major alterations were made between 1700 and 1720 when the present brick façade was built round the timber-frame. It is a rare sight in the heart of a market town. Another fine sight is the Alford tower-mill, one of the most attractive in the county, and recently restored.

Alford's church is chiefly 14th century work, restored and partly rebuilt in 1869 when the tower was heightened and an outer north aisle added. The south porch has an upper room, and shelters a fine old traceried door with a wicket.

The interior is impressive because of its great width and its big array of pillars and arches in the three arcades. (The capitals of the two old arcades have beautiful carving of foliage.) There are three splendid 14th century sedilia with crocketed gables, and of the same period are fragments of glass in chancel and vestry windows. The restored chancel screen is late 14th century work, and the richly-carved pulpit is Jacobean, with modern support and stairway.

On their great marble tomb in the chancel lie the alabaster figures of Sir Robert Christopher and his wife, with their heads on tasselled cushions. The town's almshouses, rebuilt in 1870, were originally founded in 1668 with a bequest by Sir Robert.

A tragic period in Alford's history began on a summer's day in 1630 when the vicar wrote in his register the awesome words "The plague begins". The scourge lingered on until the following February, having in those dread months carried off no fewer than 132 of the townsfolk. A link with those unhappy far-off days is to be seen under a weeping ash on the lawn of the old manor house at Tothby (a thatched farmhouse now, north of the town). A stone about a yard square—doubtless the base of an old cross originally—it was used as a plague stone during the pestilence, probably on the road to Spilsby. The countryfolk would bring their produce from the villages and lay it on the stone, and the townsfolk would purify their money by dipping it in vinegar in the hole cut in the stone.

Algarkirk. Its name recalls Earl Alfgar, who fell in battle at Stow Green while successfully defending South Lincolnshire against the Danes in 870. It tells, too, of a fine mediaeval church.

Standing on the edge of a park, its central tower and leaded spire rising above embattled walls and beautiful traceried windows, the church underwent costly restoration in 1850, with Richard Carpenter as architect, at the expense of Basil Beridge, who was rector here for nearly 60 years. This restoration gave the 13th century tower its belfry windows and pyramid spire, and the chancel its east window and rich colour scheme; the north aisle was restored and the south porch rebuilt, new roofs were fixed, and the interior was given its oak furnishings.

Striking is the great array of windows, all of them (except those of the clerestory) shining with a medley of colour blending well with the golden-tinted stonework. The long lines of the nave clerestory, with 10 three-light windows on each side, and the clerestory of the transepts, are 15th century. The rest of the windows are chiefly 14th century, and some of them, like the great windows of the transepts, have the beautiful flowing tracery typical of the close of the period.

The double aisles of the transepts are a remarkable feature for a village church. Their arcades, and those of the nave, are 13th century, some of the nave pillars being carved with nail-head and others with carving of leaves.

The chancel has its 13th century double piscina and locker, and the south transept a handsome canopied piscina of the 15th century. Other links with the past are a few glass fragments in the vestry window, the font bowl of Purbeck marble on a rebuilt base, five bells of 1662, the stone figures of a priest in his robes and a 14th century civilian, and the brass portraits of Nicholas Robertson of 1498 and his two wives. Nicholas, a merchant of the Staple of Calais, wears a furred gown, with a purse hanging from his girdle; his wives are slender figures in tightly-fitting gowns with girdles.

A mile south of the village is a disused woad mill, a long brick building now used for farm implements, a reminder that woad was once grown in the rich land hereabouts. The mill ceased to work in 1921.

Alkborough. Rich in natural charms is this village, for it stands on the high Cliff ridge overlooking Trent Falls, where Trent and Ouse become the Humber. There are splendid views into Yorkshire (with York Minster coming into the picture), and a delightful Cliff walk above the river to Burton-on-Stather. Half a mile along the road to Burton on the left stands old Walcot Hall (Walcot Manor), a charming house of Tudor and later times, with lovely gardens and magnificent trees. On the opposite side of the road, hidden behind a stone wall, is Walcot Hall, a charming house of Georgian and later periods.

In the south-west corner of the village is the site of a Roman camp—originally a square enclosure with fosse and vallum—known as the Countess Close, after the Countess Lucy, wife of Ivo Tailbois, who owned the manor in Norman times. Another survival from ancient times, and much rarer, is a maze called Julian's Bower. It is not a puzzle formed of tall hedges, like the famous maze at Hampton Court, but a tortuous pattern cut in the turf, as at Hilton in Huntingdonshire and Wing in Rutland. Alkborough's maze, 44 feet across, is believed to have been made in the 12th century by the monks of a small cell established here as a cell of Spalding Priory. The turf has been re-cut to show the outline of the maze, but a plan, in black-and-white stone in the floor of the church's fine oak porch, is a perpetual reminder of its character.

The story of the church goes back to the middle of the 11th century, when Thorold gave it to his priory of Spalding; and the lower portion of the fine unbuttressed tower may be of his time. Serving as a foundation stone for the north side of its tall, narrow arch is a stone with lattice pattern, believed to be part of a Saxon or early Norman cross; it may be seen by lifting a loose stone.

The rest of the tower, with its great gargoyles, belongs chiefly to the 13th century, when much of the church was rebuilt. The lovely south doorway enriched with billet and dog-tooth moulding, and the fine nave arcades, all belong to this period. The aisles have later mediaeval windows, and above one of them (outside) is a huge stone grotesque. The font has a Norman bowl, and there is also a massive old stoup.

The dignified chancel was rebuilt in 13th century style in Victorian times and has lancet windows framed in the decorative arcading of the walls. Glowing in soft colours in the triple-lancet east window are Our Lord in Glory, St John the Baptist, and the Madonna; and in the top of the window is a picture of the ancient maze.

Old yews grow like green pyramids in the churchyard for the gravestones have been removed to reveal a fine green sward pierced by the shaft of an old churchyard cross with marks made by the sharpening of scythes, swords, and other implements.

Allington. East and west have met here (East and West Allington) and now the twain are inseparable, forming a secluded village near the Leicestershire border, with two towerless churches.

St Andrew's of East Allington, a simple little building with some 13th century remains in its walls, now stands dilapidated and forlorn. Holy Trinity of West Allington is happier in its pretty setting in the grounds of the hall. This church, which has a 12th century arcade and a Jacobean pulpit, had the poet George Crabbe as rector for about 25 years; but he can seldom have ministered here, for he lived at the parsonage of his other living—Muston, across the border—and too often left a curate in charge of both parishes.

Althorpe. A busy Trentside village, it is close to the Keadby bridge, which has carried road and rail across the river since 1916. This colossal steel structure has a lifting span 165 feet long and weighing 3600 tons; it is operated by two electric motors, each of 115 horse-power. Farther downstream is the village and port of Keadby, where the Trent is joined by the New Idle River, and by the canal which runs across the Isle of Axholme and links the River Don with the Trent.

Althorpe's fine church, by the river, comes from the 15th century, the nave with its tall, leaning arcade being a little earlier than the tower and the chancel built in 1483 by Sir John Neville. His arms (with those of Newmarch and Mowbray—all now worn) are on the tower, which has a lovely west doorway with an ogee arch enriched in its hollow mouldings by carved leaves and flowers and human faces; between the doorway and the west window is a band of flowers and heads.

The chancel has a 15th century screen (much restored and with a modern canopy), three lovely sedilia with projecting and crocketed ogee canopies looking like crowns (one of them vaulted), slender pinnacled buttresses, and a band of flowers under the embattled cornice. Beside the sedilia is a simple trefoiled piscina. The font, adorned by a band of flowers, is another 500-year-old relic.

During the restoration of the church in 1868 several coats of white-wash were removed from the bench of the sedilia and it was found to be a stone slab with the fine little brass portrait of a 14th century rector, William de Lound, wearing a flowing robe with four-leaved flower ornament on the collar.

Alvingham. Inseparable from this village is North Cockerington (though between them run the River Lud and the canal joining Louth with the sea), and the reason is that their churches both stand in Alvingham's tree-fringed churchyard, hidden away behind an old farmhouse and a watermill, and looking across fields which stretch to the coast 6 miles away.

The story of this curious (but not unique) circumstance of two churches in one churchyard goes back to the 12th century when a Gilbertine priory was founded at Alvingham. The church of St Mary was the priory chapel, and was given at an early date to the village of North Cockerington, whose own church had fallen into ruin. The second church, St Adelwold's, has always been the village church of Alvingham.

Restored in 1841, St Mary's Church has a low 18th century tower, a chancel arch and small nave arcade of the 13th century, and the head of a Norman window in the north wall of the chancel. The font, set on the base of a Norman pillar, comes from the beginning of the 14th century, and so does the battered figure of an armoured knight, with the lion on which his feet once rested. The nave is filled with trim box-pews.

For a hundred years St Adelwold's Church was closed and neglected, but in 1933 it was beautifully restored in memory of Robert Armstrong Yerburgh, MP, who died in 1916. A fitting tribute it is, for in the church chest were found documents showing that the Yerburghs had been associated with Alvingham for 800 years. Most of the old work in the church is 14th century. The embattled tower has a richly-moulded arch on corbels, the 14th century font is on an inverted 13th century capital, and there are three little sprays of leaves in old glass. The modern woodwork is in pleasing harmony with the simple interior.

No other church in England is dedicated to the Saxon saint Adelwold (or Ethelwald), who became Bishop of Lindisfarne. He was a monk at Ripon before he went to live a solitary life where St Cuthbert had lived, in a cell on the island of Farne. There he spent 12 years, and once, the venerable Bede relates, calmed a storm which was threatening some of his visitors. He was laid to rest beside St Cuthbert at Lindisfarne.

Ancaster. An attractive stone-built settlement set in pleasant wooded countryside midway between Grantham and Sleaford, it was an important place in Roman Lincolnshire and still has things to show which make the battered mediaeval cross in its street seem young.

Standing on Ermine Street (hereabouts called the High Dyke, and very well defined), it was the last Roman town on this famous old way before Lincoln was reached. Believed to be the Roman Causennae, the defences enclose nine acres, its rampart and ditch well marked and seen at its best at a corner opposite the church. Thousands of coins have been found here, 2000 of them in one spot, like a miser's hoard; many Ancaster people are said to have traded with them in the 18th century.

Excavations to study and date the Roman defences have been undertaken by Nottingham University and an extensive Roman cemetery has been found in the modern west cemetery.

Among other remains unearthed here and in the neighbourhood were a mosaic pavement, a fragment of Roman wall 7 feet wide (near Ancaster Hall), and a kiln with some pottery and coins north of the village, by Ermine Street. Clay moulds for the production of Roman coins by casting have also been found. A small altar, a milestone of

Constantine I, and some Roman sculpture are in the museum at Grantham.

Ancaster has fame apart from its Roman story, for it has given its name to the stone which has built many of our old churches and many modern buildings, too. This limestone, notable for its special quality of hardening soon after exposure, is quarried here and in greater measure at Wilsford nearby.

The vicarage and the church (striking with its elaborate panelled parapets) are both of this native stone, the house a centenarian, the church going back 800 years. The chancel has a Norman corbel table outside, under its roof, and the 14th century tower has the slenderest of 15th century spires. Between the clerestoried nave and north aisle is a massive Norman arcade with round pillars and cushion capitals. The fine font with its interlacing arches is late Norman work.

In the restored nave roof are eight old wooden figures with shields and musical instruments, and, facing each other in the porch, are two much-worn stone priests, one with a chalice, the other at prayer.

Anderby Creek. This is a fine place to laze in upon a summer's day—a restful, unspoiled little seaside resort with a fine stretch of golden sands. Two miles inland is Anderby village church, built in the 18th century, it has chancel and apse of Victorian times. In the churchyard stands part of an ancient cross.

Anwick. A quiet village of the Fens. The 13th century church has a tall tower and spire of 14th century.

The north doorway, with nail-head ornament on its capitals, and the north arcade, with dog-tooth moulding on its four arches, belong to the 13th century. The south arcade is a little later, but both are on clustered piers and decorated with little mediaeval heads. In the tracery of some of the aisle windows are a few fragments of ancient glass, and by the chancel arch is a headless mediaeval sculpture of the Madonna and Child, found when the rood-loft doorway was opened up during restoration last century. A Norman pillar piscina is another point of interest.

A brass inscription tells of Samuel Pogson, who served as church-warden for 50 years and died in 1922; he saw much change here—the chancel completely rebuilt, the spire restored after being struck by lightning, new oak roofs given to nave and aisles. In the church-yard is a fragment of an ancient cross.

Appleby. A pretty village on Ermine Street, it has a little elm-shaded green and a lovely church (partly rebuilt last century) with a rich array of battlements, pinnacles, and gargoyles, as well as a great variety of flowers, animals, mediaeval folk, angels, and dragons carved on its corbel table.

In the west wall of the nave (near the tower) is herringbone masonry of Norman days, and there is also a fine Norman font with bold interlaced arcading. The tower is mainly work of the 13th and 15th centuries, and the nave has 13th century arcades, the clustered pillars on each side having "hold-water" base moulding. The chancel arch is 15th century. Crowning the nave is a fine modern roof with rich wall-plates and 14 angels on the hammerbeams.

A happy blending of old and new is the pedestal pulpit; it has a pinnacled canopy like a rich crown, and fine panels with carved coats-of-arms and 15 sacred scenes, including the Nativity, the Flight into Egypt, and the story of Joseph. These are believed to be Flemish of the 16th century.

The chancel has richly-carved altar-rails and a traceried tomb. The east window, with leaf tracery, shines with the brilliant colours of Capronnier's glass, showing the Crucifixion and two Old Testament scenes. A Kemp window in the south aisle has figures of Noah, St John the Baptist, and Moses, with pictures of the Ark, the Lamb, and the Tables of Stone.

A clock in the tower is notable because it has no face and merely strikes the hours on the big bell. It was given by a farmer churchwarden who wanted the men in the fields to hear the passing hours but said that if other people wanted to know the minutes they could look at their own clocks.

Asgarby. An attractive village east of Sleaford, looks up to a massive 15th century tower with a spire seen from far across the neighbouring Fens. The tower has a rich parapet decked with a row of grotesque animal heads and shields, and from its pinnacles spring flying buttresses to support the crocketed spire.

The aisle and the clerestory which floods the church with light are also 15th century; the nave is 14th, and the chancel, with its priest's doorway and piscina, is 13th. Halfway up in the splay of this doorway is a chalice-shaped recess with a little hole at each side, suggesting that a chalice was kept here, locked up by a bar; it is a little mystery.

The church has its mediaeval font and ancient chest, and on a wall is a painting of a kneeling figure still clear after five centuries. Above the tall tower arch is a 17th century fresco with emblems of man's mortality—skeleton, crossbones, and hourglass—and the admonition "Redeem the Time". One of the windows has 19th century glass portraying the Supper at Emmaus, and another has modern glass of Jesus ascending into Heaven, guarded by four angels.

Asgarby Hall stands south of the church and is an attractive 19th century Gothic building.

Ashby-cum-Fenby. Over a field and past a fragrant lime is the way to church in this quiet village at the foot of the Wolds. By the churchyard, set in charming gardens, are the little red almshouses built of brick in 1641 by Lady Frances Wray.

The south wall of the nave, with a plain Norman doorway, is the oldest part of the church. The tower is chiefly 13th century, and dog-tooth ornament enriches its two-light belfry windows. The nave arcade, with its three round arches and clustered shafts, was built at the close of the Norman period, but its pointed arch is 14th century. The chancel is chiefly 14th century work, and two of its windows have a little of their original glass.

A mediaeval oak screen is across the tower arch, there is a 15th century font adorned with roundels of tracery, and an old iron collecting-box is set in a Norman shaft piscina with a scalloped capital. The oldest monument lies under the tower, the early 14th century figure of an unknown knight in chain-mail and bearing sword and shield; his legs are crossed and a lion is at his feet.

The aisle has the splendid monument of Sir William Wray of 1617 and his lady Frances. There they lie, under a great stone canopy supported by 10 classical columns. Sir William, wearing light armour and a ruff, with a book between his hands, and his lady resting her head on an embroidered cushion. By her side is a daughter in heavy drapery, and lying placidly at Sir William's feet is a little child in bonnet and dress trimmed with lace. Almost hidden between pillars is their son, kneeling on one knee and holding a tall hat with a high crown. Susanna Drury, a sister to Lady Frances, has a monument in the chancel, with her figure on a marble table supported by greyhounds, and wreaths and cherubs adorning the great arch above her.

Ashby-de-la-Launde. Once belonged to the Knights Templars of Temple Bruer. The gabled hall, an Elizabethan building, was much altered in the 19th century but is an attractive house. The church stands aloof at the end of an avenue of elms and chestnuts and beeches.

One of four English churches, all in Lincolnshire, dedicated to St Hibald, a missionary who helped to spread the Gospel in these parts some 13 centuries ago, it was rebuilt last century. But the plain 13th century tower still stands (with 14th century parapet and slender spire); and there is a 13th century doorway enriched with nail-head and tooth ornament, and a 14th century north arcade which has been walled-up, though its pillars and arches are free. The font, with its band of four-petalled flowers, is as old as the arcade.

Once there were monuments here to the de la Laundes, the

family who acquired the manor in the 14th century by marriage with the Ashbys, and whose name gives this village its distinction from the other Lincolnshire Ashbys. Sir Thomas de la Launde was one of the two Lancastrian leaders who were executed at Stamford after their defeat in the Battle of Losecoat Field, fought in 1470 near Empingham in Rutland.

But all trace of the de la Launde memorials has vanished and the walls of the church now pay tribute to the King (or Kinge) family who succeeded them as lords of the manor. Chief among them is that of Edward Kinge, builder of the hall in 1595, and restorer of this church in 1605, 12 years before his death. The figures of his monument have parted company and are now on opposite walls of the chancel, the brass inscription belonging to them being on the chancel arch. In one niche we see Edward kneeling in armour, one wife before and another behind him; and in another niche are his four daughters, three kneeling, and one in her cradle.

A later and more distinguished holder of the name was Colonel Edward Kinge, whose history is inscribed on a brass set up two centuries after his death by John William King, last survivor of the family, who was vicar of this church for 53 years and paid for its rebuilding in 1854. This tribute to his illustrious ancestor tells how Colonel Edward Kinge, MP, Lord of the Manor, "in time of the General Rebellion espoused the side of the Parliament, and became a prominent commander in the army". Living to deplore its excesses, he sought to avert the danger that impended HM's person, and for these efforts was seized upon by order of the House, October 21, 1648, as for an offence "of dangerous consequence to the army under Lord Fairfax", and was cast into the tower.

"Refusing to acknowledge the powers that followed, he resisted payment of taxes during all the time of the Commonwealth. In January 1660, being returned to Parliament MP for Great Grimsby, he was (as related by the learned Dr Calamy) the first in the House of Commons that moved for the Restoration of King Charles II. The evening of his life was spent in tranquillity here, receiving and befriending the ejected ministers, until his death. He died 1680 and was buried with his ancestors in the chancel."

Ashby Puerorum. Its name means Ashby-of-the-Boys, and had its origin in the fact that an estate here was assigned long ago for the support of the choirboys of Lincoln Cathedral. A tiny place it is, in a delightful part of the Wold country, and reached by deep, winding lanes.

The village church is a sturdy little building of Spilsby Sandstone with toadflax growing from the crannies of its rough stone walls, and, though much restored, still shows its antiquity in the two arches and short round pillar of its 13th century nave arcade. The tower with arch soaring to the roof beams, some of the windows, and the font are 500 years old.

Here in enduring brass is a family of early Tudor days who lived at Stainsby Manor (now a farmhouse) east of the village; they are Richard Lytlebury of 1521, his wife Elizabeth, and six sons and four daughters. Another brass has a fine portrait of a knight in plate armour and mail shirt; and on a floorstone under the altar is a 14th century incised slab to a priest with the figure under a canopy.

North-west of the village is Holbeck Manor, a charming 19th century house in 70 acres of park-like grounds with three lakes. It stands in delightful surroundings developed from an old sandstone quarry.

Aslackby. A quiet and scattered farming village, called by its own people Azelby, it lies by the road from Bourne to Sleaford, where the high lands begin to drop down to the Fens. It has known more important days, for here long ago was a castle, and here the Knights Templars had one of their five preceptories established in Lincolnshire during the Norman period. A mile or so west of the village, too, is the historic spot called Aveland, surrounded by what was once a moat, and giving its name to the Wapentake; here the Thane held his court in Danish or Saxon times, and here, too, the sessions were held under an oak till late in the 19th century.

A few grassy mounds and trenches in a field behind the church keep green the memory of the castle, said to have been built by one of the de Wakes; and fragments of the preceptory are preserved in the grey walls of Temple Farm almost facing the church. When the Templars were suppressed, the preceptory and its lands passed to the Knights Hospitallers. Part of its round church lingered on till the dawn of last century; in 1891 its 14th century gatehouse-tower was pulled down.

The parish church of St James, with its handsome panelled parapets, has a 19th century chancel with 13th century windows. The tower and nave are 15th century. It has lofty and graceful arcades with moulded arches on tall clustered piers, a narrow tower arch reaching almost to the ancient roof timbers, an old font enriched with tracery, shields, and Tudor roses, and a piscina and an aumbry in each of the wide aisles. The south aisle has a doorway to the former rood-loft.

Aswarby. Set in gentle wooded country, its few grey 19th century cottages with square stone chimneys are picturesque against their leafy background near the entrance to the park where once stood the home of the Carre and Whichcote families. The church has a fine 15th century tower and spire, and a nave and south aisle a century older. The chancel and porch are 19th century, but the doorway within the porch is Norman, its arch enriched with bands of zigzag and dog-tooth; and the font, its great bowl on shafts with foliated capitals, is 700 years old. Nave and aisles are filled with high-backed pews, and at one end of the aisle, facing the pulpit, is the even higher manorial pew. High above the 12 clerestory windows are 14 old stone corbels bearing up the roof, each one with a mediaeval face or grotesque mask.

On the nave wall is a 19th century memorial to Marian Whichcote with a charming figure of a woman holding a book inscribed with the Lord's Prayer. Sir Thomas Whichcote, also of the 19th century, has the east window as a memorial with four scenes in the life of Our Lord, and nine angels in the tracery.

A son of the village who also deserves a memorial was George Bass, born here in 1771, who was apprenticed to a surgeon at Boston and became a surgeon in the Navy. He sailed to Sydney in 1795, explored the coast of New South Wales, and in 1798 sailed round Tasmania, proving it to be an island. The channel between Tasmania and Australia is called by his name, Bass Strait.

Aubourn. A quiet place with an ancient story, it lies in the flat lands below the Cliff, where the River Witham turns eastward to receive the waters of the Brant. Where a shady lane sets off to the hamlet of Haddington, across the river, stands a 19th century cross-shaped church with a shingled oak spire; it is in 13th century style, with an apsidal chancel. It is no longer used for worship.

Close to the Hall is the parish church. Only the chancel is left (restored and still used), its walls raised about the year 1200, and still having the original priest's doorway and a lancet window. The east window, a window in the south wall, the open timber roof, and the font with carved shields in quatrefoils are all 14th century work, the font having traces of the locking arrangement fitted in an age which believed in witchcraft. On a wall is a small kneeling figure of Anthony Meres in Elizabethan armour and ruff, his hands gone; and near him is the sculptured bust of Elizabeth Nevile who died in 1745.

There was a church here at the time of Domesday Book (and also a fishery mentioned as worth 1000 eels a year), and Aubourn Rectory was part of the endowment of Belvoir Priory, which appointed the vicars from 1219 until the Dissolution. The list of vicars goes back to 1076, one of the most recent being F. Willan, who was incumbent here for 55 years last century and saw the new church built. The earliest name is that of Geoffrey, of whom little is known save that he witnessed a deed by which 30 sticks of eels were paid yearly out of the rent of Aubourn Mill to the prior of Belvoir as additional endowment.

Down by the River Witham still stands the mill, a picturesque red-brick building with an ancient story. The old wooden cog wheels are still there though it is many years since they have turned.

Aunsby. It is a tiny village, and an old one, for its church, though much rebuilt last century, still has some work of the Normans. It was they who built the sides of the chancel arch, and the north arcade with its elaborate foliated capitals. The font, with two tiny heads carved sideways among its ornament, is also Norman. Very carefully was the restoration made, for the tower was taken down and rebuilt stone by stone, each in its former place, so that it stands as strongly as in mediaeval days, its base 13th century, the top storey and spire 14th, and the unusual finial crown with the words Ave Maria a 15th century addition.

Aylesby. This quiet little place between the Wolds and the Humber has an old church with great sycamores about it.

The tall tower of the church, adorned with pinnacles and hideous gargoyles, is 15th century, and the porch has windows of that time. To the 13th century belong the nave arcades (with wide stone seats round the pillars of the south side), and the fine font like a pillar adorned with shafts; the modern font cover has a handle engraved with birds, a fish, and a lamb. The 14th century chancel has a tall niche at each side of the east window, two big tomb recesses, and a piscina. As old as the chancel are a floorstone to a rector, and the stone figure of a lady in flowing gown and mantle and draped head-dress, her hands at prayer, and a little dog at her feet. High box-pews of 1759 in the nave add to the simple charm of the interior.

A window showing the Sower and Our Lord with a reaping hook is a tribute to Richard Lowish, churchwarden for 30 years; and there are windows with the Presentation and the Ascension in memory of Captain Francis McAulay, who fell in action in the First World War.

It was in memory of Captain McAulay that Aylesby was given its almshouses—a fine, gabled block of dwellings with dormer windows looking out on beautiful gardens.

Bag Enderby. A tiny Wold village midway between Alford and Horncastle, it lies under Warden Hill, and has on its little green a great tree with hollow trunk and spreading branches under which Wesley is said to have preached. The poet Tennyson and his many brothers and sisters must have known this tree, for Bag Enderby is close to Somersby, and their father was rector of both places. They would also have known the Old Hall (now a farmhouse) with its Jacobean staircase, and the 15th century church which can be dated by an inscription to Albinus de Enderby whose gifts built the bell-tower of the church. He died in 1407.

23

The oldest of many interesting things in the church is the iron boss of a Saxon shield, found in a field and now fixed to the ancient door. Parts of the simple oak screen remain and there are fragments of old glass, including the knives and scourges of Crowland Abbey. In their wall-monument we see the kneeling figures of a 16th century family who knew this place—Andrew Gedney, his wife Dorothy, and four sons and daughters.

The treasure of the church is the font, notable for its exceptional and quaint carvings; among them are David playing his harp, a hart turning its head to lick the leaves of the Tree of Life growing from its back, and St Mary with her dead Son.

Bardney. A thriving little town it is—between the Cliff and the Wolds—but no visitor sauntering in the long high street that runs down to the Witham could ever guess that once it was a place of pilgrimage famed throughout the land. Yet such was the case.

The great abbey of Bardney, founded in the late 7th century, and dedicated to St Peter and St Paul, was one of the earliest Benedictine houses in our land, and the richest among the many established in this part of the Witham valley. It is sometimes said that it was founded by Ethelred, King of Mercia, and Ostryth his queen, and that may be true; but it is certain that the abbey existed in their time, and that within its hallowed walls Ostryth laid the remains of her uncle Oswald, King of Northumbria—years after he had been slain by Penda at Oswestry. Many pilgrims flocked to his shrine, and the name of St Oswald was added to those of St Peter and St Paul.

Five years after the murder of Queen Ostryth in 697 Ethelred renounced the crown and retired to Bardney, dying here in 716. Queen Ostryth is said to have been buried in the abbey, but it is believed that King Ethelred was laid to rest in King's Hill, an ancient barrow in a field east of the abbey site, near the railway line.

The abbey was destroyed in 870 by the Danes, who murdered some 300 monks and brethren; but, about the time that Domesday Book was being compiled, it was rebuilt and richly endowed by Gilbert de Gaunt, Earl of Lincoln, with the aid of Bishop Remigius. The new abbey (which bore the old dedication to the three saints) grew in wealth and importance, and its abbots sat in Parliament as Lords of Lindsey. Henry of Bolingbroke stayed at the abbey for a few days in 1406. At the time of its suppression six Bardney monks were condemned to death because of the Lincolnshire Rising, and after the Dissolution (when it was valued at £429 a year) the abbey was granted to Sir Robert Tyrwhit.

The abbey stood to the north of the town, its great buildings covering 6 acres and enclosed in a moated space of 25 acres. Excavation between 1909 and 1912, under the guidance of the Rev. C. E. Laing (vicar of Bardney), laid bare the ground plan of the monastic church (nearly 260 feet long and 61 feet wide) and also the foundations of the Norman cloister and surrounding buildings which included the refectory and infirmary. The great gatehouse of the abbey was discovered to the west of the church.

Among the interesting things revealed were the fine bases of Norman and later clustered pillars, and many tombstones and carved stones, some of which are now in Bardney parish church. The rest of the abbey remains brought to light by the excavation were covered up again in 1933, and now the moated grassy mounds alone indicate the site. In a field of Abbey Farm (a thatched house near the abbey site) Roman remains have been dug up, including a coin of the time of Constantius. A Roman lock found at Bardney is now in Lincoln Museum.

Bardney's imposing church is chiefly 15th century work, with a brick chancel, and all of it much restored last century. Its tower has catlike gargoyles, and its nave has tall arcades. The finest of the monuments unearthed from the abbey site and now preserved here is that of Abbot Richard Horncastle, who died in 1508. Set against the south wall of the church, his stone is 8 feet long and half as wide, and is said to weigh three tons; it shows the abbot in his vestments standing under a pinnacled canopy, with two angels above his head bearing his shrouded soul to heaven.

A charming sculpture of St Lawrence in the chancel, found headless in the ruins, has been restored in memory of a vicar, Walter Thomas French; about 3 feet high, it shows the saint holding his grid, book, and pen, and wearing a robe embroidered with flowers. The ancient altar stone with its seven crosses, now the high altar, is reputed to be the body-stone of King Oswald; and among the other abbey relics at present in the church are carved stones—capitals, bosses, two great keystones of arches, the head of a ram, the face of a Norman knight, and many more.

Barholm. Its grey cottage and farm buildings line a winding byway, blessed by a tranquillity which the noisy 20th century seems to have passed by. The centuries have been kind to its church also, and even during the Civil War time and money were found to build it a new tower, with a quaint inscription asking

> *Was ever such a thing*
> *Since the creation?*
> *A new steeple built*
> *In the time of vexation.*

But long before this tower was built in such vexatious times, even long before its 13th century predecessor, there was a church here. Just to the right of the porch, and easily overlooked, is a Saxon doorway, now filled in, but with the long-and-short masonry of its jambs plain to see and cut with fragments of crude ornamentation. That is the sole evidence of a Saxon church, but of the Norman shrine much remains. The 13th century porch shelters a splendid Norman doorway with three orders of zigzag and a diapered tympanum; over it is a modern statue of St Martin with the beggar.

In the nave is a massive arcade with three more Norman arches, handsome with chevron and other ornament, a curious spectacle being the pointed tower arch similarly adorned. The rest of the church is largely 13th and 14th century, the chancel, watched over by eight big angels with coloured shields, still having its old sedilia and piscina; the chancel also has a fine Dutch candelabra of bronze.

Striking is the Norman font bowl, decorated with carved foliage, rosettes, and other pattern; it came from the church of the neighbouring hamlet of Stowe, pulled down in the 18th century. It was serving as a big flower vase in a garden just before being brought into the safety of this church.

Barkston. It is one of Grantham's little northern neighbours, with a fine 15th century spire rising above a 700-year-old tower on the edge of Syston Park. The 14th century south aisle has a panelled parapet of little shields in quatrefoils, and the 15th century porch has a Latin inscription to Thomas Pacy, lord of the manor in those days.

The arcade has 13th century arches with nail-head ornament, and in the chancel are mediaeval sedilia, a founder's recess, and piscina, revealed during restoration last century. The screen is modern, but has finely-carved vine pattern, roses, and tracery, and graceful ironwork gates. On either side is a peephole to the altar, one of them mullioned like a window with three lights. Built into the nave wall are two figures carved in deep relief, one of a priest, the other of a man with an angel on either side.

Barlings. A tiny cluster of roofs and hayricks, with an outlying farm or two, it lies scattered among fields and woods in a three-cornered patch of the county bounded by a stretch of the Roman road from Lincoln to Horncastle, the River Witham, and its tributary, the 12-mile-long River Langworth.

The small church, lonely in a field, has a chancel rebuilt last century in Early English style, but still keeping two simple Norman doorways in the old walls of the nave, and a plain 13th century font.

About a mile away, and reached by a rough track across the fields, is the site of Barlings Abbey, which came to the same tragic end as most abbeys did four centuries ago. Founded in 1154 by Ralph de Haya for Premonstratensian canons (who followed the Augustinian rule of life, but were robed in white), the abbey had a great church 300 feet long, with a splendid tower 180 feet high.

Now all that is left is a great jagged piece of grey stone walling about 30 feet high, with a built-up arch between two clustered piers with foliated capitals. Fragments of stone lie scattered in the grass, and other fragments—stone pinnacles and tracery and corbel heads —are in the walls of neighbouring cottages and of a barn.

All else is gone; the glory is departed! But to the few stones of this once-proud abbey clings the memory of its last abbot, Matthew Makarell.

Matthew Makarell, educated first at University College, Oxford, was later at Cambridge and Paris universities, from each of which he received the degree of doctor of divinity. Before reaching here he was abbot of Alnwick, and there preached the funeral sermon on the Duke of Norfolk, who had signalised his release from the Tower by winning the Battle of Flodden.

The Reformation had already begun to extinguish the smaller monasteries, and Makarell bestirred himself in the movement which, with the beautiful name of the Pilgrimage of Grace, was a dangerous rebellion, aimed at the reversal of religious reform, the restoration of monastic properties, the removal, or worse, of Cranmer and Latimer, and the abolition of new laws affecting taxation of private estates.

The Lincolnshire rebels found their leader in Makarell, who took the field in 1536 at the head of 20,000 men. The man to defeat him was the Duke of Suffolk, who appears in Shakespeare's Henry VIII, brother-in-law of Henry, the grandfather of Lady Jane Grey.

Carried to London, the abbot vainly pleaded that he had been compelled to feed the rebels. But he had been the brain and inspiration of the movement in the county, and he was hanged, not at the abbey gate here, as tradition asserts, but at Tyburn, in March 1537.

Barnetby-le-Wold. Important for its railway junction and busy with its market, this big village has an old church and a new. The old, used for burials, and sometimes for summer services, stands high on the hillside in a churchyard screened by trees and presents a rather gaunt exterior of patched walls and low Norman tower. The Saxon origin of the church is revealed in part of its south wall where there is a built-up doorway and nearby is a Saxon keyhole-shaped window with a crudely-carved cat on its horseshoe arch.

Built into the north wall are remains of an arcade from the close of the Norman period. The arch of the chancel, its lancet windows, and its priest's doorway are 13th century; and the screen has a plain base made two centuries later.

The chief possession of the church is the Norman font. One of some 30 lead fonts in England, it is the only one in Lincolnshire, and is enriched with three bands of scrollwork and leaf patterns. This rarity was recovered some years ago from the church coal cellar. It has now been transferred to the new Church of St Barnabas.

Barnoldby-le-Beck. From its little upland above a stream flowing from Croxby Pond, this pretty village looks over the flats stretching to the Humber estuary 5 miles away.

In a field, facing two great limes guarding the churchyard gate, stands a granite column set up in memory of William Smith, a popular huntsman of whom we are told that his gallant horsemanship and management of hounds were unsurpassed. It marks the spot where he was thrown in 1845, receiving injuries from which he died.

Restoration has robbed the church of much of its old work, but the lower part of the tower is 12th century work, and the nave arcades, on clustered pillars, were built early in the 13th century. The font has a bowl with intersected arcading possibly late 13th century, and in the south aisle is another old font bowl on which it used to stand.

In the east window of the south aisle is some 14th century glass showing the Crucifixion, St Mary, and a medley of fragments—all under canopies, with old roundels in the tracery above. More old fragments are in the other aisle, and in the east window of the chancel is fine modern glass with figures of St Helena, the Madonna and Child with a lamb, and St Hugh with his cathedral and pet swan.

Barrowby. A rapidly developing village, 2 miles from Grantham. Its church stands in a commanding position overlooking the fertile patchwork quilt that is called the Vale of Belvoir. Most of the church, including its fine tower and spire, is 14th century, but the doorway (approached by an avenue of yews), and some lancet windows are a century older. In the south wall of the chancel outside is a piece of Anglo-Saxon interlace sculpture. The elaborate panelled font is 600 years old and its bowl rests on a hollow shaft in which lurks a strangely-carved monster. The traceried pulpit is old, and parts of a 15th century screen are worked into the new.

There are brass portraits of the Deenes who lived here in the 15th century—Nicholas with his wife Katherine in butterfly headdress, and nine sons; and Margaret in heraldic mantle with three daughters. Tablets to two 19th century rectors reveal successive ministries covering almost a century; Jonathan Kendal served Barrowby for 47 years, from three years before Trafalgar until 1849; George Earle Welby followed him for 51 years, and the lychgate commemorates his golden wedding.

An earlier parson was Dr Thomas Hurst, who was a chaplain to Charles I and suffered much for his loyalty; but he lived to see the Stuarts back on the throne, dying here 20 years after the Restoration.

Barrow-on-Humber. Memories of far-off days cling to this big village lying by a stream flowing to the Humber 2 miles away. At the haven are impressive earthworks, known as "The Castles", a Norman motte-and-bailey castle and part of its old butter cross in the marketplace. Barrow is an ancient Christian site, for here in the 7th century St Chad founded a monastery on land given him by Wulfhere, King of Mercia. The monastery was destroyed by the Danes and never rebuilt, but stone coffins and other relics have come to light.

The attractive village church is for the most part 15th century. The north arcade of the nave comes from the close of Norman days, and the south from the 13th century; the porch is 600 years old. There is much 15th century work in the skeleton screen, and enclosed by the massive 19th century railings of the little baptistery stands a 700-year-old font. The chancel has an old piscina and aumbry, and its modern east window is a fine group of three lancets, their arches enriched with dog-tooth ornament and resting on clustered shafts. The sundial in the churchyard was made 200 years ago by a brother of the famous clockmaker John Harrison (1693–1776) who lived here as a child. He invented the famous Harrison chronometer that revolutionised navigation at sea in the 18th century.

Three miles south of the village is the hamlet of Burnham, which is one of a number of places which claim to be the site where the important Battle of Brunanburh was fought in 937—the desperate struggle in which King Athelstan routed the enemies of Wessex, killing five kings, it is said, and certainly going far to establish the unity of England.

Barton-upon-Humber. Saxon in name, and possessing one of the finest Saxon towers in the land, Barton was once the biggest port on the Humber. But Hull grew up across the estuary, taking away Barton's cargoes and old importance, and leaving it a little market town a mile from the waterside. Crowding round two remarkable churches, Barton's narrow streets seem to echo with the clatter of the horse-coach in spite of all their modern bustle—there is an air of another century about them as they thread their way between the houses, some of which, indeed, are 300 years old.

Barton has much to show a traveller. A sailless black windmill, shortly to be restored, rises behind the marketplace; and two others on Caistor road and down Waterside, both without sails. A school stands on earth ramparts dug round Barton in the Middle Ages; and a wide ditch called Castle Dyke completes the ancient defences. There are many attractive streets with good Georgian houses; outstanding examples of individual houses of the period are Bardney Hall and Baysgarth Park. Tyrwhitt Hall is a 17th century house worthy of notice.

In the lovely garden of Cobb Hall (a charming house of mellowed brick in Priestgate) is a great beech by a rose-bordered path; but the wonder of this surprising place is a magnificent weeping elm with a spread of branches sheltering the garden like an enormous umbrella. The garden wall is 5 feet thick, and in it are many alcoves. The house itself is said to be on the foundations of a 12th century Moot Hall, and in one of the windows are roundels of 17th century heraldic glass. Baysgarth Park, a Georgian house with pedimented doorway, once the home of the Nelthorpes and now belonging to the town, is in a fine little park with magnificent trees and shaded walks; its fine iron gates are between pillars crowned with unicorns' heads.

Barton's two old and well-restored churches are in a pleasant setting at one end of the town, with a pond and the road between them. St Peter's, which is always known as Old St Peter's, consists of a Saxon tower, 70 feet high, and a tall, gabled narthex (like a tiny nave) built on to its western side. The tiny chancel which completed the Saxon church was on the east side of the tower and was destroyed in the 14th century when the ancient tower and narthex became the west end of a fine new church (with nave and wide aisles, chancel, and two porches) which stands today, with the 15th century addition of the nave clerestory and the chancel windows.

Square and massive Barton's tower stands, one of the most remarkable examples of Saxon architecture in all England. The greater part of it is believed to have been built in the 10th century, and the top stage in the 11th, either just before or after the coming of the Normans. On the north side is a pointed doorway, and on the south is a round-headed one. Between the long-and-short quoins the lower walling is enriched with arcading, round-headed below and triangular-headed above, and very striking; but the remarkable thing about this arcading is that what appear to be just stone strips are in fact solid blocks of stone, with their full length embedded in the walls and only their edges projecting from the rubble. In the tier of gabled arcading are little round-headed double windows with beautifully worked balusters; above these are similar small windows, but with gabled heads; and in the top stage are round-headed windows of greater length. Except for a 14th century window in the west wall, and a small pyramid roof, the tower stands as its Saxon builders left it, and seemingly still as sturdy.

A tall, rounded arch in the west wall of the tower leads to the narthex, which is thought to be even older. It has long-and-short work at the corners, some windows splayed both inside and outside, and two circular windows in the west wall; one of these round windows is unique in still having a fragment of the oak shutter which was opened and closed by Saxon hands. In the east wall of the tower is the original chancel arch, tall and rounded, and having above it a flat stone carved with a head of Christ in relief.

The door below this face leads from the Saxon twilight of Old St

Peter's into the brightness of 14th century St Peter's—into the spacious nave where the elegant clerestory of nine traceried windows on each side makes two long continuous lines of light. The nave arcades are enriched with carved capitals (some having dog-tooth ornament and some having beautiful foliage), and with stone portraits; these include a simpering Edward II, a jester wearing a mask, a caricature of a friar, and a life-like lady in a crown, believed to be a portrait of Elizabeth I added two centuries later to this little sculpture gallery. (The church registers, in 20 volumes, go back without a break to Elizabeth's young days; the many quaint entries include one of a shilling paid to "pacify Sharp's wife".)

Across the wide arch between the nave and the comparatively short chancel is a handsome 15th century screen which was restored and given its beautiful vaulted canopy (with rich cornice and cresting) last century. Also 500 years old is a small oak chest bound with iron strips. On a windowsill are five pieces of armour which Barton men buckled on to fight for Parliament during the Civil War.

A charming feature are the windows of this church. One with flowing tracery (at the east end of the north aisle) lost its glass when the organ was built behind it, but has a special interest because it is enriched with stone figures of St Mary and St John, and of Our Lord on the Cross (this being barely discernible now).

In the east window of the south aisle are two shields in 15th century glass. In the east window of the chancel are two 14th century pictures; one shows St James as a pilgrim in a flowered coat, with a badge in his broad-brimmed hat and a scallop worked on the scrip hanging from his shoulder-strap; the other has St George in shining armour, with jewelled sword and short spear, and a red cross on his shield. Other bits of mediaeval glass make a shining star.

In striking contrast to the simple Saxon tower of St Peter's Church is the massive one of St Mary's, built in the 13th century and given its pinnacled parapet two centuries later. Below the parapet is a band of small corbels of faces and foliage; the lovely west doorway and the fine windows of the tower are all shafted, and the arch to the nave is enriched with capitals of overhanging foliage.

Most of this lovely old church is 13th century work, including the graceful south arcade (its arches on pillars with elegant clustering shafts), and the beautiful south porch with its shafted entrance and three empty niches. But the chancel and its chapel of St James are for the most part early 14th century, the clerestory is 15th century, and the north arcade of the nave with rich chevron pattern on its arches, was built at the close of the Norman period. (One tall, pointed arch is a little later.)

Complete with sedilia, piscina, and aumbry, the chapel is divided from the chancel by a striking 14th century arcade with foliage capitals, and above the pillars are stone portraits of Barton folk who helped to build it. A piscina in the north aisle has a trefoiled projecting drain and carvings of leaves and a man's head.

Some of the fine array of windows lighting St Mary's are richly moulded outside. The east window has heavy mullions and unusual tracery, and in it is a curious medley of mediaeval glass fragments, including a figure of Christ in golden crown and blue tunic. Under the altar is the ancient altar stone with its five crosses, and under the tower is a 7-foot oak chest with four heavy locks hollowed out of a solid trunk 500 years ago.

Among the monuments are two mediaeval brasses. One has the half-figure of a 14th century lady. The other shows Simon Seman, vintner, alderman, and sheriff of London, who died in 1433; as large as life, he balances himself on two casks of his wine.

Bassingham. Close to the Witham, it is a big village with a goodly company of red-brick cottages on a network of byways and a church much rebuilt but still keeping much of its Norman and mediaeval work.

The exterior of the church is enriched with a gallery of quaint carvings—gargoyles on the battlemented clerestory, tiny heads on its pinnacles, and more heads by the windows, among them a lady in a wimple, an ape pointing to its teeth, a frog with bulging eyes, a curious animal twisting to bite its own tail, and a dog not unlike Walt Disney's famous Pluto.

The battlemented tower, long ruinous, was rebuilt in the 18th century, and the following century saw the rebuilding of part of the 13th century chancel and the north arcade with its three round arches only the westernmost of which is original Norman work. The four arches of the south arcade are 13th century, one of the capitals being enriched with carving of ferns and shells. The nave is illuminated by the light of 10 clerestory windows, and a striking sight is the east window with its modern glass portraying a celestial company of angels in gorgeous raiment.

Roses adorn the 500-year-old font, and there is a fragment of mediaeval screen in the narrow tower arch. In the south aisle, at the east end, are two stones with Anglo-Saxon interlaced cable moulding.

Bassingthorpe. It is a tiny hillside village with a church going back 800 years, and a manor house of Mary Tudor's time. The Normans built the church, with its massive round chancel arch, and the tower and spire were added in the 13th century. There is a mediaeval font with traceried sides, and the east window has pleasing modern glass of Our Lord as the mystical Fountain of Life. In the churchyard is a stone with this noteworthy epitaph: *The Grave— Kind Reader—To a level brings Beggars, Heroes, Galley Slaves and Kings.*

The solid, grey manor house behind the church, attractive with its stepped gables, tall chimneys, and panelled oriel, was built in 1568 by Thomas Coney, High Sheriff of Rutland, and one of the richest wool merchants of his day. Ten years previously, when the English lost Calais to the Duke of Guise, he had been captured and held prisoner for two months until ransomed.

Baston. It is a Fen village with a medley of brick and stone houses, some of them thatched, strung out for half a mile. Lying between a Roman road (King Street) and a Roman canal (Carr Dyke) its story is ancient, and Saxon pottery and other remains have been unearthed here.

The mediaeval church has been much restored and is curious for having a bellcot at the west end of the south aisle, though it no longer echoes the knell of parting day, the bells being in the embattled tower. The porch, with a niche over its arch, is 14th century, and the wide chancel arch and the eight graceful arches of the clerestoried nave are 13th century. There is a pleasing simplicity about this white-walled interior. There is the plainest of mediaeval fonts, and nave and aisles still have their old wooden roofs.

Since the drainage of Cowbit Wash several years ago Baston Fen is the only area capable of flooding and is now the main venue for skating in south Lincolnshire and the national skating championships are held here. It is a fenland nature reserve.

Baumber. A neighbour of Horncastle, it lies on a low ridge of the Wolds, with the River Bain bounding it on the east, and looks down on villages and hamlets nestling in valleys and hollows; on a clear day the towers of Lincoln can be seen.

The church, ringed by trees and standing in a field, had much of its old stonework faced with brick in the 18th century and appears essentially a Georgian church. However, the tower still has its massive Norman base with a carved west doorway, and a low arch, striking in its severe simplicity, built of massive stones and lacking capitals or ornament. The narrow opening to the large tower suggests Anglo-Saxon origins.

The nave, with its mediaeval arcades, was once longer, and at the entrance to the modern brick chancel are fragments of 13th century clustered piers. Between nave and chancel is a screen of painted wood, with a coat-of-arms and other decoration above its three arches.

Beckingham. The road from Newark to Sleaford enters Lincolnshire at this pleasant village on the River Witham which treasures a beautiful church with its roots in Norman England.

Set on a little rise above the twisting road, the church has a sturdy 15th century tower with battlements and eight tall pinnacles, and a 13th century south porch with a doorway of rare beauty, surpassed only by that of the inner doorway of the same period. Deeply recessed, this inner doorway has an arch adorned with dog-tooth and zigzag carving and resting on shafts with rows of dog-tooth between. The round-headed north doorway was built by the Normans and is enriched with zigzag, quaint faces of men and women, grotesques, and a prancing animal.

The 13th century nave arcades have slender clustered shafts and carving of nail-head and dog-tooth. The aisles were rebuilt six centuries ago when Thomas of Sibthorpe was rector; he founded chantries in the aisles, and the old brackets for statues are still here. The richly-moulded chancel arch is 700 years old. The wide tower arch soars so high that the lofty flat roof of the nave takes an upward sweep, like the prow of a ship, to meet the tip of the arch; it must be a unique feature for a church.

To the 14th century belong the traceried font and the much-worn figure of a lady in flowing gown lying in the tower, her name forgotten. The tall, traceried oak screen is modern, and so is the richly-carved oak reredos with the Crucifixion scene.

Beelsby. A tiny village of the Wolds, it has a hillside church looking almost new outside because of 19th century rebuilding, but still keeping some interesting mediaeval remains within.

Now an aisleless building with a little spire on its bell-turret, it has the arch of a vanished tower built into the west wall, and the fine arcades of lost aisles showing in the walls of the nave. The north arcade, with its eight-sided pillars is 14th century, and the south arcade, with one round and one clustered pier, is a century older. The chancel has a modern arch dividing it from the nave, and a mediaeval arch leading to the vestry on its south side. The font has a mediaeval bowl, and there is an old panelled pulpit. Remains of an old stoup are in the porch. Beelsby House is a Georgian building.

Belleau. This little place below the eastern foothills of the Wolds is as pretty as its name—said to be derived from the copious spring which comes to life here and helps to feed the Withern Eau. Just below the village church is a great eight-sided brick dovecot which belonged to the old moated manor house, other remnants of which survive in the farmstead still lower down, where there are blocked 16th century windows in a barn, and a stone arch (in an outbuilding) with the stone bearded head and bust of the wild man of the Willoughbys at the top. By the farmhouse door runs a never-failing supply of the sparkling spring water.

The old mansion belonged to the Lords Willoughby de Eresby, and was used after the Civil War by the younger Sir Henry Vane, who left England in search of religious freedom, became Governor of

Massachusetts, and returned to take his place as one of the chief Parliamentary leaders. He was executed for treason after Charles II came back, and was buried at Shipborne in Kent, but his connection with this corner of Lincolnshire is commemorated by a marble stone within the church. Placed here in 1915 by English and American admirers, it tells that Sir Henry was a man of noble and generous mind, a defender of civil and religious liberty.

Surprisingly fine for so tiny a village is the church. The tower and outer walls were entirely rebuilt in 1862, on the old foundations, but the fine 14th century nave arcades survived, as well as the old rood stairway. In the spacious chancel are three 13th century relics—an aumbry with a shelf, a richly-carved image bracket, and a bracket-piscina with trefoiled and crocketed arch. Mediaeval, too, is the sculptured knight, cross-legged and wearing armour and surcoat; battered angels are at his head and a big lion nestles at his feet.

Belton. A big village in the Isle of Axholme, it has a handsome 15th century church, with demon gargoyles on its embattled and pinnacled tower, and battered angels on its porch. Between the soaring arches of the clerestoried nave are heads of two women in square headdress, and on one of the pillars is an old hourglass stand. The chancel has three sedilia with cinquefoiled canopies, and a piscina. There are two fonts—one Norman, and the other 15th century—and among other old relics are a 14th century tomb and a still earlier battered coffin stone with the bust and feet of a knight.

Little more than a mile from the village is the estate of Temple Bellwood which once belonged to the Knights Templars of Balsall in Warwickshire; some remains of their old house are built into a farmhouse in the grounds.

Standing in beautiful grounds between Belton and Crowle is Hirst Priory, a splendid house near the site of a 12th century Augustinian monastery founded by Nigel d'Albini as a cell to Nostell Priory in Yorkshire.

At Sandtoft (west of Belton and near the Yorkshire border) was a small cell founded by Roger de Mowbray about 1150 and attached to the Abbey of St Mary, York. Here was a considerable settlement of Dutch and Flemish workmen brought over by Cornelius Vermuyden; the chapel built for them here was destroyed by rioters who were opposed to his scheme for draining the Isle of Axholme.

Belton. Stately trees line the approaches to this little neighbour of Grantham, nestling on the edge of Belton Park, ancestral home of Lord Brownlow. Many generations of his family have lived here, building comely cottages, founding almshouses, planting noble trees on every side, enriching the little church with splendid memorials.

The village is an example of imaginative estate management.

Attractive limestone houses and cottages are pleasantly grouped around the village cross.

Completely charming it is. The grey stone houses are all well-built and well-kept; and a modern cross finely carved, with a shaft 30 feet high, faces Dame Alice Brownlow's 17th century almshouses and village school on which Latin inscriptions offer a home to the pious aged and the gift of true knowledge to the young. Belton disputes with its neighbour Syston (and with Staunton in Notts.) the claim of being the original of Scott's "Willingham" in the *Heart of Midlothian*. Be that as it may, its claims to a place among the loveliest villages in this green and pleasant land are undeniable.

The splendid park of nearly 700 acres is 5 miles round. Across the long vistas of the great avenues of elms and limes are fascinating glimpses of lakes fed by the Witham, and of wooded slopes. The eastern entrance to the park is spanned by a triumphal brick-built arch of 1750, called Belmount Tower, and the wonderful view from its summit shows not the dull, flat Lincolnshire of tradition, but a well-wooded and well-watered stretch of country with slender spires rising here and there, and the "soaring loveliness of Grantham spire" close by.

The great house and its ornamental gardens (where two descendants of Newton's famous apple tree still flourish) can be glimpsed from the churchyard. Designed by Sir Christopher Wren, it was finished in 1689, and the park was planted and enclosed soon after. About 80 years later, James Wyatt made alterations to the house, giving it a new south entrance, and replacing the cupola built by Wren. Grey and impressive, with tall roofs, and pedimented north and south fronts, great windows all round, and an attractive court-yard at one side, it is in plan like the letter H and the repository of many treasures. There are tapestries, and family portraits by great English artists; and rarer still are the carvings by Grinling Gibbons adorning the cedar-lined private chapel and some of the rooms—festoons of fruit and flowers and game which are masterpieces of the carver's art.

A short sketch of the family history is necessary for a proper appreciation of the monuments which fill the church. The first of the family to own the Belton estate was Richard Brownlow, a rich lawyer of Elizabethan and early Stuart times. His great-grandson, Sir John Brownlow, the builder of the present great house, died in 1697, his brother William inheriting the lands. Sir William's son John Brownlow, who became Viscount Tyrconnel in 1718, made many alterations to the house and grounds and built the Belmount Tower four years before his death in 1754. He had no children and Belton passed to his sister Anne, who in 1717 married Sir Richard Cust, and thence to their son Sir John Cust, who became Speaker of the Commons in 1761. Sir John Cust's only son (who commissioned

James Wyatt to make alterations to Belton House), on being raised to the peerage in 1776 because of his father's public services, took the title of Baron Brownlow. That is the title still held today by the owner of Belton.

As already stated, their memorials fill the village church and are its chief feature. But its walls were raised centuries before a Brownlow ever came to Belton. The oldest work in the church is seen in the font and the nave's twin-arched arcade, both from late Norman days. One of the arches is plain and the other has carved zigzag ornament; the massive pillar is adorned with a deeply-cut diamond pattern covering its entire length. The tower is 13th century, with a top stage of 1637; the rest of the building, including the chancel, is early 18th century work, with a transept chapel added in Victorian times.

The font is a fine example of Norman work, the sculptures under its round-headed arcading being vigorous, primitive, and quaint. Experts have suggested differing meanings, but their story can vary according to the fancy of the beholder. Some of the scenes are perhaps from the story of a priest; a man is pulling at two bell ropes for his induction; dressed in a cope, he is seen reading; and again with his hands raised in benediction. There is a delightful prancing steed with a forked tail, and two gruesome pictures show a headman and a hangman at the gallows with a vulture hovering near, and a gleeful demon waiting for the soul of the wretched victim. For lack of space the primitive craftsman has dispensed with the legs of the figures, attaching a tiny pair of feet to the upper part of the body with comical effect.

The Jacobean pulpit has a carved back and high canopy and the stone steps leading to it are contrived in the angle cut into the lofty chancel arch and a nave pillar. The modern reading-desk is of original design, supported by brass lions on a black marble base.

The reredos is modern, too, with a gilded background and angels with musical instruments on each side of the figure of Our Lord, all in harmony with the exquisite gold embroideries of the altar hangings; above it the turrets of the Heavenly City stand out in gold and ivory against the crimson and blue lights of the east window.

The church has been well called a Museum of Monuments. Some are in the chancel, others in nave and aisle, and many more in the raised chapel, beautiful with fan-vaulted roof and ornamental brass screen. The earliest is the coloured figure of Richard Brownlow, died 1638, the first of the family at Belton and Prothonotary of the Court of Common Pleas. He is in a niche, holding a scroll. Then comes his son Sir John Brownlow, who is with his wife, the Lady Alice who built the almshouses, where her portrait is still treasured. A gracious comely pair they are, in white marble, hand in hand, and brave in curls and lace collars and cuffs.

In the north arcade there is a long inscription to the later Sir John "who built this noble house from the ground", and another elaborate marble memorial with a mourning woman and a medallion portrait of his nephew Sir John Brownlow, Viscount Tyrconnel, on whose death in 1754 the Belton estates went to his sister Anne, wife of Sir Richard Cust.

The Cust family, soon to revive the title of Brownlow, went on adding to the wealth of monuments here. On the chancel wall is that of Sir John Cust, Member for Grantham for nearly 30 years, and Speaker of the House of Commons from 1761 till his death nine years later. He died in harness at the early age of 52, two days after he had begged the House "to excuse him from further service", and his carved panel by Tyler shows a graceful woman with the Journals of the House at her feet. His only son, the first Baron Brownlow, has a monument by Westmacott with a woman's figure expressing grief at the foot of a broken column. He died in 1807 and was succeeded by his eldest son John, the 1st Earl Brownlow, whose imposing tomb is in the middle of the chapel. His stately figure wearing the coronet and ermine-trimmed robes of his rank, was sculptured by Marochetti, who was born in Turin, studied in France, and was driven by the Revolution of 1848 to make his home in England. The memorial to the earl's first wife is by another Italian sculptor, Canova; she died at 26 in the fourth year of her marriage, leaving "three infant children to deplore her loss", and her lovely altar tomb bears a huge white marble figure of Religion. The earl's second wife is portrayed on a carved panel, seated as if resting during a woodland ramble, a peasant's cloak about her shoulders, lilies in her hand, her hat and staff flung carelessly on the ground; cherubs swarm above her.

A Calvary in a rich canopied recess of alabaster is to the memory of the 2nd Earl Brownlow, whose "short life was spent in love and charity to all men". There is a bust of the 3rd Earl Brownlow, Lord-Lieutenant of the County for 54 years and aide-de-camp to Queen Victoria, King Edward, and King George; and there is also a marble bust of his wife Adelaide in a rich setting of coloured marble. Below the west window of the aisle lies the robed figure of Henry John Cockayne-Cust, JP, one of the editors of the *Pall Mall Gazette*. It is raised on pillars of porphyry and onyx, and a bulldog, doubtless a pet, droops his head in grief below the hem of his lost master's robe; the simple inscription reads, "High heart, high speech, high deeds."

Four other memorials to sons and daughters of the family have still to be mentioned. One is a sculpture by John Bacon of a young girl kneeling at play with her dog, and commemorates Etheldred Cust, who died in her teens in 1788; another is a little marble copy of Donatello's St George set up in memory of Elizabeth Cust, a young girl who died in 1913. Dean Richard Cust, rector here for 54 years last century, has a wall memorial with a relief of St Peter kneeling at the feet of the Good Shepherd; and a bronze tablet showing a cruiser at sea is a tribute to Arthur Purey-Cust, who went down with his ship during the First World War.

In its great array of family monuments this little Lincolnshire church is matched by few village churches in all the land.

An entry in the church register is an echo of the unhappy far-off days of the Civil War when Cromwell was gaining experience as a cavalry leader in the neighbourhood of Grantham. There was fighting here, and the entry in the register reads, "May 1643, buried three unknown soldiers, slain in Belton fight."

Benington. A big and pleasant village within two miles of the sea, with the hamlet of Sea End a mile nearer still. It has a stately church testifying to the skill of our mediaeval builders.

The tower, with its cornice of flowers and leaves and a west doorway between canopied niches, is 15th century work. From the 14th century come the nave of six bays with lofty arcades, the aisles with richly-moulded windows, the restored porch, and the lovely deeply-recessed doorway within it. The nave roof, adorned with carved wooden angels, the fine clerestory, and the splendid font are 15th century. The octagonal font has a bowl richly carved with saints and the Holy Trinity under pinnacled canopies; there are angels in a band of grape and vine under the bowl, and more canopied saints are on the stem.

The chancel has something of all three mediaeval building periods. To the 13th century belong the aumbries, a double-arched recess which may have served as an Easter Sepulchre, and the lovely lancet windows on the north side. The sedilia and piscina are 14th century. The windows in the east and south walls, and the base of the restored oak screen, are all 15th century work.

At a corner of the nave is a turret with a tiny spire, in which the newel stair once led to the rood-loft. By its entrance in the church are a piscina and a tiny trefoiled niche. There is also a quaint old chest shaped like a trunk.

The east window has fine glass in memory of Canon Walter Fallows Hodge, who died in 1938 after being rector for a quarter of a century. It shows Our Lord preaching by the sea; St Paul with a sword and writing in prison; and John Wycliffe above an angel with an open Bible.

In the pretty churchyard is the grave of James Rheson, with a marble headstone telling of his bequest to the church. James Rheson lived in one of the 18th century almshouses close by, and when he was nearing his end made a will leaving all his worldly possessions to start a fund for a clock in the church tower. He declared he had "nowt to leave." But after his death 1100 halfcrowns were found in an old chest among his belongings—an unexpected and surprising windfall for the church, and an adequate sum for providing the church tower with a clock in his memory.

Benniworth. There are lovely views of fields and hills from this Wold village to the distant Cliff. The old Grange of mellowed brick is a farmhouse now, and up the hill is a small church, hiding among trees, which dates from Norman times and has the rare dedication to St Julian. About a mile away is a fine 8-acre pond well known to fishermen.

The Norman church had the shape of a cross, but the present chancel and transepts are a rebuilding of 1875, when the rest of the church was restored. Part of the south wall of the nave belongs to the original building, and there is still a striking west doorway the Normans built, its arch rich with zigzag and roll mouldings and a hood of horseshoe arcading. The font has been built up round a fragment of the Norman one.

The chancel screen is a skilful combination of 15th and 20th century craftsmanship—part of the framework being mediaeval, the rest new. The spandrels of its traceried bays are adorned with heraldry; the rood-beam has rich carving of vine leaves and grapes, and on brackets between the bays are figures of saints and angels. Aidan is here with a stag nestling under his robe, Hugh of Lincoln with a swan biting the end of his garment, Julian of Mans with mitre and crozier, his hand raised in blessing, and Augustine with a shield on each side, one of them showing King Ethelbert in a font.

On a wall of the low tower is a touching memorial to a cripple who was sexton here for about 30 years before they laid him in the church-yard in 1928. He was Charles Hobson, affectionately known to the village children as Hobbie.

Bicker. Once stood on the famous Bicker Haven and takes its name from the neighbouring Fen, across which run the Hammond Beck and the South Forty Foot Drain. A road divided by a stream leads to it, adding to the pretty picture made by the church, the houses with creepered walls and pantiled roofs, and a fine avenue of trees.

Its great heritage is a Norman and mediaeval church, altered a little in the 16th century, and restored in the 19th century, but still impressive in the richness of its ancient adornment. There are stones with Anglo-Saxon interlace in the porch and north and south aisles.

The original Norman church had the shape of a cross, with a central tower. The tower and the chancel were rebuilt in the 13th century, and the tower was given its top stage two centuries later. The Norman transepts were absorbed into 14th century aisles, but the Norman nave of two bays still stands in all its massive strength and richness of decoration. The round piers of its imposing arcades are crowned with scalloped capitals shaped like crosses, supporting arches enriched with varied carving of zigzag under hoods of billet moulding. The windows of the clerestory are seen, outside, to be set in the middle bays of triple arcading, and above them is the Norman corbel table.

It is fine to look along this Norman nave to the work of the 13th century builders, the stately arches of the tower carrying the eye to the fine chancel beyond, with its three tall lancets lighting the east wall, elegant arcades opening to aisles, an old timber roof, three fine sedilia, and a bracket piscina.

Parts of the old screen have been worked into some of the seats and among other relics of the past is a lovely 700-year-old font, on a base of old gravestones. Of unusual design, the font has a square bowl made round within four shafts, of which the capitals are carved with leaves trailing on to the bowl.

Bigby. From its charming setting on the western slope of the Wolds there are lovely views over the Ancholme valley; and the village has the added attraction of gay gardens and fine trees.

In a churchyard ringed with tall limes and chestnuts stands a church with a goodly array of monuments and brasses. It is for the most part a restored 13th century building, with a 14th century south aisle, and a north aisle (like a narrow passage) rebuilt in 1779. The old, low tower has a corbel table adorned with heads, and there is an oak porch. The nave and chancel are under one continuous roof.

Among the church's possessions is a Jacobean table with a cupboard, and there are two fonts, one modern and the other with a carved bowl on a new pedestal. This old bowl came back to church in 1876, it has nine sides; it still has the remains of the old staple fastening for a cover. The chancel has three stepped sedilia, and in the south aisle is a piscina.

Some of the monuments here are to the Tyrwhits who lived at Kettleby over a mile away. The moated site of their old home is still to be seen, with an 18th century farmhouse (Kettleby House) beside it.

Kneeling in the sanctuary, in a wall-monument with arms painted in lively colours, are Sir Robert Tyrwhit and his wife, Lady Bridget Manners, who is now headless; she was a Maid of Honour to Elizabeth I, and made a runaway marriage with her husband. On a great canopied altar tomb dominating the chancel are the splendid alabaster figures of Sir Robert Tyrwhit of 1581 and his wife; he wears armour and lies on a mattress to which the wild hairy man at his feet is clinging; she has a lion at her feet. Round the tomb are the words of the 128th Psalm and the figures of their 22 children—a strange collection; there are eight sons in ruffs, nine daughters, two babes in tiny cradles, and three others in swaddling clothes.

A floorstone in the chancel has the small brass portrait of Elizabeth Skipwyth of 1520, wearing kennel headdress; she was a Tyrwhit before she married. Near the altar lies the sculptured figure of a Skipwyth lady of about 1400, wearing a wimple and finely-carved robe. Another Skipwyth lady (she died in 1374) is finely engraved in stone in the south aisle, and though the monument is rather worn the folds of her gown are plainly seen, and so is the dog with bells on its collar at her feet. In the same aisle is a tiny 13th century floorstone with a floriated cross.

One of three brasses set into the back of the sedilia shows Edward Naylor, a rector who died in 1632; his epitaph states that he was "a faithful and paineful minister of God's word". A kneeling figure with beard and moustache, he wears a gown and a ruff and has his wife and seven children grouped about him.

Billingborough. One of about a dozen English places bearing the name of the Billings, a famous tribe of Northern invaders, it lies on the edge of the Fens with the Roman Carr Dyke close by—more like a little town than a village, with its long street of houses, shops, and old inns.

Hiding behind its wall and its trees is the handsome Hall of Tudor days, with grey stone walls and tall chimneys; and in a quiet byway is a fine church with slender spire soaring to 150 feet. The tower rises at the west end of the north aisle, and has a fine vaulted roof, and pinnacles linked to the spire by delicate flying buttresses.

Like the tower, most of the church is 14th century, but there are traces of slightly earlier work in the south aisle (still with its old aumbry and piscina). The chancel was rebuilt in 1891, and the most impressive part of the building is the nave with four great arches on each side and the light streaming through the 12 windows of a 15th century clerestory.

The great west window, also 15th century, has modern glass with a richly-coloured portrayal of the Resurrection, and the east window has the Crucifixion, set up in memory of the Duke of Clarence. There are also a few fragments of old heraldic glass, but the finest glass is in the east window of the south aisle, which has attractive modern figures of Gilbert of Sempringham, St Andrew, and the Madonna, above figures of Stephen Langton and John the Baptist.

Billinghay. This big workaday village is in a bleak stretch of Fenland. A wide dyke runs between green banks alongside the main road to join the River Witham about three miles to the east.

A slender spire linked to the old tower by flying buttresses crowns a church coming chiefly from the 14th and 15th centuries, though restoration and rebuilding have taken many of the old features. The long nave, however, still has its mediaeval south arcade, its four arches borne upon clustered pillars. Above the arches are the windows of the 15th century clerestory, and the original roof adorned by bosses with foliage and faces and still bearing traces of old colouring.

West of Billinghay, half a mile along the road to Digby, is the site of Catley Priory, founded in the middle of the 12th century by Peter of Billinghay for nuns and canons of the Gilbertine order. It ranked third in importance among the Gilbertine houses, and covered 5 acres; all that is left of it are green mounds in a field.

Binbrook. Once it was a market town with two old churches; now it is a growing community with a fine 19th century church keeping a memory of the earlier two in its dedication to St Mary and St Gabriel. One thing has remained unchanged—its setting in a valley with a fine stream running through it and the charming Wold scenery all around. The green is on the side of the hill.

The broach spire of the church rising above the trees and the red-pantiled roofs of the houses makes an attractive rural picture; and pleasing, too, is the little market square, redolent of other days. The old cross, with finely-foliated arms, stands proudly in the churchyard now, a rare survival of the 13th century; and near it is another cross, with a carving of a crusader's sword, in memory of men who died for their country.

The modern church, built in the styles of the 13th and 14th centuries, is lofty and spacious, and has graceful arcades with clustered pillars. Across the fine arch leading to the apsidal chancel is an oak screen in 15th century style, and under the impressive tower arch is a 700-year-old font on modern shafts.

Bishop Norton. Well known for its fine 18th century house, known as Norton Place, set on the edge of plantations in a once spacious park. The house and lake make an attractive setting. Two lovely copper beeches are companions of its church, much rebuilt last century and of little interest to the traveller except for one splendid thing. Set into the west wall of the tower is a Norman tympanum, enriched with a mass of unusual carving. Under the round head are five roundels; along the foot is a line of interlaced circles; and in the space between is a weird group of what appear to be men's heads, a dragon, and a man fallen down, with the head of a lamb in the midst.

An ancient stone coffin stands under the tower.

Bitchfield. Here flows the little River Glen, swollen by a brook from neighbouring Bassingthorpe and flowing south towards old earthworks.

The church is a simple one with a 13th century tower capped by a younger spire, and a 14th century porch sheltering a Norman doorway. The three round arches in the nave are also 12th century Norman work, and in the south wall are some traces of herringbone masonry even older.

The 600-year-old font has a fringe of leaves and roses, and a shield with emblems of the Passion. In the modern nave roof are foliated bosses and six musical angels, relics of a former roof.

Blankney. Halfway between Lincoln and Sleaford it lies, a model village with trim stone cottages by the roadside. Innumerable elms cast their shade on the pleasant scene, and all around is spread the matchless beauty of an English park, with the charm of rolling grassland, of wood and coppice, and of stately trees standing in solitary splendour.

A lychgate designed by G. F. Bodley leads to the church, rebuilt last century, but still keeping a few ancient features. The handsome pinnacled tower is decked with bands of quatrefoils and wide-mouthed gargoyles; in it hangs a peal of eight bells given by farmers as a thank-offering after the First World War.

The archway of the porch and the arcades of nave are survivals of the mediaeval church, and other relics from it are the 15th century font, with its band of four-petalled flowers, and a tombstone in the chancel floor with the stern features of one John de Glori, carved beneath a heart-shaped opening at the top. The wooden eagle lectern is a fine example of modern craftsmanship.

A white marble figure of Lady Florence Chaplin, wife of the famous Henry Chaplin, is a work of charm and feeling. The sculpture shows her kneeling in a long graceful robe, hands clasped and face upturned, a lovely girl in all the bloom of youth. The sculptor was Sir Edgar Boehm.

Blankney Hall, a mansion spaciously built of grey stone, until recent times the seat of the earls of Londesborough and before them the home of Henry Chaplin, the famous Squire of Blankney, has recently been pulled down.

Born in 1841, Henry Chaplin was a romantic figure and he figured in a strange romance. He became engaged at 23 to Lady Flora Paget, who just before the wedding day left him at one door of a London shop while she passed out by another door into the arms of the Marquis of Hastings, whom she forthwith married.

Three years later the Squire won the Derby with his horse Hermit, a result which beggared his successful rival. Chaplin was 35 before he married the Duke of Sutherland's daughter Florence, and she died only five years later.

Entering Parliament as a Conservative, he was a friend of both Disraeli and Gladstone, and for many years he was the last of the Protectionists in the House of Commons, a redoubtable Tory Die-hard. That fine Liberal journalist, A. G. Gardiner, in a masterly but slightly malicious essay, wrote of him:

"Age cannot wither him, nor custom stale. He lingers on into these drab prosaic times, a glorious reminiscence of the days of the dandies, defying the machinations alike of time and of the Radicals, cheerful and debonair, his ample hat sitting on his head with just a suspicion of a sporting angle, his cambric peeping from his breast pocket with a subtle suggestion of gallantry, his eyeglass worn as if to the manner born; a kindly simple-hearted gentleman, with the spacious manners of an earlier day slightly exaggerated; a mirror in which we may see the England of long ago and the Toryism that is dead."

He was in 1916 created Viscount Chaplin of St Oswald's, Blank-ney, and when he died in 1923 he was laid to rest by the side of his beloved wife under a big elm in the trim churchyard of St Oswald's, Blankney.

Bloxham. It is a tiny place sequestered in a byway skirting the grounds of the Hall, which has recently been demolished. It was a dignified three-storeyed house of stone with dormer windows, built nearly 300 years ago and enlarged early last century. It was long one of the homes of the Manners family, some of whom rest in the little church close by in the Hall grounds. The arms of this famous English family (with unicorn supporters and peacock crest) are on the house and also on the church porch, rebuilt with the chancel in 1812 by General Robert Manners, who also gave the 15th century tower its battlements. The nave of the church belongs to the early 14th century.

Blyborough. Hall and church and rectory are close companions here in tranquil setting. There are many stately trees all around, and the long avenue leading to the hall is of splendid oaks.

The church, dedicated to the Northumbrian saint Alkmund, was almost rebuilt last century, but there is old work remaining in the tiny tower, the west wall, and the 13th century chancel arch. The nave arcade (its capitals carved with stiff leaves) is also 13th century, and was opened out to a new aisle after being built up. There are three big mediaeval niches adorned with heads, an old font with flowers and leaves at its base, and a Crucifixion (on the rood-beam) carved by Flemish craftsmen six centuries ago.

Lying on a windowsill are fragments found in the restoration—the head of a wimpled woman, a crude figure with outspread hands, stones shaped by the Normans, and some red tiles. On his tomb in

45

the chapel, is the stone figure of a 15th century priest, Robert Conyng, his features worn by time.

One of the stained windows is in memory of two Luard brothers who fought in the Peninsular War and at Waterloo, and a tablet tells of four of their descendants who fell in the First World War. Near a 200-year-old yew in the churchyard is a memorial to "all who gave their lives for this country and freedom".

Blyton. A strange spectacle awaits the traveller who enters its church—a spectacle to which kings and presidents have contributed —an impressive display of the flags of the Allies in the First World War.

It began with a mother whose son died in France; she wanted a French flag for the church. Then the mother of a son who fell in Belgium wished for a Belgian flag. So it was that the vicar of those sad years set himself the task of collecting the flags of the Allies for his church.

King Albert sent the Belgian flag, and the French President sent the Tricolor. Admiral Beatty sent an ensign flown at Jutland, and the Viceroy of India, and the Governors of Australia, Canada, New Zealand, and South Africa sent Empire flags. The Kings of Italy, Serbia, and Rumania responded, and so did the Emperor of Japan, whose country was a friend of Britain then. The American flag came from President Wilson, and the Portuguese flag came with special affection from the President of the republic, for it was from Blyton that Sister Margaret went out to be matron of the Portuguese hospital in France, where she was decorated with one of Portugal's ancient Orders.

The flags hang above arcades six and seven centuries old. The chancel, though much rebuilt last century, has its original east window of about 1300, its old piscina and aumbry, and a 15th century window; and part of the old rood-beam is still over its arch. The tower was first built by the Normans, and the font, with carved panels and embattled top, is a handsome example of 15th century craftsmanship.

A link with Shakespeare's day is a brass in the chancel, inscribed:

> *In expectance of the Resurrection here quietly*
> *sleep the little bodies of William and Elizabeth,*
> *two of the children of Sir John Wray of Warton and*
> *the lady Griselda, his wife, having only seen the*
> *world and left it.*
>> *Whom scarce the world yet saw, say, cruel Death,*
>> *Why didst of each sex one deprive of breath?*
>> *That either parent might in heaven have one,*
>> *To be their pledge till they in person come.*

The great Hebrew scholar, Thomas Coleman, was vicar in those days. It was he whom Cromwell chose to preach at the signing of the Solemn Covenant between England and Scotland.

Bonby. One of the string of villages on the western edge of the Wolds, it has the memory of a priory founded here in the time of King John as a cell to the abbey of St Fromond in Normandy. It also has a church with some remains even older.

With a fine sycamore to keep it company, the quaint little building looks over the wide plain to the Cliff. Its brick tower with a pyramid cap was built about 1700, but much of the old work in the church comes from the 13th century, and there are two doorways probably built at the close of the Saxon period; both of them have long-and-short work. The south doorway is round-headed and is now built up; the north doorway is gable-headed within the church, but has been given a flat head on the outside at a later time.

The nave is aisleless now, but in the north wall the three bays of a 13th century arcade can be seen—one of the arches framing the ancient doorway, and two framing 15th century windows. Other original windows are a lancet and an early 14th century window in the south wall of the nave. The font is an ancient square bowl. A neat modern oak screen divides nave and chancel, but the only remnant of the old chancel arch is a respond on the south side.

Boothby Graffoe. A small village high up on the Cliff road south of Lincoln, it looks far across the plain through which the rivers Brant and Witham flow. The church stands a little aloof from the cottages, ringed by sycamores and beeches and comparatively young. It is the third on the site, the first having been "extirpated by a hurricane" in the year of London's Great Fire (as recorded in the register of the neighbouring church of Wellingore), and its successor pulled down and rebuilt in 1842. Little remains of earlier days except for the arches of tower and chancel (which are partly mediaeval work), and a 17th century tablet to Christian Beresford.

Antiquity is more evident in the ruins of Somerton Castle, at the end of a narrow road nearly two miles to the west. Built by Anthony Bek in 1281, a few years before he became Bishop of Durham, it was originally a fortified manor house, built round a quadrangle 330 feet long and 180 feet wide, with round towers at the corners. One of the two remaining towers is joined to an attractive farmhouse of Elizabethan times; the tower is 45 feet high, with small lancet windows, and in front of the house are a huge grassy platform and a deep dry moat. In the orchard is the other tower, a ruin with two doorways, arcaded walls adorned with worn heads of kings, and a very fine vaulted ceiling with 12 arches growing from a central column. By it is a moat still full of water.

47

Bishop Bek gave his house to his royal master, Edward I, and it remained with the crown for 300 years. For several months in the years 1359 and 1360 it was the scene of the lavish entertainment of King John of France and his son Philip, who had been taken captive at Poitiers by the Black Prince.

Boothby Pagnell. An attractive little place in richly-wooded country, with the River Glen flowing placidly by, it has a church standing partly as the Normans left it, and, something much rarer, an unfortified manor house which is one of the oldest domestic buildings in the land.

The 12th century manor house is in the grounds of the modern Hall. It has thick walls, a vaulted undercroft, and an upper floor with two rooms, reached by an outside staircase. One of the rooms has a huge fireplace.

The church, wholly restored in Victorian times, still displays its 12th century origin in the arcades (with massive piers) and in the Norman doorway and arch of the tower. The 14th century chancel is notable for some fine modern windows. The east window has fine glass by Clayton and Bell with little Bible scenes and big figures of Matthew, Andrew, Luke, and John, their emblems being among angels in the lovely tracery. In the side windows of the chancel are the archangels Gabriel and Michael and 12 other canopied saints, Hugh of Lincoln, St Alban, and St Winifred among them. There are more Saints and Virtues in the aisle windows, and a chapel window with many Biblical characters is a tribute to W. E. Newcombe, rector here for 50 years last century.

On a wall is a monument with busts of a 17th century rector, Abel Litchford, and his wife. A more distinguished 17th century rector, who is not commemorated, was Robert Sanderson, chaplain to Charles I. It was this tragic king who said of him, "I carry my ears to hear other preachers, but I carry my conscience to hear Dr Sanderson". He was a famous Bishop of Lincoln, and he is also remembered as the author of the second preface to the Prayer Book.

Boston. In all Lincolnshire there is no town more famous than this; and in all the land there is no church steeple more renowned than Boston Stump, which through the centuries has been a landmark to men travelling across the flat lands or sailing in ships along the coast. But the fair fame of Boston is not confined to England. It has been blazoned far across the seas. It was carried by doughty adventurers, like Matthew Flinders, who set sail from the port for the other side of the globe and wrote their name indelibly on the map of Australia. It was carried across the Atlantic by those brave Puritan emigrants who in 1630 followed in the wake of the Pilgrim Fathers and founded a new Boston. This new Boston—Boston, Massachusetts—has long since surpassed the Lincolnshire Boston both in size and importance, but the close links are never forgotten by Americans, and the old mother town is ever a place of pilgrimage for them.

Boston is Botolph's town, and its earliest history—shadowy, it must be confessed—is inseparably associated with this saint, a Saxon monk, who travelled far and wide as a protagonist of Benedictine Monasticism. His home was at Iken in Suffolk, but there are relics of him in Denmark and Norway. Nearly 80 English churches are dedicated to him and Boston has the most famous of them all.

We know all too little of Botolph, but certain it is that this old Lincolnshire town, a few miles from the sea, has grown up round the name of this man of God whose reputation for wisdom and sanctity has come down the years; and Boston's wonderful old church, with its rare lantern tower looking out over a third of Lincolnshire, is known to be the successor of another church of St Botolph in Domesday Book, but their early church is given there as one of two belonging to the Danish settlement of Skirbeck—the parent parish of the town to which it now belongs.

In Norman and mediaeval times Boston became one of the chief commercial ports in England. Trade sprang up between its port on the Witham and ports in northern Europe, Flanders, and the Rhineland. England had become a wool-producing country and was growing rich, and the Witham was Boston's highway to the sea and to the Continent. Foreign merchants opened business houses here, buying English wool and selling their own goods. Boston's trade was next to London's, and, indeed, was second to none in the land at the close of the 13th century.

In times of great prosperity the merchants built Boston's great church. In the 14th and 15th centuries they had no fewer than 15 guilds, and, growing rich on trade with Flanders, built a fine church to accommodate their chapels, giving it a superb tower after the fashion of those at Antwerp and Bruges.

King John gave the town its first charter, in 1204, and it was incorporated in 1545 by Henry VIII. In addition to the guilds, friaries belonging to the four chief orders had been established in the town, and though only a few fragments survived at the Dissolution, their sites (and those of some of the guilds) live on in street-names.

Boston's prosperity began to decline in the 15th century, and it is recorded that early in the 17th century the corporation petitioned that "their borough might be put among the decayed towns". Much has been done since then, however, and the silting-up of the tidal river bed which brought decay to the port has been overcome by modern engineering skill. The straightening of the bed of the river last century quickened its flow, and with the building of a new dock in 1882 trade has greatly increased. Covering about seven acres, the dock is 825 feet long, and 450 feet at its widest, and can safely accommodate ships of 3000 tons. Once busy with the coal trade, there is now only one coal-hoist; there are huge warehouses for storing grain; another has been adapted for the shipping of cattle, and there is up-to-date machinery to speed the moving of cargo. There is also a riverside quay with additional berths. The port is among the busiest for its size on the east coast with a very large timber and fruit import trade and is undergoing extensive development. Apart from all this, Boston is the chief agricultural centre of this fertile county, and widely celebrated for its markets and fairs.

Much of old Boston has been swept away, or survives only in fragments; but St Botolph's Church remains the same magnificent testimony in stone to the skill of 14th and 15th century builders. Its crowning glory is, of course, the tower, 272½ feet high and famous the world over as Boston Stump. The highest and loveliest mediaeval lantern tower in the land, it would seem to merit a better title than "Stump"; but the name is most apt when the tower is seen from afar, for then the exquisite octagon lantern seems to give the whole a blunted, unfinished appearance.

For five centuries Boston's lantern tower has been a guide to travellers by land and sea, and in former times a beacon light shone at night from the octagon. From its summit (reached by about as many steps as there are days in a year) there is an amazing panorama embracing Tattershall Castle, the towers of Lincoln 30 miles away, and Hunstanton across the wide stretch of the Wash.

The tower was built during the 15th century—it was finished in 1460—but its foundations, 36 feet deep, are said to have been begun in 1309 and to be the oldest part of the present church. Other 15th century work includes the two eastern bays of the chancel (the east window is an addition of 1853), the upper room of the south porch, and some of the pinnacles and parapets which are such an attractive feature of the exterior. The end windows of the aisles have tracery marking the transition from the 14th century style to the 15th; but the rest of the structure belongs entirely to the 14th century, and is a striking example of the development of the architecture of the period. Between the two World Wars the nave and aisles were given splendid panelled roofs, enriched with bosses and gay with colour after mediaeval fashion; and at the same time the 18th century wooden vault of the chancel (which retains mediaeval bosses) was painted red and green.

Projecting slightly from the west wall of the tower is a 14th century porch with splendid old double doors; it was brought forward when, with the rest of the church finished, the long-delayed building of the tower was resumed above ground. Carved on the porch are stone figures of two men reading (one with a lion on his back and the other with an eagle), a man playing a harp, and a woman with a demon on her shoulder.

The walls of the tower are enriched with bold panelling, and its three stages are lighted by great windows, the huge eight-light west window being one of the biggest in the kingdom. Panelled buttresses climb in steps to the delicately-carved parapet, ending in fine turret pinnacles from which pairs of flying buttresses spring in support of the elegant lantern. With its eight long, transomed windows, its parapet of pierced carving like an edging of lace, and its buttresses ending in a ring of eight pinnacles with gilded vanes, this lantern is indeed a fitting crown for the majestic tower.

Low down on the west wall are marks showing the level of record high tides, for Boston has suffered much from floods in days gone by (as well as from plague). On the north side of the tower is a knight carved in stone; and from his embattled pedestal on the south side St Botolph surveys his town.

The stone groining within the tower, 137 feet above the floor, is said to be the highest in England, except for that above the central crossing in Liverpool's new cathedral. The keystone in the centre, with a carved Holy Lamb, is reputed to weigh more than five tons. Carved on other bosses are leaves and flowers and angels. Seen from far below this vault has the appearance of a great spider's web. It is the newest part of the tower, for although it was provided for in the original design the work was not carried out until the 1853 restoration. The base of the tower is separated from the nave by an iron screen placed there in 1934; from 1743 it had stood at the west end of the nave until it was taken in 1853 to form the entrance to the Grammar School.

The town's best views of this gently-tapering tower are from the south end of the marketplace and from the two bridges between which it soars. Most stately it looks from the water's edge, and the rest of the church is well worthy of its place in this picture. Rich parapets adorn the chancel, the aisles, and the clerestoried nave with its noble range of 14 windows on each side. The parapets running east to west are solid, and those at the eastern ends pierced —chiefly with quatrefoils; the eastern parapet of the north aisle, however, is of more intricate design, and spaced along it are three charming pinnacles with statues in niches. The great pinnacle at the end of this parapet is perhaps the loveliest of all, but there is another of special note at the west end of the south aisle. On the nave gable is the old sanctus bellcot.

The beautiful south porch (14th century below and 15th above) has buttresses enriched with canopied niches and crocketed pinnacles. Above its entrance archway (and under a quatrefoiled parapet with a sundial in the centre) is the window of the upper room where is kept the church library founded in 1635 by the then vicar, Anthony

Tuckney, with considerable encouragement from Archbishop Laud. But it is the great oak double door within the porch that fascinates visitors, for its two halves are dove-tailed into each other in a rare and probably unique manner; it has fine tracery and a wicket entrance, and must be one of the finest of the mediaeval doors remaining in our churches. Another splendid old door opens to the north aisle, and at the foot of the south stairway of the tower is a door with a fine old bronze handle-ring of lizards in a lion's mouth.

Spaciousness is the outstanding feature of the interior of Boston Church. Its length, including the tower, is 283 feet; the width 100 feet, though there are no transepts; and the total area 20,270 square feet. Built above the foundations of a small Norman church—they came to light in the 19th century restoration—the nave of seven bays is 155 feet long and 68 feet high; the arcades have slender clustered piers leaning slightly eastward, and above is the fine clerestory. Raised high on four steps in the great open space at the west end is a fine 19th century font by Pugin, its bowl encircled with intricate carving of trailing flowers and leaves. Crowning it all is the richly-panelled roof.

For this nave roof, and for those of the aisles, the people of Boston raised £23,000 in three years, and part of the story of how it was done is carved on the bosses of the south aisle. A white elephant recalls a sale of unwanted treasures that raised hundreds of pounds; St Hugh tells of grants made by Lincoln; David plays his harp as a reminder of many concerts held. The vicar, the verger, the choir, the children all have their own bosses; so have the villages which helped, and also the farmers who one market day had a sale for the cause.

Among the carvings on the nave bosses are the Dove, a gateway of the old town, a pilgrim, a sheep (recalling the wool trade), a life-boat, and the *Mayflower* (here only as a reminder of many Boston folk who became Pilgrim Fathers, for the *Mayflower* did not sail from here).

More fragments of Boston's history are recorded on the north aisle bosses. Here can be seen King Ethelmund, St Botolph, a Viking, King John, the Friars, Dame Tilney who helped to lay the foundation stone in 1309, a merchant weighing wool on the steel-yard, one of 17 ships Boston sent to fight the French in the reign of Edward III, a Fair man with his dancing bear (recalling Henry VIII's charter), and Death with a scythe—a reminder that the Black Death took toll of half the population. Here are portraits of Mary Tudor and Philip of Spain, and of John Cotton, Boston's famous Puritan vicar. Here, too, are children of the Bluecoat school, emblems of the Boston guilds, and the Boston coat-of-arms with the date 1630, the year when Boston, Massachusetts, was first named. Truly the bosses in Boston's church are a fascinating collection, reflecting the town's storylike engravings in an old history book.

The chancel has an 18th century wooden ceiling (with mediaeval bosses and modern colours), 18th century altar-rails, and a modern screen. Its most outstanding features, however, are a wonderful array of mediaeval stalls and an astonishing reredos erected 1890–1 and completed in 1914 by the addition of the statuary. Extending right across the east wall, and soaring 32 feet, the reredos is a massive work in English oak, shining with many golden canopies, and adorned with a host of carved and coloured figures in niches and in scenes of the Bible story. Above the Last Supper are the Crucifixion and Our Lord in Glory, and there are smaller scenes showing Abraham's sacrifice, Elijah's ascension, Moses lifting up the serpent, and Jonah and the whale. The Disciples stand in canopied niches, and in dainty niches on the buttresses are 38 small saints.

The stalls, among the finest in the land, were made about 1390, except for the elaborate canopies which were added last century. There are 64 of them, and all but two have their original hinged seats—a series of carved misericords unsurpassed in quality of workmanship even by those of Lincoln Cathedral which, however, has a greater number. Many are carved with animals, real and fabulous; others have scenes beloved by mediaeval craftsmen. Among the carvings on the south group of stalls may be seen an armoured knight on horseback picking up a horseshoe; two sailors in a boat listening to a siren or mermaid; a woman chasing a fox which is carrying off a cock; bear-baiting; two winged lions sharing one head; a man threatened by his wife because he has returned empty-handed from the hunt; and a wolf in clerical garb (attended by a fox) preaching to geese.

Among the quaint carvings on the north side can be seen a bear playing an organ, while a chained bear blows for him (perhaps the earliest English carving known of organ-playing); a man with bellows, a cauldron on a fire, and a woman with basin and ladle; St George and the Dragon; a hooded baboon with his legs crossed, pouring water from a pitcher into a bucket held by a fox; and a choirmaster birching a boy who protects himself with his book. Among the misericords on the return-stalls can be seen a bishop on his throne, a rector reading, and a man lassoing a lion. Fine carving on the elbow-rests portrays an eagle scratching its foot, a fox eating a chicken, a beggar asking alms, a woman with bellows reviving a fire, an old man feeding his dog, a fox in a cope taking a jar of water from a baboon, a hound chasing a hare, and a cat after a mouse.

The eastern end of the south aisle, still with its plain old piscina and lovely sedilia, was originally the chapel of the Guild of St Mary (their hall, now the Guildhall, still survives in South Street).

Founded in 1260, it was the oldest and richest of Boston's many guilds, maintaining seven priests, a choir, a school, and almshouses. Opening from the west end of this aisle, and adjoining the porch, is the little 14th century Cotton Chapel. Originally it belonged to one of the smaller guilds, but it was restored by Americans in 1857 as a tribute to John Cotton, the Puritan vicar who served here from 1612 till he sailed with many of his congregation to Boston in Massachusetts. That was in 1633 three years after the daughter-city had been so named, and he ministered there faithfully till his death in 1652.

Modern glass in the Cotton Chapel's west window shows St Botolph, with this church above him, and a missionary bishop with Chinese converts below; St Francis of Assisi, and Boston Bluecoat children singing in this chapel; St Mary with Lincoln Cathedral above her, and members of St Mary's Guild below, leaving their hall to come to church; and St Nicholas, who stands below Skirbeck Church, with Boston crusaders to the Holy Land below him. The Disciples and emblems of the guilds are in the tracery.

In the north aisle (the east end of which is the chapel of the Guild of St Peter and St Paul whose restoration was completed in 1951) are portrayed other figures and scenes in the story of Boston Church. In one window are four archbishops: Thomas Becket, who sailed through Boston when fleeing from the king; Henry Chichele, who came here when the tower was being built; William Laud, who founded the library; and Cosmo Gordon Lang, who came here in 1931 to receive 55,000 dollars for the restoration of the tower and the recasting of the 14 bells—the gift of the people of Boston overseas. Another window has four patron saints of Boston guilds, and a picture of the Musical Festival of 1807 when Handel's Messiah and Judas Maccabeus were performed in the church; here also is shown the opening of the Cotton Chapel, with the Bluecoat boys as choir, and portraits of notable people who attended the ceremony, including Bishop Jackson and Pishey Thompson, the local historian whose memorial is on the south wall.

Among the fittings of the church is a Jacobean pulpit. It also has several old chests, and some of the rare books and manuscripts from the library are displayed in a glass case in the north aisle.

Boston Church is not rich in monuments, and the finest are the alabaster figures of a 14th century knight and lady lying on tombs in recesses of the south aisle wall. She is a frail figure with a flowing mantle over her gown; her head, in mitred headdress, rests on a cushion held by angels, and two dogs are at her feet. The knight has a Maltese cross hanging from the chain round his neck, and his sword hangs from an embroidered belt. In another recess in this wall are two coffin lids—one a child's; and in yet another is a stone coffin complete with its carved lid.

At the west end of the north aisle is a black gravestone with the engraved portrait of Wisselus Smalenburg, a German merchant who died at Boston in 1340. He is in a long gown with wide sleeves, and a dog lies curled up between his feet. This stone was found on the site of the Grey Friars' church, near the Grammar School, and for a time was built into the wall of a house.

On a floorstone at the east end of the nave is the engraved portrait of a priest, whose head and hands, and his chalice, were once here in brass. Of these rare memorials, part stone, part brass, there are no fewer than 11 in this church (more than half of all that exist in England), but most of the brass parts are missing.

Two splendid brasses are in the floor of the chancel, one on each side of the altar. On the north side is a Flemish brass showing Walter Pescod, a 14th century merchant whose home still stands in the town. He is portrayed in his long embroidered gown, but without the wife who once was here beside him. Above him is a series of elaborate canopies, supported by shafts bearing Apostles in niches. The brass on the south side is the portrait of John Strensall, Rector of Boston, who died in 1408; his cope is adorned with canopied figures of Apostles. (John Strensall's portrait also appears on one of three newly-painted old corbels on the arches of the Cotton Chapel.)

A tiny brass on a pillar of the south arcade has a group of six children, and another has three; they belong to a stone below, with the matrices of a man and two wives. Another incomplete canopied brass with the figure of a woman is on the south wall. On the north aisle wall is the brass of Thomas Lawe, 1657, thrice Mayor of Boston; it shows him wearing a skull cap and a gown with puffed sleeves.

Looking down from a wall is a bust of Herbert Ingram, MP for Boston, 1856–1860, sculptured by Westmacott. This famous son of Boston is also commemorated by a statue on the lawn outside. He is looking into the marketplace, and one of his hands rests on volumes of the *Illustrated London News*, founded by him in 1842, the first paper of its kind. Herbert Ingram was drowned with his son Hugh in 1860 in a shipwreck on Lake Michigan, but his body was brought home and buried in the cemetery here. Over his grave is a medallion portrait of the son, whose body was never found.

Two other monuments, both in the tower, merit special mention. One is a tablet bearing the names of five men connected with Boston who became governors of Massachusetts. The other is a tablet set up in proud memory of men of Boston and nearby who shared in the discovery and exploration of Australia.

Who are these men whose memory both Lincolnshire and Australia are so proud to honour? There is George Bass, a Lincolnshire boy who served his apprenticeship to a Boston surgeon. In 1796 he explored the coast of New South Wales in a small whaler, and in the two succeeding years sailed right round Tasmania in a 25-ton sloop and discovered the Strait which put his name, literally, on the map for all time. Then there is Sir Joseph Banks, Squire of Revesby, whose passion for botany took him round the world. He sailed with Captain Cook in the *Endeavour*; and with him were Peter Briscoe of his village, and James Roberts of Mareham-le-Fen. Next is Joseph Gilbert, an astronomer of Wrangle, a few miles from Boston, who with Robert Rollett of that town, served on Cook's second expedition, when he discovered New Caledonia, and called at Tahiti.

Finally, there is the great Matthew Flinders, a son of the fenland town of Donington, who commanded the sloop in which George Bass made his great discoveries and, two or three years later, made his wonderful survey of Australia's shores in the *Investigator*. This was a voyage packed with adventures, and they were shared by his brother, Samuel Flinders, by Robert Fowler of Horncastle, and by a young cousin from Spilsby—John Franklin of immortal memory, whose parents were married in Boston Church.

These Lincolnshire–Australia worthies were "honoured in their generations and were the glory of their times". Englishmen and Australians still honour their names today.

So snugly has Boston grown up around its church and its river that almost all that is interesting for the traveller can be found within easy walking distance. Except for the Municipal Buildings of 1904 in West Street (repository of the civic insignia and of charters granted to the town by Tudor and Stuart monarchs) all that is notable lies on the east side of the Witham, scattered along or near the two roads running roughly north and south from the spacious and irregularly-shaped marketplace. The north road begins as Strait Bargate, opens out into Wide Bargate, where the cattle market is held, and comes to Bargate End, from which point can be seen the fine Maud Foster windmill with five picturesque sweeps, which has recently been preserved by Boston Frozen Foods (part of the Ross Group) whose works adjoin it.

On Bargate Green is the town's war memorial, a shaft of Portland stone set on a great pedestal and surmounted by a cross 28 feet above the ground. A few yards from the memorial, Park Gate leads between the Post Office and the Savings Bank to the Central Park, which has attractive iron gates showing the rising sun and a wavy sea with fishing smacks, and two mermaids of the Boston arms. The new head office of the East Midlands Trustee Savings Bank in Wide Bargate incorporates an elegant house built about 1790 by a member of the Tunnard family. At the end of Mitre Lane (which runs off Bargate) is the old Pescod House, home of the 14th century merchant prince whose brass lies in the church. Now it is a warehouse, but its gabled front of rich red-brick and timber still bears witness to its original beauty.

Back in Marketplace, with the church close by, it is well to see the interesting buildings round the Close and to note the quaint narrow lanes leading off with names such as Petticoat Lane and Dolphin Lane. Looking up to the great tower from the corner of Church Street is the black-and-white house—now a shop—known as Church Key, with a hanging iron sign of a lantern and a key. Between Wormgate and the river is a fine modern vicarage facing the north side of the church. On the other corner of Wormgate is the old Church House which was part of a grant of Mary Tudor and Philip of Spain to the town; charming it is with its walls of dark brick, its Dutch gable, and its rich motley of roof tiles. Next to it is the old vicarage, now used as offices, then the Sessions House, and its dignified neighbour the County Hall.

In Marketplace, probably on the site now occupied by the Rum Puncheon Inn, stood the birthplace of John Foxe, author of the *Book of Martyrs*, that monumental work of English prose which once ranked next in influence to the Bible and *The Pilgrim's Progress* and had a place in most of our churches. He was born here in 1516, and was a friend of John Taverner of Boston, "the good musician", one of the greatest of early composers of music for the Church.

Running south from the marketplace, parallel with the river, are South Street, South Square, and South End. The first building of note in South Street is Shodfriars Hall, rebuilt in 1874. Its western end was on the site of an old timber-framed building, and some of the old timbers were used in the modern building which is a complete fake. It is said to have been given its name from the Dominican Friary whose site was near by, and of which there are fragments to be seen. Opposite the Rum Puncheon are the Georgian Assembly Rooms built on the east bank of the river in 1822 and recently restored inside to their former magnificence after a fire which destroyed the roof. The view from South Street of the Town Bridge, the white-walled Assembly Rooms, and the "Stump" is a favourite one for visitors to the town. The marketplace has recently been given pleasant treatment to a scheme of decoration devised by the Corporation's architect with the co-operation of the traders. An interesting group of buildings on the south side of the marketplace, built in 1772 and known as the Corporation Buildings, was formerly used as the Town Hall. In Spain Lane close by is Blackfriars, originally the refectory of the friary but recently restored as a theatre, arts centre, and meeting-rooms to meet a much-felt need in this part of the county.

Spain Lane took its name from the de Spaynes, a rich merchant family, and in it were many great cellars used for storing cargoes of wine brought from abroad; some of them were rented by various abbeys. Leaving Spain Lane it is but a few steps to the Guildhall in South Street, the long 15th century hall of the rich Guild of St Mary. The stone mullioned window of its banqueting hall in the gabled west front contains its original glass with 10 figures of saints and two roundels with emblems; at the opposite end is the old minstrel gallery, approached by a quaint stairway. Adjoining the hall is the courtroom, now housing a small museum, and next to this what used to be called the Red Room, with the magnificent old linenfold doors of an archive cupboard, and the portrait of Sir Joseph Banks who was recorder here. On the ground floor is the kitchen with its old fireplaces, complete with spits, turned by a fan in the chimney. But it is the iron-grated cells which are of special historic interest, for they are a link with the men of the *Mayflower*.

In these cells were imprisoned William Brewster and William Bradford, together with others of that band of heroes who were later to become the Pilgrim Fathers of immortal memory. They had embarked on a sloop at Boston intending to sail to Holland, but had been betrayed by the skipper and brought here for trial. Here still are remains of the newel stair up which they climbed to the court room above, there to be tried by the magistrates. In the following year Brewster and Bradford were more successful and, sailing with their followers from Hull to Amsterdam, began that undying series of adventures which 12 years later was to land them on the shores of New England, with freedom to worship as they chose.

In the undercroft of Boston's historic Guildhall is a doorway from the house in South Square on the opposite side of the road in which Jean Ingelow lived as a child. The house in which she was born in 1820 was burnt down in 1823 and her father removed his banking business next door to the house known as "Ingelow House". He went bankrupt in 1826 and Jean later left the town. She is specially remembered for her poem, *High Tide on the Coast of Lincolnshire*, which tells of the terrible storm and flood of 1571 when Boston and a great part of the county was devastated.

In her vivid description of the disaster Jean Ingelow tells how warning was given by the Boston bells:

> *The old Mayor climbed the belfry tower,*
> *The ringers ran by two, by three;*
> *"Pull, if ye never pulled before;*
> *Good ringers, pull your best," quoth he.*
> *"Play uppe, play uppe, O Boston bells!*
> *Play all your changes, all your swells,*
> *Play uppe 'The Brides of Enderby'."*

But there were no "Brides of Enderby" when Jean Ingelow wrote her verse. She chose the title of her song for the Boston bells from the pretty name of Mavis Enderby up on the Wolds, and the tune afterwards played on the church chimes was composed as a tribute to the poem.

Next to the Guildhall is Fydell House, built in 1726. Admirably set off by its fine wrought-iron gateway, it has a pilastered front with balustraded parapet, and is attractive inside with its panelled walls and fine staircase. An old candelabrum for 18 lights hangs from the richly-moulded ceiling of the entrance hall. Belonging now to the Boston Preservation Trust (who also own the lease of Blackfriars) Fydell House houses Pilgrim College, an adult educational branch of Nottingham University. One room is dedicated to the use of visitors from Boston, Massachusetts.

Beyond Fydell House is the Grammar School, standing back from South End and reached by Greyfriars Lane. Attractively grouped with the modern buildings is the fine old schoolroom with walls of dark red-brick and a projecting window with stone battlements. Built in 1567, and restored, it is now the library of this celebrated school which was founded in mediaeval days, probably as early as the 13th century. In the north window of the hall are portraits of Lord Burghley, Elizabeth I, Francis Bacon, and Francis Drake.

By the school playing-fields stands the gaunt red-brick ruin known as the Hussey Tower. It is all that remains of the old home of Lord Hussey, a former favourite of Henry VIII who was executed on a charge of complicity in the Pilgrimage of Grace.

A description of Boston would be incomplete without mention of its bridges. The oldest, the Grand Sluice Bridge, where the sluice gates prevent the incoming tide flowing farther up-river, was opened in 1766. It was this occasion which prompted a guest, dissatisfied with the hospitality offered after the ceremony, to quote:

> *Boston, Boston, Boston, thou hast nought to boast on*
> *But a Grand Sluice and a high steeple,*
> *A proud, conceited, ignorant people,*
> *And a coast where souls get lost on.*

A quarter of a mile downstream is the Town Bridge opened in 1913 to replace an earlier iron bridge built by Sir John Rennie, and downstream again is the fine new Haven Bridge opened in 1966 to carry traffic to and from the Docks.

Bottesford. Here the church is all in all. A beautiful building shaped like a cross, it is for the most part a legacy from the 13th century, with the 14th century represented by the south aisle windows, and the 15th century by the windows of the north aisle and the buttresses and parapet of the tower. Far older than all else here are two sundials, believed to be Saxon, which came to light during restoration last century; one is outside and the other is within the south porch, which also shelters a lovely doorway.

It is the 13th century chancel, glowing with golden light, that makes this church notable, for its nine deeply-splayed lancet windows, adorned with dog-tooth moulding, are believed to be the longest and narrowest lancets to be seen in any English village church. Above the three in the east wall are two more lancets and a small round window. Triple lancets with round windows above them light the transepts, and lancets alternate with round windows in the nave's 13th century clerestory. Other fine examples of Early English work are the nave arcades, with stone seats round their lovely clustered piers; the fine tower arch—like a great lancet; the handsome triple sedilia, double piscina, and three aumbries in the chancel; the restored shaft-piscina in the north transept; and the font, with nail-head ornament.

Two of the memorials here (one with a table to the Morley family, and another with an inscription of 1677) were formerly altar stones. Notable among the church's relics is a great 17th century chest carved with flowers and curious animal heads; another is the small bronze sanctus bell (in the chancel) which was found last century embedded in the west wall of the church.

Bourne. A rare little town looking eastwards to the flat and fertile, black-soiled fens, and westward to delightful wooded uplands, it has a place in history that must be called remarkable. Here the Romans brought their King Street on its way to Sleaford, and here also they brought the Carr Dyke, one of the greatest engineering feats carried out in Britain during the Roman occupation, an immense dyke catching the drainage from the hills for 56 miles, holding it from the low fens and discharging it into the River Nene at Peterborough and the River Witham near Lincoln and at the same time providing a waterway for the transport of grain from the Fens to the north. Among the best places for seeing it are here at Bourne, by the church of the neighbouring village of Thurlby, and in the hamlet of Dyke, which gets its name from the great Roman canal.

That is one visible witness to the past greatness of Bourne; but there is an invisible one that makes it a cradle of the English language. It is no small claim, but it can be made for Bourne. It was Robert Manning, says Professor Freeman, who gave our English language its present shape, and Manning was a man of Bourne, or Brunne, as he called it. He was the first man to write English as we read it now; and the fine old church here belonged to the abbey in which he lived and wrote. The town has named one of its roads in honour of Manning, but he was better known as Robert de Brunne because of the long years he spent as a teacher at the abbey. It was here that he wrote his *Handlyng Synne* (a translation from the French), which has in his preface:

For men unlearned I undertook
In English speech to write this book,
To all true Christians under sun,
To good and loyal men of Brunn,
Robert of Brunn now greeteth ye
And prays for your prosperity.

In the long pageant of English history no mean part has been played by this little town which began as a cluster of dwellings on the banks of the Carr Dyke, and is now gathered about a marketplace and roads reaching it from the four points of the compass. It was a Roman station (Roman pottery kilns were found when the Grammar School was rebuilt in 1959); it was a Saxon stronghold; it had a Norman abbey and a moated Norman castle. Behind West Street is the site of this once-famous castle, now little more than grassy mounds and traces of moats. The Romans may have had a fort here to guard their road and canal, and here lived the Saxon Morcar, Lord of Bourne, who fell fighting the Danes at Threekingham in 870.

But its heyday was as a castle of the Norman lords, the Wakes. There was Hugh, who married Baldwin FitzGilbert's daughter, and later on Margaret de Wake, who married a Plantagenet, her daughter Joan marrying Edward the Black Prince and so becoming the mother of Richard II. The Wakes claimed descent from Hereward the Wake, who made a great stand in the last struggle against the Conqueror. The legends which have grown up round this hero make Bourne his birthplace, and Charles Kingsley made it the scene of his story. We know that Thomas de Wake entertained Edward III here, and we know that nothing but mounds and the moats remained in the time of Elizabeth I, though a tale persists that the castle was destroyed by Oliver Cromwell.

The Norman castle is said to have been a massive keep with square towers, with a moat surrounding its low mound, and another moat enclosing the bailey covering 8 acres. The moats were filled by Bourne's famous spring which comes to life here at a spot called Well Head, or Peter's Pool. Issuing from a natural fissure in the limestone, it flows past the church, makes humdrum corners of the town picturesque, and then flows eastward on its way to become the little river called Bourne Eau, flowing across the Fens and joining the Glen at Tongue End.

Baldwin FitzGilbert, or his son-in-law Hugh de Wake, founded in 1138 an abbey for Augustinian Canons, the abbey where Robert Manning wrote his all-important works. Little is left of its buildings, however, except the church, which escaped destruction at the Dissolution by becoming the parish church. Serene in its setting, it is reached by quiet pathways, and displays two very striking features in its nave and west front. The west front, reflected in the waters of the passing Bourne stream, was begun early in the 13th century and is a vista of lancet arcading and windows. In the centre is a 15th century doorway, still with its ancient door, and on either side is a tower, that on the north (with flat roof) being unfinished, while its companion, with a pinnacled top stage added in the 15th century, is more than twice as high.

Entering the church through the embattled 15th century south porch we come to a nave which is the only surviving fragment of the original Norman church and is an impressive spectacle, with four round arches on each side borne up on massive piers with scalloped capitals. Above each arcade are four windows of the 15th century clerestory, and beyond them is the wide and lofty chancel, rebuilt and now without arch or screen. Both of the Norman aisles were widened in the 15th century, and the north aisle has been much altered again in modern times. The interior at the west end of the church is made impressive by the great arches of the twin towers and has a passage like a triforium running in front of the lancet windows.

To richness in glass and brass and monument Bourne Church has small claim, and its roofs and seats are all modern. The font, with an inscription meaning Jesus is the name above all names, is 15th century; there is a fine brass candelabrum with 24 branches made in 1742; and above the north arcade is a memorial tablet to Thomas Rawnsley, who at his own expense raised a troop of Light Horse Rangers when Napoleon threatened England; he was the great-grandfather of Canon H. D. Rawnsley, author of *Memories of the Tennysons*, and W. F. Rawnsley, who wrote *Highways and Byways in Lincolnshire*.

Three other buildings of great historic interest has Bourne. One is the Red Hall, 17th century, charming with its gables and weather-beaten sundial, its mullioned window, and two-storied porch, and its grey mossy roof. Once it was the home of Sir John Thimbleby, the great Roman Catholic leader, and then of the Digbys. When the railway came the estate was sold to the railway company. Another building is in the marketplace, next to the 19th century town hall, prominent with its pillars and pediment and clock turret, on the site of an ancient guildhall; this is a house, now the Bull Inn, with four dormer windows overlooking all the bustle of market days, and it is famous as the birthplace of that William Cecil who became Lord Burghley, the great statesman of Elizabeth I and founder of the fortunes of the illustrious Cecil family. The third is the remains of the old late Elizabethan Grammar School, founded in 1603 and now found among trees in the churchyard.

Two lesser names in the history of Bourne are Job Hartop and William Dodd. Hartop, born here in 1550, sailed with Sir John Hawkins, spent 10 years in the galleys and 13 in a Spanish prison, but came home safe at last to end his days in his native town. William Dodd, son of a vicar of Bourne, and born here in 1729, was man about town, popular preacher and king's chaplain in turn, but, falling into debt, signed Lord Chesterfield's name to a bond for £4000 and was hanged for forgery.

Bourne has some richly endowed charities, and to these its young people can give thanks for the Abbey Lawn (one of the best sports grounds in Lincolnshire, with a splendid swimming-pool) and some of its old people can give thanks for the modern Bede Houses in West Street, a charming group of single-storeyed houses of warm-looking brick, with rounded doorways opening on to a central garden. In addition, the Bourne Charities help to maintain the Schools, the Memorial Gardens, the Well Head Fields, and the mounds both of Bourne Castle and Hereward's Castle. A more curious Bourne charity is associated with White Bread Meadow. Ever since 1770, it has been let from year to year by an auctioneer who starts a number of boys running for a certain distance. As soon as they have set off, the bidding for the field begins. The bidding can only go on till the boys return, and then the highest bidder holds the meadow for a year; the rent goes to buy bread for the poor, according to the bequest of Richard Clay.

Most students of Early English agree that the Lincolnshire monk, Robert Manning, who died about the time Chaucer was born, had more than anyone else to do with putting the ordinary speech of the English people of his day into a written form still recognisable.

What is known of him is nearly all told in his writings. He went to Sempringham Priory, 6 miles north of Bourne, in 1288; he must then have been 24 years old according to the rules of the House. In 1303 he there began to write.

He never wrote anything quite original. He translated the writings of other men into English rhyme from French rhyme. But if as he translated he knew anything more about the subject than the author, or anything that would illustrate a point, he added it in his own words. We should call his rhyme doggerel, but the people who read it in his day could understand it; their language was his own native language, he knew that rhyme is most easily remembered, and he wanted to give simple, unlearned people knowledge and advice and amusement. He hoped his writings would be, he said, "solace in their fellowship as they sat together".

His first and best book is called *Handlyng Synne*. It is a translation of a poem in bad French by a William of Waddington, whose writing is far inferior to Manning's. The results of pride, envy, anger, idleness, and other sins are illustrated by 65 stories. He discusses a wide variety of subjects which picture the life of that period, such as witchcraft, tournaments, games, and dress; and the great value of his book is that it gives glimpses into the ways and thoughts of our

63

countrymen 600 years ago and, even more, shows us the language then in common use. His influence in standardising that language was very considerable, for the East Midland dialect in which he wrote took the lead of others and eventually became national.

Thirty-five years later he began to write in rhyme his *Story of England*, chiefly a translation of a chronicle compiled by a canon in Bridlington Priory. Manning had left Sempringham and was a canon of the Sixhills Gilbertine Priory near Market Rasen. His chronicle has no historical value except where it touches the reign of Edward I and so overlaps his own experience. It is a collection of legendary records, so its value is much less than the writings that picture contemporary life, but from the point of view of English as it was used it remains deeply interesting.

Robert Manning was an earnest man, intent on doing good through a rather narrow piety—as might be expected then; but he had a sound knowledge of the people and in his own way was one of the most practical of popular educators. He tried to give the people material for talk and thought, and while adopting their own language he sought to extend its scope. He wrote, as he said, "in simple speech for love of simple men".

Braceborough. As a health-giving spa it once had a measure of fame, and it still has mineral springs yielding their bounteous daily flow. But fame has passed on its way, leaving the village its sequestered charm, enhanced by a few thatched cottages. The church, with big ivy-mantled porch, aisleless nave, and tiny apsidal chancel has largely been rebuilt; but the sturdy 13th century tower with soaring broach spire still stands, and another witness to antiquity is the Norman font, its square bowl carved with arches, zigzag, and diamond pattern. Yet another is a big stone with the impress of a brass to Thomas de Wasteneys, who died here of the Black Death in 1349.

Braceby. A little cluster of red-tiled cottages and haystacks, it has a tiny church with a double bellcot dwarfed by the neighbouring sycamores. This humble place of worship has a 13th century chancel arch and north arcade, a plain round 14th century font, and a 15th century clerestory. In the south wall are the three arches of a vanished aisle, and by the pulpit is the old iron stand of a vanished hourglass.

Bradley. At a charming tree-bowered corner of this quiet retreat near Grimsby stand a small church and manor house. The church is of stone and Norman in origin; the house is a lovely brick building of 1689 with creeper-clad walls, set amid delightful gardens. Close to one of the garden paths is the fragment of an old cross, and another cross with embattled head stands on three steps by the church's little porch.

The unbuttressed tower of the church is partly Norman, but its upper part has two-light belfry windows showing early plate tracery of the 13th century, and the battlements are later. Traces of an early arcade can be seen outside in the north wall of the nave.

The interior is quaint. The stout walls are panelled, and the tiny pews all have extremely tall fleur-de-lys poppyheads, from every one of which rises a dainty wooden candle-holder. The big font, made in the 14th century, has a richly-moulded stem supporting a bowl adorned with a continuous band of quatrefoils, and bears a black-letter inscription which runs:

> *Pater noster ave maria and criede*
> *Leren ye child yt es nede.*

The glass of the east window, showing the Ascension, is a tribute to John Caley, who became rector here after serving as a missionary in India for 35 years.

Branston. A rapidly growing village on the longer of two roads from Lincoln to Sleaford, it has a fine old church standing on the highest point in the village, and with nine centuries of history. It is a splendid building, spacious and light, with a happy blend of mediaeval and modern styles. A disastrous fire in 1962 made necessary a complete restoration and rebuilding of the nave roof and chancel.

The oldest work in the church is some Saxon long-and-short masonry seen outside at the south-west corner of the nave. The striking tower, crowned by a 15th century parapet and spire, was probably built soon after the Conquest, the Normans giving it a tall west doorway with a tympanum enriched with trellis pattern, and adorning the walling on each side with round-headed arcading; their belfry windows preserve the Saxon style of coupled lights divided by baluster shafts. Four Elizabethan bells, with two of the 19th century to keep them company, ring out from the tower.

The lofty 14th century arch from tower to nave was opened out in 1876, when Sir Gilbert Scott restored the church and gave it a new outer north aisle. The original aisles and lofty nave arcades, with foliage on the capitals, are also 14th century, but the clerestory is 15th. The 13th century is represented by the north and south door-ways, and the font with its bowl resting on a central shaft and four pillars. The chancel, though much rebuilt in 1864, also has its original 13th century sedilia and piscina with four mediaeval faces on their arches. The chancel received a new roof in the 1964–66 restoration and follows the 15th century outline, but the treatment is modern; the inner ceiling is a wood barrel vault. A fine new east window with glass by Keith New (1965), depicts the "Glory beyond the Cross" and provides lively colour and interest. The free-standing altar-table is of oak and a tall wrought-iron cross is placed behind it.

All the pews have poppyhead ends, and about 40 of them have been here since the 15th century; most of them have tracery and foliage, but a few have figures such as fighting monkeys, a man with bagpipes, and a fox with two dancers. The old foreign glass making a medley of colour in a north aisle window was collected by Lord Leven; among its fragments are the lion of St Mark and an angel in gold.

A striking feature of the church is the new organ built in 1966 on a detached gallery in the western part of the nave.

The oldest memorial is a 13th century stone in the chancel tran-sept, carved with a cross, and bearing a Norman–French inscription to rector Richard de Thistleton. The strangest monument is that of Sir Cecil Wray, who died in 1736; raised in his lifetime, it has his sculptured bust, with a turban, separated from that of his wife by a tall marble obelisk; prosperous-looking they are, and both double-chinned.

The Curtois family had a remarkable connection with Branston Church. For 211 years a Curtois was rector here; there were six of them from 1680 to 1891, and one of them built the old rectory in 1765, a dignified Georgian house by the church.

Brant Broughton. Old houses gathered about the roads, a manor house at one end and a beautiful church at the other, close to where the Sand Beck is flowing to the River Brant—that is Brant Broughton, a village with much to delight the traveller who can tarry awhile. Well may this village be proud of its church, a splendid mediaeval building which owes much to the skill and generosity of a 19th century rector, and also to the Coldrons, from whose lowly little forge close by iron wrought with magic skill into forms of exquisite beauty has gone into our cathedrals and churches up and down the land.

The church is notable for much excellent stone carving adorning its walls and the mouldings of its windows and doorways—a rich profusion of flowers, leaves, grotesques, and animals peeping out here, there, and everywhere. Most of the church is 14th century, but the lofty nave arcades, the chancel arch, and the south doorway are 13th century; and the aisle windows and the fine battlemented and pinnacled clerestory are 15th century. The restoration saw the chancel worthily rebuilt in 14th century style and the north aisle set up on old foundations.

Lovely is the 14th century steeple, from the ground to the tip of the graceful crocketed spire 170 feet above. The tower has handsome mouldings round the base, double buttresses stepped and gabled, and battlements with tall, leafy pinnacles.

The two porches are also handsome with canopied buttresses, gargoyles, pierced and carved parapets, and fine stone-vaulted roofs with carved bosses. The north porch has a corbal table with a strange procession of kneeling people and animals, one of them showing a fox running off with a goose; and on one of the roof-bosses is a Pelican in Piety. The charming doorway within this porch has mouldings dotted with flowers. Most of the figures enriching the south porch have lost their heads, including one in a niche over the entrance.

The lofty modern chancel has a decorated parapet, and its ceiling is a wooden vault, painted and gilded, with carved bosses. The 15th century roof of the nave, restored and repainted in its original colours, displays ten angels with golden wings outspread; it rests on clustered responds which enrich the walls between the clerestory windows.

Stained glass in all the windows fills the interior with dim, religious light. Portraying a host of saints, disciples, and prophets, it was nearly all designed and made in this village by Canon Sutton, the oven he used still being at the rectory. There is some more of his work in Lincoln Cathedral. Another of his gifts to this church was the carved and gilded reredos with figures of the Evangelists.

The oak stalls, the screen, and the font-cover are tributes to Canon Sutton's memory. Like a richly-pinnacled spire, crowned by an angel with a scroll, the font-cover is a fine example of oak carving, and has a door which opens to show carved and coloured figures of St Agnes, St Michael with the dragon, and St Nicholas with three children in a tub. The screen has fan-vaulting and figures of Mary and John by the Cross; its graceful iron gates, and the iron candlesticks and candelabra about the church, are the work of the Coldrons.

Two old treasures are a silver-gilt paten made about Armada time (perhaps in Germany), and a worn carving of the Trinity on a stone bracket in the vestry.

William Warburton, a famous 18th century Bishop of Gloucester, was rector here for some 50 years, though he lived here for only about half that time. It is said that he used to sit up half the night studying, and it was here that he wrote his most famous controversial work, *The Divine Legation of Moses*.

The Old Vicarage is now a Youth Service Residential Training Centre—Brant Broughton House—administered by the Kesteven Education Committee.

Bratoft. It lies secluded in a maze of narrow lanes below the southern edge of the Wolds. Except for the 200-year-old tower of brick, the church is mainly 14th and 15th century work, restored and partly rebuilt in 1890. Among its old features are the 14th century nave arcades, a low-side window and a piscina in the chancel, and a fine 14th century font with grotesque faces under a bowl enriched with arcading and Passion symbols. A rare feature is the double archway of the tower, the western (and bigger) arch being as wide as the nave.

Spanning the chancel arch, and enclosing chapels in the aisles, are traceried 15th century screens with carved fruit and flowers among their decoration. On the modern chancel seats are 18 poppyheads of the 15th century, with carved men, angels, and birds. The richly-traceried modern pulpit also has a 15th century panel.

A curiosity here is an old painting on wood, kept in the tower. It shows the Spanish Armada as a red dragon stretched between the shores of England, Scotland, Ireland, and France, while a little English fleet and soldiers massed on the coast await the enemy. A crude jingle below tells how the devouring dragon was defeated.

The east window was restored in memory of the Bible commentator, Thomas Scott, who was born here in 1747.

Brattleby. Sheltering below the Cliff 6 miles north of Lincoln, it has a few little red-tiled cottages with big flower-gardens, and a church, all in a bower of tall trees. Trim is the churchyard, too, with its ancient cross and the shade of stately-spreading cedars soaring as high as the little lead spire.

Most of the church was rebuilt last century, but as tokens of its antiquity the base of the tower and nave arcade still stand. The tower has a 13th century doorway, with a comic stone head at each side, and a Norman arch to the nave; the arcade has two 14th century arches with foliated capitals; and the chancel still has its mediaeval credence shelf with leafy canopy and a carved head on either side.

Brigg. From a fishing hamlet by the River Ancholme it has become a quaint little town, reached by tree-lined roads and busy with its markets and fairs, agriculture, and food factories. Its greatest charm is, perhaps, where the trees and the warehouses go down to the water's edge, and the bridges span the old river and its straight new cut. Between the town and the Humber this straight New River Ancholme has the Weir Dike running beside it.

Brigg (or Glanford Brigg, to give its name in full) has a church of 1842 on the site of an older one. It also has a Grammar School founded in the time of Charles II by Sir John Nelthorpe; its old red-brick building, now part of a fine up-to-date range, has a curious bulging chimney, and a coat-of-arms above an old doorway.

In 1886, when excavations were being made for the gas-works, an

St Peter's Church, Barton-upon-Humber

Algarkirk Church

Belton House

ancient boat was unearthed here. Shaped out of an enormous oak tree, it was between four and five feet wide, three to four feet deep, and nearly 50 feet long, and it could carry up to 50 men. This rare treasure, dating from the Late Bronze Age (c. 1000 B.C.), was sent to Hull Museum and was destroyed by enemy bombs during the Second World War.

A second interesting discovery found here in the bed of clay in the brickyard in 1884 was a causeway fashioned of huge oak logs set on a layer of oak, hazel, and yew boughs. A third was an oak raft, some 40 feet long and over 5 feet 6 inches wide; a model of it is in the City and County Museum at Lincoln. Both may belong to the Early Iron Age.

Brigsley. A pretty company of cottages and little orchards and a tiny patched-up church, it clings to a gentle slope above a stream winding to the Marsh and to the sea at Tetney Haven.

Reached by a lane with grassy banks, the church has a tower with a 15th century top, adorned with ugly gargoyles and battlements from which ivy and persistent elder-bush are growing. Except for a 15th century west window, the base of the tower is Norman, its simple round-headed arch now filled with a door and a grille.

Nave and chancel are chiefly 13th century work, with some windows a century later, and traces of old arcades in the nave walls. The chancel has its old sedile and piscina, and a few fragments of old glass; the font is mediaeval, and the old pulpit has a quaint low canopy on two fluted panels between which the parson enters. Among the church plate is a tiny Elizabethan chalice.

Brocklesby. Here is a setting of great beauty. It is the home of the earls of Yarborough, descendants of a branch of the Pelhams, the famous family whose Buckle badge can be seen in many a Sussex church. Some of them rest in the delightful 13th century church in Brocklesby Park, a gem of weathered stone in rich setting.

The church's old embattled tower has a lead spire built in 1784. Nave and chancel are impressive in their height, and the arch between them soars without capitals to the roof. The windows are notable for their beautiful Victorian tracery (some of it in the chancel still with fragments of old glass) and also for their modern glass. Shining in a medley of colour in the east window is a Jesse Tree, and in the nave are fine figures of the Madonna, Paulinus, St Hugh of Lincoln, St Alban, St Helen, and St Botolph of Boston.

The church possesses massive altar-rails with octagonal balusters, a fine chair with a carved fan-shaped back, box-pews, a panelled chest, and a 19th century alabaster reredos, coloured and gilded, and showing Our Lord in Majesty and six Saints. The register is complete from 1538—the year their keeping was made compulsory by

Thomas Cromwell. The organ of 1773, festooned with flowers and carved with instruments of music, was in the Hall of the Pelhams before it was brought into the church.

The church is indeed a sanctuary of the Pelhams. The founder of the Brocklesby line, Sir William Pelham, one of Elizabeth's great military commanders who died in 1587, has a fine alabaster wall-monument. It shows Sir William and two sons wearing armour and ruffs, another small boy with a skull on his cushion, and his wife and three daughters in flowing gowns and beautiful ruffs.

Facing the founder of the house is the alabaster altar tomb of Sir William Pelham who died in 1629. On the front of it is an exceptionally fine family group: a father with eight grown-up sons and two boys, and a mother with two grown-up daughters, two maids with skulls, and three babes in swaddling clothes, Sir William is the armoured figure on the tomb, with the proud Pelham peacock at his feet, its tail outspread; with him is his wife, wearing long cloak, hood, and ruff, her head on an embroidered cushion. On the shield at the top of the monument is the Buckle which is the Pelham badge.

Thereby hangs a tale. To explain the significance of this symbol we have to recall the great Sir John Pelham who lies in an unknown grave at Robertsbridge in Sussex, not far from Bodiam Castle. For it was Sir John who, having fought so bravely at Poitiers, and there having captured King John of France, was given as a reward for his courtesy the right to wear the king's buckle as a badge of honour. So it is that the buckle adorns this noble tomb at Brocklesby.

In a black marble recess with carved flowers and foliage is the lovely white figure of Marcia, Countess of Yarborough (died 1926), sculptured by Sir William Reid Dick. A loving mother, she is portrayed looking down at two little boys who cling to her. She was a peeress twice in her own right, and at her marriage she brought more than 150 quarterings into the family's heraldic arms.

Another beautiful modern memorial was sculptured by Charles Jagger and is set in the wall by the chancel arch; it is to Charles Sackville Pelham, Lord Worsley, who fell in the First World War and lies at Ypres. He is shown kneeling on a sandbag in a trench, his cap in front of him, his sword on the ground. In memory of the 4th Earl of Yarborough, who died in 1936, there is a big wall-monument with a coat-of-arms and his portrait.

Brocklesby Hall, ancestral home of the earls of Yarborough, stands in a great park entered on its western side by a fine classical arch set up by tenants in memory of the 2nd Earl. A road made beautiful with lily ponds leads to the Hall, one of the stately homes of England, and storehouse of treasures, including a gallery of sculptures, and pictures by Titian, Lely, Romney, and Reynolds. Originally an early 18th century house, it was extended to include picture galleries and has recently been reduced in size and restored.

Beyond lies as fair an estate as man could desire—the park 3 miles long and half as wide, with a view of an immense area of rolling country, and an almost incredible wealth of trees.

In a ring of fine cedars at the southern end of the park (near the village of Great Limber) is the mausoleum designed by Wyatt in 1794 for Sophia, wife of the 1st Lord Yarborough, and daughter of George Aufrere of Chelsea, whose collection of paintings and sculpture are among the many treasures of the Hall. Built like a Greek temple, with a circular colonnade and a flat-topped dome, it enshrines a statue of her by Nollekens. Keeping her company are other sculptured monuments of the Pelhams.

The mausoleum stands on an ancient burial mound; rings, combs, and beads have been found here, as well as Roman urns with charred bones and ashes. Close to the park (on its south, east, and north sides) are the sites of three religious houses founded in the 12th century: an alien priory at Great Limber, a Cistercian nunnery at Nun Cotham, and at Newsham what is believed to have been the first English abbey of Praemonstratensian or White Canons.

One more tale has to be told of Brocklesby—the almost incredible tale of the planting of millions of trees by the lords of Yarborough. Part of the story is written on Pelham's Pillar, which rises 128 feet from a high ridge of the Wolds and is symbolically guarded by two stone lions, one watching while the other sleeps; the result of it all is to be seen in the magnificent curving belt of woodlands stretching from the park to the Pillar, only a mile and a half from Caistor.

One of Nelson's admirals, Lord Collingwood, when his sea-going days were done, used to go up and down the country sowing oaks from the bag of acorns he carried, so that England should never lack timber for her wooden walls. For over 150 years the lords of Yarborough have been making sure, at Brocklesby and Manby, that whatever forests fall in England, there shall always be new trees springing up in Lincolnshire.

They began the task of growing trees for use and beauty at Brocklesby two years before the French Revolution, and they have planted trees every year since then—by the thousand, the ten thousand, and the hundred thousand.

In the first of their great enterprises 40,000 saplings were planted, and the planting went on in increasing volume. In the year of Nelson's victory off St Vincent the planting reached a total of 668,801 trees. After that it fell off, till in the year before Trafalgar the number of trees sank to a beggarly 10,652. But then it increased again and in the year after Waterloo it touched a record of 680,451.

Pelham's Pillar, soaring so proudly in this Lincolnshire domain of the Pelhams, records the astonishing feat of the 1st Baron Yarborough, who between 1787 and 1823 planted 12,552,700 trees! But the work has been nobly continued by his descendants, notably by the 4th Earl of Yarborough, who died in 1936; in the 60 years of his stewardship he planted nearly half of the mighty total of over 30 million trees grown on these estates.

Of course, these are not merely woods of grandeur and loveliness, but an area where a great scheme of scientific forestry has matured. There are trees of every kind: oak and ash, acacia and Spanish chestnut, beech and hornbeam, fir and pine, larch and spruce, elm and cedar. Hardwood and conifer are their main classifications, which admit of the introduction of many special kinds of trees for experiment, such as Japanese larch, Chinese birch, Caucasian wing-nut, or the giant Sequoia bought as a seedling for £5 in 1856 and now more than 100 feet high.

The age and condition of the trees are as carefully noted and kept as are the particulars of the human population at Somerset House. There are acreages of trees all under 20 years of age, and other areas for trees under 40, or between 40 and 80.

That is the astonishing story written enduringly by the tree-loving earls of Yarborough. And it is pleasant to record that it is an unfinished story. Year by year the good work still goes on. Long may it continue! Long may these trees climb upwards to the sky, spreading their branches graciously over these abounding green acres of Lincolnshire!

Broughton. Neighboured by woods which are fragrant in spring with lilies-of-the-valley, it lies by Ermine Street, and the discovery of tiles and coins and fragments of pottery suggests there was a Roman settlement hereabouts. Certainly Saxon and Normans were here, and some of their work survives in the village church—a fine building neighboured by old white cottages and a blacksmith's forge.

The upper part of the church tower is 15th century work (with modern battlements); but the lower part, with its big patches of herringbone masonry, primitive little doorway, and small windows on the south side, was built by the Saxons and was probably the nave of their church. The semi-circular turret on the west side of the tower (enclosing a newel stair to the belfry) was added later, perhaps by the Normans.

The chancel (partly 13th century) still has much masonry and part of a Norman window in its walls; at the foot of two pillars of the 14th century nave arcades are stones carved by Normans. The clerestory and the aisles are 15th century, much restored; the porch is modern.

On a richly-carved altar tomb in the chancel lie the alabaster figures of Sir Henry Redford and his wife—a 14th century knight with a lion at his feet, and a lady in a mantle held by a rich clasp. Serving as a canopy for the tomb is a most unusual arch, splayed out, and adorned with tracery and ballflower ornament. On the chancel floor is a fine brass portraying another 14th century knight and lady, probably of the same family.

By the arch above the tombs, and similarly carved, is a little doorway opening to a chapel built in the 17th century by the Andersons, who succeeded the Redfords as lords of the manor. It enshrines a great monument, elaborately enriched with garlands, bearing a reclining figure of Sir Edward Anderson, who died in 1660. Here, too, is preserved a fragment of a Saxon cross with interlaced carvings.

Among the old relics of this church are a cupboard and a chest with linenfold panels, and another cupboard with three carved panels from an Elizabethan pulpit.

In the hamlet of Gokewell, across the woods, a Cistercian nunnery was founded eight centuries ago; it has long since vanished.

Broxholme. A friendly cluster of cottages and barns and hayricks, it is among the flat pastures by the River Till, here flowing southwards to join the Witham near Lincoln; in the eastern horizon the Cliff ridge is seen riding towards the cathedral towers, a noble sight for villagers who rise at dawn, or plod homeward wearily at dusk. The church, with an octagonal turret and heads of a bishop and a priest by the porch doorway, was rebuilt in 1857; thus did it lose an early Norman doorway and all other marks of antiquity.

Bucknall. Standing in an attractive churchyard with a Queen Anne rectory as neighbour, its church is partly 13th century, with a chancel restored last century, and a tower restored in our time. In the low, sturdy tower hangs a mediaeval bell.

The base of an ancient cross is by the timber porch, which shelters a 13th century doorway. Facing the 700-year-old arcading on the north side of the nave is an arcade of the 14th century. The octagonal font was originally square and is a link with Norman times. The altar-table, the carved pulpit, and a chest with a band of carving have come down from Jacobean times.

A modern oak figure of St George in triumph over the dragon was given by two friends of Langton Benson-Brown, a rector's son who fell in France in 1916, and whose tablet here has St Paul's words:

We thank our God for every remembrance of you.

Bullington. It has little to show of its long history save the moated site and a few stones of a once-famous priory which rose among the woods about a mile from the village, where a stream flows towards the little Barlings river. Founded in the reign of Stephen by Simon de Kyme for canons and nuns of the Gilbertine order, it had seven Lincolnshire churches among its rich endowments, and was granted at the Dissolution to the Duke of Suffolk.

The scattered fabric is in the walls of neighbouring farms, and the last remaining stones have been collected and built into a pillar some 8 feet high which can be seen from the road leading to Stainfield.

Burgh. A quaint little market town on an outpost of the Wolds, it looks over the Marsh to the sea. Conspicuous on its little hill it stands on a Roman settlement from which coins and pottery have been unearthed. Anglo-Saxon objects and earlier mesolithic flints and Roman pottery have been excavated from Cock Hill, a grassy mound which is a wonderful viewpoint near the church and was used in mediaeval days for cock-fighting.

Two windmills are here, one, dated 1833, recently purchased by the Lindsey County Council and restored. Time was when the town could boast two churches; only one still stands, however, a splendid sight, as it has been for nearly 500 years, and a landmark seen far out to sea.

The nave has a carved parapet to its gable, and an embattled clerestory with 10 windows on each side. The tower has a stair turret, canopied niches, big belfry windows, a parapet richly carved with tracery and shields, and pinnacles with finials added about 1600. This tower has a grand peal of eight bells, and the long climb to the top is rewarded by magnificent views.

Within the church is some fine old woodwork. The nave has its old roof with moulded beams and floral bosses. The screens of tower and chancel embody much of the 500-year-old woodwork in the former chancel and aisle screens. From Jacobean days comes the lofty canopied font-cover with its rich carving, double doors, and gilded dove which holds in its beak an inkhorn for entering the baptisms and a sandsifter for drying the ink. Another Jacobean treasure is the pedestal pulpit with a mass of carving and a handsome canopy.

The lectern, an impressive wooden eagle with half-closed wings and powerful beak and claws, was carved last century by a local man, Jabez Good, and given in memory of William George Tozer, the missionary bishop who was vicar here from 1858 till 1863, and gave the church its organ.

St Paul's School built in 1860 is a fine brick building with a chapel added in 1890

Burgh-on-Bain. It lies on the road from Wragby to Louth, here winding smoothly along the slopes of the Wolds and giving fine views of the rolling hills. There is a neolithic long barrow at Burgh Top and neolithic leaf-shaped arrow-heads and other Bronze Age flints have come from Baxter Square Farm. Perched on a bank where the road goes down the hill is its little church of golden-tinted stone, restored and enlarged last century.

Among its old remains are the narrow tower arch and the blocked doorway in the north aisle, both early Norman. The fine south arcade is 13th century, and the north arcade is a modern copy of it. The chancel, with its low, massive arch, is chiefly 15th century work.

There are monuments in the tower to 18th century owners of Girsby Manor, and a tablet in the chancel records the restoration of the church in memory of Flora Fox who lived there in the 19th century.

Girsby Manor, which has now been demolished, came into the news in our time with the accidental discovery there of a rare treasure—one of only two known copies in existence of the Shakespearian Quartos of 1619, a pirated attempt at a collected edition which was never completed. The other copy is in the Folger Library, Washington. The one found at Girsby was sold for £1000.

Burton. A well-wooded park here clothes the slopes of the Cliff Road and screens Burton Hall, once the home of the Monson family, but now demolished with the exception of the handsome south range of 1768 which has been restored. The village, now a pleasant residential suburb of Lincoln, has some attractive modern houses that agree well with the earlier buildings.

Its church, rebuilt in the closing years of the 18th century, but still with a Norman doorway and one or two old memorials. One is a 17th century group showing Christopher Randes kneeling in armour at a prayer-desk, his wife facing him in a pretty veiled headdress, four sons kneeling behind the father and three daughters behind their mother, and a baby in swaddling clothes. The Lindsey County Council has designated the village as a Conservation Area.

A modern window in memory of a rector shows the Madonna with the Child on her knee, and an aged Elizabeth bringing John the Baptist to see Him. A tablet tells of Colin Chappell, whose ancestors lived long in the village; Colin died in Flanders in 1915 while trying to save a wounded friend.

Dipping sharply down to the village is a group of almhouses, founded in 1651 by Sir John Monson for poor widows, rebuilt in 1879, with grey stone walls and lichened roofs. There was a Roman villa on this site and extending down the hill-slope.

Burton Coggles. A delightful spot on its own winding byway, it has an ancient though much-restored church, the tower with its lancets and blunt spire being 700 years old. The font is also 13th century, and the porch and arcades only a little younger.

In the porch lie two stone figures of armoured 14th century knights, both found under the floor and both without feet. On a wall within are three portrait brasses of Shakespeare's time. The long-haired knight with plumed helmet at his feet is probably **Sir**

Henry Cholmeley, the lady in embroidered gown his wife, and the man in fur-trimmed gown and ruff a kinsman. In the chancel are two windows with modern glass telling the story of St Thomas Becket, to whom the church is dedicated.

Burton-on-Stather. Attractively placed on the short range of Cliff high above the last few miles of the Trent, it has magnificent views and is the starting-point of a charming 3-mile walk along the ridge to Alkborough. In the great expanse of Yorkshire that comes into the picture even the towers of York Minster are visible on a clear day. From the village church, set commandingly on the edge of the Cliff, the road drops steeply down to the Stather—the name of the landing place for the ferry crossing to Garthorpe in the green Isle of Axholme. Not far away the Trent and the Ouse unite to form the Humber.

The ancient church has been much restored, but its massive unbuttressed tower is chiefly 13th century work, with later battlements; within the 19th century porch, too, is a lovely doorway as old as the tower, with rich foliated capitals crowning the three shafts at each side.

In the spacious and light interior the north arcade of the nave is a most impressive feature. Its two western bays are late Norman and the third is early 13th century. The arches are decorated with ball and billet ornament and a band of chevron, and stone faces between them look across to another face on the mediaeval south arcade.

In the chancel are three beautiful old sedilia, with rose-tipped and crocketed canopies; and there also is an old trefoiled piscina with a modern drain inscribed: *I will wash my hands in innocency*. Other old relics are an almsbox, part of a coffin-lid with a floriated cross, and a Civil War cannon-ball.

The oldest of the many monuments of the Sheffield family is a badly mutilated figure of a 14th century knight (brought from Owston Church). A monument to Sir Charles Sheffield who died in 1774 has a much-draped woman leaning on an urn; and another commemorating Sir John and Sir Robert Sheffield (who both died in 1815) has a kneeling woman sculptured by the younger Bacon. A window in the north aisle, showing the Madonna and Child, Anna, and Simeon, is a tribute to Charles Sheffield, vicar from 1822 to 1882.

The most famous of the family was John Sheffield, 3rd Earl of Mulgrave, a friend of Pope and Dryden and a prominent figure during four reigns. He lies in Westminster Abbey, but a reminder of him here is an inscription stating that he rescued the venerable remains of five of his ancestors from the danger of oblivion, and brought them here from Owston. It tells also that Charles II made him a captain at sea and a colonel on land, King James made him Lord Chamberlain, King William made him Marquis of Normanby, and Queen Anne Lord Privy Seal and Duke of Buckingham.

A mile-long beech avenue leads to the hamlet of Normanby, where cottages nestle by the fine wrought-iron gates of Normanby Park, the great domain of the Sheffields. Built in the Italian style, from designs by Smirke, their great house was enlarged early this century. With the threatened need to undermine the park for iron ore, the Sheffield family moved to Sutton-on-the-Forest, north of York, in 1963 and leased Normanby Hall and Park to Scunthorpe Borough Council for a term of 99 years. House and grounds are now open to the public and represent a great enhancement of local amenities.

Burton Pedwardine. Lonely among the fields it stands, a village little more than a hamlet, with a towerless church little more than a chapel. Part of its story is in its name, for to this small place on the edge of the Fens came the Pedwardines of Herefordshire six centuries ago. Of the church they found here only a few fragments are left—a group of Saxon, Norman, and Early English stones with knotwork and other entwined ornament, built into the west wall. Of the cross-shaped church which Sir Roger Pedwardine finished by 1340, only the north transept remains, the rest having been twice rebuilt last century.

It is a small and simple church with a little bellcot in which a 17th century bell hangs, and its interest for the traveller is all in the old transept. Under an arch in the north wall is a grey marble slab with a Norman-French inscription to Dame Alice, wife of Sir Roger Pedwardine who built the mediaeval church. Against the west wall is the fine monument of Sir Thomas Horsman who died in 1610; he lies here in his armour, both his hands and one of his feet gone but otherwise well-preserved, and his bearded face looks up to a pillared canopy adorned with his heraldry. His nephew Thomas Horsman, who raised this monument, has only a humble floorstone from which the brasses have vanished.

Two miles west of the village are the base and shaft of a 15th century cross. It is between the railway and the Roman King Street, hereabouts called Mareham Lane after the moated Mareham Grange which stood near the cross.

Burwell. The road from Louth to Spilsby runs through this pleasant village among the upland pastures and cornfields of the Wolds. It gathers round a green, along which a stream flows on its way to the Great Eau. Once it was a market town, and there is still the early 18th century red-brick butter cross to indicate its old importance; for some years it served as a dovecot. Of the small alien priory for Benedictine monks founded here in the 12th century nothing remains.

A leafy tunnel leads to a hillside church that has seen much change wrought by the centuries. Restoration has left a striking Norman chancel arch adorned with chevron moulding, and with two horses carved on one of its capitals. Above the arch is a fragment of old wall painting showing a woman's crowned head. The lofty 15th century tower arch reaches the traceried and gabled roof of the nave.

From mediaeval days come the double piscina and the font, the font having an inscription telling that Thomas Fitzwilliam gave it in 1460; its bowl has carved quatrefoils and shields. There are three wooden figures of angels under the tower roof, and the painted pulpit is Jacobean with its hourglass stand. At each side of the east window (shining with modern glass of St Michael in golden armour) is a richly-carved old stone bracket.

An inscribed stone in the chancel commemorates Robert Christison who paid for the church's 20th century restoration. An explorer and pastoral pioneer of north-west Queensland, he was born in 1837 and was laid to rest at Foulden in Berwickshire in 1916.

On the eastern side of the highway are the lovely Haugham and Burwell Woods, and the 200-acre park in which stood until 1958 the great house. It was sad that this fine building was totally demolished. Known as Burwell Hall, it was a great building of 1760, on the site of an older house which Sarah Jennings, Duchess of Marlborough, knew. In one of the letters of the famous duchess she refers to staying "at the peaceful Manor House of Burwell at times".

Buslingthorpe. Its modest little church, standing in a field, has two treasures from the past—memorials of the De Buslingthorpes who were lords of this manor three centuries before the Tudor Dynasty.

One of the memorials is the stone figure of a cross-legged knight wearing mail armour with surcoat and spurs; angels are at his head, and a lion is at his feet. Believed to represent Sir John de Buslingthorpe who died late in the 13th century, this remarkably well-preserved knight was found face-downwards in the floor near the pulpit, where he had served as a paving stone.

The second memorial is a brass showing the half-figure of Sir Richard Buslingthorpe, set in a coffin-shaped stone against a wall. The knight is in chain mail, with hauberk, coif, and surcoat, and remarkable scaled gauntlets; he holds a tiny heart, and round his stone is a worn inscription in Norman-French. Believed to be early 14th century, this famous brass is the oldest in Lincolnshire and one of the oldest in England.

Except for its stone tower and the chancel arch (both 13th

century) and some 15th century windows, the church dates from 1835. A shield of old glass is in the east window.

Butterwick. A marshland village between Boston and the sea, it has an old church of brick and stone much restored in the late 18th century. The church has a low tower, an old sanctus bellcot crowned with a cross, and a quaint little brick rood-loft turret with a stone spirelet ringed by quatrefoil windows. The little door to the stairway within the church is carved with tracery.

The nave arcades, and the font with a restored bowl on the old cluster of shafts, are 13th century. The traceried oak screen, repainted in red and green and gold, is chiefly 15th century work, and there is an old pulpit adorned with shields.

Cabourne. A mile along the road from Caistor to Grimsby, in a hollow of the Wolds, stands this pretty village. In the woods to the north, over a mile away, soars Pelham's Pillar, 128 feet high and commemorating the astonishing feat of Charles Anderson Pelham, 1st Baron Yarborough, who planted no fewer than 12,552,700 trees on his Lincolnshire estates. The story of this fine achievement is told at Brocklesby. From the Pillar are magnificent views of wood stretching without a break to Brocklesby Park, and, farther away, the broad silver streak of the Humber enfolded by the curling arm of Spurn Head in Yorkshire.

Cabourne's church has an ancient story, but in the big restoration last century the nave and chancel were partly rebuilt and the porch was added. The unbuttressed tower, believed to have been built before the Conquest, was then raised 12 feet and given its pointed tiled roof, and the belfry windows were restored. The west doorway of the tower has a solid stone tympanum, and above it is a little horseshoe-shaped window; the arch leading to the nave is exceedingly tall and has square capitals of single massive stones.

The nave has a round-headed doorway, and the chapel a 13th century lancet window. Other old possessions are a low-side window in the chancel, a piscina (only its arch is original), a 15th century chalice, and the Norman font with crude interlaced arcading and a rim of double cable moulding, recovered from under the floor and standing now on another font turned upside down.

Cadney. An attractive farming village between the Wolds and the Cliff, it has a bright and airy church, restored but with its roots in Norman England.

The fine nave arcade with round arches and massive pillars is Norman, and so is the tub-shaped bowl of the font. The chancel and the tower are 13th century work; the east window of the chancel and the battlements of the tower are 15th century.

Other old relics are a trefoiled piscina (with nail-head) and a low-side window in the chancel, a cinquefoiled niche with a bracket held by a man carved in stone, a 13th century floorstone with a fine floriated cross, and a piscina in the south chapel. Enclosing two sides of this chapel is richly-traceried screenwork of the 15th century, with two little wickets and a tiny carving of two cocks drinking from shells. Across the chancel arch are remains of another 15th century screen, much restored.

On a bank of the Ancholme, a mile from Cadney, stands Newstead Priory Farm, a grey stone house on the site of a small Gilbertine house founded here by Henry II. Incorporated in the house is a big chamber with round-arched vaulting, possibly part of the refectory of the 12th century priory. Another room has a 15th century window.

Caistor. Roads from all round the compass lead to this attractive market town, set high on a western spur of the Wolds. It has a fine old church, many springs gushing out of the chalk hillside, and a story telling of its importance long centuries ago.

It has grown round a Roman walled town; some portions of the walls and associated bastions may be seen. Excavation has helped to determine the plan which encloses 7–8 acres and the line of the defences form a polygon about 850 by 525 yards. An interesting theory is that Roman Caistor may owe its origin to a spring with health-giving properties—a Roman spa. In Saxon times it was still an important place, known as Tunna-Ceaster or Thong-Caster, and outside the town are mounds supposed to mark the site of King Egbert's victory over the Mercians in 829; but it is a peaceful scene that the old town looks down on today, over the great plain criss-crossed by river and streams and dykes, with the sight of the distant towers of Lincoln Cathedral on a clear day.

In the very heart of the town stands Caistor's church. Its walls are of golden stone, and it has something to show of Saxon and Norman times and of the three great mediaeval building centuries. Of all these periods there is evidence in the splendid tower. The base is chiefly Norman, with zigzag carving on its worn doorway, but its plain round arch (with big imposts) is thought to have belonged to the Saxon church. The second stage is 13th century work, and the rest 14th century, with battlements and pinnacles added a century later still.

The lovely south doorway, with its clustered shafts supporting arch mouldings enriched with dog-tooth ornament, comes from the 13th century, other remains of that time being the chancel and its arch, and the nave arcades with stone seats round their pillars and capitals on the south side carved with nail-head. The south aisle windows are from the close of the 14th century.

Under an arched recess in the north aisle is the tomb of Sir William de Hundon, who accompanied Edward I on the last Crusade—an armed knight in chain mail and surcoat, with a dog at his feet. Under another arched recess, richly cusped, lies Sir John de Hundon, Sheriff of Lincolnshire in 1343, wearing plate armour and also well-armed. A lady with a wimple, thought to be his wife, has battered features but is still a slight, graceful figure with a lion at her feet. On a coloured wall-monument kneels a third armoured knight with a queer medley of feathers scattered about him; he is Sir Edward Maddison of Unthank Hall, Durham, who died in 1553 in his 100th year.

A strange old relic preserved in this church is a gad whip, which, with a silver penny of Edward I, recalls a curious ceremony by which land at Raventhorpe (near Broughton) was held. For many centuries a man from that village would come to this church on Palm Sunday, crack his whip while the first lesson was read, and then, kneeling down, would wave the whip three times over the minister's head during the second lesson. After this, the whip (to which was attached a purse containing 30 silver pennies and three pieces of wych elm) was placed in the seat of the Hundon manor pew. The rite was last observed in 1846, and the whip preserved here (a stout affair with a cruel-looking lash) is said to be one of four still in existence: another is in Lincoln's Museum.

Opposite the church is a spreading chestnut tree, planted when the chapel behind it was built in 1842. By the chapel is the 17th century grammar school, a simple oblong building with embattled walls of golden stone, mullioned windows, pantiled roof, and pretty doorway. A section of the Roman wall is in the headmaster's garden. The school (now part of a modern range) has had many famous pupils, including the poet Sir Henry Newbolt.

Cammeringham. Set amid the fields that slope down below the Cliff road, 7 miles north of Lincoln, it is a small and tranquil village with about 30 cottages gathered about an ivied church. Once it had a priory, founded in the 12th century and attached to an abbey in Normandy; but that has long since vanished, and even the church is smaller than of yore. Now it has nave and chancel only, like one big room, very simply furnished and with round and pointed arches of a former arcade built up into a north wall. Serving as a step to the west doorway, below the bell turret, is a Saxon stone with carved interlace decoration, suggesting an antiquity that is nowhere else apparent here.

On the chancel wall is a 17th century monument recording the proud achievements of an old family. It has a sculptured bust of curly-headed Jane Tyrwhitt in a garland of flowers, and a lengthy catalogue of her family's eminence. There was brother Robert, who died at Hampton Court in 1641, an eminent servant of Charles I: there was Thomas, the King's chaplain, and Edmund, Gentleman Pensioner; there was Francis Tyrwhitt, who commanded in the Irish Wars, Sir Robert, who was an admiral of Henry VII, and another who was Queen Mary's Master of the Horse. After this recital of Pomp and Circumstance it is refreshing to read that Jane Tyrwhitt's own greatness was in the humble virtues, "her humility, chastity, piety and charity, for which she and her religious mother were incomparable patterns to their sex".

Canwick. Set on a steep hill on the south side of Lincoln Gap, it rejoices in splendid views of the city spread out below the soaring cathedral.

It is a charming walk from the village to Lincoln, the road dropping down the Cliff by the edge of South Common, that green oasis in a workaday part of the city. The Common is a favourite haunt of the city folk, and the tree-lined walk running along the top of the ridge shares with Canwick the splendid views of the valley and the cathedral. It is said that Southey's first sight of the Minster was from this spot, and of it he said, "Never was an edifice more happily placed; it overtops a city built on the acclivity of a steep hill, its house intermingled with gardens and orchards. To see it in full perfection it should be in the sunshine of an autumnal evening, when the red roofs and red brick houses would harmonise with the sky and the fading foliage."

Canwick's own little church stands in the middle of the estate, now the property of Jesus College, Oxford, near the Hall, built early in the 19th century; it is the ancestral home of the Sibthorp family, whose name has so often been inscribed within the church. One of them was Humphrey Waldo Sibthorp, vicar of neighbouring Washingborough for nearly half of the 19th century; later and more famous members of the family were the much-travelled botanist John Sibthorp, one of the founders of the Linnaean Society, the notorious Tory politician Col. Charles Sibthorp, and his brother Richard, whose conversion to the Roman Catholic faith was a sensation in early Victorian times. Canwick Hall, Canwick House, and the Dower House, once the homes of a dozen or so people, now accommodate 30 families in flats. Interesting styles of contemporary architecture are a feature of the parish.

It is a church of great interest, for the Normans built it on the site of a Roman villa, using the tessellated floors for its foundations. Time has wrought its changes, and nothing Roman can be seen today, but the hand of the Norman is still evident in the nave arcade, with its two round arches on massive pillars with scalloped capitals, and in the chancel arch with its chevron ornament. From the 13th century comes the font on four pillars, and the arcaded stone reredos in the side chapel now used in a vestry. Some of the windows are 14th century work, and the 18th and 19th centuries left their mark here in hatchments, inscribed wall-monuments, and little wooden gallery at the west end. There are some early 20th century box-pews.

Careby. Nearby is a small oval earthwork with ditches possibly of Iron Age date. Trains rush past it on urgent journeys north and south, and the River Glen winds slowly by, passing close to its secluded church. The church has a sturdy Norman tower with a staircase in the thickness of the wall, a 13th century spire, a nave with three 15th century arches on each side reaching almost to the clerestory windows, and a chancel with three Norman windows and a Norman doorway. Sheltered by the porch is a splendid door six or seven centuries old; it is about ten feet high and has a fine handle ornamented with a pair of lizards.

The great possessions of the church are its fine old monuments, and an altar frontal preserved in a glass case. Made from a 15th century cope, the altar frontal is of red velvet with lovely embroidery showing the Entry of Mary into Heaven, surrounded by angels, six-winged seraphim, and many slender double-headed eagles. On the vestry wall is one of the rare heart shrines of long ago, a stone with a carving of two hands holding a heart. In the chancel is a finely-preserved stone figure of a knight in chain mail, a dog at his feet and a headless lion at his head; it is believed to represent a lord of the manor who lived here 600 years ago.

Two other interesting memorials are in the aisles. One has the 14th century figures of an armoured knight and his wife, side by side, their hands clasped in prayer, a shield below them. The other is a modern monument to the Stopfords, set up by Mrs Evelyn Perry in memory of her mother, father and brother; it is a copy of an ancient Greek relief in the Street of Tombs outside Athens, and portrays a family parted by death, the son holding his mother's hand, and the father beside them.

Carlby. A tiny place near the Rutland border, it has an attractive church standing with a fragment of an old village cross in a leafy churchyard. The tower with its tall spire is 700 years old; and so are the aisles, though their arches, round on one side and pointed on the other, were built about 1200 when the Norman style was passing.

A windowsill serves as sedilia, and there is a stone by the door, other survivals from the ancient church being the font with its leafy border, and two gravestones enriched with crosses. The nave roof still has its old beams, but the other roofs are modern, those of the aisles being handsome with gilt and coloured shields and foliated bosses. In the chancel is a tablet to Thomas Toller Hurst who died in 1844 after ministering here for 53 years. After falling into a sad state of disrepair the church has been finely restored in our time and is as light and graceful as a village church should be.

Carlton-le-Moorland. A tranquil village of the byways between the River Witham and the Brant.

The imposing parish church has evidence of an Anglo-Saxon tower embodied in the later battlemented 15th century tower which rises above an Elizabethan nave built up with the materials of vanished aisles. The chancel is 14th century, and its restored screen, with narrow traceried arches, is almost as old. There are a few old pews, an old iron-bound chest, and a 13th century font enriched with interlaced arcading and nail-head ornament. The north chapel, now a vestry and organ chamber, was used for a time as a schoolroom.

Brass inscriptions recall Disneys of Shakespeare's day, and a tablet tells of James Pearce who was headmaster and chorister here for 45 years. There is a small Baptist Chapel (now closed and used as a grain-store) which was one of the 5-mile limit chapels of the late 17th century.

Carlton Scroop. A village on the Cliff ridge, passed by both road and rail running between Grantham and Lincoln, it has a little grey church screened by tall trees, the lower part of its tower with massive round arch into the nave being Norman. Most of the chancel, the porch, and the two big arches on each side of the nave, are 13th century, the aisles and the top part of the tower 14th. Part of the tower fell in 1630, damaging the nave, but as John Palmer's wall tablet proclaims, it all was put right by him within three years. The old rood-loft stairway is still in the wall, and the pulpit close by, resting on a base with little round arches, is Jacobean.

The big traceried font is over 500 years old, and the chancel has its ancient piscina and sedilia. But the rarest sight here is the fine old glass glowing in the 14th century east window; at the top is a figure of Christ holding the globe, and below are kneeling figures of the donor of the window and his wife, both holding shields; the donor is shown as a knight in chain mail and crimson cloak, and his wife is in a blue gown—a strange figure, because a later age gave her a priestly face brought from another church.

Castle Bytham. It has the attractiveness of all hillside villages —a little stream in the valley, flowing to the River Glen, the houses on one side climbing up towards the hilltop church, and on the other side the great earthworks of a castle. The castle, built by Norman lords, has vanished; the church, begun in Norman days, has lived on to be enriched through the years.

Boston Church

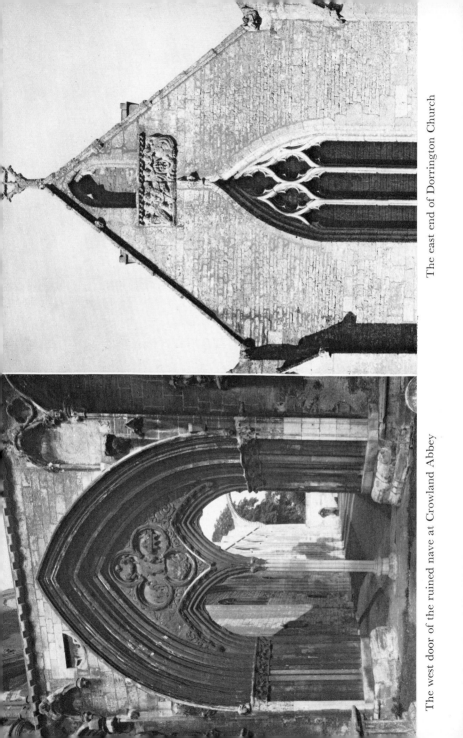

The west door of the ruined nave at Crowland Abbey

The east end of Dorrington Church

Shaped like a cross, the church has a sturdy tower with 13th century lancets, 15th century battlements, and an 18th century sundial inscribed with the old pun, "Bee in Thyme". The nave is part of a Norman church and has an arcade of three round arches on octagonal pillars, built when the Norman style was waning. The chancel, striking because it is longer than the nave, is 14th century, and has a fine east window, a piscina, and a canopied recess handsome with trefoiled arches, pinnacles, crockets, and ballflower ornament. The recess has been used as an Easter Sepulchre, but was probably the tomb of one of the Colvilles who owned the castle after it had been besieged by Henry III.

There is a fine brass candelabra dated 1810, and in a corner of the nave is a ladder which once played a part in the customs of Merrie England, an inscription stating that *This ware the May Poul, 1660*. Having ended its career on the green it became a ladder for climbing up to the belfry.

One of the vicars who often walked along this yew-bordered pathway early last century was Thomas Middleton, who became a famous Bishop of Calcutta.

The huge, grassy earthworks of the castle are still an impressive spectacle, and it is not difficult to picture a strong fortress standing here. They date back to the Norman invasion of Saxon England. The Saxon owner of this bold site was Morcar, a Northumbrian earl who vainly tried to resist the Conqueror in the Isle of Ely, and died in prison; his name lives on in Morkery Woods which lie westward by the Rutland border. His successor here was Drogo, brother-in-law to the Conqueror, and his castle, finished by the Conqueror's own half-brother, Odo, stood here until swept away in the Wars of the Roses.

Castle Carlton. Once it was a little market town; now it is but a scattered group of farms and cottages. Its small 15th century church stood till 1902, but nothing is left save a few tombstones and the base of an old cross. At Castle Hill, close by, are earthworks marking the site of a castle belonging, it is said, to Hugh Bardolf, a 12th century Chief Justice. It is said, too, that the hayward (or cattle-keeper) of the castle had the right to stop a salt-cart going through the town and to take from it a handful for himself.

Caythorpe. A big village on the road from Grantham to Lincoln, it has a fine mediaeval church and a 19th century Hall standing where the old home of the Husseys stood before it, a grey stone house with pillared entrance, in high-walled grounds where there is one of the oldest mulberry trees in the land.

The big church is a legacy from the 14th and 15th centuries, and is notable for its unusual plan and its remarkable steeple. Rising from four lofty arches on clustered pillars, the central tower has a parapet of pierced trefoils, and four pinnacles linked by flying buttresses to a crocketed spire which was rebuilt by Sir Gilbert Scott after it was struck by lightning in 1859. Now it climbs to 156 feet, but the original 14th century spire was even higher.

An extraordinary feature of the church is the double nave, divided from end to end by a 14th century arcade, which begins between two windows at the west end and ends in a half arch above the western tower arch. North and south of the tower are shallow transepts which once were chapels, each having still its old aumbry. The plain eight-sided font is 600 years old.

Over the chancel arch (or eastern tower arch) are faded wall paintings of the Last Judgment and St Michael weighing souls, and among the monuments is one with the head of Sir Charles Hussey of 1698. An ancient scratch dial is on the porch, and a much-worn figure of Our Lord is over the ancient door within it. On two of the buttresses at the west end of the church are carvings of the Annunciation and the Crowning of the Virgin, and in the churchyard is the old cross, restored, its new head having sculptures of a bishop, a saint, the Madonna, and the Crucifixion.

Caythorpe Court is now used as Kesteven's College of Agriculture; originally 17th century, it was rebuilt at the end of the 19th century.

Chapel St Leonards. Its fine air and splendid sands bring increasing favour as a seaside resort to this village defended by a sea-wall of concrete replacing fine dunes swept away in 1953. There is a good view of the stretch of sands from Chapel Point.

A white bridge over the Orby Drain leads to the neat little church with red-capped tower and an open-timbered roof crowning the nave. It was built in 1794 out of the ruins of the old church, but the 19th century saw the chancel rebuilt, and the addition of porch and vestry. The tower followed in 1901, and in 1924 the chancel was enlarged.

Cherry Willingham. A rapidly growing dormitory of Lincoln near the Witham, 3½ miles from the city. High on a mound stands the church of St Peter and St Paul built in classic style in 1753. The church is square with an apsidal east end and contains a notable monument of John Becke who had the church built. An outstanding feature of the church is its cupola restored to its original condition in 1967.

Claxby. Flanked on both sides by woods, the farms and snug cottages of this Wold village near Market Rasen are charmingly placed. Fine fossils have been dug up from its ironstone beds, and near the church the remains of a blue and white tessellated pavement have been found, suggesting that a Roman villa stood here.

The little church, neighboured by great beeches, stands in a pleasant setting opposite a wooded hill, with a lake gleaming in the fields below. It was built in the latter part of the 14th century, and much restored in the 19th, when the windows and the top of the tower were renewed; the north arcade of the nave is mediaeval, and the south modern. Still here are the great stone corbels which once supported the rood, carved with heads of amazing ferocity; one has its long tongue out, the other has hands pulling open a great angry mouth.

John Witherwick, who died on Christmas Day in 1595, has a canopied monument in the chancel, showing him in armour and cloak. His two wives are with him, one without her head. Within a recess in the sanctuary lies a tapering floorstone of the 13th century, enriched with a floriated cross and a coat-of-arms, perhaps commemorating a founder of the church.

Claxby. It is close to Alford, a tiny but charming village in a dell, with woods all about it, and a small mediaeval earthwork close by. Its wayside pond, overhung with trees, is filled by the Burlands Beck which springs from the rocky hillside. Hiding among trees at the top of a steep little hill are the 18th century Hall and the church which was rebuilt on the old foundations in 1846. It is in Norman style.

Claypole. It lies by the River Witham, with the Shire Dyke close by separating the county from Notts. Seen for miles around, its crocketed spire soars nobly above the 700-year-old tower of a noble church finely restored in 1892.

The big, cross-shaped church is for the most part an example of the rich, flowing style of 600 years ago, with a south transept which is chiefly 13th century. The east window and the battlements and leafy pinnacles adorning all but the chancel are 15th century.

The south porch has a deep image niche among its rich decoration, and shelters a fine old studded door with traceried panels and a wicket entrance. The splendid arches of the nave, with their lovely foliated capitals crowning clustered piers, make the interior an impressive sight. Above them are tall clerestory windows and newly-carved wall-plates of the old flat roof, handsome with carved beams and bosses.

The chancel is notable for the beautiful flowing tracery of its windows and for the exquisite carving of its canopied sedilia, piscina, and aumbry. Projecting from the moulding of the chancel arch are two quaint sculptures of a man's head and a woman with a wimple and gloved hands; they once served as brackets for a rood-beam.

The south transept has a lancet window, and its original sedilia and double piscina under a 15th century window; and in the sacristy on the north side of the chancel, built about 1400 and entered by a richly-moulded doorway, is the old altar stone with five consecration crosses. The most westerly window in the north wall of the chancel contains some fragments of early glass and on the south wall, just within the altar-rails is a hook and ring for the Lenten veil.

The 15th century chancel screen with traceried bays has been given new fan-vaulting and a border of vine and grape. The splendid pedestal pulpit is largely 15th century work, too, and its fine old canopy and its desk (resting on the stem of a brass processional cross) were made long ago from the former rood-loft. The tall and stately 14th century font has six sides adorned with window tracery under leafy gables and finials; its corners are buttressed, and it has the old staple fastenings.

Clee. This village is now absorbed into Grimsby. Old Clee preserves its village aspect, though it is seriously threatened by modern building. It stands among trees, a mile from the sea, with many charming houses both old and new; one of them, a farmhouse now, is the 17th century Clee Hall, picturesque with white walls, Dutch gables, and clustered chimneys, and containing some fine old oak panelling.

Renowned in a county famous for its churches, the old cross-shaped church of Clee is for the most part a rich legacy from the 11th, 12th, and 13th centuries, restored and partly rebuilt. The chancel, the porch, and the low tower over the crossing are all modern, and the very early 13th century transepts have been largely rebuilt; but the beautiful nave comes from the Norman period, and the tower at its west end is Saxon. It is an 11th century tower (with 15th century parapet) in the Saxon tradition, built of rubble with roughly-dressed quoins, and with the typical coupled windows in its belfry.

The old south door of the church opens to reveal a compact array of fine old arches—those of the nave all round-headed, and those of the central tower and transepts pointed. The two eastern bays of the north arcade, adorned with bold roll moulding, are early Norman work; the western arch with its fine display of zigzag is later. The south arcade is a beautiful example of later Norman work; its two great arches (enriched with cable, billet, and roll mouldings) reach nearly to the roof.

Just within the south door stands the fragment of an early cross, and in the modern chancel is a fine 13th century double piscina. Another early piscina is in the north transept, and there is a massive Norman font with a rim of cable ornament.

On the round pier of the south arcade is an ancient tablet with a

Latin inscription telling of "the dedication of this church by Bishop Hugh of Lincoln in 1192". As the nave had been completed many years before that time, it is thought that Hugh's dedication was of the transepts and chancel. Below this are two modern tablets—one telling of the church's 1878 restoration, and the other of the restoration completed in 1937; this included under-pinning of the foundations, made necessary by shrinkage of the ground.

The old custom of "rush-bearing" is still kept up in this church on Trinity Sunday. On this day the floor of the church used to be strewn with rushes, but, as the field from which they came is now built over, the rushes have given place to grass from the churchyard.

Cleethorpes. A fishing hamlet which has grown to a town of 35,000 folk, it is famed throughout the land as a holiday resort.

Every summer it is invaded by a great crowd who find here the bracing air, the splendid sands, and all the other attractions dear to the hearts of seaside holiday-makers. Here they can delight in a pier, a high sea-wall stretching for a mile and a quarter, a long promenade of cliff gardens, a boating-lake winding under little bridges, and one of the largest open-air bathing pools round our shores; and if all these, as well as the spacious sands, are not enough, they can hie them to Sidney Park (given by Sidney Sussex College, Cambridge) and there find winding walks among flowers, a paddling pool for the children, and bowling greens and tennis courts. There is also a golf course and attractive zoo.

Not the least of the town's attractions is the clear view of the Yorkshire coast, with Spurn Head's revolving light 6 miles away; and always, of course, there is the fascinating spectacle of ships passing to and fro, coming home to port, or putting out to sea.

Clixby. A neighbour of Caistor on the edge of the Wolds, it has a tiny church, hidden by trees, which was in ruins till 1889 and is now merely the old chancel with a modern bell-turret of brick. In the west wall is a 13th century doorway enriched with dog-tooth ornament and flanked by the remains of the old chancel arch. Close by are the responds of vanished arcades, with nail-head on their capitals.

Two 14th century windows in the chancel have hoods adorned with carved heads, and under one of them is a blocked doorway with an ogee arch. In the floor is the gravestone of a 14th century priest engraved with a cross and a chalice and a Lombardic inscription.

The churchyard cross, with the Crucifixion and the figure of St Mary in its head, stands tall and graceful against a background of beeches. Only the base and part of the shaft are ancient.

Coates-by-Stow. A tiny place near the River Till, it has a church hiding among splendid trees—a surprising little treasure-house, finely restored last century.

Much of the old work is 15th century, but the church still has two Norman windows (one blocked), a plain Norman font, and a Norman south doorway adorned with bold dog-tooth. In the north wall of the nave is a cinquefoiled recess with a deep aumbry beside it; and in the west wall is a blocked arch (almost pointed) with a square-headed window set in it. In the chancel north wall is an Easter Sepulchre with rather poor figures of Christ risen and one angel; the rest have been destroyed. The altar slab is believed to be unique with six incised crosses.

With its homely brick floor, its old open roof of rough timbering, and its old brass candelabra, the interior is very quaint. In a chancel window are two tiny saints in old glass, and other fragments are in the nave, which has seven old poppyhead benches and a Jacobean box-pew. This church can boast a 15th century pulpit said to have been rescued from a barn; but the rare treasure here is a beautiful carved oak screen which, though much restored, still has a great deal of its original 15th century work. Supported by a very deep vault (which has a cornice of delicate vine carving), the rood gallery has its original framework, and is enriched with tracery and a little projecting bay; it is reached by the old stone stairway lit by a tiny two-light window in the nave wall.

A monument in the chancel has the half-figure of Brian Cooke of 1653, and there are also brasses (1590 and 1602) of William Butler, portrayed in armour with his wife in embroidered gown and babe in swaddling clothes, and Charles Butler with his wife and eight children.

Coleby. A quaint Cliff village, high as the Heath across which the Ermine Street runs, and looking far over the valley where the Brant and the Witham draw near to their meeting, it has a many-gabled Hall built in Charles I's day, and a church with a tower raised in Saxon times.

The gabled Hall was built in 1628, on the foundations of an old manor house, by Sir William Lister, the first of many Listers to live here. One of them was Thomas Lister, a colonel of the Parliament in the Civil War, and a member of Cromwell's Council of State. One of the commissioners for the trial of the king, he was marked down for execution at the Restoration, but on the plea that he sat at the trial only once, his enemies were content to spare his life and send him into exile. In the 18th century the house was enlarged, and two classic temples were built in the grounds, both designed by Sir William Chambers. One is a domed pavilion, the Temple of Romulus and Remus, placed at the end of the avenue; the other, on the terrace, was built in memory of Lord Chatham, the elder Pitt. The gateway is a ruined Roman arch and was no doubt inspired by Lincoln's Newport Arch.

The earliest work in the church is the lower part of the un-buttressed tower, which has stood since Saxon or very early Norman days. Its arch to the nave (a lofty arch on small pilasters with plain capitals) was rebuilt at a later period, but part of the original arch can be seen within the tower. The top of the tower, with its battle-ments and eight pinnacles and graceful spire, was built early in the 15th century.

The 14th century porch shelters a doorway from the close of Norman days, its rich nail-head and chevron carving a fine frame for a door five centuries old and heavily studded with nails. As old as the doorway is the nave's massive north arcade with narrow beading on its two round arches, and also the font, one of the finest Norman fonts in Lincolnshire, its drum-shaped bowl enriched with interlaced arcading. The south arcade of the nave, its capitals carved with stiff foliage, is 13th century; and so is the chancel, with a filled-in arch in each of its side walls, and lancet windows filled with fine modern glass; in these lancets are figures of the Mother of Jesus, the Cruci-fixion, St John, Hugh of Lincoln, St Barbara, and St Thomas de Cantelupe who was rector here before he became Bishop of Hereford. Among other relics are several old seats with worn poppyheads which were once in Hackthorn Church, and a Jacobean chest carved with flowers.

The church was well restored in the first year of this century, and the chancel was "set in order" in 1864 as a memorial to Thomas Trevenen Penrose who was its vicar 33 years; a brass is inscribed with a tribute to him written by Sir John Coleridge, justice of the queen's bench and nephew of Samuel Taylor Coleridge. *From Early manhood to a ripe old age* (it reads), *in health and sickness, in strength and decay, within these walls and in this house he ministered humbly, earnestly, tenderly, lovingly: Here he fed us with the Bread of Life, by God's Grace here he taught us how to live and how to die.*

Colsterworth. A big stone-built village on the Witham, it has a story going back to Roman days—the museum at Grantham has the remains of a furnace worked here in Roman times. After the Romans left there were Saxons here, and they built a church which the Normans pulled down and rebuilt. The church still has some-thing from those early days, but its pride is in the memory of a New Year's Day many centuries later when a baby was brought here from the hamlet of Woolsthorpe and christened Isaac Newton!

The 15th century doorway through which they brought him has a scratch dial which must have interested him greatly as he grew up, for he was to make sundials of his own, one of which is here for all to see. They christened the week-old baby at a font of which only the mediaeval stem now remains, and a page in the register records that great day with the entry: "Isaac son of Isaac and Hanna Newton, January 1, 1642–3." In the Newton Chapel, rebuilt in the scientist's memory, sleep three generations of his people; and here in an alabaster frame (below a corbel on which his portrait is carved) is a sundial which he cut with his penknife when a boy of nine, a young scientist fluttering his wings.

This church of Newton's boyhood also has great architectural interest, for although the chancel and the Newton Chapel were rebuilt last century, it displays elsewhere the mark of Saxon and Norman builders as well as those of all our great church-building periods in mediaeval times. The north arcade of the nave is Norman, and above its three round arches is Norman herringbone masonry pierced with three round openings lined with pottery, possibly to amplify the preacher's words. By the chancel arch is a fragment of an Anglo-Saxon cross, 30 inches high and carved with interlace.

The south arcade, with its pointed arches and clustered piers, is 13th century work; the tower, aisles, and spacious porch are 14th century, and the clerestory and several windows are 15th century. Colsterworth can truly boast a church of great historic interest.

Coningsby. A charming neighbour of Tattershall, lying by the River Bain, it has old houses with pantiles and thatch, and a grey church of Ancaster stone with a handsome 15th century tower standing on tall arches open to the churchyard.

The tower's unique feature is a great clock dial, 16½ feet in diameter and gaily coloured; it is the largest in the world with only the single hour-hand. Before the middle of the 17th century clocks had no minute hands; but such clocks are now very rare. In this case the dial is so large that it is possible to tell the time to within five minutes by carefully noting the position of its hand.

This clock was long silent, but it was put in order again by a Nottingham firm of clockmakers soon after the Second World War. The mechanism has some queer features, the framework being made up of oak beams to which the iron bars forming the bearing for the wheels are attached by wedges instead of screws. The wheels themselves are of wrought-iron, and the teeth were cut by hand with a chisel and a file. The pendulum, which is so long that it swings across only once in every two seconds, does not hang on the clock at all, but is suspended from a bracket set in the tower wall some distance from the main mechanism, and is linked to the clock escapement by a long connecting rod. The clock-weights are big blocks of stone, which now hang on the ends of steel-wire ropes, though they undoubtedly were originally hung from large hemp ropes.

The porch of Coningsby Church is as old as the tower; it has a big stoup and an old oak door with starry decoration in delicate wrought-iron which leads to its upper room. The spacious nave is mainly 13th century work and is crowned by an open-timbered roof with rough old beams. The chancel is a 19th century apse, but retains its 14th century arch with remains of a mediaeval oak screen. The eight-sided font is 700 years old.

The Old Rectory has recently been recognised as a mediaeval hall with 16th and 18th century additions. It has a fine timber-frame.

Two 18th century rectors of Coningsby have a place in literary annals. One was Laurence Eusden, probably the least-distinguished Poet Laureate this country has ever had. Fulsome flattery of the Lord Chamberlain secured him the appointment, and he proceeded to celebrate the honour with a coronation ode likening George II to the Deity, and containing these ridiculous lines:

> *Thy virtues shine peculiarly nice*
> *Ungloomed with a confinity to vice.*

Eusden, who according to Thomas Gray "turned out a drunken parson", died here in 1730. As parson of Coningsby he was followed, some 20 years later, by John Dyer, a Welsh lawyer's son, who had lived as a wandering artist-poet, painting his way to Italy and back and writing songs which made something of a stir in his day. Dr Johnson wrote of him disparagingly, thinking little of a man who departed from artificial convention and called his fellows back to Nature; but Wordsworth paid him tribute in a sonnet beginning:

> *Bard of the Fleece, whose skilful genius made*
> *That work a living landscape fair and bright.*

There are attractive brick, gabled houses—the Elizabethan House with interesting decorated brickwork and the Hall.

A mile upstream from Coningsby is the pretty village of Tumby, sheltered on the east by 100 acres of beautiful woods renowned for their oak and larch and wild lilies-of-the-valley. From the highway between the two villages a road leads to the old Lea Gate Inn. On one corner of the house is the old iron bracket which held the beacon light to guide lost travellers in the days before the fens were drained; and on the lawn are stone fragments brought from a hermitage in the Witham valley where Archbishop Becket is said to have sought shelter when he had fled from the wrath of Henry II. The name of the inn (on a swinging sign) recalls a former toll gate, and painted on the wall of the inn is a picture of a mounted highwayman jumping the gate.

Conisholme. Hidden on a twist of a bridle road among the reedy ditches in this tiny place 2 or 3 miles from the sea is a 13th century church which was once much bigger. A humble building it now is, but it shelters a rare treasure.

Two restorations last century brought to light the 700-year-old arcade now exposed in the north wall of the nave, and two arches of the same period in the north wall of the chancel. There is also a built-up arch in the south wall of the chancel, and another blocked arch in the east wall—these two arches, together with the one into the nave, supporting the theory that the present chancel was formed from a former central tower.

There are old moulded beams in the roof of the nave, and the tub font is Norman. A finer treasure is a brass in the nave floor, with the portraits of John Langholme of 1515, his wife, and 14 children. John wears armour with dagger and sword, his wife is in kennel head-dress and gown with fur cuffs, and their nine daughters and five sons are below, all alike as peas in a pod.

The church's rarest possession, however, is the Conisholme Stone, as it is called, which was dug up in the churchyard and is now on a windowsill. In the form of an Anglo-Saxon wheel-cross, much battered, it has in the middle an erect figure with arms outstretched, clearly a small, primitive crucifixion. Above his head is an inter-lacing serpent (symbol of eternity), and at the sides are three discs meant perhaps for symbols of the sun-god. It may be a sunstone used in worship on Midsummer Eve.

Corby. This was a place of no little importance in bygone days; the church registers reveal a variety of occupations—peruke-makers, apothecaries and stay-makers, saddlers and tailors—which point to the town having been a centre for the surrounding country. In 1239 Henry III granted permission to hold weekly markets (which con-tinued until the end of last century) and an annual sheep fair. The spacious marketplace contains an ancient market cross probably erected in the reign of Edward III, and visitors are astonished at the number of inns.

The church, occupying a commanding position on the hill, is a large 14th century building incorporating Norman remains. Over the south porch is a parvise or priest's chamber reached by a worn stone staircase. The communion rails of Archbishop Laud's time are particularly fine. One of the bells is dated 1629 and bears the poetic line, "Not noise but love sounds in the ears of God," and the church also has several fine specimens of mediaeval stained glass, including a crowned Madonna and a quaint figure of Saint John, its Patron Saint. But its rarest possessions are its wall paintings.

When the church was being cleaned and restored in 1939 dis-covery was made of mediaeval colour under the peeling coats of limewash. Mr E. Clive Rouse was called in, and after skilful investigation and treatment (nearly 1200 square feet of plaster were involved) revealed one of the most extensive collections of mediaeval mural paintings in the country.

On the north wall are life-size paintings of Saint Anne, mother of the Virgin Mary, teaching her Child to read, and of St Michael weighing souls at the Last Judgment. The Archangel holds in his hand a large balance. In one of the pans is a Soul being weighed, while the Devil sits astride the beam to weigh the scales in his favour. His efforts are frustrated by Our Lady of Mercies, who is sheltering numerous souls in the folds of her cloak and lets the beads of her rosary fall upon the scale to weigh it down for mercy. On the same wall is a remarkable pièta in which the Virgin Queen of Heaven sits enthroned, bearing on her lap the dead body of Christ. Around her are numerous men being tempted by devils to specific sins, and beneath this is a 13th century painting of St Christopher bearing the Christ child on his shoulder. On the clerestory walls are large representations of King Herod, the Wise Men, and Shepherds, and the whole Nativity series is crowned by a beautiful Madonna and Child.

The Doom over the chancel arch is unfortunately but a fragment of what must have been a magnificent painting. Nevertheless, upon it are still to be seen angels sounding the last trumpet call, the twelve Apostles with their emblems, royal figures waiting to enter Heaven, and tortured souls being thrown into a boiling cauldron while Hell's mouth gapes to receive them. On the north wall are represented the Heavenly Jerusalem with its pinnacles and temples, and the general resurrection wherein shrouded figures emerge from their stone coffins. Altogether, these paintings form a wonderful little picture gallery straight from the Middle Ages.

The old manor house at Corby, for more than 100 years the Rectory, is a fine Jacobean house with some Elizabethan portions. Another historic building is the picturesque Grammar School founded in 1669 under the will of Charles Read. The present building dates from 1673 and has recently been carefully restored by the Earl of Ancaster in memory of his son (Lord Timothy Willoughby de Eresby) and is known as The Willoughby Memorial. It has a library and gallery for exhibitions. For 240 years this school educated the more prosperous sons of the countryside until it was closed in 1909, being inaccessible for modern transport.

Corringham. The little River Till comes to life hereabouts; not far away is Wharton Wood, where herons nest; and across the high-road, in a small park studded with stately trees, is the partly-Elizabethan Somerby Hall. In a field west of the house is the site of a mediaeval earthwork.

Corringham's grand old church, finely restored, has an unbuttressed tower with coupled belfry windows which are Anglo-Saxon.

Its massive round-headed arch to the nave, however, is certainly Norman work, and its embattled parapet is a 17th century addition.

There are said to be more Saxon stones at the foot of a pillar of the nave's north arcade, which has two Norman bays and a pointed eastern bay which, like the arches of the south arcade, is 13th century work. The carved capitals of both arcades are interesting for their display of the development of natural foliage. The chancel is chiefly work of about 1220, and is divided from the nave by a fine 19th century screen, incorporating parts of a mediaeval screen. The east window, the clerestory, and the north transept are all 15th century.

There are old stalls with men's faces carved on their arm-rests, some old glass in the north aisle, and a stone coffin in the south aisle. The font is a 19th century copy of the lovely 700-year-old font at Thorpe St Peter. In the chancel is the recessed tomb of William de la Gare, prebendary of Corringham in the 13th century; and there is a brass showing one of his 17th century successors—Henry Clifford, with his wife and three sons. A second brass has a lengthy inscription in memory of Robert and Thomas Broxholme; it was put here in 1631 by their brother Henry and their sister Mary and states that all four of them had "lived together above sixty years and for the most part in most brotherly concord".

A window showing Jesus as the Good Shepherd and the Madonna with two children in a wood is a memorial to Miss Mary Beckett of Somerby Hall who paid for the costly restoration of this church last century.

Covenham St Bartholomew. Almost one with Covenham St Mary, this remote little village lies in the green flats below the Wolds. It has a small church built of stone and chalk; but of the small Benedictine priory founded here in mediaeval times there is no trace.

The church, hiding among the trees, is chiefly 14th century and lost its cruciform shape when the north transept was destroyed. The quaint little bell-tower is covered with slates and has an odd-looking fowl for weathercock; from the porch a great worn head looks down.

The fine brass of Sir John Skypwyth of 1415 shows him in armour with sword and dagger and gauntlets. Another fine possession is the 15th century font, its stem encircled by angels, wing to wing, and its octagonal bowl like a little sculpture gallery with figures of the Twelve Apostles holding books and emblems, the Madonna sitting on a bench with the Holy Child, and God in Majesty with the Crucifix between His knees. It has an old, pear-shaped cover in red and black.

A reservoir, constructed by the North-East Lincolnshire Water Board, is approximately ¾ of a mile square and has a water surface

of some 200 acres. It will be used for a variety of recreational purposes including water sports.

Covenham St Mary. Adjoining its twin village on a twisting
stretch of road crossed by a stream and embowered with trees, this
pretty place is graced by a church with a slender embattled tower.
Built for the most part in the 14th century and much restored in the
20th, it has a fine array of mediaeval windows filling the interior
with a blaze of light and all framing pictures of the churchyard trees.
Very charming the whole scene is, and the rich flowing tracery of the
east window and the cinquefoiled tomb recess in the north wall are
particularly attractive.

The font is almost as fine as that in neighbouring St Bartholomew's
church; the rim of the bowl is dotted with flowers, and below are
panels bearing shields with Passion emblems.

On the list of rectors from 1219 is the name of John England Rudd
who ministered here for more than half of the 19th century.

Cowbit. A few miles from Spalding, it lies to the east of Deeping
Fen, looking over Cowbit Wash—a long, broad expanse used as
grazing land in summer and until recently flooded by the Welland
in winter. This Wash (stretching from Spalding to Peakirk) has been
known to be under water for eight months of the year, and in time
of severe frost it was thronged with skaters. This winter sport has
now been transferred to Boston Fen.

Standing below the level of the road (which has a deep dyke on
the other side) is a church with a tower and chancel built in 1487 by
John Russell, Bishop of Lincoln. A band of quatrefoils adorns the
sturdy tower, and a turret climbs to its embattled parapet. The
walls of the chancel are of rougher stone, and its roof rests on corbels
carved with grotesques and foliage. The font and piscina are old,
and above one of the doors of the brick nave is a carved stone fish.

In a garden at Brotherhouse (between this village and Crowland)
is one of the stones, part of the shaft of a cross, which marked the
boundary of the famous abbey. It is known as St Guthlac's stone,
and bears a Latin inscription.

Cranwell. It has been on the map of Lincolnshire for many
centuries, but not until this Flying Age has its name been known
in every corner of the world. In all parts of the British Commonwealth are flying officers who served as cadets at Cranwell Royal
Air Force College; and it has been truly said that here is the heart
and centre from which the Royal Air Force derives its vitality.
From Cranwell it recruits its strength year by year and renews its
inspiration. The College was founded in 1919 and the magnificent
buildings with a prominent tower feature were designed by Sir

James Grey West in 1933. It is surrounded by fine spacious lawns.

Although the great RAF College has inevitably wrought much change in the life of the village, an old-fashioned air of tranquillity still abides at the corner where stands the ancient cross and village church.

That the Saxons knew this place is shown by four fragments of a cross-shaft enriched with interlace, found early this century and now standing in the aisle; and by about 10 feet of long-and-short masonry at the north-east corner of the nave, now under cover of the organ chamber. For the rest, the church is a mixture of many centuries, with a Norman arcade on thick round piers, several 13th century lancets, a 15th century east window and porch, and 17th century bellcot, itself shaped like a bell.

The plain 700-year-old font is still here, the chancel has its mediaeval traceried screen, and a tiny 13th century lancet at the west end of the aisle is filled with a mosaic of ancient glass—leaves, canopies, angel wings and other fragments. Two 13th century lancets in the nave have modern figures of the Good Shepherd and St Andrew, and four 19th century lancets in the aisle have figures of St George, St Christopher, St Martin, and St Catherine.

Creeton. Its highway crosses the River Glen and a rough track climbs from it steeply up the hillside, to end in a farmyard close to the little church. In the sloping churchyard are two bits of Saxon England, the broken shafts of two crosses with roundels and scroll and interlacing patterns, each several feet high. Other links with a remote past are several coffin-shaped stones with raised crosses, believed to mark the resting-places of monks from the vanished Cistercian Abbey of Vaudey (God's Vale) in the heart of the neighbouring Grimsthorpe Park.

The church comes chiefly from the 14th and 15th centuries, and once was bigger, for the pillars and arches of a north arcade were found in the wall during restoration. The tower has a broach spire with dormer windows, and the south transept, built probably as a chantry, has an ancient piscina. The church has little to show a traveller, but in the transept are two curiosities—a little wooden model of the church, and a Bible of 1611 in which the printer made the strange mistake of putting *Judas* instead of *Jesus* in the 36th verse of the 26th chapter of St Matthew, the story of Our Lord with the disciples in Gethsemane.

Croft. One of the finest of the marshland churches belongs to this lovely village. The noble tower soaring among the trees, the south doorway, and the spacious nave with its arcades and clerestory, were built in the 14th century; the aisles and the great chancel in the

15th. Restored in the 17th century and again in the 19th, the tower is of four storeys, with angels at the corners of its embattled and pinnacled crown; and its walls of ashlar contrast strikingly with the green sandstone of the rest of the church, patched here and there with brick.

A big porch with stone seats and an old roof of rough beams leads to the interior, where walls and arches and windows are all dazzling white. The chancel has great windows, a windowsill as sedilia, and a trefoil-headed piscina niche. The 15th century chancel screen has a modern cornice in place of the vanished rood-loft, but still has traces of its old colour and gilding, and is graceful with leafy arches and pattern of open trefoiled tracery. There are birds for crockets above the doorway, and in spandrels on the base of the screen are many quaint little figures, among them a lion, a hare, a fox with a bird, a monkey with a bottle, and a squirrel with a nut.

The traceried screens enclosing chapels in the aisles, and the poppyhead benches with little doors and wooden latches, are other fine examples of the work of 15th century woodcarvers; and a fine altar-table in one of the chapels, the south door of 1633, and the pulpit all testify to the skill of the men who followed their craft in Jacobean times. The south door, beautifully panelled and with a wicket, bears the words *God Save the King*, carved in raised letters. The richly-carved and canopied pulpit was given in 1615 by the vicar, Dr Worship, in memory of his wife Agnes, whose brass inscription in an aisle reads that she was matchless "for wisdom and godlyness".

Superbly set on a great stone platform is the graceful 15th century font, its ribbed stem supporting a buttressed bowl with panels of tracery and shields; under the bowl are little figures and rosettes. A rarer treasure is the brass eagle lectern which was recovered from the moat of the Old Hall. It stands almost as high as a man. It is of a type common to East Anglia. The eagle has wings with a spread of 2 feet, and is in perfect preservation except that its silver claws have been stolen; at its round base are three small lions. An entry in the register 300 years ago tells that the charge for "scouring and furbishing the eagle was half a crown by the year".

The earliest monuments are a brass, a coped gravestone of the 13th century, and another of the 14th century with a cross engraved on it. The brass is the half-figure of a knight of about 1300, and the oldest in Lincolnshire except for one at Buslingthorpe. It shows him with his hands at prayer, wearing banded mail, with a tunic over the hauberk.

To the Brownes who lived at the Old Hall there are two sumptuous monuments in the chancel, both having shields of arms and kneeling figures. One shows Sir Valentine Browne of 1606 with his wife and 15 children, and the other has their second son John with one of his two wives. The men are in armour and the women in rich gowns with bonnets and ruffs.

On the wall by the chancel arch is a pillared monument with a shield of arms and a skull set up in memory of William Bonde, a "most kynd father", who died in 1559. One of his two sons, Nicholas, was president of Magdalen College.

Crowland. Lying on the edge of Deeping Fen, close to the meeting-place of Lincolnshire, Northamptonshire, and Cambridgeshire, this remote little market town is a place of wide renown. Only just above the level of the Fens today, it was once an island in the midst of a vast swampy countryside, traversed only by little boats. Although streams have been diverted and the swamps drained Crowland still has the feeling of remoteness and the splendour of the abbey rises majestically above the high-banked modern flood banks, and wide streets.

Fame came to Crowland because of its great Benedictine abbey, founded in memory of a saint. It was in AD 699 that a little boat came to rest by this patch of dry ground in the dismal morass which gave the place its name—for Cru-land means soft, muddy land. In the boat was a young Mercian noble, named Guthlac, over whose shrine was to rise Crowland Abbey.

St Guthlac, who was born about AD 673, belonged to a family from which had sprung the kings of Mercia. After a wild youth, however, during which he was a leader in lawless fighting and plunder, he decided to abandon his wealth and military career and devote himself to religion.

For about two years he was at Repton Abbey in Derbyshire, where he studied assiduously. Then, when he was about 26, he determined to live a life of still greater solitude and austerity, and, setting off in his boat down the River Trent, he came eventually to Crowland. Here he built himself a hut and little chapel, and for the rest of his days lived on simple and meagre fare, clad in the skins of animals, but happy amid the dreary waste as a follower of God and a student of Nature.

Here at Crowland Guthlac was sought by men in need of spiritual counsel; and here, in flight from his cousin Ceolred, came the future King Ethelbald, to be assured by Guthlac that he would gain the crown without bloodshed. Guthlac died in 714, and was buried in his own little chapel, which soon became a place of pilgrimage. Two years later Ethelbald became King of Mercia, and, true to his promise to Guthlac if his prophecy should be fulfilled, founded the abbey in remembrance of his friend and protector. Such were the romantic beginnings of Crowland Abbey.

When, many centuries later, the melancholy swamps that Guthlac knew had become fields of golden corn the glory of the abbey had passed away. Three times in its long history it was destroyed by fire, and three times it was rebuilt, ever with increasing splendour, until it eventually became the wealthiest mitred abbey in the county. After the Dissolution the monastic buildings and cloisters (which lay on the south side of the church) were largely destroyed, and the church lost its choir, transepts, and central tower; but all that lay westward was left to serve as the parish church.

By the middle of the 18th century the south aisle had been taken down and the nave had fallen into ruin (weakened perhaps by Cromwell's bombardment of the abbey in 1643, when it had been fortified by the Royalists) leaving the north aisle to serve as the parish church—as indeed it had always been, and is still, with the grand old tower at its west end, and a short chancel added in 1897.

This aisle and tower are the only complete survival of the old abbey; but grouped with them are splendid fragments—the ruined nave with its glorious west front, the lovely west arch of the central tower, and a portion of the west front of the old south aisle. To the west of this aisle walling, in the churchyard, is the site of the cell in which St Guthlac lived his hermit's life; and about a mile away, by the road to Spalding, is Anchor Church Field, where he is said to have landed. (It was on St Bartholomew's Day that Guthlac came to Crowland, and both saints have a place in the abbey's dedication.) Of the abbey's first wooden buildings there is, of course, nothing to be seen, but grave-diggers in the churchyard have come upon the oak piles on which they were set.

A century and a half after its foundation, Crowland Abbey was burned by the Danes, who murdered its abbot (Theodore) at the altar. In the first half of the 10th century rebuilding was begun by Abbot Thurcytel (a kinsman of Edward the Elder), who founded the Crowland library and obtained from King Edgar a charter still extant. He it was who set up stones to mark the extent of the abbey's domain; and in a garden at Brotherhouse (4 miles away, near the Asen Dyke) still stands one marking the boundary between Crowland and Spalding, and proclaiming (in Latin) "This rock, I say, is Guthlac's utmost bound".

It was Thurcytel, too, who gave the abbey a huge bell called Guthlac; and according to Ingulphus, the abbey chronicler, a better bell could not be found in the land. Abbot Elgeric, who went on with rebuilding after Thurcytel's death in 975, is said to have added six bells and so made the first peal in England. Whether that be true we know not; but it is certain that the six bells now in the old abbey tower have made Crowland Abbey known to countless folk who have never seen it, for their fine peal has been carried by radio far and wide. One of the bells is 15th century, and another sounds the curfew at 8 o'clock every night, followed by a number of rings corresponding with the day of the month.

In the time of Edward the Confessor, Abbot Ulfketil restored some of the wooden buildings and began to build a new church of stone, having found a generous benefactor in the famous warrior-earl Waltheof, the only man ever condemned to death by the Conqueror. Waltheof's body was allowed burial in the abbey, and miracles are said to have been wrought at his tomb. In 1091, while Ingulphus the historian was abbot, the abbey was destroyed a second time by fire—this time, it is said, owing to the carelessness of a plumber. The whole library of 700 manuscripts perished in the flames, and what little of the building survived was pulled down in the time of Abbot Joffrid of Orleans, who began the next rebuilding in 1113.

The massive Norman church built by Joffrid and his successors had the shape of a cross, with transepts and central tower, and although it was damaged by earthquake in 1118 and was partly burned down in 1143, some remains of it are still to be seen. There is Norman work in the remaining portion of the west front of the south aisle, enriched with arcading in which are clearly seen the old masons' marks—among them a pair of compasses, a circle with the four points of a star, and a circle with rays. On the eastern side of this wall is a blocked Norman arch. The most striking feature of the Norman remains, however, is the western arch of the vanished central tower; richly adorned with zigzag, and set on its two lofty piers, it stands out like a graceful bow against the sky, defying Time. Beneath the arch is a 15th century stone screen, pierced with two doorways, and carved and panelled on its eastern side, where an astonishing detail is the marks of a fire lit one day in the 18th century when the squire decided to roast an ox for his son's coming-of-age.

Next in order of time to this Norman work is the west front of the nave. It has all the richness of a cathedral front, and is almost complete except for its vanished gable, the tracery of its vast window, and some of the splendid statues in niches which adorn it from top to bottom. The lower portion of the front is 13th century work, and the rest was rebuilt early in the 15th century after it had been blown down. In the tympanum of the richly-moulded double doorway is a bold quatrefoil showing five carved scenes (now very worn) from the life of Guthlac—his boat landing at Crowland where a sow and her litter are resting; his ordination by the Bishop of Winchester; his compelling of Satan to bring stone for the abbey; his body being prepared for burial; and his elevation to Heaven by two angels.

The statues are in five tiers, occupying the whole front except for the space taken by the doorway and window. With the three figures believed to have been on the missing gable there were 29 in all; now there are 20. Highest of all are saints and apostles, including Philip with three loaves, James the Greater with staff and wallet, Andrew,

Peter, James the Less, and Jude. The second row, divided by the head of the window, has King Ethelbald, the two patron saints (Bartholomew and Guthlac) and Richard II in whose reign the abbey was refounded. (Guthlac is shown holding the three-thonged whip which he is supposed to have obtained in answer to prayer, for warding off the "fiends" which assailed him at Crowland, one of which is shown here at his feet.)

The first statue of the third tier is either Kenulph (the first abbot) or Thurcytel; then come William the Conqueror and his Queen Matilda, and Abbot Ingulphus holding a volume of his history. Below them are the Conqueror's Archbishop Lanfranc, King Wiglaf, who found refuge at Crowland and was buried here in 825, Earl Waltheof, and Abbot Joffrid. By the doorway is the one remaining Evangelist.

Except for three stately bays of its south arcade, little is left of the rest of the nave, which, together with the old north aisle and the tower, belongs to the great 15th century rebuilding under the three abbots who ruled from 1393 till 1469—Thomas Overton, Richard Upton, and John Lytlyngton.

The tower (which was given its two-storied west porch and its stumpy spire with four dormer windows early in the 16th century) has a great six-light west window with fine tracery, an arcaded top stage, and panelled buttresses rising to a plain parapet. Its interior is a glorious lantern, with enormous arches framing windows with panelled sides. There are four galleries at various levels, and a great panelled arch leads to the old north aisle which through the centuries has been the people's church. With its great windows and its fine vaulted roof of stone, this old aisle is a lovely sight from the tower, giving a vivid impression of the beauty and dignity which the complete church must have possessed. One of the roof's six golden bosses, showing a staff over a tun, is the rebus of Abbot Overton in whose time the abbey was mitred.

The fine 15th century oak chancel screen, enriched with tracery and still retaining some of its original colour, once enclosed the lady chapel in the north transept; in the spandrels of its lower panels are leaves and flowers, a man in a boat, a bat-like grotesque, a fierce dragon, and a man's head with golden hair. Here are also two fonts —a traceried one of the 15th century, and a round font of Norman times set in an arched and vaulted recess in the south pier of the tower arch. Two of the three old chapels on the north side of the old aisle are vestries now, and in the rector's vestry stands a solid oak chest five centuries old. Gathered together in a south window is a mosaic of old glass fragments, including two little angels in white and gold.

The upper room of the west porch is used as a chapel, and within the porch is the entrance to a dark little room where the abbots of old may have sheltered people who claimed sanctuary. Some fragments of old stonework are preserved within it.

Against the inner wall of the tower is a fine tombstone with the engraved portrait of William of Wermington, the 15th century master of works responsible for much of this splendid architecture. Standing under an elaborate canopy, he holds the instruments of his craft, a pair of compasses and a square. Nearby hangs a miniature stone coffin-lid—the top of a heart-burial casket.

One other ancient sight known far and wide has Crowland. Standing at the crossroads in the middle of the town is the famous Triangular Bridge, a relic unique in the land. Built when these streets were waterways, it is like three halves of bridges meeting at a centre and climbed by three flights of steps. Built in the second half of the 14th century, it replaced a wooden bridge mentioned in a document of 1000 years ago, and may have served as the base of a great cross, as well as a three-way bridge. For about 200 years the bridge has been adorned by a crowned, seated figure of Our Lord holding an orb. It is believed that this statue was originally on the missing gable of the west front of the abbey church, where it perhaps had figures of St Mary and St John for company.

Henry VI, who gave the town its charter for a market and a fair, landed here when he came to stay with the abbot in 1460, and some years later Edward IV stepped from the bridge on to a boat that was to take him to Fotheringhay Castle.

Crowle. Busy with agriculture and brick-making, it is a remote little town of the Isle of Axholme, lying near the Yorkshire border.

A church dedicated to the Northumbrian St Oswald was here in Saxon times. This was succeeded by a Norman church, substantial parts of which can be seen in the present one, still bearing the ancient dedication.

The tower has a tall Norman arch, a late 13th century west window, and a round opening in which a beacon light is said to have shone. The clerestoried nave is much restored, but its south wall is still Norman in part, with the jamb of a Norman window visible inside, and (within a modern porch) a Norman doorway with richly-carved arch. Two of the arch's four orders are roll mouldings; a third is of zigzag edged with balls, diamonds, and tiny faces; and the fourth is of diamond lattice. It frames an old panelled and studded door. Adorning the exterior of the south wall is a gallery of grotesque corbel heads.

The church has a pillar almsbox and a chalice, both of the 17th century, but its great treasure is a thousand years older. Known as the Crowle Stone, it is 7 feet high, and is believed to be part of the stem of an Anglo-Saxon cross. In the carving on the front of the stone are crude figures of two men facing each other, another man on horseback, and a Runic inscription almost worn away; on the back are interlacing ornament and an entwined serpent.

It is thought that the two men represent the Northumbrian kings Oswald and Oswy, and that the cross was perhaps set up by Oswald's niece Ostryth (queen of Ethelred) to commemorate the saint's body passing through Crowle after he had been slain in battle by the pagan King Penda.

The Norman masons used the Crowle Stone as a lintel for their tower arch, and not until the 19th century was it taken out. It is a precious relic of early Christianity in this country, and a copy of it is in the British Museum.

Croxby. A tiny village in a steep dip of the Wolds, it has a quaint and interesting little church with a story eight centuries old.

Originally built towards the close of the Norman period, it is now only 30 feet long and 16 feet wide, but was once considerably bigger. The arcades of its former aisles can still be seen, built up in walls which are bowed in unusual fashion in order to exhibit them more fully. On the south side are two massive Norman arches. The pointed north arcade is 13th century, with richly-moulded capitals crowning fine clustered pillars. These blocked arches frame 14th century windows, and in the chancel wall are traces of an arch which led to a lady chapel.

The simple, rugged chancel arch and the doorway within the 13th century porch are Norman; and Norman, too, is the fine font with interlaced arcading and a band of nail-head and plaited ornament. Eight old traceried bench-ends are still here and have served as models for the rest.

A stream from Thoresway runs through the village and goes on for a mile before filling Croxby Pond, a charming sheet of water in a fine plantation, and a haunt of many water-birds. Beyond the Pond it joins another clear stream from Kirmond Top, and together they reach the sea at Tetney Haven.

Croxton. It looks over the fields to Kirmington's green spire and to Brocklesby's grand woods; and on the wooded height west of the village is the great earthwork known as Yarborough Camp, where many Roman coins have been found, though the date of the earthwork may be earlier.

The old work in the tiny restored church is chiefly 13th century, though the top of the tower, the blocked south doorway, and some of the windows are from later mediaeval days. There are original lancets in the chancel and the aisle, and the 13th century north arcade still stands with its arches on fine clustered pillars. Surprisingly high for so small a church, this arcade dwarfs the low arch of the tower. Remains of the south arcade are seen built-up in the wall. The old font is like a cup with massive bowl and short stem.

There is a panel of early 14th century glass in a south window depicting the Crucifixion. The stained glass in the east window, with representations of the Incarnation, the Crucifixion, and the Lord in Glory, is a memorial to an airman who crashed in 1943 when returning from Berlin. A Lancaster bomber is cut on the headstone marking his grave by the porch.

Cumberworth. A mile from Mumby and reached by narrow twisting lanes, this village has a small church with a quaint lead-covered turret and spire springing from the nave roof. Restoration has left it a 15th century doorway, some 14th century windows, an old piscina, mediaeval floorstones down the middle of the nave, and a fine font with 500-year-old carving of flowers and leaves and shields with Passion emblems.

Cuxwold. Tiny and remote, and prettily set in a hollow of the Wolds, it has a little church on rising ground, with a great sycamore standing like a sentinel at the churchyard gate.

The church lost most of its ancient bearing last century, except for the low tower, the lower part of which was built in the 11th century and has its original Norman arch opening to the nave; its top stage, with lancets in the belfry, is Early English. There is also a Norman font with simple arcading round the top of its huge bowl, and outside, in the north wall of the nave, traces of a pointed arcade can be seen.

Dalby. It is all tranquil and charming. Church and Hall nestle in a quiet hollow of a park, with trees all around and a grand avenue linking them with the highway. The Hall is the successor of the one which was burned down in 1841 and was the home of Tennyson's aunt Mrs Bourne. The little church was also rebuilt last century, but still has some of the old monuments. In a delightful monument above the pulpit is the tiny figure of Juliana Llanden who died in 1617; kneeling at a desk she wears a black gown and a white ruff. Kneeling in another monument are her husband's parents, William and Alice Llanden. There is also a little 14th century font, carved with leaf-tipped quatrefoils.

In the hamlet of Dexthorpe, north of the village, Roman coins and pottery of the 3rd and 4th centuries have been found.

Dalderby. It has only a few farms and cottages, but the manor house built in Georgian style is well worthy of notice. Its church is reduced to grassy foundations in a field; but it has proud remembrance of sons who have served their country well.

By the roadside is a gabled-headed cross (with carvings of the Crucifixion and the Madonna), of which this tiny hamlet may well be proud, for it was put up in 1915 in honour of the Dalderby men who volunteered before conscription was introduced. Eleven of them there were, from a population of about a score; and it is said that no village in the land sent a bigger proportion of volunteers. Ten of the eleven came back from the war; the other—one of four brothers who fought—sleeps in

> *. . . some corner of a foreign field*
> *That is for ever England.*

Six centuries earlier another son of Dalderby was serving his church and building himself an enduring memorial in stone. He was John de Dalderby, who as Bishop of Lincoln completed the central tower of the cathedral.

Dalderby's quaintest possession was unfortunately burnt down some years ago. It was a one-roomed cottage with a thatched roof reaching to the ground; with a jutting window for a handle and a chimney for a spout, it was known for many miles around as Teapot Hall.

Deeping St James. This big Fen village joins hands with Market Deeping, and only a road-sign marks where the one ends and the other begins. The busy main street which links them runs alongside the River Welland and is crossed at Deeping Gate by a fine old bridge of three arches.

The great possession of Deeping St James is the fine church, which has room for 800 worshippers and a story going back to 1139. It was the church of the small Benedictine priory founded here as a cell of Thorney Abbey by Baldwin Wake, or FitzGilbert, founder of the abbey at Bourne.

Spacious as it is, the church was once bigger, and a built-up arch tells of vanished transepts. The tower, with arcaded parapet and lofty spire, is 18th century work, but the rest is a rich legacy from Norman and mediaeval times. The massive 13th century porch has a sundial on its gable and dog-tooth ornament on its arch, and the aisle to which it leads is notable for its fine array of traceried 14th century windows.

The impressive feature of the interior is the nave arcade. Its seven bays display the merging of the Norman and the Early English styles of architecture, for the arches, though round-headed, rest on clustered piers; above them are the thirteen pointed arches of a triforium with the slender lancets of the clerestory behind them—all 13th century work. The arcade, like the north wall of the nave, leans outward as though overburdened by the passing centuries.

Other survivals from the Norman church include some graceful wall-arcading in the chancel, and two round-headed windows in the same wall, framed by a lovely transitional arcade of richly-moulded arches on clustered shafts. In the 14th century window set in the blocked Norman arch in the nave's north wall are figures of Baldwin de Wake (founder of the priory) and Richard de Rulos, the Norman lord of the manor who first drained the fenland hereabouts and made a wilderness blossom as the rose.

The huge tub-shaped font, which has its remains of the old staple fastenings for a cover, is a Norman relic. To the 13th century belong two piscinas and a 14th century floorstone with traces of the figure of a knight. Other old relics include a chest with three locks, and a sentry-box shelter once used by the parson when conducting funerals in the rain.

Near the church are two more links with days gone by—a fine tithe barn 36 yards long, and a stone lock-up with three alcoves for seats, and chains for fastening the prisoners. The early 19th century lock-up was originally a 15th century market cross, and its huge base is enriched with traceried panels and set on two great steps.

Dembleby. It is a tiny old-world village with a 19th century church built throughout in Norman style, trim and beautifully kept, with a saint in each of the five deeply-splayed windows of its rounded apse. As token of the village's antiquity it preserves a round Norman chancel arch and uses a Norman stoup for a font, both from the demolished church.

Denton. Set in a hollow near the Leicestershire border it has the undeniable charm of well-built cottages with warm brown stone walls and mellow red roofs, and a great house in a park approached by a splendid avenue of horse-chestnuts. The present house built in 1962, replaces an earlier 19th century building of which the gate-house survives. In the park is a spring called St Christopher's Well, filling a group of lakes; and north of the park flows a stream which fills another big lake serving as a reservoir for the Grantham Canal.

The light, clerestoried church stands in a lovely position looking over one of the park lakes. It comes mainly from the 15th century, though largely rebuilt, and still keeps many old features, including the sedilia, the piscina, and the font with the carved rosettes. The 15th century screen has been fashioned anew, and the rest of the woodwork in the chancel is entirely modern, including six angels with outspread wings looking down from the roof. Modern glass in the east window shows the scene at the empty grave of Our Lord, and twelve angels in gorgeous raiment above. Four golden-haired angels are among old fragments in a side window.

Five stone heads look out from each of the arcades, and lying in his tomb in the south aisle is John Blyth, an Elizabethan in tunic breeches, and long cloak; kneeling on the side of his tomb are his wife, three sons, and three daughters, the name of each child inscribed above its head. In the other aisle is the wall-monument of Richard Welby of Queen Anne's day, with two cherubs crowning his bewigged head, and two infants mourning him below; the inscription is a catalogue of his virtues (modesty, humility, courtesy, probity and universal charity) and describes him as forbearing landlord, prudent master, and invaluable friend. The oldest memorials are floorstones which have lost their brasses, and another engraved with a much-worn figure of an unknown priest.

Close to the church are the Welby Almshouses built in the 17th century and in the village the 17th century manor house should be noted.

In Grantham Museum is a drawing of a tessellated Roman pavement unearthed here in the 18th century; a portion of the pavement is in the Lincoln Museum.

Digby. Known to most visitors because of its important RAF station. Among its old attractions are a striking wayside cross, a little round village lock-up, and a church going back to Saxon times. The evidence of a Saxon church is the long-and-short masonry seen outside at the south-east corner of the nave.

The doorway carved with zigzag is unmistakably Norman; the chancel, with its sedilia, aumbry, and two piscinas, is 13th century; the arcades on clustered pillars, and the pinnacled tower, are 13th and 14th century; and the crocketed spire and clerestory are 15th century. Thus did mediaeval builders enrich this church through the years.

Notable among the church's old possessions are a few pews with poppyheads and traceried ends, a traceried chancel screen, a chest with three locks, a tall font with carved flowers, an Elizabethan chalice and paten, and a Jacobean pulpit.

Doddington. Set in a delightful patch of the county where English oaks abound, it is one of those charming villages where trees are more in evidence than cottages; and its charm is enhanced by a little grey-walled church nestling under the wing of the mellow red-brick Hall.

The old church, with quaint lead spire above its pinnacles and battlements, was almost rebuilt in 1771 by Lord Delaval, but the splendid Hall where this family lived stands much as it stood in Elizabeth I's day, though a great deal of the interior decoration (including oak panelling, a fine staircase, and marble chimney-pieces) was also the work of Lord Delaval.

Doddington Hall, which has come through the years so graciously, was built by Thomas Taylor, registrar to the Bishops of Lincoln, who bought the estate from John Savile in 1593. Three storeys high and shaped like the letter E, with projecting wings and lofty central porch, it is 160 feet long and is notable for its many windows, its flat cornices, and the three eight-sided turrets with leaden domes which crown it. It looks out on beautiful grounds with flower gardens and cedar-shaded lawn, and is approached through an attractive Tudor gatehouse with three mullioned windows and Dutch gables above its entrance. Little remains of the original interior arrangements; the present rooms are 18th century.

After the death of Thomas Taylor's son during the Commonwealth, this fine inheritance passed to his niece, Lady Hussey, whose husband had been fined £10,000 as a Royalist. His great-uncle was the Lord Hussey beheaded by Henry VIII for his share in the Pilgrimage of Grace, and whose portrait is one of the many fine pictures treasured here. The last of the Delaval men to live at Doddington was Edward Hussey Delaval, who made a famous set of musical glasses, won the gold medal of the Royal Society for various scientific experiments, and was laid to rest in Westminster Abbey in 1814.

Of the Jarvis family who have lived here for more than a century there are many reminders in the little church, as broad as it is long, and with nave and chancel undivided. The stained windows they have given as memorials dominate the scene. Well drawn, but in flamboyant colours, they depict such scenes as The Nativity, Suffer Little Children, the Good Samaritan, The Supper at Cana, The Crucifixion and the Ascension, and altogether make a striking gallery of sacred art.

There is a tablet to Henry Jarvis who died of fever in the West Indies about a century ago, and there are attractive wood carvings by Colonel Payne Jarvis, who served in the Peninsular War and sleeps here. One shows Peter and John at the Gate Beautiful, with life-like figures of the cripple on the floor, St Peter holding his hand, women passing with baskets on their heads, and a small boy with two birds; the other has the scene of St Paul preaching on Mars Hill.

Amid so much that is modern the 13th century font, with carved leaves and roses, seems singularly ancient.

Donington. An old market town of the fenlands that has been most attractive in its day. It lies at the meeting of two important roads, one running north from Spalding, the other on the line of the old Holland Road—the Salters' Way made by the Romans to link the Midlands with the Wash. A few miles west of Donington runs the Carr Dyke, made by the Romans as a canal along which to convey grain to the north and to assist in the drainage of the fens. Between the town and the Carr Dyke are the South Forty Foot Drain and the Hammond Beck, which have also played a part in the re-claiming of the Fens.

Donington was long famed as the centre of the trade in the flax and hemp which were grown hereabouts, and even up to the 19th century there were three hemp fairs here every year. Now it is busy with farming.

On the cobbled market square are two little blocks of houses and shops; and round it are old brick houses with pantiled roofs and Georgian houses with bow windows. Sheltered by tall limes, not far from the square, are the fine buildings of a school which has grown from the old grammar school founded in the 18th century by Thomas Cowley, for "twenty poor children to be taught to read English and write". The old building is still here with the new, its walls of mellowed brick new-roofed, and the old portico still has its sundial of 1719. The founder's gravestone in the church states that he died in 1721 at 96.

The church is a great landmark, and splendid testimony to the mediaeval builders, the oldest portion being the 13th century chancel which was given finely traceried windows in the 15th century. The great east window is of five lights, and three similar 15th century windows light the west front of the church.

But the glory of this church is the 14th century tower with a spire rising more than 200 feet. The spire has three tiers of traceried dormer windows and is crowned by an imposing golden ball and weathercock. The tower has gabled buttresses climbing to the battlements, and its base, with groined roof, buttresses enriched with canopied niches, and handsome doorways, serves as a porch. The inner doorway has four shafts on each side supporting a richly-moulded arch, and in a fine niche above it is a figure of Our Lord. Among the grotesque carvings by the other niches are two men in a boat, and a dragon attacking a woman.

The fine embattled clerestory, the big rood turret, and the north aisle, are all 15th century work. The spacious nave, still with its old roof, and the south aisle are 14th century, the aisle being notable for its lovely windows with shafts and moulded tracery, both inside and out. The lofty arcades are an impressive feature of the interior, adorned by a gallery of carved heads of mediaeval folk between the arches, and with big corbels at the ends showing a man supporting the arch, two men fighting, and heads of men with shields among foliage.

The chancel has its 13th century priest's doorway adorned with nail-head, an old piscina with a floral drain, a window seat for sedilia, a curious arched recess with three steps or shelves, and a 16th century doorway on each side of the altar. The old rood stair-way and a large bracket for the rood are also here.

A quaint sculpture in the church portrays a boy kneeling on a wall; and a stone panel against a pillar of an arcade shows a child kneeling before a chalice on a table.

Among the many memorials, is one of outstanding interest—a tablet in the chancel to Captain Matthew Flinders, the famous explorer, who was born in the town in 1774 and died here after a short but adventurous life. Carved in low relief on his tablet are sailing ships at sea, symbolic of the pioneering voyages which inscribed his name indelibly on the map of Australia.

Donington-on-Bain. The high Wolds encompass this village and its tiny 700-year-old church with squat, unbuttressed tower. The arcade of a vanished aisle is built-up in a wall of the church, and from the moulding of one of the capitals peeps an odd little face. The chancel, partly rebuilt last century, has two old lancets and a 15th century east window; and its crooked old entrance arch has slanting pillars and capitals carved with nail-head ornament. In the south wall of the nave are a 13th century lancet and a big window inserted two centuries later. Shaped like a cheese, and resting on what seems to be part of a moulded capital, the Norman font is enriched with interlaced arcading and bands of cable moulding.

An early 17th century brass to the memory of a rector has a quaint epitaph stating that:

> Both Chrysostom and Polycarp in one
> United lye intered beneath this stone.
> This one a Phoenix was all eminent,
> The learned, prudent, pious Thomas Kent.
> Late rector of this church as whilome were
> His good old father and his brother deare,
> Fame hath his praise, ye world his life well spent,
> His spirit Heaven, his bones this monument.

Dorrington. Several pretty cottages grace its long street, and in a garden stand the shaft and base of the old village cross. Alone on a little rise is the ancient church, its massive tower a gaunt spectacle by the roadside, unadorned by battlements or spire.

Like most of the old work in the church, the tower is chiefly 14th century, but its curious arch (with one capital adorned by carving of stiff foliage) is a century earlier. Other remains of the original 13th century church are the chancel arch, two lancet windows in the chancel, and the nave arcades of two bays. The arches on the south side look heavy for the low, frail pillar supporting them; the arches on the north rest on a lovely central pillar enriched with dog-tooth ornament between its clustered shafts. A queer little head peeps out above the capital of this pillar, and on the wall above is a pouting face. The clerestory was added at the close of the 15th century.

The east end of the chancel is notable work of about 1330. The east window has moulded mullions and reticulated tracery, and at each side of it is a niche with shafts and leafy capitals supporting a trefoiled canopy with finial. A third niche enriches the east end, outside, together with a vigorous sculpture of the Last Judgment, a beautiful gable cross, and gabled buttresses with a gallery of gargoyles, including a demon pulling a man's ears.

Dowsby. A tall stone Elizabethan hall, a few cottages, and red-tiled farm buildings here keep company with a church largely rebuilt last century.

The low, battlemented 15th century tower still stands, and four stones with cable moulding built into the last wall of an aisle reflect the church's Norman origin. The nave, with big pointed tower arch at one end and wide chancel arch at the other, also looks venerable though both of its own arcades have been rebuilt. The plain round font is centuries old, and in the chancel is a brass almsdish of 1503 with an engraving of two men carrying a huge bunch of grapes on a pole. In a recess is a 14th century stone figure of Etheldreda Rigdon in long, tight-waisted gown.

From the churchyard, with a row of yews, and a monkey puzzle tree shading its gate, there is a good view of the Elizabethan Dowsby Hall, picturesque with tall gables and a row of nine chimneys. It was probably designed by John Thorpe for Sir William Rigdon.

Driby. The road from Louth to Boston runs over Driby Top, 286 feet up on the Wolds; below, in the remote and pretty valley where the headstreams of the Great Eau gather, is the tiny village. It was an important manor centuries ago, and the earthworks and moat (still wet in winter) of an ancient manor house are visible behind the old farmhouse called Driby Manor, itself of Elizabethan date.

The little stone church was completely rebuilt last century. It has an open oak bellcot and a fine doorway adorned with dog-tooth ornament. Within are brass portraits of James and Alice Prescot who lived here in Elizabeth I's time.

Dry Doddington. Charming is its setting in the countryside near the Nottinghamshire border; there are wonderful views from the little church on the edge of the green crowning the hill.

Like much of the old work in the church, the sturdy tower and its short broach spire (both leaning at an alarming angle) are early 14th century work. The south doorway, with its simple zigzag carving, comes from the close of Norman days, and the low nave arcades, with a little nail-head pattern on one side, are nearly as old.

Dunholme. A pleasing village picture is here—of an old church in a churchyard shaded by chestnut and beech, and a stream passing by on its way to the little Langworth river. A source of spring water, bored in 1892, and 100 feet deep, was restored by public subscription in 1963.

Restoration has not robbed the church of all its antiquity, and 13th century work is displayed in the massive embattled tower with its eight low pinnacles, and the nave arcades, each with three arches on clustered columns and decked with three serious little heads. The quaint font with its much-worn carvings of flowers and seated men, some with staves and others with books, is also 13th century. From the 16th century comes a rare treasure found in the chancel some years ago and now preserved behind glass; it is a leather case used in mediaeval times for holding sacramental vessels, adorned with foliated pattern and looking not unlike a miniature hatbox.

In the chancel is a stone carving of a parishioner who died in 1616 and remembered his poorer fellows in his will; he is Robert Grantham, kneeling in robes at a little prayer-desk, his features worn. The chancel screen, with its linenfold panels, delicate tracery and bold Crucifixion figures is fine modern work.

Dunholme Church is dedicated to St Chad and there is a statue of him in a niche of the modern porch. This saint of Lichfield appears again in a north aisle window in company with Hugh of Lincoln, each holding a model of his cathedral church. The window is a memorial to Samuel Wild, vicar here for 35 years of this century. The east window is notable for the restrained colours of its Crucifixion scene.

Dunsby. A village on the edge of the Fens, it has the base of a mediaeval cross where its three roads meet—the merest fragment opposite a smithy—and a grey embattled church tower by the wayside with a figure of Our Lord in a niche.

The tower, like most of the church, is 14th century, but the south doorway with heads of a man and woman at the sides, the chancel arch, and the four pointed arches in the nave, are a century older. The 500-year-old font has an obscure inscription which has been interpreted as "In the beginning Jesus Christ, born of Mary, is He the Baptist". The modern glass of the east window has an attractive picture of the Adoring Shepherds, with the Archangels Michael and Gabriel kneeling above, and St Nicholas and St George below.

Dunston. Its church was rebuilt last century, and its antiquity is apparent only in the mediaeval tower, and in the porch, which has a Norman doorway with a row of dog-tooth ornament above, stones with zigzag carving set in its walls, and an inner 14th century doorway with foliated capitals and two carved heads. For the rest, it is an attractive village church, with graceful nave arcades and a striking east window with figures of Our Lord and the Four Evangelists.

What is known far and wide as the Dunston Pillar stands 4 miles away beside the Heath road to Lincoln. A great square pillar 92 feet high, it was reduced in height in 1940 and the huge Coade Stone statue of George III, erected in 1810, was removed and is now in the Museum of Lincolnshire Life in Lincoln. It was originally a land lighthouse with a lantern 15 feet high, set up in the days when travellers on the lonely heath were not only at the mercy of highwaymen but often completely lost. That was in 1751, the public benefactor being the eccentric Sir Francis Dashwood, then owner of Nocton Hall.

Eagle. The preceptory of the Knights Templars founded at Eagle Hall by King Stephen has vanished, and the ancient church has been rebuilt, though the 13th century tower still stands. At the rebuilding of the ancient church bosses and shields for the interior of the roof and "Jerusalem" and a "St John" crosses were mounted on the exterior as a reminder of its association with the Order of St John of Jerusalem and were provided by the Order. An important officer of the Order bears the title of "Bailiff of Egle" [*sic*]. Within the rebuilt church is the defaced bowl of a Norman font.

The stone gateway of the churchyard, with statues of a Knight Templar and Knight Hospitaller is a memorial to eight warriors of the First World War who left this peaceful Lincolnshire village for evermore.

East Barkwith. It lies on a green-verged patch of the highway from Wragby to Louth, still keeping a few objects of mediaeval date in its much-rebuilt church.

The 19th century saw the chancel and the upper part of the tower made new, and the north aisle added to the nave. The porch, however, with a carving of the Madonna and Child in a niche, is 15th century work, and the fine south arcade of the nave is of the same period, except for its one round 13th century pillar.

Another 13th century fragment is a lancet window at the west end of the south aisle, which was found during restoration and had not hitherto been glazed. It is thought it may have been an opening from a hermit's cell in bygone days.

The 15th century font has carvings of quaint heads, leaves and flowers, and shields with instruments of the Passion. Two old bench-ends make a seat in the chancel. The modern pulpit is of ironwork, gleaming with gold, and has filigree borders and panels of vine.

A mile nearer Wragby is West Barkwith, with a tiny church made new this century, when its old tower was saved from ruin.

East Halton. A long, straggling village near the Humber, it has an old church (chiefly 13th century) standing a little way off, its walls a patchwork of weathered stone. The chancel is interesting for its array of windows coming from Norman and 13th and 14th century days. One window in the south wall has plate tracery, and one reticulated, and in the opposite wall are a lancet window and a mediaeval arch, both blocked.

There are some fine 15th century bench-ends with embattled tops and carving of tracery and foliage, and a Jacobean chest. In the tower (which has a plain parapet and is but slightly higher than the nave) is a grand old ladder with sides fashioned from a tree-trunk split in two; here, too, stands an old sanctus bell. In the churchyard is the battered bowl of a Norman font.

East Keal. An attractive village on a winding highway, it stands high on the southern slope of the Wolds, looking far across the Fen countryside. Boston Stump, 15 miles away, is visible on the horizon.

The church, much rebuilt last century, still has its 13th century south arcade with clustered pillars, and 14th century north arcade. The modern tower has a striking interior; its three windows with plate tracery are framed by curtain arches on slender shafts and all round them is fine dog-tooth ornament; its west doorway is also adorned with dog-tooth. Quaint old carved stones have been preserved in the south doorway—men with crossed arms, two tiny draped figures, a kneeling girl, a dog with a bone, and a creature never seen on land or sea.

The font with its carving of flowers and foliage and grotesque heads is 14th century work. The modern pulpit has fine figures of St Hugh of Lincoln and St Helen.

East Kirby. This village in attractive setting under the southern slope of the Wolds has an old church of unusual charm, enhanced by fine restoration early this century.

Built of greensand and Ancaster stone, it is mainly 14th century work; but the sturdy tower (with a mass dial by its doorway) has a two-light window from the close of the 13th century and a later embattled parapet, and the chancel has 15th century windows below its modern clerestory. The east window is 14th century and two others, fine examples of this period, are the east window of the south aisle and the west window of the nave.

Soaring arcades with slender pillars, roofs with a fine mass of timbering, and rich carving in stone and wood help to make the interior of the church even more attractive than the exterior.

In the north wall of the chancel are two things of note. One is a little two-light low-side window with a tiny quatrefoil in its head.

The other is a remarkable recess looking rather like an Easter Sepulchre but actually a credence and a piscina combined. The bowl (with a drain) projects from a narrow shelf under a reredos richly carved with diaper of flowers, two branches of foliage, and canopied half-figures of three women, probably the three Marys, holding heart-shaped caskets; immediately above this recess are two trefoiled arches under a cornice of flowers. On this same wall, but outside, is a piscina belonging to a vanished chapel. In the south wall of the chancel is a finely-traceried arch, perhaps part of a window.

Between the nave and chancel is a 15th century oak screen enriched with delicate tracery. There are also remains of other mediaeval screens which enclosed chantry chapels, and 18 old bench-ends with worn poppyheads. The fine font, with flowers and heads carved in its traceried bowl, is 15th century.

The south aisle has a piscina, a 14th century stone with heads carved at the corners (perhaps an altar bracket), and a floorstone with a graven cross in memory of Robert Sylkestone, who founded a chantry here 600 years ago. An old altar stone found in this aisle during the restoration now lies under the floor of the vestry, but can be seen by opening a trap door.

In a house near the church is a stone carved with the letters L.G. and the date 1544. It is thought to be a link with the Goodrich family, and is a reminder that this village was the birthplace, towards the end of the 15th century, of Thomas Goodrich, Bishop of Ely and Lord Chancellor of England, and a staunch supporter of the Reformation.

Consecrated Bishop of Ely in 1534, Thomas Goodrich had a leading part in reforming ecclesiastical laws; he caused the new religion to be expounded in all the colleges and churches of Cambridge; and he shared in the translation of St John in the revision of the New Testament. As Edward VI's Lord Chancellor he had an important share in the Prayer Book of the young king, and opened the Parliament which made it the law of the land.

With the death of Edward he acted on the council during the nine days of Lady Jane's reign. His name was included in the list of persons for trial for high treason, but was struck out by Mary, partly, as a later historian says, on account of his sacred character, and partly on account of his insignificance.

Thomas Goodrich did homage to Mary at her coronation and was allowed to retain the see of Ely. He died at Somersham, Huntingdonshire, in May 1554 and was buried in Ely Cathedral.

East Ravendale. Tree-bowered roads lead to this little place among the wooded valleys of the Wold country. By the village school, which has a fine black raven for a weathervane, stands the village church, rebuilt last century in 13th century style and with only nave and chancel. On a wall is a tablet to John Wilson Henry Parkinson who lived at the 18th century Ravendale Hall among the trees not far away; he was Administrator-General of Kenya Colony and died at Mombasa in 1923. In a window glowing with the rich colour of Burne-Jones a man in blue raiment is giving a drink to one fallen by the wayside, while a woman in green offers cloth to one in rags.

Half a mile away is the hamlet of West Ravendale, where a quarry has bared the white cliff in the wooded hillside. Here are only a farm or two and a few cottages, and the ruin of a tiny chapel 8 yards by 4. Standing on a knoll in front of a wayside farm, all that remains are roughly-built fragments of walling rising to 12 feet at the east end. It belonged to a small Praemonstratensian priory founded here in 1202 as a cell of an abbey in Brittany. Later it formed part of the dowry of Henry IV's queen, Joan of Navarre.

Edenham. It lies in pleasant country—gently broken into hill and dale, wooded by a remnant of old Kesteven Forest, and watered by the Eden stream twisting southward to join the River Glen. Reached by a road from Bourne, it is an attractive village with stone houses.

The church standing on a raised mound is handsome—with pinnacled tower rising high above the clerestoried nave—and beautifully kept; it is also notable because every century down from Saxon times has contributed to its architecture or its enrichment. Of the Saxon church, which most likely stood where the chancel now is, only a few vestiges remain. There is a fragment of a Saxon cross in the nave, with interlaced ornament and a crude seated figure; and in the south aisle, built into the wall above the arcade, are two Saxon roundels with scrollwork.

From the 12th century church there remains a massive arcaded font with shafts of Purbeck marble. The graceful nave arcades, with all their arches borne up on clustered columns, are 13th century work; and so also is the fine south doorway with its dog-tooth moulding. The porch sheltering it is 14th century, and adorned with two quaint carvings: an imp holding its mouth open with its hands, and a man holding an animal by its tail.

To the spacious 15th and 16th centuries the church owes its fine tower, 84 feet high, the chancel and its delicately traceried roof, and the nave clerestory and roof. This nave roof, restored in this century, is one of the splendours of the church, enriched with eight wooden angels bearing coloured shields, and with green dragons in the centre of the beams; a curious fact is that the roof is 3 feet higher at the west end than the east, and 18 inches higher on the north side than on the south.

Some of the pews have traceried ends, and are a legacy from the mediaeval church; a few have humorous carvings, such as two bearded heads joined together. A window in the south aisle has 15th century figures of a pope and a mitred bishop, with the arms of Elizabeth I below, at the west ends of the aisles are ancient windows with Saints Catherine, James, and John. A rarer relic is a 15th century brass, 18 inches high, with a figure of an archbishop holding a crozier and with the other hand raised in benediction; now brought indoors for shelter, it is believed to represent Thomas Becket, and is unique because it was once outside on the west wall of the tower in a panel which can still be seen to the right of the clock.

A fine Norman doorway, from a chapel associated with Vaudey Abbey, that once stood at Scottlethorpe, has now been built into the church for preservation.

Among other valuable possessions of Edenham Church are three carved chairs in the chancel, and a set of rare old Continental altar plate, richly embossed, and all gold-plated.

Nothing here is more remarkable, however, than the array of monuments. Under the tower are a fine 14th century knight and a lady. Their figures rest on a 15th century altar tomb (once in the chancel and later in the churchyard)—the knight in armour with a lion at his feet, the lady with her cushioned head under a remarkable canopy supported by angels and a dog at her feet with two little figures who twitch the hem of her robe, quaint and appealing. Under the tower also are three ancient and worn figures in long gowns, a lady with a boldly-carved angel at each side, and two others, possibly of priests.

From this sleeping assembly it is a far cry to the grandiose display of monuments in the chancel and manorial pew, paying tribute to members of the noble family whose home is Grimsthorpe Castle, a mile away. Here are sculptured portraits of this family from the time of Charles I—a family which for over 300 years has held the office of Lord Great Chamberlain of England.

The earliest of their monuments here is to Robert Bertie and his son Montagu, 1st and 2nd Earls of Lindsey; it is above the family pew, a mass of inscriptions, heraldry, guns, gauntlets and other war trophies befitting to these men of war. Robert Bertie, 13th Lord Willoughby d'Eresby, went with an expedition against Spain and was at the Siege of Amiens, and while living for a time in retirement in Lincolnshire he drained a stretch of the Fens. It was in 1626 that Charles Stuart made him Lord Chamberlain and created him Earl of Lindsey. Ten years later he was Lord High Admiral, and in 1642 he fell fighting for the king at Edgehill. He died in the arms of his son Montagu, the 2nd Earl, who was taken prisoner there; the son fought at Naseby after being exchanged, and lived to sit at the trial of the regicides in 1660.

Montagu's son Robert Bertie, 3rd Earl of Lindsey, has an extra-ordinary monument in the chancel—a black sarcophagus on white claws and supporting a white urn, and, above this, a tall black marble screen on which are seven white marble corbels. Each corbel bears a bust, all sculptured to look like Romans and with a marked family likeness, the earl being here with his wife Elizabeth, his daughter Arabella Lady Rivers, and his four younger sons Pere-grine, Philip, Norreys, and Albemarle (who set up this rather pompous monument four years before his death in 1742).

The 3rd Earl's eldest son, Robert Bertie, 4th Earl of Lindsey and first Duke of Ancaster, has a pretentious monument reaching to the chancel roof; his is a life-size figure by Scheemakers, in Roman toga under a huge pediment in classical pillars. His son Peregrine, the second Duke of Ancaster, is also draped as a Roman, and leans on an urn while a cherub holds a medallion portrait of his wife. Another towering structure has a life-size but not ungraceful figure of the 3rd Duke, "the most Noble Prince Peregrine Bertie", also in Roman costume, a cannon by his side. The inscription tells us that "His Grace having raised a Regiment of Foot for His Majesty's service during The Rebellion in Scotland in 1745 was promoted to the rank of a General". It tells also that he lived with "Magnificence and Liberality", but died of "a lingering bilious disorder". By this warrior duke's side sits his son Robert, the 4th Duke, arrayed in ducal robes, and with his right hand resting on a medallion portrait of his mother.

Two other memorials, both of the 19th century, belong to this family statuary. One is a marble pedestal with a bust of Lord Gwydyr, who married Priscilla, Baroness Willoughby de Eresby, a sister of the 4th Duke of Ancaster. The other is to Clementina, Baroness Willoughby de Eresby in her own right, joint hereditary Lord Chamberlain of England; her monument is a medallion carving of her profile, as charming as Whistler's portrait of his mother.

All this pomp and grandeur is reflected a thousand-fold in the family's ancestral home, Grimsthorpe Castle. It is Lincolnshire's finest country house, a huge mansion standing on a rise just over a mile from the church and easily seen from the road. The magnificent park of 2000 acres is 16 miles round, stretching from the village of Edenham to the River Glen and Little Bytham 4 miles away; for much of the way runs a chestnut avenue which is claimed to be the longest in England, and to be rivalled in splendour only by the one at Hampton Court. There are innumerable majestic oaks, horn-beams, and mistletoe-bearing hawthorns, and there are herds of fallow and red deer for which Grimsthorpe is famed. There are streams flowing to the Eden, one filling a lake of 100 acres. Not far from the southern end of the lake are a few fragments of the old

Cistercian abbey of Vaudey (Vale of God), founded in 1147 by William, Earl of Albemarle, and colonised by monks from Fountains Abbey who came to this spot after settling first at Castle Bytham.

The massive, embattled south-east tower of the castle, called King John's Tower, has walls 7 feet thick and was built early in the 13th century. But the early history of the building is obscure. In Tudor times Grimsthorpe was rebuilt by Charles Brandon, Duke of Suffolk, for the manor of Grimsthorpe, part of Lord Lovell's forfeited estates, had been granted to the 10th Lord Willoughby d'Eresby on his marriage to a Spanish lady in attendance on Catherine of Aragon, and Charles Brandon had married their 16-year-old daughter and heiress, Katherine; this was after the death of his third wife, who was the king's sister, Mary, widow of the King of France. This young Duchess of Suffolk, Katherine, was a witty, merry-hearted woman and she helped to make history. She was foremost in support of the Protestant faith, and made Hugh Latimer her chaplain; despising Bishop Gardiner, she called her dog by his name, but when the persecuting Bishop of London became Queen Mary's agent Katherine fled abroad with her second husband, Richard Bertie, whom she had married in 1552. During their exile, awaiting the end of Mary Tudor's reign of terror, their son Peregrine, famous as soldier and diplomat, was born at Wesel on the Rhine. We read of him at Spilsby where he was buried, like so many of his maternal ancestors.

To these stirring days belong the east side of the castle, with its four attractive Elizabethan bay windows, and the graceful south or garden front, with its many gables and its tall chimneys. The dominating feature of the building, however, though by no means the most pleasing, is the north front, built in 1722 by Sir John Vanbrugh in his ponderous, ornate style.

Perhaps the best view of Vanbrugh's building is through the rich iron gates of the forecourt, which like the castle itself are surmounted by the Bertie arms, with monk and savage as supporters. In the centre of this great front, all built of stone quarried in Grimsthorpe park, is a pedimented doorway with three round-arched windows on each side and seven more above, framed by two pairs of massive columns supporting a plinth with classical sculptured groups. The roof is balustraded and on each side is a massive three-storied tower wing, also balustraded. One of these wing towers has a dining-hall with a wonderful ceiling by Thornhill of the Muses, Arts, and Sciences, valuable 17th century Brussels tapestries on its walls, and a vaulted chamber below, converted into an entrance hall; the other wing contains an ornate chapel with windows on three sides and a gallery on the fourth.

Between the wings is Vanbrugh's magnificent hall, 110 feet long, with a double staircase at each end, behind colonnades. Each of its four sides has two tiers of round arches. Some of the arches frame family busts, while the top tier along one side, above the fireplace, has dark paintings of seven kings to whom this ancient family owes much: William the Conqueror, Edward III, Henry V, Henry VII, Henry VIII, William III, and George I.

There are of course many other magnificent rooms in Grimsthorpe Castle, such as the State Drawing-room, Blue Drawing-room, King James's Drawing-room, Chinese Drawing-room; and all these rooms, together with the corridors, and galleries, enshrine fine family portraits by Lawrence, Reynolds, and other famous masters. Among the treasures is a splendid portrait of Charles I and his family by Van Dyck, and the actual dress worn by the king in the picture is still treasured at Grimsthorpe.

Among the official possessions of successive Lord Great Chamberlains treasured at the Castle are chairs and canopies used at coronations, coronation robes worn by sovereigns from the time of James II, and gold plate of great value and interest; and it is worth recalling here that Edenham Church has blue carpet used at the coronation of George VI. Among historic pieces are the House of Lords clock which ceased to tick as George III ceased to breathe, the table on which Queen Victoria signed her accession oath, and many others which have figured in State ceremonies in the royal palaces and at Westminster on occasions forming milestones in our national story.

When all is said and done there is a display of magnificence here unmatched in Lincolnshire and surpassed in few places other than our royal palaces.

Edlington. Fine trees embower the winding lane to the church, which has for company the modern hall and a churchyard yew that must have been growing here for 200 years or more.

The church has been rebuilt, except for the lower part of the tower, which has a Norman arch to the nave. A mediaeval arcade of three bays is built up in the north wall of the nave, and among other relics of the past are a Jacobean chest and a 16th century font enriched with arcading.

Elsham. Here, secluded among the lovely foothills of Elsham Wolds, was once a priory of Austin canons; all that visibly remains of it is the old fishpond, now in the charming grounds of the 18th century Hall, which was extensively reshaped by Guy Elwes in modern times.

The pretty village has an old church, restored but chiefly 13th century, with earlier remains in the base of the small tower, which has a 12th century arch with Saxon opening above it. The base of the tower serves as a porch, and is entered through an unusual mediaeval doorway which is its most splendid feature. Some of its rich mouldings are continuous to the ground, and others rest on groups of shafts with capitals delicately carved with flowers and leaves. At each side of the doorway is a remarkable stone panel on which are figures sculptured in high relief, one figure rising from a stone or a coffin. The modern doors are enriched with fine tracery.

The chancel has its 13th century piscina, and lying in the tower are the bowl and stem of the old font, rescued from a village garden. High on a corner of the tower is a stone which may have been a mass dial. On the west buttresses of the tower are unusual reliefs dating from the 13th century.

Epworth. A small market town which has taken Haxey's place as the little capital of the Isle of Axholme, it has an abiding place in the hearts of all Methodists. To this place in 1696 came Samuel Wesley as rector; and here many of his 19 children were born and passed their early years. Immortal John Wesley, the 15th child, was born here in 1703; his brother and faithful lieutenant Charles, writer of more than 6000 hymns, four years later.

Epworth's present rectory, a building in Queen Anne style restored by the World Methodist Council in 1956-57, is not the one in which the young Wesleys first saw the light. Their birthplace, which stood on a site close by, was burned down in 1709 by an angry mob of objectors to Samuel Wesley's political sympathies. It is said that at midnight Hetty Wesley was wakened by wood falling from a blazing ceiling and burning her feet. The rector was roused and managed to rescue a nurse and some of the children; and his wife, a sick woman at the time, broke through a wall of fire into the garden. All seemed safe when suddenly the shrill cry of a child was heard coming from the burning house. It was 6-year-old John, overlooked in all the excitement!

To reach him by way of the blazing stairs was impossible, but when all hope seemed lost a man, standing on the shoulders of another, lifted young John out of the bedroom window. A moment later the roof fell in, and the rector of Epworth, with ruin all about him, joyously exclaimed: "Come neighbours, let us kneel down; let us give thanks to God! He has given me all my children; let the house go; I am rich enough!"

Samuel Wesley was rector here for 39 years, and from 1722 till his death was also rector of Wroot a few miles away; and there John assisted him as curate for two years after being admitted to Holy Orders. In 1735 Samuel fell into his last sleep and they laid him to rest in his churchyard, under a table tomb on the south side of the chancel. It was on this tomb that John Wesley stood preaching to a big crowd in 1742, night after night, when he had been denied the pulpit within the church.

Epworth Church is approached by a fine avenue of lime trees and set on a hill with grand views over the countryside. It has been little altered since the time of the Wesleys. The tower, the aisles, and north porch are 15th century work; the chancel is chiefly 14th century (with a modern east window); and the nave has a Tudor clerestory and 13th century arcades. Also 15th century is the vestry (once a chapel), still with its narrow old door; and other old relics include the 14th century font, a 16th century chest, a reading-desk with some old screen tracery in it, an Elizabethan carved chair, and the chalice from which John Wesley, aged 8, first received Communion. A tablet tells of John Matthews, chorister for 62 years.

A rare treasure which used to belong to this church but is now in the British Museum is the Epworth mazer, a 15th century bowl of maple wood and silver. Some 8 inches in diameter, it is encircled by a broad band of silver engraved with zigzag. In the centre of the bowl are two figures, probably St Andrew and St John, with the cross of St Andrew between them.

Two steps in Nonconformity are fittingly marked in this town. One is the fine stone chapel built in 1889 in memory of John Wesley and his brother Charles; the other is a chapel built in 1860 in memory of Alexander Kilham, founder of the New Connexion of the Methodists, who was born here in 1762. It is now a youth centre. The chapel of the Wesleys, attractive with its tower and spire, its manse and Sunday school and its lawns and neat yews all round it, has an east window showing Our Risen Lord and His Disciples, and the portraits of John and Charles in a roundel above.

In the marketplace are the steps of the old market cross, time-worn reminder of the town's right to hold a market (and two fairs a year), procured for it in the 14th century by Thomas Mowbray, Duke of Norfolk. Nearby is another link with the old days—the court house—rebuilt in 1806 and now used for other purposes, but still containing the old straight-backed bench of the magistrates.

The shining name at Epworth, as it will be for all time, is that of John Wesley, founder of the Methodist Church.

Wesley was born at the rectory here on June 17, 1703, the 15th child in a family of 19. From his great-grandfather downwards the Wesleys had been educated at Oxford, and there went John in the first stage of a distinguished career. In his 23rd year he was a fellow of his college, and a year later was Greek lecturer, holding the post while he was curate to his father at Epworth.

During his academic life there was a period when he had time for a reasonable degree of physical activity and amusement—in riding, swimming, active games, and an occasional dance. He was fond of company and had a merry wit. Cheerfulness, indeed, was his natural disposition, and it came forth afresh in his old age when his life had become a serene conquest.

But spirituality was equally natural to him, and showed itself throughout his whole life. At Oxford he and his brother Charles, George Whitefield, James Hervey, and other young men met regularly for religious talk and devotions, and received the nickname of Methodists long before it was accepted as descriptive of the Church system introduced by John Wesley. In those days Wesley was distinctly a High Churchman, following a strict routine of two daily services, fasting, confession, and frequent communions.

When he was 32 John Wesley went out to Georgia as a missionary among the Indians. He had a troublesome time. On his voyage, too, he had been unsettled by meeting Moravians aboard who in a stormy sea did not share his fears. He felt they had a faith he lacked. When Wesley returned to England he sought further contact with the Moravians, and it was at one of their meetings that he experienced the change of heart which he described as conversion and afterwards made the chief aim of his ministry for other men.

Wesley had been a preacher for nearly 13 years before he gave himself up to the impulse "to save souls", as he phrased his life's work. His surrender was complete, and his labours were incredible. The Church of England had no room for work such as his. So, while still regarding himself as a Churchman, he went outside the Church, and with masterly skill organised the results of his work into a separate Church. In the 52 years that followed his conversion, he travelled 250,000 miles and preached 40,000 sermons. He went into every part of England and Wales; he crossed the Irish Channel 42 times; his visits to Scotland numbered 22. Wesley counted on travelling 5000 miles each year and preaching 15 sermons each week. His usual manner of travel was on horseback. Much of his preaching was carried on in the open air, for churches at first closed their doors against him, and later the churches were too small to hold more than a fraction of the crowds that gathered to hear him.

At first he suffered from persecution and disdain; he was not respectable, he was a renegade, and he collected the riff-raff. And then the real riff-raff were set on to pull down the chapels his followers had built. But all this opposition passed away and John Wesley saw the time when his entry into a town was like a royal procession, and the entertaining of him a coveted privilege.

He preached nine days before he died in his 88th year, his task accomplished, his long day done. He lies in the City Road graveyard of the great Christian community which he founded.

The story of his preaching, and of his constructive skill in welding his work into a firm unity, does not exhaust his labours. He wrote and published books on all kinds of subjects helpful to his ministerial colleagues, including commentaries on the whole of the Old and New Testaments. From his literary work he made £30,000 profit, all of which he distributed in charity. John Wesley was a **very** great man—great in spirit, great in his labours, and great in **influence.**

Evedon. A tiny place near the Old River Slea, it has a church lonely in the fields, reached by a track through a farm, its low tower looking out from a hillside. The little building has seen much change for only the arch remains of its 14th century south chapel, and its 700-year-old north arcade was built up early last century, one of its two arches being opened up again some years later when a small transept was built.

The nave has a 15th century font with worn shields and sacred monograms, and the chancel has ancient sedilia into which an amazing medley of pillars, bits of arches, praying figures and other carved stones have been built for preservation. On a wall is a 17th century brass of Daniel Hardeby kneeling at a desk with his wife and 13 children; Daniel was a Justice of the Peace and another brass below has his epitaph, proclaiming that

> *Just did this Justice live, and dying just,*
> *As all good mortals ought, sleeps here in dust.*

The manor house, once a seat of the Bertie family, is a 17th century house remodelled in the 19th century.

Ewerby. This pleasant place on the western edge of the Fens has cottages well spaced-out, with a thatched one here and there to emphasise its charms, and part of an old cross as evidence that it was once a small market town; it is set on six round steps on the little green by its splendid church.

Set on a hill, it is one of the fine company of churches near Slea-ford, and one of a trio outstanding above the rest, Sleaford and Heckington being the others. All three are thought to have been built by one architectural genius who flourished in the later part of the 14th century, and are notable for the rare quality of their stone carving in window tracery, mouldings, and other ornament. Ewerby Church, well restored and lovingly tended, is indeed a great possession.

The tip of its lovely broach spire is 172 feet above the ground, and crowns a fine west tower from which the music of 10 bells rings out over a wooded countryside that seems to enhance its grey dignity. Only one other church in the county (at Grantham) has so many bells in its peal; four of Ewerby's bells come from between 1616 and 1783, and the rest were the gift of the Earl of Winchilsea in 1896.

The tower stands on three arches with massive piers opening to the nave and aisles, and has a stone-groined roof. Below it is the 14th century font, its beautiful six-sided bowl enriched with tracery and resting on the upturned bowl of a Norman font lightly carved with interlaced arches. Near it is an ancient stone with two iron rings, probably a relic of bull-baiting days.

The porch has a trefoiled arch, and the nave has arcades on clustered piers enriched with foliage. Nave and chancel are under one roof, their only division being a handsome mediaeval screen with seven richly-traceried arches. The chancel has its old sedilia and piscina, a canopied niche in the opposite wall, and an aumbry behind the modern altar of Fen oak. Fine old screenwork separates chancel from the north chapel, which keeps its old altar stone and piscina. A few old benches with small poppyheads are here, and a mediaeval chest adorned with tracery and roundels. All the windows have modern glass, the most attractive being six scenes from the Life of Christ in the east window.

Three monuments here are of special interest. One is a remarkable Saxon gravestone, carved with a cross and an all-over pattern of knotwork; the others are the sleeping figures of two men who gave of their riches to this church. The older benefactor, lying in a recess of the chapel he founded, is Sir Alexander Aunsell, who died in 1360, in his helmet and chain-mail, much worn and without arms. The later benefactor is the 12th Earl of Winchilsea and Nottingham, who died in 1898 and lies in the chancel, his monument showing him in his ermine-trimmed robes, a dog at his feet.

Nearby is the site of Haverholme Priory, a Gilbertine House founded in 1139. A Gothic house was built in the late 18th century which was rebuilt in Tudor style for the Earl of Winchilsea in 1835. Only the centre portion remains.

Fenton. In this lonely spot, a mile and a half from the River Witham and the Nottinghamshire border, a church and a house have long been good companions. The house (old home of the Lucas family) was built in Tudor times, but it suffered from fire in the 18th century and is a farmhouse now, with creeper and roses and clematis draping its walls. The gabled ends, the mullioned windows, and the stone coat-of-arms dated 1597, all belong to the old dwelling.

The church has come down from Norman days, and has a sturdy arcade of that item leading to the north aisle. The south arcade is chiefly 14th century, and so is the low south porch. The chancel was rebuilt last century, but has an old arch leading to the chapel.

The 500-year-old tower and spire rising above the trees make a lovely picture. The spire is lighted by dormers, the tower by big two-light belfry windows and a quatrefoil window in the second stage; under the parapet of tall battlements and crocketed pinnacles is a carved band of lattice design, and at the corners are great demon gargoyles.

There is a Norman shaft piscina with a scalloped bowl, and the font may be 12th century. The traceried pulpit is 500 years old and there is old screenwork in the chancel. Several old bench-ends here have served as models for the 19th century ones.

Fillingham. This charming village, with its red-roofed stone cottages among trees at the foot of the Cliff, has a niche in the story of the English Church; for to this place came John Wycliffe, having given up the mastership of Balliol College at Oxford to become rector here. Here it was that the Morning Star of the Reformation began his career as a man of the Church. He was at Fillingham from 1361 to 1368, years during which he "broke forth into open heresy", as his enemies said, denouncing tribute to the Pope and preaching Protestantism 150 years before Luther practised it at Wittenberg.

The church John Wycliffe knew stands at the end of a fine avenue of limes. It was almost rebuilt in 1777. The tower (standing on open arches) and the chancel are of that time, but each has kept its 14th century arch to the nave, and the tower has a round-headed doorway from the close of Norman days. The nave has lost its aisles, but the 14th century arcades which led to them are visible in the walls, still adorned with wimpled women and other heads; in their lofty bays are the 14th century windows of the vanished aisles.

Among the monuments is a tablet to Sir Cecil Wray, who built Fillingham Castle on the hill four centuries after Wycliffe passed this way. He enclosed it in a park, and in so doing blocked a right-of-way beloved by Squire Whichcot, MP, who lived at Harpswell. Indignant at being thus robbed of his right, the squire used once a year to come over in his coach-and-four, bringing his labourers with him to pull down the wall; then he would drive through the breach, across the park and back again, and go home well satisfied with his outing. Every year Squire Whichcot would pull part of the wall down, and every year Sir Cecil Wray would build it up again. So the battle went on and on till the old squire died, when, there being no more breaches in the wall, the right-of-way lapsed.

The mid-18th century Gothic castle is rectangular in plan with circular towers at the angles and crenellated parapets. The park is enclosed by a stone wall with gateways and Gothic lodges. Nearby is the site of a Roman settlement.

It is in this park that the River Ancholme comes to life, and then dives underground to reappear near Spridlington. There it begins its journey north, and, after a few miles, flows into the Humber.

One other building in Fillingham is worthy of special mention: the 17th century manor house, which looks out on a 40-acre lake known as Fillingham Broad.

Fishtoft. Lying between Boston and the Wash, this big village is near the great Hobhole Drain, which has reclaimed 40,000 acres of marshland and runs into the River Witham 2 miles away. This navigable stretch of the river below Boston is a canalised waterway known as the Haven.

The beautiful church has come down from Norman days, and its spacious chancel is still partly Norman, with later alterations. Except for the modern vestry, the rest of the building is 15th century.

In a canopied niche above the west doorway of the tower is a small statue of St Guthlac, the Saxon saint of Crowland Abbey to which this church was given by Alan de Creon. Outside, too, is seen the turret of the rood stairway.

The church interior is dignified and simple, with walls of irregular stonework and windows with clear glass framing views of the countryside. The clerestoried nave has arcades with clustered pillars, and a modern oak roof with golden bosses adorned with carvings of angels and faces. The chancel has windows from the 12th and 13th centuries, and a 14th century east window with formal tracery. One of the windows cuts into an old aumbry. There are fragments of old glass in the clerestory.

Two fine 15th century oak screens are in this church, one being the original chancel screen; the other, in the tower arch, is from the neighbouring church of Freiston. The pulpit is made up of old woodwork, and there is a carved 17th century chair with scrolls and roses and an inscription, *Praise ye the Lord*.

Prominent at the west end of the nave is the handsome 15th century font, mounted on a flight of three steps, and adorned with rich tracery on bowl and stem.

Fiskerton. A village by the Witham, opposite Washingborough, which has grown recently with the arrival of light industry.

The church was given to Peterborough Abbey by Edward the Confessor, and the living is still in the gift of the Dean and Chapter of that city. One of the rectors was Simon Gunton, whose name is remembered for the notes he collected about Peterborough Cathedral. Son of the diocesan registrar, he was able to delve at will in the cathedral archives and even as a boy he had copied down the inscriptions on the cathedral tombs, many of which were afterwards defaced by Roundhead soldiers, so it is said; he came here in 1666 and was buried here 10 years later. Ten years after his death a history of Peterborough Cathedral based on his painstaking collections was published. A rector of our own time was Thomas Vines, who had ministered here for 52 years when they laid him in the churchyard in 1928.

The church, partly rebuilt in the 15th century and much restored in 1863, has a bold 500-year-old tower with eight big open-mouthed creatures below the battlements, and rounded walls within, suggesting a round tower of earlier times.

The oldest part of the church is the north arcade with two round Norman arches enriched with billet ornament in the nave, and two simpler Norman arches in the chancel. The north doorway is also Norman, though with a flat arch instead of the original one. From the 13th century come the south doorway, the south arcade (its two arches on clustered columns with richly-foliated capitals) and the square font with nail-head ornament. A rarer feature is a band of carved leaves and flowers along the south aisle wall. Supporting the old nave roof are eight big stone heads—a lion, a bear and six solemn mediaeval folk.

Two of the memorials are about 500 years old. One is a tomb recess with mediaeval heads on each side of its arch and on two of its three leafy pinnacles. The other is a big brass of a priest in his cope, engraved about 1490 and probably a portrait of Thomas Dalyson; it was found last century by Bishop Trollope in a Lincoln shop and returned to this church from which it had long been missing.

Three striking relics of Fiskerton's more remote past are treasured in the British Museum. They are three highly ornamental silver-gilt pins, notable as examples of fine Anglo-Saxon art. A fine hoard of Bronze Age socketed axes was also found in the parish.

Fleet. It is now some 8 miles from the Wash, but its name is a reminder that once it stood on a creek, and close by are clear signs of the sea-bank.

Approached through a delightful thatched lychgate which has four tree-trunks for support, the church is for the most part a 14th century building, much restored in the 19th; but its nave arcades are a century earlier, and the huge west window is 15th century.

Said to have been built by the monks of Castle Acre, it is a stately church, and is remarkable for its detached tower and spire. Standing a few yards from the south-west corner, the tower is imposing with its bold stair-turret, its buttresses stepped and gabled, its unusual gargoyles of men, women, and grotesques, and its em-battled parapet with pinnacles from which flying buttresses spring to the spire—a rare feature for a detached tower.

The church interior is exceptionally light, the only colour in the windows being the tinted glass at the west end, and the lovely modern glass of the east window showing the Madonna and Child, Our Lord crowned, and His appearance to Mary Magdalene. Most of the attractive window tracery is in the flowing style, and the side windows of the chancel have hoods formed by the arcading in the walls. On the north wall is a little carving of the Lincoln Imp.

The nave has fine soaring arcades with tall leaning pillars, and its neat, modern hammerbeam roof rests on old corbels carved with a quaint gallery of mediaeval folk. The chancel keeps its fine old sedilia and piscina with crocketed canopies, Jacobean altar-rails, and a brass chandelier which is probably Flemish work of the 18th century. The 15th century font stands proudly at the west end of the nave, where there is a worn floorstone carved with a childlike praying figure.

Flixborough. Great steelworks are a landmark close to this small village on the green ridge of the Cliff, but they do not mar the fine views over the Humber into Yorkshire and across the broadening Trent.

Close to the little green on the hilltop is a 19th century church, successor to one which was built in 1786 to replace the ancient church, which stood half a mile south. The Norman font, with a huge bowl, and several fragments of old carved stones in the churchyard wall are all that remain of the old house of prayer below the hill.

Near the site of the old church once stood the hall where Sir Edmund Anderson was born in 1530. He was a judge who took part in the trials of Mary Queen of Scots and Sir Walter Raleigh, and was notorious for his severe treatment of the Puritans.

Folkingham. Set on the high road between Bourne and Sleaford, it was a place of some importance in coaching days. It is now receiving special consideration as a place worthy of conservation. The main street is broad and flanked by attractive houses. The spacious market square, with its Queen Anne coaching inn of mellow red-brick, wears a pleasant and leisured air. Towering over it is a fine church with a handsome steeple.

It is a big church, well restored and worthy of a city. The 15th century tower has niches in its buttresses, a panelled doorway with roses and foliage, and lofty stone vault. The porch is also vaulted, and over it is a room with a fireplace. The aisles and lofty arcades are 14th century, but the chancel is largely 13th century, and an arch in its north wall has a Norman pier. Six centuries old are the sedilia and piscina, and in a north aisle window are small panels of ancient glass with heads of three golden-haired men. But the finest old possession of the church is its dark oak screen, with tracery, roses, and vine pattern richly carved 500 years ago; it is among the best screens in the county. At the side are the rood-loft stairs. Also preserved in the church are the old stocks and whipping-post, with six holes for the legs of malefactors and two iron rings for their arms.

Shading the churchyard gate is a fine horse-chestnut with a trunk about 14 feet round.

Folkingham was one of over 100 Lincolnshire manors bestowed by the Conqueror on his wife's nephew, Gilbert de Ghent. The Norman castle was rebuilt in the 14th century but destroyed by the Parliament men during the Civil War, and only the grassy mounds remain. At the foot of the Castle Hill are the remains of the former House of Correction built in 1825. The present building is the gatehouse with stone front and brick back and sides.

Fosdyke. It is a marshland village near the mouth of the River Welland, here crossed by a 20th century iron bridge which took the place of one designed by Rennie in 1814 and built entirely of oak.

The church, built in 1871 at the cost of a beneficent rector of Algarkirk, Basil Beridge, is in 13th century style and of red-brick with stone-lined interior; it has a tower and leaded spire, fine arcades with rich, leafy capitals, and a group of three lancets in the east wall.

A few stones from the old church are in the porch, and two fine pieces from it are within the church. One is the 14th century font, with carvings of angels and St George and the Dragon on its bowl, and a queer gallery of human and grotesque figures below. The other is the lofty oak font-cover, enriched with tracery and pinnacles 500 years ago—a rare treasure. In the fenland is a long row of almshouses endowed some 350 years ago by Sir Thomas Middlecot of Boston.

Foston. The old highway from Grantham to Newark is by-passed here, leaving the village its quietude. The church was heavily restored in the 19th century but includes earlier features.

The tower is 13th century, except for its 15th century embattled and pinnacled top; its west doorway, enriched with dog-tooth ornament, is now blocked, with a window set in it; but it has a striking arch, tall and narrow, opening to the nave.

In the modern porch is a battered but richly-moulded 13th century doorway, with two mass dials beside it. One of the nave arcades is as old as the doorway, and the other comes from the close of the 12th century. Earlier still is the Norman chancel arch, handsome with chevron moulding. By the arch is a peephole. The old stocks with iron clasps are by the old font, which has an oak cover with a figure of St Nicholas in red and gold, holding a book. There are many interesting slate headstones included among the monuments in the churchyard.

Fotherby. From this village of the foothills, near Louth, a track climbs the Wolds to Fotherby Top, 350 feet high, with its wonderful views of a long stretch of the Marsh and of the sea as far as the Humber and Spurn Head in Yorkshire.

The broach spire dominating the village belongs to the neat little church rebuilt in 1863, its walls of chalk and sandstone lined inside with red-brick and stone bands. Its ancient possessions are three 17th century bells, a 15th century font, and a mediaeval piscina with a deep flower drain.

A marble monument like a scroll commemorates Thomas Jacob Freeth, 47 years vicar, through whose efforts the church and the vicarage were rebuilt.

Doddington Hall

The House of Correction at Folkingham

Gainsborough Old Hall

The Angel and Royal Hotel at Grantham

Frampton. This is a distinguished and large village not far from the Wash and fine trees make a charming setting for a lovely old church. Facing the church stands Frampton Hall, a Queen Anne house, built by Coney Tunnard, with a delightful garden and a small park, and at one end of the village is another attractive old house, Frampton House, with low stone gables and a Roman Doric porch.

The church has come gracefully down the centuries, standing much as it stood in mediaeval days, except for the loss of its north transept and the addition of two porches in a careful restoration in 1891. Its glory is its steeple, the lower stages of the tower having been built at the close of Norman days, and the rest, together with the remarkable broach spire, in the 13th century. The exterior of the tower is decked with an array of carved heads, and its three arches are a striking feature of the interior.

The old doorways sheltered by the new porches have ogee arches, one resting on pairs of shafts and the other on jambs carved with trailing leaves. The slender pillars of the nave arcades are 13th century work, but they rise from the foundations of the Norman church, and they support 14th century arches. All the roofs, though modern, are of good English oak, the barrel roof of the nave still having its old tie-beams and carved stone corbels.

The 14th century chancel, shortened in restoration, now has only one sedile—with dainty ogee hood and trefoiled arch. Near it is a beautiful doorway, and in the opposite wall is another fine doorway, leading to the vestry. There is an Easter Sepulchre. Here, too, is a handsome tomb recess with pinnacles and leafy hood and a stone that once bore the brass portrait of a priest. In the transept, where the ancient altar stone rests under the present altar, is the stone figure of a 14th century lady in a long gown.

The font bowl, with interlaced arcading and nail-head carving, comes from the close of the 12th century; and among the other old possessions of the church are a restored 15th century oak screen, an ironbound chest, and a Jacobean pulpit bought from Bourne Church in 1890 for £3 3 0. There is also a remarkable 18th century candelabrum with 26 candlesticks and, below its mass of curved branches, this inscription:

> *The gift of Coney Tunnard for an example to all*
> *pretenders of love to the church which by their acts*
> *don't show it. Let your light so shine before men.*

At the top of his gift sits a rabbit—a play on his name. Coney's candles are all lit at Christmas-time, Harvest Home, and other festivals.

Outside, on a gabled buttress of the transept, is a stone head of a man. He is Richard-in-the-Corner, and a merry-looking fellow, though a quaint inscription informs the passer-by that he is there because he forswore his faith.

Freiston. Its name comes from the colony of Frieslanders who are said to have settled on this spot, where the big village has grown up between the Hobhole Drain and the sea. Once the sea came up to it; today it is 2 miles to Freiston Shore, and the sea is still receding, leaving the old salt marsh like a channelled carpet of sand grasses and wild flowers, washed only by the high tides.

Freiston's pride and glory is its church, the remnant of one which belonged to the Benedictine priory founded here in 1114 by Alan de Creon, and which became a cell of Crowland Abbey 16 years later. The original church had the shape of a cross, but its three eastern-most arms are gone, leaving the splendid nave of nine bays (six of them Norman and three 13th century), the south aisle which still corresponds in style with the nave, but has had its windows renewed, the 15th century north aisle of brick, and the noble clerestory and west tower which were added in the 15th century. The quaint little north porch has a 13th century entrance arch, and shelters a curious doorway which is under a blocked Norman arch and has an old traceried door.

The most striking feature of the exterior is the clerestory, with eight great windows on each side. Above them are the old Norman corbel tables of wavy pattern (removed from their original place when the clerestory was built) and also an array of ugly gargoyles. By the east window, outside, can be seen the pillars which supported the western arch of the Transitional-Norman tower; within the church the fine arch is complete with its rich mouldings and zigzag ornament. Round the east window of the south aisle is the built-up pointed arch which led to the transept on this side.

The Norman doorway in the south aisle is a reminder of the vanished buildings of the priory which stood on this side of the church; it once led into the cloisters.

Within the church the two arcades running from end to end in long, uninterrupted lines of grand simplicity make a memorable picture. The three pointed 13th century bays of the nave are at the western end, and halfway along the Norman portion of the north arcade, in a pier different from the rest, is the old rood-loft stairway. The 15th century oak screen which marked off the part of the nave used as the chancel is now in Fishtoft Church, but the two contemporary screens which enclosed chapels in the aisles are still here, and there is a chest of Elizabethan days with iron bands and three locks.

In noble setting at the west end, and mounted on three steps, is the 500-year-old font, with attractive carving of tracery and quatrefoils on bowl and stem. Its beauty is enhanced by the original oak cover, which is a rare and remarkable treasure. Shaped like a spire about 12 feet high, and crowned with a figure of the Madonna, it is a mass of intricate carving of tracery and pinnacle work, and still has some of its old colour and gilt.

Freiston Priory, south of the church, is mainly 17th century with Georgian alterations; White Loaf Hall with its stepped gable is also 17th century.

A valuable experiment has been carried out at Freiston, where from 1935 to 1963 Borstal authorities established their North Sea Camp as headquarters for many of their boys who reclaimed 600 acres of salt marshes by the construction of a dyke. The Camp is now used as a Detention Centre for young short-term offenders.

Friskney. A big village between the Marsh and the Fens, within 2 miles of the coast and the great stretch of the Friskney Flats, it has a name derived perhaps from the Frieslanders who settled hereabouts. Its other name, Friskney-Bolington, is a reminder of an old religious house founded here in connection with Bullington Priory; its site is still marked by the dry-moated grassy mounds known as Abbey Hills.

At a tree-shaded corner is the village churchyard, notable for an old 18-foot-high cross which is whole and sound, its top having been discovered under the church floor last century. The head has sculptures of the Crucifixion, and the restored shaft rests on a worn 13th century base with carved symbols of the Evangelists.

Though it has some remains of earlier times, the spacious church is for the most part 15th century work, with aisles, porch, and many windows partly rebuilt in the costly restoration of 1879. The tower climbs through four centuries, having a base from the close of the Norman period, a 13th century stage with lancet windows, another stage with simple Geometrical tracery of the early 14th century, and a 15th century top storey. From the beautiful, lofty arch of the tower, six steps lead down to the nave. The north aisle has a restored late Norman doorway.

The great chancel has fine windows filling it with light, buttresses with canopied niches adorned by leafy hoods and quaint human and grotesque figures, a priest's doorway, three splendid carved sedilia, and a piscina and aumbry with trefoiled arches. On the north side of the chancel are traces of a vanished sacristy.

The chancel screen and the two screens enclosing chapels in the aisles are all richly-traceried work of the 15th century. The south chapel screen has three tiny openings to enable those kneeling there to see the high altar. The north chapel also has a peephole to the chancel altar. The old rood stairway is enclosed in a turret beside the chancel arch, and the fine carved pulpit of 1659 has a six-sided canopy hanging from an arch of the south arcade. One of several mediaeval floorstones has a floriated cross in memory of a 14th century rector, John de Lyndewode, and a brass inscription in Norman-French tells of Piers Jonson and his wife. Lying on a stone coffin is the battered stone figure of a 14th century knight of the Friskney family, wearing armour.

The lofty nave has a grand old roof of open timbering, some of its spandrels having pierced tracery and others bearing paintings of censing angels and figures of the Annunciation; on one of the beams is the old pulley frame for lifting the cover of the big 15th century font.

On the clerestoried walls above the tall, leaning arcades is a fine series of 15th century wall paintings uncovered at the restoration, faded now, and hard to unravel without the aid of the framed pictures of them hanging in the church. The subjects on the south side (from west to east) are believed to be: Melchizedek's offering of bread and wine to Abraham; The Gathering of Manna; The Last Supper; King Aethelred entering Bardney Abbey; and the Stabbing of the Host by the Jews. On the other side the subjects are: The Annunciation, Nativity, Resurrection, Ascension, and the Assumption of the Virgin.

Hanging round the church are a number of paintings picturing the sacred story. Some of the figures are portraits of local folk, and the paintings were the work of the wife of John Pacey Cheales, who ministered here, as curate and vicar, for over half a century before resigning in 1940. The illuminated list of vicars, and the figures (copies of old masters) painted on the vestry screen, were also her work.

A curious relic preserved in the church is a Georgian sentry-box in which the parson used to shelter in bad weather when conducting funerals at the graveside. There is another at Pinchbeck.

Fulbeck. Serene and fair to look upon it is, with houses nestling among fine old trees on the steep hillside and looking up to a handsome church mellowed by many centuries. The old village cross, with a shaft 25 feet high, has been finely restored. Near the church are splendid iron gates leading to the dignified stone Hall built in 1733 as the home of the Fanes. Earlier they had lived in the manor house, a 17th century residence but much restored. A distinguished member of this family was Sir Francis Fane, one of the early members of the Royal Society, and another was his dramatist son, also Francis.

The church tower, with traceried parapet and noble crown of eight leafy pinnacles, is 500 years old, and so is the clerestory, studded with fearsome gargoyles. The aisles were built in the 14th century, and the arcades in the 13th. The chancel has been much restored but still has its ancient piscina, sedilia, and tomb recess;

and the splendid font, from the end of the Norman period, is carved with interlaced arcading itself enriched with cable, nail-head, and dog-tooth moulding. The modern stained windows making this old church so sombre are mostly gifts by the Fanes; perhaps the best of them is the east window showing the Last Supper and Crucifixion.

Among the big array of wall-monuments four are notable for records of long service in this village. Thomas Sharp, who died in 1825, was surgeon here for 44 years; Charles Smith was surgeon here for 50 years last century; and the rector who saw the passing of both, Edward Fane, was minister for 55 years. The fourth good and faithful servant was Thomas Ball, who waited on Sir Francis Fane for half a century, dying in 1673. His memorial tells us that he travelled with his master "into Holland, Denmark, Germany, Lorraine, Switzerland, Italy, Naples, France, and Flanders, where he considered ye courts and camps of most of ye European princes, their splendour and mutabilitie, concluding, with ye preachers there was nothing new under ye sun and yet all was vanity, and only one thing necessary, to fear God and keep his Commandments. *Soe doth F.F. who fixed this stone.*"

Fulletby. Its position high in the rolling Wolds gives fine views across Salmonby and Tetford and for this reason it is always worth a visit.

The village's old story was echoed last century by the finding of some Roman urns, but the church has lost most of its antiquity in rebuilding. One mediaeval treasure, however, it still possesses—14th century sedilia skilfully restored. There are two seats, their leafy arches, richly moulded and crowned by fine finials, resting on delicate clustered shafts with capitals from which mediaeval folk look out—one holding leaves, another holding a sprig of oak with an acorn, and a third with bell and staff. Rich carving in wood is seen in a Jacobean chair in the chancel.

Henry Winn, described on his memorial as Poet and Antiquary, was for more than 76 years parish clerk here, dying in 1914, when he was 98. His is surely a record of long service. He left behind him a book telling the full story of this village from as far back as it is known. The text is in his own beautiful writing, illustrated by photographs and drawings, one of which shows the church as it was in 1834, with a thatched roof. Some of his papers are deposited with the Lincolnshire Archives Committee; others are in private possessions.

Fulstow. Notable for the many springs hereabouts, it has a plain little church, rebuilt last century, with a great bell swinging in an enormous bellcot. Of the old building there are the remains of arcades in both sides of the nave, a mediaeval font with its bowl on a cluster of shafts, and the figures of an old knight and his lady in flowing gown and wimple.

Gainsborough. An ancient market town threaded by narrow streets, it looks across the Trent into Nottinghamshire. A great array of wharves, warehouses, and works are huddled along the front of the river, and astride it is an 18th century bridge.

A low, wooded ridge rises sharply above the town, sheltering it on the east, and there is pretty countryside close at hand; but Gainsborough itself is a workaday place, with agricultural engineering works, factories, timber-yards and shipyards, extensive seed-crushing mills, and a considerable river trade. In the 18th and 19th centuries it was an important river port, carrying on a flourishing trade between the great seaport of Hull and the Midlands industrial towns. However, the construction of railways took away this traffic from Gainsborough, which then turned to agricultural engineering as its main source of employment.

Though the Humber is some 20 miles away, the tides are felt every day at Gainsborough, and at Spring tides the curious tidal wave known as the Bore, or Aegir, comes rushing up sometimes at the height of several feet, to continue some way beyond the town with its force greatly reduced. The phenomenon is described in George Eliot's *Mill on the Floss*, in which Gainsborough is called St Ogg's; and although this mill has been pulled down, her vivid description of the river and town still holds good—"the broadening Floss hurries on between its green banks to the sea, and the loving tide, rushing to meet it, checks its passage with an impetuous embrace. On this mighty tide the black ships, laden with fresh-scented fir plank, with rounded sacks of oil-bearing seed, or with the dark glitter of coal, are borne along to the town of St Ogg's, which shows its aged, fluted red roofs and the broad gables of its wharves between the low wooded hill and the river brink, tingeing the water with a soft purple hue."

Gainsborough has been an important place ever since Saxon times. It was here in 868 that King Alfred married Ealswitha, daughter of the chief of the Gaini; and it was here that Sweyn, King of the Danes, died in 1014, a year after coming up the river with his son Canute. The Danes overran this countryside, but the defences at Castle Hills—above the town at its northern end, on the edge of Thonock Park—so often described "Danish Camp" are a post-Conquest motte-and-bailey castle. King Sweyn is said to have been buried in the big tumulus by the camp, but his body was afterwards embalmed and sent to Denmark and buried, according to his wishes, in the cathedral at Roskilde which he himself had founded.

In the early years of the Civil War Gainsborough was a centre of bitter strife. On July 20th, 1643, when Robert Pierrepont, Earl of

Kingston, was holding it for the king, the town was surprised by Lord Willoughby of Parham; and while the earl was being taken as prisoner down the river to Hull he was killed by a Royalist shot from the bank. At the beginning of the war the earl had determined to remain neutral, saying he hoped that if ever he took up arms for either side a cannon-ball would divide him between them. So it befell, for it is said that the cannon-ball did literally cut him in two.

During the Royalist attempt to retake the town Cromwell had one of his early successes. The brilliant young cavalry leader, Charles Cavendish, had come up with reinforcements and on the 28th July Cromwell met him at Lea, 2 miles south of the town. In the skirmish that followed Cavendish was defeated and killed. (The story is told more fully under Lea.) Later, Parliament had to abandon the town, but was holding it again during the winter.

Gainsborough is not rich in material evidence of its old history, for, except for the tower of the parish church, there is only one old building of any architectural note. This is the Old Hall, and in its possession the town can take real pride, for it contains a fine example of a mediaeval baronial hall. This has been well restored under the supervision of the Ministry of Public Building and Works.

In mediaeval times the powerful de Burgh family became lords of the manor. Devoted to the Yorkist cause, they saw their old home destroyed by the Lancastrians about 1470; but 10 years later, their fortunes restored by the triumph of the White Rose, they were building the baronial hall which in Tudor times was to become the central wing of a stately home built round three sides of a great quadrangle with the fourth side probably closed by a gatehouse and wall. The site occupied nearly half an acre of land.

Built of brick, with massive oak framing, the long hall of 1480 runs east to west, and links the later wings. Admirably set off by the lawn of the quadrangle, the south front is a charming picture with its patterned walls and gables, and its modern lantern rising from the red roof. On the north side is an embattled stone oriel with transomed windows and pinnacled buttresses such as is commonly found lighting the main halls of domestic houses of this period. Near the oriel, at the north-east corner of the house, is a sturdy embattled brick tower and turret, with a winding stone stairway, built about 1500. From the top of the tower there is a grand view over the valley, almost to the Humber.

The striking feature of the long hall's interior is its fine open roof with arched beams growing from the walls, tie-beams, and wind-braced rafters. At the west end of the hall is the great brick kitchen with huge bread ovens and two fireplaces big enough for roasting an ox.

Since the lords of the manor made Thonock their home Gainsborough's Old Hall has had a chequered career. It has been used as a linen factory, a theatre, and a machine workshop—and even as an auction room. In 1952, the Friends of the Old Hall Association was formed and much voluntary effort has gone into making the hall a centre for cultural activity and a museum of bygones has been established.

All that remains of Gainsborough's mediaeval church of All Saints (believed to have been built at the close of the 12th century) is the embattled and pinnacled 15th century tower, with the Tudor Rose in the spandrels of its doorway. The nave, aisles, and apsidal chancel were rebuilt in 1745 in the classical style, and the two vestries flanking the tower are 20th century additions.

Lighted by a double range of round-headed windows, and enriched outside with pilasters and a balustraded parapet, the church is spacious and lofty within. Corinthian colonnades link the nave with the aisles and support a coved ceiling. The imposing font is of Frosterley marble, and the lectern is a finely-carved oak eagle. The pulpit is of wrought-iron—the work of a local blacksmith—set on a marble base. In one of the vestries is a woodcarving of Leonardo's Last Supper—also the work of a local craftsman; and over the altar is an Italian artist's copy of the same famous picture. Hanging in the chancel is a handsome 18th century three-tiered candelabrum.

By the church stands the John Robinson Memorial Chapel. This is a Congregational chapel built in 1896 as a tribute to the great Pilgrim Father. It was believed at the time that John Robinson was born at Gainsborough, but the truth is that, like all the other organisers of the movement (except William Bradford) Robinson was a Nottinghamshire man, and was born at Sturton-le-Steeple. The chief meeting-place of these religious pioneers was at Scrooby in Nottinghamshire, and their only connection with Gainsborough is that the little band would sometimes walk here on Sundays to worship under the Revd John Smythe, a Baptist. They never had their own chapel in this town.

Among the distinguished names associated with this town are William of Gainsborough, Simon and John Patrick, and Thomas Miller. William of Gainsborough, staunch upholder of the doctrine of Papal Infallibility, was Bishop of Worcester from 1303 until his death four years later. Simon Patrick, born here in 1626, was Bishop of Ely for 16 years and was one of the five founders of the Society for the Promotion of Christian Knowledge; and his brother, John Patrick, also an outstanding theologian, was one of the translators of Plutarch.

Thomas Miller, born at Gainsborough in 1807, was brought up in poverty by his mother, his father having vanished without trace during London riots in 1810. Having served his apprenticeship at basket-making, he went to Nottingham, met the poet Thomas Bailey, and was encouraged by him to publish some poems, the profits from which enabled him to set up shop as a basket-maker. When 28 he sent some fancy baskets, enclosing poems, to Countess Blessington, then in the heyday of her beauty and social success. At her house he met many distinguished literary men, including Samuel Rogers, the banker-poet, who enabled him to start in business as a bookseller, an occupation allowing him leisure for writing.

For the next 30 years Thomas Miller's pen was busy with poems, pastoral sketches, works on flowers, birds and animals, novels, miscellaneous writings on historical subjects, and various aspects of London life and legend. An honest, unwearying toiler, always known as the basket-maker, he was never far removed from penury, however, and he died a poor man—in London in 1874.

Gate Burton. One of Lincolnshire's gems, it is a place of great charm, with its few cottages set here and there along the road going north to Gainsborough, the Hall delightfully situated in a park and facing the Trent. There is an 18th century prospect temple over-looking this view. A drive across the park, where oaks and elms and chestnuts stretch out ample branches, leads to the modern church and the dignified 18th century Hall built by William Hutton with later 19th century north wing and other 20th century additions.

The church, built in 1866, is a small Gothic building of stone lined with brick. Slender catlike imps look out from the corners of a pinnacled tower in which six steel bells hang; and the simple interior is graced by a neat western gallery fashioned from oak grown in the park. This gallery, and the reredos with its four gilded saints and Annunciation and Nativity scenes, are memorials to John Drysdale Sandars, lord of the manor. A relic of the former church is an ancient font adorned with round arcading, foliage and little faces.

Gautby. The former rectory and the tiny brick church with tower and slender spire, neighbours in a leafy setting, here making a pleasing picture.

The church is in Georgian style, and so are the pulpit, the horse-box pew, and the fluted wooden pillars by the chancel arch. But there are monuments going back to Stuart days (some of them brought from St Mary Woolnoth in London) and a mediaeval font with carved quatrefoils, from Laughton near Gainsborough.

One of the monuments is to Lord Mayor of London Sir Thomas Vyner. Set up by his son in 1672, it shows him in his robes, holding his chain of office, his hair curling under a skull cap. He had the distinction of being a friend of Charles I, being knighted by Cromwell, and being made a baronet after the Restoration. On a monument of 1673 cherubs guard another Sir Thomas, who reclines on his elbow, wearing flowing robes, an SS collar, and a wig.

An inscription commemorates Sir Robert Vyner, banker to

Charles II, who spent £30,000 to replace the Court jewels which had been sold or pledged during the Civil War, and advanced great sums during the Plague and for the wages of the Army and Navy. He also was a Lord Mayor of London.

In the chancel is a floorstone in memory of Frederick Grantham Vyner, who was captured by Greek brigands near Marathon in 1870. The Greek government, having promised to send a ransom, sent soldiers instead, whereupon Vyner and three of his companions were murdered. They left diaries showing how manfully they had sustained one another in captivity. The chalice of the church was given by Frederick Vyner's mother and bears the arms of William Weddell the antiquary who built Newby Hall, Yorkshire, that became the home of the Vyner's descendants.

Gayton-le-Marsh. A small place near the Great Eau, it lies below the level of the sea—a few farms and cottages clustered among trees and dominated by the impressive 15th century tower of the church.

Except for this tower and the mediaeval arcade, the church was rebuilt in red-brick a century ago. A curious feature of the interior is the level of the nave floor—raised so high that the pews reach up to the capitals of the arcade. This low arcade is in striking contrast to the huge tower arch which soars to the roof; and odd, too, looks the chancel arch, overpowered by the big expanse of wall above it and squeezed in between two wide flat buttresses. There is an old chest with three lids, and the plain font bowl is thought to be of the time of Edward the Confessor, whose wife gave this church some land still in its possession.

Gedney. A scattered village in a great parish extending to the Wash, it has one of the renowned churches to be seen along the road which divides the Fens and the Marshes of southern Holland.

Successor to one of Norman times, the church belonged to Crowland Abbey and was restored near the end of last century. It was built before the Fens were effectively drained, and lack of firm foundations probably accounts for the great west tower having an odd little spirelet set on a base designed for a fine spire. Rising 86 feet to the top of its parapet, the tower is splendid both in its proportions and in its decoration. The two lower stages are 13th century work and have single lancets and windows of two lights, all enriched with dog-tooth and with arcading between them; transomed windows of two lights make a lantern of the 15th century top stage.

The fine south porch, built late in the 14th century, has an upper storey (the dividing floor is gone) reached by a turret stairway, and shelters a magnificent old door. Across the top of its wicket-door are four worn coats-of-arms, with a small ivory Crucifixion in the middle; above these is a Latin inscription in beautiful raised letters, wishing Peace to the church and all who dwell within it. On the bronze double-lock is inscribed this pearl of wisdom: *Beware before, avyseth John Pette.*

A grand feature is the late 15th century nave clerestory, with 12 three-light windows on each side—two long lines lighting up the carvings, flowers, grotesque faces, and ecclesiastical emblems on the old beams and bosses of the roof. The shafts supporting the roof rest on stone corbels with carvings of people and animals. Below is a great array of arches—the lovely Early English tower arch with dog-tooth moulding and six arches in each of the 14th century nave arcades. The chancel is chiefly 14th century work, with a fine east window, richly-carved sedilia and a piscina, and a 15th century low-side window. Also 14th century is the north aisle, and there is much of the old material in the rebuilt south aisle.

There is a peephole to the high altar from the vestry, where the registers (beginning in 1558) are kept in an 18th century chest. In a jumble of brilliant mediaeval glass in the five-light east window of the north aisle are figures and fragments, with King Solomon wearing a red robe and golden crown. Elsewhere in this aisle are canopies and flowers in old glass, and there is a little more in the tops of windows in the clerestory.

The oldest monument here is the battered figure of an armoured knight of 13th century, who owned land here seven centuries ago; it lies on a great 15th century altar tomb in the south aisle. In the floor of this aisle is the brass portrait of a lady who died about 1390; a little belled dog looks up from the folds of her girdled gown. A finely-coloured alabaster wall-monument, set here in 1605, has kneeling figures of Adlard and Cassandra Welby. An old stone coffin stands in the north aisle, and in the nave is a font dated 1664, though its bowl, with shields and angels and the Madonna carved under a canopy, is 15th century in style.

A memorial in the chancel tells of Richard Lawson Gales, a 20th century vicar who won a measure of fame as a poet and essayist. One of his 16th century predecessors, not commemorated here, was Richard Hakluyt, author of the epic *Principall Navigations, Voiages and Discoveries of the English Nation*. He died in 1616, and was laid to rest in Westminster Abbey.

Gedney Hill. A straggling village near the Cambridgeshire border, it lies remote on one of the long straight roads of the rich flats of the Bedford Level, and in spite of its name there is no sign of a hill for miles round.

The church here, about a dozen miles from its mother church at Gedney, was almost rebuilt last century; but its embattled tower is old and mellowed, and there is a rare feature within—a nave with wooden arcades. Four stout oak pillars are on each side of the nave, supporting the plain timbered roofs of the aisles and the black-and-white roof of the nave, with old moulded and embattled tie-beams.

Three or four miles away is another straggling village, Sutton St Edmund, with a small church of brick and stone rebuilt in 1798. In it are the old box-pews, and a fine brass candelabrum from the days before electricity came to these lonely Fen villages.

Glentham. It lies on the road from Gainsborough, with the Seggimoor Beck flowing through it on its way to the Ancholme. The road comes to Glentham from Caenby Corner, where it is crossed by the Ermine Street, and goes on to Bishopbridge—a small hamlet where the Ancholme is joined by the little River Rase and is spanned by the bridge which gives the place its name. The bridge was built in the 14th century by a Bishop of Lincoln, and was rebuilt about a century ago. At this spot the river begins its journey north-ward through the Carrs along the new straight bed that was cut to make it navigable to the Humber at Ferriby Sluice, passing through Brigg on its way. (It is navigable now only from Brigg.) Known as the New Ancholme River, this deep cut acts as a drain for the waters coming down to the valley between the Cliff and the Wolds.

Much of Glentham's church has been rebuilt; what is left of the old is chiefly 15th century, including the battered porch, which has a niche with a fine little sculpture of the Madonna holding the crucified Jesus. Above the niche are the arms and crest of the Tournays, who for centuries lived at Caenby, half a mile away, in a grey, moated house still standing near the Paunch Beck, and in which Henry VIII slept on his journey through Lincolnshire. It is a farmhouse now.

The old door in the church porch still has its closing ring, and opens to an interior with tall, tilting arcades and old box-pews. Under the gallery at the west end lies the stone figure of one of the Tournay ladies, wearing draped headdress. Old Molly Grime was the nickname of this figure for many years; it is said to have been a corruption of Malgraen, the local word for the washing of Holy Images, and this old figure was a link with the ancient custom of washing a figure of Our Dead Lord for a portrayal of the Entomb-ment. Every Good Friday until 1832 seven old maids were given a shilling each to wash the figure of Molly Grime with water from a spring near the village.

There is a much damaged brass half-figure of Elizabeth Tournay who died in 1452.

The church has a 500-year-old chest with carved tracery and roundels; the font and pulpit are modern memorials to Sir Montague Cholmeley of Norton Place (2 miles away) who fell in France in

1914. Another tribute to him is a striking window showing St George in golden armour trampling down a blue and green dragon; it was designed by Christopher Whall, who did much to raise the standard of stained glass in England at the beginning of this century.

Glentworth. Lying in a hollow below the north Lincolnshire Cliff, this compact village has added to its charms during the last few years by the cultivation of bulbs. In the Spring some of its fields are ablaze with the colourful beauty of tulips and other flowers. It has a church going back to the 11th century, an 18th century vicarage with an acacia of the same time in its garden, and memorials of Sir Christopher Wray, who was Lord Chief Justice and Speaker of the House of Commons in Elizabeth I's time. Elizabeth's most trusted judge, he presided over or shared in many historic trials, including those of Babington and his fellow conspirators, of Campion the Jesuit, and Davison, the Secretary of State who was made the scapegoat for the execution of Mary Stuart.

Posterity condemns the sentences on Campion and Davison, but otherwise Wray's judicial career was unblemished; he was on the whole an upright judge—in the words of Coke, "a most reverent judge, of profound and judicial knowledge, accompanied with a ready and singular capacity, grave and sensible elocution, and continual and admirable patience".

Of the great house Sir Christopher built there remains only part of the old stone walling, attached to the big red Georgian Hall built by the Lumleys, Earls of Scarbrough. This is also now in ruins but the Hall stables have been made into fine dwellings for the villagers, The almshouses Sir Christopher built for three poor women are close to the ancient church but they, too, are unoccupied and in bad condition. And in the church, where Sir Christopher was buried in 1592, is his monument of rich marble and alabaster.

Sir Christopher lies in his fur-lined robes, with ruff and hat and collar of SS, and his wife is beside him in costly dress with jewelled girdle, ruff, and a remarkable hood like a canopy. In a small recess above them kneels their son William, in armour, and below are four pretty daughters in ruffs and farthingales.

Sir Christopher rebuilt the chancel in which he lies, and the nave was rebuilt in 1782; but the chancel has its late 12th century priest's doorway, and the jambs of the chancel arch are as old, crowned with capitals which are a fine example of stiff leaf carving.

The strong church tower, with its rubble walls and stone quoins, stands much as it did when first built—at the close of the Saxon period—and has its original arch to the nave. The parapet and west window of the tower are 15th century, and its doorway is later.

Gosberton. This is a growing and busy community. Its glory is

145

its church, standing in a trim churchyard just off the busy road. Big enough for more than 800 folk, it is a noble building of the 15th century, finely restored 50 years ago, when the chancel was rebuilt and lengthened.

Shaped like a cross, there is evidence by excavation of its Norman origins. It has a lovely central tower, with a lofty crocketed spire linked to the tall pinnacles by delicate flying buttresses. A curious, and perhaps unique, feature is an elephant gargoyle. On the west gable of the nave is a figure of Our Lord in Majesty, and there is a worn figure in one of the three canopied niches adorning the porch. There are more canopied niches by the inner doorway.

The interior is an impressive sight. The clerestoried nave has arcades with continuous mouldings and embattled responds. The tower has fine arches, and a groined roof with bosses of foliage and quaint corbel heads. Across the arch from the chapel to the south transept is an ancient oak screen with modern cornice, and over it is a fine rood-loft with figures carved by Belgian refugees of the First World War; the old rood stairway is also here.

Two stone figures have been here since mediaeval days. One is a cross-legged knight in chain armour, praying with shield bearing a cross; he lies in a recess handsome with a cinquefoiled arch, a leafy hood, pinnacles, and censing angels and may be the donor of the church. The other is no doubt his wife. Near them is an old piscina, and above this is a striking window with moulded mullions and transoms.

Set up against the chancel wall is part of an old altar stone with consecration crosses, and among many old carved stones lying loose is one showing a wimpled woman. Other relics from the past are the traceried 15th century font, and a chest with iron bands.

The pulpit, with carved figures of St Peter and St Paul and two bishops, is modern; and so is the reredos with its striking painted panels—copies of Old Masters. Saints and apostles from Fra Angelico are there, with the Madonna of his assistant Gozzoli, angels by Botticelli and the Annunciation of Lippi—all painted by Mrs Welby-Everard of Gosberton House, a Georgian house in lovely grounds, now a Holland County Council school.

Nearby, the site of Cressy Hall is marked by mediaeval moats. It was the home of the Cressy family and burnt down in 1791. The present house was built soon after.

Goxhill. A scattered village in the flat, green countryside by the Humber, it has a fine old church restored last century and some attractive old cottages and houses. About 2 miles away is a small port called Goxhill Haven. The proximity of the Hull ferry has influenced the growth and character of the community.

The massive church tower was built in the 15th century, and is notable for its lovely embattled parapet with eight panelled and crocketed pinnacles; angry-looking gargoyles are below. The north porch has old beams in its roof, and shelters a fine 15th century doorway adorned with flowers and foliage, odd little faces, the bust of a woman, and a quaint bird-like man—very fat, but with sparrow-legs. The door itself is modern, but swings on the old strap-hinges.

The south porch has a richly-moulded inner doorway of the 15th century (still with its old studded door), and a big recess for stoup. When this porch was being made into a vestry in 1936, there came to light on its east wall an old painting of the Crucifixion. Though worn, it is clear and is said to be "the only complete subject in any porch in England". Traces of another painting, showing the head of a saint, can also be seen.

The stately interior is full of light. The spacious nave is 14th century work, crowned by a later roof with fine moulded beams and gables filled with tracery. From the 15th century come the aisles, the fine clerestory, and the east window of the chancel, with a vesica above it. Part of the chancel is 13th century work, including the gable-headed aumbry and the beautiful double piscina with a pillar. The pulpit is Jacobean and there is an old ironbound chest, the font is modern.

A knight with crossed legs, in the chancel, is thought to be a De Vere who died about 1300; in chain armour and surcoat, he has a big shield, and his arm is raised in the act of drawing his sword. A simple inscription tells the sad story of the two children of Edward Skinner: their son died one Monday in 1669, and his sister, "bewailing ye loss of him even to admiration, followed him on ye Sunday".

The best of the church's modern glass is in the east window, and shows Joshua and Melchizedek and scenes in their lives. Another window has Our Lord appearing to Mary Magdalene, His tomb guarded by two shining angels. A third has Faith with a cross, Hope with an anchor, and Charity with a child in her arms and two in the folds of her crimson gown.

A mile away, at Littleworth, is a building known as Goxhill Priory. It is 14th century and of two storeys, the lower one stone-vaulted; the upper one reached by a newel stairway climbing to the roof. It has big windows (pointed and round-headed) now built-up, and is used now as a farm building. It may have been a manorial chapel of St Andrew belonging to the De Spenser family who held the manor, and to have been served by a hermit appointed by them. It has also been suggested that it was a domestic hall.

Grainsby. It has its own quiet corner near the Grimsby road, and 300 acres of ploughed out parkland belonging to Grainsby Hall, a Victorian building, which is now empty and used as a store.

Standing among trees, the aisleless church has a tower which has stood since the 11th century, though its west lancet and the double lancets of the top storey belong to the 13th century, and the battlements are later additions. The nave has stout, sloping walls perhaps as old as the tower, with a Norman doorway on the south side.

Notable among the church's woodwork are low oak benches, a restored 15th century screen dividing nave and chancel, two old chairs with men's heads carved on the arm-rests, and modern stalls with fine poppyheads and arm-rests adorned with an eagle and a pigeon.

Grainthorpe. Once it was a little port, and there is Grainthorpe Haven running to the sea more than 2 miles away. Its ancient story is told by the salterns still seen on the coast, for they came into the Conqueror's Domesday Book; today it straggles along in the flat country where a reed-grown dyke runs beside every road.

Grainthorpe Hall is a good Georgian building but the greatest attraction is its church, finely embattled outside and spacious and airy within. Much of it is 14th century, but the north arcade of the nave has 13th century responds, and the grand tower is early 15th century. The tower's west doorway has traceried spandrels and its buttresses climb the four stages to the battlements and leafy pinnacles; two of the three bells are mediaeval.

The nave and its extraordinarily wide aisles have restored old roofs, and the aisles have panelling made from old box-pews. Each aisle has a piscina, and one also has an aumbry. The old entrance to the rood stairway is by the chancel arch, and there is a plain mediaeval font. The old altar stone, 7 feet 6 inches long and with three of its consecration crosses, was found this century when the church was being restored.

The rarest possession of this church is a 14th century brass cross in the floor of the chancel. It is probably to Stephen de See, rector c. 1380–90. The stem is gone, but the head and the base are here, showing that it was originally 7 feet long. Lovely in design and detail is the head, its cusped arms enriched with leaves and finials and enclosing a quatrefoil filled with foliage. The base of the stem rests on a rock rising from a sea in which quaint fish are swimming.

Grantham. It has always been an important place in the eyes of travellers, for, until the construction of the bypass for the A1, it stood astride one of our greatest highways and has a station on one of our most important main lines; because of its central position it is for some express trains the only stopping-place between London and York. But the traveller—whether he comes by road or rail, whether he tarries or passes on his way—must always gaze in admiration at the soaring spire of Grantham's fine church. It is a noble sight.

Gunby Hall

Holbeach Church

Lincoln Cathedral and part of Castle Square

Grantham is old, but shows age only in its church and inns. Once it had a castle, and perhaps it once had town walls; but all traces of the castle have long since disappeared. Today Grantham is an industrial town, and looks it—its streets agog with cycles and cars and lined with busy shops. But the spacious marketplace is still picturesque, and the shaded green before its Guildhall is a pleasant place indeed. Here and there an old-world corner remains, notably near the splendid church, where an overhanging storey or a colonnaded porch bespeaks a more leisured age. For the rest, it only half lives up to Evelyn's description of "a pretty town environed by ascending grounds and for pleasure comparable to most inland places in England".

Grantham was a royal manor when Domesday Book was compiled, and before the Conquest belonged to Editha, the Confessor's queen. King John was here twice, the second time in 1213 when he held his court at the Angel Inn, in the room still called the King's Chamber. Here, too, was the first resting-place of the body of Queen Eleanor, who in 1290 had died at Harby in Nottinghamshire on her way to meet Edward I in the north of England. Her body was carried to London at the mourning king's command, and at each place where the funeral procession stayed for the night he set up a beautiful cross to her memory. The Grantham Cross, on St Peter's Hill, was wantonly destroyed during the Civil War.

Edward IV was another royal visitor; he was here in the first year of his reign, when he made a grant for the Grammar School. Two years later he made it a corporate town. Perhaps a more exciting time in Grantham's history, however, was when Cromwell distinguished himself as a cavalry leader on Gonerby Moor outside the town. The Royalists had captured the town in 1642, but Cromwell reoccupied it in 1643, and on May 13 reported, "God hath given us this evening a glorious victory over our enemies."

Grantham's crowning glory is the grand tower and spire of its old church of St Wulfram, a landmark for miles round. Though the spire is slightly lower than Louth's steeple or Boston's Stump the surroundings make it look higher than either. A turn from the High Street leads to Swinegate, where amid pleasant open spaces the traveller has his first glimpse of the west front and soaring spire. In the 7th century there was a Saxon church here, but no trace of it is left, and of the succeeding Norman church there remain but six pillars in the nave—late 12th century work, with detached shafts and rare leaf decoration. From then onwards, generation after generation has lavished wealth and skill and devotion on this splendid church.

In the last quarter of the 13th century the nave was lengthened, the north doorway and north aisle built, and the foundations of the tower laid. But the greatest architectural beauty grew up in the

14th century: the south aisle and its graceful continuation in the lady chapel, with its lovely six-light traceried window; the north porch with open arches at each side, so spacious that it served as a chapel; the double vaulted crypt; and the splendid steeple. The last great enrichment was in the 15th century, when the Corpus Christi Chapel was built to correspond with the Lady Chapel on the other side of the chancel and make the church symmetrical. The little chantry chapel of St Katharyn was also built then.

The tower soars 140 feet, and as each stage was slowly added so the decoration changed. On the lowest stage its ballflower ornament, varying in detail and depth, makes a rich setting for the west doorway and central window. There are bands of arcading and quatrefoils above, and the third stage has deeply set double lights. A newel staircase in one of the pinnacle-crowned buttresses leads to the belfry, where there are 10 bells mellow and rich in tone. Four tall octagonal turrets, completed by pinnacles, carry the eye still higher —to the graceful crocketed spire rising another 145 feet.

More rich adornment of the exterior of Grantham's church is to be seen below the battlements of the nave, where there are hundreds of little faces peering down, and long gargoyles stretching forward from the walls, staring or grinning. But if the exterior of the church is impressive, the interior is hardly less so. The tracery of all the 14th century windows, varied and graceful, the six pointed arches on each side of the nave, and the lofty tower arch borne up on massive piers, give an appearance of spaciousness befitting to a cathedral.

The fine, vaulted crypt, entered from the lady chapel, still has its original door and ironwork, with a secret bolt opened by pressing an iron stud. The east end of the crypt is a chapel and has an early stone altar, and a wide and deep recess beneath it was probably used for the relics of St Wulfram which were later removed to a chamber built above the north porch. Part of the beautiful 13th century stone doorway was cut away to make the floor of the room, and a traceried window looking into the church was made at the same time, probably to display the relics to pilgrims visiting the shrine.

A narrow spiral stairway in the wall of the aisle leads to a room above the south porch which was formerly the dwelling-place of the priest. It has a fireplace with raised hearth-stone and a sink in a recess for washing. On the inner wall is a little oriel window commanding a view of the whole church and of the high altar. Here the priest could keep watch over the altar vessels and the shrine and relics above the north porch opposite.

The chained library in this room was left to the church in 1598, by Francis Trigg, rector of Welbourne. About 150 of the books were once chained, and the original chains are still fastened to 83 of them. The oldest is a book on law printed in Venice in 1472 by John of

Cologne, and among the other books preserved here are the complete works of Dr Henry More, a Grantham boy who became a distinguished Cambridge scholar of Philosophy and a friend of John Milton.

Few great English churches have lost more of their ancient fittings than Grantham's. The 15th century font has survived, however, and is an impressive sight with its modern tabernacled cover, resplendent in gold and colour and rising nearly as high as the arcades. Canopied saints adorn the pedestal, and the eight panels of the bowl have Biblical scenes, much mutilated. There are also two old chests—an alms chest, and another large chest which once held the church plate and various documents.

Nor can the church boast a rich array of ancient monuments. Two canopied recesses decorated with angels hold the tombs of Richard de Salteby and his wife, 1362, and of John Harrington, a benefactor of the church, 1403; and there is the marble-topped tomb of Francis Malham, a Yorkshireman who fought for the King in the Civil War and died here on his way home. A huge monument with a mourning figure and a cherub holding his medallion portrait commemorates Sir Dudley Ryder, Lord Chief Justice, who died in 1756; and another memorial of the same period, with a marble panel of a sea battle, is to William Cust, Commander of the *Elizabeth*, who died at 28 in the expedition to St Louis, 1747.

Truly, as in so many English towns, the church is Grantham's finest building. Nevertheless, the town has one or two other buildings which claim attention because of their architectural or historic interest. One of these, immediately east of the church, is Grantham House, which now belongs to the National Trust. Parts of it, including the central hall, date from the late 14th century. There are Elizabethan and later additions and alterations. Princess Margaret, daughter of Henry VII, stayed here in 1503 while journeying north to marry James IV of Scotland.

Another old neighbour of the church, even more famous, is the Grammar School, now known as the King's School. Separated from the churchyard by a narrow lane, it was built about 1450 by Bishop Fox, who was born at Ropsley (where his story is told). The 15th century building is little changed and is still used as a hall and chapel, though the school, of course, has moved into roomier and more modern quarters close by. A picturesque sight it is, with its high-pitched stone roof and mullioned windows; and within it, cut in the windowsills, are the names of hundreds of boys who decided to make their mark here even if they failed to do so in the great world beyond.

The most-prized name here is that of Isaac Newton. He first came here in 1654, a bright and inventive boy of 12 who soon became head of the school. Four years later, his mother, widowed a second time, took him away to help her to manage her farm at Woolsthorpe; and so instead of attending Grantham School he attended Grantham market, selling the farm produce and taking home the groceries—tasks in which the budding scientist had little interest.

About a quarter of a century after Newton left Grantham School another name destined to become famous was entered on the school roll. It was that of Colley Cibber, actor, poet laureate, and writer of plays. In his *Apology for the Life of Colley Cibber, Comedian*, he tells how, "At little more than ten Years of Age I was sent to the Free school of Grantham in Lincolnshire, where I staid till I got through it, from the lowest Form to the uppermost. And such Learning as that School could give me, is the most I pretend to. Even there I remember that I was the same inconsistent Creature I have been ever since, always in full Spirits, in some small capacity to do right, but in a more frequent Alacrity to do wrong."

Among other famous pupils of the Grantham school may be mentioned Elizabeth I's great Treasurer, Lord Burghley; and John Newcome, Dean of Rochester, who in 1710 bequeathed his library to the town.

As the halfway stage on the coaching routes between the north and south of England, Grantham has always been noted for its inns —and they are many. But the best-known are the George and the Angel and Royal, on opposite sides of the High Street. The George, much modernised, was a famous house of call in the 18th century, Charles Dickens wrote of it in *Nicholas Nickleby* when "two of the front outside passengers, wisely availing themselves of their arrival at one of the best inns in England, turned in, for the night, at the George at Grantham" while the rest of the passengers, including Nickleby and Squeers, "wrapped themselves more closely in their coats and cloaks, and leaving the light and warmth of the town behind them . . . prepared again to encounter the piercing blast which swept across the open country."

The Angel and Royal has many claims to fame: the former is one of the oldest inns in the country, it is one of the rare remaining mediaeval hostels established by the Knights Templars for the use of travellers, as at Fotheringhay and Glastonbury, and it has preserved much of its ancient charm. The fine 14th century archway has the carved heads of Edward III and his Queen Philippa at the terminals of the arch. An oriel window above rests on a stone corbel, and the battlemented and quatrefoiled parapet extends along the whole front. Interesting features are the stone vaulted roofs of the deeply recessed windows on the ground floor and in the great room on the first floor, scene of historic events. In 1796 a curious will was made by a landlord of the inn, one Michael Solomon, who left the sum of forty shillings for a sermon every year against drunkenness to be preached in the parish church. Every year since then, in November, his wish has been carefully carried out.

Though Grantham does not live in the past—it is as go-ahead as any town in the country—it does take a real pride in its links with the past and with famous men. The visitor is reminded of this again in the pleasant green space in front of the Guildhall, a fine 19th century building. On this spot, where once stood the Eleanor Cross, now stands the statue of Sir Isaac Newton, High Priest of Science, "looking on a troubled world of science misapplied". His figure, unveiled in 1858, is of bronze, 12 feet high and weighing nearly two tons, part of the metal having come from melted cannon. Near him is another bronze statue of one of Grantham's 19th century MPs, Frederick Tollemache, standing hat in hand. In 1897, when there was some reluctance on the part of councillors to become mayor, Grantham woke up one morning to find this statue decorated with a mayoral chain of office, and a card attached stating "The problem solved".

The Museum and Library are close by, housed in a graceful 20th century brick building. In the Museum the contents of the modern display cases, attractively designed in "shop window" style, include many local archaeological discoveries arranged to show the history of Grantham and its neighbourhood from earliest times. Other cases are devoted to the civic, social, and industrial history of the town. The reserve collections of the Museum include many fine examples of Bronze Age vessels, beakers, and urns, which the interested visitor may see by arrangement. A group of Roman remains from excavation in the neighbourhood is of great interest, among them being a sculpture of three goddesses from Ancaster, and fragments of a blast furnace found in ironstone works at Colsterworth with bits of the original charcoal fuel and iron that was smelted.

One other Grantham relic of bygone days has still to be mentioned —the stone conduit in the spacious marketplace, set here in 1597 to protect the water which had been brought from springs at Gonerby by the Grey Friars in the 14th century. There are small obelisks above the buttresses, and, carved with the trade emblems of the Grantham wool-staplers, are the words, "Let the Fountains be dispersed abroad." The stream of water flows from a ram's head.

Grasby. Winding between old farms and cottages, the village street drops down from the highway which runs along the western edge of the Wolds and gives magnificent views of the countryside— of a great sweep of the Wolds to Caistor and beyond, and of the vast plain with its patchwork of woods and fields and farms and distant hamlets.

Endowed with memories of the Tennysons is Grasby, for here Alfred's elder brother Charles was vicar for about 40 years. He came here in 1835, a few years after he had changed his name on succeeding to the estate of his great-uncle Samuel Turner of Caistor. To this village in 1837 Charles Tennyson Turner brought his young wife Louisa, a niece of Sir John Franklin, and sister of Emily Sellwood, who, attending the wedding as a bridesmaid, was 13 years later to become the wife of Alfred Tennyson. Charles and Alfred, when mere boys, had published the first fruits of their genius together, *Poems by Two Brothers*, to which their eldest living brother Frederick had also contributed a few pieces.

While Charles was vicar the 13th century church was rebuilt. It has a sturdy tower which until recently carried a spire and a peal of four bells, one having been ringing since 1500, and two since 1869, when they were given by the Sellwood sisters. To the old church belong the nave arches on clustered pillars, the south doorway with its hood of dog-tooth ornament, the little font, a lead paten, part of an old cross-shaft from the churchyard, and a floorstone with a floriated cross.

Lord Tennyson gave the glass of the east window showing 10 scenes in Our Lord's Life (from the Annunciation to the Ascension), and he set up in the nave the white marble tablet in memory of the poet-vicar, kindliest of men, and his beloved wife. They died within a month of each other and rest side by side at Cheltenham. Of Charles we read in his memorial here:

True poet surely to be found
When Truth is found again.

Those are two lines from the poem *Midnight*, in which Alfred laments the death of his beloved brother:

And through this midnight breaks the sun
Of sixty years away,
The light of days when life begun
The days that seem today;
When all my griefs were shared with thee
And all my hopes were thine,
As all thou wast was one with me
May all thou art be mine.

Charles Tennyson Turner rebuilt the village school, and also the vicarage, a square house standing in grounds now famous in literary history. Here Charles, who shared his more famous brother's love of nature, wrote many poems, coloured by the experiences of his daily life hereabouts. He was a great master of the sonnet and

altogether wrote nearly 350 poems in this form. These are the concluding lines of one, called *The Pastor's Prayer*, which is extremely
reflective of his life at Grasby:

> *He prays at noon, with all the warmth of heaven*
> *About his heart, that each may be forgiven;*
> *He prays at eve: and through the midnight air*
> *Sends holy ventures to the throne above;*
> *His very dreams are faithful to his prayer,*
> *And follow, with closed eyes, the path of love.*

Grayingham. It is a small village with a small church, dedicated to St Radegund, which was rebuilt in the 18th century and
restored in our own. It has kept a massive 13th century tower with
a grand west doorway and a striking arch. The doorway is enriched
with three shafts at each side, and carving of dog-tooth ornaments
in its arch of three orders, and has a 15th century window above it.
The great horseshoe arch is almost as wide as the aisleless nave to
which it leads.

Great Carlton. Trim yew hedges and stately trees here line the
way to a fine oak lychgate and a churchyard of beautiful lawns; and
a delightful peep of the gardens and orchard of the neighbouring
house enhances the approach to the church—an approach unsurpassed in all Lincolnshire.

The church was all rebuilt in Victorian times, except for the 15th
century tower, which bears the quaint inscription:

> *For Robert Schadworth saul ye pray*
> *Who for yis fote makying did pay;*

The tower arch rests on quaint corbels of bearded men looking
wide-eyed at each other. The reredos of colourful mosaic has a scene
of the Last Supper, with Judas absent, and there is a finely-carved
oak pulpit with panels of wheat, grapes, figs, flowers, and foliage.

Great Coates. This village is now part of Grimsby. Its 500-year-
old tower rises finely above the churchyard trees, its two stages of
rust-coloured stone in striking contrast to the grey ashlar of the battlemented belfry.

The rest of the church is chiefly 14th century work, though the
east end of the chancel has been rebuilt and the nave arcades
are early 13th century, with arches supported by tall clustered
pillars. The font, with shields in traceried panels, is 15th century,

and under the tower is a 13th century floorstone with a floriated cross.

The colourful east window, displaying Our Lord in Glory, St Mary, and St Nicholas, is fine modern work. Modern, too, are the finely-panelled roof with gilded bosses, the oak reredos carved with Passion emblems and guarded by two angels, and the brass eagle lectern.

The outstanding memory here is of the Barnardistons, who obtained this manor by marriage with the Willoughby family in the 14th century and held it till the 17th. They came originally from Kedington in Suffolk, where many of them are buried; but the moat of their old home in this Lincolnshire village can still be traced in the Hall Close field by the church, their quartered arms are among a medley of old glass in the north aisle, and several are portrayed in brass in the nave and chancel floors.

On a quaint brass of about 1420 is Roger Barnardiston's wife Isabella, wearing a long robe and square headdress; a faithful little dog with bells on its collar is at her feet. A remarkable brass of 1503 shows Sir Thomas Barnardiston kneeling with his wife and their 15 children, including a priest and a nun. Above them is an odd Resurrection scene showing Our Lord sitting on the edge of the tomb, one soldier looking on, another peering into the tomb, and a third sleeping. Coats-of-arms add to the enrichment of this brass.

One further reminder of bygone days here is the name of Butts Close, a field by the church where men once practised with their bows and arrows.

The most recent addition to the church is a fine clock, taken from North Willingham Hall and bearing the date 1806, it was fixed in the tower as a generous gift in 1968.

Greatford. Standing not far from the county's farthest south it is a charming village, with the River Glen flowing leisurely past its grey stone cottages and the garden of the Hall, where a noble cedar almost as high as the neighbouring spire casts its shade on Elizabethan gables and oriel.

In a well-kept churchyard, reached by a little bridge across the river, roses line the pathway to a beautiful church, stone-roofed and shaped like a cross, the southern arm of the cross being the attractive tower with broach spire, a grinning face at every corner. Tower and spire, like almost the whole church, are 13th century (the porch having capitals with the graceful foliage of that time), but the north transept and several of the windows are a century younger. The absence of arcades is unusual in these parts.

The chancel has its old piscina and aumbry, a recess enriched with ballflower, and its rood-loft stairway. Under the tower stands a huge mediaeval gravestone, enriched with a cross. In a square, traceried opening by the north transept arch is a hollow with carved foliage, thought to be for alms.

In this transept is a monument to a doctor whose skill helped to shape history. It is a Nollekens bust of Dr Francis Willis who cured George III of his first fit of madness. He lived to be nigh on 90 and before they laid him to rest here in 1807 the king had been cured a second time by the doctor's two sons, John and Robert Willis. Robert's monument tells of this cure "at a moment pregnant with events"; and brother John's monument shows him on his own death-bed, with attendant angels. Another wall tablet here is to their mother, Mary Curtois, who had been married to old Francis Willis for 40 years when he treated the king.

Odd chance brought to this church another link with the medical profession and the years when Francis Willis was growing to man-hood. An attractively painted board in the nave tells how two doctors in our own time have given money to the poor in gratitude for the refuge England gave to the Huguenots, and particularly to their own ancestor Elias Lafargue, rector here for 30 years of the 18th century.

Francis Willis, who was buried at Greatford, was born in 1718, son of a clergyman at Lincoln Cathedral. He took orders at Oxford University, but in spite of family opposition qualified as a doctor. He helped to found and conduct Lincoln Hospital, then settled here, to specialise in the treatment of insanity.

So marked was his success that patients were brought to him from afar, and when in 1788 George III first fell a victim to madness, Willis, now 70, was summoned to Court, where his appearance was fiercely resented by the State physicians.

Willis saw that the case could be cured if the severity of the patient's treatment was modified, and, by insistence on his theory, had the king out walking within five days. Fanny Burney in her Diary describes him as: "a man of ten thousand; open, honest, dauntless, light-hearted, innocent, and high-minded. I see him impressed with a most animated reverence and affection for his royal patient; but it is wholly for his character, not a whit for his rank."

Willis returned here on the recovery of the king, built a second home for the reception of patients, and was still active in his work of mercy when he died in 1807. Later his sons attended fresh out-breaks of the king's insanity, but could not stave off the final break-down.

Great Gonerby. Its grey spire can be seen like a beckoning finger from the northern outskirts of Grantham, for the village is set on a hill looking over the Vale of Belvoir. The hill, once known as the steepest between London and Edinburgh, has been considerably cut down and has lost the terrors Sir Walter Scott attributed to it in the *Heart of Midlothian*, where Gunnerby Hill is called "a murder to post-horses". The village is now bypassed by the A1.

The church has a lofty 15th century tower and spire, clerestoried nave, and aisles with panelled parapets, the south arcade being 13th century, and the north 15th, with one earlier arch. The eight-sided font bowl is 600 years old, the lower part of the screen and the woodwork of the pulpit 500. A copy of Perugino's Martyrdom of Sebastian is a reminder that this church is one of only two in England dedicated to this saint.

Great Hale. A pleasant place in blossom time, and, indeed, at any time, its church, which belonged to Bardney Abbey 600 years ago and lost its chancel about the time of the Civil War, is a striking building with simple, rugged tower, long aisles and spacious porch. The tower is its great feature except for its 15th century parapet and leafy pinnacles it was built by Saxons, probably a century before the Conquest. Largely of rubble, it has the usual Saxon belfry windows, deeply-splayed and with a dividing baluster shaft, and an arch into the nave probably built by the Normans. At the north-east corner, in the thickness of the wall, is a turret staircase about 15 inches wide, its steps worn by the impress of feet through a thousand years.

The spacious nave, its east end serving as a chancel, has five pointed arches on each side borne up on slender 13th century pillars. Both aisles still have their mediaeval piscinas and aumbries, and north aisle and chancel have ancient screenwork incorporated with new. Part of the rood-loft stairway remains, and the fine font with quatrefoils and niches on its eight sides has been in use for 600 years.

There are two notable memorials to the Cawdrons who came to live here in the 17th century and saw the chancel, long ruinous, finally demolished. One shows Robert Cawdron, who died during the Commonwealth, with his two wives and ample family; nine sons and seven daughters, are behind the parents, and five more children in swaddling clothes lie in the foreground. Another Robert Cawdron, who died in the year of the Great Plague and was probably one of those 21 children, has a sculptured memorial showing him kneeling at a prayer-desk with one of his three wives, while the other two kneel discreetly in their long dresses and veils in separate compartments below.

Great Limber. Charmingly placed by the southern woods of Brocklesby Park.

The pond on the green belonged to the alien priory founded here as a cell to a Normandy abbey; and the pretty thatched house close by, with a fine cedar in front, has all that remains of the old building, for it has grown round the old priest's house, some of the stone walls (now faced with brick) being 7 feet thick.

The church, with a fine modern lychgate and low sturdy tower, is chiefly 14th century, restored in Victorian days; but there is a Norman entrance to the porch, which shelters a fine 14th century doorway. The chancel has been partly rebuilt, but some of its old walling is seen outside, and it still has its original 13th century arch opening to a very wide nave with 14th century arcades and narrow aisles.

The oak screen has rose-tipped tracery and panels of linenfold, and its wide loft has traceried panels and a vine cornice surmounted by the Crucifixion; both screen and loft are tributes to men of the First World War, whose portraits are in the church. The tapering turret stairway climbing to the loft is in the south aisle, where there are fragments of old glass. The fine font, with dog-tooth ornament on its bowl, is 700 years old.

Great Ponton. It stands by the A1 and has a tower that is a landmark for miles. It was built in 1519 by Anthony Ellys who lived in the grey stone house with a stepped gable that is now the rectory just by the church. When Calais was still an English town, and the port through which all our wool entered Europe, Anthony turned wool into gold, and legend says that he sent gold home to his wife in casks labelled Calais Sand. The tower, doubtless a thank-offering for those golden fleeces, has eight leafy pinnacles, double buttresses with canopied niches, bands of quatrefoil and other carving, and gargoyles grim and gay, a spectacled head among them being an unusual sight. On three sides are Chaucer's words, *Thynke and Thanke God of all.*

The last of the 15th century builders raised the rest of the church, but there is a 600-year-old arch between chancel and chapel. Still to be seen are the rood-loft stairway, an aumbry and sedilia; and the square font is believed to be a legacy from Saxon times.

Anthony Ellys is buried somewhere in the church but his altar tomb has vanished although three shields built in the north chapel wall may have been part of it. The tower remains as his real monument, looking as impressive as when he built it.

Great Steeping. Another of the small farming communities in the rich marshland, 3 miles south-east of Spilsby. There is a brick Georgian church, approached down a lane across a disused railway. It is no longer used for worship and has been superseded by a new church built in 1891. Still more important in religious history is the Baptist Chapel at Monksthorpe (on the edge of the disused airfield at Great Steeping). It is well kept and used for worship on alternate Sundays. Of special interest is the outside baptistry. The story of the chapel goes back to the Act of 1664 when all religious worship was forbidden within 5 miles of an established Church of England. The Burgh-le-Marsh Baptists had to close their chapel; but they would not give up their faith and continued to worship at Monksthorpe, while a member of the congregation kept watch from a tree nearby to warn of the approach of soldiers. The ground was given to the Baptists and a chapel built. The deeds go back to 1701 but the building may be earlier. It was thatched at first but in 1848 the roof was tiled.

Great Sturton. On a slope of the Wolds above the River Bain it lies, a cluster of dwellings near a little church now being restored.

The north aisle and the old tower were pulled down long ago, their stones being used for the churchyard wall, but the old arcade can still be seen built up in the wall, both inside and outside the church. In two of the bays are 14th century windows.

Striking is the interior, with its gleaming white walls and colourful nave roof enriched with bosses of red and gold. Rough old oak beams are in the chancel roof, and an old oak arch rises from the nave floor to the roof. On the north wall are traces of an old painting.

Greetwell. Lonely amid rough green pastures by the River Witham, it has a delightful view of the towers of Lincoln soaring up on the Cliff 2 miles to the west. The foundations of a Roman villa were uncovered during ironstone mining in the parish in the 19th century, and the Normans gave it a church. In a field the little house of prayer still stands, neighbour to the old Hall which is Jacobean but now a farmhouse. Time has wrought its changes to the church, and it has a new apse built in the Norman style, but the low, much restored, 13th century tower still stands as token of its great antiquity. In the chancel is a stone to Robert Dalyson, a Justice of the Peace in the terrible days of Mary Tudor.

Grimoldby. This marshland village is spread out along the road but has a handsome church. From the lychgate there is a fine view of Louth's lovely spire against the distant Wolds.

Built about 1380 (when the 14th century Decorated style was waning), but with a chancel partly rebuilt in 1876, the church presents a dignified picture with its three-storied tower, its clere-storied nave, and its fine array of battlements and gargoyles. One of these gargoyles is a fine old bearded man with calm expression, and another is a man in a brimmed hat who looks down with seemingly lively interest.

The north porch has its old roof and original door with a border of tracery and three long strap-hinges; another old door is in the south porch, and there is other fine old woodwork within the church, including the roof of the north aisle, and the nave roof supported by big wooden figures. The chancel screen has roses and quaint faces among its tracery, and projecting a foot on its western side are striking buttresses with pierced carving of window tracery. Old bench-ends have been used in making a table in the chancel, and others are in the pulpit. The 19th century lectern is a great oak eagle, keen-eyed and with powerful-looking talons.

In the north aisle are old glass quarries with yellow flowers and diamonds, and other fragments showing six letters of the inscription *Love God wyth al youre herte*. By one of the pillars of the north arcade are the rood stairs, an open flight leading to the opening above which now frames a figure of St Edith holding a crucifix. The 14th century font has a bowl with quatrefoils and shield on a traceried stem.

Grimsby. It is the biggest town in Lincolnshire and the first fishing seaport in the kingdom, and according to tradition it has all grown out of the kindly deed of a fisherman who saved the life of a king's son. The story, which is believed to have first been written during the period of the Danish invasions, tells how Havelok, son of Gunter, or Birkabeyn, King of Denmark, was treacherously put to sea in a boat after his father had been assassinated, and was rescued and brought up by a poor Lincolnshire fisherman named Grim. When he grew up, Havelok, a man of heroic physique, bravery, and attainments, succeeded in regaining his kingdom and bestowed great riches on his rescuer. With his great rewards Grim settled here and founded the place which still to this day bears his name. One of the town's ancient seals shows Grim with sword and shield and Havelok wearing a crown.

Grim's little settlement is now the premier fishing port of the world; but it was also important in early days, for history records that Richard I held a parliament here, and that King John came here twice and also gave the town its first charter. Henry VIII came here, too, during his Lincolnshire progress.

As a port Grimsby began early to decline, through the silting-up of the harbour; but it was able to contribute 11 ships and about 170 seamen for the Siege of Calais in the time of Edward III. Its phenomenal growth in modern times began when the little River

Freshney was diverted in 1800 into the silted-up Haven to form a new dock, now part of the Alexandra Dock. With the coming of the railway, linking the town with the great centres of industry, a new era of prosperity began. Another great step forward came at the end of last century when steam-power took the place of sail for the fishing fleet.

From the time when the first stone of the Royal Dock was laid by the Prince Consort, in 1849, the docks have steadily grown. Their present acreage is enormous—the three fish docks alone covering 64 acres of water—and they are equipped with the most up-to-date machinery for loading and discharging cargo. The covered fish market is a mile and a quarter long; and there are timber wharves, warehouses, and ice-factories. Those who love the sights of a working town may mount the stately brick tower (about 350 feet high and a landmark for miles) which provides hydraulic power for opening the dock gates and locks; they can then look down on a scene which surpasses anything of the kind to be seen elsewhere.

So far as fishing ships are concerned, Grimsby has hundreds of every type, from the latest deep-sea trawler fitted with radar to little open motor boats; and the number of fishermen working on these vessels is over 3000. Although the distant water and the North Sea fishing accounts for the great bulk of Grimsby's trade, there are still a few little inshore fishing boats.

Grimsby is, in fact, the most complete fishing port in the world. Vessels sailing from the port land everything from cod and haddock from the Arctic to cockles and shrimps from Tetney Haven. In consequence the market is the most varied in this country. Grimsby merchants dispatch parcels of all sorts of fish to customers in almost every part of the British Isles. In addition to the Grimsby ships, every year a considerable number of Iceland, Norwegian, and Danish fishing vessels land their catches in Grimsby.

It is hard to appreciate the quantities which are landed in Grimsby. In 1968 4,665,392 cwts. were landed, with a value of £23,195,144 including British and foreign landings.

Grimsby is not a great herring port. There is no longer a herring season at Grimsby.

On the other hand large quantities of herrings are brought to Grimsby both for further distribution and for curing. Thousands of cwts. of haddock and herrings and other fish are cured and sold during the course of a year. Since the war great strides have been made in the new process of the quick freezing of fish, enabling it to be kept fresh for months and to be sold when landings are short. Grimsby now has the greatest capacity for sub-zero storage in Europe. This includes vegetables as well as fish.

Large quantities of cod-liver oil are also produced and condemned fish, bones, tails, and scraps are converted into valuable fish manure and cattle feeding stuffs. All this means that the ancillary trades on the docks employ even far more men than work on the ships themselves. Hundreds of women, for example, are employed in the highly skilled operation of net-braiding, a thing which has to be done by hand.

Though the town of necessity wears a workaday dress, it reaches out to a green countryside. At Nun's Corner is a charming little Garden of Remembrance for 2100 Grimsby men who fought in the First World War, with a cenotaph of white marble rising from steps of Norwegian granite. Not far away, on the Welholme Road, is the People's Park given to the town by Lord Heneage in 1883; its 27 acres of lawns, gardens, lake, and playgrounds are enclosed in a beautiful avenue of trees in the form of a giant horseshoe.

Centuries ago Grimsby had an abbey, several smaller religious houses, and two fine churches; but the only historic structure that remains is the church of St James. The town hall of 1863 is in the Italian style—surmounted by a cornice and open balustrade, and with an open portico of Ionic columns. Adorning the front are six roundels with busts of Queen Victoria, who opened the Royal Docks, and the Prince Consort, who laid its foundation stone; John Whitgift, Elizabeth's Archbishop of Canterbury who is counted Grimsby's most famous son; Edward III; the Earl of Yarborough, High-Steward of the borough; and Gervase Holles, who fought for Charles I and was imprisoned by Parliament, but lived to collect materials for a seven-volume history of this, his native town.

Opposite the town hall are the municipal offices, set off by a narrow lawn. Facing the Dock Offices on the Cleethorpes road is a fine bronze statue of the Prince Consort holding a sceptre.

The church of St James has undergone much change, and bombing caused great damage during the Second World War. Shaped like a cross, it became the parish church when the church of St Mary was abandoned in the time of Elizabeth; and when that fine old building was taken down, about 1620, some of its materials were used to repair St James's.

In the year 1110 the original church of St James was given by the king to Wellow Abbey, a house of Austin canons which stood about 500 yards south of the church. It is believed that the canons were responsible for the rebuilding of the church about 1200, and much of the old work remaining is of this early pointed period of architecture. In 1365 the tower was rebuilt above the crossing by John Ingson, whose name is inscribed on one of the piers; the splendid 13th century arches supporting it are on piers adorned with 15th century panelling.

The nave has its old arcades of six bays, with richly-moulded arches on slender clustered piers; and above them is the triforium arcades which is enriched with clustered shafts, and has some of it-arches raised at intervals for the insertion of small clerestory wins dows. The transepts and chancel also have a triforium.

During unhappy alterations in the 18th century the chancel was reduced to half its length, the aisles were rebuilt in Georgian style, and the nave and aisles were cut off from the eastern part of the church by the bricking-up of their arches. The transepts actually became a roadway, and as time went on were used for such secular purposes as the election of the mayor, as a school, and for storing the fire-engine. During the several restorations of the 19th century the south transept was much rebuilt, the upper part of the west front (together with its three lancet windows) was renewed, and the chancel was lengthened. The south transept has a fine doorway with a hood of dog-tooth above its rich mouldings; the porch of the south aisle was built with old materials in the 18th century.

Early this century the aisles were given new windows with stone tracery, new buttresses, and new oak roofs. In 1904 the Lady Chapel (or Chapel of the Annunciation) was built on old foundations, opening from the north transept by two new arches set under two lofty ones of the 13th century. In this chapel lies a knight in armour, a fine 13th century figure with a lion at his feet; representing Sir Thomas Haslerton, it was brought here at the Dissolution from St Leonard's Nunnery which stood nearby, and which Sir Thomas had helped to rebuild after it had been destroyed by fire.

On the south side of the chancel is the lovely Chapel of the Resurrection, built on the site of a mediaeval chapel and entered by 13th century arches from chancel and south aisle. It is a war memorial and was designed by Sir Charles Nicholson.

The 700-year-old font has an 18th century cover, and the church also has two Jacobean chairs with carved backs, a curious old seat adorned with flowers and scrolls, and an old panelled chest with a band of ornament. The low chancel screen with panels of delicate pierced carving is a notable example of modern craftsmanship, and so is the splendid oak pulpit, enriched with flowers and foliage. A rare possession is a beautiful iron sword-rest at the Corporation pew. In the churchyard (near the south transept) is a worn pillar with clustered shafts, rising about 10 feet from an arcaded base.

The centre of Grimsby is undergoing great changes with modern planning and development. A splendid new public library in a modern four-storey building was opened in 1968; the Law Courts in 1969 are the first phase of a new shopping precinct adjoining Victoria Street in 1970.

Gunby. It is Gunby near Burgh—a pretty village at the foot of the Wolds. Its church, twice rebuilt last century, and the fine brick and stone Hall built in the reign of William and Mary for Sir William Massingberd, stand together among the grand trees of the park, looking across to the sea and the Norfolk coast beyond the Wash. Gunby Hall, which has about 1500 acres of grounds, belongs now to the National Trust, and its beautiful gardens are thrown open at times for all to see. The house has a fine staircase and attractive panelled rooms.

A path from the busy highway, for more than 100 yards a green tunnel of trees, opens to the church shaded by the mighty arms of a cedar which soars higher than the tower. Lighted by seven dainty candelabra, the church is notable for fine modern glass in its east window, and two splendid old brasses.

The window, showing St Cecilia and a choir of angels, is to Margaret Massingberd, whose portrait is seen in a little bronze plaque on the wall. An earlier member of this old Lincolnshire family was Sir Thomas Massingberd, who died about 1405, and whose brass here shows him with his wife Joanna, both lying under canopies and wearing SS collars. Sir Thomas is in armour, with camail and pointed bascinet; he has a great sword, his feet are on a lion, and his hands are clasped in prayer. His wife has a graceful gown and mantle, and a veil over her netted hair. In 1522 this brass was used for another Sir Thomas Massingberd, and given a fresh inscription.

The other brass has a portrait of William Lodyngton, who died in 1419, showing him in his judicial robes as Justice of the Common Pleas.

Gunness. A Trent-side village that has gained in importance as it stands at the east end of Keadby Bridge on the A18 where there is growing dockside and wharfing activity. Linked with the adjoining Burringlam it forms a thriving and growing community. A modern church erected in 1957 is dedicated to St Barnabas. It contains an interesting survival from the Commonwealth—a date-stone (1657) of a small chapel-at-ease.

Hacconby. Its name links it with marauding Danes of long ago, but for the rest it is as English as an April shower, a cluster of houses on a Fenland road, clinging like children to the apron strings of the mother church. Modern farming has brought an atmosphere of busy mechanised activity. There was a church here when the Domesday Book was compiled, but that has long since vanished, and the present building comes chiefly from the 13th and 14th centuries. Its oldest relic is a plain round Norman font, and its most striking features the nave arcades on their slender piers, and the graceful spire soaring so finely above the clerestory battlements and looking far over the flat lands which stretch away eastward as far as the eye can see.

The restored chancel still has a priest's doorway, an aumbry, and a piscina; and the 15th century north chapel, its walls a mass of windows, has stone seats and a piscina. Yet another piscina is in the south aisle, where there are two 13th century floorstones with carved crosses. A big time-worn chest is also here, and another smaller one with tracery, foliage, and six dragons carved six centuries ago. The east window has beautiful modern glass portraying Our Lord in Green Pastures, between the Reaper and the Sower, with fine figures above of St Guthlac of Crowland and St Gilbert of Sempringham.

Near the church is a fine gable and Jacobean house, Hacconby Hall, once the home of General Fynne, aide-de-camp to Oliver Cromwell. Two miles westward is the hamlet of Stainfield, known to the Romans; many of their coins have been unearthed there.

Haceby. A declining little farming community with a little church to match, now disused, but still with its plain Norman chancel arch, 13th century tower, and eight-sided mediaeval font. In the simple chancel a tablet to John Lucas-Calcraft who baptised all the new arrivals in the village for 55 years last century.

Many Roman remains have been unearthed hereabouts, and in an orchard by the main Grantham to Boston road, about a mile from the church, is the site of a Roman villa, now covered and over-grown with weeds.

Hackthorn. An avenue runs to it from Ermine Street, over a mile long and shaded all the way with canopies of fine English elm and sycamore, chestnut, beech, and ash. It is a delightful approach, and the scene at the end fulfils all expectation—great house so serene in its park, the church so well-cared for, the cottages so trim, the trees rising everywhere and casting impartial shade on one and all. Truly it is a place to remember.

The Hall is a late 18th century house built attractively of stone and the rebuilt church displays little evidence of antiquity. Reached by an embowered road skirting a lake in the park, it is an impressive building, its tower ennobled with quatrefoiled parapets, many gargoyles, and eight richly-crocketed pinnacles. A doorway in Norman style, with three deep rows of chevron ornament, leads to a lavishly furnished interior dignified by the lofty soaring chancel arch and nave arcade. Here too is great richness of ornament, for 14 angels bear up the nave and chancel roofs, and about 50 corbel heads of kings and queens and commoners adorn windows and arches and walls.

The old benches from the earlier church are now in Coleby Church, and the present modern pews are of carved mahogany, a timber used also in the altar-rails, reredos, and western gallery, all richly traceried, and in sumptuous harmony.

Hagworthingham. A big village with narrow, twisting lanes among the little hills, it has a churchyard overlooking a hollow in the Wolds, and, across the valley, a grassy barrow that is a far older burial-place.

The church was largely rebuilt last century, but some rough stonework and the great beams of the timber-framing in the low, sturdy tower may be Saxon, and there is a flat buttress perhaps as old. To an earlier church—between 1180 and 1200—belong the pillars of the nave arcade (the arches are 15th century work), and the lower part of the tower, which has a ring of eight bells.

A shaft piscina leaning against one of the nave pillars is Norman, and the font, with its bowl resting on a cluster of shafts, is 13th century; the chancel has its old low-side windows, and in the nave are two ancient, crude stones, one hollowed out.

Hainton. For 700 years it has been the home of the Heneages. The belts of stately beeches shading the highway are within the fine 145-acre park, landscaped by Capability Brown, which surrounds their ancestral home. The 17th century Hall has been much altered and the west wing was rebuilt in the early 19th century and the whole house faced with stucco. There is a 19th century chapel in the grounds.

The neighbouring church reaches still further into the past, for the lower part of its tower, with key-hole window and massive arch, comes from early Norman or even Saxon days. The slender spire is a later addition. The nave arcades are 13th century, and the aisles and the chancel chiefly 14th century, with nearly all the windows made new.

Most of the monuments are in the Heneage Chapel—a veritable gallery of art, enclosed by attractive iron gates. Some are brass portraits, and some are of stone and alabaster, radiant with colour and gold and so well preserved that they might be fresh from the hands of the sculptor.

Set in the floor are the brass portraits of John Heneage, 1435, with his wife Alice in a long-sleeved gown and horned headdress. A brass inscription of 1530 commemorates another John and his wife. Against the west wall is the painted stone tomb of a third John Heneage, who died in 1559, kneeling in armour at a table with his wife. Fine coats-of-arms adorn this memorial and above are spurs and a helmet.

Another great heraldic display is on the splendid alabaster tomb of Sir George Heneage (who died in 1595) in the middle of the chapel. He is a striking figure with his jet-black hair and beard and his richly-gilded armour, with his sword by his side, and an alert grey-hound at his feet. Exceptionally fine is the detail of this monument, showing even the stitching of the narrow strips of matting on which he rests.

Sir George's brother William, who was his heir and died in 1610 when 91, has a sumptuous wall-monument enriched with carvings and Latin texts; it shows him kneeling in armour with his two wives Anne and Jane. Jane served Elizabeth I 24 years, "in her bed-chamber and in her private chamber". Two sons and two daughters are kneeling below, and above the flowered canopy is a fine coat-of-arms crowned with a trumpeting angel. At one side Adam and Eve are under an apple tree, and on the other Our Lord is shown rising from the tomb.

Among other monuments in the chapel is one to Sir George Heneage, who died in 1660. Another has the busts of an 18th century Sir George with his two wives and an inscription extolling his many virtues, including "a perfect knowledge of mankind and of the manners of the politest countrys in Europe".

The chancel has the fine traceried altar tomb of Sir Thomas Heneage, who died in 1553, bearing splendid brass portraits of himself and his wife and daughter, all decorated with heraldic devices.

Haltham. Prettily set between the Haltham Beck and the River Bain, in the wooded country south of Horncastle, it is a small place with a thatched Elizabethan inn and a fine church with some good woodwork.

Three bells ring out from a low wooden belfry which is supported by an extraordinary box-like structure filling the west end of the nave. Its oldest possession is the south doorway of early Norman days, its massive tympanum enriched with the crudest carving of flowers, diamonds, knotwork, and cross. The nave has 14th century windows and a fine 13th century arcade with round arches; the pillars have stone seats round the base, and are crowned by capitals of overhanging foliage. The six-sided font with a band of flowers is six centuries old.

Except for the 15th century windows in its side walls, the splendid chancel displays the rich flowing style of 600 years ago—in its remarkably fine east window, and lovely priest's doorway, in its sedilia and aumbry. There is also a low-side window which has a mediaeval floorstone for roof and still keeps the old iron staples for shutters; and set in a window splay is a corner piscina with two trefoiled arches.

A rich store of 15th and 17th century woodwork gives this church one of the quaintest of interiors. One block of old oak benches looks eastward to a three-decker pulpit, and a bigger company looks southward to it from the aisle and the nave. Round this bigger group of seats is fine 15th century screenwork which itself encloses two pews, and there is also a simple box-pew adorned with parts of an old chancel screen. More parts of old screenwork are in the pulpit.

Halton Holgate. A charming village on the southern edge of the Wolds, between Spilsby and the River Lymn, it looks far across the Fens to Boston Stump, 15 miles away. Its name is descriptive, the "holgate" or "hollow-gate" being the road as it drops down to the valley—a deep cutting through the greenish sandstone.

Under a gabled shelter by the wayside is an attractive painted sign making puns on the words Halton and Holgate; it shows a horse and dray halting on the steep road by the church, and a red four-barred gate with a hole through it.

Except for its fine porch of Ancaster stone and its quoins of stone from Clipsham, the walls of its lovely 15th century church are of the local sandstone. Handsome outside, and spacious and lofty within, it was not marred by the three restorations of last century, during which the tower and chancel were partly rebuilt and many windows renewed.

The tower has stepped buttresses, great belfry windows, and a fine ring of bells. The porch has a doorway with spandrels of quatre-foiled tracery, and a parapet adorned with quatrefoils, quaint little heads, flowers, and tiny barrels. The nave has a clerestory with a grand array of 16 three-light windows, lighting up a fine roof enriched with shield-bearing angels and many ornamental bosses.

Many of the seats in nave and aisles have 15th century bench-ends, and others, work of a local carpenter, are excellent modern copies of the fine old bench-ends in Winthorpe Church. Old and new have splendid poppyheads with a great variety of carving—angels, owls, double heads, a man with a pitcher, and foxes running off with geese; round the base of one poppyhead are six monkeys and a crouching figure held by his hair. The church also has an old pillar almsbox.

The oldest monument is the 13th century floorstone of Sir Walter de Bec (with a Lombardic inscription); two other things older than the present building are the 14th century font (with worn carvings of tiny faces) and the splendid figure of a 14th century knight, cross-legged and with one lion at his feet and another on his shield. A quaint little brass on a wall shows Bridget Rugeley (hand on heart and book in hand), who died in 1658 at 21.

In the north aisle is a modern oak screen recording the names of rectors, churchwardens, and parish clerks who have served this place; carved at the foot of the screen are fish of all kinds swimming in a net.

A noteworthy son of this village was Thomas Grantham, a zealous leader of the General Baptists and a man who, like many others of his faith, was much persecuted in the years following the Restoration. He died in 1692, at the age of 58, and was buried in St Stephen's, Norwich. Another eminent divine believed to have been born here was John de Halton, who as Bishop of Carlisle from 1292 to 1324 was constantly embroiled in the wars against William and Robert Bruce.

Hameringham. From the road near this small village on the southern foothills of the Wolds there are sweeping views, with the towers of Lincoln in one direction, and Boston Stump in another.

Its neat little church has a modern bell-turret, and a nave rebuilt after falling down in 1893, but it still preserves some antiquity. The arcade, between nave and aisle, is 13th and 14th century work. Its pillars being in striking contrast to the later arches of green sandstone. Two of the capitals have overhanging foliage.

The fine font, with shields and tracery on the bowl and four canopied figures on the stem, is 15th century. The simple pulpit is Jacobean and still has its original hourglass in the stand to remind the preacher of passing minutes.

Harlaxton. Cottages with tall chimneys here nestle at the foot of a great park; on the little green stands the old cross, finely restored and decorated with shields and tracery; and near the church a quaint group of timbered houses look out serenely on their garden courtyard. In the lovely wooded park which climbs the hillside is an imposing mansion designed in Jacobean style by Anthony Salvin in early Victorian days. From 1966-69 it was the home of Stanford University in Britain but it is now standing empty. It is a most extravagant conception on the grand scale, with ornamented gables and a wealth of oriels and turrets. With the rise of this house came the destruction of the old; but a gateway of it remains and a graceful stone balustrade still adorns the lovely grounds of its successor.

At the old manor house lived the De Lignes, the first being Daniel, who sought refuge here from persecution in Flanders, was knighted by James I, and became High Sheriff of Lincolnshire. His black marble tomb is in the church, together with many memorials of his descendants.

The church is spacious, and reflects many changes through the centuries. The base of its tower is 14th century; the rest, with the spire, 15th century, a strange feature being the extension of the stairway into the spire by way of one of the pinnacles. Six pointed arches on either side of the nave make a brave array, and above them are 10 stone angels, praying or holding shields as they bear up the roof. The north arcade of the nave was built when the Norman style was passing, and the south arcade when the Early English style was developed. At the east end of the south aisle is a stairway from which a passage led to the rood-loft.

There are two mediaeval chantry chapels, and in a corner of the older one is a beautiful canopied niche with a bracket. In the north chapel, lying in a canopied recess adorned with angels and foliage, are 15th century alabaster figures said to be Sir Richard Rickhill and his wife in long-sleeved robes, their features very worn.

Among the other old possessions of the church are aumbries, a piscina, an old oak pillar almsbox, a battered old stone coffin, and a tall 600-year-old font which has among its varied carving a figure of Our Lord, crowned and holding a chalice.

The east window has modern glass of the Resurrection and Last Supper, and on either side of it is a niche, one with a statue of the Madonna, the other with St Peter.

Harmston. Serene among innumerable trees on its high place on the Cliff, it looks far west over the valley where the Brant falls into the Witham and the Roman Fosse Way is nearing Lincoln. On the eastern side of the village is Ermine Street.

Village and church are by the spacious park of Harmston Hall, which is now a hospital and has grown rapidly in recent years. It was built for Sir Charles Thorold in the early 18th century. The church is for the most part a mediaeval church made new in the 18th and 19th centuries, but its fine peal of eight bells ring out from a tower that has stood (except for the top) since the 11th century, and may even be Saxon. Tall and square, with the typical baluster shafts in the belfry windows, it has winged gargoyles looking like cats and demons, and its wide round arch to the nave has capitals carved with leaves. A fine fragment of a Saxon cross, 40 inches high, is also treasured in the church; found built into the walls of the manor house, it is carved with knotwork, the Crucifixion on one side and a much-worn Resurrection on the other.

Among the memorials to the Thorolds is a brass inscription to Margaret, who had 19 children and lived to be 80, dying in 1616. Her eldest son, who died the same year, has another brass plate. Sir George Thorold, Lord Mayor of London in 1720, has a chancel monument adorned by his bewigged head, a praying cherub on one side and a weeping cherub on the other; and his brother Samuel has a similar monument on the facing wall. Modern glass in the windows makes a fine gallery of saints with figures of Cecilia, Catherine, Peter, Andrew and Edward the Confessor; St Hugh is also here with two other Bishops of Lincoln, Robert Grosseteste and the beloved Edward King.

In the churchyard lies John Willson, who cast in Coade stone the gigantic statue of George III set up in 1810 to mark the king's jubilee on the top of Dunston Pillar which stands, although reduced in height, on the edge of the heath about 2 miles away. His grave-stone has a rough carving of the pillar and the inscription:

> *He who erected the noble king*
> *Here laid low by Death's sharp sting.*

In recent times his statue of the king has also been laid low, and awaits restoration in the Museum of Lincolnshire Life in Lincoln.

Harpswell. Reached by the road running east from Gains-borough, it has the wooded slope of the Cliff for background, and an ancient church on the steep hillside, with two great limes shading its entrance.

The tower, with 15th century parapet and a 13th century lancet in its west wall, has stood since the second half of the 11th century, the belfry having the typical two-light windows with baluster shafts. From the close of Norman days comes the arcaded font. To the 13th century belong the chancel (with blocked low-side window) and the south nave arcade. There is a fine west window in the aisle with late 13th century plate tracery. An inscription on the tower marks the presentation of a clock (not the present clock) in 1746 in honour of "the victory over the rebels" at the Battle of Culloden. There are a few old pews, and the oak beam between the nave and chancel has the date 1642.

The oldest memorial is an engraved floorstone with a Norman-French inscription and the portrait of John Gere, parson here in the time of Edward I, in his robes, his hands clasped in prayer. A figure of William de Harrington, a 14th century rector, lies in the chancel.

Sir Thomas Whichcot, who restored the church in 1891, belonged to a family prominent here ever since John Whichcot married Margaret Tyrwhit in the 15th century. Two brasses, showing a knight in full armour and lady, date from the late 15th century.

Harrington. Rebuilding during the 54 years' ministry last century of rector Robert Cracroft has left the church little of its antiquity save for its mediaeval tower arch and font, an old chancel seat with carved poppyheads, and a goodly array of monuments of people who knew this place in days gone by—Harringtons, Cople-dikes, and Amcotts. The richly-carved 15th century font was the gift of the Copledikes, the bowl having their shields held by grotesques and other figures.

The oldest monument in this trim, well-cared-for church is the striking figure of a knight, lying cross-legged under an arch in the nave wall; he wears fine chain-mail and is thought to be Sir John Harrington of about 1300. The earliest Copledike memorial is the shining brass portrait of Margaret of 1480. Under the canopy of a tomb in the chancel are the 16th century brasses of Sir John and

Ann Copledike, both kneeling at desks. Sir John's brother Francis has a canopied wall-monument showing him as a kneeling alabaster figure in armour, with his wife in a farthingale, and two children; and a stone to Francis's nephew, Thomas Copledike of 1658, ends their story with an inscription proclaiming that "of ancient stock here lies the last and best".

The home of the Copledikes stood close to the church, and was rebuilt in 1673 by Vincent Amcotts. It has an impressive brick front, part of which is Elizabethan, with a projecting porch as high as the house, and a sundial over the doorway with the date 1681 and the arms of the Amcotts. A later generation of these Amcotts were warm friends of Tennyson's father, and we may be sure that Tennyson as a boy knew this place well, and that his imagination would be stirred by its old panelled walls and their quaint carving, by the walled-in garden, and by the rooks flocking in from miles round; and, indeed, to quote Canon Rawnsley's *Memories of the Tennysons*, "it is not straining the force of early association too far to imagine that Tennyson had this garden and the quiet rookery beyond it in his mind when he wrote"

> *Birds in the high Hall-garden*
> *When twilight was fading,*
> *Maud, Maud, Maud, Maud,*
> *They were crying and calling.*

The picturesque Woodman's Cottage has recently been restored and rethatched.

Hatcliffe. It is charmingly set in a lovely Wold valley where a stream flows swiftly by to the Marsh and the sea. The village is attracting new building with consequent change. The little church is much restored but the plain south doorway and the font tell of its Norman origin. The tower has 13th century lancets in the bell-chamber, and its west window and its arch to the nave are 15th century work. The chancel keeps its old entrance arch, and in its north wall is an arch (leading to the modern vestry) which was part of the mediaeval arcade now built up in the north wall of the nave. Other points of interest are two floorstones with worn portraits of 16th century Hatcliffes, and a pre-Reformation bell.

Haugh. An attractive picture awaits all who come to this tiny place on the eastern slope of the Wolds—a line of ancient yews leads to a Tudor manor house the home of the Bolle family.

The little church (less than 50 feet from east to west) was restored in 1873, but still has a Norman chancel arch and a Transitional-Norman doorway in the north wall of the nave. Among its old relics are a piscina and a traceried font.

There are also two old monuments of interest. One is an inscription with coats-of-arms, set up in 1590 to Charles Bolle and all his four wives, the first lady being a Dymoke of "broad Scrivelsby" and the last a Dymoke of Friskney. The other, a fine monument with double canopy and cornice, is to his son, Sir John Bolle, who kneels here with his wife and eight children. (The eldest of the three sons raised a regiment of foot for Charles I.)

Sir John Bolle, who built Thorpe Hall, near Louth, was a gallant Elizabethan captain who was with the Earl of Essex at the Siege of Cadiz in 1596.

Haugham. A pleasant village in a typical Wold setting. Across the highway are the lovely Haugham and Burwell Woods, and the charming "Haugham Pastures" which are now ploughed over. From the tree-lined road leading to the highway a great mound can be seen in a corner of a field; it was a Bronze Age burial mound.

The village church stands in a field, sheltering in a clump of trees and with a cottage for company. Rebuilt in 1840, it is in 15th century style, and notable for its decorated stucco work. The gables of nave and chancel have parapets of open quatrefoils, and the tower has a pierced parapet with tall, turret pinnacles from which traceried flying buttresses spring to the richly-crocketed spire. Within the church is a 15th century font with carved tracery and shields.

Of the small Benedictine priory founded here by Hugh, 1st Earl of Chester, little trace remains. In the reign of Richard II its possessions were transferred to the Carthusian priory of St Anne, near Coventry.

Hawerby. From the hill above its great house, Hawerby Hall, the mouth of the Humber can be seen in the distance, with the faint line of the Yorkshire coast.

In a corner of the park near the Hall is a small church crowned by a double bellcot. Chiefly restored 13th century work, it has three arches and one capital of its old nave arcade visible outside in the south wall, with the old doorway and an original lancet window set under two of them. The chancel has its old low-side window, and, in front of the altar step, an old coffin-lid with a foliated cross. The bowl of the font is Norman, and one of the two bells has rung out since the Middle Ages.

Haxey. In days gone by this little market town was the capital of the Isle of Axholme, and fragments of crosses marking the sites of its old markets and fairs are still to be seen. One is on the Misterton road; another is on the little green, sheltered by three sycamores and carved with the arms of Mowbray, the exiled Duke of Norfolk who comes into Shakespeare's *Richard II*; and a third is outside the churchyard.

Standing impressively at the top of the long street, the church is for the most part restored 15th century work. The 500-year-old tower is 100 feet high, and has a ring of seven bells renowned in this fertile countryside. The oldest fragments of the church are the pillars of the north arcade, which, together with one pillar on the south side, are of the Norman period. The rest of the arcades is 13th century work, and so are the arches of chancel and chapel. The nave has a grand 15th century roof with moulded beams and floral bosses.

On a recessed tomb in the chapel lies an old stone figure of a priest; and on the wall above hangs an ancient charter of 1336, granting a gift of land from Maud, wife of Walter de Brunham of Haxey.

The tower screen, altar table, and stone pulpit were the work of John Johnstone, a 19th century vicar, Notable among his predecessors were John Lamb who ministered here for half a century, and Spencer Madan, who was chaplain to George III and went from Haxey in 1792 to become Bishop of Bristol.

Two notable mediaeval customs are still observed here. One is a peculiar game—called Haxey Hood, or throwing the Hood—played on the sixth of January. It is akin to Rugby Football, with grand scrimmages in which twelve "boggins" or ploughboys and a "fool" try to keep a hood or sackcloth while the rest of the people of Haxey and the neighbouring parish of Westwoodside take part with great zest and try to seize it and take it to one of the local pubs. The other is an ancient system of farming known as strip cultivation, the land being divided into parallel strips each 16½ feet wide and covering half an acre.

Healing. Leafy roads add to the charm of this big village between Grimsby and Immingham, and a lovely avenue leads to the church and manor house. The overspill from Grimsby is changing the character of the place with new building.

The church is a mediaeval one, partly rebuilt and much restored last century, when the chancel was given its open oak roof of trussed beams. The old tower still stands, its west doorway beautiful with rich mouldings under an ogee hood adorned with fine crockets, tall pinnacles, and finials; its doors are studded and have panels of fine tracery. By the tower lies an old stone sundial.

By the road to Riby Gap is Healing Wells, a spring long thought to have the quality of healing and to have given this place its name.

Heapham. Lying in the byways, with the headstreams of the River Till flowing round it, it has a tower windmill now without sails and a small church standing lonely in the fields.

Restored in 1868, the church reveals its long history with a tower thought to have been built just before the Normans came. It has the Saxon two-light belfry windows, and has been given buttresses to support it in its old age. A little elder-tree flourishes on the top of the tower, and down below, its original crude arch, cut in a wall 3 feet thick, opens to a nave which is shorter than the chancel.

The low tub font is Norman though it stands on a 15th century embattled capital. The 13th century is represented by some lancet-windows, the chancel arch, and the nave arcade on which are two quaint heads upside down. The altar-rails are old, and near them is a modern chair with a carved panel showing Heapham's ancient tower among the trees.

Heckington. Everyone who wishes to appreciate fully how greatly the charm of rural England is enhanced by the nobility of its churches should visit Heckington; for here unquestionably is one of the most perfect examples of a 14th century church, not only in Lincolnshire, but in all the land. This big village on the edge of the Fens, not far from Sleaford, has also a magnificent tower windmill with eight sails. It is dated 1830 and the gear was brought from an old Boston mill. It is now maintained by the Kesteven County Council. It also has a green bordered by an inviting group of 19th century almshouses. But when all these have long since been forgotten by the traveller, its wonderful church will be remembered.

Heckington had a church in Saxon times, which the Normans rebuilt, but the present one is no patchwork of the centuries. It was completely built during the 14th century as it stands today, and it owes its magnificence largely to the rich Abbey of Bardney, which already had a chantry here when in 1345 it obtained a royal licence to appropriate the church. The monks proceeded to build up an enduring monument of English architecture at its best; that is its distinction—that, and the fact that although it is the third church on the site, it embodies none of the features of the earlier two, save perhaps their foundations.

The church is 150 feet long from east to west, and 85 feet across the transepts. Time has mellowed the fine stonework, and it has been well and reverently restored. The north aisle and transept were already standing when the abbey took possession, but the nave and chancel, the west tower and spire, and then the porch, all followed within the span of about 35 years, built with a steadily pursued completeness between 1345 and 1380. Everywhere outside there is rich carving—in buttresses with canopied niches, pinnacles, turrets, parapets, gargoyles, and window tracery.

The stately tower has four tall pinnacles like turrets, rather tending to dwarf the grand spire, with its three tiers of gabled lights, which soars 182 feet. The fine porch has its original timber rafter roof, many canopied niches, and a small figure of Our Lord enthroned among the wavy tracery below the gable. At the east end of the nave are two turrets enclosing the staircases which led to the rood-loft.

Within the church the wealth of ornament is confined to the chancel, though doubtless the walls were once glorious with paintings. But it is a noble interior, and it is good to stand below the timber gallery from which the belfry is reached, and to survey the symmetry and beauty of the scene—the four fine, pointed arches on clustered piers each side, linking nave and aisles, the lofty clerestory above, the taller arches of the transepts beyond, and the great chancel arch opening to the chancel. It is an impressive scene and a wonderful testimony to the genius of our 14th century architects.

Outstanding among the windows are those of the transepts, and the east window of the chancel, magnificent with its seven lights and rich flowing tracery. This east window, 19 feet wide and nearly 36 feet high, ranks with the finest 14th century windows in England, and it is filled with modern glass portraying Our Lord in Majesty surrounded by angels, prophets, martyrs, apostles, and saints. The Benedicite is in the tracery, and figures symbolic of the continents are gathered round in praise, Europe being a portrait of William Little, the 19th century farmer to whose memory this Te Deum window was inserted.

The chancel, its beauty so enhanced by this east window, was built by Richard de Potesgrave, who could boast not only of being vicar here but also of being chaplain to Edward III. So highly did the king esteem this priest that he chose him to take charge of the removal of his father's body from Berkeley Castle to Gloucester. Fittingly enough, Richard de Potesgrave was laid to rest in his chancel; his stone effigy, showing him in his rich vestments, is under an arch in the north wall and is well-preserved, though the face is damaged. He is portrayed again in the fine modern glass of a south transept window, clad in rich purple among a company of men and women in fine mediaeval raiment; he is showing a model and plan of the church of Henry de Beaumont, who was tenant here under the king.

Next to Richard de Potesgrave's monument in the chancel is his Easter Sepulchre, surpassed in its rich decoration by only one other example in England—at Hawton in Notts. Both of these Easter Sepulchres, and probably the other fine example at Navenby in this county, were the work of the same sculptor. All the figures of the Easter story are here. The Roman soldiers asleep in their armour are below; the three Marys and an angel are on each side of the recess where the Host would lie from Good Friday to Easter morning; and Our Risen Lord is above the recess with an angel at each side. All the figures are under rich foliated canopies with fine finials, and the panels at the top are carved with foliage in the flowing style. The three canopied sedilia and double piscina in the opposite wall were doubtless by the same sculptor and form another fine composition with lavish decoration. The three trefoiled and gabled canopies of the sedilia are adorned with a mass of delicate foliage, and above them are figures of Our Lord, the Madonna, and four saints, being crowned by tiny angels in the cornice.

Approached by steps from the chancel is the old sacristy, used now as a vestry; it has a double piscina, and below it is a low vaulted crypt which was used as a skull house. The north transept has two piscinas and an aumbry, and the south transept has three sedilia, a floorstone with the bust of a 14th century man in a deeply sunk quatrefoil, and another stone with the impress of the brass portraits of a 15th century knight and his lady. Both transepts also have their ancient roofs, and so have the aisles. In the west window are some fragments of old glass making a mosaic of colour, and standing high on three steps is the six-sided font looking a little weary of the burden of six centuries. Out in the churchyard are the base and shaft of an ancient cross.

Heighington. From its hilltop the towers of Lincoln Cathedral can be seen in all their majesty.

The little church was built as a "chapel of ease" for the convenience of the villagers when the weather was too bad for the journey to the parish church at Washingborough. Originally built in Norman times, it had fallen into disuse by the time of James I. It was then that Thomas Garratt, who had bought land here, founded a school and fitted up the old chapel for the purpose. The school was for the youth and children of the inhabitants of Heighington, Washingborough, and Branston. So it remained until 1868, when a new school was built alongside and the old building became a church once more.

And that is why the village church stands in a school playground, and gargoyles on the 13th century tower look down on children at their play. The tower has a parapet pierced with quatrefoils, and one solitary pinnacle carved with a ring of imps; at its base is a massive Norman arch with a man's head at each side.

Helpringham. It is a big village on the edge of the Fens, with red-tiled and slate-roofed cottages scattered on the edge of the fields, lining the broad highway, and gathered round the chestnuts on the green. At the heart of it is the mediaeval church, one of a splendid company for which Kesteven is famed.

The chancel, with its triplet east window and lovely trefoil-headed sedilia and piscina, comes from the closing years of the 13th century. But the rest is younger—the tower, nave, and aisles 14th century, the clerestory and spire 15th. The west front is a splendid sight. The great buttresses of the tower climb to bold pinnacles which are linked by flying buttresses to the lofty crocketed spire. High-pitched roofs of the aisles flank the steeple on either side, and fine windows and a lovely recessed doorway with four depths of moulding all add to the richness of architectural design.

The interior is also impressive, the tower opening to the nave and aisles with three great pointed arches, and the nave having four more arches on each side, resting on clustered columns and adorned with six little heads, a bishop and a king among them; higher still, the light streams in through eight clerestory windows. Both aisles have aumbries and piscinas (one of them graceful with a trefoil-headed canopy and small heads of a man and woman), and the 13th century font is enriched with lancet arcading, nail-head, and a rough carving of the Holy Lamb. In a turret at a corner of the nave is the stairway which led to the rood-loft.

Old woodwork adds to the charm of this place. There are plain, workmanlike benches of the 16th century in the nave, a simple oak pulpit a century younger, a 15th century screen with seven traceried arches, and a chest with iron bands. Modern symbolical figures of Faith, Hope, and Charity shine in the east window of the chancel, and the east window of the south aisle has an attractive picture of the Annunciation.

Hemswell. Time has wrought its changes, and a tall pole with a fox for a weathervane stands where the maypole of Merrie England once stood. The old church has changed, too, for in the 18th century the 500-year-old tower was rebuilt and the mediaeval south aisle was destroyed. Among the late 14th century work still remaining are the nave arcade, the bowl of the font with the arms of Monson (on a modern stem), and the sedilia adorned with trefoiled arches, leafy gables, and heads of a wimpled woman and three men in flat caps.

Heydour. It has a spacious church displaying architectural styles of many centuries. The base of the tower is Norman and has a small doorway with dog-tooth ornament. The chancel is 13th century, the nave and stone-vaulted porch 14th, and the clerestory and spire 15th. The chancel has fine sedilia, a founder's tomb, and two peepholes from a chantry chapel; on either side of its arch is a doorway to a rood-loft stairway. There is an oak chest perhaps 450 years old, finely carved with three heads set in roundels, and a 600-year-old font with the tracery on one of its eight sides incompleted.

Several 18th century memorials pay tribute to the Newtons who lived a mile away at Culverthorpe Hall, a handsome 17th century mansion with a great lake in its grounds which borders the highway.

One of the memorials is by Scheemakers, and shows Lady Anne Newton with a cherub on each side; another, with figures of two mourning women, is to Sir Michael Newton; and a third, by Rysbrack, praises the virtues of his wife, Countess of Coningsby.

But the great treasure of the church is the old glass in two north aisle windows, given by Geoffrey le Scrope, a 14th century prebend of Haydor. One window has splendid figures of Edward the Confessor in armour of silver and gold, St George with shield and spear, and St Edmund with sword upraised. The other has beautiful glowing figures of St Vincent, St Lawrence with a big silver gridiron, and St Stephen holding stones of his martyrdom.

In a field west of the church are traces of the moat of a castle believed to have been built here in the 12th century. The priory south of the church is a 17th century building.

Hibaldstow. It is the village of St Hibald, who is thought to have been Abbot of Bardney, though he is a shadowy figure and nothing is known of him save a reference in the Venerable Bede's writings of one Hygbald, "a most holy man", who went from Britain on a visit to a Father Egbert in Ireland, there to discuss the lives of the former saints and rejoice in imitating them. Here he is said to have been laid to rest.

When the nave was rebuilt in 1875 the old tower fell, it was rebuilt in 1958–60 and reflects 15th century details; it has a pyramid roof. The tower arch is 13th century but heavily restored. Apart from this, the 15th century bowl of the font (enriched with flowers, faces, and angels) is the only old relic left in the church of St Hibald.

Between Hibaldstow and Kirton was the deserted village of Gainsthorpe, on the line of the Ermine Street, and there are mounds which belong perhaps to a Roman settlement, for Roman coins and remains of tessellated paving have been found close by.

High Toynton. The old church was rebuilt in 1872, but its Norman origin is displayed in the remains of two arches above the tower doorways. One of the two bells is probably mediaeval; it was brought back to the church in 1934 after being at the Queen Elizabeth Grammar School, Horncastle, since 1772.

Holbeach. A bright little market town midway between Spalding and the Wash. It lies on a stretch of highway notable for its range of fine old churches. It came into Domesday Book, and evidence of Roman occupation comes to light from time to time, and considerable settlement has been seen from the air.

The charter for the town's market and fair was obtained in 1252 by Thomas de Multon, whose family became lords of Holbeach in the 12th century. After them came the De Kirtons, and it was a

John de Kirton who founded here a hospital in 1351; it stood opposite the parish church, where the Chequers Inn stands now, and its ruins were taken down at the end of the 17th century by the father of the famous antiquary William Stukeley.

Standing in a churchyard shaded by magnificent trees and carpeted in spring with wild hyacinths, the stately church is a fine example of the rich flowing style which prevailed towards the close of the 14th century, and has been well restored. Many of the windows have the typical flamboyant tracery, and some (in tower and clerestory) belong to the early 15th century period.

The tower has huge stepped buttresses, great five-light windows, and a shallow west porch with a traceried roof and a gable cross. The spire, soaring to 180 feet, has four tiers of louvre lights. The splendid embattled clerestory has 14 windows on each side. The nave has a sanctus bellcot, and a corner turret with the rood-loft stairway. The chancel has great windows deeply-moulded and beautifully traceried, stepped buttresses with traceried heads, and a priest's doorway. The south porch has a remarkably tall and narrow entrance arch and a gable as high as the aisle roof; it shelters a fine old door. Even more remarkable is the great north porch with traceried entrance arch and flanking embattled turrets; one of these turrets is groined, and the other has a stairway which led to an upper room before the dividing floor was taken away. It is thought that this singular porch was brought from Moulton Castle when that fell into decay five centuries ago.

Bright and spacious is the interior of the church. The tower has a vaulted roof, and a huge arch leading to a nave with lofty, leaning arcades. Their arches, seven on each side, are supported by clustered pillars, and between the clerestory windows above them are old stone heads of men and grotesques carrying a fine modern hammerbeam roof with two angels at its eastern end. The east and west windows add a happy touch of colour with the Last Supper and the Ascension.

Below the east window is a carved and coloured oak reredos, with scenes of the Nativity, the Crucifixion, and the Ascension, and dainty statues of saints and bishops and angels. The much-restored sedilia and piscina have rich decoration, and the ancient font is adorned with angels.

On his sumptuous table tomb in the north aisle lies the figure of Sir Humphrey Littlebury, who lived at Penny Hill Hall and is said to have been slain during the Wars of the Roses, about 1400. The figure is finely sculptured and portrays Sir Humphrey in rich armour with a handsome belt of medallions; his feet are on a great lion, and his head rests on the life-sized head of a man in a netted hood. On a stone tomb near Sir Humphrey's is the brass of a 15th century lady, Joanna Welby, showing her in draped headdress, long flowing mantle, and heavy girdle. On the floor between the two tombs is the brass of a headless knight with sword and dagger, his feet on a lion. An 18th century wall tablet, in memory of Jane Davey, who died at 24, is notable for these quaint words:

> *Life is a journey of a winter's day;*
> *Where many breakfast, and then post away.*
> *Some few stay dinner, and depart, full fed,*
> *Few be that sup, and then retire to bed.*

Among the names on Holbeach's roll of fame are William Stukeley and Henry Rands. William Stukeley, an attorney's son born here in 1687, was a man in whom intense love of learning was mingled with old superstitions. He was a zealous student of the Past, and is remembered as one of the founders, in 1717, of the Society of Antiquaries. The house where he lived is now the local Council offices. Henry Rands, one of the compilers of the Prayer Book, called himself Henry Holbeach on entering Crowland Monastery. He became Bishop of Lincoln in 1547, but brought discredit on himself by surrendering the estates of his See to the Crown for personal gain.

A third native of Holbeach was the dramatist Susannah Centlivre, born about 1667. She is supposed to have been the daughter of a man named Freeman who suffered in the political and religious persecutions following the Restoration. Susannah was only 23 when she wrote her first play, six years before her marriage to Joseph Centlivre, who became chef to Queen Anne and George I; and she followed this with practically one a year until her death in 1723. She had rich powers in comedy, in the invention of comic plot, and in humorous dialogue. One of her plays gave Garrick a favourite rôle.

Holton. Sometimes called Holton Beckering, to distinguish it from other Lincolnshire Holtons, it takes its second name from the nearby hamlet across a stream.

An avenue of yews leads to its church, well restored last century but made rather sombre with painted walls and stained windows. What is old is chiefly 15th century work.

The chancel has a tall oak screen, modern and richly traceried, and a reredos of shining mosaic, showing the Crucifixion and the Four Evangelists. The plain old font has a modern cover richly adorned with ironwork.

Holton-le-Clay. A village changing rapidly with modern bungalows. Its small church, a patchwork of brick and stone, was almost rebuilt last century, and only the tower, from the top of which the sea can be glimpsed, bears the impress of antiquity. The lower part of this tower was built before the Normans came, and primitive indeed it looks, with its rough stone walling, small west window, and tall arch opening to the nave. The top storey, with its fearsome gargoyles, is 14th century work.

A stone altar, a piscina by the chancel arch, and a battered Norman font enriched with herringbone, plaited ornament, and interlacing arches, are other tokens of the church's age. Standing by the font is a cracked 14th century bell.

Holywell. A little Lincolnshire gem in a hollow near the Rutland border, it has all the beauty of steep, winding lanes, a shimmering lake with sheep and cattle browsing on its tranquil shores, and the shade of immemorial trees. From a bridge there is an enchanting view of the lake, with the fine 18th century Hall in its wooded grounds beyond, and the church tower peeping above the trees.

The little church, standing serenely by the lawn of the Hall, was built early in the 18th century and has stones in its walls brought from the ancient church at Aunby a mile away. Two pillars helping to support the tower are Norman, the doorway with clustered shafts and foliage capitals is 14th century, and there is a carved chest of Charles II's time. In the east window is some old Dutch glass showing men feasting, and also a curious medley of 15th century fragments found buried long ago in the neighbouring village of Careby.

Honington. An attractive village with grey stone walls and the shade of innumerable trees. It has a pretty church in a delightful churchyard with rose-bordered path. It has history, too, for it boasts the largest Iron Age fort in the county. Situated on the heath, it commands the important Ancaster Gap and its elaborate and well-preserved triple defences testify to its strength and strategical importance. An urn containing Roman coins was found within the defences and this may indicate further use of Honington Camp by the Romans. A mile walk from the village to this site also gives its reward of fine views, into which comes Boston Stump.

In such a corner of ancient Britain a mediaeval church seems comparatively new; nevertheless it goes back to Norman days. The tower is 13th century and its quatrefoiled parapet and pinnacles were added 500 years ago. The chancel is as old as the tower, but traces of the round Norman arch can be seen above the pointed one. On one side of the arch is the rood-loft stairway, and on the other is a peephole with a renewed arch in Norman style with zigzag moulding.

The massive arcade, with big round pillars, is also Norman, and on one of its capitals is a grotesque face. High above, six angel corbels support the old nave roof. The aisle is 15th century and so is the font with Moses and John the Baptist among the little figures on its pedestal.

Among the memorials is a stone engraved with the figure of William Smith in doublet and hood of Henry VIII's time; there is also one with the bewigged marble head of 17th century Thomas Hussey.

Close by is Honington Hall, built in the Victorian period—lovely and gabled and grey, and with a tower taller than that of the church.

Horbling. Lying where the road from Bourne turns eastward for its journey across the Fens, it is an attractive village with charming old cottages, an ever-flowing spring shaded by chestnuts, and a cross-shaped church built long ago by the monks of Sempringham.

Venerable is the low late Norman central tower with its pointed arches leaning outward, weary with age. Ever since it was built it has given trouble because of poor foundations; iron bars help to support it, and it bears the mark also of partial rebuilding in mediaeval days. Its pinnacled top is 15th century. The work of the Normans is also seen in the remains of arcading on the west front, and also in the chancel, with its two narrow Norman windows on each side. The three lancets of the east window are modern, but underneath is a Norman stringcourse with zigzag. The four pointed arches on each side of the nave are 13th and 14th century work and the great west window (with modern glass of 15 saints and apostles), and the clerestory, with eight windows on each side, are 15th century.

The font has the Instruments of the Passion, carved on its bowl nearly 600 years ago, and in the north transept is a mediaeval recess with a shield supported by an armoured knight and a lady with butterfly headdress; they are believed to be the parents of Thomas de la Laund, who was killed at the Battle of Loosecoat Field near Stamford in 1470. The monument has been used as an Easter Sepulchre, and above it is a small sculptured group showing St Thomas looking at the wounds of Our Lord.

Horkstow. It is one of the string of villages on the north-western edge of the Wolds which are notable for their lovely views. From its quiet churchyard can be seen the long smooth line of the Cliff bounding a view of the Carrs through which, close at hand, the Old and New River Ancholme and the Weir Dike are on their way to the Humber.

A noble elm and other great trees add to the charm of the church's setting. It is for the most part a mediaeval building, restored in the 19th century, and has a 13th century tower wearing a later pantiled cap. Earlier than the rest is the north arcade of the nave with slightly pointed arches and round pillars from the close of the Norman period.

An arresting feature of the interior is the extraordinary effect given by the chancel. From the west end it looks rather like a cavern, with its walls bridged by three arches and its ten steps rising in three stages to the altar—six from the nave, and then in pairs. The rise is caused by the Shirley vault below.

One treasure from Horkstow has joined others in the British Museum. It is part of a Roman pavement found here in 1796; it was in three sections, and included a fine portrayal of a chariot race and another scene of Orpheus taming the beasts.

Horkstow is also famous as the place where George Stubbs dissected horses during his anatomical studies leading to his fine horse paintings.

Horncastle. This pleasant little town, lying where the Wolds come down to the Fens, was a walled town in Roman Britain and also played a decisive part during the Civil War. Long celebrated for its great August horse fair (once the biggest in the land), Horncastle has a niche, too, in English literature; for George Borrow's *Romany Rye* has several chapters telling of his experiences after he had wended his way to this "small town, seemingly ancient and crowded with people and horses". Fascinating chapters they are, too, telling how he sold his fine steed at the horse fair and of "half a dozen cautions" from the ostler at the inn who the previous night had informed him that his master was busy drinking wine with some of the grand gentry and couldn't be disturbed "for the sake of the like of you"; and of the evening he spent listening to the extraordinary tales of the jockey from Suffolk and the gentleman from Hungary.

Busy with much traffic to and from the North Sea coast, Horncastle stands on the banks of the River Bain and the Waring, and their meeting forms the horn-like tongue of land from which the town takes part of its name. The Romans built here a walled town enclosing an area of 7 acres. It is thought that they called it Banovallum, the walled place on the Bain. Excavations have revealed a fine length of the Roman wall on the site of a new Branch Library alongside the canal. Bastions have been found by excavation and a portion of Roman wall still exists in the foundations of a building in a coal-merchant's yard at South Bridge. There is also a long stretch skirting an alley at the south-west corner of the churchyard; other portions, 6 or 7 feet high, are in the walls of a school close by.

It was in the autumn of 1643 that Horncastle became involved in the Civil War. The Cavaliers were besieging Hull, and the Roundheads advanced to its relief from Boston, besieging Bolingbroke Castle by the way. Fairfax had occupied Horncastle for Parliament, but 75 troops of Cavaliers and 5000 foot soldiers were coming from Lincoln to check the Parliament men, so Fairfax fell back and concentrated with Cromwell, who had 37 troops of horse with about 6000 foot. The battle, however, was determined by the horsemen.

They met at the hamlet of Winceby, on the high ground between Horncastle and Spilsby. Though his men and horses were weary after their travels, Cromwell charged at once. The royal dragoons fired two volleys, the last at pistol-shot distance, and then the Ironsides were upon them. Cromwell had his horse shot dead under him, and, on struggling to his feet, he was charged again by Sir Ingram Hopton, a doughty Cavalier, who called on him to surrender. They were swept asunder, however, and Cromwell, seizing another horse, joined in a second charge which sent the Cavaliers helter-skelter through Horncastle and Lincoln, only to draw rein when they reached Newark. At once Bolingbroke surrendered, the Royalists raised the siege at Hull, and all Lincolnshire became a Parliamentary recruiting ground. The Winceby battle, in which Cromwell came so near to death, had sealed his fame.

In the rout which followed the second charge Sir Ingram Hopton was slain, and the next day Cromwell rode into Horncastle, sought out the churchwarden, and arranged with him that his doughty antagonist should have honourable burial in the church. Such was the chivalrous tribute paid by the "arch-rebel" (as Sir Ingram's hatchment in the church rather meanly describes Cromwell) to the memory of a beaten foe, fallen in battle. That night Cromwell slept in a house that has since been destroyed; it was in West Street, next door to the one now called Cromwell House.

Horncastle's mediaeval church has been much restored and partly rebuilt. The tower, crowned by a 19th century leaded spire, is 13th and 15th century, and is notable for an arch with responds merging without capitals into the mouldings. The nave has 14th century arcades, with stem and leaf carving on the two western capitals; the clerestory running through nave and chancel is late 15th century; and the nave has a Tudor roof with moulded beams, resting on angels of oak and stone.

There is 13th century masonry in the east wall of the chancel, but its east window with leaf tracery is modern. In the north wall of the sanctuary is a little barred window, once open to the daylight, but now looking into a vestry; and on the other side of the chancel is an old shaft piscina with a crocketed ogee head. The traceried screen-work on both sides of the chancel is chiefly 15th century, with modern embattled cornices.

The church possesses a chest of 1690, and also some old chained books in a case. A rarer sight is the collection of 13 scythe blades which may have been used in the Winceby fight or else in the Lincolnshire Rising in defence of the monasteries.

A brass on the north aisle wall is of great interest because it shows the Champion of England—Sir Lionel Dymoke, 1519—kneeling in the armour he wore as he rode into Westminster Hall to challenge in battle any who denied the monarch's right to the crown. The figures of his two sons are gone, but those of his three daughters are still here, and in the floor below is a much-worn brass showing Sir Lionel in his shroud.

On a stone tablet let into the chancel arch are the names of Thomas Gibson, vicar, and John Hamerton, churchwarden. An inscription in the south chancel chapel states that Thomas Gibson was "four times by the rebellious powers carried away from his congregation", and once was "exchanged into the garrison of Newark for a dissenting teacher". But he lived to see the Restoration and in the end he became a prebendary of Lincoln Cathedral. John Hamerton, his churchwarden, was probably the man interviewed by Cromwell when he sought honourable burial for Sir Ingram Hopton.

Facing the chancel is a gabled brick building of 1778 which once housed the grammar school founded here in Elizabethan times. (This school has fine modern buildings on the Lincoln road.)

A few paces from the church is the marketplace, where stands a stone monument with plaques bearing the portrait and arms of Edward Stanhope (MP for Horncastle) who held government posts under Disraeli and Lord Salisbury.

In a corner near the marketplace is the many-windowed Sellwood House, once the home of Emily and Louisa Sellwood, daughters of a Lincolnshire solicitor, and nieces of Sir John Franklin. It was from this house in 1836 that Louisa with gladness in her heart went forth to Horncastle Church to wed the poet Charles Tennyson Turner, then a curate at Tealby. (He had a little earlier taken the additional name of Turner—that of a great-uncle who had bequeathed some property to him.) Emily also went, a bridesmaid rejoicing in the crowning happiness of her sister; and at the wedding she, too, found her own happiness, for it was on that day that Alfred Tennyson fell in love with her.

Alfred Tennyson had met Emily once before—in 1830, when the Sellwoods had driven over from Horncastle to Somersby Rectory. Arthur Hallam, who was staying with his friend, asked Emily to go for a walk with him, and at a turn in the woods the poet came upon them suddenly. He was enchanted by the sight of the beautiful 17-year-old girl in her bright dress, moving "like a light across those woodland ways", and he called out to her "Are you a Dryad or an Oread wandering here?" Six years later, attending his brother Charles's wedding here at Horncastle, he found himself leading her into the church. As a bridesmaid she seemed to him lovelier than ever.

They continued to write to each other, but their engagement was not announced for four or five years later, and a long, weary wait it was for both of them before the success of Tennyson's poems made marriage possible—in 1850. Then their dreams came true. "The peace of God came into my life," Lord Tennyson used to say to his children of that June day when, in Shiplake Church, he married Emily Sellwood of Horncastle.

Hougham. Sheltered by trees at the end of a quiet lane, and close to the Witham flowing by on its unhurried journey to the Wash, stands its church, built of clean grey stone and full of light. Grotesque gargoyles, and the fine pinnacled 15th century porch with gabled image niche and sundial make the south side of the church an impressive sight.

The lower part of its tower is largely 14th century work, but the west window has a hood of chevron, and its fine arch, of three orders, is 13th century. The south arcade of the nave is Norman, with stout, round-headed arches on capitals enriched with nail-head and leaves. The north arcade and the clerestory date from about 1400. The chancel has been rebuilt, but its arch is 15th century work, and so is its chapel, divided from the north aisle by a fine modern screen of stone. Crowning the nave is a handsome old roof.

There is a late Norman font with interlaced arcading, and over the south door (inside the church) is a long, carved stone believed to be part of a Norman churchyard cross. The oldest monument is a 600-year-old stone figure of a knight in mail armour, with sword and shield. (The arms on the knight's shield are also on one of the corbels between the clerestory windows.) He belonged to the De Bussey family who lived for generations in the old moated manor house, part of which still survives in the stone farmhouse east of the church. It has some interesting mediaeval architectural features worthy of study.

Hough-on-the-Hill. Its story is an old one, and although nothing is left of the small alien priory founded here by Henry I for Austin canons, and in which the miserable King John took refuge just before reaching Newark to die, the tower which the Saxons gave to their church still stands secure.

The top stage of the tower, with its striking crown of tall, leafy pinnacles, is a 15th century addition, but the rest of it is Saxon; roughly built it is, with two prominent string-courses and a rare semi-circular turret attached to its west wall. The turret has a number of small lights of various shapes, and contains a remarkable newel stairway winding round a splendid stone post which is about 18 inches thick for the greater part of its length. The turret is reached by a square-headed doorway inside the tower, and its old stone steps climb to a gable-headed doorway now leading to the bell-chamber. There are two Saxon windows in the second stage of the tower; another, gabled and now blocked, is in the nave, and yet another has been set into the porch, where there are stone seats engraved after the fashion of solitaire boards, with lines and hollows for playing games.

The rest of the church, including the lofty nave arcades and the arches leading from the chancel to the vestry (which was once a school), was largely built in the 13th century, but the clerestory and the roofs with their carved and moulded beams are 15th century work. The font, enriched with round-headed and pointed arcading, is more than 700 years old, and on the floor is a 14th century grave-stone adorned with a floriated cross.

Near the church is an ancient artificial mound called Castle Hill, and above the village the site of Loveden Hill has been proved by excavation to be a pagan Saxon cremation and inhumation ceme-tery rich with associated grave goods including fine hanging bowls and other ornaments. On a little green at Gelston, a mile from Hough, is part of an old cross on its massive base and steps.

In the hamlet of Brandon, 2 miles away, is a small restored church with a Norman doorway under a tympanum diapered with stars; by its side is a mass dial. The pillars and responds of the nave arcade are 13th century, and some of the windows 15th century. The plain tub font is perhaps 700 years old. In the tiny chancel chapel is a gabled niche with pinnacles and finial and a medley of old stonework.

Howell. An attractive village in the byways a few miles east of Sleaford, it has a towerless church full of interest. In the churchyard is a broken cross with an inscription to John Spencer who was rector here 500 years ago, and in the porch is an Anglo-Saxon coffin-lid with a cross.

The plain doorway within the porch is Norman, and so is the nave arcade, its round arches borne on massive round piers with bases like millstones. The chancel, with its projecting aumbries, its piscina, and its altar stone with five consecration crosses, is 14th century, and from the same period comes the font, decorated with heraldic shields.

By the altar is a stone with the engraved figure of Rector John Croxby in his 15th century vestments, and under a low arch with hanging tracery is the bust of a 14th century woman, her child sculptured in a sunken trefoil below. An Elizabethan monument shows Sir Charles Dymoke kneeling in his armour with his wife, now headless.

In a lancet window is a modern figure of this church's St Oswald, arrayed in red, and in the 14th century bellcot is a bell with an inscription recording its making by Tobie Norris in the year of London's Great Fire.

Humberston. The masts of a radio station, visible for miles, soar high above the many fine trees lining the 2-mile road from the highway to the village. They strike a modern note which is further emphasised by modern seaside building developments; but this village, not far from the sandy shore at the mouth of the Humber, has a long history; it saw the coming of the Danes more than 1000 years ago, and the founding of an abbey 800 years ago.

The only evidence of antiquity here, however, is the massive tower of its strange-looking church—a 15th century tower of grey and amber stone, attached to a huge brick oblong built in 1710 and lighted by seven windows with latticed panes and iron bars.

The church has an oak lectern—an alert-looking eagle on a finely carved stem—and a monument with the figure of a sorrowing woman and the bust of a local philanthropist, Matthew Humberston. The son of a foundling, Matthew was educated at Christ's Hospital, prospered exceedingly, and left money for the rebuilding of this church as well as for almshouses and a school. The church has recently been refurnished through the generosity of Mr F. A. Would.

Another memorial rings out from the tower—a chime of eight tubular bells given by pupils of a school in Kent to commemorate a vicar who was once their master.

Humberston "fitties" near the beach has been extensively developed for holiday facilities and in 1960 a narrow-gauge railway, the Lincolnshire Coast Light Railway, was opened. It is operated by enthusiasts and provides a daily service in summer.

Hundleby. Almost one with Spilsby, this pleasant village has a 15th century church much rebuilt in 1854. Between its clerestoried nave and the aisle is an old arcade of greenstone arches on sandstone pillars, and the old rood stairway can still be seen. In the east window are two old fragments of glass showing a bishop in red and a saint in blue. There is also an old seven-sided font with a 17th century cover.

Huttoft. From a little height in the salt marshes the trim village looks across to the grey North Sea, 2 miles away. On the coast hereabouts, and, indeed, on many parts of the coast between the Wash and the Humber, have been found tree-stumps that are evidence of a submerged prehistoric forest.

The restored village church has a lofty 13th century tower with single lancets in its base and double lancets above enriched with dog-tooth ornament—each pair under a hood which also encloses a vesica window. From the 15th century come the belfry windows and many of the windows lighting the rest of the church, those in the south aisle having hoods dotted with flowers. Of the same age are the two doorways of the porch, both with foliated mouldings; the inner doorway has its old door, panelled and studded and with a wicket. The rest of the old work is mainly 14th century, including the chancel arch, with its corbel heads of a man pulling the ends of his mouth and another with a dog and a hare beside him.

The font is a magnificent example of 14th century sculpture, nearly 5 feet high. On the bowl are the Holy Trinity, the Madonna and Child, and the Twelve Apostles in pairs; round the stem are eight saints; eight winged angels support the bowl, and at the base are symbols of the Four Evangelists. The fine modern cover of this rare font is like a traceried tower with a crocketed spire. The church also has a 600-year-old chest.

The pulpit, the stalls, and the chancel screen (with coloured rood figures) are modern, and a chapel has been screened and furnished in tribute to the men who fell in the First World War. One of the stained windows is in memory of George Bryan, who was vicar for 50 years last century.

By the churchyard stands the village school, where a quaint custom survived until after the First World War. On Clerk Thursday (the day following Ash Wednesday) the headmaster would be locked out of his school by the boys; if they could keep him out until midday they had a holiday in the afternoon. The boys often won this annual battle of wits.

Immingham. The 20th century has made it what it is—a port with a deep-water dock on a land-locked harbour, entered by a deep-water channel through which the largest trading vessels can pass. The population is now 15,000 and the dock covers 1000 acres, having a mile of quays and a great expanse of railway sidings. Here come timber and grain from across the sea; and a line of coal-hoists is able to deal with hundreds of tons an hour. The coal trade has fallen away but chemical fertilisers, manufactured iron, and building road materials are exported. The latest development is a cross-sea car and passenger ferry service to Amsterdam and Gothenburg.

No part of Lincolnshire has changed more than the Humber Bank. Frozen food factories, enormous chemical works, and oil refineries now occupy the skyline and bring thousands of workers into this area. The village, 2 miles inland, has been completely absorbed in new development associated with the dock, but has kept its old church with fine 15th century tower, crowned by battle-ments and eight pinnacles. The rest of the old work is chiefly 15th century (restored) but the north arcade of the nave was built at the close of the Norman period; and the tower arch, the chancel arch, and some of the lancet windows are 13th century. Between the windows of the later clerestory are curious 18th century oil-paintings of six of the Apostles.

The old font has shields adorned with flowers, crosses, and fleur-de-lys, and there is an old pewter flagon in the sanctuary. On one side of the chancel arch is the White Ensign, and on the other hangs the Stars and Stripes given by American sailors who were at Immingham Dock in the First World War. The pulpit and the lectern are among a number of things used at the Dock Naval Church in those dark days.

More stirring, however, to the imagination than anything else here is a granite monument by the muddy shore of the Humber, recalling a little ship and a few men who faced the unknown more than three centuries ago. In the town is a granite monument commemorating the fact that from South Killingholme the Pilgrim Fathers set sail in 1609 in search of religious freedom. From here they sailed to Holland, beginning the great adventure which, 11 years later, was to take them across the Atlantic and was ultimately to lead to the foundation of the United States.

Set up in 1925 by the Anglo-American Society, the monument is a tapering column on rough granite blocks, and at the very top, about 20 feet from the ground, is a granite stone cut from Plymouth Rock in New England—the very place where those brave souls first trod their Promised Land.

Ingoldmells. It is Lincolnshire's Farthest East—comprising a large holiday camp, acres of caravans and a trim village loved for its delightful sands and standing on the site of a Roman settlement. The evidence was seen when the concrete defences were constructed and still earlier activity is seen in Early Iron Age salt sites which show as red circles in the clay exposed by certain tides.

The church lost its chancel early in the 18th century, and there are plans to build a new one. The rest, well cared-for, is chiefly mediaeval, the three great building periods being represented in the three stages of the tower, which has fine buttresses, a big lancet window in the base, and a splendid arch. Low and wide, and with fine foliaged capitals, this arch opens to a nave which is exceptional in being of two levels, the western end two steps lower than the rest.

The fine porch has its entrance dotted with flowers and heads, a quatrefoil window in each side wall, and a niche at the side of the finely-moulded inner doorway. The massive pillars of the beautiful 13th century nave arcades have varied capitals, some of them bell-shaped, others cross-shaped and carved with different forms of early overhanging foliage. The clerestory, and the windows with flowing tracery in the aisles, come from the close of the 14th century. The external south wall is an attractive picture of gabled buttresses and windows with delicate mouldings.

The font is 600 years old and of unusual design. Its bowl is enriched with sunken circles of tracery and flowers; under it are heads both human and grotesque, and the carved stem rests on a square base with grotesques at the corners. Set in the floor by the font are fragments of mediaeval gravestones. Among others which have remained whole are a 13th century coped stone carved with a cross, one to John Hyltoft of 1473, and another to William Skegness of 1508. A rare little memorial in the floor of the south aisle is the brass portrait of William Palmer in a long-sleeved gown; he was a cripple who died in 1520, and at his side is shown his crutch, "ye stylt", as the inscription calls it. Most of the fine old woodwork once in the church has gone, but there are remains of old benches with simple poppyheads and some of the original ledges for books.

Ingoldsby. It has no association with the famous Legends of Richard Barham, its name being, it is said, a link with a Danish chieftain of old, one Ingold. Its church, watching over the village from a high knoll, comes chiefly from the 15th century but has an arcade with three big Norman arches. The mediaeval font with carved shields is still here and there are two ancient doors, the massive one in the porch having tracery. Old roofs still protect the tower and nave.

About a mile away, by Ingoldsby Wood, is Round Hills, a circular earthwork 500 feet across: it has a single bank and ditch. Its date is not known.

Irby-upon-Humber. So called to distinguish it from Lincolnshire's other Irby, though the Humber is 8 miles away, it is graced by a fine pond in the hollow and an ancient little church standing proudly on the hilltop.

The plain unbuttressed tower and the chancel are for the most part 15th century work, but each has a 13th century arch to the nave. The nave has two Norman arches on each side, and the oblong bowl of the font is also Norman. Each aisle has a built-up peephole, and the south aisle has its old piscina and the blocked-up rood-loft doorway.

One of the floorstones has the engraved portraits of John Malet of 1493 and his wife Elianora, charming in long robes and hoods, and resting their heads on tasselled cushions. Elianora's hands are at prayer; John's are tucked into his sleeves.

By the 700-year-old doorway in the tiny south porch is a scratch dial with part of its iron gnomon.

Near the end of Elizabeth I's reign there was born to an Irby couple a son remembered for his bravery in the first great battle of the Civil War. He was Edward Lake, who for love of Charles I threw aside his lawyer's gown and followed the king to Edgehill. Sixteen wounds he received in battle but with one hand useless he fought on with his sword in the other. He ended a prisoner, but managed to escape, and, living on to see the Restoration, was made a baronet. He was buried in Lincoln Cathedral and a photograph of his memorial there hangs in this little church.

Irnham. This is a village that should be visited. Its friendly stone cottages, spacious old church, and Elizabethan Hall on the edge of a wooded park make an attractive picture of neighbours in harmony.

The oldest part of the church is the lower part of the tower, with massive arch, from the 12th century. From early in the 14th century come the north aisle and its arcade, the chancel with its sedilia and founder's recess, and the chantry chapel. In the floor of the chapel is the old altar stone with five consecration crosses.

The round font is 700 years old, but the chief treasure here is a beautiful piece of sculpture now by the east wall of the chapel. It is clearly an Easter Sepulchre but in a strange position. It is reminiscent of Heckington and has exquisite 14th century carving, a mass of delicate tracery and foliage with broken figures of the Madonna and Child on the central finial of its three arches, and a Crucifixion scene at one side. Above it is a fine modern window of Charity. The east window is a striking and realistic representation of the scene of the Crucifixion.

Two brasses in the floor are links in the story of the manor, which belonged in early mediaeval days to the Luttrells and by marriage passed to the Hiltons. Sir Andrew Luttrell, 5th Baron of Irnham, is a brave figure in late 14th century armour with his feet on a lion. A smaller brass of a knight without feet is probably Sir Geoffrey Hilton of the 15th century.

Irnham Hall, with its mellow walls of grey stone, its mullioned windows, battlements, and tall chimneys, is a charming picture from the leafy churchyard. Built more than four centuries ago by Sir Richard Thimelby, who married the heiress of the Hiltons, it was a Roman Catholic house and has a relic of the days of religious intolerance in a hiding-hole for priests, approached from an attic passage. In another secret place, discovered in 1858, there were found a straw palliasse bed, a crucifix, and a Prayer Book; and from the hall to the garden runs an underground passage that may well have been used as a way of escape.

The old Griffin Inn is picturesque indeed, and near it is a massive weeping willow standing where the markets were held of old.

Keddington. Its few dwellings are by the lazy River Lud and the 18th century canal linking Louth with the sea at Tetney Haven. Just across the river is Louth Park, with slight remains of an abbey bounded on one side by the Monks' Dike. It is thought that some carved stones in the arch leading to the organ chamber in Keddington Church came from the abbey.

On a bank by a narrow lane, and looking over meadows to Louth's exquisite spire, stands the tiny church. Restored last century, it has walls of mottled stone and a brick bellcot. The south doorway is from the close of Norman days and has capitals carved with leaves and flowers. There is also a deeply-splayed Norman window with a grotesque animal creeping under its arch. The arch into the organ loft is 13th century and came probably from Louth Abbey nearby. A rarer possession is the 15th century lectern—a fine wooden eagle, black with age. There are only about six in all England.

Keelby. Between the Wolds and the Humber it lies, a big village with a fine 600-year-old church. Set behind a beech hedge with four fine archways is a village institute with tower and gables.

Restoration of the church in this century included the opening out of the old blocked-up arcade to a new south aisle; like the north arcade, it has big arches on low pillars. The tower is adorned with a band of quatrefoils, and the ribs of its vaulted roof within meet in a boss. An open roof of trussed timbering crowns the nave and chancel, marking their division with a cinquefoiled arch.

There is a 15th century font enriched with tracery on bowl and stem, and there is good modern glass in some of the windows.

In the dim north aisle is the medallion bust of Alice South, who died in 1605; her hands are clasped in prayer and she wears a ruff and a great hood. Another alabaster tablet is to John Smith, 1591. Set in a wall is a 13th century stone with a decorated crosshead.

Another building in Keelby worthy of note is a remarkable 14th century manor house made almost entirely of chalk. Chalk buildings are very rare in Lincolnshire.

Kelby. A grey stone village with a duckpond, it lies secluded in the byways between Grantham and Sleaford. The church has stood since Norman days, and although the tower and spire were rebuilt after falling last century, the base of the tower is Norman still. The chancel has a Norman piscina. The two round arches of the north aisle come from the close of the 12th century, the font is 13th, and the south aisle, with stone-vaulted roof and grotesque corbels, has three handsome 14th century windows.

The clerestory is 15th century work, and 10 benches of that time, with poppyheads and traceried ends, were brought here from the ruined chapel of the neighbouring Culverthorpe Hall. Perhaps the most notable feature of the church is the austere appearance of its chancel, its flat ceiling whitewashed and its walls bare of ornament or monument.

At Oasby, a mile to the south, is a delightful 15th century stone manor house with 17th century additions.

Kelstern. Coming from the high road to Kelstern the traveller passes one of the round barrows in which Bronze Age settlers buried their dead, and there is another one on the way to North Elkington.

Set on a ridge in a field, with two big ponds below it, is the church, partly rebuilt last century but keeping much of its old walling, with late 14th century windows in the nave. It has preserved, too, a 16th century chalice, a mediaeval eight-sided font, and six old traceried bench-ends, two of them with quaint carvings of a dog chasing a sheep, and a fox with a goose meeting a snarling dog.

A more charming relic of far-off days is the monument to Lady Elizabeth South, whose life ended a year after Elizabeth I's. In her hood and ruff and tight-waisted dress, she sits, looking out from an arched recess, holding a broken hourglass and resting one foot on a skull. With her lies a hooded babe, and two cherubs, with spade and torch, keep them company down the years.

Three fine modern windows to the memory of the Sleight family are by Sir Ninian Cowper.

Kettlethorpe. Situated in a remote position, this pretty village in its leafy domain in the Vale of Trent keeps green the name of Ketel, a Danish invader, and is linked, through its manor, with illustrious names in England's story.

Facing the church is a modern red-brick house, standing behind a massive 14th century gateway, with the old mounting-block close by. It is historic ground, for this stone gateway and part of the moat are all that remain of the old Hall where the Swynfords lived for 150 years. Sir Hugh Swynford belonged to the retinue of John of Gaunt, time-honoured Lancaster, and after his death in 1372 his young widow, Catherine Swynford, went through the old gateway to be governess to John of Gaunt's children. Catherine's father was Sir Payne Roelt, who came to England with the retinue of Queen Philippa, and her sister Philippa is said to have married no less a man than Geoffrey Chaucer, Father of English Poetry. In 1396 Catherine married John of Gaunt in Lincoln Cathedral, where, seven years later, she was laid to rest.

One of their sons, half-brothers to King Henry IV (they were born before the marriage and legitimised a year later), was Henry Beaufort, Bishop of Lincoln at the time of the marriage, and who later became the powerful Cardinal Beaufort. Another was John

The nave of Lincoln Cathedral

THE ANGEL CHOIR
OF LINCOLN CATHEDRAL

(a) The Lincoln Imp corbel
(b) Some of the angels

Beaufort, first Duke of Somerset, father of Margaret Beaufort and grandfather of our first Tudor king, Henry VII. So is this remote and quiet village linked with great figures in the nation's story.

Except for the 15th century battlemented tower rising among clustering trees, the humble church was all rebuilt in 1896. Its great treasure is a magnificent pulpit of black oak which was the work of a craftsman from Brittany of the 17th century. Rounded in the shape of a tulip, it has five panels, each bordered with leaves and shells, and all showing vivid scenes from the Passion—Our Lord before Pilate (soldiers guarding Him), scourged as He bears the Cross, stumbling under the burden, and passing His mother and touching her hand.

Among the men who have so faithfully served this church were Gilbert Hall, rector for half of the 18th century, and the Elizabethan John Becke, whose tablet has a quaint but feeble rhyme playing on his name.

The old churchyard cross was restored as a war memorial.

Kingerby. On a great circular mound surrounded by a fosse with a square embankment outside stands its 19th century Hall. Nothing remains of the house associated with the earthworks.

In charming sylvan setting opposite the wooded grounds of the Hall stands a tiny church. Its tower (like most of the old work remaining) belongs chiefly to the 13th century; but its west window was inserted a century later, and its doorway to the nave in the 15th century. There is a Norman doorway into the south aisle. A grand old ladder climbs to the bell-chamber.

The rugged porch has a lovely 13th century entrance arch enriched with nail-head and dog-tooth, and shelters a simpler doorway opening to the white-walled interior. The two arches which led to a vanished north aisle are visible outside in the nave wall, and one of the pillars is seen within. The chancel has an original lancet, low-side window, and a 14th century east window. Also 14th century are a window in the nave and the east window of the aisle—this having an image bracket in its splay, a sill cut as if for an altar, and much old glass, including a Crucifixion and figures of St Catherine with her wheel and St Cecilia with her organ. Among the old relics are a font (with an old pointed cover), a priest's seat made from old pew-ends, and a 17th century pillar almsbox asking a mite for God's Treasury. The nave still has its Jacobean roof with decorated beams.

Lying on low tombs in the aisle are two battered knights, belonging perhaps to the Dyves family. One is in early 14th century chain armour and surcoat and has dogs at his shoulders and feet. The other is wearing late 14th century plate armour, a tabard emblazoned with dragons, and a belt richly ornamented. Against the chancel wall is a remarkable coffin-shaped stone commemorating one of the Disney family. About 600 years old, it displays the bust of a man under an ogee canopy, and his feet in another opening below; in the space between are two shields and a cross, and two more shields are by his head. A similar stone is in Norton Disney Church.

Opposite the church gates is the base and shaft of a cross inscribed and dated 1451. It refers to the PONS EPISCOPI, i.e. Bishop Bridge across the River Ancholme east of Glentham.

On the roll of vicars (which reveals that Kingerby had a priest and a church at the time of Domesday Book) is the name of Joseph Stockdale, who ministered here for 63 years of last century. In the 17th century Thomas Bell, a native of this place, presented the church with a silver chalice and paten engraved with the Crucifixion. He also founded the village almshouses, and a dedication stone states that he was an apothecary of London. The almshouses have been demolished but the trustees are to build five new flatlets in the village for old people and the dedication stone will be retained. The great city may have claimed him, as it has claimed countless others, but it is pleasant to know Thomas Bell never forgot either the village of his birth or its church—the first he ever knew.

Kirkby-cum-Osgodby. Two villages half a mile apart, their church stands by the roadside at Kirkby, an attractive picture with tall trees about it and several pantiled cottages close by. The sturdy tower with its worn gargoyles is 13th century work, with a 15th century parapet; the chancel is chiefly 13th century, with later windows; the nave was rebuilt in 1825; and the whole church was restored in 1900 and has recently received further attention.

The chancel retains a single and a double piscina, and two well-preserved and richly-carved monuments commemorating John Wildbore of 1398 and his mother. John is wearing plate armour with helmet and a rich belt, and has a wild boar at his feet. His mother is a graceful figure with embroidered mantle, square head-dress, and long chain; her slender hands are at prayer, a small dog is at her feet, and angels guard her head, which is under a rich cinquefoiled canopy.

A 13th century coffin stone is in the south wall of the nave, and in the churchyard is the base of the old cross.

There is an interesting late 18th century house in Osgodby built by the Youngs of Kingerby with a wing, the top floor of which is used as a Catholic Chapel. It may be identified by a cross on the gable end.

Kirkby Green. A tiny place 8 miles north of Sleaford, it has a church with a bellcot, and a stream flowing below it through pastures where sheep and cattle graze. The neat little church, built in 1848 on the site of a mediaeval place of worship, is lighted by 10 lancet windows and still has the Elizabethan chalice, a wooden chest, and a piscina with a pointed arch which belonged to its predecessor.

Kirkby-la-Thorpe. Its 13th century name was Kirkebi et Leitorp.

In days gone by, this small neighbour of Sleaford must have been of more consequence, for it had two churches and probably a chapel-of-ease as well. But the church of St Peter was pulled down long ago, and all that is left of it are green mounds close to the finely-wooded grounds of the 19th century rectory, though fragments of its grey walls are said to be in an old stone cottage in the village. Another cottage has two small oak panels on which are inscribed the Creed and the Commandments, relics possibly of the vanished chapel.

The church of St Denis remains, brother now to the church of Asgarby across the fields, one of 12 to be seen from the top of the 14th century tower. It is an ancient building (though its chancel was rebuilt last century) and its walls and arches lean outwards at a dangerous angle; but heavy buttresses have made it safe once more —safe, it is believed, for many centuries. The nave has a Norman arcade on low round pillars, and a Norman doorway sheltered by a spacious 15th century porch. The aisle, like the tower, is 14th century, and each has a window with fragments of its original glass. Three bays of the 15th century chancel screen are now in the tower arch, and there is also a mediaeval lectern.

The church can boast two ancient fonts—a traceried font which has been here since the 14th century, and a 15th century one with quatrefoiled shields which belonged either to St Peter's Church or the vanished chapel; it was brought here for preservation after being in the school grounds for many years, and for countless years before that it lay in a field. Built high up in the wall of the church, too, are two fragments of Anglo-Saxon interlace work.

Kirkby Underwood. It stands serenely in the byways and lives up to its name, for there are woods all around. The small church on the edge of the village, reached by a long path between hedge-rows and guarded by an ancient door with three-foot hinges and huge lock and key. There are fragments of Anglo-Saxon interlace in the outer chancel wall. It has an embattled tower five centuries old, and a 13th century arcade, with foliated capitals, leading to the south aisle. The north aisle is gone, but its arcade (also 13th century and with clustered piers) is seen built up as a wall. The old rood-loft doorway is still here, and there are a few old stalls with high poppyheads and a plain mediaeval font. The panelled pulpit is Jacobean.

Kirkstead. It was here, in the fertile land by the Witham, that in 1139 Hugo Brito, son of a Lord of Tattershall, founded a Cistercian abbey which was colonised by monks from Fountains Abbey. Big and impressive its buildings must have looked in these quiet fields, for extensive foundations can be traced. But all that is left above ground is the gaunt, lofty, and impressive corner of a transept built about 1160.

Just outside the old precincts, however, stands a link with the old abbey—the tiny chapel of St Leonard, rightly famed as one of the loveliest examples of 13th century architecture in our land. It is thought to have been a "chapel outside the gates", which the Cistercians sometimes provided for use of the lay-folk, and it was spared when the abbey surrendered in 1537. From the time of George II till 1812 the chapel was used by the Nonconformists, and after becoming ruinous was closed for worship in 1877. It came into its own again in 1914, when it was restored by the Society for the Protection of Ancient Buildings.

In plan it is a simple oblong, with a small open bellcot on the ridge of its roof. Its windows are narrow lancets. The west front has a beautiful recessed doorway with elegant shafts, capitals enriched with delicate foliage, and fine dog-tooth ornament in the outer moulding of its arch. In it hangs the old door, with fine old ironwork, and above it is an arcade of three arches, the middle one being pierced by a vesica window.

Lovely indeed is the interior, and still lit by candles in two fine hanging candelabra and wall brackets of brass and iron. From a low stringcourse round the walls rise short shafts with delicately carved capitals, and from these spring groined vaulting adorned with dog-tooth moulding and three great bosses at the crossing of the ribs. The vaulting frames the lancets in the north and south walls. There is dog-tooth enriching the triplet of lancets in the east wall—a charming group with clustered and banded shafts and capitals which, like all the capitals in this chapel, are exquisitely carved with foliage.

The old altar stone from the abbey is now on the floor, and there is a Norman font (with a ribbed bowl) which lay for a long time in a farmyard. But the rarest thing here is the screen before the sanctuary, for the trefoiled arcading of its open bays is 13th century work and thought to be the second oldest timber screenwork in England. (Compton in Surrey has the oldest.) The top rail and the case are modern, the work of a local craftsman.

A notable memorial is the figure of a knight who lies here with a surcoat over his suit of banded mail. Wearing a cylindrical flat-topped helmet, with a long slit for the eyes, he has his sword and shield, and is thought to be the 2nd Lord Tattershall, who died about 1212. It is certainly one of the earliest military monuments in England.

During the early part of the 18th century these walls must often have resounded to the eloquence of Dr John Taylor, who was Nonconformist pastor of St Leonard's for 18 years. A remarkable man he was famous on three counts: as a classical scholar, as author of a masterly Hebrew concordance, and as a brave man who challenged the stark bitterness of Calvin and his doctrine. He is celebrated as a hero by no less a man than Robert Burns, in his *Epistle to John Goudie* acclaiming the defeat of superstition. Here it was that the worthy doctor pondered these works of scholarship and enlightenment, to win a name renowned not only in old England but in New England across the sea.

The church looks out on a white, gabled farmhouse neighboured by a towering chestnut tree, and catches a distant glimpse of another farm; but apart from the lone fragment of the lost abbey it has the horizon to itself.

Kirmington. Not far from the many richly-wooded acres of Brocklesby Park, it has an ancient church rebuilt last century but still keeping its weatherworn 13th century tower, crowned by a bright green spire of 1838 recently re-covered in a darker shade. A timber spire covered with copper, it rises within the tower's odd parapet of iron rails, and is a striking spectacle above the roofs and trees of the village. It was a notable landmark for navigating to nearby airfields during the last war.

The nave has kept its mediaeval arcades—the south arcade plain, the north a fine legacy of the 13th century with its arches on sturdy clustered pillars and its capitals enriched with a strange gallery of sculpture. A man with a pained expression, and a head with three faces sharing four eyes are carved on one capital; another is adorned with busts, and a small head among leaves, a third shows a bishop with his hand raised in benediction. On this same capital is the head of a woman with plaited tresses and a crown; she may represent the church's patron saint, St Helen, for she holds a broken shaft of what may have been a cross. Other heads are carved between the arches of this arcade.

It is interesting to note that a music-room was added to the large house, formerly the vicarage, by an incumbent for his wife who was Tennyson's "Claribel", a friend of the family and a notable musician and writer of popular songs.

Kirmond-le-Mire. Memorable is its charming setting on the slope of a Wold valley through which a fine stream from Kirmond Top runs to its meeting with another beyond Croxby Plantation.

The road going west from the village to the lofty height of Bully Hill crosses the High Street, the Roman road which rides in fine and inspiring isolation between Caistor and Horncastle, rising to a height of more than 500 feet and giving the traveller wonderful and ever-changing views of the Wold countryside.

Kirton-in-Holland. A big village noted for agriculture and horticulture on the road from Boston to Spalding. It was once a market town and can boast a town hall, as well as an old church which would adorn any town.

The brick-built town hall, which commemorates the coronation of George V, stands on land which was the gift of William Dennis, whose bronze statue in front shows him seated, his hands resting on his walking-stick. On the pedestal below his statue are three panels illustrating his chief activities: the growing of wheat and potatoes and the draining of the land.

Kirton Church was altered in 1805 when the present west tower was built out of materials of a collapsed crossing-tower. The transepts were demolished and the chancel shortened. Traces of these lost portions of the church can be seen.

The present handsome west tower of four stages has an embattled parapet with tall pinnacles, a band of quatrefoils halfway up, and statues of St Peter and St Paul on buttresses. Splendid, too, outside and in, is the 15th century clerestory, with its long lines of 12 windows on each side, under embattled parapets carved with tracery and adorned with pinnacles.

There are two old porches—the north sheltering a fine 13th century doorway with a richly-moulded arch on groups of shafts, and the south porch having an inner doorway from the close of Norman days, its three shafts on each side supporting an arch carved with zigzag and lattice and other ornament. At the west end of the south aisle is another ancient doorway, its plain tympanum under a head of two curved stones.

From the 13th century comes the nave of six bays, its tall slender pillars supporting arches with spandrels beautifully panelled. Above is the splendid 15th century roof (finely restored), and on its principals, rising from stone brackets between the clerestory windows, are canopied niches with 26 figures of angels and saints. The late 14th century windows of the south aisle have rich, flowing tracery, and in the clerestory and the north aisle are old glass fragments showing shields and pinnacle work.

The chancel, now only two bays of its original length and looking much rebuilt, has a new wagon roof with bosses, and a finely-traceried modern screen and coved rood-loft with a deep cornice of angels with crossed wings. The carved and coloured reredos has panels showing Our Lord in Glory, and eight saints. The old canopied piscina has been set by the tower arch; some old beams remain in the north aisle roof, and the font, carved with tracery and plain shields, asks a prayer for Alan Burton, who gave it to the church in 1405.

The base of an old village cross is in the churchyard. By the church are four 17th century almshouses, and on the fringe of the village is another neat little group, built in the 20th century.

A grammar school was founded in 1493 by Edmund Kirton, who became Abbot of Peterborough. There are records of the appointment of masters up to 1624 when Sir John Middlecott of Boston was empowered to set up a grammar school. The school continued until 1917 and the building is at present used as an Agricultural Institute and Experimental Horticultural Station.

Kirton-in-Lindsey. A small but busy town with a maze of little streets, it stands finely on a slope of the Cliff and has wonderful views towards the Wolds and over the wide plain to the Trent. It was anciently an important place, for the Conqueror gave both manor and church to Bishop Remigius towards the endowment of his new cathedral at Lincoln, and among the famous people who held the manor and soke subsequently were Piers Gaveston and the Black Prince. Until the end of the 18th century it belonged to the Duchy of Cornwall.

Kirton's dignified church has a fine 13th century tower with lovely belfry windows, a west doorway with dog-tooth ornament and shafts with leafy capitals, and an unusual and attractive double arch. The 17th century south porch (now a baptistery with an elaborate modern font) shelters a lovely 13th century doorway similar to that of the tower.

The north arcade of the nave comes from the 13th century, the south arcade from the 14th, and the clerestory and aisles from the 15th. The chancel was partly rebuilt last century, but retains some of its original lancet windows, deeply-splayed. It has a gabled aumbry, and a priest's doorway with a Norman head, its arch carved with a zigzag and its tympanum with honeysuckle.

Lying on a tomb is the defaced figure of a knight in chain-mail, his legs crossed and his feet on a dragon. Sparkling modern glass in one of the windows portrays St Cecilia with her organ, Bishop Remigius with his cathedral, and St Hugh with his staff and swan.

In the marketplace is the 19th century town hall, built partly with the materials of the demolished prison. Kirton also boasts a windmill, sail-less now and worked by an engine. On Spa Hill (north of the town) is an old whipping-post, still with its iron clasps.

Knaith. A loop of the broad Trent separates this little place from Nottinghamshire, and the calm of the river makes up for the rush of traffic passing along its road to Gainsborough. Close together on the river bank stand the small church and the long, low Hall.

The old Hall, charming with black-and-white walls and clustering old chimneys, was built in the 16th century but greatly altered in the 19th century when the black-and-white timbering was added. It is notable as the birthplace of Knaith's most famous son—Thomas Sutton, who for a quarter of a century served Elizabeth as her Master of Ordnance in the North, and in his old age founded Charterhouse School and Hospital in London. Here, too, lived Lord Willoughby of Parham, leader of the Lincolnshire troops who fought for Parliament in the Civil War; he it was who gave the church its fine silver communion plate.

The village church enshrines a fragment of the church of Heynings Nunnery, a Cistercian house founded here in the 12th century and dissolved in 1539. Alterations in the 17th century and restoration in the 19th converted that old fragment into the present quaint and fascinating little building—a simple oblong (with a two-gabled roof and little bellcot) curiously divided by an arcade of three bays stretching across the nave. The old fabric is late 14th century work and has big windows with elegant tracery of that time, cut short inside by the Georgian roof. In the west wall outside are several fragments of early herringbone masonry.

On one side of the chancel are Jacobean seats, and on the other side is a Jacobean two-decker pulpit with a reading-desk of the same period. There are three engraved mediaeval floorstones: one with a worn chalice and inscription; the second with the portrait of a wimpled woman with angels at her head; and the third showing William Darcy, of 1454, wearing a full gown with open sleeves, and a little dog peeping out at his feet.

The tall font is a fine 14th century type; round its rim is a gallery of quaint heads expressive of many moods, and round the base of the bowl are demon heads and ballflower ornament.

Laceby. This big village, now bypassed by the main road into Grimsby, has an old church with the memory of a rector who won fame throughout the land. He was the fearless John Whitgift, who became Elizabeth's Archbishop of Canterbury in 1583 and lived to place the crown on the head of James I. Born in 1530 at Grimsby, 4 miles away, he was buried in 1604 at Croydon, where he founded almshouses and a school which keep his name evergreen.

The plain, unbuttressed tower of the church Whitgift knew was built at the end of the Norman period; its top stage, adorned with eight pinnacles, is a 15th century addition. Within the porch are two little Norman windows and a Norman doorway with a mass dial engraved on it. The nave has a north arcade with four 13th century arches, and another arch from Norman times enriched with zigzag carving and adorned on the nave side with key pattern, and with rosettes on the side facing the wide aisle. In the side walls of the chancel are shafts which may have belonged to vanished arcades.

Fragments of carving are built into one of the walls, and there are two mediaeval bells. The font is modern, carved with patterns and emblems in mediaeval fashion. The church register dates from 1538, the year Thomas Cromwell made their keeping compulsory, and an entry of 1546 tells of the execution of a witch who was "devoured"—presumably by fire.

Langtoft. A long village astride the high road between the King Street of the Romans and their Carr Dyke, it belonged in Saxon times to the Abbey of Peterborough and was burned by the Danes when they destroyed that town a few decades before the Conquest.

Langtoft's first church was founded by the mother abbey and shared in the general destruction later. The present one has seen the changes of 700 years but is still impressive with its great array of battlements and its tall western steeple, unusually placed at the end of the north aisle instead of the nave. The steeple is 13th century in its lower stages and 15th century above, its spire, with a cross above each of eight gabled lights, looking far across the flatlands. Impressive, too, is the lofty clerestoried nave, with its great window almost filling the west wall, and its graceful 14th century arcades resting on clustered pillars a century older. The arches are adorned with little heads of mediaeval men and women, and on the wall-plates of the roof, high above them, are 10 finely-carved wooden figures.

The chancel and its south chapel are chiefly 14th century, and the capitals of the arches between them have lovely foliage and quaint carvings of a comic man on his haunches and another with his hands to his ears. The winding rood-loft stairway is still here, and by the arch between south aisle and chapel are two peepholes, one filled in. On the other side of the arch is a piscina, and there is another piscina in the chapel, with a lovely canopy and two little heads.

A brass candelabrum of the 18th century has 25 branches, the dove of peace above them; and the old pulpit has panels inlaid with flaming suns and sacred monograms. A curiosity is its sounding-board, fashioned into a vestry table, six-sided and very handsome. Kneeling in a niche high up in the chancel is Elizabeth Moulesworth, in black Stuart gown and ruff; she died in 1648, three years before Sarah Walcot, whose brass inscription in the floor speaks poignantly of her bereaved husband's anxiety to join her.

Langton-by-Horncastle. Tall trees near the church here make a green tunnel of the road, and frame a sail-less windmill. The church, a simple red-tiled building, was much restored in 1890, but its 14th century arcade (which once led to an aisle) can be seen projecting from the north wall within.

One of two old floorstones by the west wall has carved crosses, and the font has a Norman bowl said to have come from old St Lawrence's Church, Horncastle, and set on a stem and base which are probably from Kirkstead Abbey. The flat oak cover of the font has quaint cherubs and a dove carved by a rector, J. Conway Walter in 1891, with a golden dove added later. The pulpit, reading-desk, and lectern were also carved by Conway Walter, as memorials of his father, Edward Walter, who ministered here nearly 50 years from 1828.

A rare treasure once preserved in this church, and now at the British Museum, is a chrismatory, a vessel in which the holy oil was kept; this one, of terra-cotta, is believed to be the only one of its kind in England. It was found in the moat at Poolham Hall, Edlington. The Hall is a farmhouse now, with slight remains of its old domestic chapel in the orchard—fragments of two adjoining walls with a doorway and a small window, all now overgrown.

Langton-by-Spilsby. Secluded in a pretty Wold valley where a stream runs towards the River Lymn, this small village has an 18th century church on a knoll. One of its cottages, with dormer windows peeping from an overhanging thatch, is notable because it is an octagon.

The red-brick church has deep overhanging eaves, and a curious octagonal bell-turret with bull's-eye windows. Its rather austere-looking exterior is graced by a mantle of trim ivy, and its interior has all the charm and quiet dignity of an 18th century period piece. Rows of high, candle-lit oak pews rise one above another in two blocks facing the middle aisle; on the south side is a splendid three-decker pulpit with inlaid canopy; at the west end is a gallery; at the east end is rich panelling in classical style; and crowning it all is a moulded plaster ceiling.

Relics of an earlier church here are a finely-traceried 15th century font and (in the porch) the head of an early 13th century cross with the worn carving of a Crucifixion.

Langton Hall, now regrettably demolished, was built in Elizabethan style on the site of a fine Tudor house which was burned down in 1822, the ancestral home of the Langton family, long famous in this country. One of them was Bennet Langton, a man who has a special niche in literary annals as one of the best-loved of Dr Johnson's friends.

Bennet Langton, who was born here about 1737, was only a youth when admiration for Dr Johnson's writings caused him to seek an introduction to their author. Johnson often visited Langton here and at the military camps where, year by year, he underwent training.

When his young friend proposed to build a school on his estate and objection was made in some quarters that education might tend to make the people less industrious, the splendid rejoinder came from Johnson that "While learning to read and write is a distinction, the few who have that distinction may be the less inclined to work; but when everybody learns to read and write it is no longer a distinction." He added that although a man who had candles might be tempted to sit up late, "nobody will deny that the art of making candles, by which light is continued to us beyond the time that the sun gives us light, is a valuable art, and ought to be preserved".

A quarter of a century after their first meeting Dr Johnson said, "The earth does not bear a worthier man than Bennet Langton." It was to him during his last illness that the Doctor gave £750 on Langton's undertaking to pay an annuity to his old friend's Negro servant. Langton, one of the original members of Johnson's club, succeeded him as professor of ancient literature at the Royal Academy. He died at Southampton in 1801.

Langton-by-Wragby. It is a peaceful, unpretentious village on the highway from Lincoln to Horncastle, but it has a shining place in England's story.

Langton's church was rebuilt in the 19th century, but its massive mediaeval tower still stands foursquare, and as further token of its long history there is a list of incumbents beginning as far back as AD 1215. The date is extremely interesting, for it was the year of the signing of Magna Carta, a momentous event with which this village is closely linked; for this is the birthplace of Stephen Langton, the man who above all others was responsible for the Great Charter of English freedom.

The origins of Stephen Langton long remained a mystery; practically nothing is known of his early life, and more than one county has proudly claimed this great champion of the people as a son. At long last, however, Sir Frederick Maurice Powicke and Canon C. W. Foster unravelled the tangled skein and established that Stephen Langton was a son of Henry Langton of Langton-by-Wragby and that he was born here about 1165. (Their findings have been published in Sir Maurice Powicke's book of his Ford Lectures delivered in the University of Oxford, 1927.)

Stephen Langton, patriot and statesman, first comes into prominence when old Roger of Wendover introduces him, "Master Stephen Langton, a cardinal priest, a man skilled in literary science, and discreet and accomplished in his manners . . . master in secular learning, doctor in theology!" Pope Innocent III, in defiance of King John, appointed Langton Archbishop of Canterbury in 1207, and then began the long contest between pope and king, which ended in the excommunication and deposition of the king, his humble submission and regaining of the English throne at the hands of the Papal legate, as the conditional gift of Rome!

In all the fierce struggles of John for the unfettered right to do unbounded wrong, Langton nobly sustained the people and inspired them with resolution to vindicate national and individual title to justice and legitimate freedom. It was Langton who, at St Paul's Cathedral, produced before the baronial council the charter of Henry I, as an indication of the claims they ought to make. Stephen Langton was responsible for Magna Carta and the signature of it by the baffled and defeated king; he, above all others, was the man responsible for the great event at Runnymede on June 15, 1215, one of the greatest days in the long story of the British people. Stephen Langton was the brain and heart of the long and dangerous struggle which emancipated the nation from the tyranny of lawless kings, and he left for future centuries an indestructible monument of the British spirit which brooks no fetters to its freedom.

Stephen Langton was an indefatigable writer, almost as voluminous, in spite of his manifold labours, as the leisured Bede; and among his most notable literary achievements was the division of the Bible into the Chapters as we still have it. He died at Slindon, Sussex, in 1228, his body being afterwards transferred to Canterbury Cathedral.

Laughton. A few miles from Gainsborough, it nestles peacefully in the green vale of Trent, with red-roofed barns and cottages clustering round a finely restored and partly rebuilt church.

The modern porch shelters a 13th century doorway; the western bay of the north arcade is Norman work, the other three bays, with capitals displaying a variety of early leaf-carving, being Transitional; the aisles and south arcade belong to the 14th century.

The fine restoration of this church at the end of last century was made possible by the generous benefactions of the Hon. Mrs Meynell-Ingram. She it was, too, who gave the stained glass of the clerestory, the coloured roofs with golden bosses, the beautiful oak rood-screen, and the oak reredos with its Crucifixion triptych.

The finest monument here is the white marble effigy of her husband, Hugo Meynell-Ingram—a copy of the one on his canopied tomb in the lovely church which she raised to his memory at Hoar Cross in Staffordshire. The earliest monuments here are reminders of the Dalisons, as the Norman D'Alencons became. One, a beautifully carved bust of a lady, was once part of a 14th century gravestone and is thought to have been brought here from Bullington Priory, of which the family were benefactors. There is also a tomb bearing a splendid brass of an armoured knight, with a fine triple canopy above his head and a lion at his feet. Also on the tomb are brass inscriptions to William Dalison (Sheriff of Lincolnshire in 1546) and his son.

The school at Laughton had its origin in the grammar school founded in Elizabethan days by Roger Dalison, precentor of Lincoln Cathedral.

Lea. Lying near the Trent, here flowing in zigzag fashion towards Gainsborough, once a charming and tranquil village but now rapidly changing with new housing estates developing in many places. It had its crowded hour three centuries ago, for here in July 1643 Cromwell fought and won a battle against young Charles Cavendish, a godson of Charles I. It was not one of Cromwell's most famous victories, perhaps, but had the battle gone against him the course of history might well have been changed. The names of two fields here, Redcoats and Graves Close, are reminders of the struggle, and the meadow into which the defeated men were driven is still known as Cavendish Bog.

Standing high on a mound, and neighboured by a magnificent sycamore and other trees, Lea Church was much restored a century ago. The tower was built about 1500, the chancel in the 13th century, and the nave in the 14th; but the chancel arch, the nave arcade, and the fine south doorway (enriched with ballflower ornament) are modern.

The aisle (with 15th century windows in its north wall) is now undivided from the 14th century chapel which opens to the chancel with its original arch and has its tall three-light east window glowing with a rare collection of contemporary glass, including a fine Crucifixion scene and a figure of Bishop Grosseteste. Other old fragments are in the west window of the tower. In the modern pulpit is some 15th century tracery with carvings of flowers, dragons, an angel, a two-headed bird, and a tiny head smaller than a thumbnail.

On a canopied tomb in the aisle is the stone figure of Sir Ralph Trehamton, a knight in chain armour and surcoat, with a lion at his feet. The moated site of the Trehamtons' old manor house (now called Hermit Dam) is a mile east of the village, not far from Thurlby Wood.

Other memorials, windows and tablets, pay tribute to the memory of the Andersons who lived at Lea Hall, a fine old house, now used as a school, standing in park-like grounds noted for splendid holly hedges. One inscription tells of Mary Anderson, 60 years Mistress of the Wardrobe at Hampton Court; she was 17 at the time of the Stuart rising, and died at 90, three years after Waterloo. Another Anderson was rector of Lea for 51 years last century. The 9th and last baronet, Sir Charles Anderson, who died in 1891 was a well-known antiquary. One of his sons was buried at sea, and the tablet to his memory is notable because it shows an ocean map and the latitude and longitude of his watery grave.

It was at this village of Lea, 2 miles from Gainsborough, that Cromwell won one of those small but desperate victories which proved what a magnificent cavalry leader he was. The battle was fought on July 28, 1643, and it was one of the most thrilling of the Civil War.

The indecisive Battle of Edgehill had been fought, and the fortunes of Parliament were at their lowest ebb. In Gainsborough the Parliamentary party held the upper hand but were being besieged by Royalist forces from the king's stronghold at Newark Castle. A gallant young general, Charles Cavendish, a godson of Charles I, was in command of the besiegers.

News of the siege reached Cromwell, just after he had taken Stamford in the south of the county; and he at once set out on a 55-mile ride to relieve the beleaguered town, picking up additional forces from Grantham and Lincoln.

Cromwell met the mounted troops under Cavendish here at Lea. The Royalists, much the larger force, were posted on a sandy plateau with the marshes of the Trent below. Cromwell's small force dashed up the steep ascent to the plateau, riddled though it was with rabbit holes, and there was a quick hand-to-hand contest with the advance guard of the enemy, who gave way.

Cromwell then saw that Cavendish had a large body of horsemen in reserve, and quickly restrained his forces from the pursuit. So, when Cavendish attacked and routed the Lincoln troopers, Cromwell and his troopers charged the enemy from behind, driving them down into the marshes, where the gallant young Cavendish was slain.

But Cromwell had to show his mettle in even more trying circumstances. When he entered Gainsborough the news reached him that the Earl of Newcastle was approaching with an overwhelming force. Cromwell's cavalry would have been wasted within the fortifications, so he retired from the town.

It was one of the most masterly retreats in his career, for an overwhelming force of fresh cavalry was at his heels. He divided his troopers into two sections, holding back the pursuit while the other section retired. Nine times had they to halt and face their pursuers but they made good their retreat with the loss of only two lives.

Gainsborough did surrender to the Earl of Newcastle, but three months later Cromwell came again with a large force and not only won back Gainsborough but cleared all the Royalist forces out of Lincolnshire.

Leadenham. A pleasant stone-walled village, it is grouped about the busy crossing of two roads—one the highway from Grantham to Lincoln, here running up the steep slope of the Cliff, and the other the road from Newark, which goes on climbing to cross the Heath and Ermine Street on its way to Sleaford.

In a churchyard shaded by fine limes and beeches stands the big mediaeval church. From the second half of the 14th century come the lower part of the tower and the lofty nave with its finely-moulded arches on clustered piers. The top of the pinnacled tower, adorned with many gargoyles and little stone heads, and the lofty crocketed spire, were built by 15th century men, who raised the chancel and the chantry a little later.

There are piscinas in the chancel and the aisles, and the old rood stairs are still here, too. The chancel ceiling was painted by Pugin in 1841. The east window has some early 16th century Flemish glass brought here over a century ago, showing a figure of Christ enthroned as Prophet, Priest, and King, with a radiant golden light about Him and the faces of many angels below; below is modern glass with eight scenes from the Life of Christ. Another window in the chancel has good modern figures of the Good Shepherd, Hugh of Lincoln, and St Swithin; and perhaps the most attractive of the many other modern windows is one in the south aisle with Saints George, Andrew, and Elizabeth of Hungary, and another in the north aisle showing Charity. The modern oak screen, tall and elaborately carved with tracery, foliage, vine, and roses, has angels painted in its canopy.

There are two old porches, the north one being notable for its gable frieze of shields and heads in quatrefoils, and for its little modern figure of St Swithin holding a model of the church. Both porches shelter 14th century doorways, one being enriched with foliage, and both doorways have traceried double doors of oak, which, like the attractive red-tiled lychgate, were fashioned by local craftsmen and set here as memorials to Colonel John Reeve, a 19th century lord of the manor.

Leadenham House, home of the Reeve family, is sited on the Cliff with magnificent views. It was built at the end of the 18th century. Leadenham Old Hall is another attractive house still earlier in date, belonging to the late 17th century and originally the home of the Beresfords whose memorials are in the church.

Leasingham. Now bypassed by the main road and screened among trees on the road north of Sleaford, this village looks up to a tower which has stood for 800 years. At its base is a Norman doorway and on each side of the belfry is a 13th century window, each with two lancets divided by a mullion rising curiously from an angular transom instead of from the sill. Above the tower rises a heavy broach spire with three rows of gabled lights, each with its pair of gargoyles; other gargoyles look out between the windows and from the corners of the tower.

The south doorway is 13th century, but the porch which shelters it is a century younger and is called the Angel Porch because on its hood are graceful figures of two angels, one bearing a scroll and the other a sheaf of corn and a sickle. The chancel arch, the nave arcade with its three arches on clustered piers and two solemn mediaeval faces above, and the aisle with its piscina and aumbry, are also 14th century work. The east end of this aisle was restored, and the chancel rebuilt, during the rectorship of Edward Trollope, Bishop of Nottingham and famous antiquary. He was rector here for 50 years, coming here in 1843, a few years after the death of Friskney Gunnis, who served here for 54 years. Trollope it was who founded and endowed the little group of almshouses near the church.

In the nave wall is a curious recess with the bust of a praying man in a quatrefoil, and on one of the nave pillars is the iron hourglass stand. But the finest old possession of the church is the font, its base and stem 13th century, and its bowl probably a 15th century copy of the original. Round the bowl are roughly-carved scenes of the Temptation, St Michael, Herodias with Salome and the headless Baptist, and Jesus entering Jerusalem, carrying the Cross, rising from the dead, and seated in Glory on a rainbow; as supporters below the bowl are four figures of women (one with a purse and another with a distaff), an eagle, and an angel holding three heads.

There are three stone houses of note. One bearing the date 1655 stands north-west of the church. Leasingham manor house and Hall stand opposite. The former a late 17th century house with 18th century front; the latter a 19th century building.

Legbourne. Lying about a curve of the road from Louth to Alford, this village is a pleasant sight with its 600-year-old church and its canopied and pinnacled stone pump given last century as a memorial to a mother. On the other side of the stream running from Bracken Hill is the site of a priory founded here in the 12th century for Cistercian nuns; a modern house called the Abbey stands on the spot today, but there are some traces of the old building close by. A little nearer Louth the road runs by the pretty park of Kenwick Hall. The present house was built to designs by Sir Albert Richardson and replaces a later 19th century building.

Built in the second half of the 14th century, and restored in 1868, the church is a patchwork of grey and green stone, and has a fine tower. The east end of the south aisle was once a chantry, and there is a floorstone to one of its chaplains, Thomas Maidenwell, who died in 1507; here is a piscina found during restoration, and here also is a broken altar stone with three crosses. The fine 15th century chancel

Steep Hill, Lincoln

LINCOLN (*a*) The Jew's House

(*b*) The High Bridge

screen (restored a little) has rose-tipped arches and lovely tracery. The font (with traceried stem, and shields carved on its bowl) is 600 years old. There are fragments of old black and gold glass.

Legbourne has one thing more—the memory of Alfred Smith, who gave his life in that search for knowledge which saves the lives of others. He was one of the immortal band of X-ray pioneers.

Legsby. Time has done little, it seems, to disturb the tranquillity of this small place in wooded country at the foot of the Wolds, with its few farms and cottages scattered along the winding byway.

A lychgate in memory of men who died in the First World War leads to a little stone church echoing the past. The tower has a modern bell-chamber with overhanging parapet and ball-topped pinnacles, but it has kept its 15th century west window and its old arch to the nave. The tiny sanctuary, with the old altar-rails across its low entrance arch, has a 15th century east window. The massive tub font is here, too, just as the Normans made it, with double cable ornament round the rim; and among the church plate there is an Elizabethan chalice.

Lenton. A village with two names, Lenton or Lavington, it has a well-cared-for church in a churchyard trim with tall firs and clipped yews.

The grey spire looks over the green fields as it has looked for 600 years, and on the tower below is a boldly-marked sundial that has told the time on sunny days since 1824. The nave, with foliage carved on one of its pillars, is largely 13th century. The chancel is 15th century work and has an elaborate wall-monument to the Armyns who in Elizabeth I's day lived at Osgodby Hall, a moated manor house about a mile away which has now been demolished. The monument is a three-decker affair of marble erected in 1605: a massive stone table with 24 small shields round its edge, borne up on six legs with carved spears and axes and baskets of fruit, and, above this, two rows of inscribed tablets and panels decked with shields and other heraldic devices.

In the south aisle is a piscina, and on a nearby bracket is a small stone tablet with a carved figure of a Roman civilian. It was unearthed here on a farm and afterwards brought into the safe-keeping of the church.

On the list of vicars is the name of Edward Bradley, who as Cuthbert Bede was author of much kindly, humorous writing, including the *Adventures of Mr Verdant Green*. He was an unwearying worker for the social, intellectual, and spiritual life of his people last century.

Leverton. This big village not far from the sea, has a beautiful church built in the 14th and 15th centuries and restored in 1892, when an 18th century clerestory of brick was replaced by the present one. The church is attractive both outside and in, and is adorned with a number of gable crosses which call to mind its dedication to St Helena, mother of the Emperor Constantine and discoverer of the True Cross.

The leaning tower and the big chancel with its graceful chapel are 15th century work, the earlier portion of the church being the nave and its aisles, divided by arcades with slender clustered pillars. Lovely indeed is the chapel, with pinnacles and many grotesques in its wealth of carved external stonework; on an interior wall is a line of four strange corbels, carved with crouching men, a monkey, and a lion's head.

The chancel has pinnacled buttresses, and three sedilia exquisitely carved; with their cinquefoiled arches, vaulted canopies, hoods adorned with leaves, and fine finials reaching the cornice of flowers and heads (surmounted by fine cresting) the sedilia are the glory of the church. At the back of the sedilia is a peephole to the chapel, and there is another in the piscina.

There is a 15th century oak screen, tall and finely traceried, and there are also the old rood stairs and two big lion-heads which supported the loft. The font with its delicate tracery and quatrefoils is mediaeval; the fine roofs with embattled beams are modern.

The name of the village is engraved in picture (a lever and a tun) on an Elizabethan chalice and paten belonging to the church; and in the chapel is a reminder of a man who knew this place when Elizabeth I was queen and won for himself a measure of fame in later years. Deeply cut on a windowsill is the name of Henry Pecham, with the date 1597. That was the year when his father came here as rector and Henry was a Cambridge graduate of 21. He is remembered as the writer of a book called *The Compleat Gentleman*, in which he described "the most necessary and commendable qualities concerning minde or bodie that may be required in a noble gentleman". It was the book from which Dr Johnson drew all the heraldic definitions in his Dictionary.

Lincoln. For the traveller who wishes to step awhile into the past there are few cities to equal proud Lincoln, this "old, confused town—long, uneven, steep, and rugged", as John Evelyn described it. For more than 2000 years Lincoln has played a part in the story of our land, and it has a stirring tale to unfold. Long before Julius Caesar landed on our shores there was a Celtic settlement, on the magnificent hilltop soaring 210 feet above the River Witham. On this same site, on the brow of the hill, the Romans built their military fortress and later walled town and gave it the name *Lindum Colonia*. Within its confines a castle and a cathedral church were subsequently to rise; and after the Romans came Saxons and Danes, holding the town in turn.

Under Saxon rule Lincoln became part of the Kingdom of Mercia, and after Paulinus had introduced the Christian faith a stone church is said to have been built within the old Roman walls. Alfred the Great had a Mint here and coins were struck during the reigns of most of the kings down to the time of Edward I. The Danes made Lincoln the chief of the Five Boroughs of their Danelagh, and street names like Saltergate, Danesgate, and Hungate still stand as witness to their sway here. Then came the Norman invaders under whose rule Lincoln became one of the most important cities in the whole realm. Here as was their custom they built a defensive castle; and here, too, the Norman Bishop Remigius built a church on the hill-top, "strong as the place was strong and fair as the place was fair" —a cathedral church which was to grow into one of the greater glories of England.

Great fires and an earthquake in the 12th century wrought destruction in the city; it suffered severely during the long struggle between Stephen and the Empress Matilda for the English crown, and again in the Civil War. But Lincoln survived all these troubles and with the passing years grew in stature and in fame. Henry II gave it several charters, and in 1158 was crowned (for the second time) outside the city boundary; and many other royal visits were made by Plantagenet and later kings—some granting privileges, and some holding Parliaments here.

At Lincoln in 1200 King John received the homage of William of Scotland, and in the same year helped to bear the body of St Hugh of Avalon to the west door of his cathedral. Eighty years later Edward I and his beloved Queen Eleanor were present on the great occasion of the translation of the bishop-saint's body to its new shrine; and in 1290 Eleanor was borne through Lincoln on the first stage of her funeral procession from Harby in Nottinghamshire to Westminster.

In 1301 Edward I held a Parliament which denied the Pope's claim to the sovereignty of Scotland; and in 1316 Parliament met here again for the purpose of providing Edward II with supplies for the war with Scotland. On his visit in 1387, Richard II gave the mayor the right to have a sword carried before him in processions, and the sword he presented is still a treasured part of Lincoln's civic insignia. Henry VII was here for three days, giving thanks for the victory of Bosworth Field; Henry VIII was here with Catherine Howard in 1541 and was regally entertained by Bishop Longland at his palace. At the beginning of the Civil War Charles I was acclaimed by a great crowd in this city, which, after being held alternately by both sides, was besieged by the Parliamentarians in 1644 and, falling to the Earl of Manchester, was stormed and sacked. James I was at Lincoln Races in 1617, and in 1695 William of Orange visited the cathedral when on his way to Welbeck. Thus has the royal cavalcade continued, down to our own times.

No English city is a more impressive spectacle than Lincoln on its hilltop. The noble triple-towered cathedral, so often slightly veiled in mist, dominates every vista near and far. No gem in England's diadem shines more brightly; certainly not one of our cathedrals—not even Salisbury or Durham—is outwardly more striking. In addition, there is a grand array of mediaeval houses and gateways in and about the cathedral close, called the Minster Yard. Close by are the castle ruins, and splendid Roman remains including the only gateway in the land which has been in constant use since Roman times. On the hill are two houses dating from Norman times.

Lincoln of course does not live in the past. Though rightly proud of its heritage, it marches with the times, and continues to play a leading part in the industrial life of the nation, as it did in days gone by when it was a great trading centre, famed for its scarlet cloth and "Lincoln Green"—the "staple" town where wool was sold, weighed, and certified before being shipped to Boston.

Below the hill Lincoln is a workaday place, and the bustle of its High Street—all too narrow for modern conditions—is heightened by the railway level crossings which constantly halt the congested traffic. Engineering, iron-founding, the manufacture of agricultural machinery, seed-milling, semi-conductors, belt production and electronic valves are among its most important trades, providing a livelihood for many of the population, which in recent times has been outstripped by that of Grimsby.

The atmosphere of bygone days clings steadfastly to Lincoln's hilltop; and in the city below also (and especially along the High Street) much that is old rubs shoulders with the new—and not incongruously. There, the rich store of old remains includes two churches with 11th century towers; the Hall of St Mary's Guild (a Norman building known as John of Gaunt's Stables); and the grand mediaeval stone gateway called the Stonebow, striding across the road which, less than 100 yards away, is carried across the Witham by the celebrated High Bridge—unique in the land because of the old timbered houses which still stand picturesquely but firmly on its western side. Farther down High Street, within the narrow Akrill's Passage, is the attractive, recently restored, timbered façade of another old house with its coved overhanging storey and three little oriels; known as "Whitefriars House", after the Carmelites who were established here in 1269 and had their house on the other side of the road, where the St Marks station now stands.

One of the oldest bridges in England, High Bridge was built in mediaeval days on the foundations of a Norman bridge whose massive ribbed arch, 11 feet high and 22 feet wide, is one of the great possessions of the city. Its range of half-timbered houses (now shops) makes an imposing sight, and, like the bridge, was carefully restored at the beginning of this century. Narrow steps lead down to the river bank, and it is from here that the great Norman vault can be seen, a view-point known as the Glory Hole.

Just beyond lies the little river port of Brayford (a picturesque sight from its south bank, with the whole length of the cathedral poised above it in full view) where barges and boats have been loading and unloading ever since the Romans brought their Foss Dyke here to link the Witham with the Trent, and cut the Sincil Dyke to drain the flood water from the area enclosed by the great right-angle of the Witham.

Brayford Pool, as the little harbour beloved of artists is called, is a reminder of the origin of the name of Lincoln. Lincoln is derived from the *Lindum Colonia* of the Romans, but they only adapted the earlier name of *Lindon* belonging to the Celtic settlement. Lin means a pool or lake, and dun or don a hill-fort, so that Lindon meant a hill-fort by the pool. The "Pool" below the hill was a great stretch of morass flooded in bygone days by the waters of the Trent and Witham, and of which Brayford Pool is now the surviving relic. Significant too is the second part of the Roman name, *Colonia*, proclaiming that *Lindum* had become a colony, a chartered town and settlement for time-expired legionary soldiers.

The Romans forded this morass with their Ermine Street, and this was joined by the Fosse Way where the South Common comes down to the road. The High Street still follows the actual line of the Ermine Street, though at a much higher level, and changes its name where it enters a narrow bottle-neck at the foot of the hill. At first it is called The Strait; above, where a hand-rail helps those going up or down, it is Steep Hill—and never was a street more aptly named. At the top is the open space of Castle Square, with the castle to the west and the cathedral to the east, and from here the road enters Bailgate for its journey north, still on the line of Ermine Street, which runs through the Roman Newport Arch and follows a straight, uninterrupted course to the Humber. Two other important roads connected Lincoln with east and west—the highway to Horncastle and Burgh, and the Till Bridge Lane which linked Ermine Street with their *Segelocum* (Littleborough) across the Trent.

From the Stonebow below to Newport Arch on the hilltop, the Ermine Street bisected the whole of Roman Lincoln; for although the first Roman town occupied only the brow of the hill, the colony rapidly grew to more than twice its original size. Its east and west walls were prolonged downhill, and a new southern boundary was made not far from the river, the Stonebow marking the site of the southern gate of this lower Roman town.

The first Roman town was approximately a square enclosure of about 42 acres—defended on all sides by a wall and deep, wide fosse—with a gate in the middle of every side. The south and east gates were demolished in the 18th century, and the remains of the west gate collapsed soon after being accidentally discovered in 1836. The north gate, however, still stands at the end of Bailgate. This is the noble Newport Arch; and it is a thrilling experience for a traveller to walk through it if he will just remind himself that he is following a path trodden in turn by Roman soldiers and civilians, Saxons peasants, and then by Danish and Norman invaders alike. It was damaged and rebuilt in 1964 after a load of frozen-food had attempted to pass through it!

Standing across the Ermine Street as it has stood for about 1700 years, the arch gets its name from the Norman suburb to which it led, though it was old and weathered even when the Conqueror rode under it on his way from York in 1068. With its foundations 8 feet below the present roadway, the central arch is 16 feet wide and 22 feet high, and its rounded head is formed by 26 massive rough-hewn stones, about 3 feet long and so ingeniously shaped and placed that they have remained in position through the centuries without mortar or other support. Of the two smaller posterns only the eastern one remains, and the head of its arch is composed of similar massive stones. Remains of a massive external tower have been found by excavation to the north-west of the gate; the site is available for visitors to see.

At the top of a steep bank in a garden (seen from the East Bight or from Church Lane) is a splendid fragment of the Roman north wall in which the arch was built; close by is a stone interval tower on the wall; and other fragments of the city walls (which were from 10 to 12 feet thick) are in foundations of houses and in gardens hereabouts, the finest being a magnificent stretch bordering the sunken garden of Eastgate Hotel which looks on to the cathedral chapter house. About 37 yards long and 12 feet high (and capped by later walling), it is part of the east wall of the city; the garden is in the fosse. Remains of the Roman east gate, consisting of a fine 3rd century north tower, with evidence of an earlier stone gate and a military timber gateway, have been exposed in the forecourt of the hotel.

Inlaid in the roadway and footpath of Bailgate are groups of round paving setts marking the site of a long colonnade; the bases of some of the pillars still exist below. It was perhaps part of a basilica and temple, divided by the east–west road. Behind a school in Westgate stands a splendid stretch of Roman wall some 30 feet high and $3\frac{1}{2}$ feet thick, with courses of Roman brick at intervals in the rough stone; it is known as the Mint Wall, and is believed to have been the north wall of the basilica. Many other Roman antiquities found hereabouts are in the cathedral library and cloister and in the City and

County Museum, one of the most interesting being a milestone (found in Bailgate) recording that *Segelocum* was 14 miles from *Lindum*.

Occupying the greater part of the south-west corner of the first Roman city, Lincoln Castle was one of many founded in England by the Conqueror. Built perhaps to impress the townsfolk as well as keep them in order, it was begun after his visit to Lincoln in 1068, and it is recorded that "166 mansions" were destroyed to clear a space for its site. Its position on the crest of the hill made it a natural stronghold almost invulnerable on the southern side, and it was a rallying point for most of the fighting that raged about Lincoln—especially in the struggle between Stephen and Matilda. At first it was held by Matilda, who settled in Lincoln when she came to England in 1140; before long it was taken by Stephen, but in the encounter of 1141, known as the Joust of Lincoln, Stephen was defeated and taken prisoner by the Earl of Gloucester. A little later he was released in exchange for the earl, who had been taken at Winchester, and by 1146 Stephen was again in possession of the castle.

Trouble continued in the time of King John, and the castle withstood a long siege by the barons who had taken Lincoln with the help of the Dauphin of France. After the death of the king, many of the barons went over to his son, and another attempt by Prince Louis and his supporters to take the castle in 1217 met with no success. In May the garrison was relieved by the Earl Marshal, commander-in-chief of the royal army, William, Earl of Pembroke. After hand-to-hand fighting in the streets, the French and the rebellious barons were defeated and the city plundered—the enormous amount of booty taken giving the battle the name of the Fair of Lincoln. In the Civil War the castle shared the fate of the city. A royal demesne in its early days, held for the king by the constables, the castle passed through the Earls of Lincoln and Lancaster back again to the crown, and was sold to Lincoln County in 1831.

Rising from a great earthen bank raised partly on the line of the Roman wall and protected by a deep wide ditch, the curtain wall of the castle encloses a roughly-quadrangular area of more than 6 acres, trim with lawns and trees. The wall, varying from 8 to 10 feet thick, and about twice as high, includes some of Norman date with fine herringbone masonry on the north and west sides. At the north-east corner is the low tower known as Cobb Hall, and on two great detached mounds on the southern side are the Observatory Tower and the shell of the Norman keep. In the middle of the eastern wall, facing Castle Square, is the principal gateway; this also is mainly Norman work, but outside the original round-headed arch is a pointed 14th century arch, and flanking the ruined upper storey are turrets of the same period. The north-west gateway or sally-port is Norman work; now blocked, it has a round-headed archway with the old portcullis groove, and above are two deeply-splayed windows and a doorway.

The two-storied Observatory Tower is Norman at its base and 14th century above; its round turret was built last century as an observatory, and there are splendid views from the top. The many-sided keep of the castle (called the Lucy Tower after the Countess Lucy who was Hereditary Constable) has more than 50 steps climbing to its entrance, and the jagged line of its ivied walls marks the beginning of a vanished upper storey.

Cobb Hall is a battlemented tower of the 14th century with loop-holes lighting its two vaulted storeys. Here prisoners were flogged, and in the walls there are still the iron rings to which they were fastened. The roof of this tower was used for public executions till 1868, and within the walls of the ancient keep are stones marking the graves of prisoners. In the green castle enclosure stands the county gaol, built in 1787 by Carr of York and now restored to serve as the offices of the Lincolnshire Archives Committee; and here too are the County Hall and Assize Courts, designed by Sir Robert Smirke and built in 1826.

Within the passage of the castle gateway are two precious fragments of old Lincoln. One is a piece of a sculptured female figure, all that is left of the Eleanor Cross which was set up near the foot of Cross o' Cliff Hill. It stood just outside the city, close to the Gilbertine priory of St Catherine where the body of Queen Eleanor was embalmed by the nuns, and was the first of the famous crosses erected to mark the halting places of the queen's funeral procession—a "fair cross of stone, raised by the monarch of the realm to Eleanor his queen". The second fragment is an exquisite oriel window. Above its three lights are ogee canopies with finials; below are pairs of dainty quatrefoils; and between are slender panelled buttresses ending in tall pinnacles and rising from four figures (one an angel) seated in a band of fine foliage. Below this is another band of foliage, and then a row of three heads; and all three bands, tapering to an angel at the foot, make a rare bracket for the oriel. It was brought here for safe-keeping in 1849, from a house known as John of Gaunt's Palace which stood where the street bearing his name enters the High Street, and was the home of his third wife, Catherine Swynford. They were married in Lincoln Cathedral, and there she was laid to rest. Immediately opposite the palace site in High Street is the ancient Hall of the Guild of St Mary, which was one of the oldest and richest guilds in the city. Known to the townsfolk as John of Gaunt's Stables, it was built about 1180 and originally formed a small court. Portions of only two sides remain. The range fronting High Street has lost most of its upper storey, but there is still the grand old entrance archway with flowers dotted in its mouldings, and under the roof runs a rich band of carved honeysuckle and other foliage, with faces and animals peeping out here and there. Within the court is a late Norman house with two-light windows in its upper storey.

St Mary's Guildhall has lost its high estate, but the City Guildhall is in the upper storey of the Stonebow, the imposing gateway that stands where the Romans set the south gate of their extended city, and where an earlier mediaeval gateway stood until the closing years of the 14th century. Begun late in the 15th century and completed in the 16th, the Stonebow spans the High Street with a wide central archway (flanked by turrets) and a postern at each side. Canopied statues of St Mary and the Archangel Gabriel adorn the south front, and between them are the Royal Arms, added in Stuart times. Battlements complete the upper storey, and on the roof hangs the Mote Bell bearing the date 1371. Through the centuries this bell has been rung in Lincoln, and it still calls the Fathers of the Council to their civic business in the council chamber over the archway—a long narrow room with a fine old roof of massive beams and floral bosses, and windows on each side that look out on the unceasing pageantry of the city's life.

In the Guildhall is Lincoln's fine collection of civic insignia. In addition to the chains and badges of office there are two maces of the 17th century, three "Caps of Maintenance", 1734, 1814, and 1937, of crimson velvet with the Tudor rose embroidered in silver on their crowns, and an Elizabethan thumb ring of solid gold which the retiring mayor places on the thumb of his successor when he is installed—as an emblem of his union with the people. Here, too, are the three historic swords of which the city is so proud: the weighty King Richard's sword, given by Richard II in 1387 when he came to Lincoln to stay with his uncle, John of Gaunt; Henry VII's sword, believed to have been presented by that king in 1487, after his victory over the Earl of Lincoln at East Stoke near Newark; and the inscribed blade of the sword presented by Charles I in 1642.

Less than 300 yards from the Stonebow the High Street enters upon its stiff climb up the street, first called The Strait and then Steep Hill, in which stand two Norman houses. The old name for the bottle-neck at the entrance was Dernstall Lock (later corrupted to St Dunstan's Lock) and the name gave rise to a baseless tradition that once there was a barrier here which was closed at sunset to shut in the Jews who lived on the hill. In Dernstall was the home of the boy who according to ill-founded legend was crucified by the Jews at one of their houses on the hill—Little St Hugh, who was buried in the cathedral in 1255. A 15th century town house has just been restored here by the Lincoln Civic Trust and appropriately named "Dernstall House". It is of the same period as The Cardinal's Hat, just below in High Street which was restored in 1953. It was named in compliment to Cardinal Wolsey, Bishop of Lincoln 1514-15.

On the west side of the Strait is the Jew's House, built about 800 years ago and now a shop with big windows instead of the loopholes with which the lower storeys were originally lighted. Its round-arched doorway has interlaced ornament, and from it springs the chimneyshaft for the fireplace in the upper storey, which still has two round-headed windows. Here, it is said, lived Belaset of Wallingford, the Jewess hanged in 1290 for "clipping the king's coin"; that was the year of the expulsion of the Jews from England, after which any Jew found was to be hanged, drawn, and quartered. Adjoining the Jew's House is a dwelling of late 12th century origin known as the Jews' Court, which may have been used as a synagogue, or perhaps for a Jewish school.

On the east side of Steep Hill, at the corner of Christ's Hospital Terrace, is the second Norman house, sometimes called (though without foundation) the house of Aaron the Jew. The most famous of all the Lincoln Jews (who were settling here in the time of Stephen), Aaron was the richest money-lender in the land in the latter half of the 12th century. Merchants, noblemen, archbishops, and other dignitaries all borrowed money from him, and he lent money for the building of many monasteries and cathedrals. The round arch of the doorway of this house is dotted with flowers and leaves, under a hood ending in corbels carved with faces; above it is the chimneyshaft, and in the upper storey is one of the original two-light windows, restored. Within the house is a winding stone stairway leading to a barrel-vaulted cellar. Near this house the south wall of the first Roman city crossed the hill, and set in the wall on the other side of the road is a fragment, perhaps a jamb, of the Roman south gateway. A few yards below it, on each side of the road, is a stone post with the carved and painted fleur-de-lys of the city arms, marking the southern limit of the Bail. In the Middle Ages Lincoln was divided into three parts, the City, the Close, and the Bail—the Bail being the district outside the Close and within the area of the Roman walled town, ruled by the governor of the castle, as the city was ruled by the mayor and corporation.

At the corner of Steep Hill and Michaelgate is an old half-timbered house, and facing the top of the hill, at the corner of Bailgate, is an even more charming one with three gables and two overhanging storeys, now occupied by a bank. Here, back in Castle Square, at the end of the climb, the cathedral and its precincts are at hand, reached through the Exchequer Gate, a fitting portal for the grandeur that lies beyond.

Just as Rome was not built in a day so Lincoln cannot be seen in a day—nor yet in a week; and it is well for the traveller to make the Exchequer Gate the beginning of a circular tour round the Close and Eastgate, seeing on the one hand a fine array of old houses, and on the other the external beauty of the cathedral unfolding step by step. If the tour is made unhurriedly it is one of sheer enchantment —a walk amid cloistered calm more than a little refreshing after the hurly-burly of the city.

Looking on to the cathedral's noble west front with its superb twin towers, and to the incomparable central tower rising beyond them, the Exchequer Gate is the principal entrance to the close, which was surrounded by a wall late in the 13th century. Edward I's licence for the wall is still preserved. Edward II gave permission for the wall to be embattled and fortified, and the work was begun about 1319: in the garden of the Chancery are two ruined turrets that formed part of the fortifications, and other fragments remain elsewhere. Of several double gateways inserted in the wall only the early 14th century Exchequer Gate remains, and this lost its outer gateway at the end of the 18th century. A lofty, three-storied building, it has a great central archway flanked by embattled turrets and two posterns. All the archways are finely groined in brick, with stone ribs and bosses, one boss in the north passage showing the Crucifixion; and canopied niches and hooded windows with corbel heads adorn the east front. The only other original gateway is the embattled 14th century Pottergate Arch, standing where the Lindum Road makes a sharp turn into Pottergate. Almost opposite the chapter house, and leading to Eastgate, is the three-arched North Gate of the Close, erected in 1816 about 10 years after the destruction of a fine double gatehouse.

The first house in the close, adjoining the Exchequer Gate on the south, is the Deanery, with a front restored last century. Next comes the Subdeanery where Archdeacon Paley wrote his *Natural Theology*. The Deanery stands on the site of a Roman hypocaust, and the south wall of the first Roman town which ran behind these houses still survives in the bank just south of the north boundary wall of the old palace grounds. Opposite the south porch of the cathedral is the much-restored Cantilupe Chantry House, built about 1360 for the priests and choristers attached to the Cantilupe Chantry. In its gable-end is a long two-light oriel window supported by grotesques; there is a big shield at each side, and a figure of Our Lord is in a niche above.

At the corner below this house is the entrance to the Vicars' Court and the picturesque ruins of the old Bishop's Palace, all on the steep slope of the hill. Begun in the 12th century, the building of the palace was carried on by the mediaeval bishops till its splendour was worthy of the cathedral in whose shadow it rose. After the Reformation it began to decay; severely damaged in the Civil War and dismantled during the Commonwealth, it became a ruin and much of its old stone was used in the 18th century for repairing the cathedral. The Ministry of Public Building and Works has now taken it into guardianship and excavation and consolidation of this interesting palace is proceeding. It will shortly be open to the public.

The grounds, serene with their lawns and flowerbeds, are entered through two embattled gateways—the inner rebuilt, and the outer bearing the arms of its builder, Bishop William Smyth, one of the founders of Brasenose College, Oxford. A few yards from the entrance stands the inner gate-tower, a fine three-storied building with a square-headed doorway and an embattled oriel, built five centuries ago by Bishop Alnwick (who once entertained Henry VI in the palace). This gate-tower (which was restored by Bishop Wordsworth) leads to the site of the Great Hall, the earliest part of the palace ruins—begun by Hugh of Avalon and completed by Hugh of Wells. About 90 feet long and 60 feet wide, it was divided into three aisles by rows of marble pillars; now it is a great open space with fragments of its east and west walls and remains of a fine porch with triple-arched entrance at the south-west corner. At its southern end are the three doorways (with clustered shafts and carved capitals) which opened to the butteries, above which was the Great Chamber. Out of their ruins a chapel was built last century when an 18th century house to the west was adapted and enlarged to make a new palace for Bishop King; the house is now a Diocesan Conference Centre and offices. Linking the butteries with the great kitchen is a vaulted bridge with two fine pointed arches, but the kitchen and the brewhouse below it are now only a great shell. To the east of the Great Hall is a lawn raised on vaulted chambers; it marks the site of a lesser hall and dining-room built by Bishop Alnwick, and retains a shafted west doorway.

More memorable than any of the ruins of the old palace, however, are the views from its grounds, particularly a near view of the south side of the cathedral soaring above the high boundary wall; and another of the city below, in an abrupt gap of the Lincolnshire Cliff, with its towers and spires and factory chimneys veiled in a haze of industrial smoke.

The entrance to the Vicars' Court is a late 13th century vaulted gateway with a wide corbelled arch under three great shields; it frames an inviting picture of the south-east porch of the cathedral, and shelters a flight of stone steps leading down to old houses attractively grouped round a green quadrangle. Built to house the Priest Vicars who took part in the choir services of the cathedral, the Court was begun late in the 13th century by Bishop Sutton and completed about a century later. Once there were a score of houses, as well as a common dining-hall, in the Court, but those that remain still make a delightful picture—a medley of stone walls, roofs of mottled red tiles, and windows and doorways mellowed with age. (It is not open to the public.) The late 13th century house on the south side has a tiny lancet above the doorway as well as some two-light windows of the 14th century. The house on the north side was the birthplace in 1786 of William Hilton, a Royal Academician famed for his historical paintings. (In the cathedral there is a monument to him and his brother-in-law, Peter de Wint, and examples of their work are in the Usher Art Gallery.)

East of the Vicars' Court is the footway known as Greestone Stairs (from the Old-English greesen, meaning steps) where little flights of stone steps ease the steep drop to the Lindum Road—still sometimes called the New Road though it dates from the 18th century. Near the top, before the steps begin, an old postern spans the narrow way, and here too is Greestone House, attractive with its stone walls and fine iron gateway.

Running parallel with Greestone Stairs is Pottergate, with its fine 14th century arch. Here begins a long row of fine old houses of stone and rich red-brick, which continues along the Close to East-gate. Facing the east end of the cathedral is the Chancery, built by Anthony Bek about 1316, but with a three-gabled front and beautiful stone oriel added late in the 15th century. Adjoining the Chancery on its north side is the twin-gabled Choristers' House, rebuilt in 1616. In the garden of the Chancery are two turrets of the old fortified wall of the Close, and a long stretch of it borders the garden of the house known as The Priory by the 19th century North Gate of the same name. The Priory has recently been restored and found to enclose another tower of the Close Wall with fine newel staircase. The house itself is mediaeval with later modifications.

Some of the mediaeval stonework of the demolished North Gate was used in the construction of the little black-and-white Rest Room a few yards away, its open door a welcome sight to the weary hill-climber. From here the cathedral is seen to great advantage, rising from the lawn of the Minster Green, where stands the great bronze statue of that English poet who belongs so specially to Lincolnshire —Alfred Lord Tennyson. Sculptured by his friend G. F. Watts, and set here in 1905, it shows the poet standing in his familiar and ample cloak, looking intently at a flower from "the crannied wall' in one hand, and holding in the other his broad-brimmed hat. Beside him is his beloved wolf-hound, Karenina.

A turn into Eastgate, and past Eastgate Hotel with the remains of the north tower of the Roman gate in its forecourt, leads to the creeper-clad Bishop's House, standing in high-walled grounds. Opposite is the old Deanery, now used as a Cathedral School, built in 1847 and hiding from view much of this north side of the cathedral. Adjoining it on the west side is an embattled wall which belonged to the earlier deanery whose ancient buildings enclosed a quadrangular court and were pulled down last century, together with their fine 15th century gate tower. From the other side of Eastgate runs James Street, a secluded little road in which are the two fine old houses known as Deloraine Court and Burghersh Chantry House. Stone-walled and red-roofed, and with mullioned windows, the Court has work of the late 12th century in one wing; it belonged to Lord Deloraine, grandson of the Duke of Monmouth, and was once the home of George Tennyson, grandfather of the poet.

Having concluded a tour of Lincoln Cathedral's precincts, the visitor should now devote time and attention to the study of the noble fane itself, the glorious triple-towered Cathedral Church of St Mary which crowns the hilltop, expressing as it has done through many centuries man's everlasting faith and reverence. From north and south, from east and west, it affords a seemingly endless succession of splendid vistas, and no man looking upon these venerable walls, whether from afar or from the nearby lawns, can remain unmoved.

Nave, choir, and retro-choir are all aisled, and each has a triforium and clerestory. The vast central transept has eastern aisles divided into chapels, and a rare Galilee porch projecting from its southern arm. Farther east is the choir transept with chapels on its east side. (Both transepts have triforium and clerestory.) Other chapels project from the aisles of the retro-choir, and adjoining the nave aisles and the twin towers are two more chapels, forming a kind of western transept behind the great screen of the west façade. Linked by a vestibule with the north arm of the choir transept are the chapter house and cloister.

Built of the Lincolnshire oolite limestone—with less-enduring Purbeck marble displayed here and there in piers and shafts within —Lincoln is the third largest of English cathedrals, only York Minster and St Paul's exceeding it. Its area is about 57,000 square feet, its internal length 481 feet, and its greatest width—that of the main transept—223 feet. The height of the central (or Rood) tower is 271 feet, and that of the west towers about 206 feet. All three were once crowned with spires, but the central spire was destroyed by a storm in 1548, and the others were taken down in 1807.

Except for some Norman remains, and for a few additions made in the 14th and 15th centuries, the structure represents in the main 88 years of almost continuous building—beginning with Bishop Hugh of Avalon's rebuilding in the pure Early English style of architecture, and ending with the completion of retro-choir (built for his shrine) which is an unsurpassed example of the Geometrical or Early Decorated period.

For a full appreciation of Lincoln's great cathedral church, however, it is necessary to know something of its history and its builders, beginning with Remigius, its founder and first Bishop.

Almoner of Fécamp in Normandy, Remigius came to England with the Conqueror, contributing, as a gift from his abbey, a ship and 20 men for the invasion. In return for this service the Conqueror is said to have promised him a bishopric, and this promise was fulfilled in 1067 on the death of Wulfwig, last Saxon bishop of Dorchester, the place near Oxford to which the united sees of Lindsey and Leicester had been transferred because of the invading Danes. Remigius succeeded Wulfwig as bishop, and instead of building a new church at Dorchester chose Lincoln as the see of his vast diocese —stretching from Thames to Humber. At Lincoln the Conqueror was already raising his castle, and by 1075 Remigius had begun to build his church, in the south-east corner of the first Roman city. (One of the cathedral treasures is the original charter given by William for the transference of the see.)

Remigius died in 1092, shortly before the consecration of his church, built in the massive and severe early Norman style and then almost complete; it had two low west towers, another tower perhaps at the crossing, and an eastern apse, the foundations of which are below the present choir-stalls. After a disastrous fire in 1141 his church was restored and greatly enriched by Alexander "the Magnificent", that great builder of castles and monasteries who was Lincoln's 3rd bishop, from 1123 till his death in 1148. He gave the west front its three doorways, its interlaced arcading, and its bands of sculpture; and he heightened the Norman west towers.

In 1185 an earthquake devastated the cathedral. A year later a Carthusian monk named Hugh of Avalon became bishop, and he it was who in 1192 began the great rebuilding in Early English style which has endured as one of the glories of Lincoln. He pulled down the Norman church, except for its west end. Hugh died in 1200, leaving as his crowning memorial an aisled choir of four bays, an eastern apse with radiating chapels (its site is shown by lines in the pavement of the retro-choir), and a transept which had its upper storey extended by one bay in the 13th century. It is not known if Hugh began a central tower, but part of the east wall in both arms of the great transept is his work.

During the next 50 years, in the time of Bishops William of Blois, Hugh of Wells, and Robert Grosseteste, the original plan of the 13th century church was almost completed; and though there is no record of actual dates of the work, it is continued westward from Hugh's choir—first the great transept, followed by the nave and its flanking chapels, and then the screen embracing the Norman west front. The chapter house was built between 1220 and 1235. When the central tower was begun is not known, but it is certain that it fell in 1237, and that afterwards the lower stages of the present tower were built by Bishop Grosseteste. To his time also belong the two lovely doorways of Hugh of Avalon's choir aisles, the Galilee porch of the great transept, and the two-storied vestry and Choristers' Song School at the south-west corner of the east transept.

In 1220 Hugh of Avalon was canonised; and in 1255, when Henry of Lexington was bishop, another great building scheme was begun in honour of the saint's memory and as a more worthy shrine for his remains. The magnificent addition of this retro-choir to the church necessitated once again some removal of the city wall, as well as the destruction of the eastern part of St Hugh's church which lay beyond his transept. The building of the new retro-choir continued under Bishop Gravesend; and in 1280, when Oliver Sutton was bishop, the work was advanced enough for its consecration, and for the translation of the body of St Hugh to its new shrine, in the presence of Edward I and Queen Eleanor.

The cloister and its vestibule were built in Bishop Sutton's time, and in 1307 his successor, John of Dalderby, began his four years' work of completing the central tower. Other work of the 14th century included the reconstruction of the upper part of the south arm of the great transept, with its glorious round window. To the 15th century belong the great belfries of the west towers, the three west windows, the fine parapet of the Galilee porch, and the chantry chapels of Bishop Fleming and Bishop Russell projecting from the retro-choir aisles. Bishop Longland's chapel, on the south side, was added in the time of Henry VIII, under whom the chantries were suppressed and the shrines in the cathedral despoiled.

Not the least of Lincoln's many treasures are windows filled with priceless 13th century glass. There is also a fine array of mediaeval screenwork—of iron and stone and timber. Here and there are mediaeval doors still with their original decorative ironwork; and there is a grand series of stalls which were part of the enrichment of the cathedral made by its Treasurer, John of Welbourn, in the second half of the 14th century. He it was, too, who vaulted the three towers and added the fine arcading to the interior walls of the Norman towers and the one remaining bay of Remigius's nave, all serving now as west porches or vestibules.

With the 16th century came the loss of much of the cathedral's treasure; and with the 17th came the Civil War which was to cause much damage to the fabric, and the destruction of innumerable brasses and monuments. In 1674 Sir Christopher Wren built the cathedral library, raising it on a colonnaded corridor on the site of the north walk of the cloister which had fallen into ruin in the 15th century. Serving as an anteroom to Wren's library are three bays of the 15th century library which was partly destroyed by fire in 1609; and there is also a modern addition. In the 18th century came other alterations: the central tower was given its open parapet (since restored); the vestibules of the west towers were built up for support, tall classical doorways being inserted, quite out of keeping with the rest of the church; and the stone altar screen was set up in front of a portion of a double screen of the 13th century.

So runs the long story of the building of the cathedral, from the days of the Norman Conquest down to our own time, when, between the two World Wars, a great restoration was undertaken at a cost of nearly £170,000, to be followed in 1964–66 by yet another major repair and restoration for which a further £250,000 was raised. With the changes of the centuries in mind it is possible to appreciate more fully the rich detail of this great heritage. The whole building repays close study.

The building periods are well defined in the impressive west front, which is 173 feet wide, 83 feet high to the wavy parapet added in the 14th century, and rises 130 feet to the cross surmounting the central gable. Set in his massive masonry are Remigius's five deep recesses. The two short outer recesses and the two loftier inner recesses are as the Norman bishop built them; but the central recess soaring high above them all was given a pointed arch framing an exquisite cinquefoil window in the 13th century. In the three middle recesses are Bishop Alexander's splendid doorways (much restored) with embattled patterns, figures and foliage, birds and grotesques among their rich ornament. Above the three doorways are 15th century windows, and above the four outer recesses runs Bishop Alexander's round-headed interlaced arcading.

Framing the Norman work is the grand Early English screen with its tiers of lancet arcading extending round the flanking octagonal turrets. The turrets are crowned with spires, surmounted by sculptured figures—St Hugh on the south, and the Swineherd of Stow on the north, vigorously blowing his horn. (This is a modern copy of the original figure which commemorated a swineherd said to have given his hoard of silver pennies towards the building of the church.) Round the pointed arch of the central recess, and in the lovely arcaded gable above it, is the "lattice" pattern proclaiming it to be work of the time of Bishop Grosseteste.

Above the central doorway is a range of canopied niches sheltering 14th century statues of 11 seated kings; and on the wall at each side is a bishop. Above the two smallest of the Norman recesses are curious bands of sculpture in bas-relief, believed to be of Bishop Alexander's time. North of the central doorway, the scenes are from the New Testament and include Dives and Lazarus, the Death of Lazarus, the Blessed in Heaven, the Harrowing of Hell, and the Torments of the Damned. On the south side subjects from the Old Testament include the Expulsion from the Garden, Cain and Abel digging, the Birth of Enoch, and below it Lamech killing Cain, scenes from the Deluge, God speaking to Noah, Noah building the Ark, Daniel in the Lions' Den (in frame), Noah and his family in the Ark, Noah leaving the Ark. Inside the Ringers' Chapel is a scene of the Deluge.

This south-west tower is known as St Hugh's tower, and its companion as St Mary's tower, and together they give a superb finish to the west screen behind which they soar over 200 feet. Above their tiers of Norman arcading (varying in pattern on the two towers) are the long double windows of the 15th century belfries with their rich ogee canopies rising to fine panelled parapets; at the angles are bold octagonal turrets enriched at the top with pedimented arcading and crowned with lofty pinnacles. Projecting from the south side of St Hugh's tower is a charming gable which, like the arcading, is of Bishop Alexander's time; a corresponding gable projects from the north side of St Mary's tower.

Two of the 13 bells in St Hugh's tower are in memory of ringers of Lincoln Diocese who fell in the First World War; another is a memorial to Rupert Richardson (died 1947) who was 14 years Master of the Lincoln Diocesan Guild of Bell Ringers. A bell in St Mary's tower sounds the curfew at eight o'clock. For more than 300 years the old Great Tom of Lincoln hung in this north-west tower; but it became cracked, and in 1834 together with the six Lady Bells of the central tower, was recast into a new Great Tom 6 feet high and weighing 5 tons 8 cwt. which has hung in the central tower ever since. (With the breaking up of the Lady Bells Lincoln lost the unique distinction of being the only church in the land with two separate peals.)

The central tower, 271 feet high, is beautiful beyond words, from whatever vantage point it is seen. It is an amazing blend of perfect proportion, grace of outline, and wealth of decoration, including an astonishing mass of leafy crockets; many of these crockets adorn the shafts of Bishop Grosseteste's lancet arcading, which is further enriched with his lattice pattern. Divided from this earlier work by a dainty band of wavy pattern, the belfry has four pairs of long, slender two-light windows under gabled canopies which reach up to the later parapet of open carving; and at the angles of the tower panelled buttresses climb to the tall pinnacles. An ascent of some 340 steps to the top of the tower rewards the stout-hearted with magnificent views; on a clear day Boston Stump and Newark spire can be seen.

Continuing a close study of the cathedral's exterior along its south side, the boldly-buttressed Ringers' Chapel and the Consistory Court are seen first. Above can be seen Bishop Alexander's richly-arcaded gable on St Hugh's tower and then the fine arcaded clerestory of the nave, supported by flying buttresses from the aisle and enriched with a fine wavy parapet added in the 14th century and adorned with six canopied niches.

Next comes the south wing of the great transept, with niches in its lofty pinnacles, and with the rare Galilee porch at its south-west corner. This is all 13th century work, except for the richly-carved 15th century parapet of the Galilee porch and the 14th century rebuilding of the gable-end of the transept, above the four lancets—

a reconstruction which made this wall, outside and within, one of the most notable parts of the cathedral. It is thought to have been done in honour of Bishop John of Dalderby (who was revered locally as a saint), and to have been paid for out of the offerings made at his shrine. Within the gable, framed by a leafy parapet of pierced carving and resting on a frieze of quatrefoils, is a five-light window with flowing tracery; and below is the famous rose window known as the Bishop's Eye, filled with exquisite flowing tracery.

Built as a stately entrance for the bishop from his palace across the Close, the two-storied Galilee porch is especially notable for its profusion of dog-tooth ornament, repeated more than 5000 times. The groined roof of the cross-shaped interior rises from fine arcading, and opening to the transept is a double doorway with foliaged arches supported by a central shaft with lizard-grotesques at the foot.

Beyond St Hugh's choir (its buttresses ending in heavy triangular heads and its windows divided by slender buttresses) comes the south arm of his transept with its apsidal chapels, vestries, and Choristers' Song School. A notable feature of this transept is the gable-end (partly reconstructed in the 13th century) with four tiers of lancets.

Next comes the retro-choir, known as the Angel Choir, that "loveliest of human works", in which the beauty and grace of this cathedral is at its zenith. Set between the highly enriched chapels of Bishops Longland and Russell is its magnificent south portal, the cinquefoiled arches of its double doorway supported by a central shaft adorned with a modern statue of the Virgin and Child. Framing the doorway is a deeply recessed and gabled arch, and in the mouldings rising from the series of canopied niches lining the lower part of the recess are three exquisite bands of undercut foliage —the foliage in the outermost band being entwined round charming little statues of the Wise and Foolish Virgins, and that of the innermost band round statues of kings and queens which may have illustrated the genealogy of Christ. (Only 12 of the kings and queens and 16 of the virgins now remain.) In the tympanum of the doorway is the representation of the Doom which gives this entrance the name of the Judgment porch. Enclosed in a quatrefoil is a sculpture of Our Lord in Glory and attendant angels (all partly restored), while on one side the righteous are being borne by angels, and on the other side the wicked are being swallowed by the gaping jaws of hell. At each side of the porch are two fine draped figures, now headless.

The buttresses of this retro-choir aisle have crocketed gables and canopied niches, and from them flying buttresses spring in support of the beautiful clerestory. On one buttress (flanking the porch) is a gargoyle sometimes called the Devil on a Witch's Back; and on the easternmost buttress are splendid but restored mediaeval statues of

Edward I and Queen Eleanor who, together with a great company, attended the consecration of this retro-choir. On the buttress next to theirs is another sculptured figure, popularly, but probably incorrectly, identified with Margaret of Valois, second wife of Edward I.

The east end of Lincoln Cathedral displays the Early Geometrical style of architecture at its finest. Admirably set off by the lawn of Minster Green, it consists of three gabled compartments divided and flanked by massive buttresses enriched with canopied niches, and crowned with crocketed pediments and pinnacles. The east window, with its circles of foils, is about 57 feet high, and above it is a fine gable window of five lights, not seen within the church. In a trefoil above this window is a sculptured Virgin and Child. Above the three-light east windows of the aisles are tiers of arcading, and more arcading runs across the whole front below the three main windows. Near the north-east buttress on this front is an old well.

In its main features, the north side of the cathedral resembles the south, though without the grandeur of the Galilee porch and the Judgment porch. Here the chapter house and the cloister can be seen, extending half the length of the church; and here, too, corresponding with the 14th century Bishop's Eye in the southern arm of the great transept, is the 13th century Dean's Eye—a grand rose window with magnificent plate tracery.

Lincoln's 13th century chapter house, linked to the cloister, is 62 feet in diameter and is the earliest example of one on a polygonal plan. Every one of its 10 sides, except the entrance, has a pair of lancets; and at the angles are buttresses with crocketed pinnacles— the pinnacles, like the quatrefoiled parapet, being a 14th century addition. An unusual feature is the ring of eight sturdy, detached buttresses, added later as an additional support for the heavy stone vaulting, and linked to the original ones by stone beams.

The main entrance to the cathedral is through Bishop Alexander's doorways into the three west porches or vestibules, which (as already told) are the bases of Remigius's towers and the remaining bay of his nave. All were completely transformed in the 15th and 18th centuries, but high in the walls of the old Norman bay two of the round-headed windows of the original clerestory are exposed; and remains of the early Norman arched recesses can be seen in the tower walls enclosed in the Ringers' Chapel and the corresponding chapel on the north side. This north-west chapel has a wall arcade enriched with dog-tooth, and leads eastwards into the Morning Chapel of St Mary Magdalene, which also has richly-arcaded walls, and a fine vault descending to a beautiful central pillar clustered with banded shafts of Purbeck marble. On the south side, next to the Ringers' Chapel, is the Chapel of St Giles which has been the Consistory Court since 1609. It has a vaulted roof, a pointed wall arcade, and a double piscina.

Above the Norman clerestory windows and round the arch of the west window in the central vestibule is the lattice work of Bishop Grosseteste's time, and under the cinquefoil window is a gallery from which there is an uninterrupted view of the cathedral from west to east—known as Sir Joseph Banks' view. (The organ on top of the choir screen is an obstruction to the view below.) Higher still, above the vaulting, is a flat arch known as the elastic stone beam because it vibrates when jumped on.

In his book on English Cathedrals Francis Bond called the nave a study in harmonies, and it would be difficult to better the description. About 40 feet wide and 82 feet high, it is divided into seven bays, the two western bays on each side being narrower than the rest. The slender piers supporting the arches are 23 feet high and vary in detail; some are solid clustered marble piers, others are encircled by detached and banded shafts, and a third type are of stone with marble shafts. The triforium has two groups of three arches in every bay—the arches on clustered marble shafts, and their tympana pierced with foils; the clerestory has triple lancets with marble shafts. The capitals throughout have foliage, and more foliage enriches the bosses of the vault. The aisles have tall lancet windows above fine wall-arcading with marble shafts and foliated bosses (and with some dog-tooth on the south side); their vaults spring from the nave piers, and from clusters of slender marble shafts on the outer sides, the shafts breaking into the wall arcade in the south aisle.

In a bay of the south arcade is the great font, with curious beasts carved on its square, shallow bowl. Made of black Tournai marble in the middle of the 12th century, perhaps by Flemish craftsmen, it is one of only 10 similar fonts in England. (Lincolnshire has another, at Thornton Curtis.)

The four great piers supporting the central tower are composed of 24 alternate shafts of stone and marble, crowned with foliated capitals, and carrying arches with dog-tooth in their mouldings. Above is Bishop Grosseteste's arcaded lantern, signed with his lattice pattern; and from it spring the shafts of John of Welbourn's rich vault, its central boss 120 feet above the ground. It is impossible to look up to these four majestic soaring arches without being amazed at the achievement of the builders of old. All their skill and all their devotion went into their labours. They built not for themselves, but for all who should come after them; and everywhere within these hallowed walls is this quality of timelessness reflected.

From the western arch, this crossing and the arms of the great transept running from it present a wonderful picture. In front is the magnificent 14th century stone choir screen, spanning the width of the tower piers; adjoining these piers are the two exquisite doorways to the choir aisles, and from these run long lines of 15th century traceried screens (all of oak except that of the Works Chantry) separating the transept from its eastern chapels. The chapels are divided from each other by arcaded stone screens of contemporary date—13th century.

The choir screen has a finely-vaulted entrance with an ogee arch and fine finial. At each side are four bays of open ogee arcading with crocketed gables and pinnacled buttresses, linked by vaulting to the diapered wall behind. Along the top runs an embattled parapet of pierced wavy carving. Ten little figures of saints are on the buttresses, and on the arch and under the brackets by the doorway are many grotesques and animals. The organ on top of the screen was built in 1898, but the organ case is older. (For nine years in Elizabeth's reign the great William Byrd was organist here.)

The screen was skilfully restored in the 18th century by one of the cathedral masons, and so were the two exquisite choir aisle doorways. Built after the fall of the tower in 1237, each doorway has an arch with dog-tooth and a broad band of undercut foliage. In the capitals of one side of the southern doorway are men slaying dragons, watched from the other side by two little owls with slain dragons beside them. In the spandrels is the bold detached trefoil copied in the 18th century from the retro-choir. The iron gates in these doorways, and the low iron screen round the nave altar are excellent modern work on the lines of the lovely 13th century wrought-iron screens between St Hugh's transept and his choir.

Lovely as they are when seen outside the two "Eyes" of the cathedral gain in splendour when seen with the pure, vivid colour of their mediaeval glass shining into the great transept—"where rainbows play from coloured windows flung". The glass in the Dean's Eye illustrates the Church on Earth and in Heaven, and is among the finest early 13th century glass in existence. At the top, and again in the small centre quatrefoil, is a figure of Christ, and all round him are figures of angels and saints and sacred scenes; one panel depicts three kings and bishops bearing the remains of St Hugh to burial. In the lancet arcading under the Dean's Eye is a mosaic of old grisaille glass and a more colourful old medley of red and blue and silver is in one of the big lancets below. Another glorious medley of mediaeval glass belongs to the Bishop's Eye and the four lancets beneath it.

Against the west wall of this transept are two embattled pillars, and the base of a third, thought to have belonged to the silver shrine set here above the tomb of St John of Dalderby, with whom the Bishop's Eye window is inseparably linked. At the end of this wall are the great doors leading from the Galilee porch.

The three chapels of the north arm of the great transept were restored by the Lincoln Regiment, the Royal Navy, and the Royal Air Force. Here are the colours of the Regiment, and its Books of

Memory. Figures of two kneeling soldiers are on the screen of the first chapel, which resembles in its design the stone screen of the corresponding Works Chantry in the southern arm. Round the entrance arch of the Works Chantry is a Latin inscription asking a prayer for the benefactors of the church. At each side of the doorway are two small figures of kneeling priests, and it frames an old traceried door. A notable feature of these two chapels is the double arcading of their east walls, the work of St Hugh of Avalon.

The ritual choir, from the rood-screen to the altar screen, consists of seven bays—the four western bays and the eastern crossing which were the work of St Hugh, and the two easternmost bays which belong architecturally to the retro-choir. St Hugh set the arches of his arcades on octagonal stone piers with marble shafts and foliated capitals, but those towards the western end were altered after the fall of the central tower, which resulted also in the erection of the screen walls on each side. In each bay of his triforium are two large arches enclosing double arches with foils pierced in their tympana, and the windows of the clerestory are behind an arcade with clustered and banded shafts.

The least happy feature of St Hugh's choir is the lowness of the vault, which springs from marble shafts on 14th century corbels, and is so oddly constructed that the ribs and cells of the two sides do not meet.

A striking feature of this part of the building is the double arcading under the lancet windows of the aisles, repeated in the Treasury and Choristers' Vestry, and (as already seen) on part of the east wall of the great transept. It consists of an outer trefoiled arcade and a pointed inner arcade, with dog-tooth enriching the pointed arches; it all rests on stone and marble shafts with capitals of fine foliage. The spandrels between the outer arches are pierced to show the tips of the inner arcade, but these pointed openings are hidden by the sculptured angels and other figures believed to have been added about 1230. (The double arcading in the Works Chantry is as St Hugh left it, without the figures, and to most people the original plan is the more pleasing.)

At the angles of St Hugh's transept and the aisles of his choir are two remarkable octagonal stone piers (one on each side) adorned with bold, curling crockets, and surrounded by eight detached and banded marble shafts—some round, some six-sided—with fine foliated capitals. At the north-west angle of St Hugh's transept is the Treasury with a fine mediaeval door with its old ironwork, and windows with its old iron-bound shutters. It is said to have been the dispensary, and high in the wall of what was once an upper storey are triangular-headed recesses where drugs may have been stored. On the wall by the entrance to this chapel are fading wall-paintings by Vincenzo Damini, an 18th century Venetian, which are notable only because they portray four bishops who were buried in this transept: Robert Bloet, Alexander the Magnificent, Robert Chesney (the three who succeeded Remigius), and William de Blois (who followed St Hugh). Facing the Treasury are the Sacristy and Music Library with 15th century wooden screens.

On the western side of the south-east transept is the Choristers' Vestry, notable (in addition to its double arcading) for its panelled stone lavatory, the hooded stone fireplace where the wafers were baked, and the fine 14th century stone screen dividing it from the choir aisle. In the diaper of four-leaved flowers enriching the screen can be seen a little dog curled up, and two birds flying about their nest of fledglings.

The great treasures of St Hugh's choir are John of Welbourn's stalls, a magnificent series second to none in England in number and excellence of workmanship. There are two rows on each side—the upper range having superb tabernacled canopies in which the statues of saints are modern. Above the stalls are the titles of the dignities and prebends, with the first words of the Psalms it has long been the daily duty of every prebendary to recite. The five eastern-most canopied stalls on the north side, and the stall at each side of the 18th century bishop's throne on the south side are modern work, and a number of the original stalls have only plain hinged seats: but there remains a grand total of no fewer than 92 late 14th century stalls all retaining their richly-carved original seats.

Some of these misericords illustrate sacred scenes and emblems; others have scenes of everyday life at home and in the field, animals real and fanciful, and exquisite carving of foliage and flowers. The Adoration of the Magi, the Resurrection, the Ascension, the Crowning and Assumption of the Virgin, and the Pelican feeding its young —all are here for the finding. On the subdean's stall is a knight, wounded by an arrow and falling with his horse; another on the south side shows a man in a tree shaking the acorns for his pigs; yet another is a representation of the legend of Alexander's flight into the sky, and shows him on a seat to which two griffins are harnessed. Among the carvings on the north side are: a fine elephant and castle; a boy astride a crane, with another crane pecking greedily from a sack; a swan with a queen's head; a mermaid with mirror and comb; a woman with bellows blowing a fire; and a fine farming scene of a ploughman with his team of four horses, a man with the harrow, and another with sacks of grain. On the poppy-head of the precentor's stall two monkeys are churning butter, and another is being hanged for stealing a pat. This story in carving is continued on the misericord of the stall below that of the arch-deacon, where two monkeys are carrying the dead one for burial.

In front of the vicars' stalls are the choristers' seats, with a fine gallery of minstrel angels, kings, and other figures on their arcaded fronts, and a wonderful (and easily missed) gallery of 102 splendid little carvings in the quatrefoils along the backs of the seats. They deserve close study. Some are of leaves and flowers and human folk, and others make an intriguing array of all manner of animals and birds. There are two men hunting a lion; a knight ready for attack; a knight who appears to be galloping to attack the dragon in the next quatrefoil; a dragon with its prey; animals riding a bird, and a bird riding an animal; a monkey riding a griffin; a fox in a pulpit preaching to geese; a bear scratching its head; a Pelican in Piety; birds preening themselves and pecking berries; a butterfly on a spray of oak; and a fine one of a frog stabbing himself. Altogether, the stalls of Lincoln make an astonishing gallery of mediaeval carving, unsurpassed anywhere in the land.

At the end of the northern range of stalls is a richly-carved oak pulpit, with figures of the Evangelists on brackets, and Bible scenes in relief. Designed by Sir Gilbert Scott, it was given as a tribute to Edward Trollope (Archdeacon of Stow and Bishop of Nottingham) for his work in the cause of archaeology and the church architecture of Lincoln Diocese. The brass eagle lectern of 1667 replaced one destroyed in the Civil War, and the brass chandelier dates from 1680. Under the Litany desk is a stone with the words Cantate Hic; it was mentioned in the Liber Niger, an ancient book of Lincoln customs, and marks a processional "station".

The two eastern bays of the ritual choir (really belonging as already stated to the retro-choir) form the sacrarium, with the 18th century stone screen which James Essex set up in front of part of the earlier one, modelling its canopy on that of Bishop de Luda's tomb at Ely. In the first bay adjoining St Hugh's crossing, on the north side, is a handsome 14th century structure of six trefoiled and vaulted bays, divided by slender pinnacled buttresses, and having the interior wall at each end carved with foliage of vine, fig, and oak, with pigs, eating the acorns below. The three eastern bays have served as an Easter Sepulchre, and show the sleeping figures of three Roman soldiers on the panels below. The other half represents a founder's tomb, and has Bishop Fuller's 17th century inscription stating that *here lie the remains of Remigius*—a statement there is little reason to doubt, and which is confirmed by the finding in the tomb some years ago of a lead coffin with the relics, a pewter chalice and paten, and part of a pastoral staff. It is believed that on the completion of the retro-choir the body of the first bishop and founder was translated to this tomb from its original burial-place in the nave, where the site (in the easternmost bay of the north arcade) has been marked since 1872 by a tapering gravestone with carving which may represent a Jesse Tree, and shows three of the figures enclosed in vesicas. (The stone was one of many removed to the cloister in the 18th century, but certainly did not commemorate Remigius.)

237

The retro-choir, popularly known as the Angel Choir because of the famous series of angels with which it is enriched, is of surpassing loveliness, an example of English Gothic architecture at its peak. Here, as in the earlier part of the church, are arcades with triforium and clerestory, aisles with arcaded walls, and vaulted roofs. But in these five eastern bays is exhibited that greater enrichment that came with the Geometrical style; and here, too, the lancets of the earlier work have given place to great traceried windows through which light streams more brightly on the beauty within. The glorious east window, reckoned the finest of its period in England is filled with 19th century glass; the east windows of the aisles shine with a brilliant medley of medallion and figure glass of the 13th to 15th centuries.

Some of the piers of the arcades are of stone, others are of marble; but all are surrounded by banded shafts, and all have rich foliated capitals of marble. In the deep arch mouldings runs a line of festooned ornament, and in the spandrels are the big trefoil ornaments copied on the choir aisle doorways. Between the arches are the long tapering corbels of exquisite curling leaves from which rise the shafts of the vault, which has ribs meeting in a line of foliated bosses; and at the foot of one of the corbels (the second from the east on the north side) is the 1-foot-high grotesque known as the Lincoln Imp.

In every bay of the triforium are two big arches enclosing pairs of trefoiled arches with pierced quatrefoils in their tympana; the hoods of the outer arches are adorned with the detached curling leaves which are so marked a feature of this Angel Choir, and they occur again in the fine clusters of marble shafts on which the arches rest. The clerestory is a beautiful range of four-light windows, and their design is repeated in an inner plane of curtain arches. There are other lavish displays of the curling leaves between the very slender shafts of the east window, on the fine windows of the aisles, and on the blind window tracery between them; and they adorn the rich wall arcade below, which, though less sumptuous, resembles the open arcading of the triforium.

Like the rest of the retro-choir, the 30 carved angels filling the spandrels of the triforium are excellent work of their period. Many carry scrolls, and others play musical instruments—harp, viol, lute, and trumpet.

The remaining parts of Lincoln Cathedral yet to be described are Bishop Sutton's cloister, Wren's colonnade and library on its north side, and the unique, 10-sided chapter house.

Fine old doors with scrolled ironwork lead from St Hugh's transept to the cloister's vaulted vestibule, whose four-light traceried windows are repeated as unglazed arcading round three sides of the cloister garth. This is all Decorated work, of the closing years of the

13th century; but on the north side is Wren's colonnade, with its attractive view of the north side of the cathedral.

A rare feature of the cloister is the fine mediaeval oak bosses of the wooden vault, carved with saints and angels, foliage, animals, a mitred bishop, and a Virgin and Child with a dove. Here also is preserved a big collection of old relics—sculptured figures, bosses, capitals, finials, stone coffins, carved shafts from the Norman west doorways, a fine gable cross, and a lead cistern. Among several enormous gravestones in the south walk is that of Richard Gainsborough, a mediaeval master mason; it is set in the floor, and has his portrait engraved under an elaborate canopy—his purse hanging from the belt of his simple dress, and his mason's square beside him. (A fine stone panel found in the cloister and carved in relief with a bearded figure of St Paul, is thought to have belonged to the original scheme of the bands of sculpture on the west front, and is now in the choir transept.) Part of a Roman pavement found in the cloister is laid at the foot of the 18th century staircase to the library; it is about 6 feet square.

Wren's library, above his colonnade, is about 104 feet long, and was built at the cost of Michael Honywood, dean after the Restoration; his arms are on the doorway. Among the valuable collection of books and manuscripts he presented to the library are first editions of *Paradise Lost, Don Quixote,* and part of Spenser's *Faerie Queene.* Among other treasured possessions are early Bibles and liturgies, some Caxtons and other early printed books, and many manuscripts of pre-Reformation date.

Two rare possessions which have been removed from the library to the cathedral Treasury are the Conqueror's charter for the removal of the see from Dorchester, and one of the four contemporary copies of the Magna Carta still in existence. (Salisbury Cathedral has one and the other two are in the British Museum.) With its 53 lines of neat, plain script, regular as print, this copy is a wonderful example of mediaeval penmanship. It has three holes for the tags to which the seal was once attached, and on the back of the copy, where it could be seen when folded, the Norman-Latin name for the city, *Lincolnia,* is written twice—proof that it was intended from the first that the copy should be deposited here. Lincoln is rightly proud of this treasure, and proud, too, that one of the county's sons was Stephen Langton, the Archbishop of Canterbury who played such a great part in the struggle between the king and the barons which culminated in this Great Charter. After long doubt about his birthplace, it has in our time been established that Stephen Langton hailed from the village of Langton-by-Wragby.

Linking the early 13th century chapter house with the east walk of the cloister is a gabled vestibule entered by a grand double-doorway with fine modern doors which were the gift of Bishop King.

Above the doorway, within the vestibule, is graceful arcading below a round window shining with a pleasing medley of modern glass. The lancet windows of the chapter house, grouped in pairs, have modern glass telling the story of the cathedral; and below the lancets (as well as in the vestibule) runs a rich, continuous wall arcade with dog-tooth in its arches, and foliated capitals on its marble shafts. But the outstanding feature of this chapter house is its stone vault, supported by a central column, and by clustered marble shafts between the pairs of lancets, rising from tapering corbels of fine foliage in the spandrels of the wall arcade. With its stone pier enclosed in a cluster of 10 hexagonal shafts of marble, fluted and banded and ending in a ring of foliated capitals like a crown, and with its vaulting ribs branching out to meet those from the walls, this central column is like a great tree superbly carved in stone.

In the chapter house is a wooden chair with a romantic history. Its canopy and back, and the lions on its arms, are modern; but the seat is late 13th century work, and is believed to have been used by the Edwardian kings who summoned Parliament to meet here. It was probably in this chair that Edward I sat in 1301 when Parliament rejected the Pope's claim to the sovereignty of Scotland. It was here in 1310 when some of the Knights Templars were tried before John of Dalderby; and it was here, too, when the leaders of the Lincolnshire Rising met in 1536 to await the king's reply to their demands.

In the vestibule of the cloister is a brass plate recording the death at Lincoln in 1837 of Elizabeth Penrose, and of her burial in the cloister (the stone in the pavement below is wrongly placed). Famous in her day as a writer of school books on English history, she was the daughter of Edmund Cartwright, inventor of the power loom; she married the Rev. John Penrose, and took the pen-name of Mrs Markham from the Nottinghamshire village of East Markham where she lived many years with her aunts. Among others buried in the cloister are Bishop King and Dean Fry.

Before leaving the cathedral the visitor is well advised to make one final tour, to inspect closely the many monuments which have not already come under notice.

The memorials of mediaeval times seem pitifully few when it is recalled that up to the Civil War the cathedral had over 200 brasses and many fine tombs. But in 1644 when the city was captured, the brasses were torn up, and only a few of the tombs survived to bear witness to what must have been a grand array.

At the consecration of the retro-choir in 1280, in the presence of Edward I, Queen Eleanor, and a great company of high dignitaries of Church and State, the body of St Hugh was taken from its tomb and translated to a splendid shrine adorned with silver and gold and precious stones. The head (which had become severed from the body) was placed in a similarly-enriched coffer which in 1364 was stolen. The thieves were found and hanged; the head was recovered, but without the coffer, and so Treasurer Welbourn provided a new one. Pilgrims continued to flock to both shrines till Henry VIII's men despoiled them. The fine arcaded pedestal of the head shrine still remains in the easternmost bay of the retro-choir, and in the middle bay (at the back of the altar screen) is an open table tomb of black marble, set up in Charles II's time by Bishop Fuller to mark the place where he thought the other shrine had stood. The site of this tomb is within the east end of St Hugh's own choir (marked by boundary lines in the floor), and it is believed now to be identical with his original burial-place. In line with St Hugh's tomb are those of Bishop Fuller (1675), Bishop Gardiner (1705), and others of his family.

Adjoining the pedestal of St Hugh's head shrine, and extending to the east wall, are two stone tombs with a series of canopied figures on their sides, including Edward III and his sons. One is the tomb of Robert, Lord Burghersh, and the other is of his son Henry, Edward III's Treasurer and Chancellor who became bishop in 1320, baptised the Black Prince 10 years later, and died in Flanders in 1340. His effigy shows him in his bishop's vestments. Bishop Burghersh and his brother Bartholomew, who succeeded to the barony, founded the Burghersh Chantry in the chapel of St Catherine occupying the adjacent east bay of the aisle. Bartholomew, who was a warrior and had fought at Crecy, was buried here in 1356; his richly-canopied tomb in the north wall portrays him in full armour, with two angels at the head of the tomb holding his shield, and two angels at the foot bearing his soul from the earth, represented below by rabbits peeping from their warren.

To the west of this tomb is that of Richard Fleming, who was bishop from 1420 to 1431. He is remembered as the founder of Lincoln College, Oxford, but also as the man who caused Wycliffe's bones to be exhumed and burned and cast into the River Swift. His effigy shows him in his robes, his hand raised in blessing, and angels at his head; and below, through the open arcading of the tomb, can be seen a corpse in a winding sheet. By the tomb is a charming little ogee-arched doorway with snails carved on its capitals and an old oak door opening to the chantry chapel founded by his nephew Robert Fleming, who was Dean of Lincoln from 1452 to 1483. This chapel, which has a fine canopied piscina, was restored in memory of Sir Charles Anderson, of Lea, who is remembered for his writings about this city and the county he loved so well.

A striking feature of the south aisle of the retro-choir are the rich fronts of the Longland and Russell chantries flanking the great south doorway, each with a canopied tomb. John Russell, founder of the chapel on the east side of the doorway, had been keeper of the privy seal and Chancellor of England; he was Bishop of Lincoln from 1480 to 1494. Bishop John Longland, who was confessor to Henry VIII, died at Woburn in 1547, having decreed that his bowels should be buried there, his body in Eton Chapel, and his heart at Lincoln.

The chapel of St Nicholas at the east end of the south aisle of the retro-choir was the chapel of the Cantilupe Chantry, founded by Joan, widow of Nicholas de Cantilupe. He died in 1355 and lies (a battered headless figure) on one of two fine canopied stone tombs in the east bay of the arcade. On the other tomb is the headless figure of Nicholas Wymbyssh, Archdeacon of Nottingham, who died in 1461. On the south side of this chapel is a cenotaph tomb of Caen stone in memory of the Lincoln painter William Hilton, and his brother-in-law, Peter de Wint. Their monument is adorned with bas-relief copies of some of their works, including the cathedral with Exchequer Gate and the gabled black-and-white house.

In the chapel of St John the Baptist (under the east window) is a tomb enriched with arcading and shields, and bearing in gilded brass a lovely canopied figure of Eleanor of Castile, with two lions at her feet. The gift of a Lincoln citizen in 1891, it is a copy of the original tomb destroyed in the Civil War, and commemorates the burial here of the viscera after her body had been embalmed by the nuns of St Catherine's Priory and taken to London for burial in Westminster Abbey.

Another modern memorial in the retro-choir is a tomb behind the altar screen; this has the recumbent figure of Dean Butler, 1894, his hands folded in prayer. In a bay of the north arcade, near the memorial to St Hugh, is the magnificent monument to Christopher Wordsworth who died in 1885—beloved bishop, eminent theologian, and nephew of the poet. Of Ancaster stone, and displaying an astonishing wealth of decoration, it has a canopy surmounted by a figure of Our Lord, and pinnacles rising almost as high as the finial of the altar screen. Canopied figures of the Apostles are round the tomb on which the bishop's effigy lies in rich cope and jewelled mitre, with angels at his head.

On the south side of the retro-choir (where it is part of the sanctuary) are the tombs of Catherine Swynford (third wife of John of Gaunt) and her daughter the Countess of Westmorland. They have lost their brasses and both were rearranged after the Restoration.

In the south aisle of the retro-choir are gravestones of Bishop Holbeach, who helped to compile the Prayer Book, and Henry of Huntingdon, the chronicler who wrote a history of England at the request of Alexander the Magnificent. In the north aisle are those of three bishops: Hugh of Wells (1235), Oliver Sutton (1299), and John Chedworth (1471). In the south arm of St Hugh's transept are simple stones in the floor with the names of three other bishops whose tombs were once here: Richard of Gravesend (1279), Henry of Lexington (1258), Philip Repyngdon (1424), and Robert Grosseteste (1253) a man of humble birth who became a great scholar and reformer, and is especially honoured here as one of the great builders of the cathedral. Like John of Dalderby, Bishop Grosseteste was revered as a saint, and his tomb became a place of pilgrimage. The chapel and tomb were restored in 1953 to mark the seventh centenary of his death.

In the south aisle of St Hugh's choir are a few fragments of another shrine—that of "Little St Hugh" who was buried here as a martyr in 1255. The story of his death at the hands of the Jews is without foundation, but it stirred up smouldering fires of hatred against them, and found its way into more than one romance, even being told by the prioress in the *Canterbury Tales*.

Among the modern memorials still to be noted is Westmacott's white marble figure of Bishop John Kaye, 1853, on his cenotaph in the north aisle, his right hand on a Bible, his staff by his side. In the south arm of the great transept is the seated bronze figure of Edward King, the saintly and beloved bishop who died in 1910 and lies in the cloister. Of Edward White Benson, the Chancellor of Lincoln who became Archbishop of Canterbury in 1882, there are two reminders—his staff on a wall in the Morning Chapel, and the massive pulpit in the nave presented by his son, A. C. Benson; it was brought here from a dismantled church built by Wren at Rotterdam for the English people there.

At the west end of the nave a fine modern brass covers the last resting-place of Bishop William Smyth, who died in 1514. A copy of the original one removed in the Civil War, it was given by the Principal and Fellows of Brasenose College, Oxford, which the bishop helped to found. There are saints in the shafts of his canopy, and in a Latin inscription at the foot we read that "he was a lover of the Clergy, for he gave sustenance to many at home and across the sea, and he founded two schools in perpetuity".

In the easternmost bay of the nave's south arcade is a beautiful memorial to Thomas Charles Fry, Dean of Lincoln, who was buried in the cloister in 1930. It is a stepped bronze cross, enriched with shamrock leaves and set in a black marble slab. On the stem of the cross is a shield, and at the foot a chalice; and the inscription states that "through his devotion, courage, and untiring labours the repair of this cathedral was begun afresh in 1921". The restoration was continued after the Dean's death, and is a splendid tribute to all concerned.

Of Lincoln's 50 pre-Reformation churches and chapels only about a quarter were left standing in the time of Edward VI. Some of these were devastated in the Civil War, and others have been wholly or partly rebuilt; nevertheless, there are still several of historic or antiquarian interest.

Nearest to the cathedral is St Mary Magdalene's, in Exchequergate. Built of stone in 14th century style, it is a descendant of the Saxon church destroyed by Bishop Remigius to make room for his cathedral church. Late in the 13th century Bishop Sutton built a church here "at a sufficient interval from the Minster Yard"; this was almost rebuilt in classical style after the Civil War, and in 1882 was again restored and transformed.

Not far off, in Westgate, is the site of St Paul's, rebuilt in 1879, closed in 1968 and recently demolished. It stood on what is popularly believed to be the site of the first Christian church in Lindsey. On this spot, it is claimed, a stone church was built by Blecca, governor of the city, after his conversion by Paulinus; and within it Paulinus consecrated Honorius as fifth Archbishop of Canterbury.

In Eastgate is the attractive 19th century church of St Peter. Replacing an 18th century church erected on the site of one destroyed in 1643, the main portion of the building is in 13th century style. In 1914 the south aisle was built in 14th century style, and in one of the windows are figures of Paulinus, Guthlac, and Botolph. The church also has a handsome oak rood-screen.

The church of St Michael-on-the-Mount (in Christ's Hospital Terrace) was erected in 1854, in place of a small church built in 1744 of materials from one destroyed in the Civil War. Its oldest possession is a bell dated 1486. Charmingly set on the brow of the hill, with the old palace for neighbour, it was built mainly through the efforts of a vicar, John Somerville Gibney, whose memorial is an engraved brass plate showing him holding a model of the church. In the vestry is another memorial, dated 1837, which has figures of two Bluecoat School boys, one weeping, and one pointing to an inscription to the Master and Matron of Christ's Hospital, their old school on the other side of the Terrace, built in the 18th century and used until the school was closed in 1883. (A house in St Michael's churchyard was the first home of the Lincoln Bluecoat School which was founded in 1602 by the bequest of a doctor, Richard Smith, for the support and education of 12 boys until they were apprenticed.) The building at present is used by the Lincoln College of Art.

A church below the hill that claimed the longest history was St Martin's, in West Parade. It was declared redundant and demolished in 1970. Built in 1873 it took the place of the old church, which stood in St Martin's Lane. A Saxon church on the old site is mentioned in the Conqueror's charter to the cathedral, and it has been claimed that Lindsey's first church was erected here, and not on the site of St Paul's.

Farther along High Street, beyond the river, is the charming little church of St Benedict. Its low tower, chancel, and north chapel are all that is left of what was once the richest church in the city, attended by the wealthy merchants of the Middle Ages. Severely damaged in the Civil War, it was restored and reopened in 1932 and is now the headquarters of the Mothers' Union. The tower rebuilt with old materials, retained the Saxon type of belfry windows, and has a panelled door with an enormous lock and key.

In the white-walled interior of St Benedict's is an arcade of two bays, its central pillar having detached shafts and capitals of over-hanging leaves; the chancel has a massive double piscina of the 13th century and a fine 14th century recess with hanging tracery. There are also some old box-pews and an old pulpit; but a more notable relic is a brass of 1620, restored to the church after long being in St Peter-at-Arches (demolished in 1932). The brass has portraits of Alderman John Becke, twice mayor of Lincoln, his seven sons wear-ing cloaks, and his wife and two daughters in broad-brimmed hats; in the folds of the mother's gown is a little maid holding a skull. A fine old bell of 1585 which hung in St Benedict's original tower, and is known as Old Kate, hangs now in the ornate steeple of St Mark's church (near the St Mark's station), built in 1872 but preserving some Saxon and Norman fragments in its walls. This church was closed in 1969 and will shortly be demolished. The parish has been united with St Mary-le-Wigford.

Close to the Central station is the church of St Mary-le-Wigford, keeping green the name by which the whole of the lower city south of the river was once called—Wickford or Wickenford. Like the church of St Peter-at-Gowts (farther along High Street), it is renowned for its tower, built in the Saxon tradition while the Nor-mans were building their castle on the hilltop. (Both towers are tall, slender, and unbuttressed, their coupled belfry windows having mid-wall shafts.) St Mary's has a lofty round-headed west doorway, and in the wall beside it is a Roman memorial stone bearing a Latin inscription to a Gaul named Sacer (son of Bruscus), his wife Cars-souna, and his son Quintus. Long after their death, perhaps a thousand years, the stone seems to have been used as a dedication stone for the 11th century church, for in its gabled head is an Anglo-Saxon inscription which has been deciphered as "Eirtig had me built and endowed to the glory of Christ and St Mary".

The tower arch is round-headed, on great imposts, and set in the foot of one of the jambs is a Saxon stone carved with intricate knot-work. From the 13th century come the fine chancel arch, the two lancets in the east wall, and the north arcade with clustered piers and capitals of overhanging leaves. The north aisle has a 13th century doorway and later mediaeval windows. The south aisle and its arcade are modern except for the 13th century doorway (with dog-tooth) and later mediaeval windows. In a recess of the north wall lies the worn stone figure of a woman; and on a respond of the south arcade is a small brass of 1525 with an axe and a fish-knife engraved at the end of an inscription to John Jobson, alderman and fishmonger. The ironwork screen and rails were wrought in the Brant Broughton smithy. Outside the church is a handsome drinking fountain adorned with tracery, niches, and carved parapet; known as St Mary's Conduit, it is said to have been made up in the 16th century with materials from the house of the Whitefriars.

St Peter-at-Gowts—the name is a reminder of the "gowts" or old watercourses hereabouts—has been so much rebuilt and enlarged that apart from the Saxo-Norman tower and some survivals in the south side little old work remains. There is long-and-short work in the fine belfry windows, and also where the tower joins the nave. This is not bonded into the tower and indicates the width of the Saxon nave. In the west wall of the tower is a worn sculpture of Christ. The tower has a round-headed arch and the modern chancel has an original triplet window in the east wall. Other Norman remains are the blocked south doorway, a south window with glass showing Mary of Bethany, and the arcaded font like a huge pillar. The two bays of the 13th century south arcade have a central shafted pier with capitals of stiff foliage. The chapel at the east end of this aisle was founded by Ralph Jolyf and his wife Amice, and under the hood of the monumental arch runs a Latin rhyming inscription. Built into the north wall is a 13th century stone with two fleur-de-lys cross-heads. An almsbox in the church has an old panel with a quaint carving of the boy Jesus hammering vigorously at a bench in Joseph's workshop.

The last of the city churches in the High Street, before Bargate (the old southern boundary) is reached, is St Botolph's, a fine cross-shaped church before its destruction in the Civil War. The small building that took its place in the 18th century has since been altered and enlarged, but the rebuilt tower retains old quatrefoil windows in the north and south walls, as well as much of the old stonework. On a windowsill is part of a sculptured Piéta, possibly from a 15th century cross-head.

The finest of Lincoln's modern churches is the 19th century St Swithin's, dominating a corner of Broadgate. (To the west is the site of the original St Swithin's, twice rebuilt but finally taken down in 1884.) For this fine church Lincoln folk owe much to the generosity of Joseph Shuttleworth and Nathaniel Clayton. Over a century ago Joseph owned a little shipbuilding yard, and Nathaniel was part owner of the steam packets that travelled on the River Witham between Lincoln and Boston. Little did they dream, when they decided to set up together as ironfounders, about 1842, that out of their small business much of the modern industrial life of the city was to grow.

The spire and tower of St Swithin's, linked by flying buttresses and soaring 200 feet, are Joseph Shuttleworth's memorial—a tribute from his son whose portrait is carved with his father's on the hood of the big west window. The tower has arcaded walls with stone seats, and its splendid arch of five orders opens to a nave of six lofty bays, lit by a fine clerestory. Capitals of overhanging foliage enrich the arcades, and splendid foliated corbels support the shafts on which the roof rests. The finely-canopied oak pulpit has figures of saints and bishops in niches. An ancient treasure is a Roman altar found during digging operations for the foundations of the tower; 3 feet high and 20 inches wide, it has bas-relief carving of sacrificial vessels, and is finely inscribed *To the Goddess, the Fates, and to the Deities of Augustus, Caius Antistius Frontinus being curator for the third time erects this altar at his own cost.*

Two churches in Lincoln's suburbs are of special interest—St Helen's at Boultham, and All Saints at Bracebridge. All Saints was restored by J. L. Pearson in 1875, when the north aisle, shallow transept, and vestry were added, and the walls of the south aisle rebuilt. The plain unbuttressed tower (with pyramid cap) was restored later, but it is still in the main the tower built in the Saxon tradition; its belfry windows are the Saxon type with mid-wall shafts, and it has its doorway and its old arch to the nave. The chancel has a narrow early Norman arch with a peephole at each side, and there is a blocked doorway of the same period reset in the north aisle. In this doorway and at three corners of the nave long-and-short work can be seen as evidence of the Anglo-Saxon nave. The finest relic of Norman times is the font, its huge bowl carved with bold inter-laced arcading. Thirteenth century work can be seen in the south doorway with dog-tooth ornament, some lancet windows, the fine south arcade, and fragments of gravestones with carved crosses outside in the south wall. Several of the windows date from the 14th and 15th centuries. The chancel still has its old sedilia and piscina, and the modern stone pulpit has the old hourglass stand of its predecessor.

Boultham's old church is in the well-wooded grounds of Boultham Park, which have become a pleasaunce with lawns and flowerbeds, shaded walks, and boating lake for the delight of Lincoln citizens and their children. A neat little church with wooden belfry and shingled spire, it was much rebuilt last century, but still has its 13th century chancel arch, and a 13th century arcade of two bays built up in the south wall. Old pews have been turned into wainscotting, and on a windowsill are two ancient fragments of sculpture showing St Lawrence with his gridiron. One of many memorials to the fine soldier family of Ellison is a brass plate showing the grave of one who was killed during the South African War. In the churchyard is a huge block of granite brought from the shattered fortifications of Sebastopol, with two cannon-balls fired during the siege, and placed here by Colonel Ellison in memory of his company who fell in the Crimea.

In Roman times there were kilns at Swanpool and Boultham, and both the Lincoln Museum and the British Museum have many examples of Roman pottery unearthed hereabouts.

The name of John Wesley calls up memories in Lincoln; he visited the city three times, and his father, rector of Epworth, was imprisoned for debt in the castle and there preached to his fellow prisoners. His followers here are numerous, and have built some fine churches. One, recently demolished, in High Street was a memorial to Dr John Hannah, a son of Lincoln who was twice President of the Wesleyan Conference and has the credit for starting the first Sunday School in the city in 1809 when he was 17. The fine Methodist Chapel in Clasketgate, built in 1836, was demolished in 1963. It was an impressive building with Ionic portico.

Of other buildings essential to the life of a thriving city only the Museum, the Art Gallery, and the Library call for some description.

The museum (in Broadgate) is housed in a building that was part of the monastery of the Grey Friars, founded here about 1230. It was early divided into two storeys and shortly after the dissolution in 1539 till the end of the 19th century the upper storey was used by a school which had grown out of a choristers' school founded towards the close of the 11th century. From 1615 till well into the 19th century the lower storey was occupied by a Jersey School, where the poor were employed spinning with the Jersey spinning wheel; and later it became the home of the Mechanics' Institute. Early this century the whole building was restored and opened as the City and County Museum.

The lower room of the museum is a charming undercroft—a museum piece in itself—divided into two aisles by a fine row of eight octagonal columns from which spring the ribs of a stone vault added slightly later to give the building a second storey. In the entrance room is the J.H. Smith collection of arms and armour and in the lower room of the Greyfriars are preserved many antiquities of prehistoric, Roman, Anglo-Saxon, mediaeval, and later times. There is a fine series of flint and stone implements, bronze swords, and palstaves. Of Roman Lincoln there are many fine antiquities including mosaics, memorial stones, altars, and milestones, including the one found in Bailgate marking 14 miles to Segelocum; another is the inscribed portion of a milestone which stood outside the Roman city and marked the road to Leicester. There is also a model of a Roman pottery kiln, and a good collection of pottery ranging from Roman times to the 17th century. An outer stairway leads to the museum's upper room, which was the chapel of the friary and still has its double piscina, a mediaeval east window under a vesica, and a fine 13th century timbered roof. Here are collections illustrating Lincolnshire natural history.

The Usher Gallery (on the Lindum Road) was given to the city by James Ward Usher as a home for the precious things he had gathered together through the years. When Sheriff in 1916, this Lincoln silversmith promised to leave his valuable collection to the city of his birth; and when he died five years later he left also a sum of money for the building and endowment of a gallery worthy of it. A handsome building in the Classical style designed by Sir Reginald Blomfield and opened in 1927, it stands on a green bank dotted with trees and starred in spring with daffodils and narcissi; and it makes a charming picture with the mottled roofs of the Vicars' Court and the towering mass of the cathedral rising above it.

Two rules guided James Ward Usher in making his collection: "never to buy anything but the best, and to buy it regardless of cost". As was natural, his chief interest was in silver, jewels, watches, and miniatures with lovely settings; and many things of beauty are here. The delight and wonder of all visitors, the watches include the smallest repeating watch in the world, set in a ring for George III; a Queen Anne repeater rich in rubies and diamonds; a watch like a jewelled beetle that opens its wings to reveal the face; a Louis XVI musical watch with tiny dancers revolving on it; a pendant musical watch; a watch that belonged to James I; and another with Mary Queen of Scots' monogram. Among the fine miniatures are portraits of Napoleon, the Empress Josephine, Madam le Brun, Marie Antoinette, Lord Byron, Joseph Addison, John Gay, Lady Chatham, and Mrs Fitzherbert. The crown of the whole collection is a catalogue with the collector's own water-colours of the choicest of his treasures, a labour of love that occupied him for 15 years.

In one of the rooms is rare old English glass from 1680 to 1860, and a remarkable collection of Pinxton and Torksey porcelain. These were both assembled by the late Mr C. L. Exley, a dedicated local antiquary. Of special interest to the Lincoln visitor are the paintings of the city by Peter de Wint and J. M. W. Turner. The gallery's extensive collection of works by Peter de Wint has been brought together to mark his residence in Lincoln and his love for the city and county.

The City Library, in Free School Lane, is a stone building with balustraded parapet, dome, and cupola, designed by Sir Reginald Blomfield and opened in 1913. In a case in the hall are many Tennyson pieces—his marriage lines, his clay pipes, walking-stick and archer's bow, copies of his works, and hand-written roughs of some of his poems. A Tennyson Research Centre has been established at the library and contains immense resources of books and papers belonging to the poet. On the other side of the hall a case contains interesting reminders of Sir John Franklin's expeditions.

Lincoln people are well provided with parks and open spaces. One is the 80-acre park at Boultham, already referred to; another is the Arboretum occupying about 14 acres between Lindum Terrace and the Monks' Road, which in former times was a common on which the freemen could pasture their cattle and is now a pleasant place with flowerbeds, many varieties of trees, a small lake, and terraces which climb the hillside and afford charming vistas. The Arboretum was opened by Bishop Wordsworth in 1872 and shortly afterwards Mr. Francis J. Clarke gave a stone lion to mark the occasion. Above the Arboretum, in a quiet retreat on the Sewell Road, are the Bede Houses designed by Pugin and built a century ago, with the little chapel of St Anne and the warden's house for company. A third delightful open space with a large lake is at Hartsholme Park in the south-west of the city.

Beyond the Arboretum, on the south side of Monks' Road, is a recreation ground with a bowling green by the little ruined building known by the fine-sounding name of Monks' Abbey. It is part of the chapel of the priory of St Mary Magdalene, founded here in the 12th century as a cell of the Benedictine Abbey of St Mary's, York; in the 13th century walls are four 15th century windows with some tracery still hanging, and to the west of the ruin is a length of walling which formed part of the domestic buildings.

Two other lungs of the city are the West and South Commons, on the latter of which the Lincoln fair is held during the last whole week in April—the pleasure fair having grown as the once famous horse and sheep fair has declined. This April fair is a survival of the one granted by Charles II, but Lincoln was also famous for its fairs in mediaeval times, and they attracted merchants from far and wide.

In the north-west corner of South Common, where it comes down to South Park near the High Street, stood the leper hospital of the Holy Innocents, founded by Remigius and known as the Malandry. Near it stood Little Bargate, one of two gatehouses set in the mediaeval wall built here along the Sincil Dyke—Little Bargate defending the road to Canwick, and Great Bargate guarding the entrance to the High Street. Bargate and Little Bargate Street are reminders of these gatehouses, and among other names hereabouts at the foot of the common which are redolent of old Lincoln are St Catherine's, recalling the priory, and Eleanor Street, recalling the famous queen who passed this way in life and in death.

From the top of this spacious South Common there is a glorious view of the cathedral. "Never was an edifice more happily placed, overtopping a city built on the acclivity of a steep hill. To see it in full perfection it should be in the sunshine of an autumnal evening, when the red roofs and red-brick houses would harmonise with the sky and the fading foliage." That was Southey's verdict on the crowning splendour of Lincoln. There can be no other!

Linwood. Set in the wooded countryside near Market Rasen, and looking over the Wolds, it has a mediaeval church with the rare dedication to St Cornelius, third century Bishop of Rome.

Secluded at the end of a narrow lane, the church is largely 13th century work, with nave clerestory, north aisle, and tower and spire of the 15th century. The chancel (partly rebuilt in Victorian times) has its old double piscina. There is a 14th century font. Survivals from Tudor times are a chalice and paten, and two of three bells.

A fine brass (1419) in the north aisle shows John Lyndewode and his wife under a double canopy, with their seven children under smaller canopies. A second brass has the canopied portrait of their eldest son John, who, like his father, was a woolstapler; he died in 1421, and is shown with his feet on a bale of wool bearing his mark.

William Lyndewode (one of the seven children on the older brass) was the Bishop of St David's who became Lord Privy Seal in 1443. He is brought to mind in this church because the figure of a bishop in old glass in a chancel window is thought to be his portrait. A great diplomat and a pillar of the House of Lancaster, the bishop was commended to the pope by Henry VI as a paragon of virtue, and he helped to found Eton College. Before his death he directed that above his tomb in Westminster Abbey there should be chained a copy of one of his learned works.

Linwood Warren is now a nature reserve administered by the Lincolnshire Trust for Nature Conservation.

Little Bytham. It has more than its share of brick walls for these parts, and indeed many of the people here are busy making bricks, its clay being specially suitable. But the hand of industry has descended lightly on it and has disturbed its serenity little more than the trains which pass by on their way—north and south.

Saxon long-and-short masonry is plainly seen at the south-east corner of the nave, outside the church. That takes the village back for nearly a thousand years; but its dedication takes it back even farther, for it is to St Medard, a 6th century Bishop of Noyon; no other church in England is dedicated to him.

Near the Saxon masonry is an early Norman doorway to the chancel; it has a remarkable tympanum with a chequered background, a tiny sculpture of a man on horseback, and three circles, two of which have reliefs of birds and are probably an allusion to the legendary eagle which spread its wings to protect St Medard from the rain. Near this doorway is a small Norman window, and on the other side of the church is another Norman doorway leading into the nave, with bands of chevron and dog-tooth ornament and a tiny squatting figure of a man above. The lower part of the tower, and its arch with an ape's head on each side, are also Norman, the upper part being 13th century work and the spire 14th. The arcade, with three round arches, is late 12th century work.

A striking sight in the church are the stone seats running right round the chancel wall (even behind the altar) and broken only by a rich 14th century recess with ballflower ornament and little mediaeval heads.

The pulpit is modern but rests on an Elizabethan stone base with a Latin inscription meaning "Pray and Plough". The eight-sided font is mediaeval, bearing traces of old colour; and there is more of this old colour on a triple recess in the nave wall which holds the church pewter. Near it is a pleasing modern window of Faith, Charity, and Hope.

Little Carlton. One of half a dozen Carltons in the county, it has an ivied mill on the stream called the Long Eau, and a rebuilt church with two yews at its gate and beautiful hydrangeas by its little porch. A great cedar in the churchyard soars as high as the dainty crocketed spire.

The church still has its fine mediaeval font, adorned with traceried panels; and another old relic is the head of a stone cross with carvings of the Crucifixion and St Mary, said to have come from Castle Carlton.

Little Cawthorpe. Lying in a hollow, with woodlands all about it, this is a charming village with twisting lanes, an ever-running stream, and a delightful old manor house facing a plain little church rebuilt last century. Built of brick, and proclaiming its age with the date 1673 under a coat-of-arms, the L-shaped house stands serenely amid its lawns; it has fine Dutch gables adorned with balls and pinnacles, and diamond-shaped chimney stacks.

A rare and pretty feature of the village is the stream, crossed by a ford below the church, and running merrily over its gravelly bed.

Little Coates. Now one with Grimsby, it has outstripped in size the twin village of Great Coates; and to keep pace with this growth its old church of St Michael, standing alone by the bridge over the River Freshney and with a fine weeping ash by its churchyard gate, has been enlarged.

Chiefly a building of the 14th and 15th centuries, the old church consists of chancel, nave, and south aisle; and the 20th century addition on its north side consists of chancel, nave, and massive west tower. Ancient and modern make one charming whole, spacious and light, the old chancel serving now as a chapel and the old nave and aisle as a double south aisle, linked by a new arcade to the new nave.

The chapel has its old roof, and is enclosed by richly-traceried modern screenwork. The old west window has figures of St Michael and St Gabriel in pleasing modern glass, and in dignified setting in the old nave stands the traceried 15th century font.

The new nave has a fine roof of moulded beams. The beautiful chancel, filled with light from the nine windows in its arcaded walls, has a vaulted roof with flower bosses, and a fine traceried screen with rood-loft and cornice of vine.

Little Grimsby. A charming little place near Louth, it has a leafy lane leading to stately Hall and tiny whitewashed church side-by-side amid the serenity of lawns and flowers and noble trees.

Built about 1700 for the Nelthorpe family, the Hall is of mellowed red-brick relieved with white windows; in front of its handsome pedimented doorway hangs a beautiful lamp of ironwork wrought like lace. Literally hidden by trees (including many fine yews), the church is 200 years older than the Hall and is one of the smallest in the county; its interior measures only 13 yards from east to west. In the branches of one of the iron candelabras hanging from its old roof beams are quaint little fawns with enormous tails. The lectern is a fine modern oak eagle, and looking down from the chancel arch are two minstrel angels carved in oak.

There is a monument to Lord Frederick Beauclerk who restored the church last century, and there is a marble bust of his wife which was sculptured by her son. In memory of Tom Wintringham, MP for Louth, who died suddenly in the House of Commons in 1921, there is unusual glass symbolising the New Heaven and the New Earth.

Little Ponton. It lies placidly on a slope between the Great North Road and the River Witham, its charming Georgian and Regency Hall hidden among trees by the banks of the river, and its church in a well-shaded churchyard above. The church is towerless and has a bell placed in quaint manner in a hole in the west wall. The Normans fashioned the fine chancel arch and two fragments of their carving are on either side of the west window. The arcade and the doorway within the porch are 13th century. There is a mediaeval aumbry, and a piscina, and the old oak screen in front of the organ was brought from Ripon Cathedral, together with two traceried choir-stalls with poppyheads. A tablet on a wall is to Pennyman Warton Worsley who gave 62 years of service to this small place, first as curate and then as rector.

Little Steeping. Between the two Steepings runs the Steeping River—the name given to the River Lymn as it flows from here to the sea at Gibraltar Point. The villages belong to the Fens but are near the southern end of the Wolds.

Aloof in the lovely river meadows, Little Steeping's church is a quaint patchwork of green sandstone and old brick, largely early 15th century work, but on the site of an earlier church.

The interior is attractive, and notable for its extraordinarily wide nave and narrow aisles. The aisle roof and chancel roof are painted. The arcades are of light grey stone, with dark green stone outlining the arches. There is no chancel arch, but the old rood brackets remain, and there is a lovely painted coved screen with rose-tipped tracery, surmounted by figures of the Rood and kneeling angels. Except for old fragments in the lower panels the screen is modern work. The font is old and adorned with an odd array of figures, including women, an angel, a saint, and a knight with a sword.

In a south aisle window is a fine portrait of Edward King, Bishop of Lincoln; and in the chancel is the stone figure of Thomas de Redyng, rector from 1318 till 1353 and probably one of the builders of this church. Two or three centuries after he had been laid to rest, his sculptured figure was taken from its recess and placed face downwards to serve as the chancel step; there it remained till 20th century restoration revealed it, little worse for this indignity.

This restoration commemorated another rector and church-builder—Edward Steere, who left this village to become a bishop in Africa. There is a memorial tablet describing him as a brave man, a devout scholar, and a seer of keen vision; and another tribute to his memory is in the east window in which, among other figures, Thomas de Redyng appears holding a model of this church and Bishop Steere is shown ordaining an African deacon.

Londonthorpe. It stands high up in byways near Grantham, looking down on the woods of Belton. It is a typical Lincolnshire village with a mid-18th century Hall and tower mill and a nucleus of farms. Its clerestoried church has been much restored and its chancel is new, but earlier work is still in evidence. The tower, except for its modern saddleback roof, and the nave arcades with graceful clustered pillars are 13th century, the arches on the south having capitals with finely-carved foliage. The font, with shields in traceried panels, is old, and parts of the 15th century screen are incorporated in the new. In a recess is a battered knight in chain-mail and a 13th century coffin-lid with foliated cross.

Long Bennington. A mile from the meeting-place of three counties, it lies by the River Witham—a big village strung along the A1, a spacious, green-verged highway. Its church is in the meadows and was restored early this century after a period of decay. There are good Georgian houses strung out along the road and just off the road the Priory House is worthy of note. The fine old church is mentioned in Domesday Book and was given to the Norman Abbey of Savigny by Ralph de Filgerus, who founded a Cistercian priory here.

The tower with its bold turret stairway, belongs to the close of the 12th century, with 15th century additions: it has a lancet west window, a pointed arch, and a vaulted roof. The handsome porch (with upper room), with the richly-moulded inner doorway framing an old oak door which has its original hinges, dates from about 1200; so do the fine nave arcades. The aisles are chiefly 14th century. The chancel, with its aumbries, piscina, big recess with crocketed arch and finial, and image bracket at each side of the east window, belongs chiefly to the 15th century; it still has its contemporary oak screen, restored but with traces of the original colour.

Long Sutton. Busy with its markets and still keeping up its ancient fairs, this little town is a place to remember. The present town has some good Georgian houses in streets off the marketplace but in the main early 19th century terraces. There is a tower mill with six sails. John of Gaunt, time-honoured Lancaster, once owned the manor, and the Red Rose can still be seen in old glass within the stately church.

Though restored, the huge church presents externally the picture of a 14th and 15th century building with an early 13th century tower and spire. Within it, however, is the grand nave of Long Sutton's first stone church, built late in the Norman period.

Its distinctive feature is the tower and spire, crowned by a gilded ball with a weathercock 162 feet above the ground. Only just attached to the south-west corner of the south aisle, the tower stands on four splendid arches long since built-up. Above these is a stage of lancet arcading, and higher still is a bellchamber with curious double windows, each having two lights outside and three lights within. The tower buttresses climb to the belfry's octagonal turrets, which are enriched with arcading and end in pinnacles (like tiny spires) leaning inwards to touch the spire. These pinnacles are of timber, covered with lead, and so is the octagonal spire, renowned as the oldest and most perfect example of its kind in existence. Boston Stump and the cliffs of Hunstanton come into the fine view from the tower.

Another fine feature of the exterior is the great two-storied south porch, built in the 15th century and enriched with battlements and stepped buttresses with niches. It has a lovely groined roof with carved bosses—one showing a pelican on her nest, and another the faces of a man and woman with two tongues, both under one head-dress. The upper room, once used as a school, is now a library.

The south doorway is early 14th century, and the north doorway (set in a panelled wall and adorned with quatrefoils) is later 14th century work, sheltered by a rebuilt porch. The west front is for the most part 14th century work, but it has some modern window tracery, and the buttresses and some of its walling belong to the Norman church.

An unusual feature is the two-storied vestry projecting from the north-east corner of the chancel. Built in the 14th century, it has a groined roof, a winding stair, and a slit in the upper room giving a view of the chancel.

The chancel is in part 14th century work, but it retains little of the original church in its north wall, and the sedilia and east window are modern. The chancel arcades of two lofty bays were built at the close of the 15th century, but the one on the south side has been renewed. The south aisle of the chancel has an old piscina, and the vestry an aumbry.

The chancel arch, set on two remarkably tall pillars, is as old as the late Norman nave, which is like a stately avenue of massive round-headed arches; there are seven on each side, set on sturdy round and octagonal piers with fine bases and scalloped capitals. Immediately above the arcades is the contemporary clerestory with its deeply-splayed, round-headed windows. This has served as a triforium since the 18th century, when a higher clerestory was built, and modern restoration has given this late addition its three-light windows in 15th century style. The nave has a fine, restored old roof with embattled beams and traceried gables; and the chancel has its fine old roof (also a little restored) with figures of 28 men and angels supporting the hammerbeams.

Other old survivals are the rood stairway (with a tiny quatrefoiled light); a cinquefoiled recess in the south aisle, its spandrels carved with two dragons and two quaint figures; the late Norman font with the old altar-rail in front of it; the brass eagle lectern with three lions at the base; a mediaeval altar stone and a 17th century altar-table in an aisle; and a 15th century floorstone with a cross and the prayer "Jesu Mercy Lady Help". Some of the church plate is Elizabethan.

A table in the vestry (a fine piece of inlaid work showing the Holy Dove surrounded by flames of fire) is notable because it was the canopy of the pulpit given to Lutton Church by the famous West-minster schoolmaster Dr Busby; it was made in 1702.

Among the memorials is one to a sexton, portrayed as he was in life and also as a skeleton; between the two figures are various emblems of his calling. A stone with the words *Alas, poor Bailey*, commemorates a Dr Bailey who was murdered on a road near the town in 1795. A brass tablet tells of three of the Winter family who served here for 122 years without a break as organists and choir-masters.

Louth. It is a pleasant country town, typical of the county to which it belongs; and its lot has been cast in pleasant places, for it lies in a green valley where the Eastern Wolds come down to the Marsh, here at its widest, and takes its name from the little River Lud which comes to the town from its source at Withcall and pursues its winding way to the sea at Grainthorpe Haven; as far as Alvingham the river runs by the canal made in the 18th century to link the town with the sea at Tetney Haven.

An ancient place busy with its market and fairs, and an important agricultural centre. Louth has known how to grow old gracefully. With its narrow, winding streets, and old inns, houses, and shops, it gathers about a marketplace of irregular shape—a clean and trim town wearing a quiet air of prosperity and self-respect. A walk round Louth is a rewarding experience and unexpected views of the majestic spire of the church are often quite exciting. The Town Hall in Eastgate, the Corn Exchange in the Corn Market, and the Market Hall (with high clock tower) facing the marketplace—they are all important in their different ways; but it is of the steeple of their old church that Louth people speak with real pride, for they know it to be outstanding in grace and beauty—one of the great church spires of England.

Of Louth's earliest history little is known, but it came into Domesday Book. Its real importance began in 1139 when Bishop Alexander, the ambitious and forceful prelate who built castles at Newark, Sleaford, and Banbury, as well as adding to his cathedral at Lincoln, allowed a colony of monks of Fountains Abbey to settle here in his park after they had found Haverholme too swampy for their liking. The fine abbey built by the monks became one of the largest of the Cistercian houses, and flourished greatly until the Black Death brought disaster upon it.

Excavation of the site (which lies over a mile east of the town) has revealed the ground plan, showing the church to have been 256 feet long and half as wide across the transepts. The monastic buildings were round the cloister on the south side of the church, with the chapter house to the east, and a great gateway at the south-west corner of the precincts. The buildings were demolished after the Dissolution, and today there are only two gaunt fragments of the chancel walling and the base of a nave pier to be seen among a bewildering maze of mounds and moats—and the ditch called Monks' Dike which carried the spring water to feed the ponds and moats.

It was perhaps partly because of the adjacent Abbey of Louth Park, and also because there were at that time many chantry chapels as well as a rich store of treasure in their parish church, that the people of Louth took a prominent part in the Lincolnshire Rising in 1536. When the monasteries were threatened with suppression by Henry VIII they riotously opposed the movement; they were goaded to open rebellion when a letter from the king to the men of Lincolnshire described them as "the rude commons of one of the most brute and beastly shires of the whole realm". The result was that several of the townsmen were put to death at Louth, and the vicar (Thomas Kendall) was hanged at Tyburn.

Many roads lead to Louth, but there is no finer approach than the road over the rolling Wolds from Wragby, giving the traveller a first glimpse of the famous spire rising from the trees that drape the hillside, and then, as it drops down into Westgate, revealing the tower and spire in all their glory. It is a perfect picture of old England.

Standing where two earlier churches have stood, the parish church of St James is almost entirely a 15th century structure—completed by 1441, and restored in the 19th and 20th centuries; but it has a few remains of its 13th century predecessor (which was dedicated to St Herefrid), and the spire was begun in 1501 and finished in 1515. From fragments found during restoration the first church is believed to have been Transitional.

Its shape is a parallelogram 182 feet long, with the tower at the west end flanked by the aisles. The chancel also has aisles, and both nave and chancel are clerestoried. The exterior of the body of the church is impressive with its great windows, fine array of battlements with 60 richly-crocketed pinnacles, and eastern gable with pierced parapet surmounted by a cross. Among the stone carvings adorning windows and walls are lions, apes, bulls, hares, swine, parrots, dogs, a man sticking a pig, a lady in a coffin, a ferocious monk, and the Louth Imp. When the two porches were rebuilt last century the south porch lost its upper chamber. Their inner doorways belong to the 13th century church, and so do the pillars of the nave arcades, though they were made longer and raised on new bases in the 15th century.

Superb in design and proportion, the tower and the crocketed spire soar 295 feet. They are almost equal in height, and completely in harmony. All three stages of the tower have beautiful windows with steeply-sloping sills. Graceful double buttresses, stepped and gabled, climb to a parapet crowned by 16 crocketed pinnacles, the four corner pinnacles, like turrets, being 52 feet high and linked with the soaring spire by flying buttresses of delicate tracery.

The spire has been damaged by lightning several times, and it no longer has the original weathercock which was fixed amid great rejoicing in 1515—a weathercock made at Lincoln from a great copper basin which was part of the booty taken from James IV of Scotland at Flodden in 1513. Among some 16th century registers and church accounts in a glass case within the church is a neatly-written account of the building of the spire between 1501 and 1515. Turner painted the spire in his picture of the Horse Fair at Louth.

The interior of the tower is another noble sight. Its mighty arch leading to the nave has massive piers with attached round shafts, and another great arch frames the west window. The arches in the north and south walls also frame windows, and below them are smaller arches opening to the aisles. Below the fine groined roof (86 feet high) runs a pierced balustrade. There is a grand peal of eight bells, and in the belfry can be seen the works of the fine clock given in 1901 by Abraham Samuel, whose 83rd birthday was announced by its first chime. There is also a curious wheel like a squirrel-cage; it was used for hauling up stone in mediaeval times, the power being provided by men walking round inside it.

At the other end of the church, seen as though framed by the great chancel arch, the huge east window of seven lights is a fine spectacle of lovely tracery and of 19th century glass shining with kaleidoscopic effect. Below it is the modern reredos of stone and alabaster and marble, with figures of Our Lord, adoring angels, and the Evangelists. The three old sedilia (restored a little) have fine vaulted canopies, pinnacles, and crocketed hoods, and the old rood stairway remains.

There is a modern font of alabaster, and in the north aisle is an early 15th century font rescued from a garden, its buttressed stem enriched with traceried panels, and its shallow bowl with foliage.

There is also notable woodwork, both old and new. Modern are the richly-carved stalls, and the oak pulpit with canopied statues of 11 apostles and a tiny figure of Judas peering from the carved stonework below. Modern, too, are the roofs, particularly fine being the early 19th century nave roof, adorned with 18 angels on its tie-beams and resting on the old grotesque corbels. In the north aisle hang two carved wooden angels and three bosses which belonged to the mediaeval roof, and at the west end of the nave are six of the old stalls with plain misericord seats. There are also several old chests and a 17th century altar-table. The unusual chest standing under the tower is believed to have been an old alms-chest and to have been hewn from a solid log of oak. A splendid piece of old craftsmanship is the cupboard chest called Sudbury's Hutch, now in the vestry. Given by Thomas Sudbury, a vicar who died in 1504, it has two doors bearing carved busts of Henry VII and Elizabeth of York. Also in the vestry is a portrait of a vicar who rejoiced in the name of Wolley Jolland; he came here in 1780 and ministered for the next 50 years.

Edward VI gave Louth its charter, but the grammar school bearing his name was only his re-foundation of an endowed school which was here as far back as 1276. Among its most notable scholars were Admiral Hobart Pasha (who ran a blockade off North Carolina in the American Civil War), Governor Eyre of Jamaica, Sir John Franklin, Captain John Smith, the founder of Virginia, and the Tennyson brothers. (Frederick Tennyson, a gifted poet overshadowed by his younger brother Alfred, was born in this town in 1807.) The school they knew was rebuilt in 1869 on its old site in Schoolhouse Lane, and this building is now part of a school for girls, the boys having gone to modern buildings in Edward Street where two relics from the old school are preserved—a bust of Captain Smith, and the original statue of Edward VI. The school also has a fine mural painting of Captain John Smith as a prisoner of the Indian Chief Powhattan. A modern statue of the young king holding sceptre and orb looks on to the school of 1869 from the back of old almshouses which were rebuilt at the same time.

On the site of the old prison, at the corner of Eastgate and Ramsgate, are the almshouses founded last century by Frederick Orme (rector of Lyndon, Rutland)—a pleasant little L-shaped group with a fine tree shading their lawn.

On the Lincoln road, nestling among fine trees above the old town, stands Thorpe Hall, an Elizabethan house with walls of mellowed brick, and many gables and chimneys. Only the west front is of the original house. It was built in 1584 by Sir John Bolle who lies at Haugh. He was the hero of the ballad of the Spanish Lady of High Degree of whom he had charge after the Siege of Cadiz, and who, because of her unrequited love for the English knight, who was already married, retired to a nunnery. Among the rich gifts she gave Sir John to take home to his wife were tapestry worked by herself, plate and jewels, and a portrait of herself in a green dress which for long hung in the Hall. The picture has gone, and the treasure has been scattered among the Bolle descendants; but the ghost of the Green Lady is said still to haunt the old Hall she never saw.

A mile west of the town the Lud winds through the wooded gorge known as Hubbards Hills, a natural park of some 40 acres given to the town by Auguste Alphonse Pahud. A beech-clad precipice on one side faces meadows sloping up to woods, and the stream runs out of the gorge beside a mill with a lovely garden. It was on the 29th of May in 1920 that a cloud-burst on the Wolds caused water to rush into this delightful vale in overwhelming torrents and sweep swiftly onwards into Louth, carrying away bridges and wrecking many houses. Many people were drowned, for the river rose 15 feet in an unbelievably short time, and it sank as rapidly as it had risen. The flood rose as high as the coping of the pretty stone bridge below the church.

Low Toynton. A tiny neighbour of Horncastle, it has a tiny church tucked away near a red-tiled cottage and a thatched farmhouse.

Rebuilt in 1811, the church has kept its Norman chancel arch and a splendid 14th century font adorned on bowl and stem with rich carving. On one side of the font is a figure seated and crowned, either the Madonna or a Majesty; two sides have angels; three more have flowers and leaves; and on the remaining two sides are four of the disciples with their symbols. The other eight disciples, all with

Louth Church

Tulip fields near Spalding

battered faces, are round the stem of the font, which is lined with lead and has remains of the old staple fastenings.

Ludborough. Standing pleasantly on the Louth to Grimsby road, it marks the site of a Roman settlement. Facing the smithy and sheltered by trees is the old white-walled Elizabethan manor house brought up to date. Beside it is the old church, partly rebuilt.

Five centuries old is the fine tower, with walls of weathered, rust-coloured stone in striking contrast to the grey of the rest of the building. The nave comes from the close of the Norman period, but the north arcade and aisle and part of the clerestory have been rebuilt. Both arcades have clustered piers.

The chancel is chiefly 13th century work, including the north doorway, some fine lancets, a double piscina, and an aumbry; its entrance arch and south windows are 14th century. The font and some fragments of glass are also 600 years old, but a rarer survival of the same age is a fine example of scrollwork painting on the sill of a chancel window; it is in red and green, beautiful in design, and wonderfully preserved. A window showing Faith and Charity is a tribute to Augustus Gedge, rector from 1853 till 1909.

Cadeby, not far from Ludborough, was the birthplace of a remarkable 16th century traveller, Fynes Moryson, who for six years or so meandered all over Europe, went on to the Holy Land, saw the cities of the East, and explored Scotland and Ireland. He came back to his native Lincolnshire to write of the places he had seen in a lengthy account which is extremely useful to the student of the social life of those times.

Ludford. It is two villages united, on the busy road from Market Rasen to Louth.

Ludford Magna has the church, a cross-shaped building of 1863, with remains of an ancient cross in the churchyard. Just beyond Ludford Parva the River Bain begins its 20-mile journey to the Witham near Tattershall, flowing through both Ludfords and then past Wykeham Hall, 2 miles away, an ancient house with some remains of an old church in its adjoining park.

Lusby. It has fine views over the Wolds, and an interesting little church, trim and cared for.

Much of it is Norman, and even earlier work can be seen in the fragment of long-and-short work in the blocked south doorway and in the worn carving of the Crucifixion on a stone above. The stumps of pairs of semi-circular shafts on either side of the chancel arch are also Anglo-Saxon. The arch of the doorway, the blocked doorway in the north wall of the nave, and the fine little keyhole window high in the chancel wall are all Norman work.

The plain round-headed arch of the chancel is modern, but in one of its old jambs is a gabled niche. Across the arch is a restored 15th century oak screen with rich tracery. There are several old aumbries. and by a nave window is the finely-carved head of a queen.

Lutton. It was once a little market town of some importance, the chief place in the district; now it is an out-of-the-way marshland village. But it is linked for ever with a great name in the story of learning.

In a house which stood where the village school stands now was born Richard Busby, one of the most famous schoolmasters of all time. He served Westminster School for nearly 60 years, and in the vestry of Lutton Church is a print showing him in his wide-brimmed hat with one of his schoolboys.

The mellow red-brick church which Dr Busby knew, clustered below a stone spire soaring over 150 feet, comes largely from the 14th and 15th centuries, though it was restored in 1859. Nave and aisles still have their fine old roofs with moulded beams; and among the old relics are the font with its tapering bowl on a leafy stem, and a floorstone of about 1400 bearing portraits of John Chelton's two wives.

But the chief treasure of the church is the massive, beautifully inlaid pulpit erected here in 1702 by the bequest of Dr Busby; on it are the date and his initials. The canopy of the pulpit has been taken to Long Sutton Church and made into a vestry table.

To have given us the greatest schoolmaster in Milton's England is the chief historic distinction of Lutton. Richard Busby was a poor genius, whose talents won him a scholarship at Westminster School, from which he proceeded in 1624, when 18, to Cambridge University, there greatly to distinguish himself in the classics and as an orator.

Returning to his old school at Westminster as headmaster, after having taken orders and served two Somerset churches, he was the outstanding figure in school education for the next 55 years. The Civil War cost him his church livings, but such was his scholastic reputation that he was not disturbed at his school. The Restoration restored his fortunes.

As a schoolmaster he was unequalled in his day. It was his boast that of the bench of bishops 16 at one time had been his scholars. Among his other pupils he had Dryden, who, writing later that Busby "used to whip boys till he made them confirmed blockheads", yet admired him so much that he sent two of his sons to study under him.

The legend of Busby's severity did not all arise after his death. Rochester, a contemporary, wrote of a "hot-brained fustian fool" whom he wished "in Busby's hands, to be well lashed at school". And Pope, who was 7 when Busby died, knew the legends, and pilloried the supposed tyrant in 10 terrible lines. Dr Johnson, born soon enough to know men who had been at Westminster under him, said Busby called the rod his sieve, and was wont to say that whoever would not pass through it was no boy for him.

Yet the friendships maintained by Busby with his former pupils till death divided them, and the affectionate tributes to him written by them, show that he was not all tyrant.

That he was pompous and conscious of his importance is assured by the story of Busby, on the chance visit of Charles II to the school, asking to be excused from removing his hat in the royal presence, lest the boys should think there was a man greater than their headmaster.

Busby died in 1695, and sleeps in Westminster Abbey, with his bust facing Poets' Corner, close to that of his pupil Dryden.

Mablethorpe. Far different is it from the place Alfred Lord Tennyson knew—the village of his day has become a popular holiday resort and is still growing—not in the most attractive way but rather a haphazard growth of chalets and bungalows with caravans and temporary seaside residences—but it still has the fine stretch of golden sands and the dunes which the poet loved in his youth, though since the great flood of 1953 immense concrete sea defences have masked and replaced many of the dunes. Here Tennyson would stand as a boy on the sand-built ridge, thinking it was the spine-bone of the world. Here it was that he and his brother Charles spent the never-to-be-forgotten day when their first book of verse (*Poems by Two Brothers*) was published, shouting themselves hoarse as they rolled out poem after poem. Again and again he would return to this Lincolnshire shore, to this old haunt beloved, but the old magic had gone and he wrote of it in after years:

> *How often when a child I lay reclined:*
> *I took delight in this fair land and free:*
> *Here stood the infant Ilion of the mind,*
> *And here the Grecian ships all seemed to be.*
> *And here again I come, and only find*
> *The drain-cut level of the marshy lea.*
> *Grey sandbanks, and pale sunsets, dreary wind,*
> *Dim shores, dense rains, and heavy-clouded sea.*

Long before Tennyson came here, wondering who could light "on as happy a shore", the encroaching sea had claimed one of Mablethorpe's churches—St Peter's. A Roman settlement and a mediaeval village lie between the tides. But the little church of St Mary still stands, half a mile inland and reached across two bridges over the deep drain which runs like a moat on two sides of it. More than

60 sycamores screen the patchwork walls of stone and brick and boulder, and make an avenue to its porch.

So steep is the chancel roof and so squat the tower that the building looks something like a Viking ship raised at prow and stern. The fabric comes chiefly from 1714, but the south doorway and the nave arcades are a legacy from the 13th century, and a few other relics of mediaeval days have survived.

The interior of the church is no less quaint than the exterior. The arcades present an extraordinary picture of many colours in stone; moreover, their low, slender pillars are dwarfed by arches which soar almost to the flat ceiling. The tower arch contributes to the oddness, for it is lop-sided and the capitals of its responds are only 4 feet from the floor.

Under the arch stands a beautiful mediaeval font with rich and varied tracery on bowl and stem. Other mediaeval relics are a floor-stone carved with a cross, three sedilia in the chancel, and a 14th century tomb with a broken helmet hanging above it; it is said to be that of one of two knights slain in a duel at Earl's Bridge 2 miles away, the stone figure of his opponent being in the church at Maltby. There are also brasses (inscriptions and a portrait) commemorating the Fitzwilliams who lived at Mablethorpe Hall centuries ago; the portrait shows Elizabeth Fitzwilliam (who died in 1522) with flowing hair, wearing a gown with girdle, her hands clasped in prayer.

Maltby-le-Marsh. A small marshland village with a disused windmill and an early Baptist Chapel founded in 1690.

The figure of an armoured knight lies in solitary state in its attractive old church. At his pillow are two mutilated angels, and at his feet a lion fights a winged dragon. According to legend it commemorates a noble lord who was laid to rest here after fighting a duel at Earl's Bridge with a knight of Mablethorpe to whom the duel also proved fatal.

The nave has some 14th century windows, and the old entrance to the rood stairway can still be seen. Near the unusual double arch of the massive west tower is a splendid 14th century font, its bowl encircled by the outstretched wings of four angels and its pedestal guarded by four Apostles.

Manby. A great aerodrome with its RAF college has brought new activity to this village a few miles from Louth. The college buildings and residential quarters have now become a familiar part of the village. It is a pleasant village and its church is shaded by fine trees—a magnificent cedar among them—and graced on its sunny side by five spreading hydrangeas which in summer make a charming array of pink blossom, enhanced by the weathered green sandstone of the walls.

The church has a fine tower crowned with battlements and pinnacles, and is about 500 years old, though its chancel was rebuilt in 1889. The walls of mottled green stone give a pleasing effect to the simple, dignified interior. The old rood stairway with its entrance and opening above is still here, and there is an old font with worn heads under its panelled bowl. On an old beam in the chancel are two quaint men, one in red and one in white, holding shields; and in a nave window are fragments of old glass. The fine modern roof of the nave is enriched with tracery.

Built into the wall near the chancel arch is a consecration cross carved in relief, and in the north wall are two splendid stones with band and cable ornament carved before the Conquest.

Manthorpe. An attractive, neat, estate village now merging with its close neighbour Grantham, and giving its name to one of that town's main highways. Like many of the cottages the church is grey, though not with age, for it was built early in Queen Victoria's reign by Richard Cust, rector of Belton, and brother of the 1st Earl Brownlow. It is a dignified building, crowned by a handsome central tower with a 50-foot spire added later.

Manton. Fine limes and sycamores surround its rebuilt church, and there are fine views from the churchyard and from the hilltop looking across to Scunthorpe iron furnaces. Two miles north of Manton are Twigmoor Woods, in which Scotch firs, larches, and rhododendrons make a charming setting for the two fine sheets of water known as the Black Head Ponds. For more than a century thousands of black-headed gulls found sanctuary here, but their numbers have diminished in recent years and breeding has moved to other "flashes" of water.

West of the Ponds is the old Twigmoor Hall, home of John Wright, one of the conspirators of the Gunpowder Plot. He was one of the first two men to whom Catesby communicated his plan early in 1604, and he died of wounds received from Sir Richard Walsh's men at Holbeach House, Staffordshire, after the plot had been discovered.

Mareham-le-Fen. A pleasant village on the busy highway running south of the Wolds, it has an attractive inn, white-walled and thatched, and a restored mediaeval church with a modern chancel.

Like most of the old work surviving, the tower of the church comes from the 14th century, but its arch with nail-head ornament (hidden by the organ) is a century older, and its battlements are modern. The south aisle has a 15th century parapet, and on one of its fine pinnacles is a carving of St George conquering the Dragon. The south doorway, with flowers and grotesques dotted in its deep hollow moulding, is late 13th century work. The 14th century nave arcades have richly-foliated capitals.

The 14th century font, carved with bold leaf pattern, and adorned at the corners with flowers and heads still has its original staple fastenings for a cover. Near the font is part of an ancient cross head.

Markby. Lying in the Marsh, between Alford and the sea, this tiny village was once a settlement of marauding Danes. Its quaint old church—the only thatched church in Lincolnshire—stands within the moat which surrounded the Austin priory founded here by Ralph Gilbert in the 12th century and dissolved in 1534.

Probably incorporating ruins of the priory church, the thatched church, which has recently been restored, consists only of nave and chancel, lighted by modern leaded windows and divided by an arch with original dog-tooth ornament. The old round-headed mediaeval north doorway is now blocked. Among its old possessions are box-pews, a few benches, a plain font, a double-decker pulpit of Elizabethan days, a 17th century altar-table, a chest with strap-hinges and remains of scrollwork, and an altar cross and candlesticks made from beams once in the priory. The church bell is said to have belonged to the old refectory, parts of which probably survive in the red farmhouse nearby.

Market Deeping. Its market is but a memory, and the rest of its name (with the other Deepings) serves as a reminder of its place in the deep meadows subject to flooding by the River Welland from time immemorial. As far back as the Conqueror's day Richard de Rulos embanked this spot, "making it a garden of pleasure out of the very pits and bogs". Fertile these lands are now, as rich-soiled as they are rich in history and legend.

The history of the Deepings is more than a little shadowy, and centres about the Wakes, the great family to which belonged Hereward the Wake, who resisted the Conqueror, and Hugh Wake, who looked after the affairs of the Forest of Kesteven for Henry III. In 300 years their house grew in power and gained great possessions scattered about England and extending into Scotland. Their glory culminated in Joan, the Fair Maid of Kent, whom we like to picture as the friend and protector of Wycliffe. Heiress of the Wake family and daughter of Edmund of Woodstock, Earl of Kent, Joan owned this place among her 26 manors, most of them in Lincolnshire. She took her cousin the Black Prince as her second husband, and one of the two sons became Richard II.

Stretching alongside the River Welland with its big suburb, Deeping St James, it is a bright little town with fine, wide streets. There are many lovely old houses, stone-walled and stone-roofed and with dormers and little bow windows; but none more charming than the rectory by the church. Claiming to be the oldest inhabited rectory in England, it was once the refectory of a priory belonging to Crowland Abbey, and it still has a fine mediaeval timber roof (with angel corbels of later time) and a beautiful Jacobean staircase.

Much of the fine church is 15th century work, including the embattled tower; but some of it is earlier, and a blocked arch in the north wall of the chancel is probably Saxon. The porch is 13th century work and shelters a modern door enriched with the original ironwork of slender leaf pattern. The nave has Transitional-Norman arcades, with round-headed arches on the north side facing pointed arches, but all set on clustered piers; above them is a later mediaeval clerestory.

The lofty chancel has its mediaeval sedilia, piscina, aumbry, low-side window with iron bars, and a recess sheltering a fine coped stone adorned with a cross. In two richly-canopied niches by the altar are modern figures of St Hugh of Lincoln, and St Guthlac (patron saint of this church) who came from Crowland more than 12 centuries ago to plant Christianity here. Ten charming medallions in two of the chancel windows tell the story of his life.

The south aisle also has its mediaeval piscina and aumbry, and another piscina is in a pier of the north arcade. Near the old rood-loft doorway is a memorial to William Goodale who died in 1716 when 110 years old. The old font has carved tracery; and the porch shelters a fine mediaeval coffin-lid with a cross, the head of another elaborately carved, and a fragment of Saxon stone (about 18 inches long) with carved interlacing pattern.

The unhappy labourer-poet John Clare came this way a century ago, bringing a few pence to buy a book in which to write his verses. It was here that the kindly stationer Henson chatted with him, and entered into a plan for printing a prospectus inviting 300 people to buy copies of his first book of poems.

Market Rasen. A small busy market town. It has a charming setting, with woodlands all around and the high Wolds sheltering it on the east. From the Wolds, at Bully Hill, the little River Rase comes to town on its way to the Ancholme.

The big church stands by the little square, with fine chestnut trees for neighbours. It has been much rebuilt, but still has a weather-worn 15th century tower with tall narrow arch opening to a nave with mediaeval arcades. Older than all else here is the richly-moulded Norman doorway within the porch. The rood-beam and its figures were set up in memory of men who died in the First World War. A tablet tells of James Walter, who died in 1845 after being vicar here 52 years. Both he and his wife were cousins of Jane Austen.

There are few other buildings of note but the Centenary Methodist Chapel of 1863, in stone and red-brick with fine stone portico with columns, looks down Union Street.

The Market Rasen racecourse now figures regularly in the national racing programme and attracts big attendances to its meetings. The Golf Course, too, is very popular and brings many visitors to the town.

The De Aston school in Willingham Road, with its red-brick walls set among trees, is another building linked with mediaeval days. Its name is that of Thomas de Aston, Canon of Lincoln, through whose beneficence a lonely hermitage on the desolate Roman road at Spital developed into a little hospital towards the end of the 14th century. The endowment still furnishes this fine modern school with funds.

John Conolly, born in this little town in 1794, is remembered for his work in bringing about a more humane treatment of the insane.

Marsh Chapel. A big village between the Louth Navigation Canal and the sea, it has three notable old buildings: a windmill without its cap, a fine Hall of red-brick, and one of the finest churches of the Lincolnshire Marsh.

Built of Ancaster stone, the church is a handsome specimen of late 15th century architecture, though its chancel was rebuilt a century ago. The tall, tilting tower has an embattled and pinnacled crown, a corner turret with a little spire, and an arch soaring to the nave roof and framing a view of the four-light west window. One of its three bells, called John, was 4 years old when the Armada set out to conquer England, and another bears the names of eight men who died in the First World War.

The big south porch has a king's head on its parapet and a cross on its gable; and above the north doorway is a Latin inscription saying that "this is none other than the House of God". The clerestoried nave has arcades with embattled capitals. A restored oak screen with leafy arches and tracery 500 years old is now in the tower arch.

Apart from this screen and a few old bench-ends, the woodwork is modern—nave seats and choir-stalls with fine poppyheads, richly-carved altar and rails, and pulpit with canopied figures of Our Lord and the Four Evangelists. The handsome roof of the chancel has carved wall-plates, hammerbeams with traceried spandrels and 10 angels holding shields with Passion emblems. The old traceried font has a pyramid cover.

Under the canopied arches of a dainty alabaster monument in the chancel Sir Walter Harpham of 1607 kneels with his wife and small daughter—a charming group, though the heads of father and daughter are gone, and the mother's wide-brimmed hat is battered.

Some of the gargoyles round the church show women in mediaeval headdress. Another is the head of a horned ram, a reminder that the draining of the Marsh has put many sheep on the land. In the middle of the 19th century about 600 acres of salt "fitties" (the outmarsh between the sea-bank and the sea) were reclaimed for Marshchapel and Grainthorpe.

Marston. It has the beauty of green meadows, with the Witham not far away, and the charm of red cottages and quaint almshouses watched over by an old church with a broach spire. Near the church stands Marston Hall, what remains of a fine old Tudor stone manor house which is the home of a well-known Lincolnshire family, the Thorolds.

The church has a tower and spire from about 1300, and a fine 15th century porch with crocketed niches, sheltering a lovely 13th century doorway. Also 13th century is the south arcade, its only adornment being a simple leaf on one capital. The north arcade is 14th century.

The chancel, largely rebuilt last century in Early English style, is lighted by richly-moulded windows with shafts and foliated capitals: the three lancets of the east window, with their wealth of dog-tooth and other ornament, are particularly striking.

The oldest of the many Thorold monuments is a canopied tomb of Purbeck marble with shields of arms. This is the tomb of William Thorold, 1569, in the south aisle. On the other side of the modern stone screen dividing the aisle from the chantry chapel is the great alabaster monument supporting the armoured figure of Sir Anthony Thorold, Sheriff of Lincolnshire, who died in 1594. Glowing with gilt and heraldic colour, it has all been finely restored.

On a tall column in the churchyard is a fine sundial.

Martin-by-Horncastle. A tiny hamlet, it has a few cottages and farms, a modern Hall among fine trees, a Georgian manor house, and a tiny church in tranquil setting.

The church has only nave and chancel, with a bell in a recess of the west wall. A doorway, restored outside, is revealed within the church, as Norman work richly carved with lattice pattern and leaves, and with serpents whispering into the ears of two curious faces.

Very striking is the chancel arch. Pointed and narrow, but nearly 3 feet thick, it was built at the end of the Norman period, and has capitals carved with scrolls and beading.

Martin. A small parish, north of Timberland, with the Roman Carr Dyke passing through the eastern part of the village. There is a Victorian Gothic church of 1876 (tower built 1911) which was designed by T. H. Wyatt of London, and restored in 1964–66. The day school, known as Martin Mrs Mary King's School, was so named after the widow of Neville King (died 1730) of Ashby-de-la-Launde, where she lived until her death in 1763. She was daughter of Richard Middlemore of Somerby, near Grantham, and the great grand-daughter of Robert Sanderson, Bishop of Lincoln (1660–63). She built and endowed a small school at Martin to provide instruction in reading and writing for 20 poor children of the hamlet of Martin. The school was rebuilt in 1842 and enlarged in 1874 by the Rev. J. W. King, the lord of the manor of Martin, who played such a prominent part in the building of the parish church of Holy Trinity, Martin and was vicar of Ashby-de-la-Launde for 53 years.

Marton. It has seen much history in the making, for it lies where the Lincoln to Gainsborough road crosses the road made by the Romans to link their Ermine Street with Doncaster.

Till Bridge Lane, as the Lincolnshire stretch of the Roman road is called, leaves Ermine Street 4 miles north of Lincoln, and here comes to the River Trent after a straight 9-mile run. Across the river in Nottinghamshire is Littleborough, once the Roman station *Segelocum*. The ford, dating from the first century, has been seen here in times of severe drought. The Romans came this way, Harold and his Saxons crossed here on their way to Hastings, and the Conqueror may have passed through when on his way from York to capture Lincoln. From time immemorial the river here has risen and fallen with the tides, and has felt the influence of the famous Aegir which rushes up the river to Gainsborough at the spring tides.

But Marton has more than mere memories of days gone by. In a churchyard fringed with limes is a church retaining work of both Normans and Saxons. Standing defiant of time, its tall, unbuttressed and tapering tower was built in the 11th century—either at the close of the Saxon epoch or in very early Norman days—and is a striking spectacle with walls entirely of fine herringbone work, right up to the bellchamber. The belfry windows are in the typical Saxon style, with two lights divided by mid-wall shafts, and above the modern west window (framed by a blocked mediaeval window) is a tiny original keyhole light.

There is much herringbone in the walls of the chancel, and its arch, with heavy roll mouldings, was made by the Normans. The north arcade of two wide bays comes from the close of the Norman period. The rest of the church belongs chiefly to the 13th century, with later mediaeval work in the brave display of pinnacled battlements, and in many of the windows.

The chancel has a 13th century low-side window and a big niche with a pedestal for a saint; and in its north wall is an ancient stone, about a foot long, with a much-worn sculpture of Our Lord Crucified; it may be as old as the tower. Built into the west end of the south aisle (outside) is a fine row of Saxon stones, some with inter-lacing and plaitwork carving.

The tall cross in the churchyard, restored as a war memorial, is said to have been an old market cross.

Mavis Enderby. The little church of this Wold village has been much rebuilt, but the tower, heavily buttressed and displaying hideous gargoyles, still has its 15th century base; and other mediaeval work is evident in the south doorway enriched with carved flowers, the Norman pillar piscina on clustered shafts in the porch, and the 14th century nave arcade. The nave windows are 14th century; the aisle windows and the font with its simple tracery are 15th.

The modern canopied pulpit has a door leading to the rood-loft, which has a golden cross and figures of the rood, and surmounts a screen with light tracery in 14th century style.

Standing amid the ornamental trees and shrubs in the churchyard are a 17th century sundial and an old cross with carvings of the Crucifixion and the Madonna in its modern gabled head.

Melton Ross. Now a popular residential area set among the rolling little hills, it has a name keeping green the memory of the Ros family to whom Belvoir came by marriage with an heiress of the d'Albinis 700 years ago. (It was a Lord Ros who became Earl of Rutland in the time of Henry VIII.)

Between the village and Wrawby stands Melton Gallows, which was set up originally by order of James I as a warning to the Ros and Tyrwhit families that their long-standing quarrel must cease.

Tucked away among trees, behind the wayside cottages, is the village church, rebuilt in 1867 but preserving two relics of the old one: a tub font in the churchyard, and a holy water stoup within.

Mere. A 17th century farmhouse, cattle browsing beyond a haw-thorn hedge, a goodly company of elms and chestnuts and beeches, a little group of cottages and haystacks by a country lane, and a lake to justify its name—these are all it has to show today. Traces of houses and streets have been found which suggest it was once a place of importance; but that was all long ago.

The Knights Templars were established here about 1200, and before half a century had passed Simon de Roppele founded Mere Hospital as a lazar house, with 13 brethren and a chaplain. The Hospital escaped the fate that overtook the monasteries and most of the hospitals at the Reformation, and the funds of its rich endow-ment were for a long time misapplied. They amounted to £1000 a year at the beginning of the 19th century. Now the charity has been regulated by chancery, and poor folk hereabouts, as well as schools and a College of Education in Lincoln, all benefit from it.

Messingham. Not a distinguished village; mainly 19th century; and modern houses and bungalows, the village church among the trees was rebuilt in 1819 and made an ecclesiastical museum by its vicar, Henry Vincent Bayley, a great scholar, who was Archdeacon of Stow and later subdean of Lincoln. But the nave has retained its 13th century nave arcades, and the chancel its old aumbry and bracket piscina. Glowing in many of the windows is a wealth of old glass, the greater part of which was brought here by Dr Bayley from other churches as far afield as Malvern and Manchester as well as other Lincolnshire churches. In the low screen, the two desks, and the pulpit is old tracery also brought here by this famous scholar.

In the red, blue, and gold medley glowing in the east window are headless figures of the Madonna and Child, several pictures of Our Lord, heads and figures of saints, shields, an angel, tiny figures leaning from embattled turrets, a Doom, and a prancing horse. More shields and fragments are in the aisles, including a figure of St Catherine with her wheel.

Metheringham. Halfway between Lincoln and Sleaford it stands, its tower mill a landmark by the main road and its red-roofed houses and shops gathered in friendly concourse. In the twisting High Street is a war memorial—a statue of a soldier with arms reversed; close by is a stone cross set up to mark the coronation of George V, and built into a wall is the stump of the ancient village cross.

A great fire in 1599 destroyed much of the old church, which was restored and dedicated anew three years later. But the tower with round-headed windows has stood since Norman days, though its arch and its doorway with tooth ornament are 13th century work and its pinnacled top was added after the fire. The nave also has its original 13th century arcades though the round pillars on which their pointed arches rest, like the clerestory windows above them, are part of the rebuilding that followed the fire. Further restoration was made in the 19th century, when the chancel was extended and the north aisle rebuilt. Sheltered by the porch is a fine Elizabethan door; it bears the date 1602 and the letters ER.

The oak choir-stalls, screen, and pulpit are all fine 20th century work, the screen having the rood figures above a band of foliage, with peapods over its central arch; the pulpit has similar adornment and a figure of St Wilfrid, to whom the church is dedicated.

St Wilfrid appears again in modern glass in a north aisle window, an attractive figure with St Ignatius of Antioch for companion. Another window, near the font, commemorates a village blacksmith and his wife, a nurse, and is full of local interest. But the finest glass is in three windows on one side of the clerestory showing six Apostles in a row clad in red and blue and green robes; they were set here by a vicar in recent times, but most of the glass is ancient.

In spite of its great fire Metheringham is fortunate enough to have its earliest registers, going back to 1538, when Thomas Cromwell first ordered the keeping of records.

Middle Rasen. The village is seen at its best from the old stone bridge on the way to the church, where the pinnacles of the tower are glimpsed as they rise above the chestnuts at the end of the road. Close to the church is a pretty thatched cottage.

There were two churches here once; but the one which had belonged to Drax Priory in Yorkshire was pulled down in 1860. The existing one belonged to Tupholme Abbey and displays splendid Norman work.

The tower has some Norman windows, and the south doorway of the nave, enriched with no fewer than 42 beak-heads as well as zig-zag key pattern and nail-head ornament, is a rich Norman legacy. From the close of the Norman period come the sides of the pointed chancel arch, with scalloped capitals and six carved roundels which project boldly and look rather like necklaces of big beads.

The aisle of the nave has been rebuilt, but the splendid early 13th century arcade still stands, its richly-moulded arches supported by stout round pillars. Parts of the tower, some big windows, the tall oak screen, and fragments of glass in a low-side window are 15th century. Two book-rests made from old bench-ends have carvings of flowers and a shield, a king, a queen, and an angel with a trumpet.

A priestly figure lying on a low tomb carved with quatrefoils is a relic from the destroyed church; wearing 14th century hood and vestments gracefully draped, and holding a chalice, he has a lion at his feet and angels at his head.

Miningsby. Its tiny church was largely rebuilt last century but still has something to show from its Norman and mediaeval days, and shelters, too, a fragment of Saxon sculpture.

The entrance of the church is a 13th century doorway under a filled-in Norman arch, and another Norman relic is a window in the south wall of the nave. The chancel though rebuilt last century, is partly 13th century work, with a filled-in vesica window above the double lancet in the east wall, and traces of old painting on its entrance arch.

Old poppyhead benches in the chancel have set the pattern for new ones in the nave, and there is a fine 15th century oak screen with tracery and pinnacles. The font, also some 600 years old, has four grotesque heads round the bottom of the bowl and rests on shafts with capitals carved into flowers.

Hidden by the chancel seats is the most ancient possession of this church—a Saxon stone about 3 feet long, with knotwork carving and a herringbone border.

Minting. The Earl of Chester founded here a small alien Benedictine priory when Henry I was king, but at the end of our fifth King Henry's reign its possessions were granted to the Carthusian priory of Mount Grace, and nothing of it remains.

The village church is a small building. It was almost completely rebuilt last century, but between the nave and aisle is the old 13th century arcade, with the shafts clustering round the pillars restored. Set into the walls are parts of the stem of a 13th century churchyard cross, one showing, within a border of nail-head, the Crucifixion group dated c. 1210; the other, carved with trailing leaves and bordered with nail-head.

Moorby. In its small church, rebuilt last century, are two interesting pieces of sculpture. One is a stone strip of carving, in the vestry, showing a man in a tunic playing bagpipes while two women and a man are dancing; the other is the bowl of a 14th century font, set on a new base, and remarkable for the unusual carving on its four sides. One panel has a picture of the Madonna and Child, in which the Sun and Moon are shown with faces; another has a group of six figures kneeling; a third panel has a man sitting with his book, a scourge at his side; and the fourth shows the dead body of the donor of the font, with two guardian angels folding a sheet. All the figures in the panels have lost their faces, but two crowned and mitred heads below the bowl are intact.

Morton. One of Bourne's nearest neighbours, it stands on a road running due east to the Fens, a prominent landmark in this flat countryside being a tower with tall pinnacles and hideous gargoyles which rises from the heart of a cross-shaped church rich in years and dignity. For five centuries this tower has stood, bold as a beacon, and for five centuries has the wide western porch faced the village street and sheltered the big door, handsome with tracery and studded with nails.

The interior is an impressive one, a grand vista of arches and pillars. On each side of the nave are four lofty arches from the early 14th century, one with eight-sided pillars, and the other with clustered shafts and rich foliated capitals; and each arcade is adorned with three mediaeval heads, smiling, snarling, serene, or comic. Beyond is the vaulted tower with arches into nave, chancel, and transepts.

The 15th century font is a notable possession, adorned with leafy canopies and eight shields with emblems of Our Lord's Passion.

There is a fine old 18th century inn and some attractive colour-washed red-pantiled cottages made from bricks and tiles produced in Brickyard Lane.

Morton. An attractive neighbour of Gainsborough, it lies by a loop of the Trent and has a fine 19th century church which was largely the gift of Sir Hickman Beckett Bacon, lord of the manor and premier baronet of England. The home of this family, Thonock Hall, now sadly dilapidated, stands in the finely-wooded 300-acre park across the highway, where there is a Norman motte-and-bailey earthwork known as Castle Hills.

Built in 14th and 15th century style, the church is adorned with fine embattled and pinnacled parapets, and has figures of St Paul and St Peter on the two porches flanking the west tower. Inside, it is notable for its striking array of Morris windows, designed by Burne-Jones.

Glowing richly in the east window is the Nativity, and another chancel window has four saints: Barnabas, Peter, Paul, and Stephen. In lovely colours in the south chapel are the Four Evangelists. In the south transept is St Paul preaching in Athens, and another window has King Alfred and two Bishops of Lincoln (Robert Grosseteste and St Hugh). The north transept has the Stoning of Stephen. In the north aisle are St John the Baptist, the Madonna, and Anna; and in the south aisle is St Martin sharing his cloak, St Edmund, St George, St German, St Nicholas, and The Good Shepherd.

The long, wide nave has a panelled roof, richly carved and painted, and the chancel has a tall oak screen with handsome tracery and figures of the Rood. The benches, stalls, pulpit, and lectern are all of oak, and the splendid font is of Frosterley marble in which are visible the marks of numberless fossil forms of shells. The fine font cover (like a traceried and pinnacled spire) has canopied figures of Our Lord and many other saints and biblical figures.

Moulton. Centre of a big parish in the fens and marshes of south Holland, it lies near the highway from Spalding to Norfolk and has one of the grand churches for which this road is renowned.

The village green forms the centre of a delightful group of buildings; a picturesque nucleus to the settlement.

Of Moulton's castle, which stood nearby but fell into decay in the 15th century, nothing remains but an oval moat in King's Hall Park; but across the highway, in the hedge of a narrow lane running north-east, stands the Elloe Stone, about 3 feet high, round which the Saxon court of assembly for this wapentake used to meet.

Moulton Church was begun about 1180, and just 200 years later were added the tower and spire for which the village is widely famed. The tower is enriched with wall-arcading, charming windows, canopied niches with statues, and double buttresses with more canopied niches which climb to the pinnacles. From these pinnacles delicate flying buttresses spring to the ribbed and crocketed spire which soars to a height of 165 feet. Many steeples are higher; few are more beautiful.

The glorious nave, built at the close of the Norman period, is like an avenue in stone, with six pointed arches on each side, supported on round and clustered piers with foliated capitals. Above the arcades is the original clerestory, but the continuity of its rich external arcading is broken by windows inserted in the 15th century. A fine roof with alternate hammer and tie-beams crowns it all.

The north and south doorways are 13th century, and the aisles 14th century, with windows much restored.

The chancel is mainly 15th century, but some of its windows are modern, and its three sedilia appear to be 13th century work and the plain Easter Sepulchre opposite is of the 14th century. Across the chancel arch is a handsome oak screen which has a fine new vault and cornice but retains much of its 15th century work below; its delicate tracery is tipped with little faces, and above the entrance are four tiny angels.

By the sill of a south aisle window is a combined piscina and aumbry, and in a nave pillar (facing the east end of the north aisle) is another piscina. Among other old relics are an old oak pillar-almsbox; a 17th century altar-table; a cupboard made from the sides of a 17th century pulpit; the bowl of the original font brought back after serving as a pump trough; and three coped coffin-lids with crosses. There are two more fonts, one modern, and one of 1719 made by William Tydd who was paid £7 3s. od. for his work. It is in the Grinling Gibbons pattern. Carved on its stem and bowl is a representation of the Tree of Life, with Adam and Eve and the Serpent, and also on the bowl are scenes of Baptism and the Ark.

Muckton. From this tiny village on the eastern foothills of the Wolds there is a wonderful view over the Marsh to the sea. All about it are lovely woods. The little church was rebuilt last century in Norman style; but it still has its original Norman chancel arch enriched with zigzag ornament, and a traceried 15th century font.

Mumby. It is 3 miles from the coast and has a fine, restored church, encircled by great trees.

The massive 15th century tower has striking figures staring down, including a young man with a round hat, and an old man with a beard. The lovely doorway within the porch has a rich array of mouldings in its arch, and dog-tooth ornament between its shafts; it is 13th century work, and so are the beautiful nave arcades with

STAMFORD (*a*) High St Martins

(*b*) Browne's Hospital

Tattershall Castle

The chancel arch of
Whaplode Church,
seen from the north transep

their massive round pillars and foliage capitals. The chancel is 19th century.

The traceried bowl of the font is 600 years old, a century older than the lower part of the great oak screen which hides the chancel arch and is enriched with rose-tipped tracery. The vaulted rood-loft with traceried panels and coloured scenes of the Nativity and Crucifixion is 19th century. The oak seats in the chancel (incorporating some 15th century tracery) and the carved oak pulpit are also 19th century.

Navenby. A large village set on a high spur of the Cliff, 9 miles south of Lincoln, it has red-roofed stone houses huddled together by its broad main street, and a fine church looking far over the wide-spreading Brant valley. There is evidence of a Roman settlement that may be the beginning of this community.

The church is chiefly 14th century work (the nave earlier than the chancel), but one of the clustered piers of the fine nave arcades (more massive than the rest) has stood since about 1180, and the western respond of this north arcade is probably as old. The clerestory with its 10 windows was added in the 15th century. The tower was rebuilt after the original steeple had fallen in 1750, but retains much of the old masonry, and its low arch into the nave is mediaeval.

The chancel, splendidly proportioned and rich in its decoration, has great windows filling it with light; those in the side walls have reticulated tracery beautifully moulded, and the six-light east window (restored) fills the whole of the wall. In the south wall are three sedilia and a double piscina; on the north side are the Easter Sepulchre and the founder's recess, with the priest's doorway between them. It is in this ancient stonework, with its profusion of rich pinnacle-work, crockets, finials, and carving of foliage, that the charm of this chancel lies. The sedilia are especially notable for their richly-vaulted canopies and their gallery of more than a score of tiny stone heads—human, animal, and grotesque.

In the foliage of the cinquefoiled arch of the founder's recess is the tiny figure of a crouching woman in a wimple; and under the arch now lies a trefoil-headed stone with a late 13th century Lombardic inscription to Richard de Lue who was priest here. Comparable (though smaller) with the superb examples at Heckington, at Hawton in Nottinghamshire, and Patrington in Yorkshire, the Easter Sepulchre has the figures of an angel and the three Marys amid the lovely foliage of the canopy; below the recess are three Roman soldiers, all erect. All the figures on the Sepulchre are now without heads.

Other stone carvings adorning the church, inside and out, include a triple-headed jester on the clerestory, a musical jester, a man with bagpipes, and a man with a viol. The old rood-loft stairs are still here, but the screen and its rood figures are modern. The brass eagle lectern is also modern, but the fine panelled pulpit is Elizabethan. A plain old font with a pinnacled outer cover has as companion a richly-carved 19th century font with crocketed arches projecting from diapered panels; a marble pillar supporting the bowl is seen through the pierced carving of the stem. There is a late 13th century slab with Norman inscription "Pray for Richard de Lue" (Louth).

Two rectors ministered here continuously for more than a century —Simon Every, 1703 till 1753, and his successor Dearing Jones who died in 1804.

Nettleham. A rapidly expanding neighbour of Lincoln with a population at present totalling nearly 3000 people. New housing estates surround the old village centre which lies between two Roman roads—the Ermine Street and another going to Wragby. An attractive brook crossed by several little bridges runs through the village on its way to Langworth River. The village green surrounded by pleasant stone-built and red-roofed houses has a fine old church to add to the picturesque touches of the nucleus of the village. An area embodying the old village centre has been designated by the Lindsey County Council as a Conservation Area.

The village has a history of no mean importance, and it has been admirably written in a book by Florence Baker. It begins with the Bronze Age. A hoard of bronze axes and other items is treasured in the British Museum and Lincoln Museum. It continues with the Roman occupation of Lincoln when Nettleham was a source of its water supply from springs known as the Roaring Meg. A dedication stone from a Roman temple was found on a new housing estate. It is in the Lincoln Museum. In Saxon times its manor belonged to Edward the Confessor's wife, Queen Editha, and in Domesday Book it appears as the property of the Conqueror, who gave its church to an abbey in Normandy.

Early in the 12th century the bishops of Lincoln became lords of the manor, and until Elizabethan times they had a house here. Bishop John Dalderby became lord of the manor in 1300, and in the following year Edward I was his guest at Nettleham while attending a Parliament summoned to the Chapter House of Lincoln Cathedral. Here in 1494 died the wise Bishop Russell, Chancellor of England under Richard Crouchback; and here soon after the Reformation lived Bishop Henry Holbeach, a fine Hebrew scholar who helped to compile the Prayer Book, but a man who for his own gain had no scruples in surrendering the estates of his See to the Crown.

Early in the 17th century licence to demolish the manor house was granted to Bishop John Williams, and, with the departure of the bishops to their palaces at Buckden and Lincoln, Nettleham settled down to a more humdrum existence. The 18th century provided one excitement in the hanging here of one of two men who in 1732 murdered a Lincoln post-boy named Thomas Gardiner; the boy was buried in the churchyard, and an inscribed stone records his tragic end. The industrial 19th century saw a rapid rise in the population of Nettleham and a corresponding rise of brick walls; it saw too the passing of many old village customs, and a little network of roads take the place of the big village green, scene of gay Mayday festivities. The 20th century has also watched the village's growth and seen it endowed with the benefits of electricity and gas, and with a bus service that has linked it more closely with Lincoln. New housing estates are being developed as a dormitory for Lincoln.

In a field are grassy mounds marking the site of the old home of the bishops. Nothing else remains, and for more satisfying evidence of the village's antiquity the church must be visited. It has been much restored, and its chancel has been rebuilt; but the south doorway with its foliated side columns, and the nave arcades with their clustered columns, reveal its 13th century origin.

In the floor at the east end of the south aisle is the old altar stone, with the crosses still visible; but almost everything else within the church is modern—the stone font and the choir-stalls, the screen and the pulpit. Eight of the stained windows are memorials of the Hood family, among them being the east window with its Crucifixion scene and attractive figures of four saints—Hugh, Mary, John, and David. Among the monuments is a tablet to three brothers who laid down their lives in the war, one being Lieutenant-Colonel Edward Hood, DSO and Croix de Guerre; below the tablet is the wooden cross brought from the military cemetery where he lies.

Nettleham Hall, home of the Hoods for almost a century; stood about a mile north-west of the church; it was destroyed by fire in 1937, but the fine 18th century wrought-iron entrance gates brought here from the churchyard of St Peter-at-Arches, Lincoln, are still standing. The Hoods now live at the attractive Grange de Lings which in careful restoration has revealed many interesting mediaeval features. It may be associated with Barlings Abbey.

Nettleton. A neighbour of Caistor, it lies charmingly in a valley under Nettleton Hill, a bold headland of the Wolds. It has seen much activity to mine iron-ore for Scunthorpe from rich deposits in the Wolds.

The most notable feature of its church is the tower, which, except for its 15th century top stage and buttresses, was built at the close of the Saxon period; it still has its old west doorway and window, its great round-headed arch to the nave, and a small window in the south wall which is cleverly bridged by a buttress that almost conceals it from view outside.

The rest of the church was refashioned last century during the 54 years' ministry of Samuel Turner, to whose memory tribute is paid in the east window. The modern marble reredos has a sculpture of the Last Supper, with Our Lord standing and holding the cup.

Nettleton's memorial to men who died in the First World War is like no other we have seen—a bungalow for one old married couple, standing by the village school.

New Holland. A workaday town at the Lincolnshire end of the ferry crossing the Humber to Hull, 3 miles away, it is busy with its small docks and with the building of ships. Like many other industrial centres, it works hard for the needs of travellers but in its own confines has little to attract them.

Newton. A tiny village of grey stone with fine trees a few miles west of Grantham, it has an old cross on its green and a church much restored last century. The lofty tower has a 13th century base with a 15th century top storey peeping over the churchyard sycamores; and there are 14th century arcades adorned with four little mediaeval faces. Other survivals from a remote past are the eight-sided font, two old gravestones with crosses, and peepholes into the rebuilt chancel, which has a founder's tomb in its north wall. There is also an ancient chest in the vestry.

Newton-by-Toft. There are lovely peeps of the distant Wolds from this tiny place, and its rebuilt church has some interesting old remains. Built into the north wall of the nave is a graceful 13th century arcade (framing new windows); between nave and chancel is a fine, stout little Norman arch; and on a modern base is the bowl of a Norman font. The nave has its old south wall, the 13th century doorway being sheltered by a modern porch. The chancel has a blocked low-side window, and two charming mediaeval stone figures in niches; one, only 2 feet long, is of a man with his feet on a headless boar; the other, even smaller, is of a woman with a dog at her tiny feet. Both have their hands clasped in prayer.

Newton-on-Trent. The spring tides come up the Trent as far as the 19th century toll bridge, which is nearly 500 feet long and links the village with Dunham on the Nottinghamshire bank. The bridge, with its four iron arches on stone piers, took the place of the old ferry by which a king crossed the river two and a half centuries ago, and was met on the other side by a duke and his retinue in fine array; he was William of Orange, coming from Lincoln on a visit to Welbeck.

The fine wide view from the bridge embraces Dunham's handsome old tower, Laneham's lovely old church, and Fledborough, with its church and its long string of arches carrying the railway across the river. All these are on the west bank, in Nottinghamshire, but North Clifton and its church, though also in Nottinghamshire, is Newton's neighbour on the east bank.

Newton's old church is a mile from the bridge, and its old embattled tower peeps over haystacks, barns, and red-roofed cottages. It was greatly restored in 1876, when a new aisle was built on the foundations of one that had been destroyed, and the charming 13th century arcade with rich foliage capitals was opened out after long being built-up. The plain round Norman or 13th century font is still here and in the tower are preserved five fragments of richly-traceried mediaeval stalls. The handsome oak tower screen is a memorial to George Clark who was born in this village in 1857 and died in Sheffield in 1926, Justice of the Peace.

Nocton. A green and pleasant place a few miles south-east of Lincoln, it has a Hall (now an RAF Hospital) which was the home of a Prime Minister, and a church which is his memorial and his last resting-place. About a mile away, on the edge of Nocton Fen and close to Nocton Wood, where lilies-of-the-valley grow in great profusion, is the site of a priory founded in the time of King Stephen.

This priory, for Austin canons, was founded by Robert d'Arcy, whose father, Norman d'Arcy, a companion of the Conqueror, was first of a family which held this manor for 600 years. In Charles II's time the estate was sold to Lord Stanhope, and then to Sir William Ellys, whose monument is in the church. Later it passed to George Hobart, afterwards 3rd Earl of Buckinghamshire, and the marriage of the 4th Earl's daughter brought it to the rising young politician who as Chancellor of the Exchequer was nicknamed Prosperity Robinson, and as Viscount Goderich succeeded George Canning as Premier. He died as the Earl of Ripon in 1859, and three years later his widow built Nocton Church in his memory. It took the place of a poor church built by George Hobart, who had pulled down the old one because it was too near the Hall for his liking.

Designed by Sir Gilbert Scott in 14th century style, and built of Ancaster stone, it is one of the most sumptuous modern churches in all Lincolnshire, with a tower and spire 130 feet high, and a porch with niched figures of the Madonna and Child, St Peter, and St Paul, John the Baptist, and John the Evangelist. The interior is dignified by an arcade on rich clustered columns, but is chiefly notable for the richness of decoration in carving, painting, and windows. The heads of Peter, Paul, and of Our Lord are in niches on the lovely pulpit of stone and marble, and the alabaster reredos (by Italian craftsmen) shows under three gilded arches Christ carrying the Cross, with an angry man about to strike Him and a Roman soldier on a rearing horse behind; the Crucifixion, with the three women and the disciples; and the Entombment, with Mary

Magdalene kneeling. On each side of the reredos the wall is arcaded, the arches being filled with engraved figures of Apostles, Evangelists, Martyrs, and Saints.

Elsewhere the walls are adorned with sacred subjects. In the chancel are canopied paintings of Apostles and Evangelists, each with his symbol, and over the chancel arch Christ appears in Glory, with a great company of kneeling angels and saints. More unusual are the paintings on the west wall of the nave—graphic illustrations of the Israelites entering the Promised Land, the Egyptians drowning in the Red Sea, and Noah with his family and the animals going into the Ark two by two, goats, asses, rabbits, and snakes among them.

The windows form another fine gallery of pictures. The east window has a central figure of St Michael with angels and a great multitude of men, women, and children round him; and 24 Elders below, casting their crowns before the Throne. One of the side windows of the nave has figures of St Hugh of Lincoln and St Theodore, and a second has Oswald and Etheldreda. A third window, showing St Aidan with the stag and the Venerable Bede writing, is a memorial to a descendant of William Brewster, one of the Pilgrim Fathers, and has smaller scenes depicting sunrise and sunset at sea and the *Mayflower* sailing the ocean.

The fine west window of the nave, with four scenes showing the gift of Isaac to Sarah, and four more of the gift of Samuel to Hannah, was the work of Clayton and Bell and is a memorial to the Countess of Ripon the builder of this church who died in 1867.

Among the monuments set up in memory of members of her family three are specially notable. The first is of white marble with an urn to her father, Robert Hobart, the 4th Earl of Buckingham, Secretary of State for the Colonies in the first years of the 19th century and the man after whom the capital of Tasmania is named. The second is to her uncle, Henry Lewis Hobart, vicar of this church for 33 years and Dean of Windsor as well—a white marble memorial with two kneeling women and cherubs above. The third is the monument she raised to her husband, the first Earl of Ripon; it is under an arch between chancel and chapel, a stately altar tomb of Carrara marble bearing a figure of the Prime Minister in a long robe, his hands folded, his fine features in repose—a beautiful sculpture by Matthew Noble, the Yorkshireman who gave Liverpool, Manchester, and London many fine statues.

The oldest memorial, now in the north porch, and the only relic of the old church, is a pompous 17th century array of marble columns, sculptured urn, helmet, shield, and Latin inscription; it is to Sir William Ellys, who built anew the Hall that Thomas Wymbish had erected in 1530, and which was visited by Henry VIII and his 5th Queen, Katherine Howard. Here she came with the ruthless king on a journey which was to end in charges which sent her, still a girl, to join her cousin Anne Boleyn in the chapel of death at the Tower.

Fire destroyed the old Hall in 1834, and the foundation stone of the new (handsome with mullioned windows, tall gables and chimneys, and terrace leading down to a lawn) was laid by Viscount Goderich's 14-year-old son, who was born in the most famous house in England (10 Downing Street) during his father's premiership. He was to be for 40 years associated with Gladstone. Later in life, when he had become first Marquis of Ripon, and a Roman Catholic, he sold the Nocton estate. He died in 1909 at his Yorkshire home, Studley Royal, and was buried there in a modern church even more sumptuous than the one in his father's memory here.

The Hall is now used as a Royal Air Force hospital. It stands in a park with many fine trees.

Normanby-by-Spital. This twin village of Owmby has a squat little church with something to show of all the building periods from the 11th century to the 15th.

Two small round-headed windows on the south side of the tower are Saxon, or very early Norman; the west window is a 13th century lancet, the two-light belfry windows are 14th century work, and the parapet was added a century later.

The round-headed arch between tower and nave comes from early Norman days, and at the west end of the north aisle is a Norman window. Below the 15th century clerestory are the old arcades, Norman on the north side, and 13th century on the south side; their capitals display bold contrast in style, those carved by the Normans having curious stiff leaves, and the later ones showing the graceful development of more natural foliage.

By the wide 13th century arch to the lofty little chancel is a blocked low-side window; the font has an ancient round bowl.

Normanby-le-Wold. The highest point of the Wolds, 548 feet above sea-level, is near this small village, and the steep climb to it by road over Nettleton Top is well worth while for the magnificent view of the great plain stretching to the Cliff, with the towers of Lincoln prominent. Recent excavation has uncovered a Middle Saxon settlement overlooking the marshland.

The church was partly rebuilt last century, but the tower is perhaps 700 years old and its arch to the nave leans wearily. The nave arches are 13th century, too, except for their modern eastern bays; and they are unusual, for their corbels are like cones with curly tails and some of their mouldings sweep round without capitals.

On the arch spanning the old south aisle is another curious corbel with a carving of a man apparently in the throes of toothache, one hand being raised to his head and the other holding his mouth wide open. The fine mediaeval font, like a pillar, is enriched with a double band of quatrefoils and wavy pattern.

Normanton. High on the Cliff road between Grantham and Lincoln it stands, with fine views of a countryside rolling away, green and gold. Its ancient church by the roadside is largely 13th century work, with a deep-splayed lancet at the west end of each aisle and four more lancets in the chancel; but the south arcade has two big round arches from the close of Norman days, the tower is 14th century, and the clerestory 15th.

The clerestory is enriched with battlements adorned by shields and roses. The tower has a row of curious animal heads below its 15th century parapet, and a west window graced with a profusion of ballflower ornament and a smiling bishop's head of stone looking out from the tracery, where there are still a few fragments of old painted glass.

This is a simple house of prayer, its walls plain and unadorned by monument, its treasures few. The plain round font is over 500 years old, and the pulpit with sounding board has been here since Stuart times.

North Carlton. It lies at the foot of the Cliff, from whose height the grey church and little cluster of red roofs look like little models, set among model trees. But as the lane dips down and approaches them they loom larger and larger until at last the village is seen in its true proportions. Across a field by the church can be seen a charming Elizabethan Hall, with grey gabled walls and red roofs enhanced in autumn by the warm glow of creeper. Here Henry VIII is said to have stayed in 1541 when on his way to Lincoln, and to have knighted his host, John Monson.

Tall elms and beeches add their touch of grandeur to a small church rebuilt in the 18th century, though its pinnacled tower is a survival from the 15th century, and the porch is an addition of the 19th. The interior has the charm of simplicity. It has recently been restored and pleasantly redecorated in pale blue and white. Its walls are unadorned by monument; its tiny apsidal chancel unscreened.

North Coates. A village of twists and turns, it has a pretty thatched cottage close to a church almost rebuilt in 1865 but still retaining some features from its ancient predecessor. The doorway with round shafts, some lancet windows, the nave arcades, the lofty chancel arch, and the font are all 700 years old.

The 19th century stained windows make the interior dark. The base of an ancient cross is in the churchyard.

North Elkington. A gated road across fields leads to this little village on the eastern edge of the Wolds, with its handful of farms and cottages and its pretty 19th century church gathered round the green.

The church is the third on this site and is in 13th century style, with an east window of three lancets, enriched with marble shafts and hoods of dog-tooth ornament. Unusual and attractive is the stone pulpit, projecting from under one of two rich trefoiled arches in the wall, and not unlike the old reader's pulpit still to be seen at Tupholme Abbey near Bardney. Unusual too is the lectern of wrought-iron, with its trailing pattern of horse-chestnut leaves. The oak reredos has painted panels showing the Crucifixion and the Three Women, and statues of the Four Evangelists in richly-carved niches.

From the Middle Ages come the octagonal font, the capital of a pillar lying by the porch, and parts of two fine floorstones built into the porch, each carved with a cross, and one especially striking with enrichment of fleur-de-lys.

North Hykeham. Now built-up and linked with Lincoln; it is a growing urban community, and has lost much of its old village aspect. It is a natural outgrowth of the city still in Kesteven and provided with fine schools and a shopping centre close to the Roman Fosse Way. However, on byways that leave the main road behind there is still a village nucleus. Its church, attractive with an arcaded west wall and a rose window in an arch on each side of the belfry, was rebuilt last century.

North Kelsey. Two gardens below the church charm all who pass this way in summer; enclosed by trim hedges, they make a glorious rose-decked corner, ablaze with colour.

The tower of the church is chiefly 13th century work; the nave and chancel are early 14th century, much restored; the porch and aisle are modern. Among the ancient stones in the walls is the head of a 13th century incised cross above the priest's doorway; and near the porch is a great Norman stone, about 32 inches by 24, with a mass of simple herringbone carving. Curiously set in a buttress near this stone is an early 13th century round pillar with base and capital, about 4 feet high. In the chancel is a coffin-lid with two dragons carved at the foot of a richly-floriated cross. There is an attractive black-and-white Tudor-style house near the church.

North Killingholme. With its close neighbour, South Killingholme, this village gives name to the marshes and the three light-houses by the Humber 2 miles away.

Tall larches guard North Killingholme's church—a patchwork of stone and plaster outside, and attractive inside with sloping walls of grey stone and its windows all aslant. A wide, decorated arch is part of the Norman base of the tower; the rest of the tower (including the west window) is mediaeval work, and so are the nave arcades.

The old porch of stone and brick has stone seats, and shelters a gnarled old door bristling like a porcupine with its mass of studs and nails. The chancel has a priest's doorway of Norman days, and two 13th century lancets in the east wall. There are 13th century floor-stones with floriated crosses in the walls by some of the south aisle windows, and another forms the step to the 700-year-old font. The north aisle has a holy water stoup and a peephole to the chancel, with the old entrance to the rood stairway beside it.

Near the church is a charming Tudor manor house of red-brick, still with water in its moat; there are fine old yews outside, and some lovely old panelling within.

North Ormsby. There are fine views over the Marsh to the sea from this tiny place in a wooded valley of the Wolds; and prettily perched on the hillside is a neat little church rebuilt a century ago in 13th century style and surrounded by chestnut trees. Its west front is attractive with porch and gabled buttresses and bellcot. Golden light from amber glass windows fills the interior, where there are two Jacobean chairs and a 14th century font carved with quatrefoils.

In the churchyard is part of an old cross and an urn on a pedestal to the memory of John Ansell and his wife.

Higher up the valley a farm with a big pond marks the site of a Gilbertine priory founded in the middle of the 12th century. In a field above is the curious White Lady, a lifesize stone figure in classical costume, said to mark the spot where a woman was killed while hunting.

Northorpe. The River Eau runs by the pleasant park where the modern Hall stands in company with an Elizabethan Hall which has fallen on sad days and now stands neglected. The old manor house, now a farmhouse, is near the church, much of which is 15th century, including the tower and the clerestory.

When the tower was built into the west end of the nave part of a 14th century arch of each arcade was absorbed, but the rest of the arcades are as the Normans built them—low and sturdy, with big square capitals all differently carved. Most attractive is one capital with its fluted leaves curling over and looking not unlike sea-shells.

The chancel has a Norman doorway, a 15th century east window, two windows a century earlier, a piscina, a low-side window, and a recess which may have been used as an Easter Sepulchre. The old roofs of the nave and chancel, with stout moulded beams and big bosses, have been finely restored. The 14th century south doorway, enriched with carving of flowers, frames a door of oak just as old and beautifully carved with trailing foliage and tracery.

There are fragments of old glass, and one of the two bells in the tower has the appeal, "Bell, send pastors pure in word and life". A brass portrait of Francis Yerburgh, who died in 1595, shows him in a fur-trimmed gown. His two wives are with him, though the portrait of one is broken, and those of his children are gone. Anthony Monson of 1648 has a brass inscription, curiously set in an old altar stone which has five consecration crosses.

North Rauceby. A grey-walled village away from the madding crowd, it stands on high ground with a neat church visible for miles. The massive tower and broach spire are not unlike those of neighbouring Sleaford, and are likewise notable for being among this country's earliest examples of a tower and stone spire; they were built in the first quarter of the 13th century. The nave has 14th century arcades, each with three arches borne up on tall clustered piers, and a 15th century clerestory with 10 windows. The aisles are also 14th century work, and the windows have a few fragments of their ancient glass. In the south aisle is a piscina, and set in an older canopied recess is a stone with a beautiful cross carved in memory of William Fraunk of 1385.

The old rood stairs are still here, but the chancel was rebuilt in 1853, replacing one built in the time of Henry VIII by William Styrlay, vicar here and canon of Shelford Priory in Nottinghamshire; his brass portrait is in the vestry and shows him in his vestments, with chalice and wafer. The eight-sided font, adorned with roses and foliage, is 15th century, and there are a score of worn bench-ends possibly as old.

In the churchyard is a much-worn figure of a 14th century priest, and the base of an ancient cross with an attractive modern shaft and finial.

North Reston. Near to a busy highway yet it is as if the workaday 20th century had overlooked what little there is of the village, and almost untrodden is the way through a field leading from the farmyard of Reston Hall to the church.

Though mainly in 14th century style, the plain little church has a late Norman chancel arch and traces of two small windows in the nave of the same period. The rest of the chancel was rebuilt when the church was restored in 1868 by Howard Jackson, lord of the manor. A brass tablet tells of John Hampden Jackson, who died in 1941 after being vicar more than 50 years, and there is a fine old font with panels of tracery.

Further along the road to Alford is South Reston's small church, rebuilt in 1864 in 14th century style. It still has its old font, with eight heads under a bowl which is adorned by great flowers in panels.

North Scarle. A pleasant village of red-brick cottages, it has a little grey church with a rugged tower at the end of a long street. Unadorned by sculpture but clean and bright within, it was largely rebuilt in the 14th century after a fire and restored in 1898 by Sir Ninian Comper. The south doorway with its four depths of moulding is round-headed but not likely to be Norman in date. A 13th century doorway is in the modern north aisle and there is another early 13th century doorway with tooth ornament in the chancel, which also has its old sedilia unusual in being on the north side and with four seats. There are traces of mediaeval wall paintings in the chancel.

Among the other old possessions of the church are an altar stone, discovered broken in the church floor at the restoration of the building, with three crosses, and now used as a side altar, a piscina beside it, the base of a mediaeval chancel screen, and a few bench-ends with carved foliage and tiny faces. New pews match the old. There is an iron parish chest in the nave formidably chained to a pillar, it has three locks, one for the rector and one for each church-warden.

One of the modern memorial windows has attractive figures of St Hugh and St Botolph, each with his church in the background. Two other windows are in memory of Alfred Stanford, who went out to be rector of Mafeking and died there a few years before its name was on every Englishman's lips; one of them shows St John, and the other has a figure of Paulinus, who was sent to help Augustine in preaching the Gospel and is counted the first Archbishop of York.

North Somercotes. A big, scattered village near the sea, with holiday amenities, it has seen its fine old church wisely restored. In 1924 the village children gave a window to complete the restoration.

Much of the dignified building is 13th century work, including the low tower and the shortened chancel with its lofty arch, priest's door-way, north doorway which led perhaps to a sacristy, and low-side window. To the 14th century belongs the south doorway with its worn door. The arches and octagonal pillars of the nave arcades are early 15th century, but the round pillars and high bases of the two western bays on each side are from the close of the Norman period.

The south aisle chapel has a trefoiled-headed piscina niche, an altar stone with three crosses, and remains of 15th century screen-work with original colour. Old bench-ends with arm-rests and poppyheads are on two benches in this chapel and others are in a priest's seat in the chancel. There is a huge chest of 1675. A floor-stone with a stepped cross and a coffin-lid are memorials from the long ago.

The church's chief treasure is the 500-year-old font, with shields of arms and emblems of the Passion carved on its octagonal bowl together with a remarkable representation of Our Lord stepping from the tomb.

Hiding among trees by the road to Saltfleet stands the old brick Locksley Hall. A 16th century house much restored, it has in its richly-leaded windows an amazing display of glass of many periods, ranging from the 14th century to the work of a 20th century owner, who, in addition to his work in glass, enriched the beams and friezes in many of the rooms with a wealth of coloured and relief carving of exotic birds and flowers and foliage. In the wonderful collection of mediaeval glass in the staircase window are saints, bishops, two angels, a figure of Gabriel from the bishop of Lincoln's palace at Buckden, and two fine complete panels which came from St Peter Mancroft, Norwich, showing St Peter and a Majesty.

Two miles or so away, at Donna Nook, are stations of the life-boatmen, airmen, and coastguards.

North Thoresby. Midway between Grimsby and Louth, it was the birthplace of two men who made themselves known far and wide. The first was Robert Mapletoft, born here in 1609, a celebrated preacher who became Vice-Chancellor of Cambridge University after the Restoration. The second was Francis Bond, who died in 1918 and whose memorial is in the village church. Born here in 1850, he went to school at Louth, and became headmaster of a college; but it is for his many excellent books that Francis Bond is remembered—writings in which he made clear not only how our churches were built, but also why and by whom, and giving the fascinating background of our architecture as well as the facts. He also wrote several authoritative books on fonts and woodcarving in our churches.

Tucked away in a corner of the big village, the church is for the most part a mediaeval building that was well restored last century and has a rebuilt chancel. The 13th century tower has a low, stout arch to the nave, and a fine 15th century embattled crown with eight lofty pinnacles. As old as the tower is the arcade built-up in the south wall of the nave. In two of the arches windows are set, and in the third is a 13th century doorway. There are 14th century windows in the wide north aisle, to which access is given from the chancel by a double arch, the first cut in the walling to reveal one of the 14th century.

The east window has old glass showing three saints (one headless);

the font is also old, and there is a fine array of poppyhead bench-ends enriched with flowers and foliage and the bust of a man.

Preserved in the nave of this church is one of the oldest pieces of carved stone in Lincolnshire—part of an Anglo-Saxon slab with interlacing strapwork.

North Witham. A pleasant red-roofed village with its spired church, set among cornfields and pastures near the source of the River Witham—here but a small stream, newly-started on its 80-mile journey to the Wash. There is a fragment of an old cross in the churchyard and in the porch of the church part of a Saxon cross with interlace decoration. From Norman days come the doorway within the porch, a bearded Norman head above, the north doorway with a double row of zigzag, and the low, narrow chancel arch with a pointed opening on each side. The interior is striking with its rough stone walls, and the floor of the old nave slopes down towards a chancel made considerably smaller last century by the construction of a new raised altar several feet in front of the east window.

Among the old possessions of this church is a cupboard with a front fashioned from two richly-carved heraldic bench-ends and a wooden head believed to be the head of Christ from the former rood. Among the notable monuments are two to Sherards of Lobthorpe who worshipped here for many generations. One is a brass with 26 Latin verses written by Roland Sherard, who died when Elizabeth I was queen; the other, set up when Charles II was king, is an arched recess with a noble figure of Richard Sherard, with luxuriant wig falling to his shoulders, his right elbow resting on three books, and his left hand on a skull, emblem of man's mortality.

Among the stained windows is one with figures of St John and St Peter and St Paul, all richly arrayed; it was designed by C. E. Kempe as a memorial to Peter Young, who was buried in the churchyard in 1902 after ministering here for 36 years.

Peter Young was a much-loved figure, and a brief tribute edited by his daughter tells why. Before coming here he had been curate to John Keble at Hursley for 17 years, and was like a son to him. He came to this Lincolnshire parish in 1861 and served it faithfully and long, holding in trust for his people his time, his money, everything he had.

Norton Disney. The River Witham flows quietly by this small place which takes the distinguishing part of its name from the Disneys, a Norman family of Isigny near Bayeux. Here in this Lincolnshire village the Disneys lived from the 13th century till the time of James II, when the last of them, William Disney, was beheaded after the Monmouth Rebellion. Nothing of their castle remains (it stood in a field west of the church), or of the manor house built from its ruins in the 17th century; but something far older than these was found here some years ago by a farmer, who, worried because Abbey Field on Potter Hill grew nothing but weeds, dug down to solve the mystery. He made a discovery of first-rate importance, for there came to light a wall dividing two rooms, some roof tiles, and two magnificent Roman pavements, one of them 20 feet long and 16 wide, designed in small cubes of coloured stone and brick. It proved to be a fortified Roman villa with a defensive ditch system and was fully excavated in the 1930s.

The Disneys are gone; but life still centres round the old church they knew, and within it are lovely monuments and a remarkable brass keeping their memory green. In its early days the church belonged to Sempringham Priory. It is a fine light building and has a 15th century tower with 16 imps and demons looking out below the pinnacles, and steps leading down to a nave and aisles divided by an arcade of three bays, two of them 13th century, and one later. The chancel, chiefly 14th century, has a north chapel. The font of about 1400 is deeply carved with shields, in the nave are some rough benches, and in the chancel some stalls with foliage and curious little men and angels back to back on their poppyheads—mediaeval faces grave and gay. The traceried screen is Elizabethan, the ample pulpit (in front of the old rood-loft stairway) is Jacobean, and the aisle has its old roof with carved bosses, some showing foliage with a man's face and a lion with its tongue out.

Most of the impressive array of monuments are in the chapel, and the oldest is from about 1300—the lovely recessed figure of Joan d'Iseney in coif and wimple, her hands at prayer, a dog at her feet. Fifty years later is the rare sculptured stone of another lady of the house, now simply Joan Disney, with a Norman-French inscription; her features rugged, her hands at prayer, and with jewels in her hair, she lies as if half-hidden by her coffin-lid, so that we see only the upper part of her figure, and her feet with a dog beside them. Kingerby Church has a similar stone to one of the Disney men.

From the close of the 14th century comes the third monument of a woman, Hantascia Disney, who sleeps with angels and a lion by her pillow, and another lion at her feet; she wears a long gown, and her hair is caught up in a jewelled net. In the chancel, lying on a tomb is a 14th century knight in armour, his splendid shield enriched with three heraldic lions.

The most remarkable memorial here is the splendid Disney brass in the chapel, displayed in a hinged oak frame to reveal both sides. It is a thick brass 3 feet by 2, divided on the front into five compartments covered with shields and two rows of half-figures. One group shows William Disney with his wife and nine children kneeling in prayer, each with its name on a scroll; the other group shows fierce-looking Richard Disney with two wives, both prettily dressed and one with many bows on her sleeve. The first wife, who has 12 children behind her, was the grandmother of Lord Hussey, who, having refused to join the Pilgrimage of Grace, refused also to raise a force against the conspirators and was beheaded by Henry VIII; the second wife was the younger sister of the immortal Anne Askew who was martyred at Smithfield in 1546 and whose story is told in this book at Stallingborough.

Two unusual features of so late a brass (it was engraved about 1580) are the helmets worn by the men, who are in armour, and the fact that the portraits are only half-figures. But the brass is notable not only as an example of 16th century art, but because it is a palimpsest, a brass reversed and used a second time. This is a Dutch brass, bearing on the back 33 lines of the original inscription, which is astonishingly completed by nine lines on another palimpsest brass at West Lavington in Wiltshire, the whole telling of the founding of a mass at the altar of St Cornelius in St Martin's Church, Middelburg, Holland, in 1518.

A modern sculpture to the fourth Viscount St Vincent shows a hovering angel bringing a victor's bays in one hand and an oak branch in the other. On the ground banners are resting against rocks, the whole symbolising the career of a soldier who, after service in the Zulu War and against the Afghans, died at Abu Klea from wounds received in 1885 in the Sudan War. The glass of the east window, showing the Crucifixion with St John on one side and a Roman soldier on the other, is also in memory of this Lord St Vincent whose title had come down to him from John Jervis, that great admiral and disciplinarian raised to the peerage after his great victory over the Spaniards in 1797 near Cape St Vincent.

Old Bolingbroke. A place of little consequence it seems—this rambling village on the banks of a swift stream among the foothills of the Wolds. Yet, as we look on the walls and rugged mounds of its vanished castle, now being opened up by careful excavation under the direction of the Ministry of Public Building and Works, we can visualise a pageant of history and summon up scenes of feudal grandeur; for here John of Gaunt—time-honoured Lancaster—once lived, with a retinue like a king's; and here grew up that son of his who was one day to be crowned Henry IV of England. The Lindsey County Council has designated the village as a Conservation Area.

The story begins with William de Roumare, first Norman Earl of Lincoln, who built a castle here eight centuries ago. Some 200 years later John of Gaunt arrived, a bridegroom of 19, newly wedded to his cousin Blanche, heiress of the Earl of Lancaster, who was then lord of Bolingbroke. Here they lived, and here it was that on April the third, 1367, their son Henry was born—Henry of Bolingbroke.

The excavations have exposed the gateway, towers, and curtain wall of the castle which appears to have been built c. AD 1240. First records appear about the same time and point to Ranulph Earl of Chester as the builder.

Dewy Hill, a nearby earthwork, may be the site of the earlier castle of William de Roumare: 12th century occupation has been found in trial excavations.

A frequent visitor to the castle in those years was Geoffrey Chaucer, a great friend and follower of John of Gaunt. Chaucer must have been here soon after the death of Blanche, for in the *Book of the Duchess* he pictures a meeting with the widower, who was "of the age of four and twenty yeere".

Bolingbroke Castle became Crown property and was occupied until the Civil War. Then, in 1643, it was captured by the Parliamentarians and dismantled. Slowly it fell into ruin, and little was visible until recently but the mounds on which it first was raised.

North of the castle site stands the church—a mere remnant of the one rebuilt in the 14th century, perhaps by John of Gaunt. It consists of the old south aisle, turned into nave and chancel, the sturdy old battlemented tower, and a 19th century north aisle. The old work is a fine example of the late 14th century period of architecture and includes richly-moulded windows with leaf tracery, a nave arcade without capitals soaring to the modern barrel roof, three sedilia with crocketed arches and finials, trefoiled piscina, and south doorway with shafts and leafy capitals supporting its rich arch. Above the doorway is a splendid quatrefoiled niche, and a stone bracket beside it has the carved head of a wimpled woman. Near the doorway is a fine old pillar stoup, and there is also an old font.

Old Leake. Midway between the Hobhole Drain and the sea, it is a big village on the road from Boston to Skegness, where the marshland has been transformed by market-gardening and potato-growing.

The church, finely restored, comes chiefly from the close of the 14th century; but the clerestory is 15th century work, and the low massive tower begun in 1490 stands as it was left in 1547, though it was obviously meant to have been much higher.

It is a handsome church outside. The great chancel has been made almost new, and is an impressive sight with its stepped buttresses rising between windows with beautiful tracery, and its parapets enriched with pierced carving of wavy pattern. The eastern gable of the nave is flanked by pinnacled buttresses, and has a parapet of open quatrefoils. The noble clerestory has six windows on each side, divided by slender buttresses which are adorned with canopied niches and climb to parapets with corbel tables displaying a wealth of extraordinary carving: foliage, animals, heads, human faces, two men by a pot, a woman sitting by a cauldron, a man with a wheat-sheaf, a man pulling at a kind of capstan, and all manner of grotesques. On the hood of a north-aisle window are two corbels curiously carved, one showing a figure with a harpsichord, the other a man playing bagpipes.

The lofty nave arcades with clustered piers are 14th century, but they retain four responds from a late Norman church. The chancel, filled with golden light from tinted glass in the windows, has the battered old sedilia and piscina, and an aumbry; the south aisle has fine single and double niches beside its east window, and a dainty niche in the splay of another window. Some old oak beams are in the aisle roofs, and there is a Jacobean pulpit, and an unusual old pillar almsbox made out of a solid stem of oak and thought to have been a box for Peter's Pence. Under an arch lies an alabaster knight of old.

A mile nearer Boston is a farmhouse known as Moulton Chantry House, on the site of one of two chantries here. A mile across the other side of the highway is the Moat House, a little stone building with remains of an old moat which fills in a rainy season. It was rebuilt in 1832, but has kept much of the old stonework, including a mediaeval two-light window with a quatrefoil in its head, two old corbel heads beside the doorway, and a 13th century coffin stone with a worn cross, built into an outside wall.

Osbournby. Standing on the high road from Bourne to Sleaford its steeple is a striking spectacle, flat-topped and lacking either spire or battlements or pinnacles to crown its rugged, 600-year-old walls. Most of the rest of the church is also 14th century work, but the north aisle and chancel arch are 15th century. Despite the absence of a clerestory it is a fine light building, for the mediaeval windows of the aisles, as well as the modern east window, are undimmed by stained glass.

Fine stone carving is to be seen within—in the arcaded inner walls of the porch, in the three canopied sedilia in the chancel (enriched with crockets, deep mouldings, and sculptures of a lion and three quaint men), and in the Norman font with interlaced arches and nail-head ornament. Fine woodcarving is to be seen, too, in the traceried lower panels of a 15th century screen, and in a collection of bench-ends just as old. There are nearly 40 of these grand old bench-ends with poppyheads, and they display a great variety of carving, mostly with rich patterns of foliage and tracery, but also with quaint birds and beasts, and such widely varied subjects as the Crucifixion. Adam and Eve, St George and the Dragon, and a fox preaching to geese.

Owmby. It is one of the long string of villages on the low road running north from Lincoln, with the Ermine Street and the Cliff ridge in the west and the more distant Wolds rising in the east. Many Roman coins, including some of the time of Constantine, have been found hereabouts.

Much of the small church is mediaeval, including the tower with double-lancet belfry windows. The only entrance to the church is through the tower. Between nave and aisle is a fine, rugged arcade from the close of the 12th century, its massive pointed arches resting on pillars with great bases and capitals carved with bold leaves. The chancel has windows with unusually wide splays, and the ancient font of this well-cared-for little place is like a rough-hewn pillar.

Owston Ferry. A Trentside village in the Isle of Axholme, it has a link with the powerful Mowbrays. Their stronghold here, known as Kinnard's Castle, was destroyed after being taken in 1173 by Geoffrey Plantagenet; only its earthworks are left, and within them stands the village church, approached by an avenue beyond a triple-arched stone gateway.

The earliest find at Owston Ferry was a Roman coin hoard discovered in 1953 and contained in a pot; there were 116 bronze coins and 4 silver denarii ranging in date from Mark Antony (31 BC) to Septimus Severus (AD 193–211).

Restoration has robbed the church of much of its ancient aspect, but ancient it is. The south arcade with nail-head ornament is 13th century, the north arcade 14th century, the chancel 14th and 15th century, and the tower 15th. Among its relics are two old piscinas, wall-panelling made from old pews, and a fine old oak chest.

One of the windows has attractive modern glass showing three Bishops of Lincoln (Wordsworth, King, and Swayne); another has Our Lord and three kneeling Disciples. Under the chancel seats is a worn floorstone inscribed to Richard Becbanke, a vicar who died in 1458.

Owston Hall is of early Georgian date with a nice staircase and stucco ceiling of the late 18th century.

In the quiet little hamlet of Low Melwood, by the road to Epworth, is the moated site of a Carthusian monastery founded in 1396 by Thomas Mowbray. On the same site there had been an ancient chapel known as the Priory in the Wood. At present a 17th century brick building occupies the site on the farm now called High Melwood.

Panton. Nicholas Hawksmoor, an architect who, in fine buildings of Queen's and All Souls colleges, added much to the splendour of Oxford, built a fine 18th century Hall here high on a hill overlooking lovely grounds, with a beech avenue nearly half a mile long. It was enlarged by John Carr in 1775 but has recently been demolished. It was for long the home of the Turnors, but in 1919 it became for a time a Franciscan college and friary, and the friars added cloisters.

The little church, now disused and neglected, was built last century in memory of one of the Turnors. It hides by a farmyard, and its entrance has a most unusual pair of doors, covered with lead and handsomely enriched with wreaths of olive and borders of cable moulding.

Built in the wall by the chancel arch is the sculptured mediaeval figure of a Knight Templar with his hands clasped in prayer and a winged angel over his shoulder; he wears chain armour and has a long shield ornamented with stars.

Partney. An attractive village on the road running north from Spilsby, and near the meeting of two streams flowing to the River Lymn, it was once a little market town; and though its importance declined after Spilsby was granted a market, its sheep and cattle fairs, of very early origin, are still widely known.

A road scheme east of the church in 1950 revealed an Anglo-Saxon barrow with elaborate cruciform brooches and other associated 6th century finds.

In the 7th century there was an abbey here, recorded by Bede; but this is believed to have been destroyed by the Danes. There is no trace either of the later hospital which, together with the parish church, was given to Bardney Abbey by Gilbert de Gaunt in the 11th century. The church, restored and partly rebuilt in 1862, still has its lofty 15th century tower, with hideous gargoyles and a sailing ship for windvane to mark the dedication to St Nicholas. It still has, too, fine 14th century arcades notable for their capitals with flowing foliage and other decoration; one on the north side has demon heads and quaint animals between ballflowers, and another has four heads with leaves growing from their mouths.

The rebuilt chancel has kept its old arch, resting on great grotesque heads, and with leaves and flowers and a gallery of heads in its moulding. Between the north aisle and the chapel is a 15th century screen adorned with tracery; and the lovely old font is interesting for tracery showing the transition from 14th century to the 15th century style.

Within the modern porch is a restored 15th century doorway with an old statue of St Nicholas crowning the finial. The churchyard has the remains of an old cross.

Partney has a small place in literary annals, for the great Dr Johnson came here on a visit to Peregrine Langton, an uncle of his great friend Bennet Langton, of whom we read at Langton near Spilsby. He was a man whom Dr Johnson held in great esteem.

When Peregrine Langton, who passed practically the whole of

his 84 years at Partney, died in 1766, Dr Johnson urged Bennet to write his uncle's biography, saying: "His art of life certainly deserves to be known and studied. He lived in plenty and elegance upon an income which to many would appear indigent, and to most scanty. How he lived, therefore, every man has an interest in knowing."

It fell to Boswell to record the facts in his biography of Johnson. A bachelor, Langton had only £200 a year, but with that he paid rent for his house and three little fields, kept four servants, a chase and three horses, and gave a tenth of his income to charity.

He lived plainly but well, and when he entertained, his table befitted a country gentleman. All his furniture, plate, and linen were bought out of income. Every Monday morning he balanced his accounts, and when he had a surplus he ordered extra clothes or linen so that his wardrobe was ample and his household supplies overflowing.

When repairs to property were necessary he did them at once and found the stitch in time highly profitable. He paid cash for everything, and his tradesmen were warned that if they gave credit in his name to any of his servants his custom would be lost. He always had ready money for his needs.

Dr Johnson respected him as a model of piety, learning, and economy. "He was one of those I loved at once by instinct and by reason", wrote the great man.

Pickworth. Flourishing elms shade the mediaeval tower and spire of its church, and ancient oak enriches its interior. It comes chiefly from the 13th and 14th centuries but its years lie a little heavily upon it; the door in the porch (with grand ironwork), the mediaeval roofs, the benches with traceried ends, the 15th century screen, and the combined pulpit and reading-desk (300 years old and still with its hourglass stand) all need the restoring hands of modern craftsmen.

The plain 13th century font, the old sedilia, and a piscina with carved leaves and ugly heads, are all still in evidence; and in the chancel floor is a stone to Isaac Wilson who ministered in this place for 60 years.

The most interesting features of this old church, however, are its mediaeval wall paintings. During the recent war, a bomb fell near the church and shook down big chunks of the whitewash. Mr E. Clive Rouse set to work, and, carefully clearing the plaster, uncovered several paintings. One of them is a detailed picture of the Last Judgment, below which is a scene of the general Resurrection. On another wall is the Ascension. Another picture shows the Weighing of Souls. Costumes in yet another picture date it to about 1380. They are all precious as examples of 14th century art and devotion.

Pinchbeck. In Saxon times it was a place of much importance, and was attached to Crowland Abbey. In the time of Edward III it was a market town, and later it shared in the prosperity which came from the trade in flax and hemp grown hereabouts. Today it is a well-populated village by the River Glen covering many thousands of acres of fenland with attractive bulbfields.

A red-brick Hall stands serenely by the roadside behind the waters of its moat; and tall lime trees not far off shade the pathway to a grand old church. The work of the Norman builders is in the lower part of the nave's west wall; the 13th century is represented by the nave arcades, the 14th century by the chancel and its north chapel, and the 15th century by the clerestory, south porch, and tower. Restoration last century included the rebuilding of the south and east walls of the chancel (leaving one original window).

The great tower, which has a rather bent appearance owing to its lower stages leaning, has stepped buttresses climbing to pinnacled battlements, a double band of quatrefoils round its base, and a lovely west doorway with cinquefoiled arch and leafy hood; on each side of the doorway is a fine canopied niche.

Outside the porch is a wooden sundial, and within it is a remarkable doorway which has four shafts on each side supporting an elegant trefoiled arch dotted with carved flowers, its crocketed head crowned by a splendid finial.

The clerestory has a range of 10 three-light windows on each side under traceried parapets. It is hardly surpassed in all Lincolnshire and lights up the fine old nave roof supported by 10 angels holding shields with the arms of the Pinchbeck family. This nave roof, the chapel roof with its carved beams, and the splendid roof of the north aisle, with its moulded beams and carved spandrels all testify to the skill of 15th century wood-carvers. The richness of the interior is further enhanced by the tower arch, reaching to the nave roof, and by the lofty nave arcades with rich mouldings and hoods of dogtooth carving, the pillars on which they rest being alternately round and eight-sided.

The north aisle has an old traceried doorway with its original door, and windows with angels and saints in old glass. The chapel has the restored 15th century chancel screen and a window with a medley of old fragments. An Elizabethan brass in the chapel shows Margaret Carr, wife of John Lambert, kneeling in her farthingale, hood, and ruff; she holds a shield, and round her are 26 other shields of her own and her husband's families, arranged in genealogical order and taking the pedigree back to the Conqueror. The marble tomb in the chapel is of Edward Walpole of 1725. In the south aisle is the fine heraldic tomb of Sir Thomas Pinchbeck who is said to have given the nave its roof and clerestory. In the trefoiled arcading round the tomb are 22 shields, including that of John

Talbot, the great Earl of Shrewsbury. The chancel was rebuilt in 1855 at the time of a general restoration by Butterfield; to him is attributed the striking east window.

The fine 15th century font similar to the one at Surfleet is a mass of rich carving. Two curiosities are a fine old weathercock which was struck by lightning in 1893, and a little wooden shelter like a sentry-box, dated 1725, which was used by the parson at burials.

Potter Hanworth. A compact little village on the edge of a fen stretching away 3 miles to the east. The derivation of the name suggests a Roman pottery but the kilns have not been located. A line of elms adds a picturesque touch to the village street and at one corner a pinnacled 14th century church steeple rises above trees and haystacks. The rest of the church, a simple well-lighted building with four arches on each side of its nave, was rebuilt last century.

By the chancel arch is a modern brass set up in honour of a 16th century lord of the manor—Richard Smith, founder of Christ's Hospital at Lincoln. Dr Smith was laid to rest in 1602 at Welton, about 12 miles away, and the church there has a memorial window showing him making his will.

Quadring. It is a fenland village with a grand church neigh-boured by the school but standing a little aloof from the rest.

A fine-looking structure with an embattled clerestory, and a spire rising from a tapering tower, the church is largely 15th century work, with a chancel almost rebuilt last century; but there are traces of an earlier building in the bases of Norman buttresses on the south wall, and there is a 14th century stringcourse above them.

A modern porch leads to a spacious interior, dignified by graceful arcades and filled with a blaze of light, only one of the windows having stained glass. By the chancel arch is a turret for the rood stairway, panelled and embattled, and with a delicate, leafy arch to its doorway.

The tower has a groined roof and an arch reaching almost to the 15th century roof of the nave, which was restored in 1904. Angels with shields adorn the old font on which is an inscription asking a prayer for the donor, Robert Perci. In the chancel is an incised slab to Richard Peresone, vicar in the 15th century. There is a fine old chest with a coved lid, and a curious tablet of Queen Anne's time with two quaintly draped figures in memory of Mary Harryman.

In the churchyard is the base of an ancient cross.

Quarrington. A village in a winding lane near Sleaford, it will be remembered by the passer-by as a charming picture from the highway—its grey church rising up beyond arable fields, neat as a cardboard model, with slender spire peeping above churchyard sycamores. The church is 600 years old, with north aisle and apsed chancel rebuilt last century, and handsome scrolled iron gates separating aisle and organ chamber. The traceried font and the little piscina are mediaeval.

Raithby. This pleasant little neighbour of Spilsby, with the River Lymn a mile away, was an earthly Paradise to John Wesley. The old Hall, an attractive late 18th century brick house, a little forlorn now and with its once-pretty park growing wild, was built in Wesley's time by Robert Carr Brackenbury and his wife, who welcomed the great evangelist into their home when he was preaching hereabouts.

In 1779 they gave him a room which he dedicated as a chapel, and it is a Methodist chapel still. An upper room in a corner of the stableyard, it is reached by two stairways (originally one for men and one for women) which meet at the pedimented entrance. With its coved ceiling, its panelled walls of pale green and white, and its contrasting dark-stained seats, this chapel in the stable buildings is dignified and bright. It is important that this place of pilgrimage should be cared for by some responsible body; externally it is showing evident signs of neglect.

The neighbouring church seems rather dim after the bright little chapel. Except for its 15th century tower, it has been rebuilt, but a fragment of the Transitional-Norman period survives in the capital of one of the nave pillars, and the plain old font is still here. In the porch is an old carved seat, and on the seat of a richly-carved old chair in the sanctuary are three roundels of Bible scenes.

Raithby-cum-Maltby. It is near Louth, snugly tucked into the foothills of the Wolds. Its rectory is in pleasant setting on the hillside, and below it is a little church with the murmur of running water about it as a churchyard stream, prettily canopied by trees, plunges under the road.

The church, rebuilt in 1839 in 14th century style, is adorned by fine parapets with open tracery and a goodly array of pinnacles, and has a great weathercock to crown its tower.

Of the old building there remain the mediaeval arcade of the nave (though partly rebuilt) and the beautiful 14th century font with a bowl encircled by quatrefoils and resting on a cluster of eight shafts. Among 11 quaint glass medallions in the windows is one with Adam and Eve under the forbidden tree; another has the Baptism in Jordan.

The organ is a barrel-organ and still has its working instructions and a list of 30 tunes.

At Maltby, half a mile up the valley, was a small preceptory of the

Templars, established in the time of King Stephen by Ranulph, Earl of Chester.

Ranby. From its hill, where the tall church tower stands like a beacon, there is a fine view across the valley of the River Bain. Ranby's original church is said to have been rebuilt in the 15th century by Ralph Cromwell, Lord Treasurer of England, and in the 19th century it was again rebuilt; but there are still two things which have come through the years: a Norman chancel arch which has become the tower arch, and a 15th century font adorned with flowers and leaves and shields.

Rand. Remote in the fields here, with rectory and farmhouse for company, stands a little church with a surprising array of notable monuments. Nave and chancel were rebuilt last century, but the arch between them is 500 years old, and the 15th century tower stands with its gargoyles as of yore, topped by new battlements.

The oldest of the stone monuments is the lovely 14th century figure of an unknown lady, lying serenely under a recessed arch in the chancel with angels at her head, a shield on her middle, and a dog at the hem of her gown. On a wall-monument kneels Sir Sapcoat Harrington of 1630, with his wife and five children; and there are more 17th century sculptures showing Charles Metham and his three wives, the first wife having eight children with her and a relief of Time with his relentless scythe above. Richly adorned with 22 shields of arms is a monument showing Vincent Fulnetby, an Elizabethan knight, and among its inscriptions we read of his little John who died at 7, "of good and rare virtue and towardness".

Among the fragments of brasses now grouped on a wall-stone are fine portraits of two Elizabethan ladies in ruffs and richly-embroidered gowns. An elaborately decorated coffin-lid, perhaps of the 13th century, is also in the church after long being in the churchyard.

Redbourne. A mile after leaving the line of the Ermine Street, the highway from Lincoln to Brigg comes to a fine stone gateway with a lion crest and four carvings portraying a milkmaid, a shepherd, a ploughman, and a horseman; it is the 18th century gateway to the 300 acres of Redbourne Park, where a lake and many fine trees make the fairest of settings for an old, creepered Hall. This was once a domain of the Dukes of St Albans, some of whom were laid to their last rest in a mausoleum built on to the church. The present Hall has an 18th century front by John Carr of York.

The village has a charm all its own, with ducks swimming on the wayside stream and a tall bower of yews leading to the lofty 15th century church tower rising in four diminishing stages. Except for the 14th century nave arcades, most of the old work in the church is of the same period as the tower.

In the windows of the aisles is painted glass of 1831 showing 10 of the Apostles. Of the same date is the glass in the east window with its extraordinary vivid picture of the Last Judgment—the Earth being rent asunder with flames and lightning, and awesome clouds rolling over the terrifying scene.

Against the chancel wall is a stone engraved with a fine portrait of Sir Gerard Sothill, who died in 1401; he was a Lord of Redbourne castle, of which the only remains are grassy mounds and a dry moat in a field by the churchyard. Of the small Gilbertine house called Tunstall Priory, founded here in the 12th century, nothing remains.

Revesby. A truly charming place it is, with its tree-lined road and its green where church, vicarage, cottages, school, and almshouses are grouped to form a compact nucleus for the village. Through fine iron gates can be glimpsed the creepered walls of the great house known as Revesby Abbey, in its splendid park; it was built 100 years ago on the site of one which was the home of Sir Joseph Banks, the famous naturalist who went round the world with Captain Cook. He is remembered in this village as a great planter of trees, and in this part of Lincolnshire generally as one who inspired great changes in agricultural practice and took a leading part with Rennie in the drainage of the Wildmore, East, and West Fens.

Earlier still there stood on this same spot the abbot's house belonging to the Cistercian abbey which was founded eight centuries ago by William de Roumare, Earl of Lincoln, and colonised by monks from Rievaulx in Yorkshire. The site of the abbey itself, now only grassy mounds, lies just south of the village, within half a mile of the church and reached by a narrow shady lane; traces have been found of a roadway which led from the abbey to the abbot's house.

William de Roumare became a monk here and was buried before the high altar of the abbey church. In 1870 his body was unearthed, together with those of his two sons, and within the old precincts lies a flat stone of polished granite marking the place where they were reburied.

Built in 1891 at the expense of the Rt. Hon. Edward Stanhope and James Banks Stanhope, in the flowing style of the 14th century, Revesby Church is the successor of one built in 1700 and which itself succeeded a mediaeval church. It has a spire rising from a pinnacled tower with a lovely pierced parapet, and a nave with beautiful arches leading to north aisle, tower, and chancel. In the floor of the chancel is part of a fine 13th century tile-pavement found in the old abbey; and round the walls of the sanctuary is panelling with carvings of trees, vines, and ivy, and mother-of-pearl inlay.

The pulpit has an old cornice, and there are old carved panels showing the Annunciation and early scenes in Our Lord's life. The oldest things here are a Transitional-Norman shaft piscina (used as a font) and a big collection of carved stones in recesses of the tower walls; among them is a fine 13th century capital.

In the aisle is a monument to Joseph Banks, who died in 1727, with a sarcophagus and a marble bust of him, impressive in his long, curly wig. He it was who built the earlier church on the site and who also bequeathed the almshouses—since rebuilt. On the monument is an inscription to a second Joseph Banks, and another to William Banks, father of Sir Joseph the naturalist.

Near the roadside, not far from the park gates, are two ancient tumuli, and north of the park is a reservoir of 40 acres which supplies Boston with water.

Riby. A village of the byways which won a name for itself some years ago because of its pedigree flocks and herds, it is graced by the fine park of Riby Grove and its long avenue of limes. On the edge of the park is a little church with walls of rough-hewn stone— rebuilt in Victorian days but still with a blocked Norman doorway in the nave, a 14th century south arcade, a 500-year-old central tower, and a fragment of its ancient font.

The interior is neat and trim, with simple oak benches, richly-traceried stalls, and fine groined roofs in tower and chancel. The stone ribs of the chancel are adorned with bosses, and rise in the sanctuary from shafts in the walls. Seen from the west doorway, the arches of the impressive crossing seem to frame the east window, showing the Disciples and Our Risen Lord, and make a pleasing picture. Another window has figures of St Edmund and St Hubert and is in memory of Henry Dudding, who was churchwarden for 36 years. His were the flocks and herds that brought fame to Riby and were sold in 1913 for more than £17,000.

Little more than a mile north of the village, at Riby Gap, one of the encounters of the Civil War took place four days after the defeat of the king at Naseby. Here it was the Roundheads who were routed. Some who fell were laid to rest in Riby's well-kept church-yard, and others (including Colonel Harrison, the Parliamentary commander) at Stallingborough.

Rigsby. From its place on the eastern slope of the Wolds, this tiny neighbour of Alford has a lovely view towards the coast. Its tiny church, rebuilt in 1863 by James Fowler of Louth in Norman style, retains its original Norman chancel arch (now leading to the vestry). The west doorway is also Norman on the inner side. The traceried font is 500 years old.

Rippingale. It lies between two highways north of Bourne, with cottages set haphazardly about a little ring of roads. The stump of its old wayside cross faces the war memorial cross in the churchyard, where a cedar spreads its shapely branches and a battlemented 15th century tower soars above the rest of the venerable, creepered walls. Much of the church is older than the tower, and a 13th century porch leads to a 14th century aisle separated from nave and chancel by an arcade of six pointed arches on clustered pillars.

Of notable old woodwork the church can boast little—an old 6-foot chest, a smaller one of 1785, and the fine oak canopy of a 15th century rood-loft, with beautiful fan-vaulting and a row of quaint animal faces. But there is a great array of mediaeval monuments.

The oldest are the sleeping figures of two knights in 13th century chain-mail, one of them very battered. They are thought to belong to the Gobaud family, lords of Rippingale, and it may be that one of them founded this church. The Gobauds lived at Ringstone on the other side of the Old Beck, where they were followed by the Bowets, Marmions, Haslewoods, and Brownlows.

Another fine monument shows the Lady Margaret Colville lying in a richly-canopied recess with two armed men at her head and a monk at her feet, all headless. On a big 14th century tomb near her is a legless knight, believed to be Roger de Quincey, with a wife on either side in a tight-waisted gown. But the rarest monument here is 700 years old—one of the few figures of deacons left in our churches. With face much worn, he lies in his robes, an open Bible in his hands with an inscription on the pages.

Riseholme. Here is a fine park of trees close to the Roman Ermine Street, running due north from Lincoln. A barrow, near the north boundary of the parish, was proved by excavation to be Roman and to contain a single cremated burial; a secondary Romano-British burial in an urn was found inserted in the south-west quarter of the barrow. The site of the mediaeval village, south of the lake has been examined by excavation and was deserted about the mid 14th century.

For about half of the 19th century Riseholme Hall was the palace of the Bishops of Lincoln, bought from the Chaplins in 1830, and sold again when Bishop King took another house for himself and his successors in the Old Palace grounds near the Minster. The bishops had a view of the cathedral towers from their home, which looks on to a lake in the lovely wooded grounds—an old grey stone house enlarged by William Railton (who designed the Nelson memorial in Trafalgar Square), the colonnade on the south side being part of his work. The Hall is now the home of Lindsey's College of Agriculture and many new buildings have been provided to accommodate the needs of the College.

The first bishop to live here was John Kaye, who found the old church a ruin and built a new one, an attractive little building in 14th century style with nave, chancel, and bellcot. It has a brass in memory of the three bishops who lived here last century, John Kaye, John Jackson, and Christopher Wordsworth, set up by William Kaye (son of Bishop Kaye and son-in-law of Bishop Jackson) who was rector here for 67 years. Two of these bishops are buried in the churchyard here: John Kaye who died in 1853, and Christopher Wordsworth, nephew of the immortal poet.

Christopher Wordsworth's father, who was Master of Trinity, was the poet's youngest brother, and his mother was the sister of Charles Lloyd, Lamb's beloved friend. Born at Lambeth, in 1807, he spent much of his youth in Kent in the company of a friend who was to become Cardinal Manning.

At both Winchester and Cambridge Wordsworth was famous as athlete and scholar and had an almost unique list of honours. After a tour abroad, which yielded his famous volume on Greece, he returned to his university as Public Orator.

For eight years headmaster of Harrow, he resigned a stall in Westminster Abbey to spend 20 years as a country parson in Berkshire. The period was fruitful, for there he produced his edition of the Greek Testament with a commentary teeming with quotations from the early fathers of the Church, of whom his knowledge was almost unrivalled.

Among much else that he wrote, including devotional verse, was his biography of the poet, in which he was markedly reticent concerning Wordsworth's early love of national and individual liberty.

Christopher Wordsworth was a most generous friend to Lincoln Cathedral, and had the satisfaction of sub-dividing his See and bringing into existence the bishopric of Southwell. Dying in 1885 he was brought here, after a funeral service in his own cathedral, to rest by the side of his wife.

Ropsley. A few red and grey cottages, a duckpond, a grey church in a field, and black sail-less windmill on the slopes above—that is Ropsley, birthplace of Richard Fox, Tudor bishop and statesman, who founded the grammar school at Grantham and Corpus Christi College at Oxford.

The humble Peacock Inn where he was born in 1448 has altered since his day, and the Fox's Brush Inn is named after the wily animal, not the bishop. But the church remains much as he must have seen it, the three massive arches of the north arcade Norman, the chancel and its arch, the south arcade, and the tower 13th century, the chapel and the broach spire 14th. At the angles of the nave is the typical long-and-short masonry of the Saxon builders.

One of the piers of the south arcade has an inscription scratched on it to tell of its rebuilding in 1380 by John Bate of Corby, and the fine porch with pinnacles and panelled parapet, built during the lifetime of Bishop Fox, bears a Latin rhyme exhorting the passer-by to *Go not away unless ye pray, an Ave Maria say*.

In the chancel is a tomb recess of about 1300, and in a south aisle recess is the figure of a 14th century lady in a long gown, with a little canopy over her cushioned head. In front of the east window of the north aisle is an arch forming a bridge from the rood-loft to the stairway, still with its mediaeval door. The font, with embattled top is probably the one at which the infant Richard Fox was baptised.

For 30 years Bishop Richard Fox, a native of Ropsley, was one of the most influential men in England.

In 1485 King Richard III objected to his being made vicar of Stepney, on the ground that he was a friend of the outlawed rebel Henry Tudor. Later in the year, Henry Tudor won the crown on Bosworth Field, and his friend Fox not only became vicar of Stepney, but, in rapid succession, a member of the new King's Council, Secretary of State, Lord Privy Seal, and Bishop of Exeter.

Astute Henry VII meant to have by his side clever men who knew the world but did not belong to the fighting nobility, whose feuds he hoped he had ended at Bosworth. So the first two names on the list of his first Council were able men who had risen out of rural England—John Morton from Bere Regis in Dorset, and Richard Fox from Ropsley, both sons of the farmhouse.

The appointment of Richard Fox to the See of Exeter was merely a way for the king to secure his services at the cost of the diocese. Fox never visited Exeter; nor Wells, of which he was made bishop later. A deputy was chosen to perform his offices as bishop while the nominal bishop was employed in advisory and diplomatic duties, at the Court and abroad. He was Henry's chief negotiator with Scotland, and with France, and in commercial agreements with the Netherlands.

When relations with Scotland became strained, Fox was removed to Durham, and there, for the first time, took up his duties as bishop. He went into residence at Durham Castle and refortified Norham Castle. When James IV of Scotland invaded England in support of the pretender Perkin Warbeck he was foiled at Norham Castle by Bishop Fox's defences. Later, Fox met the Scottish king, and not only negotiated Perkin Warbeck out of Scotland, but also fixed up a marriage between James and the English king's daughter Margaret —a marriage which resulted, just 100 years later, in the union of the crowns of Scotland and England, when James VI of Scotland, a descendant of Margaret, succeeded Elizabeth I.

With Scottish affairs safely settled, Fox was moved southward, nearer the centre of government, and was installed in the rich See of Winchester. He also became Chancellor of the University of Cambridge, and, somewhat later, Master of Pembroke College there.

After the death of Henry VII Fox retained all his offices and power for a while. He had baptised Henry VIII in his infancy, and he was one of the trustees of the will of the young king's father. He and Henry VII had worked harmoniously together for 24 years. They had been of one mind in saving money and avoiding strife; and the country had prospered accordingly and had emerged from the ruin and disorder left by the Wars of the Roses.

Fox had been an economist in the right place at the right time; but it was his sense of economy which led to a gradual separation between him and the new king. When Henry VIII began to covet adventure in war, and to launch out in lavish, showy expenditure, Fox remained aloof, and the king went for sympathy to Wolsey, a younger, bolder, more ambitious spirit. Fox resigned the Privy Seal and retired to Winchester; and spent his dozen last quiet years, as devoted bishop and educationist.

Bishop Fox's educational benefactions were widespread. First, and foremost among his great works, he founded Corpus Christi College at Oxford. He did this with his own money, generously given, and not by robbing others. And in doing this, with infinite vision he gave a lead to the revival of learning. He also built and endowed the grammar school at Grantham, where Sir Isaac Newton was later educated, and so gave a better chance of education to the boyhood of his own native district. Similarly, he built and endowed the grammar school at Taunton.

Richard Fox also made additions to Winchester Cathedral, and helped in the restoration of St Mary's, Oxford, and was a benefactor to Pembroke College, Cambridge, Magdalen College, Oxford, and the Abbeys of Glastonbury and Netley. In Winchester Cathedral he prepared his own chantry and was taken there daily for prayer during his last years when he had lost his sight. He died in 1528 at the age of 80, and was laid to rest in his cathedral.

Rothwell. In a dip of the Wolds it lies, with a stream running through its street. It is a well-managed, neat and prosperous parish and Rothwell House, a Victorian building, reflects this feeling.

The church has a magnificent Saxon tower, rising massive and unbuttressed at the west end of the nave. It has small round-headed slits, with two-light belfry windows above, a tall and narrow doorway with plain tympanum, and a lofty arch. Among a medley of ancient glass in one of the tower windows are two heads of men and an angel.

Impressive are the nave arcades, built by the Normans. Their great round pillars are crowned with scalloped capitals, and the arches are enriched with roll mouldings, which, in the western bay on each side, are clasped by zigzag carving.

The much-restored chancel has a neat modern oak screen adorned with tracery and vine, and a dainty cresting of trailing foliage and Tudor flower. Nearby is a Jacobean carved chair.

Roughton. Here, flowing through the wooded country near the southern end of the Wolds, runs the River Bain. Above it, the village is gathered pleasantly round a delightful Georgian Hall, a charming white rectory, and a little church shaded by giant elms.

The base of the low brick and stone tower, built just before the Reformation, serves as a porch and has the square-headed stone-built doorway typical of the period. Within the tower is a splendid old ladder climbing to the wooden belfry.

Traces of 13th century work remain, and the chancel has two late 13th century windows. A few poppyhead bench-ends have survived from the 15th century, and the pulpit and the cover of the round Norman font are Jacobean.

No old painting adorns these walls, but some curious types of mediaeval art are preserved here in a small case. Found buried under the pulpit early this century, they include broken glazed vases with handles, and coloured pigments such as would be used in the painting of wall-pictures in our churches long ago. There is red and black pigment in two tiny vessels, and yellow and white in some of the pottery.

Rowston. Its steeple has been described as being like a candle with an extinguisher, and indeed it must be one of the smallest in the land for, inside, it measures only 5½ feet across. Built 700 years ago and given a spire 200 years later, its most astonishing feature is its arch, remarkably narrow and so tall that its point reaches to the nave roof.

At the base is an attractive modern screen enriched with coloured shields of landowners from the times of the Knights Templars, and near the top can be seen the floor of the belfry, borne up on four modern stone figures of angels. Built into a wall is some extraordinary Norman carving clearly a tympanum (*see also* Haltham), with a Maltese cross, knotwork, serpents, a wheel, and lion's head. It was found during a restoration of the church and its width fits exactly into a small Norman doorway in the north wall. Another interesting old stone is in the south-east window of the nave. Found in a cowshed some years ago, it bears on one side a carved head of Christ crowned with thorns, and on the other a crowned King, possibly Our Lord.

The three doorways of the church are 13th century, and so is the arcade, with one round pillar and two clustered, and arches enriched with foliage. From the 15th century come the screen between aisle and north chapel, enriched with oak leaves and acorns; and the font with carved foliage and flowers on its panels.

There is a most unusual painted reredos, now in the north aisle and vestry. It is dated 1741 and was removed in a 20th century restoration. It is worthy of attention and should be reassembled.

The manor house in stone is mid 18th century.

Roxby. The Romans knew this Cliff village and its fine views of the Humber, for it lies near their Ermine Street, and here in 1699 a Roman tessellated pavement was unearthed in a field. A cottage garden, on the south side of the churchyard, covers this fragment now, but in the church is a copy of William Fowler's coloured engraving of it—astonishing in its minute detail, and showing the pavement patterned with cable, key, knotwork, and flowers.

The church is 600 years old, but lost much of its old work during 19th century rebuilding. The low, unbuttressed tower still stands, however, and on each side of it, in the west wall of the nave, are massive stones which belonged to a Saxon church. There is a small Saxon window in the tower.

Within the porch is a simple doorway with two worn heads, and there are old windows notable for their unusual tracery. The chancel has its old piscina, and two striking sedilia with traceried ogee canopies, tall pinnacles, and finials. The south aisle also has a piscina, and an arched recess sheltering the fine stone figure of a priest wearing embroidered vestments with an elaborate collar. In the churchyard are time-worn carvings of two other men.

Ruckland. An exhilarating ride over the Wolds from Scamblesby, with majestic views on every hand, brings the traveller to this tiny place perched on a steep hillside.

A great company of magnificent trees hide the farmhouse and church at the end of a grassy track. Rebuilt last century, it has only a nave and chancel, 30 feet long and half as wide, lighted by four windows with coloured glass. It shelters a fine little tapering coffinlid of mediaeval days, carved with a beautiful cross, and another old relic is a small stoup.

Ruskington. One of Sleaford's thriving and growing neighbours, it has ancient roots, for a Saxon cemetery was found here and the work of Normans is still to be seen in the church. The remnant of the Norman church is the fine tower arch with bold scalloped capitals, now back in its rightful place after long being in the south wall; it was moved in early Stuart times when the present massive tower took the place of the original steeple, which had fallen.

The south doorway and the nave arcades with clustered pillars are graceful examples of 13th century building, the doorway having three orders of moulding with rows of nail-head ornament. The south arcade is a little earlier than the north and more richly adorned, two of its columns having upright bands of nail-head. The 700-year-old chancel was lengthened last century, the three slender lancets at the east end being modern; but it still has its old sedilia, piscina, and aumbry. The traceried screen, with carving of vine and roses, is also modern, and so is the reading-desk with carved acorns, passion flowers, and crown of thorns. The east window of the south aisle has beautiful figures of Jesus and two angels in pale modern glass.

The church still has a 16th century chest with iron bands, and a 15th century font with shields, roses, and sacred emblems. Out in the churchyard is a coffin-lid with a portrait of a priest who ministered here 600 years ago.

Saleby. It has a few scattered houses, a church rebuilt last century, and an old moated manor house of 17th century which is now a farm.

The base and shaft of an old cross are in the churchyard, shaded by huge elms. In the chancel is an effigy of an armoured knight with a lion at his feet—William de Hardreshull, who died in 1303.

Saltfleet. A market town in days gone by, it came into Domesday Book as one of the royal ports. Now it is a most attractive place for those who love a quiet holiday by the sea, with an astonishing stretch of sand at low tide, when the sea is a mile or two away and hardly visible from the land. Part of the old town and its church are said to have been washed away by the sea, and the folk go to worship at Skidbrooke, a mile away. Stones believed to be part of a church are sometimes washed up on the shore, and there is a story that one day in a fisherman's net was found the big clapper of a bell long silent. In the rather forlorn red-brick 17th century manor house by the road Oliver Cromwell is said to have slept after the Battle of Winceby.

Saltfleetby All Saints. Standing with a clump of trees like an island in a flat sea of hedgeless grassland is its spacious old church, originally Norman, but entirely rebuilt early in the 13th century and a little refashioned two centuries later. The chancel was restored in 1873.

The lower part of the tall tower, which leans noticeably, is 13th century, and the rest of it, with the fine gargoyles and big buttresses, is 15th century; it has kept its lancet windows but lost its vaulted roof. Also 15th century are the north windows and doorway, and the south porch (patched with brick) with a worn Latin inscription telling of its building by John Grantham.

The south doorway and the impressive nave arcade are 13th century. The lofty chancel arch, and the curious double arcade (a single arch in front of two narrower ones) leading from chancel to south chapel, are also 13th century work, but their responds and the central pillar are survivals from the Norman building.

Oak screens of the 15th century, almost stripped of their ornamentation, span the chancel arch and enclose the chapel. The nave has its old roof with carved bosses and was repaired in 1611, and the south aisle a restored old roof with moulded beams. In the aisle stands a disused Jacobean pulpit, and there is a 14th century font, ringed with quatrefoils, resting on what appears to be an upturned 15th century font adorned with tracery and four faces.

In the chapel is a 13th century floorstone with an inscription in Lombardic capitals. Here, too, is a rare possession—a fine stone reredos from the time of Edward I, its shallow trefoiled recess rests on a stringcourse, and at the top is a big traceried pinnacle supported by corbel heads.

Saltfleetby St Clement. The smallest of the three Saltfleetbys, and the nearest to the sea, it has a small church partly built from the ruin of a 700-year-old house of prayer which stood on another site and was pulled down in 1885. Among the 13th century remains are some lancet windows, the south doorway, the west doorway of the tower, and the beautiful little arcade leading to a narrow aisle. There are also some 15th century windows (one is finely moulded outside), an old font with its bowl on a cluster of shafts, and part of an ancient cross-shaft in the vestry.

Saltfleetby St Peter. Across the fields is the tower of its vanished 13th century church, and close by, another tower known as Prospect Tower, which appears to be a folly; at the crossroads is its Victorian church, resembling the old in style except that it has a bellcot instead of a tower. Parts of the old church used again in the new are the 13th century nave arcades, one window of the 14th century, and others of the 15th. The old piscina is in the vestry, and there is an old font with a bowl like a great stone cauldron. Glowing with rich colour in the three lancets of the east wall are the Crucifixion and figures of St Peter and St John.

From 1744 to 1905 this village had only three rectors, a fine record of long and faithful ministration. Joseph Smith was here for 58 years, John Bond for 54 years, and then William Richard Watson for 49 years before resigning in 1905.

Sapperton. A tiny spire like a dunce's cap peeps above the tree-tops here, crowning a tower built 700 years ago. The church has been largely rebuilt, but in the north wall, framing later windows, can be seen the arches of a vanished 13th century aisle. Other ancient possessions include a plain Norman font, a worn stone carving (in the floor) of a mediaeval woman in hood and wimple, and old hourglass stand. On a wall are 17th century tablets and another to William Bland, who preached here for 57 years of the 19th century. There is a nice L-shaped 17th century manor house.

Saxby All Saints. A captivating village on the western slope of the Wolds, it looks down on the Carrs where the Old River Ancholme makes a big curve; between the village and the river's new cut and the Weir Dike is the straight Land Drain with its attendant grid of waterways.

The village's charm comes from splendid trees, trim houses with cream walls, and meadows sweeping up the long wooded hill. By the roadside is a drinking fountain set up to commemorate 60 years of Victoria's reign and the lifework of Frederick Horsley, for 42 years agent to the lord of the manor.

Designed by Sir George Gilbert Scott, the neat little church was built in 1849 and follows the line of the steep hillside. The tower, with its pyramid roof, was added in 1873. Round the pulpit are niches with figures of the Four Evangelists. The traceried oak screen with its cornice of vine and grape was carved in the village and set here in 1904. Some of the church plate is 400 years old.

Saxilby. A big village of the border where Nottinghamshire juts into Lincolnshire, it has noble views of the grey towers of Lincoln soaring majestically into the eastern sky. It has, too, the more mundane sight of barges slowly passing by; but even this commonplace scene is touched with the magic of history, for the watercourse is the Foss Dyke made by the Romans to connect the Witham and the Trent and deepened for more ambitious traffic by the Conqueror's son, Henry I. From its bed at Saxilby came the magnificent Roman silver statuette of Mars now in the British Museum.

The fine light church comes largely from the 15th century, but the windows were mostly renewed last century, the heavily-buttressed tower was rebuilt in 1908, and there has been more restoration since.

The seven-arched chancel screen has some 15th century tracery, and new work skilfully blended has kept it a thing of beauty. From a few of the wooden bosses in the nave roof quaint old faces look out, but most of them are good reproductions made after the deathwatch beetle had done its worst.

On a mediaeval altar tomb lie the marble figures of a nameless knight and his lady, their features worn away. He is in armour with surcoat laced at the side, his head on a helmet, his feet on a lion. His lady has a long cloak with rich brooches and a jewelled headdres-like a crown. Loose beneath the tower is a Saxon stone with inters lace decoration.

Preserved in a wall-case are some sheets of music 500 years old—a setting of the Creed in curious notation, and a rare treasure for a village church.

Scamblesby. In pleasant setting among the little ups and downs of the Wolds it lies, with a well-cared-for church at the end of a deep, narrow lane.

Almost completely rebuilt last century, the church has kept its 13th century nave arcades, with their arches on clustered shafts. One of the pillars, re-used from the demolished church at Cawkwell, is entirely covered with zigzag carving and encircled by five detached shafts and indicate Norman–Early English transition. The font, brought back in 1931, has a massive and unusual bowl—round at the top and eight-sided below and is a relic from Norman days. There are 18 bench-ends from mediaeval days, with faces peeping from fleur-de-lys poppyheads.

Scampton. It has attractive stone-walled cottages dotted along a road dipping down from the Cliff road north of Lincoln. Recent new building has changed its character and a massive RAF station dominates the scene. South of the village the Roman Till Bridge Lane runs westward from Ermine Street towards the Trent. A Roman villa was found on the ridge in the 18th century, with traces of thick painted walls, many coloured pavements, and foundations extending over 200 square feet.

The church was originally built in Norman times, enlarged in the 13th century, and largely restored last century, when chancel and aisle were rebuilt. But the 13th century nave arcade still stands, with one of its arches adorned by a quaint head. Up in the old battlemented tower are three bells which must have tolled for the death of Elizabeth I, and in the chancel are brass inscriptions to Sir John Bolle and his wife, who lived here in Charles I's troubled reign, members of a distinguished family prominent in the story of Haugh and several other Lincolnshire villages.

This Sir John Bolle, whose son Sir Robert was one of the jury in 1660 which tried the men who had sentenced Charles I to death, was himself the son of a man who defied James I—Sir George Bolle, Lord Mayor of London in 1617. Conscious of the dignity of his office and of the privileges of London, Sir George challenged the right of James I to send his carriages clattering through the City during the time of Sunday service, and promptly stayed their progress. The matter was reported, and James in a fury said he had thought there were no other kings in England than himself. He sent a warrant ordering Bolle to let the royal vehicles pass, whatever the hour or season, and the Lord Mayor replied that "While it was in my power I did my duty, but, that being taken away by a higher power, it is my duty to obey." King James, apparently impressed by this diplomatic answer, rewarded him with a knighthood.

A modern house has taken the place of the old home of the Bolles, west of the church. It stood on the site of a grange of Kirkstead Abbey, and became a ruin after the death of the last baronet early in the 18th century, but its Jacobean gateway still stands.

Scartho. A village that has become a growing suburb of Grimsby, it is memorable for its tiny church—an attractive patchwork of coloured stone and boulders with one of the finest Saxon towers in the county.

This ancient tower is built of rubble stones irregular in size and shape, except for the hewn stone of the quoins; many of the stones show signs of fire, suggesting that they belonged to a still earlier Saxon church which was perhaps ravaged by marauding Danes. The west doorway has a round head of great stones on massive sides, and above the tall, narrow arch to the nave is a small window. Under the Saxon arch is a bell-ringers' gallery. Above the bellchamber, with its typical two-light windows with mid-wall shafts, is a 15th century parapet; and in the south wall of the tower is a 13th century doorway giving entry to the church.

The nave is chiefly 14th century, but in its north wall are big blocks of sandstone which may have belonged to the Saxon church. A 13th century arcade of two fine bays leads to the 15th century aisle, but the chancel is little more than a centenarian. The east window has beautiful glass by A. K. Nicholson, showing the Wise Men offering their gifts. The church also has a few bits of old glass, an old holy water stoup, and a Norman font bowl.

Scawby. Once a delightfully secluded village, Scawby is now a dormitory for Scunthorpe with new housing estates and roads widened for increasing traffic.

Reached by a trim path, the rebuilt church is one of three hereabouts named after St Hibald. Its tower is 13th century work at its base and 15th century above, and one of its bells has been ringing here for 500 years. There are many memorials to the Nelthorpe family of the late 17th century gabled, red-brick Hall, one is the bust of an armoured Jacobean knight with his wife and children about him.

Scopwick. Grey walls and red roofs and a stream running by the roadside make it an attractive picture, enhanced by a creepered, well-cared-for church. Much of the church has been rebuilt during the last 100 years, but the massive tower, the south doorway, the arcades with clustered columns stand as they have stood for seven centuries. The font has been here through all those long years, and so perhaps has the floorstone with the figure of a cross-legged knight.

Scothern. Six miles from Lincoln, it is noted for continuing a mediaeval custom involving the ringing of the "Pancake Bell" at 11 a.m. on Shrove Tuesday. Originally known as the "Shriving Bell" it became the "Pancake Bell" after the Reformation when the practise of confession was discontinued. It has an ancient church robbed of much of its venerable aspect by rebuilding. But its mediaeval tower still stands unspoiled, with a crown of eight pinnacles and a doorway through which the villagers have passed to and from their Sabbath devotions for more than six centuries. Among the church plate is a 16th century chalice, and in the aisle is an old coffin-lid with a handsome floriated cross.

Scotter. A big and busy village midway between the Cliff and the Trent, it presents an attractive picture with its handsome old church set finely above the red-roofed houses. The market granted to Scotter by Richard I is a thing of the past, but the village green is there and the three-day feast of St Peter and St Paul is still observed.

The story of the church goes back to the 7th century, when Wulphere, King of Mercia, gave it to the Abbey of Peterborough. The oldest fragment of the present structure is the fine south doorway with its round-headed arch enclosing a plain tympanum, for it is believed to be Saxon work within a Norman frame. Traces of a Norman window can be seen outside in a wall of the chancel.

The embattled tower is 15th century work, and so are the windows of the aisle and the clerestory. The nave has on its south side a 13th century buttress, a 14th century window, and a later embattled recess. The 13th century north arcade has beautiful clustered pillars. Nave and aisle both have their old roofs.

The chancel has a 15th century recess with ogee arch and finial, and the chancel screen is of the same period with old traceried bays.

The font, handsome with tracery, flowers, and shields carved on its eight sides, is 600 years old. An ancient altar stone that was used as a memorial to a 17th century rector has been set up again in the aisle.

Two relics from Elizabethan times are the Ringers' Rules (in black and red lettering and probably the oldest in existence in verse form) above the tower doorway, and a brass on the nave wall showing Marmaduke Tyrwhit with his wife and 10 children.

Scotton. Built around a network of roads, with the little River Eau nearby, it has a church dedicated to the little-known St

Genewys—an ancient building on which Time has laid an ungentle hand.

It was a fine church when it was "beautified" by the Nevills, Scotton's mediaeval lords. It suffered in Reformation days; in the time of Elizabeth I five of its altar stones were broken up for paving-stones; and in 1820 Archdeacon Bayley took some of its treasures to enrich his church at Messingham. Among the old glass he took from these windows were four shields of the Nevills, and he also made the church smaller by pulling down the west ends of the aisles.

The tower, which shelters the old village stocks, is chiefly 14th and 15th century work, but its arch to the nave is Norman, though blocked now. The chancel also has a fine Norman doorway, now filled in, but more unusual features are two 15th century windows above its arch to the nave. A lancet window in the chancel, the north doorway with its dog-tooth ornament, and the north arcade of the nave are all 13th century work. The south arcade is a century later.

Among old memorials in the aisles are two worn figures from the 14th century—a knight with a lion at his feet, and a tall wimpled woman with her feet on a dog. In the quatrefoil of one of the ancient gravestones is the likeness of a curly-headed priest wearing an embroidered collar.

Scredington. A peaceful village of the byways, it has a venerable two-arched packhorse bridge and five even more venerable moats, three of them still perfect and full of water—curious sights in the neighbouring fields.

The little church with slender spire was rebuilt last century; but it has kept its narrow 13th century doorway and plain round font, a 14th century arcade, and two 15th century monuments. One is an altar tomb enriched with quatrefoils and bearing a brass inscribed to William Pylet, 1403; the other is a richly-canopied recess with a worn stone figure of Thomas Wyke, in his robes as he ministered here 500 years ago.

Scremby. A pretty little village near the foot of the Wolds, it has its Hall in a small park and its brick church with sandstone dressings of Georgian days set on the hill, with thatched cottages and ivied house for company. Restored in 1884, the church has four bells of 1740 in its tower, and monuments to the Moodys, Dymokes, and others who knew this place in days gone by. A plain old font stands outside by the tower, and southwards through the churchyard trees there is a fine view of the countryside. A mile away is the old hamlet of Grebby, with its late Georgian Hall in a park. From the high ground there are fine views of the wooded landscape and across the marsh to the sea.

Scrivelsby. This pleasant leafy place 2 or 3 miles south of Horncastle is closely associated with one of the most ancient hereditary titles in England. Ever since the Conquest it has been the home of the King's Champion or Hereditary Grand Champion of England.

The office of King's Champion, which is peculiar to England, was first conferred by William the Conqueror on Robert, or Roger, Marmion, whose ancestors had been hereditary champions to the Dukes of Normandy. Together with this privilege the Conqueror gave him the manor of Scrivelsby. The Dymoke family came to the hereditary championship in 1350, when Sir John Dymoke married a great granddaughter of Philip Marmion, who had died leaving no sons. Since then, to this day, Dymoke has succeeded Dymoke as a monarch's Champion.

At recent coronations members of the Dymoke family have carried one of the Standards. But in former times it was the duty of the King's Champion to ride, clad in full armour, into Westminster Hall at the Coronation, and challenge to single combat anyone who should dare to deny the new king's right to the throne. History, however, does not record that anyone was bold enough to accept the challenge.

The full colourful ceremony was last performed in 1821 at the coronation of George IV, and a writer of the time describes how the Champion entered the Hall with a small procession.

First came two trumpeters with banners on their trumpets depicting the Champion's arms, then came a serjeant trumpeter bearing a mace, next two serjeants-at-arms also with maces, then came the Champion himself in a complete suit of bright armour with a plume of feathers in his helmet and riding a richly-caparisoned horse. On either side of him were two esquires, one carrying his lance and the other his shield.

Finally came a herald who read out the challenge that "If any person of what degree soever, high or low, shall deny or gainsay our sovereign Lord George the Fourth . . . to be the next heir . . . here is his Champion, who saith he lieth, and is a false traitor, being ready in person to combat with him, and in the quarrel will adventure his life against him on what day soever he shall be appointed."

After that the Champion threw down his gauntlet. When no one picked it up as a sign of acceptance of the challenge, the herald handed it back to the Champion. The ceremony finished with a gold cup filled with wine being presented to the king, who drank to the Champion. The cup was then presented by the king's cup-bearer to the Champion, who, after bowing low, drank to His Majesty and, bowing again, departed, taking the cup as his fee. At Scrivelsby a number of these gold coronation cups have been preserved.

By the road to Horncastle which bounds the western side of the family's 360-acre park at Scrivelsby is the arched gateway set up about 1530 by Robert Dymoke, who lived during five reigns and was Champion at the coronation of Richard III, Henry VII, and Henry VIII. Surmounting the gateway is a crowned heraldic lion, and set in the wall beside the archway is a stone tablet bearing coats-of-arms at each side of an oak tree, the branches of which are hidden by a shield representing Robert's surname in picture. The gateway was much restored in the 19th century and the lion replaced.

Scrivelsby Court, ancestral home of the Dymokes, has gone; the 18th century house was destroyed by fire; its 19th century successor pulled down. The present Champion, Major J. L. M. Dymoke lives in the gatehouse. Among the family portraits is one of the Champion who performed the last full ceremony at the coronation of George IV.

Scrivelsby's little church is a Valhalla of Kings' Champions. Although most of the windows are modern, and the tower and spire date from 1861, it is in the main an ancient building, the nave arcade, the chancel, and the chancel arch all being 13th century work. There is a fine old traceried screen of oak; but the chief treasures of the church are its monuments of the Dymokes.

The oldest of the brave array are two figures in the aisle, each lying on a separate great stone. The cross-legged knight is believed to be Sir Philip, last of the Marmions, who has lain here since 1292; he has a surcoat over his chain-mail, his good sword (now broken), and a shield on his arm. The lady, believed to be his wife, wears a gown of graceful folds and a wimple; her hands are clasped in prayer and at her feet is a dog.

On a tomb carved with quatrefoils and tracery is the brass portrait of the Robert Dymoke who built the Lion Gate. Wearing fine armour and spurs, and standing on a lion, he is rather an odd-looking knight with small head huddled between big shoulders. The inscription is curious in describing him as Knight and Baronet, though the title of Baronet was not used in his day. The words may be later restoration of the original, Knight Banneret, bestowed on Sir Robert by Henry VIII.

There is a brass tablet for Sir Charles Dymoke, Champion to James II, who was buried here in 1686; and in a wall-monument with serpents and flaming torches is the bust of Lewis Dymoke, Champion to George I and George II, who "enjoyed his office till his 91st year". Another tablet tells of John Dymoke who dared the world for George III.

Scunthorpe. The hamlet (Escumetorp) that appeared in Domesday Book is today a thriving and rapidly developing industrial centre. **The modern town** is founded on five small settlements,

Crosby, Scunthorpe, Frodingham, Brumby, and Ashby. Archaeological evidence shows that there was a considerable population in
the Early Bronze Age, c. 2000 BC but this did not grow rapidly and
at the 1861 Census the combined population for the five villages was
only 1,423.

Set in the Cliff country above the Trent valley, Scunthorpe owes
its rapid growth since 1859 to the rediscovery of rich beds of Lower
Lias ironstone, lying beneath the sandy warrens of this area, that
had not been worked since Roman times. At first, the ironstone was
transported to Yorkshire for processing but in 1862 work began on
building local ironworks and by 1864 the production of pig iron
had begun to be followed in 1890 by steel. By 1921, with the
building of new steel plants and the spread of ore mining into the
surrounding countryside, the population of the villages had reached
27,790.

In 1919, the constituent authorities became the urban district of
Scunthorpe and Frodingham and there was a lot of discussion as to
which settlement should have precedence. By 1935, the population
was 37,170 and in the following year the town received its Charter
of Incorporation as the Borough of Scunthorpe. At the time of the
Second World War, Scunthorpe was producing 14 per cent of the
country's pig iron and 10 per cent of its steel. Since the war both
population and production have increased. The population in 1967
is estimated at 70,980 and 15 per cent of the country's pig iron and
11 per cent of its steel comes from Scunthorpe—2,700,000 tons and
3,000,000 tons respectively.

Scunthorpe's late development has meant that many of the pit-
falls of industrial development have been avoided. There is still
some evidence of Victorian industrial expansion with its depressing
effect particularly in the east of the town. The ironstone bed, with
its open-cast mining, is to the north and east and all the heavy
industry is concentrated in that area. The best approach is from the
west from which direction the modern, attractive open development
is seen at its best and the town looks well in a dominant position on
the escarpment on which it stands. The dominant feature of this
belt is the Civic Centre, opened in 1963, in a bold contemporary
design. The entrance hall has a magnificent Roman pavement from
about AD 360 built into its north wall, a reminder that at Winterton,
5 miles north of the Civic Centre, there flourished a Romano-
British settlement of considerable importance. The Civic Centre is
set in pleasant gardens on the fringe of the Central Park which
includes a miniature golf course, paddling pool, and children's playground. Other features of this green belt that immediately catch
the eye are the North Lindsey Technical College, opened in 1954
and since extended, the John Leggott Grammar School established
in 1964, and the Quibell Athletic and Cycling Stadium opened in

1965. A 14-storey block of flats towers above the brow of the hill providing a striking vertical feature.

Another attractive group of buildings in the town centre consists of Frodingham's St Lawrence's Church and the Borough Museum and Art Gallery that has as its nucleus the old Frodingham Vicarage set in delightful lawns, flowerbeds, and surrounded by mature beech trees. St Lawrence's dates back to 1236 and was probably preceded by a Saxon church on the same site. A new nave and chancel were added on the north side in 1913. The old chancel, now the south chapel, is Early English and the tower is of the same period. There is an interesting 12th century arcade between the old and new naves.

The Museum, which is the Regional Museum of North Lincolnshire, moved into its present premises in 1953 and extensions have taken place in 1962 and 1965 giving more room for modern display and providing an Art Gallery and Lecture Theatre. The old stables and courtyard of the house have been attractively equipped to show farm wagons and implements to illustrate the agricultural folklife of this part of Lincolnshire. Another aspect of local life is seen in the Victorian cottage built of ironstone, rescued during the redevelopment of the old town and re-erected in 1963 in the museum grounds. There are also rich collections illustrating the geology and archaeology of the region.

Reminders of the rapid growth of the town are seen in the churches. Scunthorpe parish church of St John was built in local ironstone in 1891. Although situated in the old, grimy part of the town it is still the most impressive of the town's churches and was the gift of the first Lord Oswald and reflects the new-found prosperity of the iron industry. St George's and St Paul's parish churches of Crosby and Ashby date from 1924. An interesting and attractive later church is St Hugh's, the parish church of Brumby, built of brick and concrete in 1939. On the opposite side of the road is St Marks, the Methodist Church, built in 1960. It has an open concrete spire. The Church of the Holy Spirit, built in 1965, again adopts the modern idiom of an open spire but this time in steel in honour of the staple produce of the town. The most recent church in this rapidly growing community is the Church of the Latter Day Saints which again adopts an uncompromisingly modern design.

There are few evidences of the old villages of the town. The stone cottages of Old Brumby Street reflect the character of these villages in the pre-industrial period. Brumby Hall, the finest domestic building left, has a 17th century porch and sundial dated 1637. The house was extended in the 18th century and is now a student hostel for one of the steel companies. At one time it was the home of the Bellingham family, one of whom, Richard, formed one of the bands of Puritans who in 1634 sailed for America and founded the town of Boston.

The natural extension of the town to the south has meant that although outside the borough boundary, Bottesford and Yaddlethorpe have become suburbs. Here the village character is retained and a delightful Early English parish church has unusual lancet windows in the chancel which are said to be the longest in any parish church in England. Not far away is the manor house built in Romantic style by Edward Peacock, the antiquary. The new Yaddlethorpe Methodist Church in contemporary style is built in the shape of a tent with the long roof lines sweeping down in uninterrupted slopes to the ground.

Outside the borough boundary but an integral part of the life of the town is Normanby Park. Normanby Hall, the principal building, stands in 43 acres of gardens, lawns, and woodland. It was leased to the town in 1964 by the Sheffield family who had been the owners of the estate since the time of Elizabeth I.

The present building, the third on the site, was designed by Sir Robert Smirke, architect of the British Museum, and was built between 1825 and 1829. Several rooms are open to the public and furnished in Regency style. Part of the house is used as an educational and conference centre. The Hall is severely classical in design. The grounds and hall are open to the public and form a pleasant amenity for Scunthorpe's residents and visitors from farther afield.

Searby. Tranquil on the western edge of the Wolds it lies, below the road from Caistor to Brigg, and coming to it down the hill we have a lovely view of the rolling hills. There are more views from the hilltops close by, and a glimpse of Lincoln Cathedral 20 miles away.

Rebuilt in white brick in 1833, the little village church stands on a mound among attractive white cottages and farm buildings. It is notable for the woodcarving by T. J. M. Townsend, vicar for 44 years last century. We see it on the ends of the low oak benches with their representations of the Apostles and the Tribes of Israel; on the altar-rails with vine leaves and wheat; on the organ case; on the pulpit branching out from the screen; and in the screen, with its pointed arches and its angels. All these were the work of his devoted hands. A nave window, showing St Nicholas as a bishop with three bags of gold at his feet, keeps his memory ever green.

In the nave is a floorstone with a Latin inscription to a 15th century vicar. A coped stone of the 14th century, enriched with a fine cross, is in the churchyard, having been used in 1712 as a gravestone for the wife of a parish clerk.

There is an attractive late 18th century manor house and 18th century vicarage.

Sedgebrook. It is a small place near Grantham and it is linked with memories of Sir John Markham, who was called the Upright Judge, when he was Edward IV's Chief Justice. He is said to have been deposed by Edward after seven years for his fearless and impartial direction of the jury during a trial of a prisoner arrested for high treason at the instance of the king.

In the course of the trial the judge laid it down that a subject may arrest for treason, but that a king may not, for if the arrest is illegal, the subject has no remedy against the king; in other words, that an English king cannot be an autocrat, but must proceed by constitutional measures to enforce the law; a fact forgotten when Charles I sought to arrest the Five Members.

The finely-kept church, with light streaming unhindered through its windows, comes chiefly from the 15th century, but the north arcade is two centuries older. In the corners of the chancel are fine canopied niches, and the mediaeval piscina and sedilia are also here. Among the other old possessions are a Norman font, three screens, stalls with quaint poppyheads, one of them with two feathered men back to back, a panelled pulpit of 1634, and a prayer-desk fashioned from an earlier pulpit.

An ancient door leads into Judge Markham's Chapel, built by him in 1468. Only the top stone of his tomb is left, shorn of its brasses and now set in the floor, but on the wall is a stone with a crudely-graven portrait of his daughter Dorothy. High up in the east wall, on each side of the altar, are two elaborately canopied niches supported by shield-bearing angels, and there are more angels on the pillars of the lofty arches between this chapel and the chancel. Nothing remains however, of the small chamber in which Sir John Markham is said to have spent his closing years in prayer and meditation.

The three bells in the tower are all pre-Reformation, one of them being inscribed *May the sweet voice of Gabriel ring to Heaven's height.* They probably tolled for the passing of the Upright Judge in 1479.

Sempringham. Time was when its name was known throughout the land, for here was the famous priory round which grew up the one monastic order originating in England. The Gilbertine order was founded here by the eldest son of a wealthy Norman knight, afterwards canonised as St Gilbert of Sempringham, and when Gilbert died, at a great age, there were in England no fewer than 13 religious houses belonging to the Order, with 700 monks and 1300 nuns.

Gilbert, who was born here in 1083, was so deformed as to be unfit for knightly deeds as they were understood in that age, so he was sent abroad to be educated as a clerkly person. He returned home pious and kindly, and so cultured that his father's view of him changed from disappointment to hope. Gilbert became attached to the Court of the Bishops of Lincoln, and was appointed chaplain to Bishop Alexander.

Gilbert believed in education even for the poorest, a revolutionary idea for the 11th century; and though, of course, his teaching of the sons of the serfs to whom he ministered was not without regard to a future monastic vocation for the scholars, he did give his parishes free schools in which secular subjects were taught.

His heart, however, was set on wider work. In a brutal and lawless age in which no woman was safe he founded retreats to which they might retire from the world. To his convents he added houses for men, who were to be canons for the instruction of the nuns, and for menials, as lay brothers, to discharge the manual labour of the establishments.

Bishop Alexander, the pope, and the king all approved, and the Order was instituted in 1131. It never took root abroad, but in England it had very considerable success. Of its founder his biographer said, "Kings and princes honoured him, pontiffs and prelates received him with devotion, kinsmen and strangers loved him, and all the people revered him as a Saint of God."

The first house was set up here, close to the present church, in 1135, and Gilbert's reputation for piety won him abundant support from wealthy families, whose crimes cried out for expiation by benevolence of this sort. One house followed another until at his death the Gilbertine order boasted 11, with 700 men and 1500 sisters. At the Dissolution this unique English order numbered 26 houses in various parts of the country.

Gilbert was a model of mediaeval piety, learning, and selfless endeavour. He risked his life to support and finance Becket against his sovereign, and was arrested. But the king honoured him, and Queen Eleanor and her sons loved him.

Death came to him when he had exceeded his hundredth year. He was buried in great honour here, wrapped in his priest's robes, between the two altars of his church. His tomb became a place of pilgrimage, at which even King John paid homage. In 1202, 13 years after his death, he was canonised St Gilbert of Sempringham.

The site Gilbert of Sempringham chose for his Priory of St Mary is near the Roman King Street, but nothing is left of its buildings and its church, though the foundations were revealed by excavation in 1938–39. The church was 325 feet long. The south side was the nun's church, long and narrow (35 feet). The canon's church was more spacious. The shrine of St Gilbert stood astride the wall between canons' and nuns' chancels.

At the Dissolution, Sempringham Priory was granted to Lord Clinton (afterwards Earl of Lincoln), who pulled everything down and built himself a fine house with the materials. This was in turn pulled down on the death of the second earl in 1616, but traces of it that have been found show it to have had great buildings ranged round a courtyard 135 feet square.

Close to the site of the priory is a church a generation older—a lonely landmark on a hillock among arable fields. It is reached by a track leading from the pleasing little village of Pointon, which has some thick-walled houses doubtless built of stone from the priory. It is the parish church of St Andrew, and it is interesting both for its Norman work and its close associations with the Gilbertine order, for Gilbert built against its north wall a dwelling for a few nuns, chosen from the maidens hereabouts.

The south doorway with its rows of chevron carvings on arch and jambs is a fine fragment of the Norman church, and it frames splendid old doors of fir wood enriched with a mass of old iron scrollwork. Sheltering it is a 19th century porch with a fine Norman tympanum in its wall that was taken from the church more than a century ago and built into a dovecot not far off; its outer arch has a band of interlaced strapwork, and it frames another design like an open fan. The nave has a massive Norman arcade, with four arches on big round pillars, leading to a north aisle which has a plain Norman doorway and four deep-splayed Norman windows in its rebuilt wall.

The fine central tower with eight handsome pinnacles was built on Norman foundations in the 15th century, but the apsidal chancel with slender lancets is modern. The 18th century men who pulled down the Norman chancel and transepts (because they decided Sempringham Church was too big for the scattered congregation) did not heed the message of the Tudor bell in the tower which bears an inscription *Be not over busie*. The font with shields on its eight panelled sides, and some benches with carved tracery of roses, are 15th century. But older than all else here is a fragment of a Saxon cross brought in from the churchyard. It has interlace decoration. There are many good slate headstones in the churchyard.

Sibsey. A big Fen village lining a long stretch of the road from Boston to Spilsby, it is notable for its fine old church, and also has, near the Stone Bridge Drain to the west, a disused windmill which is shortly to be restored.

A grand peal of eight bells rings out from the church's lofty 13th century tower, the mediaeval belfry windows of which are enriched with clustered shafts and a wealth of dog-tooth ornament.

Great height is an impressive feature of the church's interior, and the nave arcades, which come from the close of the Norman period, have extraordinarily tall pillars. The clerestory and the bellcot on the eastern gable are 15th century work. In the big restoration of 1855 the spacious 15th century chancel and the aisles of the nave were partly rebuilt; but the north aisle still has a Norman doorway, and the chancel has remains of its three sedilia and piscina. The old font has a carved bowl on a cluster of shafts, and in the chancel is a fine brass candelabrum for 20 lights.

Silk Willoughby. The road going south from Sleaford leads to this small place with green fields all round, a pond by the wayside, a grand old church, and the shaft of an old wayside cross set on a base carved with signs of the Evangelists. Its name is really Silkby-cum-Willoughby, Silkby once being a separate hamlet.

The church is a great possession. Except for the chancel, it was almost entirely built in the 14th century, when the style was well-developed. The tower is of excellent proportions with canopied buttresses and decorated animal heads and roses below the traceried parapet, which like the spire with its flying buttresses and two tiers of lights, is a little younger than the tower itself. The beautiful south doorway in the spacious porch is adorned with ballflowers and worn heads of a king and bishop.

The old nave has three lofty arches on clustered columns; the chancel (rebuilt last century) has vaulted sedilia, a piscina, and a tall niche for a processional cross. The south aisle has a double aumbry and a piscina; the old rood stairway and a fragmentary painting on the north wall have come to light in restoration. The font, boldly carved with cable pattern and interlaced arcading, is Norman.

The church has much fine woodwork. Nave and aisles are filled with fine benches, many of them with traceried 14th century ends and tall poppyheads. There is an old chest, a panelled Jacobean pulpit, and eagle reading-desk, and a tall 14th century screen with carvings of various creatures—an eagle, a lion, dragons, a monkey fighting a dog, and a fox with a bird in its mouth.

Sixhills. Hereabouts the switchback road from the Roman High Street reveals lovely glimpses of the Wolds, culminating in a magnificent panorama of the countryside on reaching Sixhills churchyard. It is a view of hills going down to the plain and rising again in the Cliff, with the towers of Lincoln clearly seen.

The little church was almost entirely rebuilt last century, and its antiquity is evident only in parts of the tower (with pyramid cap and tall pinnacles); and in the 13th century arcade now built up in the north wall of the nave.

In the walls of Grange Farm, below the village, are a few old corbel heads from the Gilbertine priory founded here in the time of King Stephen—two wimpled women, a woman with her hair dressed in loops, and a man in a cap. On one of the outbuildings is a carving of a curly-headed queen.

Until the Dissolution the priory stood where the farmhouse still stands, and within its walls, in 1306, Edward I shut up Robert Bruce's sister, the Lady Christina Seton, after he had hanged her husband as a traitor. Here, too, a few years earlier, he sent a daughter of Davydd III, last native prince of North Wales, after her father had been executed at Shrewsbury for revolting against the king; and here she lived on as a nun for half a century.

Skegness. From the tiny fishing village which Alfred Lord Tennyson and his brothers knew so well it has grown into a town beloved of holiday-makers. Skegness is famous among holiday towns, and it well deserves its fame. It is spaciously planned with broad tree-lined streets.

Holiday-makers come here by road and rail and plane; and they come here to delight in the bracing air, the splendid stretch of firm, clean sands, the safe bathing, the gardens with their thousands of rose bushes and their boating lake, the long pier, the golf courses and bowling greens, tennis courts, and riding schools, and all the attendant pleasures of a modern seaside resort—everything, in fact, that young and old in search of recreation on holiday can desire. A great holiday camp has been established just outside its borders in Ingoldmells and fine caravan sites are provided.

Half a mile inland, and hidden among gardens and orchards away from all the modern hurly-burly, is the old church of St Clement. Standing in a beautifully wooded churchyard, it is a quaint little 15th century building with an earlier arch in its squat, sturdy tower and a simple aisleless interior of rough stone walls protected by a low-pitched roof with stout old beams. The font, carved with tracery and shields, is 500 years old.

The aerodrome of Skegness is near the Roman Bank—a misnomer as it was a mediaeval bank raised to protect the marsh from flooding.

The creation of the Gibraltar Point-Skegness Nature Reserve is a fine achievement. It is managed by the Lincolnshire Trust for Nature Conservation and embraces the finest stretch of the whole Lincolnshire coastline: more than 1200 acres of sandy beaches, mud-flats, sand-dunes and salt-marshes. It has recreational and educational aims and attracts over 100,000 visitors a year.

Skendleby. It can be counted as one of Lincolnshire's most charming villages. Set in a valley where a stream runs to the River Lymn, it has all the grace which thatched white cottages, old ivied manor house, and ancient church can bestow. There are fine views from the 18th century Hall (a modern building standing in lovely grounds), and also from the churchyard, where a cedar spreads its ample shade.

Skendleby came into the news in the 1930s, when the mound known as Giant's Hills (north of the village) was excavated and a long barrow revealed. Built about 1800 BC, the barrow was found to be 200 feet long and the burial-chamber contained eight bodies. Built of timber and wattle and earth, it had two double lines of timber posts running its whole length, and another row of posts across each end. It had a great ditch in which later settlers "squatted". A twin barrow to the south has been almost levelled by ploughing.

Nearly 3000 years after the long barrow was built there was a church at Skendleby. It came into Domesday Book, and Skendleby itself was important enough for a friend of the Conqueror, Gilbert de Gaunt, to live here. He gave the church to Bardney Abbey. Time and restoration have left little of its antiquity visible, except for some mediaeval windows, two piscinas and an aumbry, and a fine 15th century font, enriched with flowers and tracery and quaint heads.

The interior is surprisingly spacious and lofty, and the oak furnishing adds to its attractions. The wide, aisleless nave has a great wagon roof with kingposts and coved sides; the neat benches and nave panelling are embattled; the massive low screen is carved with tracery; and the pulpit has buttressed panels. Attractive, too, is the modern glass of the east window.

Skidbrooke. It stands in isolation in the fields. In the Middle Ages this was a thriving port but the deposit of silt has built up at this point leaving the village behind. More than a mile from the sea, stands the old village church with a massive tower rising from a girdle of trees.

The south doorway with its hood of dog-tooth is 13th century work, and the spacious nave, though chiefly 14th century, has 13th century pillars and capitals in its south arcade. The chancel has a 14th century arch, a plain sedile, a big bracket with grotesque carved head, and slight traces of a vanished chapel in the south wall. From early Stuart times come the carved pulpit with backboard and canopy, the altar-table with its deep lockers, and the pyramid cover of the 14th century font. There is also an old chest.

Skillington. It is hidden away near the Leicestershire border, still with a fragment of an old cross on its green. The abbey, west of the church, is a small stone 17th century manor house.

Evidence of the long story of the church can be seen in the Saxon long-and-short masonry outside, at the south-east corner of the nave. The rest of the church is largely work of the 13th and 14th centuries, though the pointed arches of both arcades rest on the round Norman columns. The font with its quatrefoils and queer faces under the bowl, and the two stones with engraved crosses set in the chancel wall, were all the work of mediaeval masons.

Two windows with mountain scenes are memorials to Charles

Hudson who was vicar here, a skilful mountaineer who went out to climb the Matterhorn—and never came back.

It was in 1865 that Charles Hudson, a practised mountaineer, left his vicarage here to join Edward Whymper, Lord Francis Douglas, with another climber and three guides, in an ascent of the Matterhorn in Switzerland, previously unconquered.

On the descent the rope snapped and let five of the climbers fall, including Hudson.

They were seen sliding down on their backs, spreading out their hands in an attempt to save themselves. Then, one by one, they fell from precipice to precipice on to the Matterhorn glacier, 4000 feet below. Death must have been instantaneous. Next day the bodies of Hudson and two of his comrades were recovered, and, after temporary burial in the snow were brought down and interred in the cemetery at Zermatt. Douglas's body was never recovered.

Whymper survived the disaster unshaken, made a pioneer exploration of Greenland, carried out wonderful climbs in the Andes of Ecuador, mastering Chimborazo and exploring the great volcano Cotopaxi. He died at Chamonix, in September, 1911, and was buried in the English churchyard there.

Skirbeck. A suburb of Boston, it has the old church of St Nicholas standing near the river, a mile from the heart of the town. The mediaeval sea-bank (Roman Bank) fringes the churchyard.

Once it was a Norman church but the nave arcades are 13th century, the tower is 15th century, and the chancel is quite modern. The finest features of the church are the lovely arcades of the wide and lofty nave, which has a clerestory of round windows much restored. The arches rest on massive pillars with clustered shafts, most of the shafts being detached and all of them crowned with capitals of rare beauty. The tower arch climbs to the nave roof, and bridging the chancel arch is a painted wooden beam with the Crucifixion scene, with St Mary and St John in robes of shining gold. Another touch of rich colour in the chancel is in the group of five lancets in the east wall, showing Our Lord in Glory with saints and angels.

The old rood-stair doorway is still here, and from Jacobean days comes the richly-panelled pulpit with its desk supported by six strange birds. Of the same time is the font-cover, shaped like a tower and spire; in its renewed lower portion are figures of St Mary with lilies and St Nicholas with bags of gold at his feet. A small font of 1662 has been made into a piscina.

Holy Trinity Church, on the Spilsby road, was designed in 14th century style by Sir George Gilbert Scott and built in 1848. It has a tablet to Dr Roy, who not only gave the site but also helped with the building. (The bell in the turret is one that was originally given to Derby by Charles I and was bought for this church by Dr Roy.) Another tablet tells of Ellen Thompson, who taught in the Sunday School for 71 years.

A mile and a half north-east of Skirbeck stands Rochford Tower, a massive and impressive red-brick tower of the early 16th century, with corner turrets and embattled parapet. It resembles Hussey Tower, Boston, and may be the old home of the Rochfords and of the Kymes who followed them. It is sometimes called the Kyme Tower. The ground-floor room is brick-vaulted. There is a circular flight of stairs leading to the first and second floors, and in one of the rooms on the first floor are traces of red wall painting said to represent the Annunciation, Mary and Anne, and other saints.

Skirbeck Quarter, south-west of Boston, has a pleasing modern brick church. Above the entrance doorway is the Madonna and Child, carved in oak, and the notable feature within is also the wood-work—benches, stalls, and screen all being of adzed oak. The screen has traceried bays and iron grilles, and above it, like a huge tympanum shining with gold and colour, are the Crucifixion with St Mary and St John and a host of angels.

Sleaford. Its name comes from the little River Slea, which divides into two small channels and runs under two narrow bridges through its main street and out to the pleasant meadows beyond. Its prosperity, and consequent air of cheerfulness, comes from its status as a market town, with a market every Monday. Its fame among travellers rests on its church, one of the finest in a countryside of fine churches.

Sleaford's early history is shadowy. However, excavations on the new housing estate in Boston Road, near to Old Place, have revealed evidence of an Iron Age settlement and a mint of the Coritanian tribe in the 1st century AD. Coin moulds of baked clay and sherds of crucibles provided abundant evidence. Roman coins and pottery have also been found in this area pointing to a settlement on the King Street, which branches from Ermine Street and passes through Sleaford. Last century when a railway extension was being made south of the town a vast Anglo-Saxon cemetery was found, with a great number of skeletons as well as many ornaments, weapons, and pottery. Many of the antiquities are now in the British Museum.

The centuries passed quietly by, and Sleaford remained veiled in obscurity until Domesday Book. From then on it was closely asso-ciated with the bishops of Lincoln. The Conqueror gave the manor to Remigius, the first bishop, and about 1130 Bishop Alexander built the castle, which stood in a field north-west of the station. King Stephen seized the castle, but it was afterwards restored to the See. King John spent a night here on his way from Swineshead Abbey to

Newark Castle, where he died, and here in 1431 died Bishop Fleming of Lincoln (founder of Lincoln College, Oxford), who caused Wycliffe's bones to be dug up. The bishop who finally surrendered Sleaford Manor and Castle was Henry Holbeach, a Lincolnshire man and one of the compilers of the Prayer Book. This was part of the spoil which Protector Somerset appropriated for the Crown. Queen Mary gave the castle and manor to Admiral Lord Clinton, and the Carre family followed him as the owners. Late in Elizabeth I's reign it was pulled down.

The most sensational historic event ever occurring at Sleaford was the execution in 1538 of Lord Hussey, who lived at Old Place. The suppression of the monasteries had been made a question of national policy by Henry VIII and his henchman, Thomas Cromwell. Lincolnshire disliked it and presently rose in rebellion. Sir William Hussey, the father of Lord Hussey, had served three English kings as an upright Lord Chief Justice, and Lord Hussey himself had given Henry VIII good service, too—and been richly rewarded. A firm Catholic, he was averse to playing into the hands of the unpopular Thomas Cromwell, and when a rising broke out in Lincolnshire headed by the abbots, Hussey did not join it. But neither was he active in suppressing it. Facing both ways, he waited. But on a charge, laid by informers, that he had said the people "would get no change unless they fought for it", he was arrested, tried, and beheaded. A few indiscreet words cost him his life, and his family his lands.

Only the mounds of Sleaford Castle remain, and Lord Hussey's home, Old Place, is hardly more than a name. Apart from its church, the town has only a few marks of antiquity. Here and there, however, amid much that has grown up in quite recent years, stand houses mellowed by two centuries and more. One of the oldest is the attractive timbered vicarage, next to the church, with the date 1568 carved on a gable; and in the walls of an inn in Southgate is a 17th century sign showing a tethered bull being baited by two dogs, a custom in the bad old days.

Another building with its roots deep in the past is Carre's Hospital facing the church, a charming group of grey stone almshouses, with a chapel and five projecting porches, built on two sides of a lawn. Founded in 1636 by Sir Robert Carre, it was rebuilt on a bigger scale in the 19th century. A similar group of almshouses, with little iron balconies between projecting porches, is in Northgate, close to the grammar school which was also founded by one of the Carres and has also been rebuilt.

The old coaching inn, the Bristol Arms, with a late Georgian front, is now converted into a shopping arcade. The offices of the Kesteven County Council are in Sleaford in a fine Victorian building of 1856. The Corn Exchange another conspicuous building is 1857.

Another notable feature of the town is the monument in South-gate set up to honour a 19th century MP, Henry Handley—a kind of Eleanor Cross with a statue of the MP standing under a rich canopy adorned with many little statues of saints and historical figures. One of his successors in the House, Henry Chaplin of Blankney, a Tory Die-Hard, was a great Parliamentary figure but found that winning the Derby won him greater fame than all his politics. A. G. Gardiner in one of his masterly essays wrote: "when Sleaford, forgetful of its long allegiance, forgetful of the lustre shed upon it by Mr Chaplin, left him in the debacle of 1906 at the bottom of the poll, he, with his long experience of the vicissitudes of fortune, took his coup de grâce with his habitual good temper and gave to Wimbledon the distinction of being represented in Parliament by the owner of Hermit."

In 1792, Sleaford Navigation made a new cut for part of the River Slea to encourage the transport of coal and other merchandise between Sleaford and Lincoln or Boston, as well as with Horncastle *via* Horncastle Navigation of the River Bain. The house where the Sleaford Navigation had its office still stands off Carre Street, and has the coat-of-arms above the door.

The crowning glory of Sleaford is its great church, dedicated to St Denis and standing four-square on one side of the marketplace. It is a noble building, almost cathedral-like in the richness of its west front and the beauty of its windows. The whole exterior is rich, but the west front is its loveliest feature, the thick-set tower crowned by one of England's earliest stone spires and flanked by the finely-decorated ends of the 14th century aisles. The lower stages of the tower were built about 1180, when the Norman style was waning, and its great doorway with zigzag ornament is pointed. The top part of the tower and the spire, rising to a height of 144 feet, was added about 40 years later. During a Sunday service in 1884 it was struck by lightning and later rebuilt, stone by stone, except that the 15th century west window was replaced by three small rose windows in line, with a row of blank lancet arcading over them. Ornamental parapets, turrets, and niches adorn the west end of each aisle; most of the niches are now empty, but one has an old headless figure of St Margaret and three others contain modern figures of Matthew, Mark, and Luke. Each of the aisles has a doorway and the north one has a gabled canopy with ballflower moulding overlapping the fine window above. The rich external decoration is continued by panelled parapets above the side walls of the aisles and the 14th century south porch, and also by slender crocketed pinnacles above the 15th century clerestory. The south porch has a seated figure of the Lord above the doorway, and a crypt below.

But the richness that raises Sleaford Church above nearly every other parish church in England is found in the rich flowing tracery of its windows. Tracery is difficult to describe except in technical language which conveys nothing of beauty, and the tracery of these windows is beautiful indeed. Each has some variation in its flowing pattern, and the big six-light window of the north transept, 18 feet wide and over 33 feet high, is unsurpassed anywhere, though similar windows at neighbouring Heckington and at Carlisle and Selby are comparable.

The sense of grandeur within the church is conveyed by its lofty nave, lighted by eight clerestory windows on each side and linked with the aisles by arcades borne on slender clustered pillars; and also by the three great 14th century arches of the tower opening into nave and aisles. A half-arch in the south aisle, and, in the north aisle, a modern double arch like the one in Wells Cathedral, help to buttress the tower. To this great array of arches the 19th century added an arcade of three more, adorned with angels, when the second north aisle (now a chapel) was built, its richly-traceried windows being those of the original 14th century aisle.

The chancel was rebuilt in the 15th century and still has its sedilia. Architecturally not notable, its mediaeval screen is a thing of beauty and one of the finest in England. Above the graceful tracery in its open bays is a projecting fan-vaulted canopy bearing up a modern rood-loft, enriched with wreaths of vine and 16 canopied figures of apostles and saints, and widening in the centre to a little five-sided bay in front of the rood figures; the rood-loft was designed by Sir Ninian Comper, and is a memorial to three brothers who fell in the First World War, the canopied figures being their father's own memorial. A staircase on each side of the chancel arch leads to the rood-loft, and a third leads to the chancel roof.

The screen is the great treasure of Sleaford Church, but there are several other notable old possessions. One is a fine specimen of 17th century tapestry formerly used as a pulpit cushion. Woven in silk and wool at the Sheldon factory at Barcheston, Warwickshire, the only school of tapestry weavers producing original designs at that time, it portrays Judith holding up the head of Holofernes, the charming background being of old English flowers and the borders finished with tiny scenes of country life.

Here also is an embroidered altar carpet of fine and elaborate needlework, mentioned in the churchwardens' records of 1628 and thought to have been made about 1620; it is carefully preserved in a frame in the north aisle. In a case close by are 15 chained books.

Up in the belfry are eight bells which were the work of an 18th century Norfolk bell-founder, Thomas Osborne; and down below, now silent, is the mediaeval "butter bell" used for the market folk, the only market bell left in the county. The traceried six-sided font comes from the 15th century and there are two fine old chests, one with strong iron bands and three locks, and the other (from Stuart times) with a carved panel of a man in a helmet.

The oldest monument here is a remarkable and well-preserved stone coffin-lid of the 14th century, or even earlier. It was found buried 14 feet deep at Leadenham when the railway cutting between Lincoln and Grantham was made, and was given to the church about 15 years ago. On it is a floriated cross, and where the arms of the cross meet the face of a woman is deeply carved in a small oval cavity; another cavity halfway down shows her clasped hands, and in a third opening at the base appear her little feet in pointed shoes. Round the margin in fine lettering is a Norman-French inscription, *You who pass by, Pray for the soul of Yveyt, the wife of W. de Rauceby, on whose soul may God have mercy.*

Other noteworthy monuments are in memory of the Carres, the wealthy merchant family of Sleaford. The earliest is a small brass of 1521 showing George Carre in merchant's gown and his wife in fur-trimmed robe. On the left of the chancel arch is the alabaster altar tomb, decorated with shields, of Robert Carre, 1599. On the right of the chancel arch is the canopied altar tomb of his son Sir Edward —a sumptuous monument with damaged figures of the knight in armour, his wife by his side; on the wall above them skulls, cross-bones, and trophies of war are assembled, and two naked cherubs stand beside the inscription, cross-legged and pensive. (Sir Edward's brother Robert was the founder of Sleaford Grammar School, and his own son Robert was founder of the almshouses.) In the transept is the black marble altar tomb of Sir Robert Carre, Chancellor of the Duchy of Lancaster; and there also is the curly-headed marble bust of his son Sir Edward, who died in 1683 when only 18. He was the last of his line.

Snarford. There are farms on every side and a narrow road leads across fields to the ancient church, shaded by chestnut trees and neighboured by a mellow red-roofed farmhouse with a duck-pond.

The tower is the oldest part of the church and its interior displays a Norman arch in each of its walls, although the only open arch is the 13th century one leading to the nave. The rest of the church belongs chiefly to the 14th and 15th centuries and counts among its old treasures an altar stone with consecration crosses and a 15th century font with the face of Our Lord, emblems of the Passion, vine ornament, and a grotesque head with tongue out.

Undoubtedly the chief interest centres in the memorials to the St Paul family, lords of the manor here in Tudor times. All have been restored and painted. The older of the great monuments is the cano-pied tomb behind the altar, bearing coloured alabaster figures of Sir Thomas St Paul of 1582 and his wife, side by side. The knight wears plate armour and helmet with an elephant and castle crest, and has one ringed hand resting on his sword and the other clasping a book; his lady, also holding a book, has a flowing robe, and a pendant on a ribbon reaching almost to the flowered cushion at her feet. On the canopy above them, borne up by six richly-carved pillars, kneel eight boys and girls, and in the centre another son kneels on a smaller pillared canopy. It is a fine memorial of an Elizabethan family.

Under an arch on the north side of the chantry we see Sir George St Paul, described by the great Lord Burghley as one of the best men in the county. He is portrayed in his armour, resting pensively on one arm. Below him is his wife Frances, her dress gay with lace and bows, and still lower is their little daughter Mattathia, with beads round her neck and a cherub on each side.

Frances, the lady on this monument, was the daughter of Chief Justice Sir Christopher Wray, and this is her tribute to her first husband, whom she married when a girl of 15. But she married again and became a countess and that is why she appears (this time with a coronet) on another monument which has busts of her and her husband Robert Rich, 1st Earl of Warwick. It was the second marriage which linked her with one of the famous love stories of Elizabethan times, for Robert Rich's first wife had been none other than the lovely Penelope Devereux, the Stella of Sir Philip Sidney's sonnets.

Engaged to Sir Philip Sidney while still in her teens, Penelope Devereux was forced into an unhappy marriage with the wealthy Robert Rich (the "Rich fool" of one of the Astrophel and Stella sonnets). In 1605 a divorce was arranged and in 1616 Rich married the widowed Frances St Paul. Rich became 1st Earl of Warwick in 1617, a few months before he was buried with his ancestors at Felstead in Essex; his widow, who spent the sunset of her life in good works, followed him there 16 years later.

But her little daughter Mattathia is here with her father, and a further reminder of her is a brass with a Latin epitaph written by the rector John Chadwick; it tells how she was cut off before she was 2, and also of her mother's poignant anguish; it ends with the parson's pious wish "that I the writer, instead of thee, had been the subject of a funeral elegy".

Snelland. A peaceful farming village in the flat countryside between the Cliff and the Wolds, it came into Domesday Book, and was held by the Conqueror's chaplain and by one of the Percys; but its antiquity is not apparent and the church was rebuilt last century. It is a tiny building with a bell-turret hiding among trees.

Reasby Hall is a fine house bearing the date 1708 and the arms of the Earl of Scarbrough.

Somerby. It is a charming little village between Brigg and

Caistor, on the edge of the Wolds, and there are fine views from Somerby Top, under which it lies.

Set on a grassy platform of the steep hill is a tiny church of simple charm, with windows deep-set in walls of mottled grey stone and a 700-year-old unbuttressed tower just peeping above the nave. Inside are neat modern oak benches, and a tub-shaped Norman font. There is also a fine figure of a smiling knight within a recess, his 14th century armour shown in rich detail; headless angels support the pillows on which he rests, and at his feet are a lion and a little curled-up dog. Found near the chancel in the 1884 restoration, the figure is believed to represent a knight belonging to the Cumberworth family. One of the church's two old bells has an inscription proclaiming that Sir Thomas Cumberworth gave it in 1431.

A big pyramid monument of grey marble, with an urn at the top, is in memory of Edward Weston, a classical scholar who became Chief Secretary for Ireland; he was buried here in 1770.

Somerby Hall, built in the early 19th century, is the successor of a house built by Sir Edward Rossiter in 1660. In a field nearby is a pillar bearing an urn and erected in 1770 by Edward and Ann Weston.

Somerby. One of Grantham's little neighbours in secluded byways, it has a church with a plain, square 13th century tower standing a little aloof from the village. Chancel and nave and traceried font are all 14th century work, and the oldest feature is a splendid Norman chancel arch with billet and scallop and chevron moulding; on each side is an old rood-loft stairway.

In the sanctuary is the stone figure of a knight, believed to be one of the De Somerbys who lived here about 600 years ago. He is a fine warrior, and at his feet is a tiny saddled horse with its head held by a hooded groom. In ancient glass is another figure of a horse, and also the arms of the Threckinghams who held the manor 600 years ago.

Among the other memorials to be noted is a brass inscribed to Peregrine Bradshaw, 1669, a kinsman of John Bradshaw who, wearing his iron hat, passed sentence on King Charles I. A tablet extolls one of his contemporaries, Jane Brownlow, for her *solid serious temper, competent stature, and fair complection*, and another tablet recalls John Myers, who was rector here for 42 years last century. One of his 18th century predecessors was Dr William Stukeley, famous antiquary and friend of Isaac Newton. He was a strange character, and one of his contemporaries described him as a mixture of "simplicity, drollery, absurdity, ingenuity, superstition, and antiquarianism".

Somersby. This is the very heart of the Tennyson country. This tiny place in a hollow of a well-wooded patch of the Wolds, with

Warden Hill rising above it, was the birthplace of Alfred Tennyson.

Hereabouts are the "Woods that belt the grey hillside", and fine ash trees with buds black "in the front of March". Here are "the silent woody places by the home that gave me birth". Here are the little hills and dales and a hundred other landmarks which inspired some of Tennyson's finest poetry and were a joy to him, in recollection, all his life.

From the hills above the village there are fine views down the valley of the Lymn, and across the Marsh towards the sea. Tennyson's early work teems with charming description of this countryside he knew so well—of the hills and valleys, the boundless open spaces of Marsh and Fen with their great breadth of sky, and the flat Lincolnshire coast where "the great waters break and thin themselves far over sand marbled with moon and cloud".

Dr George Clayton Tennyson came here in 1808 as rector, and rector also of Bag Enderby, one of the "four hamlets" of which his poet son Alfred wrote in *In Memoriam*, telling how he listened to their Christmas bells, which "from hill to hill answer each other in the mist".

At Somersby 10 of Dr Tennyson's children were born, and the home in which they played and grew up is still here, facing the church; but it is no longer a rectory, and gone are many of the trees of which the poet wrote in his *Ode to Memory*:

> *The seven elms, the poplars four,*
> *That stand beside my father's door.*

On the lawn, however, still stands a copper beech which is perhaps the one he had in mind when he wrote:

> *Unwatched, the garden bough shall sway,*
> *The tender blossom flutter down,*
> *Unloved, that beech will gather brown,*
> *This maple burn itself away.*

The rambling old house is attractive outside with its pantiled roof, its oriel window and little balcony, and the unusual dining-room (with tall windows and gables) which Dr Tennyson added. Of the family's deep love for their home there are many glimpses in Tennyson's poems; *In Memoriam* tells how his friend Arthur Hallam would join them here at Somersby.

> *O joy to him in this retreat,*
> *Immantled in ambrosial dark,*
> *To drink the cooler air, and mark*
> *The landscape winking through the heat:*

> *O sound to rout the brood of cares,*
> *The sweep of scythe in morning dew,*
> *The gust that round the garden flew,*
> *And tumbled half the mellowing pears!*
>
> *O bliss when all in circle drawn*
> *About him, heart and ear were fed*
> *To hear him, as he lay and read*
> *The Tuscan poets on the lawn:*
>
> *Or in the all-golden afternoon*
> *A guest, or happy sister, sung,*
> *Or here she brought the harp and flung*
> *A ballad to the brightening moon:*

Halcyon years indeed for the poet and his brothers and sisters were those years at Somersby.

The family stayed on here for six years after their father's death, leaving in 1837; and *In Memoriam* tells of their sorrow at the departure:

> *We leave the well-beloved place*
> *Where first we gazed upon the sky;*
> *The roofs, that heard our earliest cry,*
> *Will shelter one of stranger race.*
>
> *I turn to go: my feet are set*
> *To leave the pleasant fields and farms;*
> *They mix in one another's arms*
> *To one pure image of regret.*

High above the road stands the squat little church where "the kneeling hamlet drains the Chalice of the grapes of God". In a grave marked by a plain tomb west of the tower Dr Tennyson was laid to rest in 1831, and in reminiscent mood one Christmas Eve when the family were no longer at Somersby, his son Alfred reflected:

> *Our father's dust is left alone*
> *And silent under other snows;*
> *There in due time the woodbine blows,*
> *The violet comes, but we are gone.*

Violets still grow and, in season, yield their fragrance on the churchyard bank.

The church, for the most part a 15th century building, is of interest chiefly for its association with the Tennysons. Alfred when a boy regularly tolled the bells in the low tower, patched with brick. Here is the plain old font at which he and his brothers and sisters were baptised; here is the small 17th century brass they must often have looked on, with its portrait of George Littlebury kneeling in prayer; here is Thomas Woolner's fine bronze bust of the poet, given to the church to mark the centenary of his birth. Each year in this church, or in one of its neighbours, a commemoration service is arranged by the rector in association with The Tennyson Society; the sermon deals with some aspects of Tennyson's life and work.

By the porch stands Somersby's rare treasure, a beautiful 15th century cross in perfect preservation and about 15 feet high. Its slender octagonal shaft has a gabled head with sculptures of the Crucifixion and the Madonna.

By the Old Rectory is a house with square towers and an embattled parapet which Vanbrugh is said to have built. In a wooded dell north of the village is Holy Well—a spring flowing from the sandstone rock.

At Somersby, on August 6, 1809, was born Alfred, fourth of the 12 children of the rector, George Clayton Tennyson, and of his wife, a daughter of Stephen Fytche, vicar of Louth.

Taught by their father, the children had the run of a fine library, but before he could read Alfred would go into the garden during a storm, and, spreading his arms, cry, "I hear a voice that's speaking in the wind", and derive a strange delight from the words, "far, far away". At 10 he mastered Pope's *Homer*, and wrote hundreds of lines in imitation, following with an epic of 6000 lines based on Scott. At 14 he wrote a play in blank verse which, published more than a century later, astonished everyone with its precocious power.

Alfred Tennyson grew up lusty and strong, beating all the villagers at throwing the crowbar, and carrying with ease a Shetland pony round the garden. Musical, he played the flute; a good actor, he portrayed comic Shakespearean rôles.

Although he was near-sighted, such was the power of his vision at close range that he once saw the moonlight reflected in the eye of a nightingale singing near; and so alert was his ear that he could detect the thin, shrill cry of a bat. Mimicry of its call brought an owl to his hand, to become a free member of the household; another of his pets was a snake. As his poems show, he was an exact botanist, and science was a passion with him always.

Entering Cambridge University at 19, he won the Chancellor's medal for English poetry with his *Timbuctoo*; and published his *Poems*, chiefly Lyrical, sounding a new and lovely note in English verse. It was at Cambridge that he met Arthur Hallam, who, outstanding in a remarkable group of brilliant young men, most affected his career. With Hallam he visited Spain and the Rhine, and often Hallam, engaged to Emily Tennyson, was a visitor to Somersby. Halcyon days they were.

His father dying in 1831, Alfred had to leave Cambridge to

become head of the family, which was allowed by the new incumbent to retain the rectory till 1837. The family capital was lost in an unsuccessful attempt to finance machine-made art furniture, and Tennyson's proposed marriage to Emily Sellwood was deferred.

In that year was published a volume which, including his *Lady of Shalott, Lotos-Eaters, Oenone, Dream of Fair Women, Morte d'Arthur*, and *Locksley Hall*, was favourably received by the discerning, but ferociously attacked by Lockhart and Christopher North. So the sensitive poet, once contemplating emigration, was silent for 10 years. During that time Hallam died, and from the poet's brooding sorrow sprang *The Two Voices, Break, break, break, Ulysses*, and *In Memoriam*; and *Ulysses*, being read to Sir Robert Peel by Monckton Milnes, brought its author a Civil List pension of £200 at 34.

From the poem celebrating his dead friend Tennyson proceeded to the Laureateship, and in 1850, with income at last assured, he married. Speaking of his wife in after life he said, "The peace of God came into my life before the altar when I wedded her." A few years later he bought his Isle of Wight home from the profits of *Maud*; later he built his Surrey house at Blackdown, changing its name, Black Horse Copse, to Aldworth in memory of a Berkshire village with which his wife had family associations.

At intervals appeared successive sections of the *Idylls of the King*, the Crimean poems, the delightful dialect pieces, *Enoch Arden*, and other compositions everywhere famous. From time to time his genius flared again into brilliance; he was 70 when he wrote *The Revenge*, the finest sea-battle ballad in the language, 79 when the second part of *Locksley Hall* appeared, and 80 when he wrote *Crossing the Bar*.

The end came at Aldworth on August 6, 1892, with the moonlight streaming over the bed where he lay clasping an open volume of Shakespeare. Five days later he was laid to rest in the Abbey, with due pomp and noble ceremony.

No poet was more lauded than Tennyson during the latter half of his life; few have been more criticised after death. But, in spite of some superficiality and complacence, and occasional absurdities, he remains an acknowledged master of lovely jewelled diction and heart-searching lyrics. Like Homer, he nodded at times, but he left us a treasury of purest gold.

Sotby. Here, on the western slope of the Wolds, a vassal of the Bishop of Bayeux held land when Domesday Book was written, and the tiny church has come down from those early times, a fine Norman relic being the massive chancel arch with heavy roll mouldings. The chancel was rebuilt in 1857 in 13th century style, but it still has its old double piscina and a founder's tomb.

South Carlton. A lane dips sharply down from the Cliff road north of Lincoln and winds round past its cottages and haystacks and church. Near the church are one or two thatched cottages, and next-door to it is the manor house, a gabled stone house with dormer windows built in the time of Queen Anne and now the home of Lord and Lady Monson.

The 13th century church was much restored in Victorian times, but its pointed arcades and pinnacled tower still display their antiquity, and the chancel has stalls and a screen 500 years old. The screen has panels ornamented with foliage, and four coloured shields over the central arch with sun and moon faces in its spandrels; the five stalls have finely-traceried ends, and carvings of angels and poppyheads with little smiling women back to back.

The chapel on the north side of the chancel is the burial-place of the Monson family, who lived here before they went to neighbouring Burton Hall from where they have since moved back to South Carlton. It has a rich modern exterior in Tudor style, with a canopied niche on each side of a door decorated with elaborate ironwork (it is studded with 34 roses). Over the door is the Monson motto (in French), Ready for my Country, and their arms supported by rampant lion and griffin; above this is a richly-mullioned window with an angel on either side. On a canopied tomb within the chapel lie the alabaster figures of Sir John Monson and his wife; he is clad in Elizabethan armour, and kneeling round the tomb are four sons (also in armour, and some headless), and seven daughters with delicate lacework on their veils.

Sir John Monson, High Sheriff of Lincoln and descendant of one of Henry V's followers, was father of Sir Thomas and Sir William Monson. Sir Thomas, who also rests in this church, was master falconer to James I and afterwards Keeper of the Armoury at the Tower, but was suspected of a share in the murder of Sir Thomas Overbury and was there imprisoned for a time until his innocence was established. His brother, Admiral William Monson, a great seaman in those days of great seamen, was knighted for gallantry at the Siege of Cadiz in 1597, but lost his command when he also became implicated in the Overbury murder.

Sir William's son, Viscount Monson, grandson of the man whose monument is here at South Carlton, was one of the many men on whom Charles II wreaked vengeance for the share in his father's punishment. He was imprisoned for life, and every year, on the anniversary of Charles I's sentence, was drawn on a sledge from the Tower to Tyburn and back, a rope about his neck.

South Cockerington. The Monks' Dike flows through this charming little village, and the church hides in tall trees near the Hall. The church is chiefly 14th and 15th century work, and to the earlier period belong the greenstone tower (patched with brick and having a bell perhaps 700 years old), two windows in the south wall of the chancel, and the font carved with quatrefoils and shields. The nave has windows from early Tudor days.

Inside the north door is a holy water stoup, and engraved on the walls inside are six or seven consecration crosses, another being on a buttress outside. The chancel keeps its old priest's doorway (now blocked), a piscina, and a recess with a projecting bracket. Across the wide chancel arch is a fine 15th century oak screen enriched with cinquefoiled arches and delicate tracery; it has been restored and given a modern cornice (with lacy cresting) in place of the old vaulting. At the west end of the church are four tiny old bench-ends of oak with poppyheads and arm-rests.

By the screen is the splendid alabaster tomb of an old knight so virtuous (we read) that a story and not an epitaph would be needed to tell of him. He is the "thrice noble" Sir Adrian Scrope, who died in 1623 and is here exquisitely sculptured in stone. He is in armour, with his helmet behind him and his mailed glove under his knee, and looks rather severe but very life-like as he reclines on his arm. Below are two daughters in mantles and flowing headdress, and a group of six sons, some in armour and some in robes; a babe lies by the knee of the eldest son (who is turning the pages of a book), and another child lies on a cushion behind one of the daughters. The coat-of-arms by the tomb came from the neighbouring Hall, the old home of Sir Adrian and his descendants which was pulled down in 1921 in favour of a smaller house.

The almshouses near the church were founded by Sir Adrian's eldest son Gervase, who fought for the king at Edgehill and received 16 wounds. Left for dead on the field, Sir Gervase was carried off by his own son and revived by the famous Dr William Harvey, who was with the Royalist army. His grandson, Sir Carr Scrope, born here in 1649, became known as a satirical poet at the court of Charles II, and a distant kinsman was the Adrian Scrope who signed the death warrant of Charles I.

South Elkington. It is a charming little neighbour of Louth, and lovely is the road between them, running by the beautiful park with a lake filled by a stream flowing to the Lud. In the park is the fine 19th century Hall in the Italian style, and on the edge of it is the church, hiding in trees and reached by a little lane.

The church has been rebuilt but has kept its 15th century tower (with a modern arch to the nave) and mediaeval font carved with shields and quatrefoils. The modern stone reredos has a scene of the Last Supper, showing Our Lord offering the cup to the kneeling disciples, with Judas grasping his bag, his head turned aside as if deep in thought.

On the site of an Anglo-Saxon burial-ground here nearly 100 burial urns have been unearthed in recent times.

South Ferriby. Clinging to the western edge of the Wolds, it is indeed fortunate in its setting. Behind the village tree-clad slopes rise like ramparts; before it the flat Read's Island, with its single farmhouse, stretches for more than a mile in the broad estuary of the Humber; and across the river are the Yorkshire hills. Read's Island, now permanent pasture on a long stretch of sandbank where wild sea-birds used to breed, has been formed partly by the Humber washing land away near Ferriby Hall, rebuilt about 1800.

On the steep hillside the church finds a perch from which to look over the red roofs and chimney-pots to a magnificent view beyond. On account of its site, the church has been singularly transformed. Its aisles have gone, and it has been given a new chancel which faces south instead of east (the nave also running now north to south). Of the old chancel, which for a time became an organ chamber, there remain only the 13th century pillars, supporting a modern arch in what seems to be the "north" wall of the nave, but according to the compass is an east wall. A brick tower has been built on this side of the church.

In the outer walls are parts of mediaeval floorstones, and over the porch is the church's oldest possession—a Norman tympanum showing St Nicholas holding his staff and blessing all who come this way. A lancet window frames a figure of St George in golden armour.

A mile west is the hamlet of Ferriby Sluice, where the old River Ancholme, the New River, and the Weir Dike fall into the Humber.

South Hykeham. Unlike its neighbour and namesake it has so far escaped the growing tentacles of Lincoln city and is a peaceful village still, with a few pleasant cottages looking across green fields, and a churchyard shaded by tall elms and chestnuts. The small church with three slender lancets lighting its apsidal chancel has been restored, but the tower and spire still soar up with all the dignity bestowed on them by their 14th century builders.

South Kelsey. A trim village of many twists and turns, it has a 650-year-old church tower of richly-tinted ironstone. The rest of the church (St Mary's) was rebuilt in 1795, and in it were used the materials of the ruined church of St Nicholas. It has recently been restored and panelled inside in oak.

It has a plain old font and two notable monuments. The earliest is a fine stone figure of a cross-legged knight, wearing chain-mail and surcoat and with his feet on a lion; it may represent Robert Hansard, one of Edward I's doughty warriors. The other memorial is a

15th century brass with almost life-sized portraits of Sir Richard Hansard and his wife; the knight is portrayed in full armour, with his feet on a lion, and his wife with mitred headdress and a dog with a belled collar at her feet.

The old Hall where the Hansards lived for centuries stood to the south of the village, and fragments of it can still be seen by the 17th century farmhouse on its site: a stone arch of the courtyard entrance, and one of the octagonal turrets of the house. The wide moat, overhung with trees, still holds water.

At Winghale, within a mile of the Old River Ancholme, a small priory was founded by Roger Poictevin as a cell of the Benedictine Abbey of Sées in Normandy.

South Kyme. It lies off the beaten track, a quiet Fen village with two bridges across the River Slea, called hereabouts the Kyme Eau as it flows through on its way to the Witham. South Kyme has known great days, and still has reminders of three great families who were its lords from the 12th century till Henry VIII's day—Kyme Umfraville, and Tailboys.

Philip de Kyme, Sheriff of Lincolnshire in the 12th century, founded here a priory for Austin canons, and a fragment of its fine cross-shaped church still survives. In the 13th century Lucy de Kyme, heiress of the manor, married the Norman knight Robert de Umfraville, and South Kyme Tower built by Sir Gilbert de Umfraville in the 14th century still stands. After the Umfravilles the Tailboys (descendants of another of William the Conqueror's henchmen) were lords of the manor, and the church has a brass inscription to the last of them, Gylbert Tailboys, who died in 1530.

The grey square tower, standing out boldly in this flat countryside, is ashlar-faced with small loophole windows, and has a room on the first floor from which the way opened to the rest of the tower, which was pulled down early in the 18th century; it is called the Chequer Chamber, its floor being of the pebbles known locally as chequers. The rooms above this have lost their floors and ceilings, but the chamber below it has its old groined roof with the arms of Umfraville carved on it.

Of the Augustinian priory that stood close by all that remains is in the church—a lofty, towerless building with the tower on one hand and a red-brick tower windmill on the other. This legacy of the past, consisting of the porch, south aisle, and part of the nave of the original church, is chiefly 14th century work, altered and partly rebuilt in the early years of last century. The south windows have beautiful flowing tracery, and between two of them is a fine gabled buttress with a niche.

The great porch has a fine entrance arch on clustered shafts, under a niche with a worn sculpture of the Coronation of the Virgin. The doorway within is a magnificent example of Norman work, with shafts supporting an arch of rich mouldings (including zigzag and diamond pattern) under a hood ending in serpents' heads. A battered stoup and a mediaeval floorstone are in the porch, and another old floorstone lies in the church, by the 15th century font adorned with shields. Older than all else here are fragments of stone in the north wall of the chancel, with knotwork and trumpet-spiral ornament carved by Saxon hands in the 7th–8th century AD.

The old brass inscription to Gylbert Tailboys, Lord of Kyme, who died in 1530, is on a tomb adorned with quatrefoils, and on a wall a stone tablet has been set up in his memory by James Getting of Ross county, a descendant of the Durham Tailboys; on it are two coats-of-arms and the motto *Taille bois*.

South Ormsby. Charmingly set on a steep and beautifully-wooded slope of the Wolds, this pretty village with its park lake is most attractive.

The massive 15th century tower of the village church rises above the trees on the edge of the broad acres of Ormsby Hall, an 18th century house with creepered walls of mellowed brick and a pillared portico. The church was restored last century, but much of it is old. The nave has a Transitional-Norman arcade built with stones of various tints; the chancel arch is 13th century; and the chancel and chapel 14th. The font, decked with carved angels was the gift in the 15th century of Ralph Bolle and his wife, whose names are on its base. At the west end of the south aisle is a doorway with a Norman head and hood; it was brought here from the ruined church of Calceby, a mile away.

Filling a window in the chapel are many roundels and figures of 17th century glass, thought to be of Flemish craftsmanship.

Two 15th century brasses are in the chapel. One shows a lady with netted hair and a little belled dog sitting on the folds of her mantle; the other portrays William and Agnes Skypwyth under beautiful canopies, with three children.

One of the church's 17th century rectors was the parson-poet Samuel Wesley, father of immortal John Wesley.

Between the village and Walmsgate is the hamlet of Ketsby, which has a water-mill worked by an arm of the Withern Eau.

South Somercotes. A pleasant place in a countryside of green flats and dykes, it is 2 miles from the sea but has a graceful 15th century spire seen from afar by sailors. With the exception of that of Louth, it is the only spire in Marshland and has earned for the church the name of Queen of the Marsh.

The low tower was built at the close of the 13th century, but it was not until late in the 15th that it was given its lovely doorway

344

with a square hood and spandrels with carved angels. The ring of three mediaeval bells (two of them 1423) is another notable feature of this steeple; they came from an unknown Lincolnshire foundry and are famous for their lettering, enriched with foliage and grotesques. A tall ladder, of more than 30 rungs, climbs to the belfry.

The chancel is chiefly 15th century work, but it has a blocked 13th century doorway in which a quaint little window is set. The round pillars and moulded capitals of the nave arcades have stood since the close of the Norman period, and on them the 15th century builders set octagonal capitals and pointed arches. Five centuries old, too, are the traceried screen and the font with Passion emblems on its eight sides and an old pointed cover.

South Willingham. This small Wold village has some delightful houses including two beautifully-thatched white cottages.

The simple little church was much rebuilt in 1838, but it has kept its 15th century tower, and has three fine mediaeval windows in the chancel, each a triple lancet with a quatrefoil pierced in the head. An old peephole is by the modern chancel arch, and there is a fine mediaeval font with a square bowl adorned by quatrefoils and resting on a cluster of shafts. The 15th century oak screen with traceried bays has lost a little of its old enrichment, but has been given a new vaulted canopy. There is a modern wood roof and new oak pews. An unusual feature is the tiny clock set on the tower battlements.

South Witham. Its name comes from the river which rises just across the Rutland border and here flows northward on its 70-mile journey to the Wash, gathering many little streams from Leicestershire on its way. To the west, between the source of the river and this straggling village, is the spot where Leicestershire, Rutland, and Lincolnshire all meet; to the east is Ermine Street.

The little church has seen much change, and its chancel was built in 1930 when the church was restored. The nave has a 13th century double bellcot with lancet arcading, and an arcade with round arches built when the Norman style was changing to Early English. The 600-year-old doorway is adorned with worn heads and ballflower ornament, and the sunk font has unusual fleur-de-lys. The oldest monument is an ancient coffin stone with an ornate cross and a quaint head of a bearded man.

The preceptory of the Knights Templars stood near to the old course of the River Witham and was excavated in 1966–67. It revealed the total plan of a manor house of the Knights Templars of the 12th century including the great hall, chapel, barns, workshops, kitchens, and a mill. The date of occupation was between AD 1164 and 1308.

345

Spalding. The last of the towns on the River Welland before it enters the Wash, it is a splendid centre for visiting the grand old churches for which the district of Holland is famed. It is also the most important town in the Lincolnshire Fens, which spread round it in almost unbroken flatness for 10 miles or more in every direction —the most fertile area in England.

Spalding is justly renowned as a centre of agriculture, today concerned chiefly with sugar beet and potatoes, and, of course, with the cultivation of bulbs. In the first months of the year flowers blossom here under a vast expanse of glass, and when spring makes its bow the fields around are carpeted with the glory of daffodils, tulips, narcissi, and hyacinths—a brilliant display of colour which attracts countless visitors. Many millions of blooms go by rail here to all parts of the country; as many as 25,000 tons have been sent away in a year. Truly, flower-growing is a great industry here; and, in addition, sugar beet grown on thousands of acres finds its way to the Spalding factory. Much agricultural machinery goes out from Spalding works.

Running through the middle of the town, with a road on either side, the Welland is an attractive feature of Spalding. Fine houses line the banks and the river in a deep, tree-lined tidal channel is reminiscent of Holland. Spalding was named in the Crowland foundation charter, and is said to have had a wooden chapel which, together with the Welland fisheries, was given to that abbey in the 9th century. In the middle of the 11th century Spalding Priory was founded by Thorold of Buckenhale (brother of Godiva). At first it served as a cell of Crowland Abbey, but after the Conquest it was enriched and transferred to the Abbey of Angers by Ivo Taillebois, with discord ensuing between Crowland and Spalding until well into the 14th century. Before that century closed, however, the priory had gained its independence from Angers, and so much did it prosper that at the Dissolution it was, after Crowland, the richest house in the country. Among the visitors entertained at the priory were Edward I, Edward II, John of Gaunt and his friend Geoffrey Chaucer.

Ivo Taillebois, a native of Angers, was a nephew of the Conqueror and carried his standard at Hastings. After marrying Thorold's niece and heiress he lived at Spalding Castle, which stood to the north of the town, between the river and Pinchbeck Street. The castle has completely vanished, and only a few fragments remain that are traditionally associated with the priory, which stood on the left bank of the river. One fragment is a stone turret projecting from an old brick building in the quaintly-named Hole-in-the-Wall Passage running from the south side of the marketplace; and in Priory Road (almost opposite the end of Hole-in-the-Wall) is a block of dwellings of fine old brick with stone buttresses and doorways, thought to have been the dormitory. At the corner of the Sheep Market (east of the marketplace) is a small stone building with a modern square room built above the original vaulted octagon. It is known locally by the quaint name of Prior's Oven and is said to be mediaeval.

West of the town, by the road to Bourne, is Monk's Hall Farm, with 16th and 17th century windows. Beyond the handsome 19th century church at Fulney (on the eastern outskirts) two roads come to the highway—one running south to the old Fulney Farm House, now offices of the Land Settlement Scheme, but retaining a vaulted chamber which was probably part of the priory dairy; and the other going north to the ruined early 14th century Wykeham Chapel built by Prior Hatfield. Once attached to a grange, it is a picturesque roofless oblong (43 feet long) with some of the tracery still left in its enormous windows, and with heavy buttresses dividing its three bays.

Chief among the many bridges spanning the river at Spalding is High Bridge (rebuilt 1838), not far from the marketplace. To cross it is to step from the busy, workaday part of the town to all that is loveliest in it; for within a triangle of roads on the eastern side of the river (Church Gate, Church Street, and Love Lane) are some of the old houses which invest this town with so much grace and charm. Here also is the parish church, one of the most interesting in the county.

At the corner of Church Gate and Church Street stands the old White Horse Inn, white-walled and thatched, picturesque and inviting. On one side of Church Street is the church, set back in a churchyard shaded by grand old limes, sycamores, and ash trees. On the other side is a lovely old house with a fine wisteria draping its mellowed walls; and next to this are Sir John Gamlyn's almshouses (rebuilt in 1844) with stone doorways, mullioned windows, and oriels looking out on the serenity of a flower-bordered lawn.

Facing Church Gate (on the river bank) is Ayscoughfee Hall, a grand old mansion of mellowed brick and stone, built originally in 1420 but modernised, and now belonging to the town; it has a long, galleried porch, and two-storied bay windows surmounted by Dutch gables. A short avenue of 14 splendid horse-chestnuts by the side of the Hall leads from Church Gate to the gardens—and also to the churchyard, for Hall and church are close neighbours, and are linked by a church walk.

The Hall gardens have come to perfection through long centuries of tending, and they are a never-failing source of enjoyment for all the townsfolk and visitors. Here are flowerbeds and lawns and shaded walks; here are tennis courts, bowling greens, aviaries, and a small aquarium; here, too, is a fine yew tunnel, and beautifully trimmed yew hedges which are seen at their best round the big lily pool with its sloping bank of lawn. At one end of the pool is the town's war memorial—a colonnaded stone shelter with the names on stone tablets. At the other end, an old ivied brick wall with beautiful iron gates is the foreground of a lovely view of the church's tower and spire.

In the 18th century Ayscoughfee Hall was the home of that singularly versatile lawyer Maurice Johnson, who in 1710 founded the Gentlemen's Society of Spalding, a social club which cultivated correspondence on scientific and literary subjects, and counted among its members such distinguished men as Sir Isaac Newton, Alexander Pope, Joseph Addison, Sir Hans Sloane, and Richard Bentley, who, before he became Master of Trinity College, Cambridge, was master of Spalding Grammar School (which moved to its site in Priory Road in 1881). Maurice Johnson, who was a keen botanist and a friend of Linnaeus, also studied and collected coins, medals, seals, armour, stained glass, and prints. He was one of the founders of the Society of Antiquaries in 1717, and he was its first librarian. The Spalding Gentlemen's Society still exists, its hall, library, and interesting little museum of antiquities now being housed in a building in Broad Street. Its fine collection of birds, from all parts of the world, is now displayed in Ayscoughfee Hall.

The crowning glory of Spalding is the old church of St Mary and St Nicholas. It is impressive both outside and in, and exceptional in its plan, for the nave has double aisles extending to the width of the transepts and making the church as wide as it is long. The tower and spire rise at the south-west corner, filling the angle made by the long and short south aisles; and there is a big chapel projecting from the south transept and occupying part of its eastern aisle.

The church dates from 1284, and at first was cruciform; but the shape was obscured by the later addition of the outer south aisle, porch, and chapel in the 14th century, and by the outer north aisle and porch in the 15th century. A lovely feature of the exterior is this north porch, with its roof of charming fan-tracery supporting an upper room reached by a winding stair. The entrance arch is enriched with pierced tracery, and the inner doorway has a richly-moulded trefoiled arch adorned with quaint figures of men, and with tiny flowers and grotesques carved on its hood. In this doorway hangs a fine old door with delicate tracery, and above, in three canopied niches, are statues of St Mary with a pot of lilies at her feet, Our Lord seated and crowned, and St Nicholas with a ship and staff.

The tower has lancets in two of its stages, buttresses climbing to the battlements, and elegant pinnacles from which flying buttresses spring to a spire probably added early in the 15th century. Spire, buttresses, and pinnacles are all crocketed, and the beauty of the spire is further enhanced by its tiers of canopied windows. Other pleasing features of the exterior are the south doorway (with a vaulted niche and angel bracket above it) and the eastern gable of the clerestoried nave, with two tall pinnacles and charming little old sanctus bellcot. Below the bellcot is a five-light window, partly hidden outside by the chancel roof but seen complete above the chancel arch within the church, where it shines with coloured glass.

The windows are well worth studying. The chancel has widely-splayed lancets (restored), and several 14th century windows; one of them with fine leaf tracery is unglazed, and looks into the north aisle added to the chancel in Sir Gilbert Scott's costly restoration. The east windows of the transepts have elegant tracery, and the great windows of the south chapel have tracery which seems a curious mixture of two styles, with upright bars and quatrefoils.

The lofty nave was given its huge seven-light west window in the 15th century, and at the same time the pillars of its soaring arcades were heightened, though they still have their original capitals. The big array of arches in the church is almost bewildering, especially when seen from the south door. Except for one flattened arch, which makes a diagonal link between two pillars of the north aisles, all of them are pointed.

Crowning the nave is a fine hammerbeam roof, adorned with 28 wooden angels and resting on stone heads and angels. The vaulted chancel screen is chiefly modern work. with a few fragments of the 15th century. The fine brass candelabrum in the chancel is 18th century, and there is a fine old chest with a carved front. At the west end is an old stone coffin from the vanished priory, and lying in a recess in the north transept is a tapering coffin-lid. (Three more coffin-lids with worn carving are upright in the old brick wall of the churchyard, by the Church Street entrance.)

The big south chapel, dedicated more than six centuries ago to St Mary and St Thomas Becket, was used for a time as a school, and was shut off from the church till the school withdrew in 1874. Now it is neatly furnished with traceried oak benches, panelling, rails, and screen. The oak altar is adorned with angels, and the oak reredos is a triptych with figures of St Hugh, St Mary, Our Lord, St Nicholas, and a bishop.

Spilsby. This pleasant hillside town at the southern end of the Wolds and looking afar over marsh and fen, has had a market since the 14th century, and at one end of its marketplace stands a graceful cross with a restored shaft and lantern head raised high on the 600-year-old steps and base-stone. At the other end of the market-place, where the crowd on market day is thickest, is a dignified bronze statue of Spilsby's most famous son—the intrepid Sir John

Franklin, who was born in a house on the north side of the central square of this marketplace. High on his pedestal stands the great explorer, holding his telescope in one hand and resting the other on an anchor; and the inscription below states simply that he was the Discoverer of the North-West Passage and died in the Arctic regions, June 1847. Other buildings worthy of notice in the marketplace are the White Hart and the former Town Hall dated 1764. The Sessions House, with its fluted Doric portico, stands west of the church and was built in 1824.

The charter for Spilsby's market was obtained by Sir William de Willoughby (near Alford), whose marriage with Alice, heiress of Baron Bek of Eresby, founded the great family of Willoughby d' Eresby. Many distinguished members of this family were buried in Spilsby Church, because for many centuries their home was Eresby Hall, which stood about a mile south of the town. With the union of the Willoughby de Eresbys and the Berties, during Henry VIII's reign, Grimsthorpe Castle in the south of the county succeeded Eresby Hall as the chief family home, and Edenham Church in due course succeeded Spilsby Church as the family's mausoleum. Eresby Hall was burned down in 1769, and all that remains of it is a gate-pier surmounted by an urn at the end of a fine avenue, and a farm-house built out of the ruins.

Spilsby Church has lost much of its old aspect; apart from its 15th century tower of green sandstone, crowned by a rather ungainly parapet with eight great pinnacles, the exterior walls were encased in Ancaster stone in 1879, when a new south aisle was added. In the curious transformation that took place in the 14th century, the south aisle became the nave, and the chapel of the Holy Trinity at its east end became the chancel, leaving the original nave to serve as an aisle, and the original chancel a repository for the Willoughby monuments. The two 14th century arcades still stand, and so do the two 14th century bays between the chapel and chancel. On the canopied oak pulpit are figures of the Four Evangelists and St James (the patron saint).

The Willoughby Chapel has been almost rebuilt, and its monuments restored. At its west end, almost filling the old chancel arch, is a heavy stone screen adorned with much heraldry and forming an extraordinary monument to Richard Bertie (died 1582) and his wife Katherine, Baroness Willoughby d'Eresby, whose first husband was Charles Brandon, Duke of Suffolk.

In arched recesses are busts of Richard and Katherine, dwarfed by weird figures of their heraldic supporters—a hermit with his staff, a Saracen crowned, and a wild man covered with leaves.

Richard Bertie and Katherine were staunch upholders of the Reformation, and often entertained Latimer at Grimsthorpe Castle. During their flight abroad from the Marian persecution a son was born to them who was destined to win great renown as soldier and diplomat. This was Peregrine Bertie, 12th Lord Willoughby de Eresby, who was sent by Elizabeth I on two delicate missions to Denmark, and later sent fighting against the Spaniards in the Netherlands. He was with Sir Philip Sidney when the poet received his death-wound at Zutphen, and, himself knighted on the field for valour, became commander of our forces in the Low Countries. With scanty forces and a few ships he prevented the Duke of Parma's fleet and army from joining the Armada, and later led 4000 men to the succour of Henry of Navarre at Dieppe.

Worn out with toil and tribulation in his country's service, he finally returned to England in 1596, and a year or so later was appointed Governor of Berwick. He died there in 1601, and was brought here for burial among his ancestors. His monument shows him as a proud upright figure in armour with helmet and gauntlets at his feet. Below him reclines the strangely-hooded figure of his only daughter, Catharine Lady Watson, with the babe who cost her her life lying in a cradle at her feet. She was the last of the Willoughbys to be buried here.

The oldest of the monuments of this distinguished family is the striking stone tomb of John, 2nd Baron Willoughby d'Eresby, who died in 1349, three years after he had fought at Crecy. He it was who founded the Trinity Chapel here. He is shown as a cross-legged knight in hauberk and surcoat, with his wife Joan beside him in a flowing mantle and tight-fitting dress. Their tomb is enriched with panels of quatrefoils, borders of flowers, and twin-pinnacles with robed figures in dainty niches.

A fine alabaster figure of their son John, the 3rd Baron, who fought at Poitiers and died in 1372, is set on a stone tomb with a cornice adorned by canopied figures of monks holding scrolls, staves, and rosaries. John wears armour with rich trappings and his head rests on a helmet; at his feet is a smiling lion.

Robert, the 4th Baron, who died in the time of Richard II, is shown with his third wife, Elizabeth Neville—alabaster figures on an alabaster tomb. In full armour he lies, with his head resting on a helmet with the Willoughby crest and his feet on a haughty-looking lion. His lady is richly gowned, and her head rests on cushions supported by figures of monks; at her feet are three charming little dogs. Robert's second wife, Margaret Zouch, is commemorated by a fine brass showing her in a richly-jewelled headdress and a rich gown with many buttons; two dogs with belled collars are at her feet.

A splendid 15th century brass with triple canopy (some of its pinnacle-work gone) has the portraits of the 5th Baron, William, and his wife Lucy—the knight richly armoured, and the lady in a high gown with full drapery.

At the west end of the church are three tablets keeping in remembrance three Franklin brothers, all born in Spilsby—Major James Franklin, who made the first military survey of India; Sir Willingham, a judge in Madras; and Sir John, who lies where no man knows. Born at Spilsby in 1786, John Franklin joined the Navy at 14, sailed with his cousin Matthew Flinders to survey the coasts of Australia, and when 19 fought at Trafalgar. At 32 he began his unprecedented Arctic career, outstanding in which were two tremendous journeys in unknown Northern America, one lasting three years and the other nearly five. His memorial (set here by his widow) has his profile in relief and tells of his death in the Arctic Seas while in command of the Expedition which first discovered the North-West Passage, and pays tribute to him and his brave companions with these fine words:

They forged the last link with their lives.

A brass inscription tells of the gentle virtues and many gifts of Sir John Franklin's first wife, Eleanor Anne Porden, who *smitten by mortal illness yet speeded her husband on his Second Arctic Expedition, and surviving his departure only six days, died 1825*. She was a valiant soul, and so, too, was the explorer's second wife, Jane Lady Franklin, who won world-wide admiration by her unswerving devotion to his memory. For years she maintained the search for the lost expedition, equipping several ships for the task at her own expense.

Spital. It has the distinction of being the only place on a very long stretch of the Ermine Street north of Lincoln, near its crossing with the road from Gainsborough to Louth. A farmhouse here was once a well-known coaching inn, and there is a medicinal spring which gave Spital a little fame in days gone by.

The hamlet's curious name is a link with a hospital which had its origin in an older hermitage founded here as a refuge for travellers along this lonely Roman road. The hermitage was absorbed into the hospital through the beneficence of Thomas de Aston, Canon of Lincoln in the 14th century, whose name still survives in that of the de Aston school at Market Rasen, founded out of the funds of this hospital charity. The grammar school at Lincoln also benefits from the charity.

Until late in the 17th century the quarter sessions for the Kirton division of Lindsey were held at Spital, and were for many years accommodated in the old chapel of the hermitage, dedicated to St Edmund. The hospital and chapel fell into decay in the time of Elizabeth (who had taken possession of the property) and were pulled down by Sir William Wray. A new sessions house built some years later still survives in a barn, which has on it two Latin inscriptions

telling of its days as a court house. On one side is *1619, Fiat Justitia*;
the other inscription, translated, runs:

> This court does right
> Loves Peace,
> Preserves the Laws,
> Detects the wrong,
> Rewards the righteous cause.

The chapel was rebuilt in 1661 by Dr Mapletoft, who helped to
put the charity on a sound basis, and his plain little building still
stands, bearing a Latin inscription with the story of the old hospital
and chapel. This is a translation:

> I was in 1398
> I was not in 1594   The House of God
> I am in 1616   and of the poor
> He who destroys this temple
> May God destroy him.

The date 1616 was a mistake; it should have been 1661.

Springthorpe. The traffic on the Gainsborough road 1 mile
away does not disturb the serenity of this pleasant village among
the fields and woods near the source of the little River Till.

Much restored last century, the church has the distinction of being
the only one in the land dedicated to both St George and St
Laurence, and is one of a group possessing a tower built about the
time of the Conquest, either by Saxons or early Normans. Severely
plain and unbuttressed, the tower has some herringbone masonry,
and in its built-up west doorway is set one of the old belfry windows,
the belfry having new ones. The handsome Norman doorway within
the porch has two shafts at each side, fluted capitals, and carving of
zigzag and chequer work.

From the 13th century come the nave arcade, a window in the
aisle, and the font bowl. Among the old relics are a chest and a cupboard, both 300 years old. The pulpit and the low screen with dainty
iron gates are modern.

In 1814 this church was the scene of a curious tragedy. It was on
Shrove Tuesday. A village girl named Mary Hill was ringing a bell
when the rope coiled round her arm and carried her up to the belfry
floor. In falling she struck the foot of the font and was instantly
killed. The tattered paper garland of rosettes in the form of a
crown hanging near the organ is her memorial.

These funeral garlands found at times in our churches are of
interest because they remind us of Shakespeare's Ophelia. The

garlands are the "crants" which were allowed at Ophelia's funeral, greatly to the indignation of the churlish priest upon whom Laertes poured his wrath with immortal words of scorn.

Stainby. A secluded village by the Leicestershire border, it looks up to a handsome tower and spire and to a company of noble beeches close at hand. The church was almost entirely rebuilt last century, but the nave still has an arcade with two slightly pointed arches built when the Norman style was waning, the central pillar having fine foliage on its capital and a bearded head above. Stained glass makes the interior dim and sombre, and it is remarkable only for the wealth of carving bestowed on it by W. A. H. Thorold, who ministered here from 1877 to the early years of this century.

All the woodwork was carved by this rector-craftsman—the chancel screen and its rood, the organ screen, traceried stalls and prayer-desk, the reredos with its canopied figures, the altar-table with painted panels of saints under traceried canopies, and the pulpit with more panels of saints and a figure of St Peter.

But the crowning effort of this gifted amateur was the cover of the modern font with its symbols of the Evangelists. This cover is 12 feet high and is adorned with carvings of the Baptism in Jordan, Christ blessing the Children, the Prodigal Son, and the Ark. An Apostle stands at each corner under a crocketed canopy, each with a musical angel above, and higher still soars the spire, an angel poised on the summit and Christ with the lamb below.

It is exceedingly rich adornment for a small village church, and it was all a labour of love. More of this devoted rector's work is in the neighbouring church of Gunby, 1 mile away, a rebuilt church which still has its pinnacled 15th century tower, and the 6-foot shaft of an old churchyard cross.

At the south-east end of the village, behind a farmyard, is an earthwork, apparently a small motte; it has been mutilated by gravel diggers.

Stainfield. Narrow winding lanes lead to this small place, set by a tributary of the Witham in a wooded patch of the county between the Cliff and the Wolds. It has no village street, its houses are scattered, and the Hall has a little church for company.

Once there was a small priory here for Benedictine nuns. Founded by Henry Percy in the 12th century, it was granted at the Dissolution to Sir Robert Tyrwhit, who built on its site a house which was destroyed by fire in the 18th century; a pillar of its old gateway stands near the Hall.

There is a story that the church was designed by Sir Christopher Wren and that the great architect stayed at the old house. The old church was rebuilt in 1711. It has a doorway such as a house might have, and the altar is at the west end instead of at the east. There is Georgian woodwork enclosing the Ten Commandments, the Lord's Prayer, and the Creed, all worked in cross-stitch; and there are three tattered banners embroidered by the Tyrwhit ladies. By the banners are gloves of mail, a sword, and a helmet with a wild man for crest.

Stainton-by-Langworth. A little village near the Roman road from Lincoln to Wragby, and on a gentle hill above the Langworth River, it has the stump of its old preaching cross in a garden and a grey church by a farmyard. Through neglect the church fell down at the end of the 18th century and was rebuilt. At the beginning of this century it was again neglected, but twice in our time it has been restored and now all is spick-and-span once more in this neatly built Georgian church with wooden gallery.

Tokens of its antiquity are the 14th century piscina and sedilia with trefoiled arches; a mediaeval bell in the little tower bearing a cross and the inscription: *Jesus be our Spede*; and the plain bowl of a 14th century font found buried in the church and now resting on the base of a 12th century pier. On the altar are a pair of 18th century candlesticks brought from a Belgian church destroyed in the First World War.

On the chancel wall is a monument to three generations of the Sanderson family who worshipped here more than 350 years ago. (Their home was Reasby Hall, by the road about a mile to the north, an attractive gabled house bearing the date 1708 but with earlier features.) Each of these Sandersons kneels in his gown and ruff under a round arch—Nicholas the father who died "very aged" in 1556, Nicholas the son who lived to be nearly 80, and Robert the grandson who "in youth left the terrestrial aire".

Stainton-le-Vale. A charming secluded hamlet in a beautiful Wold valley. A narrow road between its Hall and church runs attractively on a ledge above an infant stream which comes from a pretty tree-fringed lake and reaches the sea at Tetney Haven. In a beautiful green churchyard stands the church, now only a fragment of its former self—a simple oblong of nave and chancel, with the reconstructed tower now at the west end and serving as an imposing porch.

Built into the south wall of the nave are the arches and capitals of a 13th century arcade, and under two of them are modern windows. A fine Norman doorway of about AD 1100 opens to a vestry.

Stallingborough. The Humber is 3 miles from this big straggling village now being developed rapidly with the industrial growth along the Humber. But the parish extends to the shore, where there is a lighthouse. The village has a a link with the Mercian King Offa, who is thought to have held his court here 12 centuries ago.

The church was built of brick after the old one had fallen in the 18th century, and has been more than once restored; and its interest lies chiefly in the monuments within, for they bring to mind the poignant memory of one who suffered a cruel death for her faith. She is remembered as Anne Askew, though she was married to Thomas Kyme and her kinsfolk buried here are known by the older spelling of the name—Ayscough.

In a recess in the chancel wall is the bust of Anne's brother Francis a disagreeable-looking man who is resting his head on his hand and holds a spear. Above the bust is the Ayscough rebus—an ass. Below Sir Francis is the magnificent alabaster tomb of his son, Sir Edward Ayscough of 1612, who lies in armour, with ruff and skull cap. Just behind him his wife leans stiffly on her elbow, wearing a farthingale and tight bodice with a ruff; below are 14 children and two babes (looking strangely like old men) in a cradle. A coat-of-arms adorns this finely-preserved monument, and above is an old iron helmet.

Another memorial of the family is a brass under the altar, engraved with the portrait of Katherine Heneage (second wife of Anne Askew's father, Sir William), her two daughters, and two boys in cradles, both named William. Under the choir seats is another brass, showing an earlier William with his lady. He is portrayed as a knight in chain and plate armour, with sword and big spurs; she has kennel headdress, and both his surcoat and her gown are emblazoned with heraldic arms.

A striking modern addition to the interior of the church is the oak screen set up in memory of three kinsmen of the Sutcliffe family who fell in the First World War. It is in the Classical style, with pediment and double-columned bays, and is enriched with shields bearing symbols of St Peter and St Paul in rich foliage.

There are two old chairs with carved backs, a font perhaps 600 years old, and, in the churchyard, part of an old cross-shaft with a later sundial. It was in this churchyard that they buried Colonel Harrison, the Roundhead leader slain at the Battle of Riby Gap in 1645, together with some of his soldiers. Others lie in Riby churchyard.

Anne Askew, a daughter of Sir William Askew, was born at Stallingborough in 1521. She received an excellent education, and from youth was devoted to study of the Bible and to discussion of doctrine with churchmen. While still quite young she was forced to marry Thomas Kyme who, when she was the mother of two children, drove her from home because her religious principles were obnoxious to him.

Apparently in quest of a divorce from him, she made her way to

London, where she was received with kindness by Katherine Parr, who was favourable to the Reformation. Meanwhile Kyme is said to have accused Anne of heresy. The Reformation had left Henry VIII a Roman Catholic in all but allegiance to the pope, and his ministers at once began a protracted series of questionings, in part intended to win Anne back to conformity, in part to convict her.

She faced one enquiry after another with unshaken fortitude, and although committed to gaol when agonisingly ill, refused to sub-scribe to the unreformed doctrine of the Real Presence in the Sacra-ment. Finally, a prisoner at the Tower, she was submitted to horrible tortures, and Lord Chancellor Wriothesley and Sir Richard Rich themselves turned the screws of the rack to heighten the torment.

In spite of her sufferings and the repeated efforts of the leading doctors of the Church to induce her to change her views, the heroic woman remained steadfast, and, maimed and broken, still argued bravely with her persecutors. She was condemned to death as a heretic, but so helpless was she after the rack that she had to be carried to Smithfield in a chair.

Anne Askew's broken body had to be supported at the stake by a chain, but to the end she was mistress of herself, and commented acutely on points with which she disagreed in the sermon preceding the lighting of the fire. She died in company with three other martyrs, on July 16, 1546. She was only 25.

Stamford. In all Lincolnshire there is no finer town than this, the county's southern gateway. It stands astride the old Great North Road, just where Lincolnshire, Northamptonshire, and Rutland meet, and where the River Welland leaves the hilly country to enter the Fenland plan. The recent building of a bypass has eased the traffic problem in its delightful streets. Its name was originally Stane-ford, the stone-paved ford, and the word stone is significant, for in addition to a stone quarry in Stamford, there are close by, at Barnack, Collyweston, Ketton, and Clipsham, famous quarries in the Inferior Oolite.

Approached from the south, through that part of the town which is called Stamford Baron and is actually in Huntingdon and Peter-borough, Stamford presents a pleasing picture of spires and towers rising above mellow houses of grey stone. This was a view of the old town painted by Turner in 1829 and now in the collection at the Usher Gallery, Lincoln. As the traveller draws nearer and crosses the old stone bridge over the Welland, the boundary between the two counties, he can appreciate Sir Walter Scott's description of St Mary's Hill as "the finest scene between London and Edin-burgh".

Though not a Fenland town, it was in early times the capital of the

Fens, and one of the five towns (Lincoln, Stamford, Leicester, Derby, and Nottingham) from which the Danes ruled Lincolnshire and the Midlands. For nearly a thousand years it has been a market town, and, in spite of changes wrought by flourishing industries, it still has many of the surprises and charms which the passing centuries have bestowed—stone-slated roofs and steep gables, little bow windows, Tudor oriels, Queen Anne houses, and Georgian mansions; and behind the unpretentious fronts of some of the old homes are lovely fireplaces, ceilings, staircases, and panelling as well as ancient vaulted crypts.

Here and there are groups of almshouses, hospitals for the sick and old, known locally as "callises", which were mostly founded by the rich Stamford wool merchants who traded with France through the port or staple of Calais. A notable one is the bedehouse near the bridge, recently renovated inside, which was built by Lord Burghley in 1597 for 12 poor men and a warden, and there is also Hopkins' callis, which has a gargoyle from an old friary built into one of its walls.

But Browne's Hospital (in Broad Street) outshines them all. Described by Leland as "a merchant of very wonderful richness", William Browne was six times Alderman of Stamford and a Sheriff of Rutland. He built the Hospital in the 1480s and richly endowed it. A fine old place it is, and well preserved; one of the best mediaeval hospitals in England.

A battlemented porch leads to the spacious buildings of Browne's Hospital, grouped round a charming cloistered garden. In the Audit Room is a magnificent 16th century refectory table, and here, too, is a case with a copy of the Breeches Bible, a charter of King John's time, and a Warden's Prayer book, dated 1662, with written corrections of the prayers for the king after William and Mary came to the throne. Another treasure is a 15th century almsbox of maple wood which was discovered (filled with fine linen) embedded in a wall. William Browne's domed-top chest is here, and a tablet recording the fact that the hospital was built according to his instructions has these artless lines:

> *The honour of the country and this town,*
> *Alas, now dead, his name was William Browne.*

In the little chapel of Browne's Hospital, consecrated in 1494, is a Tudor screen in perfect condition; and there are also carved bench-ends and misericord stalls, and some fine 15th century glass with figures of the Trinity, the Madonna, and various saints.

Another building, not so old, but with a dignity befitting this historic town, is the 18th century Town Hall, on St Mary's Hill. Among its treasures are portraits of James II and the great Lord Burghley; and there is also a valuable collection of plate and regalia, including a silver punch bowl which holds five gallons and three fine maces—two of Charles II's time and another even older.

The Stamford school is another source of pride among local people. A very ancient school, it was re-endowed by Alderman William Radcliffe in 1530, and when many of the old foundations were destroyed in the time of Edward VI it escaped their fate because it had a friend at court in Lord Burghley. He had been a pupil here, and it was he who saved the endowments for his old school and further enriched it.

The chapel in the grounds near the extensive modern buildings of the school was part of a 12th century church, dedicated to St Paul. It was long used as a schoolroom but was later re-consecrated as a school chapel, in memory of old boys who gave their lives in two World Wars. Surviving parts of the Norman church are the flat buttresses, the parapets, and the stringcourse on the outside. There is a 13th century arcade and some 14th and 15th century windows. Over the west doorway is a mutilated head of St Paul—called the Old Scholar—which was at one time ceremoniously kissed by every new scholar.

A curious chapter of educational history is recalled by a pointed archway in a wall of the school premises. It is called Brasenose Gateway and was part of the Brasenose Hall here which was occupied by students who seceded from Oxford in the 13th century and established halls of learning first at Northampton and later at Stamford. Their differences with the University authorities were at last patched up, and in 1335 the students returned to Oxford. The brass knocker, or closing ring, which they had brought from Oxford remained on the doorway here until 1890, when it was sent back to its original home in Brasenose College; it is still preserved there.

Another fine mediaeval gateway, now the entrance to the Infirmary grounds, was part of the monastery of the White Friars. It has empty canopied niches above the buttresses, and weatherworn shields carved with the arms of England and France. The Grey Friars and the Black Friars also had religious houses here, and near the fragmentary postern gate which has survived from the Grey Friars monastery is the last resting-place of Joan, the Fair Maid of Kent, who married the Black Prince. Of the Black Friars Monastery no trace remains, but a 15th century lead coffin was discovered on its site.

The oldest building in Stamford is the ruined chapel of St Leonard's Priory, standing just off the Spalding road, in a meadow shaded by sycamore and chestnut trees. Founded in the 7th century by Wilfrid, Bishop of York, it was rebuilt in 1082 by William of Carilef, the great Norman architect of Durham Cathedral. Its little west front is rich in detail and exceptionally well-preserved. The three lower arches have finely-carved and varied mouldings; above

359

them is a slender arcading of seven bays, three of them pierced. Five arches of the nave arcade and part of the clerestory also remain.

There are also ruins of a castle originally built by the Normans in the south-west corner of the walled town on the spot where the Danes had their stronghold. Part of a wall still stands, and there are also three pointed arches and a 13th century gateway that were part of the Great Hall. Below the castle ruins, where a stream flows on its way to the Welland, is the King's Mill, a 17th century building with its roots in pre-Norman times.

The finest piece of the old town wall is a 13th century bastion in Petergate; but in the garden of a house on Barn Hill is a gate built about 1743 in the town wall by Dr William Stukeley, the famous antiquary, who was at one time vicar of All Saints' Stamford. In this house, which was Dr Stukeley's residence for many years, Charles I was in hiding on the night of May 3, 1645. He escaped on the following night with his faithful companion Dr Hudson, who was afterwards killed by the Roundheads at Woodcroft House in Northamptonshire. Charles joined the Scottish army at Newark and remained in their hands till they surrendered him to Parliament the next year.

Six of Stamford's churches have an ancient story written in their walls.

The exquisite 13th century tower of the mother church, once called St Mary's on the Bridge, is crowned by a 163-foot spire which was added a century later. The tower is adorned with five rows of elegant arcading, and canopied statues of the four Evangelists deck the corners below the spire. The 13th century west doorway is unusual; it has a round arch with a tympanum enclosed by a slender pointed arch, and above this are three round carved panels —the middle one filled with a delicate carving of a serpent devouring its own tail (symbol of Eternity) and the outer ones with trefoil pattern.

The tower arch and the roof-high chancel arch are also 13th century work; so, too, are the responds of the nave arcades, though most of the nave was rebuilt in the 15th century. The beautiful 15th century north chancel chapel was the chapel of the wealthy Corpus Christi Guild, and here on the Feast of Corpus Christi they used to perform a miracle play. An inscription round the walls, below the roof, proclaims that it was the gift in 1467 of Alderman William Hickham and his wife Alice. It has been called the Chapel of the Golden Choir because of the lovely painted roof studded with stars of gold; each star frames a face gay or frowning or grotesque. A great treasure here is a big 14th century statue of the Madonna, full of grace, and on a tomb under a window framed by a very graceful trefoil arch lies an alabaster figure of a 14th century knight in armour.

Beneath an arch between the chapel and the chancel is the splendid monument of Sir David Phillip, who fought at the Battle of Bosworth Field and became a gentleman usher at the court of Henry VII and steward to the king's mother, Lady Margaret Beaufort. He also held the office of Keeper of the King's Swans in all the waters of Lincolnshire, Northamptonshire, Cambridgeshire, and Huntingdonshire. Sir David is shown in armour, and his wife, now headless, is with him. His tomb and its magnificent canopy are covered with royal carvings and a deep band of undercut foliage forms the upper frieze; on each side of the tomb are three weepers and a shield-bearing angel.

A modern east window by Christopher Whall completes the glory of the Golden Choir; it portrays the Madonna with an archangel on either side, and, in the two outer lights, Adam with a spade and Eve with a distaff.

The octagonal font of St Mary's, with slender stem and trefoil-headed panelling, is 500 years old. Three of the eight bells were cast by Tobie Norris, a worthy 17th century bell-founder of Stamford.

St John's Church has been called an almost perfect example of a small 15th century town church. Its pinnacled north-west tower and its lofty clerestory, chancel arch, and slender-pillared arcade are all equally fine. Of the same period is the beautifully-carved font. The painted roof of the nave is supported on wide-winged angel brackets and grotesque corbels, while wooden figures with gilt shields and books support the chancel roof. Round the chapels of the chancel are rich 15th century screens of black oak.

There is a "pulpit cloath" with the date 1701 embroidered in white silk; but the chief treasure is the 15th century glass. Only fragments remain, but they give some idea of the earlier glory of the windows. They are arranged in the upper lights of the aisles, and the subjects include the head of King Edmund the Martyr, Faith and Hope, Bishop Blaize, St Leonard, and St Peter. A few odd pieces, including a mitred head, also make a lovely patch of colouring in the chancel south window.

Less pleasing is the glass in the huge and richly-traceried west window. It portrays the Entombment and Resurrection and was given in 1851 in memory of Richard Newcomb, owner of the *Stamford Mercury*, the second oldest provincial newspaper in England. It first appeared on January 3, 1712. There are also two modern memorial windows to a rector, Walter Hiley. One of them, by Clayton and Bell, has incidents in the Life of Christ, one of the figures in a group being a portrait of the rector. In another Clayton and Bell window (below mediaeval fragments) are scenes typical of Charity.

Among the monuments are portrait brasses of a priest who died in 1487 and of Alderman Nicholas Byldsdon (with his wife and nine children), who died a few years later. A wall tablet is to the family of James Whitley, "a player" of the 18th century who built the old Stamford theatre and was proprietor of theatres at Worcester, Wolverhampton, Nottingham, Derby, and Retford. A memorial to a boy of 7 shows Grief and bears the pathetic words, "He never gave his parents grief but when he died." In the churchyard is an inscription in memory of an inn-keeper named Pepper—one of those punning epitaphs 18th century mourners could not resist:

> *Tho' hot my name, yet mild my nature,*
> *I bore good will to every creature,*
> *I brewed fine ale and sold it too,*
> *And unto each I gave his due.*

All Saints' Church, on one side of Stamford's old marketplace, has a handsome exterior; rare 13th century arcading with carved capitals and deep arches which once encompassed the building still decorates the south and east sides, below the finely traceried windows. Battlements further enrich the 15th century aisles and clerestory, and above them rises a fine 15th century tower with panelled sides, magnificent belfry windows, and corner turrets grouped round the delicate crocketed spire 152 feet high. The tower and spire were part of the restoration which was the gift in 1470 of William and John Browne, who both rest in the church. The merchant mark of this old Stamford family is on a shield above the lofty chancel arch, and they also founded a chantry here that was served by the Warden of Browne's Hospital.

The 13th century arcades of nave and chancel have beautiful capitals, with wide bands of foliage deeply cut on the under side. The most impressive spectacle in the interior, however, is the timbered chancel roof, adorned with great gilded bosses and painted angels with outstretched golden wings. The wide 15th century roof of the nave, with gilded bosses, rests on 18 big stone corbel heads, and there is another fine 15th century roof over the Lady Chapel.

All Saints' has a 15th century font of marble, and also some fine brasses commemorating the generous Browne family. The oldest, 1460, shows John Browne and his wife Margery, the woolpacks on which he stands being a symbol of his trade. A similar brass has the portraits of his son William (founder of Browne's Hospital) and his wife Margaret; and a third shows another son, John Browne, with his wife Agnes. Other brasses are to Henry Wykys, 1508, a vicar (in cope, but headless); a lady with a crescent-shaped headdress, 1471; and a civilian and his wife of about 1500.

There are two fine modern windows by A. K. Nicholson. One has canopied figures of Raphael, Michael, Gabriel, and Uriel; and the other shows the Four Evangelists with their symbols in gold above their heads.

In another rich window are golden figures of the patron saints of Lincolnshire and three neighbouring dioceses. There are four warriors (Joshua, St George, Michael, David) in the memorial window to those "who died that England might live", and in a thanks offering window from a vicar are figures of St Patrick, St Columba, St David, and St Augustine.

Descendants of the devoted men who gave so freely of their wealth have come in recent years from their homes in the United States to enrich still further the church of their forefathers. In 1888 Edward Browne of Boston, Massachusetts, set up new glass in the big and richly-traceried 15th century west window; it shows six saints with the heraldic devices of Stamford and of the Staple of Calais. In 1921 Henry Browne of Philadelphia gave a silver chalice and paten.

Standing apart in a quiet square is St George's Church, with a plain embattled tower bearing a quaint sundial. It is a 13th century building, much altered through the years, and its chief interest lies in its glass. One of this church's 15th century benefactors was William de Bruges, 1st Garter King-at-Arms, and it was he who gave a series of unique and wonderful windows for the chancel. They represented Edward III and the first 25 Knights of the Garter (including the Black Prince and Henry, Duke of Lancaster) together with scenes from the life of St George. These, alas, were removed during the 17th century. A series of photographs of the drawings made of them by Dugdale in 1641 is framed on a transept wall, and further reminders of their vanished glory are the few fragments that have been found and pieced together. In a chancel window are 15th century figures of St Katharine and St Anne; and below are the heads of an abbot and Sir John Lisle. Modern figures of St George and St Paul flank the mediaeval saints. In the opposite window are 200 little quarries bearing the Garter motto, *Hony soyt qui mal y pence.*

A monument by Bacon (1779) to Sir Richard and Lady Cust of Belton-by-Grantham has the life-sized marble figure of the wife standing by the bust of her husband; their son John was a Speaker of the House of Commons. There is also a tablet of bell metal to Tobie Norris, the Stamford bell-founder, who was buried here in 1676.

St Michael's Church was entirely rebuilt last century, and a Norman arch in the crypt below the tall, pinnacled tower is all that is left of the ancient building. A few of the old fittings have also survived—an hourglass bracket, a 15th century font, and an oak figure of Our Lord blessing the children. The Communion plate was given in the 17th century by the Trollope family, and in the vestry is a pewter inkstand dated 1798. This church is now closed for services.

The sixth old church of Stamford is St Martin's, in the southern part of the town, close to the fine old coaching inn which so boldly displays its sign across the road. It is the parish church of Stamford Baron, the part of Stamford which lies south of the Welland and is officially in Huntingdon and Peterborough.

Watching over the dignified grey houses that line the hill climbing southwards out of the town, stands its stately tower, handsome with pinnacles and battlements and panelled parapet. Fine 15th century work is this tower, as indeed is the whole church of St Martin's, from end to end, having been built in 1480 of stone from the Barnack quarries 3 miles away. The man responsible was John Russell, Bishop of Lincoln, whose arms are on a corbel in the nave and in one of the windows; the arms of the See of Lincoln are on the boss of the great south porch, which has a priest's room over it.

It is a noble interior. The lofty nave has four arches soaring on clustered pillars on each side, angels in their spandrels. Fourteen clerestory windows fill the nave with light, the aisles with their old roofs add to the impression of spaciousness, and the modern oak screen in the tower arch gives an extra touch of beauty with its carvings of angels and of St Martin dividing his cloak with the beggar. The font near this screen is 600 years old.

Five windows in the chancel and its south chapel glow with mediaeval glass. With it is some modern glass, but most of it is 15th century and much of it was brought to St Martin's 200 years ago from the Lincolnshire church of Tattershall. It is an astonishing medley of heraldic devices mingled with angels, bishops, saints, abbots, and little groups of heads. The best of all the windows (the one next to the organ) has a bewildering variety of colour and design showing small figures in Bible scenes, including Moses striking the Rock, David disposing of Goliath, Samson carrying away the gates of Gaza, and the Crucifixion.

The Burghley Chapel is on the north of the chancel and is richly decked with monuments of the Cecils, whose home is close by. Here is the effigy of the first Lord Burghley, William Cecil, lying on his marble and alabaster tomb. As befits this great man who was a pillar of State during three reigns and did so much to shape England's history during its Golden Age, his monument is richly carved and painted and fills the arch dividing the chapel from the chancel. Lord Burghley may have seen it, for it was designed before his death in 1598. It shows him in his armour wearing the gorgeous scarlet mantle of the Garter, a noble figure nobly arrayed, his head on a pillow of gold brocade, his wand of office in his right hand, and a lion at his feet. His father and mother kneel at a prayer-desk on the wall close by; they are Richard and Jane Cecil and have three children with them. The father died in 1552, little dreaming of the eminence his son was to attain.

Another imposing monument, carved in Rome by Pierre Monnot,

is a marble group in memory of John Cecil, 5th Earl of Exeter, a traveller and collector who inherited Burghley House and in the 17th century brought to it many of its fine possessions. His monument shows him reclining on the tomb with his countess, and there are symbolical figures of Grief and Victory at the sides. Among the wall tablets is one to the Dutch artist Willem Wissing, who painted many portraits for the Cecils and died in 1687 while painting at Burghley House.

In the churchyard of St Martin's lies Daniel Lambert, the biggest man in our annals. Born at Leicester in 1770, son of the Earl of Stamford's huntsman, he succeeded his father as keeper of Leicester gaol; but early in his twenties, in spite of the fact that he was a great walker and a great swimmer, and in spite of the fact that he drank only water, he was compelled to resign his post owing to the size and weight of his body. He now (at 23 years of age) weighed 32 stones, and was henceforth to live as a human curiosity. A special carriage was built for him, and he was brought to London, where people called to see him from twelve to five at a house in Piccadilly. His portrait appeared on tavern signs, and thousands of people called to see him, this biggest man in the world, only 5 feet high but weighing nearly 53 stones. He died at the Waggon and Horses Inn in Stamford on July 21, 1809, and was buried in a coffin containing 112 square feet of elm. (Some of his clothing is in the possession of the Stamford Corporation and can be seen by arrangement; his chair is in Leicester Museum.)

A short distance from St Martin's Church is the gate of Burghley Park, historic domain of the Marquess of Exeter. Through his courtesy part of the great park surrounding the magnificent Elizabethan house built by Lord Burghley is open to all, and no words can reflect the beauty of its stretches of woodland, the avenue, the lakes, the deer-haunted glades, and the enchanting vistas; and for those who dwell in this fair town of Stamford, which many consider as lovely a little town as England can show, it is a never-failing source of delight.

Stapleford. Stapleford Wood, now extensively planted by the Forestry Commission, but roadside rhododendrons add their touch of summer's blaze of colour. A stream flows through this small village of russet cottages and farm buildings, and then meanders, willow-fringed, through the fields to join the Witham just beyond the church.

A tiny church, with walls of brick newly-raised 200 years ago and wooden window-frames, it still has its 13th century tower with tiled pyramid roof probably from the restoration in 1903–04. A reminder of the Norman period is seen in the pillar piscina and a Norman capital.

365

Stenigot. Up hill and down dale runs the road to this small place on a wooded slope where the great house stands in grounds watered by a stream flowing down to the River Bain.

Neighboured by two tall beeches on the edge of the park is a little red-brick church, built in 1892 but having in its keeping two monuments and a 15th century font brought from the old church within the park. (Of this old church only the chancel is left, with a Norman chancel arch and window.)

One of the monuments shows the kneeling, robed figure of Francis Velves de Guevara, a Spaniard who married an English maid and settled here in Elizabethan days. The other monument has the armoured figure of his son John, who, despite his Spanish name and ancestry, held the honoured post of Deputy Warden of the East Marches of England.

Stewton. A market-garden village in the unspoilt countryside near Louth.

The tiny, 50-foot-long church has been much restored and altered, but has some remains revealing its ancient origin. The nave has a deeply-splayed Norman window, and from early in the Norman period come the chancel arch with its massive stones, the arch of the blocked north doorway, and the primitive-looking south doorway (now leading to a vestry) which has a mass dial beside it. The outer arch of this doorway has a big plain tympanum. More ancient stones and part of a churchyard cross can be seen outside, built into the east wall.

The porch at the west end (with two doorways in Norman style) is modern; so are the oak benches, the east window, and the font with an oak cover like a little spire.

Stickford. This Fenland village on the Spilsby–Boston road has two towers. One is a war memorial clock tower; the other is the fine west tower of its church, which stands, in company with a shapely sycamore, facing the village inn.

The church has been much rebuilt, but its tower, with deeply moulded doorway, has stood since the 15th century; its tall arch is still open to the nave, but the arches in its north and south walls are blocked. The porch is also partly 15th century work, and has a shield-of-arms on each side of its entrance arch.

Some old masonry and 14th century windows remain in the north aisle, and the nave has leaning arcades of the 13th century. On the north side are bell capitals crowning clustered pillars, and on the south side are capitals with nail-head surmounting octagonal pillars.

Other interesting items are the 14th century font, with plain shields and flowers in traceried panels; an old chest carved with flowers and foliage and heads of men; 21 old bench-ends with fleur-de-lys poppyheads; and a massive old bell, now silent, on the floor of the tower.

Stickney. Strung along the highway between Boston and Spilsby, amid the market-garden crops of the West and East Fens, it has a big church much rebuilt last century. A yew-shaded path leads to it.

The chancel, the porch, and the nave clerestory are all modern. But, except for the 15th century west window, the base of the tower (with tall lancet arch) is 13th century work; and so are the nave arcades with their finely-moulded capitals, some of which are adorned with nail-head.

In the aisles are 15th century windows, and one of these has a charming scene of Our Lord with children of our day, some playing games and others with their pets. This window is in memory of children of Stickney, especially those who have no other memorial.

Stixwould. Its church was built anew after the Dissolution from the ruins of a Cistercian nunnery founded here during the reign of King Stephen; and in the churchyard, shaded by stately trees, are a few reminders of this ancient nunnery: the stump of an old cross, a mediaeval floorstone, and some broken stone coffins. In 1831 the church was again rebuilt, in 15th century style, with quatrefoiled battlements and fearsome gargoyles crowning its attractive tower. But in its walls the venerable stones still play their part.

From the old church, too, come the oak screen, and a few bench-ends with quaint carvings of bearded and long-haired men. The modern bench-ends match the old and display heads of a Roman soldier, a farmer and his wife, a man and woman with their tongues out, and men with hairy faces. There is also an old stoup which for many years was a drain for the school pump.

The finest relic here is a 14th century font adorned with a wealth of carving. On four sides of the bowl are representations of the first four months of the year, and on the other four are the names and symbols of the Evangelists.

A mile from the village stands the old moated Halstead Hall, now a farmhouse. What remains is a wing of an L-shaped brick building of the early 16th century. It has been considerably restored.

Stoke. It used to be said that there was not a poor person in all Lincolnshire, and although this may not be true today most of the villages have an unmistakable look of well-being. Stoke is certainly no exception and is undeniably attractive, serene as it is in its setting between two wooded parks, and sheltered from the hurly-burly of the A1 which divides them.

The park to the north of it belongs to Stoke Rochford, since 1650 the home of the Turnor family, and before them of the Rochfords. Long before that there was a Roman villa on the site and its remains were unearthed early last century. The park on the south is that of Easton Hall, for three centuries the home of the Cholmeley family. Stoke Rochford is a big mansion with many gables and tall chimneys, largely in Jacobean style, but built in the middle of last century. Near it is an obelisk set up in honour of Sir Isaac Newton, who was born at Woolsthorpe close by—a tribute to the scientist from Canon Charles Turnor. The house is now the Kesteven College of Education and there has been much building to provide additional accommodation for the College. Easton Hall is another impressive house, largely modern though its gables and oriels reflect the spacious Tudor age. It stands high above the Witham and a great feature of its lovely garden is the long flight of steps going down from the terrace to a graceful two-arched bridge across the river.

The church stands pleasantly on a knoll, sharing a shady winding lane with the humbler houses of the village. Most of it is 15th century but the tower is a legacy from the 13th and 14th centuries and even greater antiquity is evident in the nave, the north arcade having Norman arches on massive round piers. The south arcade also has round arches, but they are set on more slender piers and have the foliated capitals of the Early English builders.

On each side of the chancel is a chapel: the Easton Chapel on the south built by Ralph Rochford in 1448, and the Stoke Chapel built a few years later. In these chapels are some fine monuments of the lords and ladies of the manors. Altar tombs of two unknowns are on each side of the high altar, and in the floor of the Stoke Chapel is a 14th century memorial stone to Sir John de Neville and his wife, showing them as knight and lady with a sheet covering all but their heads and the animals at their feet. On the north wall is a huge 17th century monument of black marble with an inscription to Sir Edmund Turnor, the first of the family to live here, and ancestor of Edmund Turnor the antiquary, who in 1829 was also buried in this church. A monument like a screen of white alabaster against the east wall of the chapel is adorned with tracery, roses, and foliage, and bears carved medallion portraits of Christopher Turnor of 1886 and his wife Caroline; figures of saints are drawn in black outline below—Augustine, Columba, Paulinus, Oswald, Aidan, Hilda, Bede, and Queen Margaret.

Against the wall of the Easton Chapel, and reaching to its roof, is 17th century Sir Henry Cholmeley's monument, enriched with heraldry and sumptuously carved and gilded. He kneels at a prayer-desk in tunic, breeches, and long cloak, facing his wife in her long, tight-waisted gown; in front of them lies an infant, and in recesses behind them are kneeling figures of two sons.

In the chancel are two ancient brasses. One has the armoured figure of Henry Rochford, 1470; the other has figures of Oliver St John in armour with his wife Elizabeth (widow of a Rochford) and eight children. This brass is historically interesting because Oliver was half-brother to Margaret Beaufort, mother of Henry VII.

The church has long been tended with loving hands and in modern times has been invested with much that is colourful and attractive. The tall font-cover is a thing of beauty, each of its three tiers being appropriately adorned with eight scenes in the Infancy and Boyhood of Jesus. Designed and given by Mr Christopher Turnor, its decoration was the work of a well-known artist, Miss Jessie Bayes, who also painted the figure of Christ in Glory filling the apex of the 14th century chancel arch, and the saints on the beautiful reredos, which has the added interest of having been designed by Mrs G. F. Watts.

The ways to Stoke are pleasant travelling and the church itself is balm to traveller and villager alike.

Stow. Legend and fact are nicely blended in the early story of this quiet old village, standing a mile from the Roman Till Bridge Lane which links Ermine Street with the Trent. In Saxon times, a pretty legend tells how St Etheldreda, staying here when in flight from her husband, King Egfrid of Northumbria, stuck her staff into the ground. The staff took root and sprang into an ash tree and a church was built to commemorate the miracle.

Traditionally, Stow's earliest church is said to have been built by Egfrid in AD 678 and to have been the Saxon cathedral of the diocese of Lindsey, formed when the Northumbrian diocese was divided. About the year 870 this church was burned down by the invading Danes and a century later the bishopric was removed to Dorchester-on-Thames. Soon after the Conquest the bishopric was transferred again, this time to Lincoln. Thus did the ancient church of Stow earn the title of Mother-Church to Lincoln—a name that clings to it this day.

However, there is no documentary evidence for a church at Stow before the 11th century. Much of this early story of Stow is, of course, shadowy—and must remain so; and we are on surer ground in considering the venerable church which still stands—a cross-shaped building with a central tower. Simple in plan, Stow Church has an austere beauty that makes it an unforgettable sight; and except for its low 15th century tower, a few mediaeval windows, and some windows renewed in the fine 19th century restoration, it belongs almost entirely to the 11th and 12th centuries.

When a college of canons was founded in the first half of the 11th century the builders did not construct the church from the foundations but "they repaired an existing fabric for whose age we have at present no certain evidence". The college of canons was founded by Eadnoth I (c. 1004–16), Bishop of Dorchester. To this period belong the transepts and the round-headed arches of the crossing. A grand spectacle this central crossing is, for when the 15th century builders set up their tower they left the original arches framing their pointed ones, and built their own piers within the angles of those of the 11th century. The bases of all this noble company of piers are shoulder-high, and the western round-headed arch is enriched with unusual loop or hairpin moulding.

The nave and the upper part of the transepts are early Norman work (probably due to Remigius, first Bishop of Lincoln). The chancel, with its rich Norman work of the 12th century, is ascribed to Bishop Alexander, who may also have given the nave its three splendid doorways—highly enriched with characteristic mouldings, including zigzag and billet.

The clerestoried chancel as seen from the nave, with the crossing as foreground, is another grand spectacle. Above the stone bench all round it, the walls are adorned with shafted arcading, enriched with zigzag; above this is a stringcourse; then come the deeply-splayed windows with continuous carving of zigzag and key pattern, and between the windows are clusters of shafts soaring to the lovely stone groined roof which was renewed in 1865 when John L. Pearson carried out a restoration. The east end with its three tiers of windows (two tiers round-headed and one circular) also belongs to the restoration, and so do the west windows of the nave glowing with pleasing colour.

In the west wall of the north transept (and leading now to a modern vestry) is a fine round-headed Saxon doorway. Near it is a mass of stone charred by fire, of which traces can also be seen on the north-west pier of the tower. In an altar recess in the east wall of the north transept are remains of a 13th century wall painting of St Thomas Becket, showing now only part of his rich vestments. It is a fresco of very high quality and similar to paintings in the Galilee Chapel in Durham. Winding up the north-east pier of the tower is the ancient rood stairway. Carved on the shallow bowl of the Early English font is a curious monster with leaves issuing from its mouth; and a similar but more massive winged creature is creeping round the font base. Six of the nave benches have some old work, including all their ends, and incorporated in the modern stalls are four poppy-head ends and a little old tracery. The church also has two old chests. The pulpit was given in the 18th century in memory of a rector who died of smallpox caught while ministering to his stricken parish.

In one of the windows is the portrait of St Hugh of Avalon, Bishop of Lincoln from 1186 to 1200. Thereby hangs a tale. Stow has close associations with St Hugh, for at Stow Park, on the other side of the Till Bridge Lane, once stood a palace or manor house of the early bishops of Lincoln. A farmhouse is on the site now, and where once the still waters of the moat reflected the peaceful scene there are now only dry dykes, overhung with trees.

Here St Hugh is said to have tended poor lepers, and to have given them hope when all seemed lost. Here at Stow appeared the fierce swan which is St Hugh's symbol. Everyone was afraid of it but Hugh adopted the bird, and it would follow him about the park and the house, poking its bill into the pockets of his robe for breadcrumbs. When the bishop was away the swan lived on the moat, but, strange to relate, it always knew the day on which he was returning and would fly up and down the moat beating the water with its wings as though to herald his approach.

St Hugh, who was the son of a French nobleman, first came to England at the request of Henry II, to build the Carthusian Order in Somerset. In 1186 he became the 6th Bishop of Lincoln and shortly afterwards started the planning and building of the choir and other eastern parts of the cathedral which remain to this day among its greater glories.

Statesman as well as a great man of the Church, and "one of the most beautiful spirits that was ever incarnated in human clay", as the historian Froude called him, St Hugh had the courage to fight tyranny wherever he found it and in so doing won the esteem of all —from the king down to his humblest subjects; and when Hugh died—in 1200, King John, whom he had often so bitterly opposed, was among those who bore the Saint's remains to their resting-place in his cathedral on the hill.

Stragglethorpe. This small village between the River Brant and its tributary the Sand Beck has attractive pantiled cottages and a charming Old Hall, basically Elizabethan but restored in the 20th century, at a pretty corner near the little church. The gables and dormers of the Hall look out on a small courtyard, and by the drive leading to it is an old dovecot.

The church is an ancient building with most of its windows restored. It has a double bellcot of the 13th century, and its simple porch has a 15th century archway and shelters a 700-year-old doorway and an ancient door with strap-hinges; by this inner doorway is a mass dial. In a buttress at the west end is a dainty 15th century niche with a modern stone figure of St Michael and the Dragon.

On this west wall (but seen only within the church) is a blocked triangular-headed doorway which is probably Saxon; and between the nave and its aisle is an arcade of two round-headed bays built at the close of Norman days. Late Norman, too, is the fine arcaded font, still with one of its old iron fastenings for a cover; and there is also a Norman pillar piscina in the sanctuary, a scalloped capital forming its bowl.

Box-pews, high-backed pews, and fine double-decker pulpit—all fitted with tall wooden candle-holders—give the nave an old-world charm. Other reminders of days gone by are a few fragments of old glass, a chest, and a marble monument with two sculptured busts. It commemorates Sir Richard Earle who died in 1697 when only 24, and the inscription extolling his virtues ends with these lines:

> *While the mother this sad structure rears*
> *A double dissolution there appears:*
> *He into dust dissolves, she into tears.*

Stroxton. Lying secluded 1 mile from the A1, it is as serene as the stream flowing through on its way to join the Witham. In a field behind a farm is a little church, restored in Victorian days but still with much evidence of antiquity. The new saddleback tower has a Norman arch with chevron ornament in its west wall and the former Norman chancel arch in its east wall. The arcades, long built-in but opened up when new aisles were built, are 700 years old, and so are the aumbry, the piscina, and a gravestone with a foliated cross near the porch.

On the chapel wall is a solitary monument with three heraldic shields in memory of William Blyth, who died here in 1648.

Strubby. A farming community in close proximity to an RAF station have contributed to this pleasant village.

Almost rebuilt last century, the church still has a few remains of 14th century work: the nave arcade leading to the aisle, the aisle's fine east window with geometrical tracery, and the finely-traceried octagonal font retaining much of its old red colour. At the east end of the aisle (a war memorial chapel) is a 17th century altar, and there are some mediaeval bench-ends with poppyheads.

Under a canopied recess in the chancel is a worn 14th century effigy of a man in a long gown. Another memorial is a tablet paying tribute to Thomas Wilson, a native of Strubby, who became a diplomat and Secretary of State in Elizabeth I's time. The inscription tells of his sufferings in Rome, and of his noble qualities; beneath it hangs his portrait. One of his titles to fame is the *Arte of Rhetorique*, a work first published in 1553, "for the use of all suche as are studious of eloquence", and one which must have been familiar to Shakespeare and his fellow-dramatists.

A third monument portrays a charming family group under a Classical canopy—William Ballett (a portly alderman of London), his two wives, and their nine children. William, who was 99 when he died in 1648, kneels here bare-headed, and his wives have little chimney-pot hats. Their home was Woodthorpe Hall a mile and a half away, a pretty Georgian house with a fine little avenue of elms.

Near the house (which has been a farmhouse for 200 years) is a wonderful oak, said to be mentioned in Domesday Book; its great trunk is hollow, and most of its mighty limbs are gone, but it is still full of life and spreading ample shade.

Sudbrooke. Set amid quiet byways, 4 miles north-east from Lincoln. This is now an area of suburban development with attractive houses of modern design. It is close to the site of Sudbrooke Holme, demolished some 50 years ago. This was the home of the Ellisons who bought the estate in the 18th century. They increased their wealth by securing the lease of the Foss Dyke navigation from Lincoln Corporation at £75 a year. They cleaned up the neglected canal and then charged 1d. a ton per mile for boats and barges using it. This brought in an income of £7,000 per annum. The last member, Richard Ellison, left money to rebuild Sudbrooke Church.

Peter de Wint was a regular visitor to Sudbrook and the Ellison's valuable collection of water-colours was left to the Victoria and Albert Museum, London.

Standing among trim firs and yews, the church was rebuilt in 1860. Modelled largely on the lines of the exquisite Norman church of Streetley in Derbyshire, its exterior walls are enriched with a wealth of ornament. The round arch of its doorway is adorned with 15 beakheads, and each of the seven nave windows has its pair of heads. Carved pillars and zigzag arches frame the windows of the apse, and below its roof are 28 more heads of men and beasts.

Within the church the Norman style is just as rigidly followed. Seven round-headed windows, with two circular ones at the west end light the nave; the chancel has four more Norman windows and a richly-carved round arch; and a further arch rich with zigzag and cable moulding leads to a stone-vaulted apse. By the plain round font is a foliated capital, the sole survival of the ancient church.

Surfleet. The little River Glen flows through this big village as it nears the end of its 31-mile journey to the Welland. It waters a countryside lovely to look on when the bulbs are in bloom.

The church stands at the crossroads, and has a curious appearance owing to its foundations having sunk. The 14th century tower and spire are leaning at an alarming angle, the top of the spire being 6 feet out of centre. No less odd is the tower within, where it seems to be lurching like a ship at sea; its floor is five steps down from the nave. Lovely ballflower ornament of the 14th century adorns the outside walls of the aisles and the porch, and the porch entrance has fine dog-tooth moulding a century older.

In the 15th century the 600-year-old nave was given its clerestory, the arcades were given some new capitals, their western pillars were stoutly buttressed with masonry, and the north aisle was shorn of its eastern bay; the window then set in its blocked arch still remains. A small quatrefoil window a century older gives a view from the tower stairway into the nave.

The chancel has a medley of old glass in one of its windows, remains of its old hammerbeam roof, and a new oak screen designed from the remnants of the old one found buried during the restoration. Lying in the chancel is a figure of a knight in chain and plate armour, his shield on his arm. He is said to be Sir Roger de Cressy, of Cressy Hall near Gosberton.

The splendid 15th century font, with rich carving of tracery and flowers and deeply buttressed stem, is like the one at Pinchbeck. Among fragments of old stones are gravestones with carved crosses.

Sutterby. An attractive little disused 15th century church now standing alone in the fields. It has a bricked-up Norman doorway. Nearby are the Neolithic long barrows known as Spellow Hills and the interesting sheep-walks at Langton-by-Spilsby are worth a visit. The southern slopes of the Wolds were sheltered and warm and no doubt used for early cultivation which may explain the terracing.

Sutterton. It lies where the busy highway from Spalding to Boston is crossed by the one running from Sleaford to Holbeach. Fishmere End and Sutterton Marsh, north and south of the village, are reminders of the nearness of the sea in bygone days.

Like neighbouring Algarkirk it had a church in Saxon times, but nothing of it remains, and the present fine building, shaped like a cross and filled with light, comes from the second half of the 12th century. Remains of that period, when the Norman style was giving place to the Early English, include two splendid doorways, the stately nave arcades of five bays, and the pillars and arches supporting the central tower. The capitals of the arcades are all differently carved, and one has heads and grotesques creeping and peeping out of foliage; the western arch of the tower has Norman zigzag carving.

The rest of the fine tower and its lofty crocketed spire is 15th century work, though the spire was rebuilt in 1787. From the 13th century come the transept arcades and the clerestory of the north transept. The 13th century chancel was rebuilt in 1862, and has plain lancets in the east wall, and the mediaeval sedilia, double piscina, and aumbry set in its tiled walls. The nave clerestory and the great west window with its flowing tracery are late 14th century work; the north transept has a 15th century window filling its north wall.

Sutterton has a fine ring of eight 18th century bells, and also treasures a 700-year-old sanctus bell with an inscription in Lombardic letters to Symon de Hazfelde who made it. In the 19th century aisle of the south transept are three coped tombs with figures of John Boneworth of 1372 in gown and hood, his wife Alice, and their son John (who was priest here) holding a chalice.

Sutton Bridge. It lies by the River Nene, in a land of reclaimed marshes spreading to the Wash. Now a small port, with quays and derelict docks, it grew in importance last century because of the construction of the long, embanked road over the treacherous Cross Keys Wash.

It was in this dangerous marshland that in October 1216 King John lost his treasure and all his baggage, and almost his life as well. About 2 miles north from the little town's long and busy main street is King John's Farm, a brick house of 1878, on the site, so the story goes, of one where the king rested for a night after his mishap. He was already a sick man, and this narrow escape from drowning probably hastened his death at Newark a week or so later.

In 1831 the Nene was given a new deep outfall for a length of 7 miles, and a wooden bridge made by Rennie and Telford was thrown across the river to give access to the road. This was replaced in 1850 by Robert Stephenson's swing bridge, which in turn was replaced in 1894 by the present hydraulic swing bridge.

The water near the bridge is deep enough at high tide to float a warship, but the town's bid for becoming an important harbour by the building in 1881 of docks covering 12 acres did not materialise, for the docks collapsed through faulty construction only a month after being opened.

Sutton-on-Sea. Known of old as Sutton-in-the-Marsh, it is today a quiet seaside resort with the natural attractions of firm golden sands. Here was the most destructive break-through of the sea in 1953 and concrete defences now replace the sand-dunes. There are attractive chalets on the sea-wall. Fine bathing, boating, and fishing are here for the amusement of holiday-makers, as well as cricket and tennis on the sands; and there are also golf links and facilities for many other games. Its special appeal, however, is a restful atmosphere noticeably absent from so many seaside resorts.

Sometimes the sands are washed away, and the underlying clay beds exposed, and at neap tides the remains of a submerged pre-historic forest can be seen. Traces of Early Iron Age salt-workings were exposed in 1953 and much mediaeval building material supported the view that the early village was lost to the sea. The present brick church, reached through a pretty lychgate, is an early 19th century building.

Sutton St James. This out-of-the-way village on the eastern edge of the flats of the Bedford Level, has a church which is something of a curiosity. Set back from the spacious road behind a little green, it presents the strange spectacle of tower and chancel standing quite separate, the nave which originally linked them having been destroyed during the Commonwealth and never rebuilt. Tall trees cast their shade where the nave once stood.

The old chancel of stone and brick has been rebuilt, but the massive tower is the original 15th century building. Its west wall is decorated with shields and flowers in a band of quatrefoils; above this is a blocked 15th century window, and below is a recess which was probably the upper part of a filled-in doorway. There are traces of the old arch which led to the nave in the ivied west wall of the chancel, and the font has an old eight-sided bowl with simple tracery.

Where the road divides at the west end of the village stands St Ives' Cross. Time has reduced it to a short length of shaft and a few fragments of flying buttresses, set on a base with four tiers of battered steps.

Swallow. In a pretty Wold valley it lies, between Caistor and Grimsby, serene with its pond by the green, a delightful little avenue leading to one of its houses, and tiny church on a high bank.

Its chancel was rebuilt last century, when the nave was given its north aisle. Of the old south aisle only the built-up arcade remains. The upper part of the unbuttressed tower has been restored, but the rest of it comes from late Saxon and Norman days; it opens to the nave with a wide and massive arch and has one of its original little windows above the Norman west doorway. Built into a wall of the tower is part of a worn Crucifixion carved in stone.

The ancient font is still here and there also is a fine Norman shaft piscina with a cushion capital on its cluster of thin shafts.

Swarby. An attractive small village south-west of Sleaford has an unusual round pump-house on its green, and a church rather drastically restored last century but still wearing its mediaeval dignity. The massive 15th century tower stands four-square to all the winds that blow, spireless in a countryside of spires, and crowned only by a low pyramid roof. The round font is 700 years old and other mediaeval features are the rood stairs, a piscina, and a beautiful small sculpture of Our Lord, showing His five wounds.

Swaton. A few red cottages peep out from little gardens here, and high above them all rises a grey church tower, crowned by eight pinnacles. The cross-shaped church is an outstanding example of 14th century architecture, displaying in striking contrast the simple work of the early part of this great building period and the more lavish style which marked its later years.

The early work is represented by the lower part of the central tower (the top is 15th century) resting on low arches and decorated in three of its angles with heads of a king, a queen, and a demon; and also by the chancel, which has six lancet windows in its side walls and a simple two-light east window with the earliest form of tracery.

The richer 14th century work is seen in the aisles and in the nave, an impressive sight with three great arches soaring up on either side and the light streaming from the six windows of the aisles and the huge window that fills the west wall so that it is veritably a wall of glass; in these windows is a great display of quatrefoil tracery.

The chancel has a big double piscina; the north transept has a small canopied piscina; and the other transept has a piscina, an aumbry, and the entrance to a rood-loft. In an aisle is a stone figure of a 14th century lady with her feet on a dog; the font, with its graceful petalled design and border of ballflowers, was new when she worshipped here. The seats in nave and aisles are decked with foliated poppyheads and traceried ends; many of them are 500 years old and the new ones were made to match.

Swayfield. A little farming community with grey stone houses and a church looking over the bountiful fields, it stands above the River Glen, with the railway running by at one of its greatest heights between London and the Scottish border.

The little church, humble but cared-for, has been largely rebuilt but still has its battlemented 13th century tower and its plain mediaeval font. The east window has Nativity, Crucifixion, and Resurrection scenes keeping green the memory of a 19th century rector.

Swinderby. A well-wooded area where history echoes along the Roman Fosse Way half a mile from this pleasant red-roofed village on the Nottinghamshire border. Modern history is seen in the important RAF station established by the roadside.

The battlemented tower of the church, neighboured by lime trees and a magnificent beech, is 700 years old. The rest of the church has been much restored, but still has a fine Norman arcade of three bays, with bold scalloped capitals, leading to a 14th century aisle enlarged in 1854. Some years later the chancel (sombre with stained glass) was given its apse and its screens of attractive ironwork.

The font with its eight carved shields is 14th century work. There are 18th century memorials to John Drake and John Disney. The modern oak pulpit, and a window with figures of the Madonna, Isaiah, and John Baptist, commemorate Charles Long who ministered here for 34 years; another tribute to him is a cross in the churchyard, with sculptures of the Madonna and the Crucifixion.

Swineshead. Lining a long stretch of the road which marks the meeting of two old highways running across the county from Grantham, Swineshead is no longer a market town, though the old market cross has recently been restored and the wooden post of an earlier cross was found; it stands in company with the broken old stocks in a little War Memorial garden. Another link with its past is the tolling of the curfew from October to March; but the finest link of all is the mediaeval church.

A noble building this church is, with lofty and massive tower standing within its west end, flanked by the aisles. The lower portion of the tower is 14th century, the belfry stage with its great windows and tall pinnacles, and the lovely embattled octagon from which the small spire soars to 160 feet above the ground, all being a century later. The tower has a stone vaulted roof, and three majestic arches opening to the nave and aisles; its west doorway, richly moulded, is a foretaste of the cathedral-like grandeur within.

Fourteenth century builders raised the spacious nave, with its stately arcades of six bays; and also the clerestory, which has big traceried windows and an embattled parapet. Notable features are the continuation of the clerestory above the chancel arch, and the fine array of corbel heads which adorn the nave battlements and the arcades. The south aisle and porch (adorned with leafy pinnacles and gables) are also 14th century work, partly rebuilt in Victorian times. The north aisle is 15th century, and the chancel was rebuilt last century. An embattled turret on the south side of the church has a stairway which led to the rood-loft and the chancel roof; its entrance doorway is within the church.

The church has some fine woodwork. A mass of old open timbering crowns the nave, the old north aisle roof has moulded beams and bosses, and the south aisle roof has rough old timbers. The chancel roof, with bosses enriching its hammerbeams, is modern, but the finely-traceried oak screen is 500 years old. The great north and south doors, swinging on their old hinges, are adorned with tracery and have wickets. In the south aisle are some old seats and bench-ends, and there is an old chest covered with a splendid lattice of ironwork.

An old stone coffin stands in an aisle, and in the nave is a floor-stone with brass portraits of Richard Benet of 1520 and his wife; twelve holes have been cut in their stone as if for a game. A third stone has an elaborate cross and an inscription to Roger Berdney of 1512 and his wife. All that is left of a fine Jacobean monument to Sir John Lockton, set up by his wife in 1628, is a panel about 2 yards long with carving in high relief of kneeling sons and daughters in ruffs and black robes, three babies in hooded cradles, and two more boys standing. Interesting for its record of exceptionally long service is a tablet to Joseph Holmes, who was vicar here from 1848 till 1911!

A mile north-west of the village is the site of a small Cistercian abbey founded in 1148. All that remains is a farmhouse built in the early 17th century with the old materials, together with a few fragments of stonework, and a stone knight in chain-mail and surcoat, still with his shield. He is set in a niche on an outside wall.

The abbey is notable because Shakespeare brings it into his *King John*, basing his story of the king's last days on a tradition that he died here after being poisoned by the monks. The legend has no foundation in fact. The king was probably ill when he left King's Lynn with his army, and became worse through the disaster which befell him when he lost all his baggage and treasures (and almost his life) while crossing the River Nene, then part of the Wash, near Sutton Bridge. It is true that he lodged at Swineshead Abbey on October 12, but he continued his journey from there, tarrying at Sleaford and Hough-on-the-Hill before reaching Newark Castle, where, on October 19, 1216, his wretched career ended.

It is Swinstead Abbey in Shakespeare, the Swin being the inlet of the Wash up which sailed the Vikings to their great encampment here, still called Man-war-ings. The head of the camp was Hubba, leader of the raiding Danes who came and conquered town after town and was killed at last in a Homeric fight with the Saxons of Devon. West of the abbey site, Manwarings is in perfect preservation, round in shape, with a diameter of 60 yards, and is surrounded by a double fosse.

A reminder of the great engineering schemes which turned the fenlands of Holland into some of the richest land in our country is seen in the South Forty Foot Drain, which is crossed by the road to Sleaford at Swineshead Bridge 2 miles away. The road from Swineshead to Brothertoft crosses the South Forty Foot at Hubbert's Bridge, named after Hubba the Dane.

Swinhope. Set in a lovely Wold valley with a stream running through, its lanes are as deep and narrow and winding as many in Devon. Secluded in a deep fold of the hills, and screened by trees within the gates of the park of the great 18th century house, stands its little church—nave and chancel, with a tiny baptistery on the south side and a tiny tower serving as a porch.

In the west wall of the tower is a lofty arch on heavy clustered shafts which looks as if it was once part of an arcade, and in its east wall is a simple 13th century doorway leading to the nave. The building still has some of its mediaeval windows and in a recess in an outside wall are part of a mediaeval floorstone and a fragment of an old shaft. At the entrance to the baptistery is a sturdy 13th century arch with great capitals a frame for the simple rugged font which is probably Norman.

In a small wood on Hoe Hill is Cromwell's Grave, a fine Neolithic long barrow, 180 feet long: another one stands in the west corner of Swinhope Park.

Swinstead. Its grey stone cottages line byways between the River Glen and the wooded slopes of Grimsthorpe Park.

At the heart of the village stands an old cross on high steps, and near it is the ancient church with hideous gargoyles looking out from its low 600-year-old tower. The nave still has a Norman arcade with three round arches, and the chancel still keeps its mediaeval piscina and its sedilia with two grotesque corbel heads. An unusual feature is the clerestory with deeply-splayed circular windows, each with three lights. There is a plain mediaeval font, borne up on four pillars. On either side of the chancel are wide openings to give a view of the altar, though one is now blocked by the organ.

Under the tower is a 700-year-old stone figure of a cross-legged knight, and in the chancel is an early 19th century marble monument with a figure of the 5th and last Duke of Ancaster kneeling by the tomb of his two wives. On the wall near it another 19th century monument, to Baroness Willoughby de Eresby, an ornate affair with her coloured coat-of-arms, elaborate canopies with four little saints, and three shield-bearing angels below.

Syston. This charming little place, 3 miles north-east of Grantham, has the River Witham on one side, and on the other a lovely 500-acre park with a big lake and plantations climbing the steep hillside.

One of the villages claiming to be the Willingham in Scott's *Heart of Midlothian*, it is the home of a very old Lincolnshire family, the Thorolds, one of whom was sheriff of the county at the Conquest. The great house (1760–1824) has gone, but the family now live in the Old Hall rebuilt in 1830 but retaining 16th century features.

The church, where many of the Thorolds rest, was restored in 1861–62, but it still has its sturdy Norman tower with splendid zigzag-ornamented arch, and a Norman north arcade with two wide arches on low piers. The Norman doorway in the porch has over it arcaded figures of nine praying saints, four of them worn, the rest restored. Eight musicians and animals bear up the nave roof.

Tallington. The main line from London enters Lincolnshire here, crossing the River Welland and the broad highway on which the village lies.

The village church, cross-shaped, has long-and-short masonry at the east end of its north aisle to reveal its Saxon origin; and there is a splendid doorway from Norman times, enriched with chevron ornament and framing a fine mediaeval door.

The walls of the church remain in all their original rugged simplicity. The nave arcades are 700 years old, and the chancel, lighted by a grand 15th century east window, has a curious Norman piscina with little side pillars and an inverted stoup for its head. The plain font with old crocketed cover is 13th century, and in the tower arch is part of the 15th century chancel screen.

The 14th century tower of the church lost its spire in the 18th century, and now its weathercock is lower than the row of limes in the churchyard. In the belfry hang three ancient bells with Latin inscriptions. In the bellcot on the eastern gable of the nave hangs the sanctus bell—silent now.

Tathwell. Charmingly secluded in a hollow of the Wolds, it has a church looking over a lake, and a century-old Hall in lovely grounds hidden among trees on the hillside opposite. Neighbouring hills with splendid views tell a far older story. On Bully Hill, an upland ridge to the south-east, are six Bronze Age round barrows; and in the north-west of the parish is a fine Neolithic long barrow with a large tree growing on it.

Originally Norman, the church was largely rebuilt in the 18th and 19th centuries; but the brick walls were raised on the foundations of its predecessor, and the old grey stonework still seen above ground is probably Norman. The tower has kept its Norman arch with capitals enriched with scallop and stiff leaf ornament, and there is an old font with a shallow bowl.

- In the chancel, and reaching from floor to roof, is a striking 17th century monument of alabaster. It shows William Hamby kneeling at a desk, and Edward and Elizabeth Hamby at another desk below, the men wearing rich robes, and the lady a flowing mantle and ruff. Thirteen children are with them, including a babe in swaddling clothes.

On the wall opposite is a marble relief showing a seated woman with her bare foot on a mask, set up 200 years ago in memory of Thomas Chaplin of Tathwell Hall; and among the other memorials is one to a grand old lady who lived into her 103rd year with unimpaired mind, wide sympathies, and a memory of the important events of six reigns. She was Jane Chaplin, a lady vigorous enough on her 100th birthday to give a dinner to her friends, and to propose a health unto His Majesty, who had sent her greetings. On her 102nd birthday, in 1913, she entertained her friends again, but before the year was out she fell asleep.

Tattershall. Standing on the River Bain, not far from its meeting with the Witham at Dogdyke, this attractive little place reflects a proud past. It is linked pre-eminently with Ralph Cromwell, who became Lord Treasurer of England nearly 20 years after he had fought for her at Agincourt. Here are remains of his castle, with its keep splendidly restored. Here is the church he built when he founded his college of the Holy Trinity. Here are the homes of charity he endowed. Here on the fine 15th century market cross is his shield, with those of Tateshall and Deyncourt. The cross has been given a new head, but it still rises from its four old high steps on the green that was once the marketplace; and though the market is no longer held the character of the market town is still evident. The modern growth is reflected in the choice of Tattershall for the fine new Tattershall Gartree Secondary Modern School built in 1962.

The first castle here was begun about 1230 by Robert of Tateshale, a descendant of Eudo, Norman lord of the manor. After the Tateshales the estates passed to the Dribys, and when the inheritance came eventually through the female line to Maud Bernak, her marriage brought the first Ralph Cromwell to Tattershall. It was their grandson, Ralph, third Lord Cromwell, who shed such lustre on this place.

One of the happy band of brothers who fought with Henry V at Agincourt, Ralph Cromwell returned home from the war in France to hold high office. Chamberlain of the Exchequer, Master of the King's Falcons, Constable of Nottingham Castle, Warden of Sherwood Forest, Lord High Treasurer of England—all these proud titles were his in turn, and for a great number of years he was a power behind the throne.

This man of many parts it was who, while he was Lord Treasurer to Henry VI, transformed the old castle of Tattershall into a magnificent home for himself, founded the college, and rebuilt the church in which he was laid to rest in 1455; and while he was carrying out this building scheme in Lincolnshire, Ralph Cromwell was expending more of his great wealth on the church at Collyweston in Northamptonshire, and a superb manor house at South Wingfield in Derbyshire, now a splendid ruin.

Excavations have recently been undertaken to discover the plan of magnificent collegiate buildings which stood on the south side of the church. Brick towers on either side of the gateway have been revealed and the enclosing wall with hexagonal towers. North of the church is the row of old almshouses (under one long pantiled roof and with pretty gardens about them) which were founded before Lord Cromwell's time but were re-endowed by him and rebuilt in 1486. These have now been attractively restored.

Built of Ancaster stone, and shaped like a cross, Ralph Cromwell's church is a striking example of the architecture of the period. Begun about 1440, it was completed by his executors, one of whom was

William of Waynflete, Bishop of Winchester, who is said to have given the north porch which bears his coat-of-arms. The tower may not have been completed until late in the century.

The nave and transepts are clerestoried, and indeed, so many fine windows has the church that they seem to take the place of walls. Their vertical tracery carries the eye to the moulded and embattled beams of the dignified old roofs and their angel supporters. There are more than 60 windows through which light streams quite unhindered, for most of the lovely stained glass once here was taken to St Martin's Church, Stamford, in the 18th century. All that remains at Tattershall has been brought together in the great east window, where it looks like a pattern in a kaleidoscope. Mingling in it are queens and angels, Our Lord emerging from the Tomb, the Holy Family, a woman in a red robe giving clothes to a beggar in rags, a fine figure of a bishop, and a man giving alms.

The chancel has its old sedilia and piscina (enriched with crockets and pinnacles, and a border with animals and flowers) and a fine stone screen with a loft which is reached by a stairway in the screen. Above the doorway (on the eastern side of the screen) is a projecting bay with two stone reading-desks; and on the nave side are pillared piscinas and recesses for altars at which mass was said for Robert de Whalley, who gave this screen in 1528 and was laid to his last rest beneath it. He was a member of Ralph Cromwell's college.

This screen divided the collegiate chancel from the people's nave; now, owing to Tattershall's shrunken population, the chancel is used for all services, and has its own pulpit—a plain one enriched with 15th century tracery and cresting, and also with the purse which symbolised Ralph Cromwell's office of Treasurer. The fine carved oak pulpit in the nave is as old as the church, but its canopy is Jacobean work. The old font is unusual, its shallow bowl (plain and tapering) set on a great traceried base.

In the north transept is a splendid brass commemorating Ralph Cromwell—a headless figure in rich armour, with two hairy savages at his feet. The brass of his wife, Margaret Deyncourt, is missing, but there is a picture showing the brass in its original beauty, with both figures complete. Like her husband, Margaret was buried at Tattershall, and so, too, were their two nieces and heiresses, whose brass portraits are here—Joan, Lady Cromwell, with jewels round her neck and six saints in her canopy; and Maud, Lady Willoughby de Eresby, wearing heart-shaped headdress, a veil and a mantle, with two belled dogs at her feet and eight saints in her canopy.

Yet another splendid brass shows a 16th century warden of the college wearing a professor's cap, cassock with fur cuffs, and handsome cope fastened with a brooch engraved with a figure of Our Lord. There are also small brass portraits of two priests—William Moor, 1456, and William Symson, 1519; and in front of the altar is the small worn brass figure of Hugh de Goudeby in long robe, his hands at prayer. He was Lord Cromwell's steward.

Ralph Cromwell's castle belongs to us all, for it was presented to the National Trust by Lord Curzon of Kedleston, whose purchase of castle and grounds in 1912 saved it, let it be hoped, for all time. Subsequent repairs and preservation included the excavation of the remains of the earlier castle and the double moat, and the restoration of the old Guard House and the great quadrangular tower or keep which had become a roofless and floorless ruin. One of the finest mediaeval brick buildings surviving in England, this tower was built to the west of the older hall by Lord Cromwell, who also added an outer ward and moat to the old enclosure. Of the original castle there remain what is now the inner moat, and the bases of two round towers at two corners of the great 15th century tower, with fragments of adjacent walling.

The Guard House is a little two-storied building with rich red walls and fireplaces and stout oak-beamed roofs. Now it is a museum in which are many things telling a silent story of life in the castle centuries ago—coins, keys, buckles, knives, stirrups, old clay pipes, many fragments of pottery made about 1600, and bits of 17th century Venetian glass.

But it is Lord Cromwell's lofty tower that lives in the memory of all who come to Tattershall. Believed to have been built to serve as his private mansion (leaving the old hall and other buildings to his great household and armed retinue), its walls are of red-brick, patterned outside with blue and black; but the windows and stringcourses, the corbels supporting the projecting and embattled gallery, and the magnificent fireplaces in the great rooms are all of stone.

With walls some 20 feet thick at their base, this noble keep is a four-storied building rising 110 feet, with octagonal turrets at the four angles climbing well above the battlements. From the parapet walk above the gallery (which is lighted by loopholes and resembles a cloister) and also from the top of the south-west turret (climbed by a winding stairway with 181 steps) there is a vast and amazing panorama over the flat countryside to Boston Stump and Lincoln Cathedral. In the great chamber of every storey is a splendid fireplace enriched with heraldic shields and emblems (including here and there the purse emblematic of Lord Cromwell's office). Round these great rooms are smaller rooms, passages, and alcoves, and there are rooms also in the turrets. The chamber on the ground floor was perhaps the guard-room, or the Common Hall. That of the first floor was the Great Hall, used as dining-room and court room; in the windows of its three alcoves is heraldic glass showing the descent of the manor.

Reached by a finely-vaulted passage in the thickness of the wall, the State Room or Great Chamber on the second floor is a magnificent apartment with five huge panels of tapestry on the walls, three fine old chests, and a long old oak table. It was probably Lord Cromwell's room, and here we may picture him in his glory. In a tiny room leading out of it is a dovecot made by a farmer after the castle had become silent and desolate; made of wood and plaster, with nesting-places for 262 birds, it is very quaint with its round holes and projecting perches. A fine feature of the third-floor chamber is the lovely vaulting of its two alcoves, adorned with tracery in its spandrels, and with heraldic bosses. Among the shields in their windows is that of the builder of the 13th century castle, Robert of Tateshale.

Ralph Cromwell left this manor and castle to the two nieces whose brasses are with his in the church, but they were with the Crown after 1471. Henry VII gave them to his mother, and Henry VIII granted them to the Duke of Suffolk. After reverting again to the Crown, they passed from family to family until this century, when the rooms were being stripped of their fireplaces and other contents, to be taken to America. There was even talk of the keep being taken down, piece by piece, and shipped across the Atlantic. Fortunately Lord Curzon stepped in, bought the castle and restored it, and then handed it all over to the National Trust. It is a great possession.

Tealby. To this lovely village under a steep slope of the Wolds came two brothers who were to win fame—the one fleeting, the other immortal. The brothers were Charles and Alfred Tennyson, whose grandfather lived at Bayons Manor. When young, they must often have worshipped in the big church standing so proudly on the hill—the church in which Charles, as curate, was later to preach. Often, too, they must have gazed out from its old stone porch at the unforgettable views both near and far. Down in the valley the little River Rase comes fresh from its source at Bully Hill, and smoke from village fires throws a gossamer veil over the homely pantiled roofs of the houses, and over the school looking rather like a little church with bellcot and spire among the trees. On the opposite slope there stood the proud towers and gables of Bayons Manor in its fine park until it was finally "blown up" in 1964 and the park gave way to modern farming techniques.

It was the Tennysons' uncle (Charles Tennyson d'Eyncourt, younger brother of their father) who made Bayons Manor a stately-battlemented house, complete with barbican and drawbridge, but enclosing parts of a Tudor house which itself succeeded a fortified dwelling centuries older. Traces of its earthworks are still to be seen. The manor belonged to the Conqueror's half-brother, Odo, Bishop of Bayeux, and the name Bayons is a link with him. A chance discovery on the estate early last century revealed another link with its early story. It was a hoard of treasure in an earthen vessel—no fewer than 600 silver coins from the time of Henry II, some of which are now in the British Museum and others in Lincoln Museum.

The story of Tealby Church, like that of the Manor, reaches back through the centuries. The lower part of the massive tower comes from the close of the Norman period, and has a low and wide arch (with huge scalloped capitals) which was opened out when the church was restored in 1872. Above the arch is a sacristan's window (round-headed), and from the hood of the west window a little head is peeping. The top stage of the tower is 15th century, with a modern parapet.

The nave, the aisles, and the chancel are partly 13th century work, the south arcade and most of the windows are a century later, and the 15th century saw the addition of the porch, the clerestory, and the embattled and pinnacled parapets. The nave roof has mediaeval beams and pendant bosses, and there is a simple Norman font with its original iron staple fastening.

The chancel has a blocked low-side window (seen outside), two niches with hoods ending in great heraldic corbels and a 15th century east window with gaily coloured heraldic glass which is modern and a few fragments of ancient glass. The other chancel windows also have some fragments of mediaeval glass. The reredos has old traceried panels and Bible scenes set in a modern frame. The altar frontal is a beautiful example of bead tapestry worked by nuns of Venice in the 17th century, and shows flowers and leaves on a silver background. The altar-table was made of oak grown on the Bayons estate.

Temple Bruer. A visit to this lonely spot, 6 miles from Sleaford, evokes memories of the Crusaders who with Bible and battle-axe went forth to hew their way to the Holy Land.

Serene in a churchyard with a yew-fringed pathway is a small stone church with a fine Crucifixion scene in its east window. But that was built in 1873, and historic interest here is centred in a grey stone tower in the middle of a farmyard, rising above the grey farm buildings and capped by a modern pyramid roof 50 feet above the ground. It has been here for seven centuries and is a remnant of one of Lincolnshire's five preceptories of that flower of Christian chivalry, the famous Order of the Knights Templars, whose houses were links in a superb chain extending throughout Europe. The tower was restored in 1961 by the Kesteven County Council with the help of the owner, Mr J. E. Mountain and the Ministry of Public Building and Works.

Six stone steps climb to the round-arched doorway of the tower, and there is a winding stair to two upper rooms. The ground floor is thought to have been a chapel, for two of its walls are enriched with the interlaced arcading of sedilia. There is an old piscina, and also a stone with a worn carving of a priest's head. The roof is finely vaulted.

In days gone by the tower was linked by a cloister to a beautiful round church, whose slight remains lie buried just to the west. The site of the church was excavated in 1833 and again in 1908. It had a circular aisled nave and apsidal aisleless chancel. In the 13th century the apse was squared and two most unusual towers built flanking it. Only four round churches survive in England—the lovely Temple church in London, one at Cambridge, another at Little Maplestead in Essex, and one at Northampton; and there is also a ruined round chapel in Ludlow Castle. They were shaped by their builders in imitation of the Church of the Holy Sepulchre at Jerusalem, and at the suppression of the Order early in the 14th century, about 24 existed in this country.

The Templars began early in the 12th century as a small company of Crusading knights vowed to the protection of pilgrims to Jerusalem, admitting to fellowship only knights sworn to poverty, austerity, and good works. With increasing membership and a widening social status, enormous estates, and riches accrued to the Order.

The proud wealth of the Templars, once sworn to poverty, incited fear and hatred against them, aroused the jealousy of the kings of England and France, and was the ultimate cause of their downfall. In 1312, when the Order was finally suppressed, the greater part of their riches and property were transferred to the Knights Hospitallers, who established a commandery at Temple Bruer.

At the Dissolution of the monasteries and religious houses, Henry VIII gave the Temple Bruer estate to his brother-in-law Charles Brandon, Duke of Suffolk. Most of the old buildings were still in evidence when the king came here with Katherine Howard, and the round church continued to withstand the buffets of time and fate until the 18th century, though by this time it had become a ruin. In the 19th century the old foundations were laid bare showing the church to have been 52 feet across (only 6 feet less than Temple Church) with a colonnade of eight round piers, and a big west porch. No trace of the round church can be seen today, but the old well, 9 feet across and never dry, is still here.

So does the past linger on in this quiet place, once the scene of strange, rapt, fierce devotion. The melancholy tower, incongruous in a scene of rustic activity, survives as a reminder of the proudest Order in the world, whose members, white-mantled and with flaming red cross on their breasts, upheld religion by the sword.

Tetford. Among the lovely wooded uplands of the Wolds it lies, gathered about roads which make a figure eight, and looking up to a hill rising boldly 468 feet above sea-level. West of the village is a fine grassy height known as Nab Hill, 400 feet high.

The church is chiefly 14th century work, on an older site, with a tower and clerestory from the 15th century, and a north aisle rebuilt in 1826. The tower has tiles worked in as building material; hideous gargoyles look out from the top and ugly buttresses reaching the battlements give it a curious stunted appearance. In the frame of a south aisle window (outside) is a niche with a leafy canopy. The porch has a holy-water stoup, and built into one of its stone seats is a gargoyle rain-water head. The lofty 14th century arcades are an impressive feature of the interior. The font is a shallow 13th century bowl on a modern cluster of shafts.

A wall memorial to Captain Edward Dymoke is a reminder of a family which has held the hereditary office of Champion to the King since the time of Richard II. It was the Champion's quaint duty at the Coronation feast to ride into Westminster Hall and, throwing down a gauntlet, challenge anyone who would dare to deny the king's right to reign. Edward Dymoke was Champion to George II, and the helmet and breastplate here are the ones he wore at the ceremony.

The early 18th century Mansion House has recently been restored and attention has been given to the interesting water-mill.

Tetney. An urn containing more than 400 Anglo-Saxon silver coins, which was unearthed here by a farmer's ploughshare in 1945, was a picturesque reminder to the people here that their village has been a dwelling-place of Englishmen for a thousand years and more.

As in most villages, however, the church is the one visible link with its remote past. Its glory is its 15th century tower of Yorkshire stone, but the rest of the building, of native sandstone, is a repository of much earlier work. When the 15th century chancel and part of the north aisle were rebuilt last century, foundations of Norman transepts were found; and in the Norman walling of the west end of the church are scorched stones, evidence of a fire. The south doorway, now blocked, is 13th century. The south aisle and the nave arcades are 14th century, one of the pillars having a Latin inscription telling that the "work was accomplished in 1363, Robert Day then vicar".

In the tower are fragments of tracery from an old screen, and a broken floorstone with a floriated cross. There also is a brass inscription recording what must surely be a record; it tells of Matthew Lakin, clerk and sexton, who rang the church bells for 84 years of last century. Two stones with finely-preserved lettering in the north aisle are memorials to 14th century Elkyntons, and there is a brass cross of 1888 in memory of the Rev. William Swaby, born at Tetney, who was Bishop of Barbados and the Windward Isles, and Archbishop of the West Indies.

Half a mile from the church, beyond the long stream from Croxby Pond, are several blow-wells, the deep pits of blue water which popular fancy declares bottomless. They are, in fact, reservoirs of artesian well water. The stream leaves the village to join the Louth Navigation Canal (made in 1763) at Tetney Lock, a hamlet 2 miles away; then both go on as one to Tetney Haven and the sea. Between the Lock and the Haven the grass-covered traces of the mediaeval sea-bank are still visible.

Theddlethorpe All Saints. Most of the farmsteads on this windswept stretch of the marshland are sheltered by brakes of trees; so is the delightful Hall of this village not far from the sea; and so, too, is the church—a landmark in this countryside, and handsome enough to have earned the name of the Cathedral of the Marsh.

The church, wisely restored, is almost all 15th century work, but some remains of its Norman predecessor are still to be seen. Its walls outside are an attractive medley of green sandstone and brick.

The lofty tower has walls nearly 5 feet thick and is of four stages, surmounted oddly by a central crocketed pinnacle covered with lead; and at one angle is a newel stairway. The stone battlements of nave and aisles are a fine feature, adorned with grotesques, and the nave gable is pierced with quatrefoils and enriched with crockets. The clerestory comes from the close of the 14th century and has five pointed two-light windows on each side.

There is much old brick in the spacious porch, which has a sweeping entrance arch and a plain old roof sheltering an ogee-headed doorway; an earlier round-headed arch is to be seen above this doorway, inside. In the wall above the north arcade are more than 60 Norman stones thought to have belonged to the original chancel arch, some carved with zigzag and some with beak ornament. Other fragments of the early church are the three sedilia and the double piscina (with new drains) in the chancel, fashioned at the close of Norman days and found in the 1866 restoration. The font of about 1400 has carved flowers and grotesques and a cover more than two centuries old.

The old rood stairway is in the north aisle, and each aisle has a chapel with a mediaeval altar stone. The south chapel has balustraded altar-rails of the 18th century, and here too is a splendid mediaeval stone reredos not unlike the one at Theddlethorpe St Helen. It is a deep recess in a richly-carved frame which has a heavy cusped arch under a fine hood formed by a double row of crockets, this being crowned by a finial and flanked by pinnacles. In a window of this aisle are old glass fragments showing two saints.

The chancel screen with its leafy arches, tracery, remains of black and gold painting, and its original gates, is fine 15th century work. Fine, too, are the screens of the chapels, made at the close of the 16th century and having among their carved scrollwork faces, angels, grotesque serpents, and the arms of the Angevine family. These arms are seen again on bosses adorning the roofs of nave and south aisle. All the roofs are old, but partly restored. The north aisle has a good array of 15th century oak seats, and there is some fine old tracery on the front and back rows of the modern benches in the nave.

There is a 14th century floorstone to Roger of Hagnaby, and another has the Angevine arms. The rarest memorial is a little brass in a chapel showing Robert Hayton, 1424, in armour with his feet on a lion. It is rare because he has a basinet with mail falling from his helmet on to his shoulders, and this is the latest known brass in which it appears. In striking contrast is a great marble monument of 1727 with busts of Charles Bertie and his wife resting on a sarcophagus.

Theddlethorpe St Helen. By the sandy seashore it lies, with a church in a bower of trees at a bend of the road. A house by the church has a cannon on each side of its gate, and not far away is the manor farm, secure behind the waters of its square moat.

In 1866 the church was almost entirely rebuilt, but the nave arcades and clerestory are mediaeval, and so is the narrow tower arch, which is unusual in having bands of flowers carved on its bases as well as on the capitals. The bowl of the font is also centuries old, but the treasure of the church is a mediaeval stone reredos in the north aisle. Deeply recessed, it is like an elaborately carved frame, enriched with wavy pattern and a graceful trefoil in its finely-crocketed head, which has a corbel head at each side. In a corner near one of these heads are tiny figures of a man and woman, perhaps the donors; below them hang two dainty festoons of flowers, and among more flowers strewn along the base and hood of the frame are many faces of men and women. The crucifix which surmounted the reredos now stands on a bracket within the recess.

In the vestry hangs a portrait of Payne Edmunds, who preached in the old church from 1810 till 1861.

Thimbleby. The declaration of the Lindsey County Council to make the eastern part of this delightful village a conservation area, highlights its neat thatched cottages along the main road. Along with the small sandstone church built in the 15th century they form a picturesque group. The church has an octagonal upper stage to the tower which carries a spire. It was restored in 1879 by James Fowler.

Thoresway. It lies in a pretty Wold valley with high hills about it, and a sparkling stream beginning a journey which ends with the Marsh and the sea; and trim and pleasant it is with its cream-walled houses and farms, and its church with tiny spire crowning the bell-turret.

The church was almost entirely rebuilt last century but has kept a north doorway from the close of Norman days, and a Norman arch (at the west end) that was once part of a tower. The chancel arch (partly restored) and the font are 14th century work; and so are the nave arcades, which were long built-up. A little older are four floorstones, three of them enriched with floriated crosses.

Thorganby. Here in this open valley of the Wolds is a link with the Civil War—the Old Hall plundered by the Roundheads. It has finely-wooded grounds sloping to a clear trout stream.

Watching over the farms and the cottages with pantiled roofs is a humble little church which comes partly from the 13th century and has been restored. Of the 13th century there remain two lancets in the chancel, the chancel arch, and the sturdy arches of the nave. A 14th century window in the nave has attractive modern glass showing St Hugh with his swan and a picture of Lincoln Cathedral. From the 15th century come nine or ten fine traceried bench-ends on which the rest of the seats have been modelled. The font is another survival from mediaeval times.

Thornton Curtis. A village of the byways a few miles from the Humber, it has its own lovely old church, an early 18th century Hall and, by the East Halton Beck 2 miles away, the fine remains of Thornton Abbey.

Except for some later windows, and for the chancel, which reveals in part its Norman origin, the village church is chiefly 13th century work, and was finely restored 60 years ago. The 12th century remains in the chancel include round-headed windows in the side walls, a stringcourse, two lovely piscinas (one with a pointed head of a later period), and a doorway with foliage capitals, curiously set in a wide flat buttress of the north wall. The south wall has another Norman buttress.

The pinnacled tower has lancet windows and a splendid arch with five shafts on each side. The stone-vaulted porch has been rebuilt, but shelters a charming 13th century doorway with richly-foliated capitals and shafts adorned with dog-tooth. Its splendid door is largely old work and still swings on old C hinges enriched with scrolls.

A lovely feature of the spacious, dignified interior are the 13th century nave arcades with arches on clustered pillars; pleasing, too, is the south arcade, with some of its capitals foliated, and others, like the shafts below them, decorated with dog-tooth. Nave and chancel are under one roof, and are divided by a tall modern oak screen adorned with tracery. The south aisle windows have the leaf tracery of the late 14th century, and the east window of the chancel is a fine patch of colour showing two saints, and Christ as the Good Shepherd and the Light of the World.

The font, though damaged, is still magnificent. Made at the close of Norman days, of black marble from Tournai in Belgium, it is set on steps forming a cross, and has a square bowl carved with fabulous animals. It is the church's rarest possession, for in all the land there are only six other fonts like it: in Lincoln Cathedral, in Winchester Cathedral, in St Peter's, Ipswich, in St Michael's, Southampton, and in two other Hampshire village churches, East Meon and St Mary Bourne.

The story of Thornton Abbey, dedicated to St Mary, goes back to 1139, when it was founded by William le Gros (Earl of Albemarle and Lord of Holderness) for a prior and 12 Augustinian canons who came from Kirkham in Yorkshire a year later. In 1148 the house was raised to the dignity of an abbey, and in 1517 it became a mitred abbey. After the Dissolution, Henry VIII refounded it as a college, dedicated to the Holy Trinity, and with his court was entertained here for three days. That was in 1541. Six years later the college in turn was suppressed and the lands given to the Bishop of Lincoln.

The abbey covered 100 acres and was surrounded by a wall and a moat; and the remains bear eloquent testimony to its former magnificence. Of the cross-shaped church, which was 282 feet long, and 128 feet across the transept, all that remains above ground is a fragment of the early 14th century south transept. It consists of a great part of its south and east walls, enriched with traceried panelling. Other fragments of the church are bases of pillars, a stone coffin, and many of its floorstones, some richly adorned, and others with evidence of vanished brasses.

There is also a fine fragment of the 14th century chapter house. Only two sides remain, but they are enough for the imagination to visualise the lovely octagon, which was 43 feet across and may well have rivalled the one at York. The walls are enriched with lofty arches framing exquisite panelling, and below them is rich trefoiled arcading. Recent excavation has laid bare the foundations of the other walls of the octagon.

There are traces of other buildings near the cloister court, and in the farmhouse to the south of the site of the church is the groined lower storey of what is thought to have been the abbot's lodging. There are also many old carved stones in the farmyard walls.

The most impressive of all these old ruins, however, is the noble gatehouse and barbican of stone and brick, built in 1382 (in Early

Perpendicular style) by Abbot Thomas de Gretham, and reached by a remarkable brick bridge over a dry moat.

Built in the time of Henry VIII, the bridge is about 120 feet long and has a round tower at the beginning of each of its long, embattled, and deeply arcaded walls. It is a rare approach to the west front of the gatehouse, which is in splendid preservation and a picturesque sight with its three archways, its four octagonal turrets climbing above the roof, and its fine array of canopied niches. In the lower row of a group of six niches above the beautifully decorated central archway is a sculpture of the Madonna being crowned by the Trinity; to the right and left of the Madonna are other statues, probably representing St John the Baptist and St Augustine.

The rich vault of the main archway has fine floral bosses and two others carved with giant heads. There are some remains of the two great oak doors, and the grooves of the portcullis can still be seen. On the ground floor are guard-rooms, and on the first floor, reached by a newel stairway, is the great hall 48 feet long and 21 wide. The hall has a fireplace 10 feet long, the opening in the wall where the portcullis was raised, and a lovely oriel window in the east wall. An altar was below the oriel, and the old piscina is still here. There are two smaller windows on this side of the hall, and on the south wall is one of four lights. Three corbel heads once supported another storey.

In the thickness of the great walls of the gatehouse are narrow passages leading to little chambers. The newel stair has a lovely vault with eight cinquefoiled ribs rising from corbels carved with little men. All who climb the stone stair to the roof are rewarded by a fine bird's-eye view of fields and woods and farms stretching to the Wolds, and to Hull across the shining Humber.

From the grassy court beyond the gatehouse, its eastern front is seen in all its glory of rare old brickwork, proud turrets, archways, and lovely windows. Above the finely-moulded central archway the exquisite oriel can be seen borne on the head and shoulders of a man, and below the plain parapet runs a corbel table of grotesques.

Thornton-le-Moor. A tiny place between the River Ancholme and the Wolds, it has a little church that may go back to Saxon times.

The church has a late Norman doorway, sheltered by a modern porch, and displays Early English work in its fine double bell-gable, in one or two original lancet windows, in one of the quatrefoil windows of a rebuilt clerestory, and in a built-up north arcade with quaint corbel heads between its four arches, under which modern lancet windows have been set.

The chancel was completely rebuilt in Victorian times but it has an aumbry fashioned from fragments of a 13th century coffin-lid and a stone with Saxon interlaced carving. The font has a mediaeval bowl and base, and a 19th century cover crowned with a rose. There is also a Jacobean chest. Among ancient floorstones is one with a floriated cross; another, now in the wall of the porch, has a worn carving of a man with hands clasped in prayer.

The chalice was the gift of John Le Neve, rector here from 1722 till 1741. He was a man devoted to antiquarian research, and after leaving Cambridge spent much of his time recording monuments and inscriptions—a veritable Hakluyt among the monuments in our churches. He published several volumes containing the results of his researches, but they were unprofitable and he found himself deeply in debt. Having taken holy orders he was presented to this rectory, but his creditors were remorseless, and for a time he was thrown into a debtor's prison at Lincoln. John Le Neve gave this chalice to his church; it is the only memorial of this man who lavished so much attention on the monuments of others.

Thorpe-on-the-Hill. Its hill is but a gentle rise, half a mile north of the Roman Fosse Way. On its summit is a pyramid-capped tower which was rebuilt in the 18th century but includes Norman work. The rest of the church was rebuilt in 1912, striking features being the barrel roof and the nave arcade with three pointed arches sweeping to the ground unbroken by capitals. The tall oak screen is a memorial to Edward King, much-loved Bishop of Lincoln.

Near the church is a red-brick Methodist Chapel built in 1909 as a memorial to John Hunt, who at the beginning of last century worked here in his teens as a ploughman, educated himself in the little leisure he had, and preached in the villages on the Sabbath. When he was 21 he went to the Hoxton College for Wesleyans, studied hard for three years, and then went out as a missionary to Fiji. For 10 years he preached the Gospel to the natives on the islands and translated the New Testament into their language, dying there as a young man of 36, a victim of overwork. His life and work is commemorated in the Museum of Lincolnshire Life in Lincoln.

Thorpe St Peter. A neighbour of Wainfleet, it has a mediaeval church sheltering among trees and reached by a path bordered by shapely yews. It is a squat little building, largely of 14th century work, though the porch and its inner doorway are a century older, and the clerestory and top of the creepered tower (with a crown of battlements and tall leafy pinnacles) are 15th century additions. In the outer walls of the chancel (partly rebuilt) are blocked arches and a piscina telling of vanished chapels.

The interior is pleasing with its tall arcades and its windows shedding a golden light. There are fine old roofs with rough-hewn beams of all shapes; a chancel screen enriched with rose-tipped tracery and eagles; and a splendid Jacobean pulpit with carvings of sea-serpents and faces with mouths from which grapes and thistles are emerging.

There is also a lovely 700-year-old font resting on part of an old altar stone; its bowl is carved with trefoiled arcading and though its supporting shafts are gone, their capitals remain, carved with foliage and heads of a bishop, a king, and a knight. At the west end of the nave is a coffin-lid with a cross and inscription.

Threekingham. A small village with an ancient story, it stands among the fertile pastures where the Roman King Street, going north, crosses the road going eastward to the Fens. Its name is traditionally a link with a battle fought in the 9th century at Stow Green close by, when the Danes were routed with great slaughter and three of their kings or chieftains were slain. Another reminder of this is a fine old rambling inn; but a more commonplace explanation of the name is that the Threcking or Thriking is a tribal name of Saxon origin.

The fine steeple soars 150 feet, the lower part of the tower and its fine arch being 13th century work, the upper stage and the broach spire 14th. The chancel and the eastern bay of the nave come from late Norman times, the chancel having three Norman windows linked by arcading in its east wall, and a built-up arch which once led to a chantry. The nave arcades are 600 years old, borne up on pillars round, clustered, and octagonal. The south porch with its arcaded walls is also 14th century and shelters a double door with fine old scrolled ironwork.

The font has an arcaded 13th century bowl on a 15th century base, the nave has many mediaeval benches with ends richly carved with tracery and foliage, and in an aisle are the combined stocks and whipping-post. At the west end of the church is a massive stone monument with a figure of a 7-foot giant in chain-mail and tunic with two lions at his feet; his wife is by his side in flowing dress and veil and with two dogs at her feet. This knight is believed to represent a 13th century judge, Sir Lambert de Threckingham, and three huge stone coffins close by, with crosses carved on their lids, probably entombed other members of his family, and not the three Danish kings as popular legend would have.

At the end of the south aisle, just to the left of the porch, is a sundial with the inscription *1688, gifte of Edmund Hutchinson, Gentleman.* Gentleman indeed, and a wise one, too, to have had the happy thought of linking his name with the sunny hours through all eternity!

Stow Green has a fame apart from its being the traditional site of the battle in which the three Danish chieftains fell, for it has one of the oldest chartered fairs in our land. It is said to have been originated in Norman days by a tinker, from whose one stall developed a horse and pleasure fair which lasted several weeks.

Thurlby. Nearly a thousand years of history are reflected in its church, and nearly a thousand more by the Roman Carr Dyke, once the principal waterway of the Fens, serving for both drainage and transport. Linking the Nene with the Witham, the Dyke was nearly 60 miles long, and though it can be traced for most of the distance, one good stretch is at Thurlby, where its few feet of water divide the vicarage from the church. Near the big village flows the River Glen, leaving its winding course to cut a straight way through the Fen to meet the Bourne Eau at Tongue End.

After the Romans came the Saxons; and although some authorities maintain that the church is not older than the Conquest, others recognise the long-and-short work at the corners of the tower as positively Saxon and the triangle-headed doorway above the arch inside also belongs to this period. It was built perhaps as a fortress as well as a sanctuary, and for patron was chosen St Firmin, first Bishop of Amiens, who was martyred early in the fourth century. It is one of the few churches with his name. The Normans came after the Saxons, writing the place down in their Domesday Book as Turolvebi.

Shaped like a cross, the church is still fortress-like, its west windows overlooking all comings and goings along the Fens as of old. The tower is a massive structure, with Norman masonry above the long-and-short, crowned by bird-like gargoyles and a short 14th century spire bristling with little gables. The Norman arch of the tower is framed by one still older, and in the wall above them is the triangular-headed doorway. The room above is reached by climbing the ladder into the belfry.

The church has two spacious and well-restored 13th century porches, one sheltering a Norman doorway, the other an ancient door and three 700-year-old stone coffin-lids with ornamented crosses. The nave has Norman arches borne on massive piers with cushion capitals, four 15th century clerestory windows on each side, and an ancient roof with massive beams. The chancel was rebuilt in the 13th century, though its big east window is 15th and its south wall has a blocked Norman arch enriched with zigzag, probably set up in later years as a canopy for sedilia. The chancel has a trefoil-headed piscina and two aumbries, each with its central oak pillar, though the doors have gone. The rood-loft stairs and doorway can still be seen, and on each side of the chancel is a chantry chapel with a peephole to the altar.

The transepts are 13th century work and are notable for their stone benches and wall-arcading, the south transept on one side only with five pointed arches, the north with four trefoil-headed arches on two sides. The font is Norman, with a low bowl divided into panels by ribs adorned by primitive heads. Other interesting features are a fine fragment of a mediaeval screen with battlemented cornice, and altar-rails and a carved chair of the 17th century.

Thurlby. It is the Thurlby not far from Lincoln—a tranquil village on a chestnut-shaded lane, with a thin line of poplars pointing the way to the church and to the River Witham flowing peacefully by. Big enough for a hundred folk to gather together in worship in its little nave and narrow aisle, the church was much restored a century ago, but the doorway through which they come and go was built at the close of Norman times. The chancel is lighted by seven lancets and the nave has a simple late 13th century arcade with low pillars. A coffin-lid, set up in the north aisle, shows in sunk relief the bust of a woman praying. The splendid 14th century font has what may be the Crucifixion carved on one side of its bowl, flowers and leaves on the others, and angels below; the stem is delicately traceried, and the base is enriched with shells and foliage.

Much of the woodwork in the church is notable, for there is an old chest with rich panels of flowers and foliage, a Jacobean tower screen with bands of foliage, and a mediaeval chancel screen remarkable because the cusps of its tracery are like greyhound heads, sharp of nose and long of ear. The modern benches are also striking for they have big poppyheads shaped like the fleur-de-lys, orb, crown, and various kinds of crosses. One of the crosses is the VC and it serves to remind us (as does the east window with its Resurrecton scene) of a village hero, Gonville Bromhead, VC, who was born in Versailles, one of a fine family of soldiers. During the Zulu War of 1879 Bromhead and his friend John Chard each won the VC at the Battle of Rorke's Drift.

Timberland. Its cottages and farms and church lie snugly together in a well-wooded countryside redeemed from bog and fen. The Romans brought their Carr Dyke close by (some of their coins have been found here) and the Normans built the first church here, a man named Lundi being the first recorded priest in a list going back to 1145. Of this Norman church all that remains is the tower arch in which the Early English builders inserted a stout pointed arch when they rebuilt the tower. The tower has since been heavily buttressed and its battlemented top storey was added in the 15th century. The chancel and its big arch were rebuilt last century, but the nave still has its mediaeval arches on clustered piers. There is an ancient piscina with four carved pillars, and the font, with quatrefoiled roses on its bowl and heads of women and animals below, is 600 years old.

Timberland will always be associated in the world of historical scholarship with Canon C. W. Foster, its vicar from 1902–35, founder of the Lincoln Record Society.

Toft-by-Newton. A tiny place between the River Ancholme and the Rase, it has a tiny church rebuilt in 1890 but still preserving some ancient carved stones in its walls. In the south wall of the nave are three 13th century fragments: parts of a foliated capital, a carved head, and a cross. In the north wall are a battered 14th century bracket and a fragment of interlacing work which may be part of a Saxon cross. Two more fragments, showing plaitwork and interlacing bands, are set on a base of old stones in the churchyard.

Torksey. Now a village much visited for its well known golf course, it came into Domesday Book as a town. The Romans developed this place as a key point at the junction of the Foss Dyke with the Trent. Extensive Roman potteries have been located by excavation at Little London. The Danes found Lincolnshire easy of attack, not only along its coast, but also inland, because they could sail all the way to Lincoln by way of the Humber, the Trent, and the Foss Dyke. In 873 the Danish invaders spent a winter at Torksey.

In the 12th century two small priories were founded here—the Priory of St Leonard for Austin canons, and the Priory of Fosse for Cistercian nuns. Nothing remains of these, but Torksey Castle, the Elizabethan home of the Jermyn family, is a substantial red-brick ruin on farmland near the river, a striking spectacle with a long line of jagged wall and many windows; during the Civil War it was occupied by the Parliamentarians till taken by Royalists from Newark.

The church (which some say was the chapel of the canons) has a humble exterior, and its best work is inside—a handsome 13th century nave arcade of three bays with arches resting on four clustered piers. There is also a huge font from the end of the 12th century, adorned with a band of leaves. Outside, at the foot of the embattled tower, are some old coffins. A stone figure of a woman, worn by long exposure in the churchyard, is now safe in a niche in the wall; it is said to be the memorial of a prioress of the nunnery.

The pottery tradition begun by the Romans was continued in the Middle Ages. Further kilns have been located south of the castle.

It was in the neighbouring township of Brampton that William Billingsley and his son-in-law made the china and pottery known as Torksey Ware—rare now, because the business ended five years after its founding in 1803. Billingsley, known for his skill in painting flowers and scenery on china, came here after working for William Duesbury at the works in Derby, and in 1808 went to Worcester. Examples of Torksey Ware may be seen in the Usher Gallery, Lincoln.

Toynton All Saints. This neighbour of Spilsby, looking out on a fine stretch of flat countryside, has cottages in pretty gardens along a deep-cut lane. An extensive pottery industry, sited on the lower slopes of the Wolds overlooking the Fens, has been discovered by excavation. Starting in the mid-13th century it continued into the 17th century. Kilns and "waster" pottery tell the story.

The church is Georgian but restoration early this century revealed the old arcades now exposed in the nave walls, the south arcade being 14th century, and the north (with pointed arches on round pillars) marking the transition from the Norman period. The windows are chiefly 15th century. The font has a shallow mediaeval bowl on a modern base.

Less than a mile away is Toynton St Peter (also known as Potter Toynton), with a neat church (restored and patched with old brick) at the end of a narrow lane. It retains its 15th century tower, a 14th century north arcade of low arches, and a 14th century font, adorned with shields and tracery. By the tower doorway are the base and 5 feet of the shaft of the old churchyard cross.

Trusthorpe. Those who knew this village 50 years ago would hardly recognise it today. Bungalows, camps, and caravans have changed the face of this quiet little neighbour of Mablethorpe and Sutton-on-Sea. Almost gone, too, are the sandhills; and the encroaching sea is held in check by an immense concrete sea defence which also serves as a promenade along the popular stretch of sands. But for those who like a restful seaside holiday with the quiet of the English countryside close at hand Trusthorpe has many attractions. On the shore, at low tide, can be seen remains of a submerged forest rooted in the boulder-clay and submerged 2500 BC.

The church has been rebuilt, but the tower of mellowed brick comes from 1606, and the chancel arch has 14th century sides. The fine traceried font is mediaeval and there is a stone inscription in the tower asking a prayer for 16th century Richard Wright and his family.

Tupholme. Two miles from Bardney, and close to the Horncastle road, are the slight remains of Tupholme Abbey, founded for Premonstratensian canons by Gilbert and Alan de Neville in the time of Henry II. All that survives, picturesque even in its raggedness and neglect, is part of the refectory wall, leaning on the gable of a row of cottages and stretching to others nearby. Between the five deeply-splayed lancets and one round-headed window in the old wall is the stone pulpit used by the reader during meals.

Tydd St Mary. St Mary is its church, and Tydd is the tide which reaches its limit up the River Nene 1 or 2 miles away. Cambridgeshire and Norfolk meet in this corner of the Lincolnshire Fen, and the two great drains which bound it on the north and south (the South Holland and the North Level) empty into the river nearby.

A lovely grove shades the road near the church, a graceful building which is largely 14th century work but in its clerestoried nave displays the fine arcades built at the end of the Norman period. The brick tower, with stone dressings and slender stone spire, comes from the close of the 15th century and is unusual for its double arch of brick and stone, opening to the nave; it is adorned outside by three little niches with quaint statues of Edward VII, Bishop Edward King, and the Madonna, all set up to mark King Edward's coronation. A fine cross crowns the old sanctus bell niche (now filled) on the east gable of the nave, and an old sundial marks the hours on the restored south porch.

The long 14th century chancel, still with its original arch, has fine sedilia with cinquefoiled arches and corbel heads of a man and a wimpled woman, a double piscina with trefoiled arches, and a blocked low-side window. The fine but battered 15th century font has on its eight sides angels with shields bearing sacred emblems. On a floorstone in the north aisle is the engraved portrait of William de Tidde, who died about 1395, showing him with his mailed head on a cushion and his feet on a lion. Eighteenth century monuments are to the Trafford family.

Uffington. Here, between the road and the river going east from Stamford, is a beautiful wooded park with a splendid avenue of limes; facing it are grey stone village buildings, a thatched hall and an inviting thatched inn among them. Opposite a gateway of Uffington Hall is another fine iron gateway opening to a churchyard where grand old trees spread their branches high above a long yew avenue.

The church comes from mediaeval days, but the nave with its three round arches on each side was rebuilt last century, when new oak was brought in for the roofs and new stone for the chancel. Much of it, therefore, is new; all of it is well-cared-for. From the 15th century come the tower with lofty crocketed spire, and the north chapel belonging to the Trollope family whose home is the delightful Jacobean Casewick Hall, a mile away. It has fine 18th century additions including the magnificent front. Among the church's fine old possessions are two chairs with carved backs, and a brass candelabra of 1685 engraved with two royal heads and crowned by two cherubs.

The oldest of a splendid array of monuments is a stone warrior, 6 feet tall, lying in a handsome panelled recess between chancel and chapel. Found built into a wall, he is a knightly figure clad in 14th century armour, his feet on a lion and his head on a helmet, and is thought to be Richard de Schropschire, standard-bearer to Thomas,

5th Lord Roos, and a constable or governor of Belvoir. On the chancel wall facing him is a grand marble and alabaster monument to two brothers who were also associated with Belvoir. We see them kneeling on rich cushions in their gilded armour, with wide ruffs, and little metal spurs—Sir Roger Manners, who was esquire of the body to Queen Mary and her sister Queen Elizabeth, and his brother Oliver, who served Elizabeth "in her warres at Newhaven" and died of the plague in 1563. By the altar is another wall-monument showing a 17th century man and wife kneeling, a quaint little girl behind each; the man is Dr Lawrence Stanton, a rector who became Dean of Lincoln.

Ulceby. A big village in pleasant setting a few miles from the Humber, it has a fine little church crowned by a tall 500-year-old spire, which on close examination shows a distinct twist.

The tower, adorned with great gargoyles, is chiefly 13th century work; and the long chancel is as old, although, like the south aisle, it has been much restored. The clerestoried nave and arcades, all remarkable for their height, is 14th century. The south porch is modern.

The chancel is lighted by windows of the 14th and 15th century and has an extraordinary arch leading to the north chapel—6 yards wide and looking not unlike the span of a bridge. There are piscinas and aumbries in both chancel and south aisle, and there is also an oak chair carved with foliage. The east window of the south aisle is in memory of a former vicar and one of the figures has a representation of his features with side-whiskers and Moses is shown holding the tablet of stone inscribed *Exodus XX*.

A striking feature is the splendid array of richly-traceried old bench-ends which, together with the 15th century chancel screen, give a touch of rare distinction to the church interior. The screen is enriched with tracery and has trefoiled arches tipped with roses. All that is left of the old churchyard cross bears an 18th century sundial to mark the passing hours.

Upton. A small village by the River Till, it has a windmill, and a church of Norman origin on a mound by the highway.

In the 18th century the tower of the church was rebuilt after the old one had fallen, and a century later the rest was much restored. But the nave still has a Norman south doorway with a big plain tympanum, and the chancel has a mass of fine herringbone masonry in its leaning south wall, as well as a little in the north wall. The great chancel arch (only slightly pointed) and the nave arcade of two bays (reopened to a new aisle after long being bricked-up) are early 13th century work. Still here, too, is the old doorway which led to the rood stairway.

Two acres of Upton land, left by two 17th century benefactors, are let to the highest bidder every year on the first of May, the rent being given to the poor.

Utterby. Here, across a shady lane, village church and manor house face each other as they have done through many centuries.

Utterby Manor, with its three-storied porch and Dutch gable, was enlarged in late Victorian times, but has on its old fabric the date 1639 and the coat-of-arms of the Elye family who acquired the manor in the 16th century. The church has a restored tower, chancel, and tiny chapel from the 14th century, and a 15th century nave. Within the porch is a dainty little doorway with crocketed hood and finial, and moulding dotted with flowers and leaves, human heads and grotesques, a fox with geese, a bearded man with a club and a monkey on a string, and a monkey holding a child. The rugged old door still has its original iron boss for a ring.

The chancel keeps its old piscina and aumbry, a statue bracket, and a windowsill serving as a sedile. By the chancel arch is a beautiful canopy shaped like a turret with embattled top, and richly carved with tracery and flowers. The screen, stalls, altar-rails, and canopied reredos are all fine examples of modern woodwork.

In the wall of the north aisle is a memorial stone to a 14th century vicar, William Cumberworth, which shows his half-figure deeply sunk in a quatrefoil, his hands clasped in prayer. Another memorial is a hatchment with the coloured arms of William Davison who died a young man in 1702. Hatchments were hung out of the window of a house where a dead person lay, and put in the church after the funeral; but it is rare to find one inscribed as a memorial.

Another rare sight is the open channel by the 14th century font, made for draining off the water into the churchyard, and in this case left uncovered.

In the churchyard is the lower part of an old cross, and by the side of the road crossing the stream below the church is a disused packhorse bridge, 600 years old.

Waddingham. A big but trim village between the Ermine Street and the new River Ancholme, it has the attractions of a big green and a wayside stream, and a windmill which has unfortunately lost its sweeps.

Long ago there were two churches here, but only one remains—much restored in Victorian times, when its 13th century chancel was rebuilt. The original chancel arch still stands, however, enriched with foliage and nail-head, and of the same age as this arch are the nave arcades, two lancets in the south aisle, and the restored south doorway. The tower with its catlike gargoyles is chiefly 15th century work, but the west window is modern.

Wainfleet All Saints. It is a pleasant market town set in the rich marshland. Formerly it was a port but is now some miles from the sea. Standing on the River Steeping, which began as the River Lymn and goes on as Wainfleet Haven to the sea at Gibraltar Point 5 miles away, the town itself is 2 miles from the marshy coast and the great expanse of Wainfleet Sands.

The town shines brightly in our history as the birthplace of the great William of Waynflete who was the first Provost of Eton, Bishop of Winchester, Lord Chancellor to Henry VI, and tutor to Edward, Prince of Wales. He obtained for the town its charter, and after giving Magdalen College to Oxford, gave this town in 1484 the finest building it has today, the Magdalen College School. Standing near the river, and sheltered by a row of chestnut trees, this lovely two-storied structure of mellowed red-brick, 26 feet wide and three times as long, is a little reminiscent of Tattershall Castle which the bishop helped to complete many years earlier, after Lord Cromwell's death. Two eight-sided towers flank the west front; one contains a remarkable newel staircase, the other an old bell. It now serves as a secondary modern school and has recent additions of classrooms and other facilities.

There are many old pantiled houses and shops along the trim roads. Two unusual terraces of High Victorian houses are to be seen in Barcumbe Street. The old cross still stands in the marketplace; but the town's two old churches are gone. Of St Thomas's church at Northolme only the churchyard is left. All Saints was pulled down in 1820, but some of its materials were used in the building of the present church on a new site near the station.

Among the remains of the old church built into the new are a 15th century window and two canopied niches in the west wall, and the fine 15th century font adorned with emblems of the Passion, figures holding shields, and other carving. There is also a Jacobean carved chair.

The splendid tomb with the figure of William of Waynflete's father, Richard Patten, which the Bishop erected in the old church, shared in its destruction, but its fragments were collected and preserved in the old school until 1829, when it was restored and placed in Magdalen College Chapel, Oxford. The College, in return, has set up a tablet to Richard Patten here. Another inscription tells of the famous William himself, but it is in Winchester Cathedral that he lies.

Wainfleet St Mary. Most of the folk here have a long walk on Sunday, for their church is a mile and a half from the village—dignified and aloof and completely hidden in a cluster of fine beeches and other trees.

It is a fine marshland church with its roots in the Norman period.
It was much rebuilt last century but still has considerable remains
from the 13th and 15th centuries. The tower is of both these periods,
and has beautiful arcading on its walls, and a low arch resting on
fluted corbels that belong to the late Norman period.

Most unusual is the 15th century doorway within the porch, for
peeping from its moulding are 10 busts of men and women—some
with happy faces, others serious, and one seemingly in great pain;
there is also an old fury with her tongue out, and another old woman
in frilled headdress is leaning over the top of the hood.

The best features of the interior are the 13th century arcades of
the nave. The north arcade has five bays and the south four, and
all the massive pillars are round except for a particularly fine one
which is hollowed to accommodate four detached and banded
shafts.

Old relics are two mediaeval floorstones with crosses, set in the
walls of the tower; a Jacobean table in the vestry; and the fine bowl
of a 15th century font with tracery and shields with Passion emblems.
The modern screen has a base of linenfold, traceried bays with gilt
and colour, and figures of the Rood.

Waithe. Where the road from Louth to Grimsby is crossed by
a stream flowing to Tetney and the sea, stands this tiny village, with
a Saxon tower to bespeak its ancient story.

Striking in its simplicity, the tower is between nave and apsidal
chancel, its rough stone slightly dressed, and its windows above the
stringcourse divided by mid-wall shafts with heavy imposts. This
tower and the 13th century nave arcades (with clustered piers) are
the only notable features of the church, which was rebuilt last
century.

Two fine cedars soar up among the many trees in the churchyard,
where there is also a modern cross set on an ancient base.

Walcot. East of Grantham, it is an attractive prospect when seen
from the neighbouring slopes, it has mellow red roofs clustered
together in friendly concourse and a lofty grey 14th century spire
soaring above them, its lines of crockets standing out boldly against
the sky.

The church is a spacious one, displaying great antiquity. The
nave arcades are 13th century, but rest on bases which were formerly
Norman capitals; and the tub-shaped font with two bands of foliage
and faces is also Norman but recut in the 18th century. The aisles
have fine 14th century windows, and more light streams in through
a 15th century clerestory. From mediaeval days come also a fine
canopied niche, a double peephole with a projecting piscina supported by a carved head, a piscina in a chancel windowsill and

another in the south aisle. There is a finely-carved oak chest and 28 bench-ends 500 years old. A priest's doorway, contrived out of a window, is decorated with a band of oak leaves.

Walesby. An old village climbing the western slope of the Wolds, it boasts two splendid churches—one old and one new. Evidence of Walesby's antiquity was a Roman villa covering an area of 100 square yards which was unearthed here in 1861. Portions of hypocausts were excavated, and in an ashpit not far away were found many other antiquities—broken bowls of Samian ware, a stone chisel, spindle whorls, and bones of sheep, oxen, and deer.

Down in the village is the new parish church—an enduring memorial to Perceval Laurence who was rector here for 34 years and, having worked long and diligently to get this new house of prayer, died on the very day in 1913 that the building was begun.

Designed by Mr Temple Moore, the church has a small west tower with a carillon of eight bells, and an attractive interior where the stately arches of a central arcade soar from slender shafted pillars to the ridge of the deep nave roof. Another pleasing effect is given by two 15th century windows set in front of modern ones in chancel and vestry, one of them making a charming frame for three sedilia. The mediaeval font from the old church is here, and there is also an old oak chest.

The old church of All Saints is away up on the hill, from where there is a glorious view across the plain to the distant towers of Lincoln. One of the finest churches hereabouts, it was long neglected and only just escaped being pulled down. Careful restoration has brought back its old beauty, and now it is open to all and occasionally in summer used for services.

Except for its 15th century buttresses and parapet, the tower is 13th century work, lighted by a west lancet and coupled lancets in the belfry; two of its eight bells were here in mediaeval days. The porch is also 13th century. The nave has massive arcades—the north from the close of the Norman period and the south from the 13th century; two of the capitals of the north arcade are fine examples of stiff leaf carving, and a capital on the south side has six quaint little heads. The canopied Jacobean pulpit (brought here from the chapel at Kirkstead) and the traceried modern screen and rood-loft are an unusual sight, for they are painted white. The old rood stairway is behind the pulpit.

The chancel was built about 1300 and still has its priest's doorway, double piscina, and ancient altar stone with five crosses. The south chapel also has a double piscina, and on a windowsill of this aisle is a tiny incised floorstone of the 13th century. Among several other floorstones is one commemorating Henry Waterland, a 17th century rector. One of his sons, Daniel Waterland—born at the old rectory here in 1683—was a learned theologian and author of a famous history of the Athanasian Creed.

Walmsgate. This delightful spot in a lovely wooded patch of the Wolds was once notable for its great house, Walmsgate Hall. This has now gone and the furniture of the private chapel, built in 1901, that stood next to the house has been used to furnish a new church at Langworth.

Waltham. The built-up area between Grimsby and Waltham is now almost continuous and the parish of New Waltham was formed in 1961. There is a fine windmill still surviving in the village.

The church has been much restored and partly rebuilt. The stone vault of the base of the 13th century tower has given place to timber groining, but the old sacristan's window still looks into a nave flanked by 700-year-old arcades with clustered pillars.

The chancel, as long as the nave, is chiefly 14th century work and has its old sedilia with crocketed gables and finials and its double piscina with a carved border of leaves. Each aisle also has a double piscina. The 15th century font is enriched with angels and flowers and tracery; and there is an old chest with three flaming suns on its panels.

On a chancel windowsill is the brass portrait of Joanna Waltham of 1420, wearing draped headdress, with her son and daughter. On another sill is a brass inscribed to the parents of John Waltham, who, born in this quiet Lincolnshire village, became known all over the land as Bishop of Salisbury and Lord High Treasurer during the reign of Richard II, with whom he was a great favourite; his own splendid brass is in Westminster Abbey, where, by order of Richard II, he was buried among the kings. No record of his birth or parentage was known until 1849, when this memento was found, broken and buried under a pew.

Washingborough. Here the Fens begin, and here the Romans brought one end of their Carr Dyke, cut as a catch-water and navigation canal between the Nene near Peterborough and the Witham at this spot 3 miles east of Lincoln. Into this great canal, nearly 60 miles long and 50 feet wide, came the water that once flooded the land and with the construction of this waterway the Romans were able not only to drain the low-lying land, but to provide part of a fine system of canals to transport grain to the north. The Dyke is now sometimes difficult to trace but there are still a few perfect stretches left, notably between Sleaford and Bourne.

At the heart of the village a modern cross stands on the steps of the old, and near it is a fine church with massive 14th century tower, heavily buttressed, and with eight imps and demons looking out below the battlements. The dignified interior has four pointed arches soaring up on each side of the nave, some of their round pillars having capitals with graceful foliage. Modern restorations have taken away much of the church's ancient look, but the splendid Norman font is here, enriched with arcading, foliage, and stars. There are two old traceried chests, old balustrated altar-rails, and an 18th century brass candelabra adorned with cherub heads and said to have belonged to George IV.

The oldest memorial is one of those rare mediaeval gravestones such as are to be seen also at Norton Disney, Kingerby, and Welby, showing only the feet and the upper part of the figure. Here the figure is of a veiled 14th century lady in her wimple, her head resting on a pillow held by angels.

Welbourn. It is a peaceful farming village on the Cliff road, halfway between Grantham and Lincoln, with the lowland stretching away westward to the River Brant, and the high heathland running eastward to Ermine Street. The church, standing a little aloof from most of the village, is approached through its iron churchyard gates which are a memorial to good King George V.

The 13th century tower is crowned by a crocketed 15th century spire supported by flying buttresses and adorned by a row of mediaeval faces below the battlements. Porch, nave, and aisles were all built in the 14th century, the porch having canopied buttresses and a niche containing a battered sculpture of the Holy Trinity. The stately nave and spacious aisles, separated by arcades with four graceful arches, are thought to have been raised by John of Welbourn, treasurer of Lincoln Minster about 1360; the fine clerestory with four tall traceried windows on each side and arched recesses between them, is a 15th century addition. The chancel was rebuilt last century and fine glass in the east window has four Bible scenes and four saints—Peter, Patrick, Chad, and Hugh.

There are two tablets to men of peace: Henry Disbrowe, rector for 47 years last century, and Frederick Melville who followed him for another 40. In the north aisle is a memorial tablet to a man of war, Sir William Robertson, the soldier who found a field marshal's baton in his knapsack. The tablet bears his coloured coat-of-arms with his motto, *Fight the Good Fight*, and an inscription saying it was placed here to perpetuate the remembrance of a great soldier who by his own indomitable energy, resource, skill, and judgment accomplished the distinction of rising from a trooper in the 16th Lancers to the rank of Field Marshal.

Welby. An attractive stone village within 1 mile of the straight stretch of Ermine Street called High Dike. Its church is on a gentle rise, as though keeping a fatherly eye on the cottages and farm buildings. The tower and broach spire are 13th century work, the porch and clerestory 15th, the south side of the nave early 16th. In the 19th century the chancel was rebuilt and other alterations were made; but the church still wears a venerable air, and the simple screen, some of the benches, the massive door in the porch and another door near it, were all fashioned by good woodcarvers of centuries ago.

Well. It is one of Lincolnshire's beauty spots—a small village on the eastern slope of the Wolds, with a grand view seaward across the Marsh.

Withdrawn from the highway, its few dwellings and its school nestle by the fine 170-acre park surrounding Well Vale Hall, a dignified 18th century house with pedimented front which takes its name from the lovely green valley opening out from the park and climbing to Miles Cross Hill on the Alford road. Larch and pine and beech are among the glorious trees of the vale, and oak and cedar and Scotch pine are in the park, where an attractive little Georgian church (in Classical style) stands on a slope facing the Hall. Two fine lakes by the Hall are fed by a copious chalk spring which gives Well its name and finds the sea at Anderby Creek.

Wellingore. The Cliff road from Grantham to Lincoln climbs steeply to the top of the ridge at this village, giving it splendid views westward across the valleys of the Brant and Witham. The popularity of this attractive site is seen in its recent growth with new houses and bungalows surrounding the nucleus of the old village. On the edge of the village are the steps and stump of a mediaeval cross, and above the clustered red roofs rises the spire of an ancient church. (The surveyor's mark at the foot of the tower gives the height above sea-level—245 feet.)

The oldest part of the present building is the chancel, which still has its late Norman piscina (restored) and sedilia with three round arches. The south arcade is late 12th century work (Transitional); the chancel arch, with brackets for a rood-screen is 13th century; and the north arcade is 14th century, though its piers may be earlier work adapted to later needs.

The tower and spire are both 14th century, and one of the bells in the belfry, bearing figures of the Madonna and two royal heads, has been ringing for 500 years. The font is modern, but has a 13th century central column. In the north aisle are a few 16th century poppyhead bench-ends with foliage, and old pillar almsbox with four locks, and a 15th century altar tomb with alabaster figures of an unknown knight and his lady. The knight wears armour and SS collar, and has a lion at his feet; the lady has rings on her fingers and a long girdled gown from the folds of which a little dog is peeping.

To the east of the church is Wellingore Hall, built in the late 18th century but greatly extended in the eighties of last century; it contains a private chapel with good stained glass.

Welton. It is Welton near Lincoln, a big village with a stream running through it on its way to the Langworth River. Recently, the village has grown and new building now provides homes for many Lincoln businessmen. The new William Farr Church of England Secondary School is a striking modern building. The Lindsey County Council has designated the centre of the village as a Conservation Area.

In the church the battlemented tower has a tablet recording its 18th century builder, Thomas Bell, and much of the rest of the church was built in the 19th century, though its mediaeval arcades still stand, adorned by five little heads, grave and gay. But amid much that is new are many tokens of the past.

The apsidal chancel has old Flemish chairs with carvings of Blind Bartimeus and the Prodigal Son. The fine traceried screen is modern, and so is the oak lectern, a memorial to William Williamson who was vicar here for 57 years.

A striking window is a memorial to men of the RAF who died for us during the First World War, a poignant sight in a village which saw so many of a new generation of flying-men go forth to save civilisation once more; it shows St George, with red wings and cloak standing triumphantly on the dragon in mid-air, aeroplanes circling round him, Lincoln Cathedral below him, and the blue hills in the distance.

Another window keeps green the memory of Dr Richard Smith, founder of Christ's Hospital in Lincoln, who was buried here in Elizabeth I's time. For nearly three centuries 11 boys from this village were fed and clothed and taught there, but in recent years his charity has been turned into scholarships. The window has a portrait of Richard Smith in a fur-lined purple gown, a panel showing some of his Bluecoat boys going under the Stonebow arch at Lincoln in procession to St Mark's Church, and another panel showing him making his will, his wife, nephew, and faithful servant by his bedside. The church also has a brass inscription set up in 1902 on the tercentenary of Richard Smith's death, and in the churchyard is a cross with carvings of the Madonna and the Crucifixion raised to his memory by old Bluecoat boys.

Welton-in-the-Marsh. It lies at the foot of the Wolds, and for the traveller who comes to the village down West Lane, passing the reservoir which supplies Skegness with water, there is a wonderful view over the vast marshland to the sea. There are fine views, too, from the lovely Welton Woods, which cover more than 500 acres between the village and Claxby.

The old village church has a mediaeval chalk base with brick upper structure and west tower. It is mainly 18th century but had new windows inserted in 1891. There is a 14th century font bowl which long served as a drinking trough for cattle.

Welton-le-Wold. High up in the Wolds it stands, glorying in its setting, with stately trees making a magnificent aisle of the steep hillside down to the church and to the rectory serene in its own mantle of trees. The church looks down on the road winding through the village below, and in richly-wooded grounds on the hill opposite is the 19th century manor house of white brick.

Except for its embattled 14th century tower the church was built anew in Victorian times. Its font, adorned with shields and quatrefoils, is as old as the tower, and has a later spire-like cover hanging from a huge iron bracket on the wall.

West Ashby. In pleasant company here on a bank by the busy highway are the church and a Queen Anne house which was used at one time by the Bishops of Carlisle. Known as West Ashby House, it has a carved and canopied doorway which is said to have come from the London house of Captain Cook, discoverer of Australia.

The church is chiefly 15th century work, much restored in 1873. The tower has a band of quatrefoils under the parapet, and fine pinnacles. The porch has a band of trailing foliage and a row of flowers and faces on its parapet; it shelters a simple Norman doorway. The arches between the nave and its aisle rest on eight-sided piers encircled by slender shafts.

The font, with bowl and stem adorned with panels of tracery, is 15th century, and the church also has a piscina of the same period.

Westborough. It is an ancient place—a settlement in Roman times—and an old-world charm still lingers about its narrow lanes and round the green where the steps of the vanished village cross stand imposingly.

The old church, set among great trees by the River Witham (joined by the Foston Beck a mile upstream), is still a fine spacious building, though its south transept has gone, and later work has marred some of its beauty. The tower was rebuilt two centuries ago, and carved on one of the corners is a quaint little portrait of one John Askew, 1849.

Within the brick north porch is a 13th century doorway, and a doorway of the same time (framing an ancient door) is within the 15th century south porch. Late 12th century work is to be seen in the nave arcades (with their soaring arches on clustered piers), and the 13th century chancel has six lancets in its side walls and remains of its original east window in the sides of the later one. The battered sedilia, the round-headed double piscina with fluted drain, and the handsome font with its interlaced arcading and nail-head, are all from the close of the Norman period.

To the 14th century belong the north transept and the lovely four-light window in the south wall of the chancel. The lean-to sacristy on the north wall of the chancel, built about 1400, still has its original stone altar. Sacristy, chancel, and nave all have their old roofs. The chancel screen, embattled and richly carved, is 15th century work; the west gallery, pulpit, and reading-desk are Jacobean. Among other features are eight bench-ends with grotesques carved on their poppyheads, there is also an old oak chest, and on the west wall are painted figures of Time and Death. A marble tablet tells of Robert Hall, rector for 52 years last century.

West Deeping. The smallest of the three Deepings on the southern edge of the county, it lies in a crook of the Welland, set back from the high road linking its neighbours. Its houses line nearly half a mile of the Roman King Street, which crosses the river here on its straight and narrow way northward to Bourne.

From the one-arched stone bridge over the river the church is seen across a meadow, a picturesque water-mill beside it. Most of it is 14th and 15th century work, its tall pinnacled tower being 600 years old and its spire 500. The dim chancel has been over-lavishly decorated with 19th century tiles—in floor and walls and even in the old sedilia and piscina—and the general effect is not happy. On the south side of the chancel is a peephole, and in the south aisle is a window with a piscina projecting from its frame and a sill serving as a seat.

Carrying its years with more grace than does the chancel, the nave has 14th century arcades with bell capitals, 16th century clerestory windows, and massive roof timbers borne on corbels with carved mediaeval heads. There is a fine 18th century brass candelabrum of 24 lights, and the font has a 13th century arcaded stem supporting a bowl a little younger and adorned with eight shields. One of the shields is probably that of the Black Prince who married Joan, the Fair Maid of Kent; she was heiress of the Wakes, whose great possessions included all the Deepings.

West Halton. A hillside village looking across green pastures to the Humber, it has a humble little church and a charming old rectory set in a lovely garden and completely mantled at one end with climbing roses, wistaria, and honeysuckle.

The church was rebuilt in 1695 after a fire, and it was again partly rebuilt last century. But one of its bells has been ringing through six centuries, and in the porch is a 700-year-old floorstone with a flowered cross now scarcely discernible. Four oak bench-ends in the chancel were carved by a 19th century rector's wife. The church register dates from 1538, the year their keeping was made compulsory. Coleby Hall, a fine 17th century house with later alterations, lies south-west of the church.

West Keal. From its high place on the southern edge of the Wolds the village church has a glorious view across miles and miles of fertile fenland to Boston's famous Stump on the horizon. A fine frame for this picture is the entrance archway of the porch, a fine old structure decked with huge gargoyles. Its vaulted roof rests on corbel heads of men and angels, and in the moulding of the old inner doorway are more tiny heads and a grotesque.

The tower and the chancel were rebuilt last century. The chancel is in early 14th century style, but still has its old arch with grotesques carved on the battered capitals. The tall, graceful tower is in the 15th century style of its predecessor, which collapsed in 1881; it is enriched with winged gargoyles, and, like the chancel, still has its original arch (restored).

The nave has long 13th century arcades with a remarkable display of carvings—bold foliage, heads of men and women, grotesques, angels, and animals—on their capitals. One has a group of men and women with an angel for company, and others show two dragons fighting and a fox with a goose. Only one original 15th century window remains in the clerestory.

An old stoup is by the south door, and in the vestry is a coloured print of Elizabeth Shaw who died here in 1683 at the age of 117, in full possession of all her faculties.

Weston. It is a fenland village lovely to look upon in springtime, when the fields are gay with tulips and daffodils; and for the traveller it has the added lure of a church which is the first of a splendid group strung along the road running east from Spalding.

Shaped like a cross, with a central and tilting tower, Weston's church is an elegant example of a 13th century building, with aisles and transepts of the 14th century, and a tower of about 1420. The porch is finely proportioned, and with its stone seats and its pointed arcading enriching the walls, makes a handsome setting for the tall inner doorway with detached shafts crowned by leafy capitals.

The east wall of the chancel is attractive with slender buttresses and three lancets with a single quatrefoil above them; and no less attractive—though dimmed by stained glass—is the interior, where fine pointed arcading with detached shafts enriches the walls and frames all the lancet windows. On each side, below the arcading, are low stone seats, and the chancel also has its old piscina, and a priest's doorway from Norman days. A fine slender arch leads to the nave.

Handsome too, are the nave arcades. The pillars supporting their pointed arches are round on the south side and eight-sided on the north side, but all are encircled by slender detached shafts linked together by capitals of rich foliage. The nave roof is barrel-shaped, supported by kingposts, and the tower arch soars almost as high.

Weston's 13th century font, with its bold carving of foliage, and its original steps with a broad platform for the priest, is worthy of the setting. A few fragments of glass, an ironbound chest, four carved chairs, and an oak seat against a wall are among this church's other interesting possessions; and above the seat are 17th century panels with carved flowers and scenes of the Nativity and the Presentation in the Temple.

There is a 14th century incised slab in the north transept. Close to the church is the base and shaft of a churchyard cross.

West Rasen. A charming scene greets the traveller where a 14th century packhorse bridge spans the River Rase. Its cobbled roadway echoes no metal hoofs, for trade goes other ways and over a modern bridge close by, and this old one with its three ribbed arches is left to those who go on foot. The lovely view from the bridge of a group of tall trees lends a touch of mystery to the half-hidden church, its tall tower, with battlemented turrets, rising airily above the boughs. Three miles west of the village the little River Rase falls into the Ancholme at Bishop Bridge, where a bridge built by a bishop of Lincoln in the 14th century and rebuilt in the 19th stands.

West Rasen's church was much rebuilt in 1829, and of its north aisle only the Norman arcade (and one pointed bay) remain, built up in the wall. The mediaeval south arcade, with stone seats round its pillars, remains as of old.

Other points of interest are a few fragments of glass, the mediaeval pillar font with old pointed cover, a 700-year-old piscina in the chancel, a Tudor bracket carved with heads of a bishop, a layman, and a monk, a floorstone of 1421 to John de Suthill and his wife, and 21 low oak benches with traceried ends. The shields from an old tomb once in the Pouger chantry are now on the wall of the 15th century clerestory, outside in the sun and the rain. But the most thrilling possession of this church is a chair in the chancel, for in it used to rest someone who had sat on Shakespeare's knee—his granddaughter Elizabeth, only child of his daughter Susannah and her husband John Hall. Elizabeth married Thomas Nash of Stratford, and when he died she left New Place, the poet's last home, to marry John Barnard of Abington Hall, Northants, whence came this armchair with its carved roundels and scrollwork.

Elizabeth was the last direct descendant of Shakespeare, and it is a dull person who is not moved by the experience of standing in this chancel and reaching across the centuries to the woman who sat in this chair—she whose name the poet wrote in fond remembrance in his last will and testament.

West Torrington. The little village church like that of the sister village of East Torrington was rebuilt last century. It has a nave with bellcot and chancel. The sadly battered figure of an ancient knight was found when this work was undertaken; now he lies within, close to the splendid font, which has a Norman bowl enriched with beaded arcading. Remains of a simple 15th century screen, brought from St Benedict, Lincoln, are also here, and in the churchyard is an old cross restored in 1880, with a Crucifixion and the Madonna and Child in its gabled head.

Gilbert of Sempringham was rector of Torrington, and there is still the moated site of the small Gilbertine house he established here.

Whaplode. A big and scattered village among the fens and marshes of southern Holland, it is graced by one of the great churches soaring up every 2 or 3 miles along the road running east from Spalding.

The splendid tower, which has a stairway turret at one angle, represents the work of three great building periods. The base, which serves as a south transept, has zigzag enriching its pointed arcading and is Transitional-Norman work: the second and third stages (with lancet windows pierced in their bold arcading) are 13th century: and the top stage, with pairs of trefoiled lights adorned with clusters of shafts and dog-tooth, is a handsome early 14th century addition.

Equally impressive is the nave—more than 100 feet long, with seven massive arches on each side, supported on piers of varying shapes. The four eastern bays are typical Norman work, and the three western bays display in their pillars and capitals the transition from the Norman to the Early English style. Of this period, too, is the west front, which has a projecting gable over a beautiful doorway resting on double rows of shafts. The clerestory has continuous round-headed arcading, broken on the south side by big windows; and above are remains of the old hammerbeam roof adorned with angels and tracery. The aisles have old roofs simple and unadorned.

The north transept is late 15th century work. The chancel was rebuilt in 1818 but still has its Norman arch with a rich hood of zigzag partly cut away for a rood-loft. (The loft has long since been removed, but the turret stairway which led to it is still here.) The canopied pulpit is rich Jacobean work.

In a 13th century doorway opening to the south aisle is an old door. In this aisle hangs a bassoon which once led the singing, and here, too, is the splendid canopied monument, recently repainted, of Sir Anthony Irby, who has a tiny place in literature because Phineas Fletcher, one of the minor poets of early Stuart times, wrote an elegy of 100 stanzas lamenting his "unripe decease". Sir Anthony, who died in 1610, is shown here in armour and baggy breeches with his wife (d. 1625) by his side in long flowing gown; by the tomb kneel three boys and two girls in rich lace collars. Coats-of-arms crown the monument, and on the wall above are a banner and helmet. (The old home of the Irbys was Irby Hall, now a mellow brick farmhouse, a mile south of the church.)

In the chancel is an ancient altar stone, and among a collection of old stones lying at the west end of the church are Saxon fragments carved with interlacing bands, a woman's head peeping from a quatrefoil under a leafy canopy, and the stump of the old church-yard cross. Here also are some stone coffins, and a fine 13th century floorstone with a leafy cross. The font, a copy of the Norman one, stands imposingly on three wide steps.

Whitton. Once an embarkation point serving surrounding areas, with jetty haven for barges and later a railway station. This village has relapsed into rural calm and all traces of its former importance destroyed or decayed. From the green ridge on which it stands there is a view across the Humber to the modern industries on its farther bank and the hills of Yorkshire beyond.

The old church was almost rebuilt in the closing years of last century, but its tall, unbuttressed tower still has some Norman work, including its simple doorway and massive arch. The arcaded font and some of the fragments of old carved stones lying in the church are also Norman.

Wickenby. A compact and homely little place, with a fine thatched house at one end and the church at the other, it lies between two streams of the Langworth River.

The church tower, rising above stately beeches, was added in a big restoration of 1878. An ancient studded oak door with old hinges and heavy closing ring leads to an interior protected by old oak roofs. The nave has an arcade from the close of the 12th century, and between nave and late 15th century chancel is a restored mediaeval screen with simple tracery. There are stone heads adorning two old stone brackets and a piscina, and the plain old font is notable for having the two staples used for securing the cover in days when holy water was left in it. In some of the windows are fragments of old heraldic glass, and in an alabaster frame is the 17th century brass of Henry Milner, bearing his arms, a rhyming inscription, and a shrouded skeleton.

Wigtoft. A quiet place in rich farming countryside, it has its inns and a fine old church among the trees by the village square.

One of its oldest features is a richly-carved window from the close of Norman days, set into the 13th century base of the tower which also has a reset Norman west doorway; other traces of Norman work are seen beside the tower arch to the nave. The rest of the steeple, with a big corner turret rising well above the parapet and beside the small spire, is 15th century work. The chancel, with its charming priest's doorway (seen outside), and the clerestory of the nave are also 15th century.

The porch is chiefly 14th century, but it has on each side remains of a Norman corbel table, and its entrance arch is 13th century, enriched with three shafts on each side which are crowned with leafy capitals. The nave (with a fine gable cross) and the aisles are also 14th century work in the main, but the arches are a century older.

The lofty and richly-traceried oak screen is 500 years old, but much restored, and there is still the old entrance to the rood-loft stairway. Other features are a piscina and aumbry in the south aisle, some fragments of glass (including a quartered shield of England and France), a Jacobean pulpit, and two chairs in the chancel with backs made from old and richly-carved bench-ends—one traceried, and the other with three saints, the Madonna and Child, and the Piéta (a rare subject for a bench-end). The canopied tomb in the south aisle, adorned with battlements and a border from which heads of men and a lion are peeping, came to light during restoration in 1891.

Wilksby. Its little 19th century church, standing alone by the wayside between Moorby and Wood Enderby, has a fine 13th century font. The eight sides of its bowl are carved with simple leaves, and at every corner, under a rim dotted with flowers, is a carved face.

Willingham-by-Stow. Attractive is this little place with its walls of mellowed brick and its church rising above the pantiled roofs of farm and barns. In summer the gardens are gay with flowers, and the churchyard is shaded by fine trees, and through every season the River Till flows gently by.

The church tower (with winged imps for gargoyles) is chiefly 14th century, but its base has stood since early Norman days. The rest of the trim little church was much rebuilt in 1880, but the head of the lofty chancel arch, and some of the arch stones, come from the close of the 12th century. The font, too, is Norman, adorned with inter-laced arcading. The low benches with traceried ends match the few old ones that remain.

Willoughby. Pleasantly situated on the edge of the Marshland, it is typical of this region. Close at hand, between the station and the

Burlands Beck, is an earthwork of irregular shape and unknown date; a group of Bronze Age round barrows nearby has been ploughed out and there are Saxon stones in its church. In English history it shines brightly as the birthplace of Captain John Smith, founder of Virginia, married to Princess Pocahontas.

Red-roofed cottages, tree-shaded roads, and a well known station that for many years secured the prize for the best-kept station, all help to make the village attractive. It has also a fine church, standing in a trim churchyard.

The church is chiefly 15th century work (with modern restoration), but its nave arcades and clerestory are a little earlier. The impressive tower has four battlemented pinnacles like chimneys and fine recessed windows. Low down in its south wall (inside) are two crudely-carved stones believed to be Saxon, and climbing to the belfry is a grand old ladder fashioned from two long tree trunks, with rough-hewn logs for steps.

The lofty porch has a splendid entrance arch with clustered shafts, and an inner doorway with continuous mouldings. A curious feature of the lofty and dignified interior of the church is the double archway between the chancel and its chapel; it consists of two stout pointed arches, one built about 1190 and the other in the 14th century, the earlier arch being a little lower and narrower than the other.

In the floor of the south aisle is a 13th century gravestone showing the worn head of a man, carved in low relief at the top, and his feet at the base. The old font has remains of the two hasps which secured a cover in olden days; the carvings of an angel, a cross, and a lamb are 19th century additions.

The registers are distinguished by their reference to one of the most doughty warriors of our race, for they tell us that "John the sonne of George Smyth was baptised the IXth daie of Ianuarye 1579". This is all the village has to show of its close association with a great Elizabethan seaman, founder of Virginia and Admiral of New England. The eldest of the three children of a small tenant farmer of Willoughby who in 1596 left him fatherless, he was at 16 proprietor of "seaven acres of pasture lyenge within the territorie of Charleton Magna".

After a brief and uncongenial spell as a clerk Smith crossed to Europe, had four years fighting in the Protestant cause, was wrecked on his way back, and, returning here to recuperate, found himself lionised as a hero. Displeased, he took his horse, his lance, and some books and retired into "a little wooddie pasture" where by a fair brook he built a pavilion of boughs, found his food in the woods, and studied philosophy and military science.

At 21 he was again in Europe, facing the Turkish advance on Vienna. Left wounded on the field, he was sold as a slave to a brutal

Turk, whom he killed in retaliation for one of many unprovoked assaults. Seizing a horse he fled and, welcomed everywhere as an escaped Christian slave, regained his native land to sail in 1607 to plant a colony in North America.

With headquarters at Jamestown he faced cowardice, treachery, sickness, fire, and famine, with constant danger from Red Indians. He alone remained undaunted; exploring, building, sowing and harvesting, and creating civilisation in the wilds. He discovered the food value of maize, and learned from the Indians to cultivate it.

But he owed his life to Pocahontas, the daughter of Powhattan, paramount chief of the Indians. While in search of a waterway to the Pacific, Smith was captured and taken before the chief, who ordered his execution. (A fine mural painting of this incident is at the King Edward VI School at Louth, where John Smith was educated.) Smith was ordered to lay his head on a great stone for the descent of the executioners' clubs. Pocahontas loved the brave, handsome Englishman, and, having vainly pleaded for his life, threw her arms about him and laid her head on his, to avert or share the death penalty. Powhattan thereupon gave the order for his release.

When the little colony was starving, she saved it by secretly sending gifts of food. Believing him dead she was persuaded to marry another Englishman, John Rolfe, whom she accompanied to England, where she again met John Smith. Pocahontas died of smallpox and was buried at Gravesend in 1617.

Smith mapped 3000 miles of coast, opened up fisheries and surveyed an immense area of New England, while selecting sites for settlement. This great yet little-known man, who was really the father and founder of Virginia from which the mighty United States eventually sprang, spent his last days in peace and died in London in 1631. He lies in St Sepulchre's Church, Holborn.

Willoughton. Another attractive village of stone cottages sheltering under the Cliff, known here as the backbone of England. The fields around have produced prehistoric, Roman and Anglo-Saxon antiquities.

Rebuilding last century has left little of the old church of St Andrew except the 13th century chancel arch, and the tomb of Nicholas Sutton, a trader who made a fortune in Tudor times. In a case on a wall are a pewter chalice and a fragment of a paten which came from a tomb at the east end of the north aisle which has now gone. The discovery was made during excavations for a new heating system at the end of last century.

The curiosity of the church is an old vamping horn, one of the earliest loudspeakers. Made in six sections, it has a trumpet nearly a foot and a half in diameter. There are only eight other examples left in our churches. Disused for 80 years, it served for more than a hundred years to call gleaners to and from the fields, to warn cowherds from the common land, and by a woman parish clerk to give out notices of banns of marriage and hiring statutes from the chancel steps, c. 1830.

Wide ditches overhung with trees in the fields round Temple Garth Farm (west of the village) are all that remains of the preceptory of the Knights Templars founded here in the time of King Stephen; at Monks Garth Farm (the old manor house on the hillside) and in the field called Swineyard are other old moats, marking the site of an alien priory which belonged to an abbey at Angers.

Wilsford. A typical stone-built village. The quarries on its heath yield a famous stone used for many churches and houses in Lincolnshire, and elsewhere up and down the land. Known as Ancaster stone because it was first quarried and worked in that neighbouring village, this Lincolnshire limestone is an excellent building stone and was used in the rebuilding of the House of Commons in London.

Much restoration has not robbed the church of all its old features, and it has a graceful soaring spire. The nave was initially Anglo-Saxon and long-and-short work survives at the south-east corner. There are two Norman pillars supporting the later arch of the north chapel, enriched with nail-head, but the north wall of the nave is probably Saxon. The north arcade is 13th century work, and the south arcade 14th. From mediaeval times also come three piscinas, a font with carved roses, and a collection of 21 bench-ends with carvings of birds, animals, and quaint little men, including one on horseback.

The chancel is largely 13th century, but its attractive east window is 15th century.

By the churchyard is the old grey wall of Wilsford Hall, built in 1649 by Sir Charles Cotterell, who was born in this village in 1612 and left it to win renown as scholar, courtier, and Master of Ceremonies to Charles II. In 1776 the Duke of Rutland converted the house into a hunting-box, and in 1918 it was demolished.

Wilsthorpe. It is a tiny place among flat meadows where willows mark the winding course of many waters, here crossed by little bridges. Close to the village the River Eden ends its meandering and falls into the Glen. A mile away the Roman King Street pursues its straight way north and south.

When the old church was pulled down in 1715 a new one was built in Italian style; a century and a half later this was remodelled in English mediaeval style. The result is a strange mixture of Classical and Gothic—a bell-turret with little shingled spire at the west end, a nave with eight big rounded windows, and a dim chancel which gives sanctuary to a fine stone figure of a 13th century knight bearing a shield with the arms of the Wake family.

Winceby. Its people are few, and it has little to show a traveller, but it has a place in English history.

It was here, on the high ground halfway between Horncastle and Spilsby, that Oliver Cromwell had one of the most exciting days of his life. It was on October 11, 1643. The Cavaliers were besieging Hull, and the Roundheads, with whom were Cromwell's newly-drilled Ironsides, advanced northward from Boston towards its relief. Thomas Fairfax had already occupied Horncastle for Parliament, but 75 troops of Cavaliers and 5000 of the King's foot soldiers were on their way from Lincoln to check the Parliament men's advance, so Fairfax decided to fall back and join Cromwell, who had 37 troops of horse with about 6000 foot.

The site of the bloody encounter, still known as Slash Lane, lies north-west of this village. Though his men and horses had had several irksome days of travel, Cromwell immediately hurled them into the fray. The royal dragoons fired one volley, and then they fired another—at closer range. But the Ironsides were not to be halted this day. Cromwell fell as his horse was shot dead during the charge, and as he rose to continue battle on foot he was knocked down again by Sir Ingram Hopton, a redoubtable Cavalier, who then called on him to surrender. But it was of no avail. The Cavalier leader and his mount were swept aside and Oliver Cromwell, quite undeterred, grabbed another horse and joined in a second cavalry charge which broke up the Royalists' defence and completely routed them.

Bolingbroke Castle, which was still in Royalist hands, immediately surrendered; the siege of Hull was raised; and practically all Lincolnshire went over to the side of Parliament. A great victory had been won.

The Battle of Winceby, in which Cromwell came so near to death, signed and sealed the fame he had already won as a cavalry leader. In the mêlée which followed the second charge Sir Ingram Hopton was slain. The next day Cromwell rode into Horncastle, interviewed the churchwarden, and arranged that his brave foe should have honourable burial in that church.

Winteringham. A long, straggling village of some character and charm which lies at the northern end of the Lincolnshire Cliff where it slopes towards the River Humber. There are fine views of the Yorkshire Wolds across the river. Although modern and Victorian buildings now predominate, there are still a number of houses and cottages dating from the 18th century and earlier. The western end of the village is the most attractive part.

Here, the Roman Ermine Street met the River Humber and found a crossing point to Brough on the Yorkshire side. The Roman station is sometimes wrongly given the Latin name *Ad Abum*, a mistake which owes its origin to an 18th century literary forgery. Excavations by the Ministry of Public Building and Works are confirming long-standing beliefs that the Roman station was about three-quarters of a mile to the east of the present village on what is now Eastfield Farm. The existence of a spring close to this site may have been one of its attractions, but probably the principal reason for selection was an inlet from the Humber which used to exist where the field called Flashmire now lies.

Winteringham slowly deteriorated in importance as a crossing point as the northern stretches of Ermine Street became covered with blown sand. By the time of Domesday, South Ferriby had already surpassed it in importance and the construction of a bridge over the River Ancholme at Brigg in the 13th century finally diverted through traffic to Barton-upon-Humber. But in 672 it was at Winteringham that St Etheldreda chose to cross on her celebrated journey southward to found a Convent at Ely. And, as late as 1143 William de Barbara, Dean of York, took this route to return home from a Council at London. At Winteringham he learned the news that he had been elected Bishop of Durham and tradition has it that he was dragged against his will to the altar of All Saints' Church to have his election sanctified.

The present Haven is comparatively recent and arises from improved drainage of the West Halton valley and land won from the Humber. In the 19th and early 20th century it enjoyed a brief period of prosperity as a small river port, shipyard, and stage for the packet service between Gainsborough and Hull. A branch of the North Lindsey Light Railway was built to the Haven in 1907, but soon afterwards trade declined and both Haven and Railway fell into disuse.

Winteringham is associated with two names known to history and literature, the Marmions and Henry Kirke White, the young Nottingham poet.

The Marmions of Scrivelsby are reputed to have been the King's hereditary Champions. At the time of the Lindsey Survey (c. 1115) Marmions held land in Winteringham partly in chief and partly in Knight's fee of Gilbert de Gant, one of the Conqueror's tenants-in-chief, who was also Lord of Barton-upon-Humber. The Marmions acquisition of land appears to have been subsequent to Domesday, and the majority of their possessions (but not Winteringham) came— possibly through marriage—from the estate of Robert Dispensator, the Conqueror's steward. In the first half of the 13th century there was a division of Marmion lands between older and younger brothers. Scrivelsby, and with it the Championship, went to the senior branch, while the Winteringham Marmion lands went to the junior branch. By the end of the century Philip, last of the Marmions of Scrivelsby, was seised of the former de Gant Knight's fees of Winteringham, and on the death of his widow, the whole of Winteringham passed to the surviving junior branch of the family. The Marmions had the advowson of Winteringham Church, and two members of the family, Roger and Robert were presented to the benefice in the latter half of the 13th century.

It is probable that Marmions actually lived at Winteringham during the 13th century, their seat being at Hall Close on the steep ground to the south of All Saints' Church, where extensive foundations and a well have been uncovered. Among these may have been Robert Marmion the Younger (d. c. 1241); William Marmion (d. c. 1275) who fought on the side of Simon de Montfort and was in 1264 summoned to Montfort's Parliament; and John, 1st Lord Marmion, who obtained for Winteringham a Charter to hold a Market in 1318, and was the first Marmion to be summoned to the King's Parliament. Robert the younger contracted an advantageous marriage which drew the Marmions away from Winteringham to West Tanfield in Yorkshire, where many of the later generations of the Winteringham branch of the family lie buried.

Henry Kirke White, the young Nottingham poet who died of consumption while still a student at St John's College, Cambridge, lived at Winteringham during 1804 and 1805 when he studied under the curate, the Rev. Lorenzo Grainger, prior to entering the University. While at Winteringham he worked too hard to produce much poetry, but tradition has it that the fragments later arranged into the well-known hymn "Oft in danger, oft in woe" were composed by Henry Kirke White after surviving a dangerous journey to Hull in a rowing boat. In his published correspondence, Henry Kirke White has left generous tributes to the beauty of Winteringham at that time, and to the kindly Lorenzo Grainger and his eccentric sister Lavinia, who used to drive through the streets in a basket carriage drawn by two donkeys and preceded by a running boy from the Sunday school.

The 17th century rectory in which Lorenzo Grainger lived forms part of the outbuildings of what is now known as "The Old Rectory", a handsome Victorian building which has in recent years been replaced by a more utilitarian building in contemporary Church Commissioners' style. The three parsonages, spanning three centuries, stand in a line on the south side of All Saints' Church, a testimony to changing architecture and standards of living in the Church of England.

Grainger's Rectory was built by the Rev. Edward Boteler, a Royalist parson and scholar of some distinction, who was rector from 1649–70. Another parson of note to occupy this house was the

Rev. Thomas Adam, rector from 1726–83, author of the religious best-seller *Private Thoughts on Religion*, evangelist, and opponent of John Wesley, with whom he entered into a spirited correspondence. Adam's successor, the Hon. John Lumley Savill, was an absentee. Born Lumley he added the name of Savill after inheriting the Savill Estates, subsequently became the 7th Earl of Scarbrough, and died in the hunting field. He was known as "Black Jack", and seems to have been a disagreeable, miserly person.

All Saints' Church stands in a pleasant tree-filled churchyard which contains a number of interesting gravestones. It has a good Perpendicular tower and a Norman-Transitional nave with fine arcades. The 13th century chancel was restored in 1849–51 by G. T. Andrews of York. It is believed that Sir Giles Gilbert Scott, who restored nearby Saxby-all-Saints in 1845–49 gave advice on the restoration. The chancel retains its old piscina, a recess used probably as an Easter Sepulchre, and another recess with a stone figure of a cross-legged knight with a lion at his feet and angels about his head. This effigy is of late 13th or early 14th century date, and tradition has it that it is a Marmion. Having regard to the probable date of the effigy, and the identification of Marmion effigies in West Tanfield Church, it seems likely that the Winteringham effigy is either William, son of Robert the Younger, or John, 1st Lord Marmion.

Winterton. An old market town near the Humber, it has no definite beginning or ending—and no signs of planning—and is altogether a charming place in which to wander.

The impressive, cross-shaped church, hemmed in by old houses, displays nine centuries of change—from Saxon times to our own. The lower portion of the massive western tower was built just before the Normans came, and the rest of it is 13th century work with modern battlements and pinnacles. The Saxon work is clearly visible inside the church, where the tower projects far into the nave and is linked with the arcades. The west doorway, too, has a broken Saxon gravestone for lintel.

The restored south porch is unusually lofty, and has two empty niches beside its entrance arch. It shelters a high 700-year-old doorway and a fine old door covered with ironwork; above the doorway is a lovely niche. More 13th century work is to be seen in the rather dim chancel, which has some lancet windows; in the nave arcades, with octagonal pillars enriched by bands of dog-tooth; and in the walls of transepts and aisles, though some of the windows are later. The chancel has a double piscina; the north transept has a simple piscina; and the south transept has a piscina and an aumbry.

The pulpit and the oak chancel screen are fine modern work, and so is the lovely Jesse-Tree glass (by Kemp-Towers) in the east window. Other glass from the same workshop has the Women at the Tomb, and Our Lord appearing to the Disciples. There is also a window of sparkling colour with figures of St Luke, Our Lord, and a shepherd boy; another, more delicate in tone, shows Faith, Love, and Hope.

On a stone in the chancel are brass portraits of the two wives of John Rudd, looking rather prim in their long, flowing gowns and kennel headdress. The figure of John himself, a merchant of Calais who died in 1504, has unfortunately been lost.

The churchyard has part of its mediaeval cross, and also a modern cross copied from the old one at Somersby. Here, too, are two interesting memorials. One is an 18th century gravestone inscribed on both sides, partly in English and partly in Latin, and telling that beneath the turf lie the "sordid atoms" of the wife of William Teanby. William cut this inscription himself, but other hands added the record of his own death in 1810 when he was 97. William kept a school in the church, and the story goes that he used this stone for a table and his own coffin for a cupboard.

The other memorial is a small stone near the porch, with the initials of William Fowler who was born here in 1761, lived here all his life as builder and architect, and died here in 1832. He is remembered for his exceptionally fine coloured engravings of various antiquities, particularly of the Roman pavements found hereabouts.

Just outside the town runs the Ermine Street, and at the foot of the Lincoln Cliff a Roman villa was discovered and tessellated pavements and other Roman antiquities have been found here and are now in the Scunthorpe Museum.

Winthorpe. Holiday camps have taken away much of the old-world peace of this neighbour of Skegness, but it is largely unspoilt and still has its fine and ancient church, possessor of much fine 15th century woodwork.

It is mainly a 15th century marshland church, much restored in 1881, though the south doorway and the nave with its arcades are from the close of the 14th century, and the bases of two pillars in the north aisle are fragments of an earlier building.

The tower, built about 1500, has an embattled and pinnacled crown with a pyramid cap. The nave has a little sanctus bellcot on the gable and a fine embattled clerestory with varied tracery in its windows. The chancel has three great windows on each side and a restored east window in similar style. The striking external feature is the porch, which has a gabled and pinnacled parapet carved with trailing foliage. On the front of the porch are a niche and two stones inscribed with a prayer for the two donors, who "payd for thys".

Within the porch is a holy-water stoup, and an elegant doorway with dainty continuous mouldings which is a lovely frame for the traceried double doors—modelled on the original door standing now by the chancel arch, still beautiful though damaged and worn.

Walls of clean stone enhance the beauty of the grand array of old benches, screens, and roofs within the church. The ends of the seats in nave and aisles have curved arm-rests, elaborate poppyheads, and slender, flower-like candle-holders. On one of the tie-beams of the nearly flat roof of the nave is the pulley-block for the rood light. The splendid mediaeval chancel screen is still here, too, though its doors have been used in a tower screen; above it are the moulded stone brackets for the rood-beam, and in the north aisle is the old rood stairway.

Fine screens enclose chapels in the aisles, but nothing here is more charming than the four stall-ends in the chancel. Nearly 5 feet high, they display a wealth of rich carving. In a mass of foliage and tracery one stall-end shows in detail the legend of St Hubert, who kneels before the stag he went forth on a holy day to kill. The hunter's bow and arrow are fallen to the ground, rising from a tree is St Hubert's guardian angel, and behind him is the foiled Satan. The poppyhead above this vivid scene shows a wonderfully carved oak tree in which are three climbing boys. Tracery and flowers add to the beauty of all these stall-ends, and at the elbows are spirited carvings of dogs and human-headed lions.

In the north chapel are six image brackets, a piscina niche, an old altar stone with three crosses, and a roof with painted rafters and carved and gilded bosses. In the south aisle are two image brackets, an aumbry, a 13th century piscina from the earlier church, and a 13th century coped gravestone with a carved cross. In the windows of both aisles are fragments of 15th century painted glass. The font, carved with delicate tracery, is also 15th century.

One brass in the nave shows Richard Barowe with his wife Batarick and their four children. Richard, who died in 1505, belonged to a family of renown long established here, and was a Merchant of the Staple of Calias; he is shown in an ermine-trimmed gown, with a money-bag at his girdle. Batarick wears draped kennel headdress, and her long girdle hangs almost to her feet. Brass symbols of the Four Evangelists are set in the corners of their stone. A second brass has the portrait of Robert Palmer of 1515, also in a long gown with ermined sleeves.

Lying in the church is the head of the ancient churchyard cross, with carvings of the Crucifixion and the Madonna and Child; it was recovered from a farmyard moat in 1910. Remains of the old shaft on the old base and steps have been restored and given a new canopied head as a tribute to men who died in the First World War.

Wispington. It lies among the rich green fields, and its church is by the wayside. Originally a small Norman building, the church has been rebuilt in the 19th century in lancet style and has a slender tower and broach spire growing from the nave roof and supported inside by triple arches. It has two mediaeval bells, two Jacobean chests, and reminders of two parsons who ministered here.

One was John Heddersett, who died in 1394; his portrait is engraved life-size on a floorstone in the vestry and shows him in his robes with a chalice in his hands. The other was Charles Pratt Terrot, vicar here from 1838 to 1886. His monument is the rich carving in stone and wood with which he adorned his church. He carved the emblems of the Evangelists on the corbels under the roof and the figure of St Margaret above the dedication stone on a wall, showing her thrusting the Cross into the mouth of a dragon. He carved the fine capitals of the chancel arch and the tower arches; and he carved the font, with its big array of animals—among them a cock and hen with chicks, a goat, horses, a camel, a sheep and a lamb, a lion with its prey, a wild boar, a snake about to strike, a bird on its nest, and a fox and its earth.

On the pulpit is more of Charles Terrot's carving: Abraham preparing to sacrifice Isaac; one of the Wise Men coming with out-stretched arms to Herod; the Child in the Manger with the Madonna kneeling, Joseph behind her, and the shepherds adoring. The oak lectern, an eagle with strong claws, is yet another piece of this parson's skilful carving.

Witham-on-the-Hill. A typical stone village built on a hill which rises up boldly between the winding valleys of the Eden and the Glen, and the spire on its summit is a prominent landmark. This crowns a tower which stands in an unusual position—in place of a south transept—and which was built in the 18th century after the old steeple had fallen: at the corners are the urns fashionable as ornaments in those days.

The church is spacious and has been finely restored. The south porch has a Norman arch with a niche above containing a modern figure of St Andrew. The doorway within the porch is also Norman and has another niche above it containing a battered saint. Through the big west window and eight lofty clerestory windows the light streams into an impressive nave with lofty arcades from Norman and 13th century days. The chancel has a graceful 15th century east window, a triangular piscina, and a 13th century pillar built into the wall. The oldest window is a narrow lancet near the mediaeval eight-sided font which has an elaborate modern cover copied from the 15th century font-cover at Freiston near Boston. On the south aisle wall are two painted panels of saints from the 15th century screen.

The church has a strong 17th century chest and an old cupboard with panels of carved foliage. More impressive, however, is the modern woodwork: the richly-carved screen with its great coloured rood, the array of light oak seats with linenfold ends, a handsome canopied pew stretching right across the west end of the nave, and the choir-stalls adorned with carved angels.

On the chancel wall is a 16th century brass inscription to Sir Robert Harington, ancestor of one who is remembered in Bourne for his generous bequests. In the time of James II the Harington family was succeeded at the Hall by the Johnsons, descendants of Archdeacon Johnson, founder of Uppingham School, and it was General Johnson who in 1831 gave the church a bell with an inscription betraying strong anti-royalist inscription.

Protected by a round stone roof at the wayside near the church are the old stocks, with holes for the feet of two wrongdoers; close by gushes a spring which has never been known to fail, even in time of greatest drought. On Bowthorpe Park Farm, about 1 mile away, is one of the wonders of Lincolnshire a giant oak with a trunk more than 45 feet round. It is impossible to estimate its age but it must have seen 500 years, and it is flourishing still, though bound by a chain to save it splitting with the weight of its heavy boughs. A great hollow in the trunk has a roof and a door, making it a room in which 39 people have stood at a time, and 13 have sat down comfortably to tea. Strange it is that Yorkshire's mightiest oak should be at Cowthorpe, and Lincolnshire's at Bowthorpe!

Withcall. Here is born the little River Lud, which gives its name to Louth 4 miles away and then follows a winding course to meet the North Sea at Grainthorpe Haven.

It lies in the heart of the Wolds, and can be reached from the highway by taking the Bluestone Heath Road—a delightful approach to the village, yielding an ever-changing panorama of the rolling hills with some of the largest fields in Lincolnshire.

The neat little church of brick and stone has few signs of antiquity, for it was rebuilt in 13th century style in 1883. The west window has pleasing modern glass showing St Martin of Tours (the patron saint) as a warrior and a bishop, with scenes of him sharing his cloak with the beggar and converting the robber in the mountains. In the rose window above is a fine picture of Tours Cathedral.

Wold Newton. Remote in the Wolds, with its road winding between gay gardens and trim hedges and farm buildings, it has an ancient story revealed by the finding of 20 Anglo-Saxon urns in a tumulus in 1828.

The church is approached by a path rising steeply across a meadow to a 20th century lychgate, and embowered in flowering shrubs and plants. Rebuilt in 1862, in 13th century style, it has an apse for chancel, and a bell-turret with a little spire. A quaint little stone man carved by Norman hands is on the porch, and on the walls within are six brackets from Norman and 13th century days, some of which were capitals of pillars. Among other old fragments on windowsills is the drain of a double piscina. Some of these have been collected from other sources.

The font bears an inscription asking a prayer for John and Johanna Curtys who gave it in the 14th century; and one of the windows has a panel of ancient red, blue, and gold glass, showing St Hugh as a bishop, which is said to have come from Swinhope.

Among the memorials to the Wrights of Wold Newton Manor are the rood-beam (with figures of the Crucifixion) and a cross in the churchyard.

Woodhall. It is the parent village of Woodhall Spa (which has outstripped it in size and importance) and has a tiny church standing in a field, with the old hall (now a farmhouse) and massive barns for companions. Much of the church is new, but it still has its curious old steeple—resting on high, slender arches supported by buttresses, and with flying buttresses springing from the pinnacles to the spire. From the hood of a 15th century window the heads of a man and a woman look down on all who come here. Inside there is an 800-year-old font bowl believed to have been brought here from a Yorkshire church.

The font-cover, the pulpit, and the reading-desk were carved by Conway Walter in memory of his father, Edward Walter, whom he succeeded in 1877 as vicar here and rector of Langton. A similar tribute from the son to the father, who served his parishes for nearly half a century, is in Langton Church.

Woodhall Spa. When engineers were sinking the first shafts for the Channel Tunnel project they found the Kent coalfield. Here in Lincolnshire, when engineers were boring unsuccessfully for coal in 1824, they found water—a spring of medicinal water which founded the fortunes of a little spa set among pine and birch woods and gorse and heather.

The water is unique in our islands for its richness in salts of iodine and bromine, and the little spa has grown into an attractive health resort mainly for the treatment of rheumatism, sheltered on the north and east by the Wolds, and with pump room and fine baths and acres of lovely gardens and woodland for all to enjoy.

Woodhall Spa is a most attractive situation with tree-lined streets, delightful woods, and public pleasure gardens and swimming pool opened to celebrate King George V's Jubilee.

There are two churches—both built in Victorian days. St Andrew's, the older church, is a small building, with walls gleaming white inside and showing to advantage the nave's fine hammerbeam roof and its 10 hovering angels looking down on pews with fleur-de-lys poppyheads. Set in the chancel walls are two mediaeval stones believed to have come from Stixwould Priory; one is a floor-stone with an engraved cross, the other has a deep recess from which a quaint long-headed man peeps out with a surprised air.

St Peter's is a brick building, spacious and light, with a lofty nave arcade of brick arches on stone pillars, and much fine woodwork. The walls are panelled in oak. There are fine traceried screens with rich cornices, and a handsome canopied oak reredos showing the three crosses on Calvary. The east window has striking glass illustrating the Te Deum, and in the nave is glass showing the Madonna and Child, and St John taking Our Lord's Mother into his house after the Crucifixion.

About 2 miles along the low road to Horncastle, besides a little wood, is a link with stirring times. It is a bust of Wellington set on a tall stone column which proclaims that this is Waterloo Wood, raised from acorns sown immediately after the battle, the bust being set up by Rd.E. in 1844. Rd.E. was Colonel Elmhirst, who waited to see if his acorns grew before hazarding a description of his wood; but a wood it is, a fine and flourishing one, and interesting because it shows clearly the rate at which oaks grow.

A veteran of the moors, to which the little town looks up, with the deference due to age, is the red-brick tower by the golf-links known as Tower-on-the-Moor. Sixty feet high, it is said to have been part of a hunting-lodge built by the Cromwells of Tattershall at the end of the 15th century.

Woolsthorpe. A trim and pretty village on the little River Devon, with a thatched roof here and there, it looks across to the wooded heights of stately Belvoir Castle, ancestral home of the Dukes of Rutland, just across the Leicestershire border.

The former Grantham–Nottingham Canal runs through the parish and although disused there are interesting lock cottages and bridges.

When it was besieged during the Civil War Woolsthorpe's old church was burned down by Roundheads quartered here, and nothing remains of it but a few stones in the old graveyard. Half a mile away stands the new church, built in early Victorian days, its walls painted lavishly, its windows filled with dull stained glass. It has a big font richly carved with heads and angels and tracery, and there are tablets paying tribute to the 5th, 6th, and 7th Dukes of Rutland. The 7th Duke, who died in 1906 completed the sturdy church tower which looks across to the towers of Belvoir Castle.

It is just a hamlet, tucked away in the quiet byways of south-west Lincolnshire, but as long as intellect is honoured among men it will be a place of pilgrimage; for here the immortal Isaac Newton was born.

Woolsthorpe has an inn named after its famous son, and a cottage which was formerly a chapel and boasts a Norman arch; but it is the grey stone Manor, hemmed in by haystacks and farm buildings, which draws the traveller here, for it is the actual birthplace of Newton. From this house it was, a little over 300 years ago, that two kindly old women hobbled as fast as they could go to the home of Lady Pakenham, a mile or two away at North Witham, to beg medicine for a weak and tiny baby who seemed likely to die. "I have often heard my mother say", Isaac Newton told a friend, "that when I was a baby I was so tiny you might have put me into a quart pot." Such was the unpromising beginning of one of the world's greatest thinkers, a man who lived to see his 85th year!

Woolsthorpe Manor is an attractive house, with mullioned windows, tall square chimneys, and great beams in the ceilings of its spacious rooms. Mellowed are its grey stone walls. They have seen the passing of centuries, and will see the passing of many more, for through the good offices of the Royal Society and the Pilgrim Trust the house will continue to be treasured as a priceless fragment of our English heritage. Safe, too, is the orchard here, where according to tradition he first received inspiration for his theory of gravitation.

Over the front door of Woolsthorpe Manor are the crossbones of the Newton coat-of-arms, and upstairs is the bedroom where the weakly infant first saw the light. On a wall is a tablet recording Newton's birth, and the famous lines from Pope's epitaph:

> *Nature and Nature's laws lay hid in night;*
> *God said Let Newton be! and all was light.*

In another bedroom is a little partitioned chamber which is said to have been used by him as a study when he was making the researches on which his fame rests.

Such is Woolsthorpe Manor, the most intimate link we have with the youth of this great Englishman whose name is now universally honoured.

The supreme mathematical genius of all time, Isaac Newton was born at Woolsthorpe Manor on Christmas Day, 1642. His father had been dead three months.

On the marriage of his widowed mother to Barnabas Smith, rector of North Witham, young Newton was left to the care of his grandmother, who sent him to school—at Skillington and at Stoke, and, when he was 12, to Grantham.

He was a bright and inventive boy. He wrote verse; he built a model windmill, driven alternately by air and mouse-power; he sent up lighted paper lanterns by kite at night, to the terror of the neighbourhood; he made a water-clock, and a hand-propelled carriage; and he made sundials, one of which can still be seen in the church at

Colsterworth where he was baptised and where for many years he worshipped.

Widowed a second time in 1656, his mother returned to Wools-thorpe, and took Isaac away from school to work on the farm. On Saturdays he attended Grantham market, selling the farm produce and taking home the groceries; but his interests were elsewhere, and he was apt to leave his duties to spend an hour with a book under a hedge, or in the garret of his old lodgings.

Rescued by an uncle, William Ayscough, rector of Burton Coggles, Newton at 18 reached Trinity College, Cambridge. Within the next six years he laid the foundations of his greatest discoveries, and the rest of his long life was spent in working them out. Galileo had established the law of falling bodies, and Kepler the law that the sun controls the motions of the planets, and the earth that of the moon; it remained for Newton to discover and explain the mechanics of the heavens.

Driven home from Cambridge by the Plague of 1665, he was sitting in his garden at Woolsthorpe when, seeing an apple fall from a tree, he sank into a deep meditation on the power of gravity. This, it occurred to him, might extend as high as the moon, and so influence its motion and retain it in its orbit.

Baffled at finding existing data as to the size of the earth at variance with the results of his calculations, he laid aside his studies until a more accurate estimate was completed by Picard. He then toiled silently at his task until he had completed the whole theory of gravitation, one of the most astounding products of the human mind.

Newton's immortal achievement was his private recreation, and might never have been given to the world had not Halley, in 1687, published it at his own expense. Next in importance was Newton's great mathematical discovery, the differential calculus, and his work on the composition of light.

Professor of mathematics at Cambridge, which he defended against the encroachments of James II, he represented the University in Parliament; and at Cambridge is his finest memorial, the statue in the ante-chapel of Trinity College, with Wordsworth's lines:

> *The marble index of a mind for ever*
> *Voyaging through strange seas of Thought alone.*

Master of the Mint, and a practical reformer of currency, Sir Isaac Newton died in 1727, and was buried in Westminster Abbey. Since then the passing years have emphasised his greatness. Time cannot wither his fame.

Worlaby. There are fine views from this pleasant village lying on the western edge of the Wolds, near Brigg, and it has an avenue of fine sycamores which led to the vanished Hall. Close to the church on the hillside is an almshouse (Worlaby Hospital) with mellowed brick walls and pantiled roofs; it was built after the Restoration by Lord Belasyse as a thanks offering for safe deliverance during the Civil War, in which he had fought for the king, and, indeed, had raised six regiments at his own expense.

The church was rebuilt last century, but its tower, built originally at the close of the Saxon period, still has its ancient and narrow arch. An unusual feature of the interior is a modern cinquefoiled arch of wood between nave and chancel.

The bowl and part of the stem of the ancient font stands by the modern one, and there is an old quern or stoup on a windowsill. The vestry table is 17th century work and among the plate is a cup of 1569. The stone figure of a woman with folded hands and a stone with engraved figures of a knight, a lady, and two dogs have both been here for 600 years.

Wragby. Its big square is a reminder that it was once a market town, the charter for the market having been granted by Charles II to the lord of the manor, George Villiers, Duke of Buckingham. Its market character has gone but it is a busy centre with a timber and plastics industry.

There are almshouses founded in the 17th century by Sir Edmund Turnor but rebuilt last century and since enlarged. The church, built in the lancet style, is little more than a centenarian. In it are a few relics from the old church, whose chancel is not far away, serving as a burial chapel. One of two old stones in the porch may have been a stoup. The old font has its old oak cover, crowned by an acorn, and with the old staple fastenings; and there is a pillar piscina which has been rescued from a garden.

Wrangle. A big marshland village from which ships once sailed along a creek that ran up from the Wash, it is grouped about a twisting stretch of the road from Boston to Skegness, and is an attractive picture with its gay gardens, trim hedges, and many trees. Its character has changed in recent years with new building owing to its proximity to Boston.

The church, which once belonged to Waltham Abbey, is a fine, lofty building, though it is a little marred by the low tower which has replaced a taller one built at the close of Norman days; the original arch remains, richly carved with diamond pattern and quaint leaf ornament. A lovely 13th century south doorway, enriched with dog-tooth moulding in its trefoiled arch, is sheltered by a big 15th century porch with an upper room and two curious corbels under its eaves; one has three men huddled together, the other has an animal being swallowed by a fearsome dragon.

The nave and its arcades are 13th century work, made partly new two centuries later. The clerestory is interesting for having in alternate windows the tracery of two different styles, showing the transition from the rich flowing tracery of the close of the 14th century to that of the 15th century. The clerestory and the aisles are embattled, and there is an old sanctus bellcot on the east gable of the nave. There are stairway turrets to the rood-loft and to the tower.

The chancel is chiefly 14th century, and has its old sedilia, double piscina and aumbry, and a fine five-light east window. The nave roof is of open timbering and the south aisle has a fine restored roof adorned with angels holding shields. The handsome pulpit, its sides arcaded and flanked by pillars with scrolled capitals, is Jacobean, and the church also has a Jacobean chest. The font is dated 1724.

A wealth of 600-year-old glass is in the north aisle, its east window having a haphazard arrangement of subjects and figures, including a Resurrection, kings, and prophets. With eight other saints in the next window are St George and St Cecilia: and there are more saints in the other windows—among them St Lucy, St Barbara, St Stephen, the Madonna, and Edward the Confessor.

John Reade, merchant of the Staple of Calais, and his wife Margaret, both of whom died in 1503, are portrayed here in brass. The merchant has a bulging purse at his waist, and his wife's rich gown with gauntlet sleeves and an embroidered girdle also reflects his prosperity. Below them are grouped 13 children and there is a long inscription ending with the lines:

> Do thou for thyselfe while ye have space
> To pray Jesu of mercy and grace,
> In heaven to have a place.

Sir John Reade, their great-grandson, who died in 1626, has a high altar tomb set up by his wife, daughter of a Lord Mayor of London. Wearing a hood and a gown with puffed sleeves, she lies just below her richly-armoured husband. Their children make a rather melancholy tableau. There are seven girls in stiff ruffs with their hair drawn primly back, and two of them hold skulls; another skull is close to the head of a baby sleeping in a cradle, and, behind it, a bare-headed boy kneels at prayer.

Wrawby. The road winds gently through the village to a post windmill now happily restored by the Elwes family, leaving the church with thriving yews and beeches round it and a duck-pond by its gate.

The mother church of Brigg, it was almost rebuilt in 1800 but still has a 13th century tower with belfry windows displaying plate tracery, and old arcades of crumbling stone. There are two brackets on the south arcade, and at a corner of the chancel are two quaint heads, one behind the other.

There is a rood-loft doorway, a peephole from the north aisle to the chancel, and a 14th century font with a carved Jacobean cover. There is also an altar tomb of the Tyrwhit family, enriched with tracery and plain shields, but without its brasses. The north porch was built in 1888 to mark John Rowland West's 50th year as vicar; he continued to minister here for another six years.

Another reminder of the Tyrwhits is by the road to Melton Ross. It is the Melton Gallows, set up originally by James I as a warning to the Tyrwhits and the Ross family that their long-established feud (which at times had led to bloodshed) must cease.

Wroot. Set in the Isle of Axholme, beside the canalised River Torne, it is Lincolnshire's Farthest West—a lonely spot looking across a great stretch of the countryside to the Cliff. It is of interest chiefly for its link with the Wesleys. While Samuel was rector of Epworth he was also rector of Wroot, and his immortal son John assisted him here as curate for two years. Of the 14th century church they knew a few fragments have survived in the little modern building. It contains a Norman stone coffin and a chalice of 1510.

Wyberton. Though the approaches to the village have been ruined by modern building, the heart is still attractive and fine trees are a welcome feature of this neighbour of Boston, lying between the road to Spalding and the River Witham flowing (as the Haven) to its journey's end in Boston Deeps. In a loop of the stream running through the village to the river are mounds marking the site of Wybert's Castle.

The Hall, an 18th century building, stands in its park. Another unusual building is a red-brick shed used until the 1920s as a woad-mill.

Standing amid a noble company of trees, the church has a bold 15th century west tower, a little brick apse for sanctuary, and modern tracery in all the windows. There are some fine mediaeval remains within, and some indication of plans for a grander, cross-shaped church which do not seem to have materialised.

The striking feature of the interior is the splendid 13th century arch which led to the old chancel and has groups of clustered shafts on each side which give it the effect of a horse-shoe. It was, no doubt, part of the crossing in the original plan for the church, for when the floor was lowered in the 1881 restoration there came to light the two similar fine bases (now part of the nave arcades) which would have supported the western arch of a central tower.

Very tall are the arcades of the spacious and clerestoried nave—the north arcade 13th century, with beautiful clustered piers, the south arcade a century later, with eight-sided piers. Above is a 15th century roof adorned with angels and bosses. The splendid font, enriched with tracery and with plain shields under leafy arches, is as old as the roof, and so is an attractive little doorway, with leafy hood, leading to the tower stairway. A fragment of old carved stonework is built into a wall, and there are parts of mediaeval floorstones with crosses lying loose. A 14th century gravestone with Norman-French inscription has engraved portraits of Adam de Frampton and his wife in long, draped robes. An old traceried bench-end has set the pattern for the choir seats.

Greatly prized are the church registers here, for they begin in 1538, the year that the keeping of registers was made compulsory by Thomas Cromwell.

The church has the rare dedication to St Leodegar, Bishop of Autun in the 7th century, and had as its rector for a short time a famous son of Yorkshire—Robert Sanderson. He is remembered as the writer of the second preface to the Prayer Book, and as the royal chaplain of whom Charles I said, "I carry my ears to hear other preachers, but I carry my conscience to hear Mr Sanderson, and to act accordingly." At Wyberton in 1618, Sanderson went to Boothby Pagnell in 1619, becoming Bishop of Lincoln in 1660.

Yarburgh. A lowland village in the valley of the little Black Dike, it has a small 15th century church with a tall tower seen for miles over the wide flat lands. The tower has a lovely square-headed doorway with the Lamb and Passion emblems graven on its spandrels, as well as Adam and Eve and the Serpent. A curious feature of this representation of the Fall are the little animals among the roots of the Tree of Knowledge, including moles peeping out of their galleries. Flowers and foliage are in the arch-mouldings of this doorway, and under its hood is the faded inscription, *Who so looks this work upon, Pray for all that yet begun.*

In the south wall of the nave is a built-up arcade, its arches now framing the doorway and the modern windows, which are copies of the finely-traceried mediaeval windows in the north aisle. Among the old possessions are the font, a dainty piscina with trefoiled head, a worn chest shaped like a trunk, some 15th century bench-ends, and a 15th century screen (now across the tower arch) with many little grinning faces about its flower-tipped tracery. The church registers date from 1540, two years after the keeping of them was made compulsory.

APPENDIX

Places of interest open to the public

(* Indicates National Trust Property)

Alford: Well Vale
Boston: Fydell House
Burgh-le-Marsh: *Gunby Hall
Castlegate: Grantham House
Doddington: Doddington Hall
Epworth: The Old Rectory
Gainsborough: The Old Hall
Grantham: Belton House
Grantham: Marston Hall
nr. Grantham: *Woolsthorpe Manor
Lincoln: Guildhall
nr. Lincoln: Aubourn Hall
Tattershall: *Tattershall Castle

LINCOLNSHIRE TOWNS AND VILLAGES

In this key to our maps of Lincolnshire are all the towns and villages treated in this book. If a place is not on the map by name, its square is given here, so that the way to it is easily found, each square being five miles.

Tallington	F16	Uffington	F16	Whitton	D1
Tathwell	J6	Ulceby	F3	Wickenby	F7
Tattershall	G10	Upton	C6	Wigtoft	H12
Tealby	G6	Utterby	J5	Wilksby	H9
Temple Bruer	E10			Willingham-by-Stow	C6
Tetford	J7	Waddingham	E5	Willoughby	L8
Tetney	J4	Waddington	E9	Willoughton	D5
Theddlethorpe All		Wainfleet All Saints	L9	Wilsford	E11
Saints	K6	Wainfleet St Mary	L9	Wilsthorpe	F15
Theddlethorpe St		Waithe	H4	Winceby	J8
Helen	L6	Walcot	F12	Winteringham	D2
Thimbleby	H8	Walesby	F5	Winterton	D2
Thoresway	G5	Walmsgate	J7	Winthorpe	M9
Thorganby	G5	Waltham	H4	Wispington	G8
Thornton Curtis	F2	Washingborough	E8	Witham-on-the-Hill	F15
Thornton-le-		Welbourn	E10	Withcall	H6
Moor	E5	Welby	E12	Wold Newton	H5
Thorpe-on-the-		Well	K8	Woodhall	G8
Hill	D9	Wellingore	E10	Woodhall Spa	G9
Thorpe St Peter	L9	Welton-le-Marsh	L8	Woolsthorpe	D14
Threekingham	F12	Welton-le-Wold	H6	Woolsthorpe (Bel-	
Thurlby	F15	West Ashby	H8	voir)	C13
Thurlby (Lincoln)	D9	Westborough	C11	Worlaby	E3
Timberland	F10	West Deeping	F16	Wragby	F7
Toft-next-Newton	E6	West Halton	D2	Wrangle	K10
Torksey	C7	West Keal	J9	Wrawby	E3
Toynton All Saints	K9	Weston	H14	Wroot	A4
Trusthorpe	L6	West Rasen	F6	Wyberton	J12
Tupholme	F8	West Torrington	F7		
Tydd St Mary	K14	Whaplode	J14	Yarborough	J5